# CONSERVATION ARCHAEOLOGY

A Guide for
Cultural Resource Management Studies

This is a volume in

*Studies in Archeology*

*A complete list of titles in this series appears at the end of this volume.*

# CONSERVATION ARCHAEOLOGY

## A Guide for Cultural Resource Management Studies

Edited by

MICHAEL B. SCHIFFER
Department of Anthropology
University of Arizona

GEORGE J. GUMERMAN
Department of Anthropology
Southern Illinois University at Carbondale

ACADEMIC PRESS
A SUBSIDIARY OF HARCOURT BRACE JOVANOVICH, PUBLISHERS
New York   London   Toronto   Sydney   San Francisco

930.1
C 755

ACADEMIC PRESS, INC.
111 Fifth Avenue, New York, New York 10003

*United Kingdom Edition published by*
ACADEMIC PRESS, INC. (LONDON) LTD.
24/28 Oval Road, London NW1          87 - 881

Library of Congress Cataloging in Publication Data

Main entry under title:

Conservation archaeology.

    (Studies in archeology series)
    Bibliography:    p.
    Includes index.
    1.    Archaeology—Research—United States—Addresses,
essays, lectures.    2.    Cultural property, Protection of—
United States—Addresses, essays, lectures.    I.    Schiffer,
Michael B.    II.    Gumerman, George J.
CC95.C66        930'.1        77-14306
ISBN 0–12–624160–0

to Annette and Sheila

# Contents

## Part III   RESEARCH DESIGN

## 9   Problem Domains in the Santa Rosa Wash Project, Arizona          135

VELETTA CANOUTS

## 10   Archaeological Research Design for the Genesee Expressway       145

NEAL L. TRUBOWITZ

## 11   Modeling Inundation Effects for Planning and Prediction         151

ERVAN G. GARRISON

## 12   Research Design in Highway Archaeology: An Example
from South  Carolina                                                   157

ALBERT C. GOODYEAR

## 27 Prehistoric Lithic Resource Utilization in the Cache Basin: A Preliminary Analysis of Aboriginal Procurement and Use of Pitkin Chert                                369

JOHN H. HOUSE

## 28 Settlement Patterns and Contract Archaeology: An Oklahoma Example                                                   379

CHARLES D. CHEEK
ANNETTA L. CHEEK
STEVEN HACKENBERGER
KEVIN LEEHAN

## 29 The Archaeology of the Logging Industry in the Little Black River Watershed                                              391

SUZANNE E. HARRIS
JAMES E. PRICE
CYNTHIA R. PRICE

## 30 Research Projects: New Melones Archaeological Project        401

MICHAEL J. MORATTO

## 31 Regional Model Building in the Contract Framework: The Hecla Projects of Southern Arizona 413

ALBERT C. GOODYEAR

## 32 Archaeological Pattern Recognition: An Example from the British Colonial System 427

STANLEY SOUTH

# List of Contributors

KEITH M. ANDERSON (43) Arizona Archaeological Center, National Park Service, Tucson, Arizona

ROBERT L. BETTINGER (217), Department of Anthropology, New York University, Washington Square, New York, New York

FRANK J. BROILO (345), Office of Contract Archeology, Department of Anthropology, University of New Mexico, Albuquerque, New Mexico

VELETTA CANOUTS (121, 135), Department of Anthropology, Southern Illinois University at Carbondale, Carbondale, Illinois

ANNETTA L. CHEEK (379), Archaeological Research Associate, Tulsa, Oklahoma

CHARLES D. CHEEK (379), Department of Sociology and Anthropology, University of Tulsa, Tulsa, Oklahoma

KEITH A. DIXON (277), Department of Anthropology, California State University, Long Beach, Long Beach, California

WILLIAM HARPER DOELLE (201), Arizona State Museum, The University of Arizona, Tucson, Arizona

STEVEN L. FULLER (227), Worland, Wyoming

ERVAN G. GARRISON (151), Department of Anthropology, University of Missouri-Columbia, Columbia, Missouri

ALBERT G. GOODYEAR (157, 413), Institute of Archeology and Anthropology, University of South Carolina, Columbia, South Carolina

GARLAND J. GORDON (43) , Western Region, National Park Service, San Francisco, California

MARK A. GRADY (259, 331), Department of Anthropology, Southern Methodist University, Dallas, Texas

GEORGE J. GUMERMAN (97), Department of Anthropology, Southern Illinois University at Carbondale, Carbondale, Illinois

STEVEN HACKENBERGER (379), Department of Anthropology, Washington State University, Pullman, Washington

SUZANNE E. HARRIS (391), Department of Anthropology, University of Missouri—Columbia, Columbia, Missouri

PATRICIA PARKER HICKMAN* (269, 351), Department of Anthropology, The University of Pennsylvania, Philadelphia, Pennsylvania

JOHN H. HOUSE (191, 249, 309, 369), Institute of Archeology and Anthropology, University of South Carolina, Columbia, South Carolina

THOMAS F. KING* (87, 351), Office of Archeology and Historical Preservation, National Park Service, Washington, D.C.

KEVIN LEEHAN (379), Archaeological Research Associate, Tulsa, Oklahoma

WILLIAM D. LIPE (19), Department of Anthropology, Washington State University, Pullman, Washington

DONALD G. MACLEOD (63), Historical Planning and Research Branch, Ministry of Culture and Recreation, Parliament Building, Toronto, Ontario, Canada

MICHAEL J. MORATTO (401), Department of Anthropology, San Francisco State University, San Francisco, California

FRED PLOG (107), Department of Anthropology, Arizona State University, Tempe, Arizona

CYNTHIA R. PRICE (391), Department of Anthropology, University of Missouri–Columbia, Columbia, Missouri

JAMES E. PRICE (303, 391), Department of Anthropology, University of Missouri—Columbia, Columbia, Missouri

L. MARK RAAB (167), Arkansas Archeological Survey Coordinating Office, University of Arkansas Museum, Fayetteville, Arkansas

CHARLES A. REHER (345), Department of Anthropology, University of Wyoming, Laramie, Wyoming

A. E. ROGGE (227), Bureau of Reclamation, Arizona Projects Office, Phoenix, Arizona

MICHAEL B. SCHIFFER (191, 249, 309), Department of Anthropology, The University of Arizona, Tucson, Arizona

DOUGLAS H. SCOVILL (43), National Park Service, Interior Building, Washington, D.C.

STANLEY SOUTH (427), Institute of Archeology and Anthropology, University of South Carolina, Columbia, South Carolina

MARILYN STEWART (107), Department of Behavioral Science, Rollins College, Winter Parks. Florida

DAVID E. STUART (73), Department of Anthropology, University of New Mexico, Albuquerque, New Mexico

NEAL L. TRUBOWITZ (145), Department of Anthropology, State University of New York at Buffalo, Buffalo, New York

MARGARET WEIDE (107), Department of Anthropology, University of Nevada, Las Vegas, Las Vegas, Nevada

*c/o Office of Lands and Surveys, Trust Territory of the Pacific Islands, Saipan, N. Mariana Islands

# Preface

*Conservation archaeology, contract archaeology, cultural resource management, emergency,* and *salvage* are all terms to designate the archaeology, or the philosophy of archaeology, that pertains to work necessary because of planned modification of the earth's surface by construction activity.

Like labels on candidates for political offices, none of these terms are satisfactory, but some title has to be affixed to the concept if we are to talk about this kind of archaeology. *Salvage* and *emergency* archaeology are terms of a, hopefully, largely by-gone era which emphasized the rapid survey and excavation of endangered sites by archaeologists. Many archaeologists of the 1950s and 1960s and some unfortunately still today operated with a "have trowel, will travel" mentality. Results of survey and excavation were seldom published and those efforts that did result in the printed page were only rarely more than a descriptive report with little attempt at synthesis and explanation. Although there is still far too much of this type of archaeology practiced today, the tide has turned and at least the philosophy of managing cultural resources within a framework of research and reporting prevails for many professionals. *Cultural resource management* as an expression gets at the philosophy of the "new" salvage archaeology, but it suffers from not having the word *archaeology* in the title, and it also evokes the image of an old man dusting paintings at an art museum. *Contract archaeology,* a neutral title, does not differentiate between archaeology accomplished because of planned land modification and archaeology done under contract for government agencies or private firms that award contracts to test devices for archaeology or that have archaeology done for interpretive or other purposes. *Conservation archaeology* as a label underscores that the emphasis is not on simply excavating to "save" the sites, but rather on protecting and utilizing the cultural remains to their fullest scientific and historic extent. It has the disadvantage of appearing trendy and it can be identified with sites or regions not endangered by construction or destruction activities. In short, the title of this volume is a compromise, but it does stress the archaeologist's responsibility to work with a philosophy of long range management of archaeological resources for the greatest scientific, historic and public benefit.

It is important for the reader to understand what this book is and is not. It was planned for the archaeologist involved in contract work, be it for a private concern, university, or museum. Those individuals in local, state, or federal positions charged with the protection or management of the cultural endowment will also find the book useful, as well as will those people in government or business who find it necessary to deal with contract archaeology. We especially hope this volume finds its way into the hands of those students and young professional archaeologists who will be held responsible for how they managed or mismanaged our cultural resources when they had the backing of legislation and the funds to do more than simply a passable job.

This volume is not unbiased; we are opinionated. We are advocating an ethic, a method and to some extent a theory for archaeologists engaged in contract work. At the same time we cannot, nor can anyone ever, prescribe a formula or formulas for accomplishing the goals of conservation archaeology. The introductory statements to the sections and the individual chapters of the book offer suggestions and guidelines. A justified fear of many archaeologists is that those people charged with protecting cultural resources and those archaeologists doing contract archaeology will work out a "system," or a suite of methods, for fulfilling the letter of the various laws impinging on archaeology, and that they will allow no deviation from that course. To permit that to happen would be to stifle the intellectual growth of archaeology, to deny the scientific validity of archaeology as a discipline, and to entrench archaeology as nothing more than a rigid technique. This is not then a cookbook, but a statement of philosophy buttressed by case studies.

The volume is biased in other ways. A book on contract archaeology cannot cover all legal, intellectual, and methodological aspects of the subject, that is, it cannot stand alone. McGimsey's volume, *Public Archaeology,* describes how to establish a state program, and McGimsey as well as Lipe and Lindsay (Proceedings of the 1974 Cultural Resource Management Conference) have outlined laws pertaining to cultural resources. A volume by King, Hickman, and Berg (*Anthropology in Historic Preservation,* Academic Press, 1977) details administrative aspects of contract work and deals with legal ins and outs.

The foundation on which this book is based is the National Environmental Policy Act of 1969 (NEPA), which championed an environmental conservation policy that demands consideration of the environmental (including cultural) effects of construction projects and the implementation of programs to reduce or eliminate those effects. The National Environmental Policy Act and the Environmental Impact Statements (EISs) it requires has had untold influence on changing all of archaeology, and the consequences and ramifications of this act have not as yet been fully determined. Government employees and archaeologists, in many parts of the country and in many positions, are still attempting to gain an understanding of the letter and spirit of the act and to place it in an operational perspective. We hope this book helps toward that goal. In some ways we have had to assume that the laws and policies, as well as the attitude and policies of firms and agencies, are remaining static. Undoubtedly there will be contradictions in some of our statements as laws and interpretations of law change. In short, to provide a point of reference and to keep the volume from becoming too long, we have had to write from the perspective of the archaeological profession rather than that of governmental agencies or sponsors of archaeological work.

We have also not come to grips with the problem of ethics in archaeology.

Concerns that contract archaeologists will have to face sooner or later involve many problems such as (*a*) the possibility of government officials dictating research problems to archaeologists, (*b*) the relationship of contract archaeology to academic anthropology programs, (*c*) the possible conflict between contract archaeologists with ethnographers or ethnic groups, (*d*) competitive bidding, and (*e*) the relationship between costs, the desire to be awarded a contract, and scientific research and publication. This volume hopefully will make some of these ethical decisions somewhat easier for the archaeologist.

Yet another bias of this work is the heavy emphasis in the readings on contract archaeological projects in the South and Southwest. Although some of this bias may result from the fact that both of us have done most of our work in the Southwest, we made every attempt to encourage participation from other parts of the country. The fact remains that the most creative and innovative contract work has been done in the West and only a few other states. In large part, this may be due to the fact that there is much more government land in the West and at present more construction—which of course means more contract archaeology. The sad fact is that with even the high-quality reports, most are in mimeographed form—50 of which have been reproduced—and of those 50, 30 are in bureaucrat's and company sponsor's files never to be read. It was a major effort to uncover the superior reports for this volume. We are painfully aware that many good reports escaped our efforts at detection.

We finally, and gladly, admit to one final bias. We feel one of the most important statements we can make is that contract archaeology has come of age. There have now been forged strong links between contract archaeology and research and between contract archaeology and so-called "academic" or "traditional" archaeology. Academic archaeology does not simply give methodological and theoretical input to archaeology, but rather, the tables are turned somewhat; contract archaeology provides creative stimulation and techniques for academic archaeology. For example, before cultural resource management it was impossible to find a single source on estimating the time and manpower necessary to do a highly intensive archaeological survey. Today, hard data are available. Cultural resource management now cuts to the very heart of archaeology and few people can deny that. And that's the way it should be.

Obviously, we owe our thanks to many people. For moral support and encouragement in the early going: Charles R. McGimsey III, Hester A. Davis, Thomas F. King, and Michael J. Moratto. For helpful comments, ideas, and advice on the Introductions: Lynn Teague, Linda Mayro, Richard Wilk, R. Gwinn Vivian, and especially Veletta Canouts, Mark Grady, and Charles M. Baker. For help in scouring various archives in search of elusive but excellent CRM reports, suggesting what to include, and for rendering other assistance: Keith Anderson, Charles M. Baker, Veletta Canouts, Rob Edwards, James Fitting, Dee F. Green, W. James Judge, Thomas F. King, Timothy C. Klinger, Alexander J. Lindsay, Jr., William Lipe, Charles R. McGimsey III, R. Bruce McMillan, Donald S. Miller, Thomas Padgett, James T. Rock, S. Alan Skinner, Lynn Teague, H. David Tuggle and Donald E. Weaver.

# Part I

# CULTURAL RESOURCE MANAGEMENT

During the mid-1970s, when the pandemonium of the new archaeology's birth rites finally abated, archaeologists suddenly awoke to the realization that the discipline had changed dramatically. No longer were granting agencies and universities archaeology's major sources of financial support. Instead, federal agencies (e.g., the Forest Service, the Bureau of Reclamation, the National Park Service, the Army Corps of Engineers), state and local governments, and even private industries were funding the lion's share of American archeology. Some investigators lamented this proliferation of contract research as an unwelcome expansion of the salvage ethic in archaeological research with all of the drastic compromises in quality that term connotes, while others hailed the new development as an unprecedented opportunity for scientific advance—if archaeologists could make the necessary organizational and methodological adjustments (cf. McGimsey 1974). It is now becoming clear that the latter appraisal, though not yet completely substantiated, seems to be more accurate.

Archaeology under the rubric of "cultural resource management" is similar in some respects to earlier public archaeology. After all, it still involves working in areas selected for nonarchaeological reasons under sometimes inflexible constraints. Yet, in more fundamental ways, cultural resource management is different. To show the ways in which it does differ—from its legislative underpinnings to its demonstrable potential for producing substantial research results—is a principal aim of this book.

Cultural resource management is more than just new jargon or a subterfuge for salvage archaeology. It is the realization of a new social philosophy for the treatment of the all too ephemeral materials that contribute to our understanding of the cultural past, as Lipe thoughtfully points out in Chapter 1. These materials, which may include archaeological sites, isolated

1

artifacts, features, historical records, modern individuals and communities, and even biotic provinces and paleontological specimens, are recognized as scarce, nonrenewable resources worthy of conservation and, in some instances, total preservation. The management of cultural resources involves determining the least loss of information concerning past lifeways (Grady 1975:1).

Actual management decision making generally resides in the public and private agencies that own or modify the land. Decision makers for the most part are nonarchaeologists who must, nevertheless, make use of information provided by archaeological investigations. Some federal agencies, such as the National Park Service or the Bureau of Land Management, can in theory accord the conservation of archaeological resources a high priority, whereas, for obvious reasons, other agencies and businesses may give archaeological considerations far less weight. The primary task of the conservation archaeologist is to provide managers with understandable information and recommendations based on sound scientific investigations (MacLeod, Chapter 3). Thus, the second major aim of this work is to demonstrate that, in compliance with its legislative underpinnings, cultural resource management studies entail sophisticated research planning, execution, and results—consistent also with the highest standards of modern archaeology.

Although cultural resource management has received considerable exposure in the archaeological literature (Chapman 1973; Cunningham 1974; D. F. Green 1975a; King 1971, 1976b; King, Hickman, and Berg n.d.; Lipe 1974; Lipe and Lindsay 1974; MacDonald 1976; Matheny and Berge 1976b; McGimsey 1972a, 1973; McGimsey and Davis 1977; Pastron, Clewlow, and Hallinan 1973), most contributions deal with transitory problems—such as setting up statewide or institutional programs, determining institutional responsibilities in conservation archaeology, developing the implications of the laws, and advocacy of performance standards. Until now there has been no general treatment of the subject from the standpoint of archaeological research. While the mutterings of every archaeobureaucrat, no matter how inane, seemingly find their way into print, there is a noticeable dearth of accessible literature on the considerations involved in actually designing a cultural resource management study written by those who have done it. The papers in this volume, we believe, partially redress that imbalance.

The movement in the United States to bring cultural resources into a management framework probably presages an international trend. It is difficult to learn exactly the directions being pursued in other countries because of publication lags and lack of suitable international forums, but some early signs are discernible. A country-by-country compilation of antiquities legislation (Burnham 1974) indicates widespread concern for protection of cultural property and illustrates government attempts to halt the trade in illicit antiquities. In addition, heroic efforts to preserve particularly significant (in an aesthetic or historical sense) sites, such as those imperiled by the floodwaters behind the Aswan High Dam (cf. UNESCO 1970), have occurred, as well as traditional salvage efforts; some, like the RESCUE program of England (Rahtz 1974), are fairly large-scale operations. Beyond these highly visible ventures, and the occasional reports of isolated projects (e.g., Derricourt, Peters, and Maluma 1976), it is difficult to chart the progress of cultural resource management in other countries. As yet, there is no worldwide compendium of environmental legislation, and only a very few dialogues on subjects of general interest have been initiated (see Schiffer and House 1977). We expect, however, that similar processes are operating in other countries that will eventually result in the emergence of an international science of cultural resource management. We believe that most of the topics treated in the present volume do have international import.

## THE FRAMEWORK OF CULTURAL RESOURCE MANAGEMENT IN THE UNITED STATES

The history of cultural resource management in the United States is intimately related to the history of legislation pertaining to cultural resources. Both the legal base and the history of investigations have been summarized in detail elsewhere (J. J. Hester, Musick, and Woolf 1973; King 1975a; King, Hickman, and Berg n.d.; Lipe and Lindsay 1974; McGimsey 1972a; Moratto et al. 1977; Reaves 1976; Scovill 1974; see also the bibliographies compiled by Kelly and Frankel 1974 and Moratto 1975a); present purposes require only a brief review in order to set the stage for more expansive discussions of the National Environmental Policy Act of 1969 (NEPA) and its implications. Our presentation is largely condensed from McGimsey (1972a), Moratto et al. (1977), and especially Reaves (1976).

Cultural resource management had its formal beginnings in the United States with the passage of the Antiquities Act of 1906 in response to urgings of archaeologists, primarily in the American Southwest, who decried the rapid rate at which cultural remains were even then being despoiled on public land. This act protects any "historic or prehistoric ruin or monument, or any object of antiquity, situated on lands owned or controlled by the Government of the United States [McGimsey 1972a:235]." It established the illegality of damaging or appropriating federally owned or controlled antiquities and provided penalties for violation. Responsible scientific institutions can gain access to federal lands and resources by means of a permit system, the details of which are spelled out in a set of regulations (reproduced by McGimsey 1972a:236–238). The greatest impact of this law was not in the conduct of American archaeology nor even in the preservation of archaeological remains (for it has been notoriously unenforceable), but in the establishment of a precedent for a national policy of conserving archaeological and historical resources.

The conservation spirit of the Antiquities Act was vastly expanded in the Historic Sites Act of 1935. The latter "authorized the Secretary of the Interior to take a leadership role in the protection of cultural resources and authorized him to coordinate interagency, interdisciplinary, and intergovernmental efforts for cultural resources preservation [Reaves 1976:18]."

This provision, which led to the initiation of the National Park Service's activities in cultural resource management, facilitated development of the Interagency Archaeological Salvage program in response to the large-scale, federal water-control programs that followed the close of World War II (Reaves 1976:19). Needless to say, this act signaled the beginnings of active federal involvement in specific archaeological investigations. An important outgrowth of this act was the belated recognition that the federal government had a responsibility to alleviate partially the disastrous impacts that it regularly inflicted on cultural resources. In effect, the federal government had taken the first step toward acknowledging that its own destructive actions were not exempt from the provisions of the Antiquities Act of 1906. In 1949 another act was passed, fashioning the National Trust for Historic Preservation, which furthered the policies set forth in the 1935 act (Reaves 1976:19).

A dispassionate evaluation of the depression-stimulated federal archaeology that flourished under the general scope of the Historic Sites Act, and the later river basin salvage work, cannot yet be undertaken. In their defense, one can point out that, as vast amounts of earth were moved, considerable knowledge was acquired of the variability in archaeological remains, and basic culture-historical sequences were erected, but it must also be mentioned that (with some exceptions) the record of analysis and publication of the results of these sometimes massive undertakings is not an enviable one. This era did provide the opportunity for archeologists to experiment with the organization of large-scale projects, as well as train many individuals who would later become leaders in the field.

The Federal-Aid Highway Acts of 1956 and 1958 took a step to further the concept of federal responsibility for mitigating adverse impacts, at least inasmuch as they occurred during highway construction. Unnecessarily narrow interpretations of these laws are responsible for the unseemly state of most highway salvage archaeology prior to very recent times. Like the earlier salvage efforts, it did have the beneficial result of forcing archaeologists to become acquainted firsthand with the entire range of cultural resources in an affected area, not just the large, early, or deeply stratified sites.

The Reservoir Salvage Act of 1960 was intended to remedy the chronic underfunding of river basin salvage. Unfortunately, sufficient money to carry out the intent of the law was never appropriated (Reaves 1976:19).

Two important laws were passed in 1966. The Historic Sites Preservation Act of 1966 reaffirmed the national policy of historical preservation. It

> placed additional leadership and coordinating responsibility with the Secretary of the Interior and directed that he expand and maintain a National Register of Historic Places. It created the President's Advisory Council on Historic Preservation and in Section 106 of the act, granted it a commentary and review function whenever properties on the National Register . . . were to be affected by Federal actions [Reaves 1976:19–20].

Although the Section 106 review procedures constitute a nightmare of red tape and place centralized decision-making capabilities in a body ill equipped to handle them, it is one of the strongest levers that can be used to insure that federal agencies have properly considered cultural resources. Although the legislative history of the act (Grady and Lipe 1976) and common sense would suggest that the National Register is a preservation, rather than a planning, tool (see also McGimsey 1972a), there are those who maintain that recommendations to mitigate impacts can only be considered for sites eligible to be nominated to the National Register (Aten 1974). Some of the issues surrounding the criteria of eligibility (which exclude no site) and the use of the National Register are discussed by King in Chapter 5, in the introduction to Part VI, and by McGimsey (1972a, 1974). A sensible treatment of the subject is provided by Grady and Lipe (1976).

The Department of Transportation Act, also of 1966, explicitly embodied the concept of considering cultural resources during the planning stages of a project to insure that destruction to sites is minimized.

The concept in the 1966 acts of involving environmental resources (archaeological and others) in the planning process is the heart of the National Environmental Policy Act (NEPA) of 1969. By many accounts, this is the most important piece of federal legislation affecting cultural resources (McGimsey 1976). For the first time NEPA and the subsequent regulations set forth a coherent and comprehensive policy for governmental decision making with respect to land-use planning and resource management. This was accomplished by requiring that environmental, historical, and cultural values be weighed against economic and technological benefits when proposed federal actions are assessed. The Council on Environmental Quality regulations for implementing NEPA, which specify that archaeological resources must be considered, spell out in detail the information that is to be included in all environmental impact statements (EIS). Such statements, prepared by the federal agency proposing the land modification project (or by private organizations requiring a federal license or permit for using federal land), must thoroughly document the probable direct and indirect impacts of a project and its alternatives on the environment (see Scovill, Gordon, and Anderson, this volume). Usually proposals are also included for mitigating adverse impacts on the resource base, although implementation of mitigation measures is not mandatory under NEPA. Those responsible for preparing an EIS do so on the basis of environmental impact reports (EIR); the latter are prepared by specialists for each kind of environmental resource.

The import of this law and its regulations, as Scovill, Gordon, and Anderson point out in Chapter 2, is that they require for the preparation of an EIS a high level of up-to-date information on the nature, extent, and significance of the archaeological resources that may be directly or indirectly affected by a proposed undertaking. Research considerations involved in meeting the specific information requirements of NEPA given archaeological meaning by Scovill, Gordon, and Anderson (1972), form the basis of Chapters 9 through 32 of the present volume. The impacts of NEPA on archaeology are many, and we shall return to them shortly.

In 1971 the White House issued Executive Order 11593 for the purpose of tying together the diverse pieces of legislation affecting cultural resources.

> The Executive Order issued three broad management mandates to Federal agencies: (1) administer cultural resources in agency control in a spirit of stewardship and trusteeship for the future (that is, get in the cultural resources management business), (2) conduct agency operations to maintain, restore, and preserve cultural resources on Federal land, and (3) conduct agency operations in such a way, in consultation with the President's Advisory Council on Historical Preservation, to assure that agency plans contribute to preservation of non-Federal cultural resources [Reaves 1976:21].

The executive order places an additional requirement on federal agencies: By July 1, 1973, they must have inventoried their cultural resources in order to determine which are eligible for nomination to the National Register. Needless to say, no federal agency has met the deadline with a complete inventory of archaeological resources. This requirement of EO 11593 makes it abundantly clear that there are conflicting provisions among the various pieces of legislation affecting cultural resources as well as discrepancies between what is required by law and what is feasible. Nevertheless, federal agencies on an unprecedented scale are contracting for archaeological surveys by which they can begin complying with the executive order. These investigations are potentially of great scientific value if they are designed, as they must be for full compliance, with loftier goals than the production of a map with dots indicating site locations. Unfortunately, some efforts undertaken have not adequately attended to the difficult problem of assessing significance.

With Executive Order 11593 and NEPA, a solid foundation was laid for cultural resource management. The only essential ingredient still needed to make it all work was money, particularly for mitigation. The Archaeological and Historical Conservation Act of 1974 (an amendment to the Reservoir Salvage Act) was intended to solve that problem by authorizing federal agencies to expend funds on preservation or recovery of significant scientific, historical, prehistoric, or archaeological information when such resources are endangered by federal actions. If the agency chooses not to contract for the work itself, it may transfer to the National Park Service up to 1% of the cost of a project for conducting the requisite investigations, or it may request (but cannot compel) the National Park Service to fund the work. Significantly, the act specifically mentions that money may be spent on analysis of materials and publication of results. The passage of this act signaled the final step in development of a national policy for the management of cultural resources. The impacts of this law, now just beginning to be felt, are likely to be far reaching as large-scale investigations are undertaken to mitigate the unavoidable adverse effects of many federal projects. What should be apparent is that the Archaeological and Historic Conservation Act and NEPA provide a legislative mandate for carrying out archaeological research that meets the highest scientific standards.

In addition to the major federal laws just enumerated are dozens of others that have implications for the management of cultural resources. These include the Community Development Act of 1974 (see Moratto *et al.* 1977), the Wilderness Act of 1974 (see D. F. Green 1975a), and Executive Order 11514 (See McGimsey 1972a:256–265 for others). To keep abreast of changes in the laws and revisions in the regulations for implementing them one may consult the *Federal Register. Anthropology Newsletter* regularly publishes information about pending legislation that may affect the conduct of anthropology and archaeology. And the *Newsletter* of the American Society for Conservation Archaeology contains timely information on recent and pending legislation.

A large part of the framework within which the conservation archaeologist works is composed of state, county, city, and even tribal laws and regu-

lations. McGimsey (1972a) provides a compilation of state-level legislation, which has been partially updated by Klinger (1975) and H. A. Davis
(1976b). California, it appears, is far ahead of most other states at virtually
every level. Not only is there a strong state-level environmental policy act
(King, Moratto, and Leonard 1973), but numerous county and city ordinances also bring private actions within the scope of the law (King 1968;
Dixon 1974). Needless to say, the rate at which archaeological projects are
being carried out in California is prodigious. It is also well to keep in mind
that many American Indian groups, such as the Hopi and Navajo, have
adopted tribal ordinances protecting antiquities. Familiarizing oneself with
the local context of laws is a necessary part of the conservation archaeologist's activities.

Inevitably, when several laws deal with the same phenomena, conflicts and
discrepancies are bound to arise. And so it is with cultural resource management law, even when federal statutes alone are considered. We have
already alluded to the problems posed by the need for federal agencies to
inventory completely their cultural resources in order to establish which
ones are eligible for nomination to the National Register (EO 11593). It is
worth noting how this provision of the executive order conflicts with
proper consideration of cultural resources in the planning procedures required by NEPA. In the first place, the Council on Environmental Quality
regulations for NEPA also require that cultural resources be evaluated for
National Register eligibility in accord with the Historic Sites Act (and EO
11593). If, however, an agency is in the earliest stages of a project, where
alternate designs are being considered and some areas of potential impact
cannot be delineated, one would be hard pressed to justify conducting a
complete inventory for eligibility determination when a sample survey
would provide the appropriate information for planning needs. Only in the
final stages of project planning, if ever, would one need to conduct a
survey of complete coverage. An inventory of resources and determination
of National Register eligibility should be the end product of multistage
investigations, not the principal goal. We also should point out, as investigators on EO 11593 surveys often discover, that for technical reasons it is
usually impossible to survey an area completely (e.g., Stewart and Purves
1975). Of course, few people now believe that EO 11593 and the search for
Register-quality sites can be implemented to the letter. To do so would
require abandoning sound principles of management and sound archaeological procedure. Other conflicts in the laws are discussed by Moratto *et al.*
(1977).

One should keep in mind that as important as the laws themselves are, (1)
the guidelines and regulations through which they are implemented by the
responsible federal agencies, (2) court decisions, and (3) additional

guidelines are designed by involved organizations and disciplines. The most important guidelines for interpreting NEPA to archaeology, based on the Council on Environmental Quality regulations, were prepared by Scovill, Gordon, and Anderson (1972). An updated version of this document is contained in Chapter 2. These guidelines have had a salutary effect on NEPA-generated. archaeology by demonstrating that high-quality research is required to meet the management needs of the sponsor agency. Had this document received the widespread circulation it deserved, it is certain that we would know a great deal more about the archaeology of affected areas. Additional guidelines have been developed, for use by archaeologists and sponsors, that also incorporate state and local legislation (e.g., King, Moratto, and Leonard 1973). It should be noted that the public (and archaeologists in particular) have the opportunity to provide input when federal regulations are reviewed. At such times investigators may furnish important guidance that will lead to better conservation archaeology (see, for example, H. A. Davis's [1976a] attempt to coordinate archaeological information on NEPA for the Council on Environmental Quality hearings). Hearings are generally announced in advance in the *Federal Register*.

## THE PROBLEM OF QUALITY

The dramatic upsurge in contract-supported archaeological activity, generated primarily by NEPA, has precipitated a second crisis in American archaeology, far different from the initial crisis of a rapidly dwindling resource base (Matheny and Berge 1976a; Moratto 1973; Price *et al.* 1975), Schiffer 1975b), as Gumerman warns in Chapter 6. Even the casual observer of the bulk of contract reports cannot help but note that there has been a marked indifference to standards of quality research. As Schiffer (1975b) has pointed out, "It is hardly necessary to document in any detail the dismal research record of contract archaeology. A glance at the bibliography of any compendium of method and theory . . . will attest to the negligible impact of contract "research" on modern archaeological thought [p. 1]." Although this statement is now dated, it was an accurate description of the general state of contract research when it was written in 1974. Individual archaeologists were not alone in demanding that contract research be upgraded. Federal agencies and other organizations began to issue various limited-edition guidelines (e.g., King 1975a), especially the then Arizona Archaeological Center (e.g., K. Anderson 1974; Scovill, Gordon, and Anderson 1972), and even some private industries began to call for guidelines to insure that they were getting their money's worth (e.g., Neuschwander 1976).

As a response to the general calls for discipline-wide action, the Society for American Archaeology (SAA), under the spur of Charles R. McGimsey

III, conducted a series of seminars at Airlie House, Virginia, in 1974. The six seminars, each involving six to eight individuals, dealt with the following topics: law in archaeology, cultural resource management, certification of archaeologists, communication, archaeologists and American Indians, and guidelines for preparation and evaluation of archaeological reports (McGimsey and Davis 1977). While all of these subjects are of concern to the conservation archaeologist, the seminars on certification and archaeological reports were particularly related to the problem of quality control.

The certification seminar recommended that a registry of professional archaeologists be established, members of which would meet minimal qualifications and adhere to standards of professionalism. In response to this recommendation several members of the SAA set up in 1976 a separate Society for Professional Archaeologists (SPA) to handle the registration process. Minimal standards have been drawn up and a code of ethics adopted; if they are uniformly enforced, one can expect the quality of contract research to improve.

The report seminar's task was to define the minimal categories of information that must be included in an archaeological report. Drawing largely on the work of Stanley South (1974a), the seminar identified nine categories of information that need to be present in any report of empirical research (from Vivian et al. 1977).

RESEARCH GOALS AND STRATEGIES should discuss the context in which the research is initiated and conducted, including place and time of implementation, personnel involved, and resources utilized. A description of the background and purpose of the research and of the sources of support should be included. Special emphasis should be placed on detailing specific research objectives.

THEORETICAL BASE should specify all principal assumptions underlying the statement of problem and its resolution. The researchers' orientation and conceptual framework, the linkage between the theoretical assumptions and problem or hypothesis formulation should be made explicit.

METHODS should describe the specific research activities and justify them in terms of research goals, theoretical base, and research constraints.

ANALYSIS should include the description, classification, and qualitative and quantitative manipulation of the relevant data.

SUMMARY OF ANALYSIS should synthesize the result of analyses derived from the data and ancillary research.

COMPARATIVE SYNTHESIS should place the summarized data in broader perspective by comparison with relevant studies.

INTERPRETATION should present the research objectives achieved. Perceived patterns should be identified and relevant processes discussed.

EVALUATION should provide for comments on the adequacy of any or all aspects of the study's research design, application, and results.

RECOMMENDATIONS should indicate areas of research potential and suggest measures for resource conservation.

Specific report types were defined in relation to sponsor planning stages, and minimal research activities and categories of information were specified. (A discussion of these report types follows). It is encouraging to note that these minimal standards are high ones that, if universally applied, would lead to improvement in conservation archæology by at least one order of magnitude. This point was recently highlighted by Leatherman (1975), who showed that in a sample of 15 contract reports written between 1972 and 1975 (which we believe are above average in quality), only 1 could be judged as adequate by the Airlie House guidelines.

The concepts of peer review of reports has been offered by McGimsey (1975) as another mechanism to raise the quality of contract research. To operationalize the concept, qualified archæologists are employed to write critical reviews of a report; these reviews are then bound with the final draft of the report and distributed with it. The peer-review experiment has been tried a number of times with considerable success (e.g., Doelle 1976; Fuller, Rogge, and Gregonis 1976; Morse and Morse 1976; Schiffer and House 1975b). One can sense that insightful criticism is now beginning to find a place in the process of archæological investigation—and that is perhaps the most stringent monitor of quality.

## NEPA: SPONSOR PLANNING AND ARCHAEOLOGICAL RESEARCH

Let us now take a closer look at NEPA. As has been noted, NEPA requires the input of information about cultural resources into the planning process. Because most projects go through several stages of planning, each of which may involve preparation of an EIS, there is an excellent opportunity for correspondence between levels of planning and stages of archæological investigation. Vivian *et al.* (1977) provide an outline of these general correspondences. They identify five general levels of sponsor planning and the necessary and optional archæological research activities that go with each (see also McMillan *et al.* 1977).

The *regional plan,* or *general design program,* is the earliest stage and does not usually involve a specific land modification proposal. This level would be equivalent to a Bureau of Land Management Planning Unit study or a Corps of Engineers basin study. The minimal archæological research activities appropriate at this early stage include summary and evaluation of extant records and literature, consultation with informants, identification of inadequacies in present knowledge of the area, preliminary estimation of the resource base, preliminary assessments of significance, forecasting of impacts likely to occur as a result of long-range regional development and ongoing destructive processes, proposals to mitigate predicted impacts, and research recommendations. The report resulting from these research activities is termed an *overview*.

At the *preliminary planning stage* a specific action is usually proposed, but not in any great detail. Archaeological research activities, generally focusing on a smaller area than for an overview, include all the activities necessary for an overview, but they will be carried out more intensively. Impact forecasts and mitigation recommendations can usually be made in specific terms. Although fieldwork generally is not conducted at this level of planning, some may be necessary if an area is completely unknown or to determine logistical requirements for future fieldwork. The archaeological report for this planning stage is known as an *assessment*.

When planning has proceeded to the *alternative design stage,* a greater intensity of archaeological research, including fieldwork, is required. Ordinarily a *preliminary field study,* or *reconnaissance,* will involve intensive surveys, by means of probability sampling, of direct and indirect impact areas of alternate projects, as well as some subsurface testing. In addition, all categories of information included in overviews and assessments will be acquired and updated. The purpose of a preliminary field study is to provide information of sufficiently high quality on the nature of the resources, their significance, and especially predicted impacts to permit identification of the least objectionable alternative—from the standpoint of archaeological resources.

In the *final design stage* one action has been decided upon, although not every component may yet have been precisely delineated. At this stage fieldwork efforts are dramatically intensified to facilitate precise estimates of the resource base, determination of significance, forecasting of impacts, and formulation of mitigation recommendations. The *intensive field study* undertaken at this stage optimally incorporates a survey of complete coverage, although not always. Subsurface testing is also expanded to obtain more definitive information about research potential and the nature of the resources. A variety of ancillary research activities may be conducted to increase knowledge of the resource base and its potential. At the conclusion of an intensive field study one should be in possession of high quality of information about the nature of the archaeological resource base, its significance in a variety of contexts, and the probable impacts of the land-modification activity on the resources. With this information in hand one can formulate responsible mitigation recommendations.

The final stage of sponsor planning is project execution. At this time, if not before, mitigation recommendations are implemented. In some cases *follow-up studies* of one sort or another may be warranted, especially to monitor the progress of mitigation (see McMillan *et al.* 1977).

In many situations, departures from this ideal pairing of sponsor planning stage and archeological research activity may be desirable. For example, in very small projects it is perhaps more economical to conduct an intensive field study at the preliminary planning or alternate design stage. Since more intensive types of archaeological investigation incorporate all of the research activities of earlier ones, no particular problems are posed by skipping to advanced stages. When this course of action is most appropriate depends upon the nature of the proposed project and the state of available archaeological knowledge. We might also note that skipping of stages may also be warranted in many cases because of the catch-up nature of much cultural resource management work. This situation sometimes results from the retroactive application of NEPA to projects already underway.

Our summary of sponsor planning stages and archaeological research activities has necessarily been brief and oversimplified. We urge that anyone intending to undertake cultural resource management studies or to evaluate reports of such investigations become thoroughly familiar with the Airlie House documents on the law (Moratto *et al.* 1977), cultural resource management (McMillan *et al.* 1977), and report preparation (Vivian *et al.* 1977).

## OTHER SUBJECTS

Several other important issues and topics also need to be included in any well-rounded treatment of cultural resource management. Because some of these issues are covered in detail in other publications and because we wish to emphasize the interface between research and management, only selected topics will be addressed here.

### Training

There has been a tendency in some universities to design graduate programs in cultural resource management that seemingly will produce only cogs for bureaucratic machines. The overemphasis in these programs on courses in law and management is quite alarming. It is already clear that most conservation archaeologists either will be doing innovative archaeological research or will be evaluating proposals for or reports of such research. If that is the case, then the primary responsibility of training programs must be to insure that cultural resource management students acquire the basic background and skills in archaeological research needed to implement and evaluate efficient, realistic, and sound scientific management studies. Many "real-world skills" can be acquired on the job, but archaeological competence can only be acquired in a university setting. Thus conservation archaeologists need to be fully professional archaeologists who have obtained additional skills (see Jennings 1974). At the University of Arizona and Southern Illinois University, for example, the training of archaeologists who possess cultural resource management expertise is carried out in the MA and PhD programs and builds upon a firm anthropological foundation.

## Communication

One major topic receiving widespread discussion today, and which occupied one of the Airlie House seminars (Woodbury *et al.* 1977), is communication. It is difficult to overestimate the difficulties conservation archaeologists are experiencing in communicating the results of their research to the sponsor, to other archaeologists, and to the general public. MacLeod's snappy paper in this section touches on some of these issues (see Chapter 3). His suggestion to include at the front of every report a management summary in language the sponsor can understand is a useful idea, one that already has been implemented by the Arkansas Archaeological Survey (e.g., Raab 1976c). This, we feel, neatly solves the problem of communicating to the sponsor (see also H. A. Davis 1976b).

The task of communicating contract research results to the community of archaeologists is not handled so easily. Several approaches are in use, but only one is without significant problems. Remarkably, some institutions, perhaps most, have no mechanism for distributing contract reports; the finished product exists in a dozen or fewer copies and molders anonymously in some bureaucrat's filing cabinet (see Schiffer 1975b for a discussion of this problem). The Arizona State Museum, Cultural Resource Management Section, gives each report, regardless of scope or quality, a number in its *Archaeological Series* and reproduces, usually at the sponsor's expense, several hundred of the longer manuscripts for limited-access distribution. Southern Methodist University distributes several hundred copies of the vast majority of its reports in an unnumbered series, also by limited access. Especially noteworthy reports may be set in type and included in one of the established publication series (e.g., Henderson 1976).

By far the most enlightened system has been evolved by the Arkansas Archaeological Survey. There, three classes of reports are distinguished.

The first consists of reports of very small projects that produce little information of interest beyond the local scene. These reports are filed and available to interested researchers. The second class usually consists of reports of more than local interest, which are rapidly reproduced from the typescript in several hundred copies and distributed as numbers of its *Research Report* to libraries and individuals with an interest in the area or topic covered (e.g., Baker 1975). The final class of reports includes documents of unusually high quality or those that might be of national or even international interest. These reports are set in type, reproduced in quantities of 1000, and issued as numbers of the *Research Series* (e.g., Schiffer and House 1975b). Publication and distribution costs of the latter two report types are in principle borne by the sponsor. The Arkansas model for handling report dissemination is basically sound and should be emulated widely.

Although the distribution of meritorious reports will raise the visibility and credibility of conservation archaeology, other channels of information flow also need to be explored. For example, conservation archaeologists should strive more often to summarize their findings in articles and submit these to established regional, national, and international journals. The appearance of such articles would eventually lead to a long-overdue recognition that some of conservation archaeology has indeed been nudging the frontiers of knowledge and help alleviate the unsupported suspicion (unfortunately held widely) that many conservation archaeologists lack scientific motivation and are merely interested in maintaining nine-to-five employment.

Communication with the public, both in terms of describing the results of investigations and discussing the nature of archaeology and cultural resource management, is also difficult. Both Lipe and MacLeod in their chapters in Part I (Chapters 1 and 3) offer useful ideas. Other insights are provided by Lipe (1975) and Woodbury *et al.* (1977). In addition, McGimsey (1973) has written a useful tract on cultural resource management for those who plan land modification projects. Presently some archaeologists are also writing nontechnical articles to explain cultural resource management to geologists, mining interests, and speleologists (e.g., J. J. Hester 1974; Pierson 1976) and to explain cultural resource management programs to nonarchaeologists in the same agency (cf. Rock 1976).

## Competitive Bidding

Other important issues simmer in the literature of cultural resource management but cannot be dealt with in detail here. One of these is the increasing role of competitive bidding for contracts (e.g., Klinger and Baker 1975; Matheny and Berge 1976a; McMillan *et al.* 1977). As McKinney (1976) has noted, however, it is futile to debate about the desirability of competitive bidding, for it already is a fact of life in cultural resource management. Competent archaeologists must insist that public agencies and private sponsors accept proposals on their scientific merits rather than on the bottom-line figure because it is always possible for greedy opportunists to do cheaper (and usually less adequate) archaeology.

## Contract Specifications

The subject of contract specifications has also received some attention (K. Anderson 1974; Carpenter 1974; Cunningham 1976; McMillan *et al.* 1977; Moratto *et al.* 1977; Schiffer 1975b). Only one basic principle is needed for guidance in negotiating a contract for archaeological research: If the sponsor is unwilling to support sound scientific research and permit the results to be widely disseminated, then one should not undertake the project. More specific issues are discussed in the works just cited and in the introductions to Parts IV and VII.

## Limitations of Archaeology

A final problem that needs some discussion concerns the sometimes poor match between sponsor needs and the archaeologist's areas of expertise. A discrepancy often arises, for example, when the archaeologist is called upon to assess the archaeological resources of an area and discovers in the process that potentially significant sociocultural, historical, or paleontological resources also exist (e.g., Skinner and Humphreys 1973). It is true that the sponsor should contract separately for assessments of paleontological resources and should also contract for an "anthropological assessment," as Stuart argues in Chapter 4. Yet, when such studies are not being conducted, archaeologists would be remiss if they failed to report resources of *potential* importance and urge further investigation by competent specialists (see King 1975a).

## CONCLUSION

This brief review of cultural resource management can do little more than acquaint the reader with some of the topics that will need to be followed up in other publications. It should be apparent, nevertheless, that enlightened legislation, such as NEPA and the Archaeological and Historic Conservation Act, forms the foundation of modern cultural resource management. The tasks which lie before us in this volume are to show how innovative problem-oriented research fits into the structure of cultural resource management and how, generally, the basic information requirements of conservation law, particularly NEPA, are met by the diligent applications of modern archaeological method and theory. We hope that, by the time the reader has finished the concluding chapters, he or she will have developed some sensitivity for the problems and promise of cultural resource management as a scientific endeavor.

# 1

# A Conservation Model for American Archaeology

WILLIAM D. LIPE

All of us in the archaeological profession are aware of the present crisis in American archaeology precipitated by the growing rate at which sites are being destroyed by man's activities—construction, vandalism, and the looting of antiquities for the market. Davis (1972) and Coggins (1972) provide thorough reviews of the problem. Many of us foresee the death of productive fieldwork in our regions during our own lifetime if these trends persist. Others foresee a few generations left at best.

Our basic problem is that we exploit a nonrenewable resource (Flinders-Petrie 1904:169–170). We are like mining and paleontology in this respect, except that our resource base is even more vulnerable, since by far the most of it lies at the very surface of the earth.

Salvage archaeology in the United States developed initially as a response to the recognition by the archaeological profession and by some members of government and business that the supply of archaeological sites was not infinite and that important sites, once lost, could never be duplicated among the supply of sites remaining, let alone be replaced. The response was to excavate sites threatened with immediate destruction—to salvage as much information as possible with the time, money, and methods available.

We are now beginning to realize that all sites are rather immediately threatened, if we consider a time frame of more than a few years. In this sense, all our archaeological excavations and surveys are essentially salvage. We can still distinguish between emergency salvage—when we know the site will be destroyed tomorrow or next year—and "leisurely" salvage—when we do not yet know the date when the site may be lost (Jennings 1963a:282). In recognition of the fact that limitations of time and money often make projects of the latter sort as frantic as the former kind, I shall refer to them as "academic" rather than "leisurely" research. They are

19

ordinarily brought into being by demands of "pure," or academic, research problems rather than by immediate threats of the loss of sites.

As I have already noted, our initial response to the threat to our resource base has been in terms of an exploitative model for the use of archaeological materials. If a site is threatened, salvage it, dig it up. There has also been a great deal of debate about how to exploit the threatened resource—such as inductive versus deductive strategies, regional versus piecemeal salvage organization, etc. (e.g., Gruhn 1972; King 1971; Longacre and Vivian 1972).

I submit that we need not only to discuss how to do salvage archaeology but how not to do it (Scovill, Gordon, and Anderson, 1972). If our field is to last beyond a few more decades, we need to shift to resource conservation as a primary model, and treat salvage, at least the emergency kind, as a last resort, to be undertaken only after other avenues of protecting the resource have failed. We must, of course, continue to excavate enough to pursue the problems raised by the discipline and to keep the field intellectually healthy.

But a focus on resource conservation leads us to a position of responsibility for the whole resource base. We must actively begin to take steps to insure that this resource base lasts as long as possible. Only if we are successful in slowing down the rate of site loss can the field of archaeology continue to evolve over many generations and thereby realize its potential contributions to science and the humanities and to society. In this context, excavation becomes only part of a larger resource management responsibility. It may be argued that archaeologists can only be held responsible for the conduct of archaeological research per se and that most of the forces causing loss of sites are outside our control. The latter is certainly true, but the body of antiquities legislation already achieved and the success of many emergency salvage programs show that society can recognize and respond to the problem of loss of antiquities. Furthermore, if we who are most concerned about this problem do not take the lead, we certainly cannot expect less immediately involved segments of society to do so. As McGimsey (1971) pointed out with respect to legislation: "To obtain such legislation and the necessary public support, a greatly increased number of archaeologists . . . are going to have to take their heads out of their two-meter pits and become involved with the outside world [p. 125]."

In the following paragraphs I explore some of the larger implications of a resource conservation model for American archaeology. My objective is to suggest some objectives and principles designed to counter the trends that are fast taking our discipline down the road to extinction.

First, I should like to discuss what needs to be done to prevent our getting into last-ditch, emergency salvage situations. Second, I will comment on the implications of a resource conservation model for the conduct of archaeology when we do choose salvage as an impact-mitigating measure. And finally, I shall conclude with a brief discussion of the implications of this model for what I have called academic research.

## POSITIVE CONSERVATION MEASURES

This area is the most important aspect of archaeological resource conservation and the one least under our control. Our goal here is to see that archaeological resources everywhere are identified, protected, and managed for maximum longevity. Archaeological resources must be accorded a higher value by society than they are now so that more projects will be designed to avoid sites.

The most important positive conservation measures we can take are in public education. We must also greatly expand our efforts to gain institutionalized and regular access to the planning process with respect to land alteration schemes forthcoming from society. And finally, we must press for expansion of our system of archaeological and environmental preserves.

### Public Education

Public education and its objective, public support, are a key to the whole undertaking. Without this we don't stand much of a chance. Individual acts of vandalism are one of the principal threats to the resource and cannot be stopped without a large-scale change in public opinion about archaeology. More stringent laws are not the answer; we have more legislation than we use now. But if increased numbers of the public understood and respected archaeological values, greater self-restraint would be exercised, land-holding agencies would find it easier to justify expenditures for archaeological patrols, and law enforcement and judicial agencies would be more eager to apply existing antiquities laws.

Furthermore, legislation and funding favorable to public archaeological programs critically depend on public support, manifested in the representation of our interests in governmental bodies. The agents of land alteration schemes in both the governmental and private sectors are also generally somewhat responsive to public opinion and especially to directed pressure from the public, as some of the successes of the environmentalist movement have shown.

If we are to have success in educating the public about the value of conserving archaeological resources, we must first be clear in our own minds about the relationship and the benefits of archaeology to society (Flinders-Petrie 1904:167–193; G. Clark 1957). Unless we are prepared to argue convincingly that archaeology is more than just an interesting game for the privileged few, we might as well check in our badges.

### *Establishing the Societal Value of Archaeological Resources*

Archaeologists are presumably convinced of the value of their discipline and of the antiquities with which it deals, but in most quarters the public, though interested in and perhaps entertained by archaeology, apparently sees it as remote from the main concerns of society. Therefore, simply making the public aware of the destruction of archaeological sites will not be sufficient to mobilize support for their protection. We must also convince a large segment of the public of the societal value of conserving archaeological sites. Since the passive value that the simple existence of archaeological sites entitles them to be preserved indefinitely is unlikely to appeal to large segments of the American public, we must stress the positive benefits to society that may flow from archaeological conservation. This positive approach requires that we convince the public that what can be *done* with archaeological sites is ultimately of value to society and that therefore a large number of sites should be preserved now so that these activities may be continued well into the future. That is, we must make the case that archaeological research and related public translations of it, such as on-site displays, museum exhibits, popular books, etc., do make significant contributions to the public welfare and that continued research and educational development will make additional future contributions. There is, of course, a danger in using this type of argument, which stresses the benefits of exploitation of a nonrenewable resource. Pressures may be generated for too rapid exploitation and hence exhaustion of the resource (Kelly 1963), when in fact the indicated policy, assuming continued evolution of archaeological methods, would be to expend the resource quite frugally in order to maximize the application of new methods and extend the period of exploitation as long as possible. I fear that we must risk overselling the exploitation argument, however, because at this time it seems to be the most workable basis for winning public acceptance of archaeological conservation.

Several positive arguments about the values of archaeology to society occur to me; I present them here as examples of the kind of thing I am talking about.

First, we need to capitalize on the obvious types of existing public interest in archaeology by finding out just what it is about the field that appeals to so many people and by using what we find to better present the case for conservation and support of archaeological research and educational activities. Outside the museum field (Frese 1960:236–237) little work of this sort has been attempted. Why do people visit archaeological parks, monuments, excavations, and museums in such droves, and what do they like and dislike about what they see when they get there? I have also not seen any good data-based explanations for the expansion of enrollments in college classes in anthropology and archaeology during the last decade or so. Nor can we characterize, in sociological, economic, or other terms, the type of person who visits archaeological museums or monuments, who gets involved in amateur societies—although Kelly (1963) has made an initial attempt at the latter—or who becomes a pothunter. I should think that the national and state parks systems could gather some of this information, and that the museums could well expand their data-gathering efforts. Archaeologists can contribute by publishing results of surveys done in classes, among visitors to sites, and in amateur societies.

Second, it seems to me that our findings are of potentially great value to one segment of our society—the Native American peoples. Grahame Clark (1957, 1970) and Ford (1973) demonstrate that archaeology has often been important in establishing group identity and pride in past accomplishments among emerging nations or newly self-conscious ethnic groups. Although some American archaeologists have worked closely with Native Americans in land claims cases, in developing museums or cultural heritage centers, and in environmental impact studies on tribal lands, there in general has been remarkably little communication between these groups and archaeologists. Since the results of archaeological research and the conservation of archaeological sites can be of great value to Native Americans, it is vitally important that we attempt to bridge the communications gap. The indicated actions on the profession's part would seem to be to ask Native American groups that their needs are for cultural heritage information, for developing the monuments of their past, and for protecting sites considered inviolate, and then to deal with these needs as well as we can in our research and educational efforts. There is also, of course, a great need for classroom teaching materials, especially at the grammar school level, that present Native American history and prehistory in accurate, detailed, and human terms. This need exists throughout the United States but is critical in the school systems where the children of these groups are being educated. Archaeologists, in cooperation with educators and representatives of Native American peoples, can play a vital role in developing such materials. Finally, it seems to me important that we recruit more Native American students into the field of archaeology. An important prerequisite is likely to be establishing greater credibility for our claim that archaeological knowledge offers something of value to Native American peoples.

Third, we can stress to the public the growing importance of archaeology to other sciences. Archaeological sites are often precisely dated repositories of many sorts of biological and geological materials that have value to specialists in other fields. Laymen are generally unaware, for example, of the potential of archaeologically derived data for the understanding of past climates, the evolution of plant and animal species, and the past wanderings of the magnetic pole. Some such findings have considerable practical relevance. Reconstruction of past climates, for example, is potentially of importance to long-term planning in agriculturally marginal areas.

Fourth, in our public role we often do not emphasize enough the contribution that archaeology has made and can make to sociocultural and physical anthropology through the testing of general theories of culture change and through the reconstructing of the cultural context in which human biological evolution occurred. Public interest in all areas of anthropology is growing; we would do well to capitalize on this by emphasizing the real and increasing linkage between archaeology and the rest of anthropology (J. M. Fritz 1973).

Finally, as Grahame Clark has so eloquently detailed (1970:1–52), archaeology provides contemporary man with a vital perspective on his place in cultural evolution and in the world ecosystem. If human society is to weather the many present and imminent crises it faces, its leaders and much of its populace must be freed of the "tyranny of the present and the local [W. R. Dennes, as quoted by G. Clark 1970:4]." Present-day man must come to see his demographic, sociopolitical, and adaptive situation as something very unusual on the scale of human history and as a state of extreme instability, hoped to be in rapid transition to a new equilibrium level (Platt 1965); and he must weigh his actions in light of this recognition. Prehistoric archaeology can provide this type of perspective.

The antiquity and evolution of human culture is one of those great discoveries of the past few centuries of science that have shaped and are still shaping a modern, panspecies world view. It is comparable to ethnology's contribution of the notions of cultural relativism and the cultural determination of behavior and to other great mind-expanding concepts and discoveries, such as organic evolution, the role of subconscious mental processes, and ecosystem relationships. The perspective furnished by prehistory is perhaps the most valuable contribution of archaeology to society. I think that the public is beginning to realize this, though generally not at a fully conceptual level, and that this realization accounts for much of the current interest in archaeology.

## Public Education Tactics

Moving now from general arguments on the societal value of archaeology to tactics, we can examine the great variety of ways the message can be conveyed to the public. The news media can be helpful if we can learn how to use them properly and do not throw in the towel at the first misquote. Of course, many of us have seen our own work turned into a treasure hunt by shallow journalism. Because of the power of the media to educate, however, our only option is to increase our efforts to get our story told properly, either by writing more popular material outselves or by spending more time educating the media people. If we withdraw from these efforts, newspaper and television coverage of archaeology will not stop; it will only be less accurate and less likely to include the messages that we want to get across.

There is much room, it seems to me, for additional discussion of archaeological conservation values in the classroom and in museum exhibits. At the college and university level, courses and texts in archaeology and general anthropology seldom treat in any depth the basic questions of the societal value of prehistory and archaeological research. Below the college level there are promising developments in grammar and high school curricular design (Bailey 1971), and anthropology and archaeology are finally beginning to find their ways into the training of teachers. Both these developments have tremendous potential value in winning public support for archaeological conservation. But the profession must insure that talented people are involved in these programs and that the programs themselves incorporate credible and in-depth treatment of archaeological resource conservation.

There is much to be done with avocational groups. They are here to stay, and it is up to the professionals to see that the tremendous energies of these groups are channeled for the benefit, rather than the detriment, of archaeology. Much of the discussion in professional circles of the role of amateur groups has to do with how amateurs can assist professionals or can attain a professional level of quality in exploiting archaeological resources. I submit that there is a very large opportunity for avocational groups to function also as educators of the general public and as advocates for archaeological conservation. We need only look at the programs and accomplishments of the Audubon Society, National Wildlife Society, and other conservation-oriented avocational groups to find models.

One of the most productive functions of avocational groups in terms of conservation payoff is a gadfly or "Ralph Nader" function. Such groups can be very successful in identifying and exposing instances of neglect of archaeological conservation by business, industry, or government. Also, they are often more effective than strictly professional groups in lobbying for needed legislation or administrative action.

The best protectors of archaeological resources are often the people who live near the sites. Almost by definition such persons generally live in nonurban areas. The inhabitants of these areas could be of great service to archaeology by refraining from pothunting; by chasing vandals away from sites, or at least reporting them; and by blowing the whistle on land alteration projects that threaten sites.

It seems to me that one of the most important things that professional archaeologists can do in this regard is to attempt to dispel the "treasure hunter from the city" image that rural and small-town people often have of them. In the areas where I have worked, the local people are aware of the economic and prestige values of museums and archaeological monuments, and they tend, with some justification, to see archaeologists as depriving them of ever having these things by digging up the local sites and carting the artifacts off to some distant urban museum. In this context local pothunters are often regarded as serving the community by getting to the treasures before the archaeologists do and insuring that the valuable artifacts remain in the area.

If the professional archaeologist can counter this kind of image, he has a much better chance of getting the local population to cooperate in conserving the archaeological resources of the area. I believe that archaeologists can effectively handle this problem only by accepting some responsibility for sharing the fruits of their labors with the communities in or near which their fieldwork is done. One way this can be done is to work with local museums if they are available or to assist in their development if they are not. Most of our institutions can spare a few items as a permanent loan to a local museum or we can somehow find time to help develop a display explaining our work.

This brief survey of public education tactics is incomplete and merely indicative of what needs to be done. The problem here is not theory but practice. Little of this type of work is being done, relative to the need. The critical variable here is professional payoff. By and large, one does not get promotion and tenure on the basis of articles in the popular press, lobbying efforts, or work with avocational groups. A recent symposium at the American Anthropological Association meetings provided a good example of this. The symposium dealt with the future of archaeology, yet no mention was made of the fact that the field is doomed unless some successful conservation measures are taken to slow down the rate of site attrition. It would obviously be self-defeating for most archaeologists to devote most of their time to public education and ignore basic research. But somehow we must make room for this type of effort in the profession and reward it professionally. Otherwise, the work will not get done because most of us are not altruistic enough to sacrifice our here and now careers for the possible benefit of future generations.

## Involvement in Planning

Archaeologists must also make strenuous efforts to acquire institutionalized access to the planning and management process whenever land surface alterations are involved. In this way projects can be designed so that destruction of archaeological sites is minimized. Legislation has been and can be more effective here than in dealing with the individual vandalism problem. As cultural resource management programs become more effective in their coverage, and more expensive, both government agencies and private industries are beginning to involve archaeologists at early project planning stages in hopes of reducing expenses by avoiding archaeological sites at the outset. Many government agencies have begun to hire archaeologists to assist them in resource evaluation and planning.

Establishing archaeologists in resource management roles so that destruction of sites, and hence emergency salvage, will be minimized creates several problems. The first is that most of our current archaeological contracting programs have been set up so that the archaeologists get paid principally for exploiting the resource—for doing salvage work. What I am proposing is that a major chunk of the money spent by businesses, agencies, or industries concerned about site destruction should go toward paying archaeologists for advice on avoiding sites and hence avoiding salvage. This will require a restructuring of many of our current modes of supporting contract archaeology teams.

There is evidence that such types of contractual arrangements between research institutions and salvage-initiating units are beginning to emerge. The Museum of Northern Arizona, for example, has recently been involved in a multistage program of assisting a private industry in planning for the location of a large plant. Several large areas were initially assessed for probable archaeological impact, concurrently with assessment of other environmental variables by other consultants. After the target area was narrowed down to one valley, brief archaeological surveys were conducted to sketch in the contours of archaeological site distribution within the chosen valley. Finally, after several specific plant sites had been designated, these areas were surveyed intensively, and the impact of the proposed construction on the archaeological resources of these specific areas was fully assessed. In this way the archaeological resource was considered in the planning process from beginning to end. Other examples of this sort of archaeological involvement in planning are beginning to appear in the Southwest and, presumably, in other parts of the country. It is encouraging that our society is flexible enough to permit the rapid development and institutionalization of such arrangements.

A second problem posed by the expansion of advisory and planning roles for archaeologists is that it may create a tendency for government agencies, businesses, and industries heavily involved in land alteration or land management to develop in-house archaeological research teams. The possible conflict of interest in such arrangements is great. If the resource base is to be protected, the archaeologist's first loyalty must be to site conservation, not his employer's need to save money or to push through a favored project. Contracting such advisory resource management work to qualified scientific and academic institutions seems the best way to minimize conflict of interest and maximize the archaeologist's independence. Private consulting teams specifically organized for the purpose of archaeological contracting and lacking a broad institutional base would also seem vulnerable to conflict-of-interest problems, although perhaps less so than in-house groups employed by the land-altering agent. This does not mean that there is no room for professional archaeologists in the employ of land-holding, land-managing, and land-alterating businesses, industries, and agencies. Such persons can perform valuable service as managers by drawing up and administering archaeological contracts, educating the personnel of their institutions about archaeology, operationalizing recommendations made by archaeological consultants, developing public education and site protection programs, and inspecting contractors' work for compliance with antiquities regulations. They may also be able to write overviews of existing archaeological knowledge, and to conduct a certain amount of continuing inventory work. But the principal research and advice on archaeological resource evaluation, impact assessment, and mitigation should come from "outside" archaeological researchers if possible.

Once the focus is on management of resources and on avoidance of archaeological sites in the planning stage of land alteration schemes, the priority of good site inventories becomes clear. These inventories are essential at the initial stages of planning, before the land-altering agent develops substantial investment in any particular location. Useful inventories must, however, provide data about where sites are not as well as where they are. The typical statewide survey, which has unsystematically accumulated data over a number of years, will seldom be of much use for this type of planning. It shows only where some sites exist and tells us little about what the blank spaces mean—whether these actually indicate absence of sites or merely reflect absence of survey. Yet the implications of doing intensive, systematic inventory surveys of any very substantial area are rather frightening.

For example, over the years, most of my research has concentrated in an area of about 3750 square miles—half of one southwestern county. If we consider as sites all archaeological manifestations down to small sherd or lithic areas and isolated petroglyphs, the target region would probably average about 25 sites per square mile. A four-person search team with members spaced 25 yards apart would have to walk about 17 miles to cover a section thoroughly. This would be at least 2 days work, 8 person-days. Plotting the extent of each site on aerial photos, recording features, noting artifact concentrations and their character, estimating the temporal position of the site, etc., would take a minimum average of 40 minutes per site, or another 8 person-days per section, for a total of 16 person-days. Even if the crew made only $3 an hour per person, the fieldwork alone would cost $1,440,000. Even if few or no collections were made, so that cataloguing and curatorial expenses were minimal, the costs of transportation, administration, typing and filing of field forms, preparation of a summary report, overhead, etc., would easily boost the cost of the inventory to well over $2 million for only half of one county.

The indicated alternative to wholesale inventory would be a multiphase sampling design. We know that the distributions of archaeological sites often correlate well with environmental features such as physiography, water supply, or vegetation zones. We would follow the lead of Binford's (1964) pioneering paper on research design and think in terms of characterizing the distribution of a population of sites on the basis of an explicit sampling design. A sampling-based inventory, plus a search of the existing literature, would provide valuable information to planners about environmental and geographic correlations of site distributions at a fraction of the cost of a 100% inventory. This would put the archaeological advisor in a position to say, for example, that sites were much more likely to be encountered in valleys than on the ridges, that grassland environments were much richer in sites than forested areas, or that the northern part of the area, irrespective of environmental variables, had a greater frequency of sites than the southern part of the area. If a specific project were broached, such general information might permit the weeding out of some possible alternative locations without additional fieldwork. Additional inventory work in the remaining alternative locations might still be based on sampling approaches, although the work would have to be much more intensive and would involve the investigation of a larger number of variables. Finally, the surviving few alternative locations could receive 100% inventory. Sampling can provide good information about the general character of distributions, but it is a poor technique for discovering rare types of sites or predicting specific locations of sites. These questions would of course have to be dealt with in deciding upon the specific location of a land alteration project, hence the need for a 100% survey of certain areas before final choices were made.

I have described the above procedure as if archaeology were to be the only variable to be considered in project location. Obviously, this will not be the case; information on numerous variables will have to be considered by any planner of a construction project or other development. The multiphase procedure I have just described can be used parallel to other information inputs. It seems the most realistic—that is, economical—way to introduce reliable archaeological information into the planning process. Furthermore, the inventory and mapping of resources, and the identification and resolution of conflicting resource demands, are established aspects of land-use planning among most of the land-holding agencies. Such procedures as I am advocating for archaeological resource management should actually fit better with established agency practices than would the *ex post facto* salvage approach, which excludes archaeology from the planning process.

Note that in my discussion of archaeological resource inventories, I have assumed that the collecting of artifacts would be minimal. Since the purpose of the inventory is planning, not research, there seems no justification for biasing the surface record at numberless sites and adding greatly to the costs of the survey by making collections. In most areas, it seems to me, inventory data suitable for planning purposes can be obtained without much collecting. It may be that in areas where surface collecting by relic hunters is rampant, professionals will be well advised to seize *any* opportunity to make collections lest all material soon be gone. We may hope such situations will become rarer as effective public education programs take hold. There is also the possibility that it will be difficult to get professional teams to undertake inventory surveys unless there is research payoff and that their research interests may require collections. In such cases the professionals must take care to collect in such a way as to obtain data useful to others and distort the record remaining on the site as little as possible. The collection of representative samples of material in terms of sampling theory should be the best way to attain both objectives. The guiding principles here are that the archaeologist himself erodes by his activities the information content of the site, that within the demands of his research needs he has the responsibility to leave a maximum of information for other researchers, and that his own collections should, if possible, be made in such a way as to be useful for future research as well as the research for which they were originally intended.

## Archaeological Preserves

A third basic conservation strategy is the establishment and protection of archaeological preserves, areas where land alteration is prohibited or at least very rigidly controlled. We currently have a number of national, state, and local parks, monuments, and wilderness areas containing important archaeological resources. The rapidly growing National Register of Historic Places also includes increasing numbers of archaeological districts as well as individual sites. All of these preserves are going to become increasingly important as arenas for problem-oriented or academic research, particularly if our efforts to slow the rate of site destruction elsewhere are not very successful. Furthermore, such areas may increasingly become the only places where groups of related archaeological sites can be studied as settlement systems and in relation to something approaching their original environmental context.

It follows that it is in our interest to promote and support the establishment of additional preserves. It is not necessary and perhaps not even desirable that all such areas be established primarily on the basis of their archaeological resources. We will probably be most successful in adding to the number of preserves if we focus on those that have wilderness or other values in addition to archaeology; this will insure us of allies in the drive to set such areas aside.

Insofar as we have to make choices regarding the establishment of preserve areas containing archaeological resources, we have to deal with the question of the significance of particular archaeological sites or groups of sites. Given several possible preserves and the likelihood that we will not be able to have them all set aside, to which shall we throw our support? Typically the answer to such questions has been that the most significant site or group of sites should be protected. The establishment of most of our archaeologically based parks and monuments, and of the National Register, has been based on this principle.

If this principle is applied, what are the implications for the future of archaeological research and educational interpretation? At some time in the future our basic usable resource for new work and new public educational efforts may be the sites in such preserves that have been set up now and will be set up in the near future. If we choose such areas on the basis of current significance to research and public interest, what do we do if these standards of significance change in the future? And they are certain to change if our field is alive and evolving, as I believe it is.

I think we can already see the conflicts that emerge as ideas of significance change. Many of our archaeologically based national parks and monuments were established on the presumption that the largest, most spectacular, and most unique types of archaeological sites were the most significant. At the time these preserves were set up, this was probably an accurate reading of both the public's and the research archaeologists' assessment of significance. Yet today many projects are designed to investigate functional variability among groups of sites, small as well as large, and there is much greater interest in the statistically typical as well as the rare and unique. It seems to me likely that the interest of the public will follow that of the archaeological profession; it is not hard to imagine a time when scattered-site displays of settlement systems will be as big a drawing card as is Cliff Palace or Pueblo Bonito. Fortunately, a number of our existing archaeological parks and monuments have been set up to cover districts rather than individual sites, so there are resources available for different research and display orientations.

From this perspective it is easy to take the next step and say that the guiding principle in setting up additional archaeologically relevant land preserves should be representativeness rather than current significance. The notion of preserving a representative sample of this country's archaeological resources should be paramount. A representative sample is designed to represent a large population of items in terms of a small selection of such items, with a minimum bias in the selection. Such a sample replicates the main features of the original population, or universe, whether these features are known in advance or not. It thus permits new discoveries about the sample that can also be reliably thought to apply to the original universe. Thus, preservation of a representative sample of this country's archaeological resources would at least theoretically permit any type of research to be carried out on the sample that could have been carried out on the original intact population. A sample selected on the bases of current ideas of significance, on the other hand, would be biased and might exclude some future research and educational possibilities. Obviously, a truly representative sample, in the strict statistical sense, is unlikely to be achievable, because of the vagaries of preservation, and the politics and economics of land acquisition. Nevertheless, I would argue that the principle of representativeness should be used instead of or in addition to the principle of current significance in selecting new archaeological preserves.

Once we begin to think of our various land preserves as possibly vital to the continuing evolution of the field of archaeology at some time in the future, it becomes evident that the whole archaeological profession has a stake in the management of the archaeological resources in such preserves. Decisions to excavate, develop, salvage, stabilize, or simply destroy archaeological sites in such areas should not be based on narrowly conceived and short-sighted management objectives. The agencies in charge of such preserves are custodians for the resources upon which major portions of the field of archaeology may come to depend for their research. Hence, it follows that management decisions affecting these resources should be subject to review by bodies representative of the profession, much as research grants are generally subject to review by committees of research peers.


## CONDUCT OF SALVAGE ARCHAEOLOGY

What are the implications of a conservation model and its implied future orientation for the conduct of salvage archaeology? (In current cultural resource management parlance, salvage would be called data recovery, and be undertaken as one type of impact mitigation. Much of what I have to say in this section also applies to research conducted for impact assessment and other management needs, as well as to salvage per se.) As I have emphasized above, the first implication of a conservation approach is that salvage should ordinarily be undertaken after all reasonable alternatives to destroying the site have been explored and when the value to society of the proposed project clearly exceeds the value of keeping the site or sites intact. How to compare such disparate types of values is of course a major question, one that I cannot deal with in the framework of this paper. This question alone should be a topic of current thinking and research among archaeologists and planners.

Assuming that salvage is dictated, what then? My starting point in thinking about salvage archaeology has been the philosophy espoused by Jesse D. Jennings (1959) for the Glen Canyon Archaeological Salvage Project, as a member of which I had my first real involvement with this type of archaeology in the years 1959–1961. Jennings's philosophy remains, I believe, a good starting point for a discussion of salvage archaeology today. He wrote:

> The operations envisioned under the Upper Colorado River Basin Project (Glen Canyon Project)—or any other salvage work—constitute a very special kind of archaeological work. The project differs in many important ways from any other archaeological project most of the staff members will ever have participated in. It is distinct in that it is not a problem study but is an area study, an area defined by law. It is a project of known duration. The field work cannot be extended beyond a [definite] period. . . .
>
> It is impossible for the technical staff to concentrate work on one problem, or one time period, or in some special aspect of a problem or time period. Total recovery is the objective; this means total sampling of all cultures, and all time periods to be found in the area. . . . Additionally, since time is the crucial factor, there will be constant compromise with the time element itself; standards of work and excavation techniques must be adjusted to the pressure of time. Salvage work, as all science has come to be, is a sampling, statistical operation, but in the course of that sampling it is incumbent upon the field observers and supervisors to gain as much objective data as possible. . . .
>
> A steady flow of increasingly competent publications will benefit the discipline and at the same time be of cumulative benefit to the project supervisors and other specialists who are writing the reports. . . .
>
> The approach to reporting, for the life of the project, will be this: Work unreported is essentially work not yet finished [pp. 681–683].

Several themes emerge here that seem to me central to a consideration of the conduct of salvage archaeology today: the possibility of an areal or regional approach, the arbitrary nature of the choice of the salvage area with respect to archaeological problems, the necessity for a sampling approach, the responsibility of the salvage archaeologist to collect data relevant to the broadest possible range of archaeological problems, and the importance of the salvage archaeologist's making contributions to the intellectual life of this field through publication. In the paragraphs that follow, I should like to expand on these points and add a few not covered by Jennings's 1959 statement.

A central problem, as Jennings recognized, was how the archaeologist is to make intellectual contributions to the field of archaeology within the constraints of the salvage format. Not only must the salvage archaeologist produce reports regarded by the profession as currently useful, but he must make observations and collections that will be useful to future generations of archaeologists. Since the body of sites he has been charged to investigate are being destroyed, his records and collections will have to serve as surrogates for these sites in the future. If these data are to function as resources for the future, they will have to meet the data needs of new research problems unthought of today. At least, this will be the case if our discipline continues to evolve, which is our fond hope.

As Jennings also recognized, in seeking to investigate a site or set of sites that is to be destroyed, the salvage archaeologist will almost never be able to apply his most intensive data collection techniques to the whole body of archaeological remains he is charged with studying. It seems to me highly unlikely that we will ever be in a position to fully excavate every threatened site, using the full battery of data recovery techniques available at the time the work is undertaken. Society is not going to support this type of investment in archaeology (unless in some way archaeology comes to be generally recognized as critical for national defense, and I am not prepared to develop the arguments for this position). Hence, we shall always have to settle for only part of the cake insofar as intensive excavation is concerned.

The salvage archaeologist is therefore in the position of having to make a research contribution on the basis of a site or set of sites selected for him by circumstance, of having to record and collect in such a way as to provide suitable data for unknown future research problems, and of having to do so on the basis of only some fraction of the data recovery that could conceivably have been undertaken.

It seems to me that the salvage archaeologist, in seeking to maximize the return on these objectives, might rely on the following devices: primary problem orientation, collection of representative samples of data relevant to other types of problems, increased use of intensive surface survey techniques in addition to excavation, application of a regional frame of reference, provision for indefinite storage of records and collections, and direct site protection techniques. Furthermore, as the problem orientations, data requirements, and data recovery techniques of the field evolve, some ways will have to be found to maintain congruence between the expectations of the contract-granting firms and agencies, on the one hand, and of the archaeological profession, on the other, with respect to what constitutes an adequate standard of salvage work.

## Primary Problem Orientation

The expenditure of large sums of money by society for the conduct of salvage archaeology is justified by the fact that at least some segments of society perceive archaeological remains themselves and the information derived from their study as being of some value. Salvage archaeology is therefore justified to the extent that it yields new information, not only by bringing forth new artifacts and exposing features long buried, but also by providing new and more satisfactory explanations of its subject phenomena. Like other disciplines, archaeology is healthy only to the extent that it continues to evolve new and more satisfactory approaches to explanation. I contend that a discipline healthy in this sense is doing a better job of discharging its responsibility to the society that supports it than is a stagnant discipline and that, furthermore, society is likely to support a basic research field in approximate relation to that field's health.

All archaeologists, whether involved in academic or salvage research, thus have a responsibility to try to make real contributions to their discipline and hence to its continued evolution and health. Furthermore, if we include surficial study and testing of threatened sites as well as actual excavation, salvage work comprises a large proportion of all archaeological fieldwork in the United States. Responsibility for the discipline's health in this country is increasingly in the hands of people doing salvage work. If salvage archaeologists do not stay intellectually alive, if they are not producing articles and books eagerly awaited and debated by their peers, if their segment of the field stagnates, then the whole field is in trouble. Jennings, in the paper cited in this chapter, argued that the salvage archaeologist should collect data useful in as many types of problem-oriented approaches as possible but that the salvage archaeologist should eschew heavy involvement in specialized problem orientations of his own. While I agree with Jennings about the archaeologist's responsibility to collect data for a broad range of problems, I believe that the salvage archaeologist must in addition to this feel a responsibility at least to attempt to make a significant contribution to knowledge in some special problem area. I say this because I believe that the nature of salvage archaeology itself provides conditions in which research may come to be done by rote and that a primary problem orientation is an antidote.

It is, of course, also possible for the academic research segment of the field to become intellectually irrelevant as well, but I think the danger is at least theoretically greater in salvage work for three reasons. First, academic research is usually justified in terms of some particular problem or problems of recognized importance in the field. If outside research funds are sought, a proposal must usually be prepared detailing the significance and innovative features of the project, and this must be approved by a committee of professional peers. Salvage, on the other hand, is generally dictated by the location of a land-altering scheme that is usually intrinsically unrelated to archaeological problems. Furthermore, the award of a salvage contract is generally a matter of negotiation between the salvage-initiating institution and the institution that furnishes the archaeological team. The proposal presented by the archaeologists generally deals more with costs and logistics than with potential contributions of the work to the solution of archaeological problems.

Second, the institutions that fund emergency salvage work tend not to be very sensitive to changes in problem orientations or in standards for data recovery occurring within the archaeological profession. Archaeological research is not their primary mission, and they generally are involved in it only because the law or public pressure requires them to be. Furthermore, contract performance standards, once agreed upon, can generally not be unilaterally raised by the archaeologists. It is often difficult to explain to an industrial business officer why standards that are adequate last year are no longer adequate, particularly if raising the performance standards requires a substantially greater outlay of money for what appears to be the same work, that is, salvaging a site or set of sites. I shall comment more on this problem later.

Third, much salvage archaeology is currently in the hands of students trained only at the BA or MA levels. This work provides fine training for them, and some may have a willingness to experiment lacked by their academic elders. But very often these people do not have the strong commitment to a problem orientation and to carving out a disciplinary reputation found in researchers who have survived the rigors of PhD training.

For these reasons I feel there is the danger that much salvage archaeology could become rote in nature and make little real contribution to the continued evolution of the field. I am not asserting that the processual paradigm in American archaeological research is more viable than the culture-historical paradigm. There is good and bad work being done in both, and also much work that cannot be classified in either paradigm. There are enough problems to go around. What I am saying is that if salvage archaeology is to continue to live up to its basic justification, it must continue to make significant contributions to the solution of archaeological problems and must move the field forward. Each worker in charge of a salvage project must actively be engaged in the intellectual life of his discipline, must be willing to stake his reputation on his ability to define and contribute to problems recognized as important by his peers.

The implication of this is that problem orientations and research designs are as important in salvage as in academic research. Whereas the academic archaeologist ideally tries to find the site or sites where best to test his hypotheses, the salvage archaeologist is confronted with the sites and must develop his problem orientation in such a way as to make the most of the raw material. Of the two approaches, the latter seems intellectually the more challenging. In the long run, however, it does not matter in what sequence the problem, hypotheses, and data get together. What matters is that they are logically appropriate to one another and that significant results are obtained.

## Data for Others

I have argued above that to discharge his responsibility to the discipline and to society, the salvage archaeologist must himself contribute to the intellectual life and continuing evolution of his field. To do this, he must concentrate on some particular problem or set of closely related problems of significance to the profession. Yet the salvage archaeologist is dealing with sites that are to be destroyed. All that will remain for others to work with are the records and collections he makes (Chenhall 1971). In a very real sense the salvage archaeologist is also working for the whole profession.

Thus he has a responsibility to be aware of problems of concern to other professionals and of the data demands of these problems. And if possible, he has to outguess the data demands of the as yet undefined problems of the future. This brings us back to the notion of maximal archaeology, applying all the data recovery techniques at one's command to the salvage work. Yet, as I have already noted, this gets very expensive very rapidly, and we can probably never expect to apply this type of approach to a very large proportion of the archaeological deposits that we have the authority to salvage. Furthermore, some types of data—village layouts, large-scale architectural patterns, intrasite stratigraphic relationships, irrigation and fortification systems, etc.—require very extensive excavation of sites. If all this were to be done with a brush and trowel so that every scrap of recognized data were retained, the process would be almost endless; thus, the large-scale features will probably get short shrift.

The only way out of this dilemma that I can foresee is for the salvage archaeologist to attempt to collect representative samples of all types of data the significance of which he is aware. In other words, his target list of variables would attempt to cover the research concerns of all segments of the profession. The target universe (the threatened site or sites) would then be sampled to obtain data on these variables representative of their distribution in that universe. Obviously, in any particular case the set of target variables and the sampling design would be further constrained by the time and money available and the salvage archaeologist's knowledge of research problems outside his own specialty.

In carrying out such a goal an explicit sampling design based on sampling theory is called for (Binford 1964; Cowgill 1964; Lipe and Matson 1971). Ideally the archaeologist would want to inventory the occurrence of all the main variables he was interested in and draw a separate sample for each variable. To do this requires considerable prior knowledge of each variable. Generally, in archaeological situations, this would probably defeat the purpose of sampling, which is to acquire reliable estimates of population parameters on the basis of a relatively small amount of investigation. In most cases, then, the archaeologist will have to carry out some type of multipurpose or compromise sampling design. In this approach data-bearing units, such as sites or areas (often quadrats, or rectangles of equal size), are chosen by some type of bias-excluding means, such as a table of random numbers. Each site or area contains data on a large number of variables. It is expected that a sample of such units will also be a good sample of the variables contained in the units, since choice is random with respect to the variables as well as to the sites or areas chosen. If the archaeologist wants to be sure to get an adequate sample of certain variables—say, for example, village sites versus camp sites—he may stratify the sample, choosing a separate sample for each type of site.

Once the sample has been chosen, data on different variables can be collected by different techniques, and subsampling can be employed. On a particular village site there is only one overall village layout, and this may have to be revealed by large-scale stripping with heavy machinery. There may be many similar house structures, on the other hand. Only a sample of these need be excavated intensively. Likewise, the contents of the one or several middens can be sampled by sets of pits or trenches rather than total excavation.

The importance of sampling approaches are that they permit estimates of total populations to be made on the basis of fractions of that population and that collections and records made on the basis of a good sampling approach may in the future provide representative data on variables not thought of at the time the data were collected. For example, if the field archaeologist today collects a sample of pottery in such a way as to reliably represent the kinds and distribution of pottery at the site, then future workers using new techniques for studying pottery may have some confidence that their results apply to the original population of pottery at that site. If, on the other hand, the fieldworker today collects only in terms of the demands of his pet problem orientation or attempts to make a representative collection on the basis of subjective judgment, the future worker will not know whether his results reflect actual conditions at the site or simply the bias of the original fieldworker.

## Intensive Survey

In seeking to get as large and as representative a body of information as possible within the limits of the time and money available the salvage archaeologist will usually be well advised to make good use of intensive surfacial investigation of sites. Surficial examination is almost never a good *substitute* for exacavation, and for many sites it gives relatively little information about what lies underground. But all sites were surface sites once. The fact that some artifacts and features lie at the present ground surface does not thereby render these phenomena devoid of information value. The return on survey work will vary from area to area, of course, but it is my impression that much progress can be made everywhere in developing methods for getting reliable information from surficial examination of sites. The much reduced costs of surfacial examination versus excavation give the former technique much appeal in a salvage situation where funds and time are limited yet where all information not recorded will be lost. In any case, if the archaeologist is attempting to obtain a representative sample of data on a site or sites that are to be destroyed, an intensive survey is almost mandatory to provide a basis for selecting sites or parts of sites to be excavated. This would hold, it seems to me, whether the choices are to be made through subjective judgment or through the application of sampling theory.

But my main notion here is that intensive surfacial investigation can be developed to be a more productive source of information, complementary to excavation (Ruppé 1966). It is my impression that in many salvage projects survey is primarily used to locate sites for excavation, rather than to supply basic information as well. Surficial examination is so much cheaper and less time-consuming than excavation that the profession needs to support studies on improving its scope and reliability. Certainly when a set of sites is to be destroyed by a construction project, the sites that are not excavated should be subjected to very intensive surficial examination and collection. Or at least a substantial sample of them should be so treated.

## Regional Framework

Some of the larger salvage projects coincide with natural regions such as river basins. Most salvage projects, however, are arbitrary with respect to physiographic, biotic, or cultural regions. Yet proper understanding of the archaeological manifestations within such an arbitrarily defined project area may often depend on relating these manifestations to environmental and cultural data occurring in the larger surrounding area. Furthermore, the value of excavating a particular site may differ when viewed from a regional, rather than a strict salvage area, perspective.

There are undoubtedly many instances in which work on a particular salvage project could be made much more meaningful to both present and future professionals through the conduct of additional survey and excavation in areas adjacent to the salvage area per se. McGimsey (1972b) suggests that research priorities be developed for each region of the country, that available funds be allocated so as to carry out these priorities, and that the regional plans be updated periodically. In salvage project areas choice of sites for excavation would be guided by these priorities. In addition, implementation of these priorities would lead to research outside of areas immediately threatened by development projects. To McGimsey, "In a literal sense all archaeology is salvage."

King (1972) urges the formation of regional archaeological "cooperatives" to facilitate team approaches to regional research designs and to permit regional organization for salvage and archaeological resource management. Such cooperatives would integrate the efforts of archaeologists from universities, colleges, museums, and avocational groups.

Such notions are appealing, for they provide means whereby academic research might be coordinated with emergency salvage proper and whereby the knowledge, expertise, and influence of many individuals from diverse institutions could be pooled. Given a conservation goal, such groups might be ideal for coordinating the type of planning inputs I have previously described as essential to slowing down the rate of site attrition. Conservation-oriented regional groups or commissions might also help us get more mileage out of salvage work by helping fit problem-derived research designs to the pool of sites available in salvage project areas. In other words, such groups might attempt to see that studies on problems of regional interest would be undertaken, insofar as possible, on sites that needed salvaging, rather than on sites safe for the time being. Such groups would also have to be sensitive to the equally important goal of acquiring representative samples of data.

A problem with such regional organization is that it might encourage a "party line" evaluation of research problems within a region. Maintaining variety in problem orientations seems essential for the continuing health and evolution of the field.

Organizers of such regional groups would have to take considerable pains to build in safeguards for variety.

Despite the problems that can be foreseen, such regional approaches seem promising to me, provided they operate within a framework of archaeological resource conservation and management.

## Indefinite Storage of Records and Collections

At some future time, we hope far in the future, archaeological sites, at least of the prehistoric period, will be very rare, and fieldwork almost a thing of the past. All that will be left for the prehistorian will be the reports we publish today and the basic records and collections that remain. Barring world chaos and catastrophe, our published reports are likely to be preserved, at least on microfilm or computer tapes, for an indefinite future, but what about the records and collections? We all know that writing a report requires us to select and abstract from and interpret our data; that is as it should be. But the report is in no sense a substitute for the basic field records and collections if someone with a different perspective, a new set of problems, or new techniques wants to re-examine our data. One of the strengths of archaeology is that even after the site is gone, the archaeologist's records and collections may be studied again with new interpretations and even new observations actually resulting (Jennings 1963b). For example, microscopic examination of the structure of animal bones from Near Eastern archaeological sites is promising to reveal important new information about early domestication; this technique can be applied to bones collected before the technique was known. My earlier argument for representative sampling is based on the point that such sampling will make our records and collections better surrogates for the sites no longer accessible to direct examination and that future new work on these materials will be thereby facilitated and made more reliable.

I submit that we should be even more concerned about the indefinite preservation of our records and collections than about preservation of our published works, however important the latter may be to scholarship. Libraries are, in general, doing a much better job of maintaining collections of books than museums are of maintaining collections of artifacts and site records. Furthermore, published works are likely to grow more and more obsolete through time and receive less and less attention, whereas the basic records and collections are likely to grow more important and be more frequently consulted through time as our supply of actual sites dwindles. Yet in some parts of this country archaeologists are still throwing away large parts of their collections after they have been given an initial study. The assumption seems to be that all possibly relevant current or future information has been extracted by this first study. Even archaeologists who do not share this assumption, which seems to me patently false, are often forced to throw away materials by the fact that their storerooms are full and they have no foreseeable possibilities of getting more storage space. And this is a one-way street. The only direction that the need for storage facilities will go is up.

Part of our archaeological conservation campaign, then, must be to convince our museums and museumlike institutions, and their financial backers, of the importance of storage. The museum's role as a keeper is at least as important to society as its role as a displayer, yet the latter usually receives more support. Storage is especially critical with respect to nonrenewable resources such as archaeological materials.

In addition to doing the educational and political work needed to increase archaeological storage space in our various institutions we can perhaps come up with innovative ways to reduce storage costs. Many archaeological facilities have too few categories of storage; many collections that are very seldom used remain in high-cost, high-accessibility storage because there are no alternatives. Many research collections, including some of great importance, may be used only once a decade or even less frequently. If we project a long life for these collections, they may be used many, many times, but the rate of use per unit of time may remain low. Such collections could better be stored in low-cost, low-accessibility "cold storage" facilities rather than in prime areas adjacent to the laboratories and exhibits.

With regard to the problem of records storage, much good advance work and trial application has been done by the librarians. Excellent systems for miniaturization of records are becoming available.

When the archaeologist is pushed into the position of having to discard portions of large collections, what principles should he use in making selections? Again, I would invoke here the principle of a representative sample over the principle of significance, as determined by current interests. Of course, there is nothing wrong with preserving materials of significance, so long as the total sample is also representative. I think the best paper on this topic is still Cowgill's (1964) on sampling large sherd collections.

## Direct Site Protection Techniques

It may be that archaeologists many generations hence will find their principal field resources in sites long buried as a result of both natural and cultural processes. Perhaps salvage archaeologists can begin more consciously to take advantage of the preservative qualities of certain types of construction to stockpile sites for the future. If, for example, a housing project or highway involves raising rather than lowering the land surface, perhaps we should in some cases content ourselves with intensive surface examination and collecting and minimal excavation, and let what remains be covered over. Such notions may seem heresy to those working within an exploitative model of archaeology, but they seem to me congruent with a conservation model.

## MAINTAINING FLEXIBILITY IN
## SALVAGE-FUNDING INSTITUTIONS

If the field of archaeology continues to evolve methodologically and if salvage continues to be an important consumer of archaeological effort, then some means will have to be found to insure that the expectations of salvage-funding businesses, industries, and government agencies are keyed to the standards of the profession. Too often now, institutions are willing to fund only minimally adequate survey and excavation and make no provision or inadequate provision for analysis and reporting. In many cases the problem is that initial contacts and contracts with a salvage-funding institution have set inadequate precedents on what types of sampling approach, data recovery techniques, analytic routines, reporting format, etc., must be funded. If the future standards of the profession require that the archaeologist put far more money into certain kinds of data recovery or analytic techniques than he had previously been doing, how does he get the salvage-funding entity to go along with this?

The archaeologist may, of course, find sympathetic ears if he merely keeps the institution that pays his costs fully informed about the reasons for his doing what he does, about the significance of his findings to the profession and to the public, and about how his publications are received by his peers. Many archaeologists have found salvage-funding organizations willing to accept increased costs if they were given full justification of the ways in which the quality of the research was thereby increased. In my opinion continuing education of salvage-funding institutions by archaeologists working under them will always be an important part of maintaining flexibility in these institutions, whatever other approaches are used as well. Archaeologists on the staffs of such institutions can also help keep their employers up to date concerning the state of the archaeological profession.

Another approach is through government agencies charged with managing federal land resources, including archaeology. These efforts are backed by numerous provisions of federal law and policy (cf. McGimsey 1972a; Lipe and Lindsay 1974). Agencies such as the United States Forest Service, the Bureau of Land Management, and the National Park Service therefore have substantial leverage already with which to set and maintain standards of performance for resource evaluation, salvage, and site preservation. Such agencies are increasingly employing administrators well versed in the activities of American archaeology. Although the agency contact with the field of archaeology seems good now, the establishment of project review panels of outside research scientists might further improve these communications and might insure that communications gaps or barriers would not develop in the future.

Finally, professional groups, such as the Society of Professional Archaeologists might function to educate and, if necessary, put pressure on salvage-funding institutions unwilling to support an acceptable standard of archaeological work. In fact, there is and probably will continue to be room for all three of the approaches just noted.

## CONDUCT OF ACADEMIC, OR PURE PROBLEM-ORIENTED, RESEARCH

I have already spent a good deal of space arguing that the salvage archaeologist must not only collect data on a broad front for the future use of other researchers but that he must also maintain a strong primary problem orientation. A strong problem orientation is necessary if the archaeologist is to contribute to the intellectual life and continuing evolution of the field. The salvage archaeologist thus differs from the academic, or "pure" problem-oriented, researcher in that he must adapt his problem requirements to the body of sites made available to him by society's decision to destroy them.

Whereas the salvage archaeologist can justify his work both in terms of his problem orientation and in terms of saving a representative sample of information for the future, the academic researcher has only his archaeological problem as justification for his work. It seems to me that from a conservationist view the archaeologist who plans to work with sites not immediately threatened has the responsibility to provide a full and explicit theoretical justification for the proposed work. Furthermore, such justification should also present evidence that the research problem could *not* be adequately investigated as part of a salvage program currently accessible to him.

In other words, I am arguing that all archaeologists need strong problem orientations. A conservationist model would further require that the data needed for these investigations be sought, if possible, from sites threatened with immediate destruction. I am perfectly willing to grant that many problems may require that unthreatened sites be worked with. But I would argue that such sites should not be attacked if ones that need to be salvaged would be adequate for the data requirements of the problem. There will of course be practical problems in bringing together the archaeologist, the problem, and the appropriate sites. Salvage-funding agencies will therefore need to maintain flexibility in awarding contracts in order to help archaeologists achieve the desired "matches."

Although archaeological research is not currently a major consumer of the resource base, we must remember that it nearly always destroys sites or parts of sites. The primary differences, then, between the salvage archaeologist and the academic researcher are that the former works with sites for which destruction is imminent, while the latter does not; that the former is responsible for gathering data beyond his problem needs, while the latter is less constrained to do so; and that the former may excavate as much as his maximal data-gathering strategy, time, and money will allow, while the latter should leave as much of the site or sites as possible for future workers.

Achieving this last objective requires a research and sampling design that makes economical use of the resource. If digging 25 rooms of a 100-room pueblo will provide reliable data for the problems of concern, why dig 50 rooms? Furthermore, maps and records must be explicit enough so that future workers can tell where excavation was done or surface collections made, and these maps and records must be archived so that future workers will have access to this information. Placing nondeteriorating markers in excavations before backfilling will be of help to future archaeologists conducting additional work on the site. The sampling design should attempt to insure that the work does not entirely eliminate some of the varieties of archaeological contexts from a site or region. In other words, all of the houses, or all of the midden, or all of the ceremonial features should not be destroyed by the project if it is possible to avoid doing so. The objective should be to leave as representative a sample of material in the project area as possible.

In conclusion, a conservation model implies that there should be no sharp distinction between salvage archaeologists and academic research archaeologists. To the extent that his research problem can be carried out on sites threatened with imminent destruction, the archaeologist is doing salvage and must accept certain data definitions and sampling responsibilities beyond the immediate needs of his problem. To the extent that his research problem requires work on sites not immediately threatened he is doing pure problem-oriented, or academic, research, and this imposes other types of conservation responsibilities.

## ACKNOWLEDGMENTS

This chapter had its beginnings in comments delivered at the Symposium on Archaeological Conservation, organized by Ray Matheny, at the 1971 meeting of the Society for American Archaeology in Norman, Oklahoma. The first draft of the present version was prepared for the Symposium on Salvaging Salvage Archaeology, organized by Tom King, at the 1972 meeting of the Society for American Archaeology at Miami Beach, Florida. A finished form of the paper was then published in *The Kiva,* 1974, Vol. 39, Nos. 3 and 4. This chapter is essentially a slightly shortened and editorially revised version of the *Kiva* article. I recognize that portions of it now appear dated, but feel that the principles articulated in it are still relevant to contemporary American archaeology.

In preparing this chapter I have been greatly helped by discussions, arguments, and correspondence with Keith Anderson; Hester Davis; Emil W. Haury; Mark Grady; Tom King; Jesse D. Jennings; Alexander J. Lindsay, Jr.; R. G. Matson; C. R. McGimsey III; Douglas Scovill; and Raymond H. Thompson. By listing these persons I am not claiming their endorsement of my views but simply recognizing their stimulus and contribution to the development of my thoughts on these issues.

# 2

# Guidelines for the Preparation of Statements of Environmental Impact on Archaeological Resources

DOUGLAS H. SCOVILL
GARLAND J. GORDON
KEITH M. ANDERSON

The National Environmental Policy Act of 1969 (NEPA) became law on January 1, 1970. By October of that year the first environmental impact statements (EIS) produced under the law were being circulated for review and comment. Analysis of these first attempts to prepare EIS's surfaced the following inadequacies in their approach to dealing with archaeological resources:

1. The use of existing records, such as state or institutional archaeological survey files, as the only data base.

2. The assumption that if archaeological resources were not already known in the area of a project's impact, there was no need to find out if any existed; that the requirements of NEPA could be met by concluding, therefore, that no known archaeological resources would be impacted by the proposed action.

3. The assumption that if archaeological resources were known to be present, the requirements of NEPA could be adequately met by enumerating the known sites that would be destroyed or damaged and by proposing an undefined and professionally unsubstantiated level of salvage as a means of lessening the effects of destruction.

Thus, a fundamental problem with the EIS of the early 1970s was its inadequate level of substantive data about the archaeological resources. Inadequate in the sense that implementation of NEPA assumes that a threshold level of real knowledge about an area is essential to undertake an environmental approach to planning and decision making, which is what the law is meant to accomplish. These earlier environmental assessments and statements implicitly denied the need for real knowledge. At least with regard to archaeological resources, they were prepared with the notion that existing data (regardless of adequacy) were all that were required. This lack of an adequate and real data base, however, precluded any real ability to meaningfully (*1*) describe, synthesize, and assess the characteristics, significance, and research potential of archaeological resources; (*2*) determine which resources would be impacted, to what extent, and with what effect; (*3*) establish the physical boundary of the area of direct and indirect impact as it applied to the archaeological resources; (*4*) develop alternatives to a proposed action that might lessen or eliminate unresolved resource conflicts; and (*5*) design realistic research strategies for the salvage of threatened resources that were relevant to the characteristics of archaeological resources as finite, diminishing comparative data banks.

As a result of these early experiences with the inadequacies of the EIS, the conceptual basis for this guideline was formed. It was first presented by Scovill in May 1971 at the Corps of Engineers sponsored Recreation and Environmental Planning Conference held at Greers Ferry Lake, Arkansas. In April 1971 the Council of Environmental Quality (CEQ), established by NEPA to administer the law, issued general guidelines to implement a federal governmentwide approach to environmental planning and decision making (Council on Environmental Quality, *Preparation of Environmental Impact Statements: Proposed Guidelines,* Code of Federal Regulations, Title 40, Part 1500, published in the *Federal Register,* Vol. 36, pp. 7724–7729, Washington, D.C., April 23, 1971). Taking the concepts expressed in the CEQ's 1971 guideline, Gordon and Scovill collaborated on interpreting its application to archaeological resources. The results came out as a draft in November 1971. The final version, titled the same as this chapter, was revised by Anderson to add substantive professional archaeological content and came out in June 1972. The coauthorship recognizes the synergism that went into the 1972 guideline. This chapter, which is a revision and reorganization of that document by Scovill, owes all of its substantive content and many of its paragraphs to its progenitor.

The current body of environmental- and historical-preservation law seems to establish two major societal goals with regard to archaeological resources: first, to preserve intact for future generations the maximum of the significant archaeological resources; and second—whenever damage or destruction of archaeological resources is the decision in response to other, competing national objectives—to recover, record, and synthesize the data these resources contain prior to their loss. Moreover, it is the intent of NEPA to provide a factually informed basis on which both government officials and the people can evaluate the effects of federal actions that impact the environment and its related archaeological resources (H. P. Green 1972:14).

The next part of this chapter provides a nontechnical discussion of the broad attributes of archaeological resources and what is involved in the study, interpretation, and understanding of them. Following this is an in-depth treatment of the concepts of NEPA as expressed in the current guidelines issued by CEQ (Council on

Environmental Quality. *Preparation of Environmental Impact Statements: Guidelines,* Code of Federal Regulations, Title 40, Chapter V, Part 1500, pp. 754–777, Washington, D.C., July 1, 1976). This section deals in specific terms on how the collection, analysis, and synthesis of substantive archaeological data ought to be handled within the conceptual framework of the NEPA approach to environmental planning and decision making. The chapter concludes with a brief statement about the relationship between the requirements of NEPA and the process of consulation with the Advisory Council on Historic Preservation specified by Section 106 of the National Historic Preservation Act of 1966.

## CHARACTERISTICS OF ARCHAEOLOGICAL RESOURCES

The investigation of the archaeological record of the American continent is the serious and scientific study of humankind over a span of time numbered in the tens of thousands of years. The study seeks knowledge—knowledge to describe, to explain, and to understand the behavior of past peoples and their interactions as integral parts of changing cultural and natural systems. Cultural history, cultural physiography, cultural ecology, and cultural processes are the current emphasis in the anthropological study of the human past through the archaeological record.

Archaeological resources predominantly consist of the physical evidences, or cultural debris, left on the landscape by past societies. They include a wide range of these cultural debris: architectural features; tools of stone, ceramic, or wood; trash dumps; campsites, villages, or towns; the often subtle remains of plants and animals exploited for food; and the interred remains of the people themselves. Of high significance to the investigation, analysis, and interpretation of cultural debris are the local and regional geomorphological sequences, soil composition, and modern biological and botanical baseline indicators. Critically essential to the methodologies, techniques, and processes of studying archaeological resources is the preservation of the undistrubed stratigraphic context of the cultural debris. Directly stated, the cultural debris of this nation's archaeological resources have no value and are of no potential for studying the past once they have been rearranged on the landscape by a bulldozer or a dragline.

Thus, the ideal objective from the perspective of the study of past cultures is to preserve all archaeological resources for measured investigation, over long periods of time, under proper circumstances, and in response to scientifically conceived and professionally executed programs of research. While not an achievable reality, this ideal should be the baseline from which to measure the impact of the inexorable destruction of the archaeological record that is occurring in this nation today. The relevance and importance of using such an ideal as a baseline indicator from which to measure and evaluate impacts should be understood in the light of one overwhelming reality: The only source of knowledge about humans on this continent from the time of the postulated first arrivals (about 30,000 years before the present) until the sixteenth and seventeenth centuries A.D. invasion of the literate "European" hordes, is the archaeological record embodied in this nation's archaeological resources. These cultural debris are a vast, unread, and as yet untranslated library of decipherable data that contain the total knowable sum of knowledge of human activities on this continent from the most ancient times until the most recent past. We have but just begun to "read" and to "decipher" this vast storehouse of knowledge. What we know now is infinitesimal, fragmentary, and inconclusive if evaluated in terms of the potential knowledge that exists undisturbed, unstudied, and as yet undestroyed in the remaining cultural debris of the nation.

For example, the antiquity of humans in the Americas and the tracing of their arrival and dispersal over the face of this continent is poorly known and considerable debate over the issues goes on. Was it 11,000, 20,000, 30,000, or 70,000 years ago? Was it a series of migrations of several populations or a gradual expansion of one population? What were the patterns of environmental exploitation and how, if at all, did they affect the natural systems? Was there a relationship between the human populations and the extinction of the mammoth, the horse, the camel, the sloth, and the bison? The list of significant questions surrounding just this one phase of the archaeological record, questions which can only be resolved through the scientific study of the undisturbed archaeological record, is substantial.

The problems of dealing with archaeological resources can be distinguished from other environmental concerns, such as air and water quality, scenic beauty, natural systems, energy extraction and conservation, or the relative merits of alternative types of created environments by several interrelated characteristics. These center on the relationship of such factors as the intrinsic nature of archaeological resources; the essential requirements of preserving the context of the archaeological record; and the theoretical, methodological, and technical tools we moderns use to conduct archaeological investigations of the past.

Foremost among these attributes is that the archaeological resources are nonrenewable. They cannot be re-created, rejuvenated, reclaimed, restored, or made whole again once the context of the cultural debris is disturbed or destroyed. In many instances the contextual relationships of the cultural debris and their related environmental evidences are both subtle and fragile. They can be easily obliterated by relatively minor modifications of the ground surface. In any event, any disturbance of the archaeological record destroys a portion of the context that is essential to the methodological processes of reconstruction of the past from cultural debris.

Archaeological resources are finite in quantity. To be sure, most resources are finite in the last analysis. The significant reality about cultural debris is that they are measurably and demonstrably finite, nonrenewable, and diminishing as a function of our society's use of this land. The quality of being finite and limited takes on added critical relevance because the location of archaeological resources is patterned, not random, and to a significant degree their location is predictable. The crucial problem of this patterning is that the resources are concentrated on the landscape in the very places where we have undertaken or where we will undertake developments to exploit the land base and its natural resources. It is not coincidence that river valleys, coastal plains, the piedmonts, and desert springs contain high concentrations of significant archaeological resources. The factors of site selection used by past humans have been similar over exceedingly long spans of time and are frequently congruent with the factors we moderns use.

Moreover, our society further intensifies the destruction of the finite archaeological resource base. Human societies that preceded ours, although they frequently occupied archaeological sites of even then ancient and extinct cultures, did not substantially destroy the evidences of the predecessor culture. Rather, they added another layer of occupation to the archaeological record for future generations to decipher. Our society, however, not only prides itself on the rearrangement of the human-created and natural landscapes, it also has the technological capacity, the economic motive, and the sociopolitical mandate to do so. Furthermore, our development techniques do not just slightly disturb the existing archaeological record and then add a new layer to it; we obliterate the cultural debris of the past, leaving only the record of our own civilization on the landscape.

The practice of archaeology also bears heavily on the effects of modern development on the archaeological resources of the nation. Archaeology is a comparative science, based on hypotheses, related methodologies, and highly specialized techniques. The archaeologist collects evidences from the cultural debris of sites, compares them, evaluates them, integrates them with comparable and contrasting data from other locations, and prepares a tentative synthesis; adjusts theory, hypothesis, and method to the tentative conclusions; goes out again to get more evidences and in turn may make more adjustments, both in the hypotheses and in the method and type of data collected; and may go through the whole process again and again until the explanations adequately account for the evidences at hand in terms of existing knowledge, current theory, and defined hypotheses.

Another consideration is that many types of archaeological evidences are very subtle, inconspicuous, and fragile. This frequently requires that the investigation of the nature and potential of the archaeological resources be done by a trained professional with considerable experiential knowledge of the content and relationships among the natural and archaeological environments of a region. Good experiential knowledge of the factors and relationships among cultural physiography, cultural history, cultural ecology, and cultural debris as well as a professional command of the published literature of a region is basic to quality archaeological investigations. The professional capability and experiential expertise of the researcher has a pronounced effect on the quality and validity of the assessment of the significance and potential of cultural debris to answer current questions about the human past and to propose questions that may be asked by future generations.

And finally, theoretical constructions are developing hypotheses that direct our inquiries into the human past along new and productive lines of cultural process, cultural physiography, and cultural ecology. Methodologies and techniques for getting more information, different kinds of information and from different perspectives have increased tremendously over the past few decades. We now have far more sophisticated approaches to the reconstruction of the factors of the daily lives of past peoples, of the environments they confronted, and how they reacted within and adapted to their cultural and environmental milieu. We collect and analyze far more categories of evidences in far greater quantity with far more precision than we did a few years ago in our quest to describe, understand, and explain the meaning and relevance of the past. The conclusion derived from this seems inescapable: The data potential of cultural debris, the archaeological resources of this nation, is far greater now than anyone would have been willing to propose 5 or 10 years ago. The reality is that most archaeological resources can be expected to have locked within them data that are potentially important to an understanding of the prehistory of this nation.

## THE NATIONAL ENVIRONMENTAL POLICY ACT

For decades the archaeological record has been subjected to indiscriminate destruction, which accelerated and intensified in the post–World War II years in concert with the unprecedented expansion of our population and our economy. The passage of NEPA ushered in the era of an environmental approach to planning and decision making as a fact of life in this nation. The requirements of this law will continue to have significant and important relevance to the conservation, preservation, and professional investigation of our archaeological resources. If properly administered by federal agencies and monitored by interested citizen groups, NEPA is a major tool in preventing the indiscriminate and inappropriate destruction of archaeological resources without an adequate level of study and recordation of the data potential they contain.

NEPA expresses a broad federal policy of a national long-range goal "to create and maintain conditions under which man and nature can exist in productive harmony, and fulfill the social, economic, and other requirements of present and future generations of Americans."[1] The act mandates a policy "that all Federal agencies, to the fullest extent possible, direct their policies, plans and programs to protect and enhance [the] environmental quality"[2] of this nation, and it establishes a procedural framework within which federal planning and decision making must operate. The main ideas expressed in NEPA can be paraphrased as follows: Each generation of Americans are trustees of the environment for succeeding generations. In carrying out this trust responsibility, present generations may seek the widest range of beneficial uses of the environment that can be obtained without degrading the quality of the environment or creating unintentioned, undesirable consequences. We should seek to maintain an environment that supports diversity and variety of

[1]From Public Law 91-190, 91st Congress, January 1, 1970, The National Environmental Policy Act of 1969, Section 101 (a).

[2]From Council on Environmental Quality, *Preparation of Environmental Impact Statements: Guidelines*, Code of Federal Regulations, Title 40, Chapter V, Part 1500.1(a), p. 754, Washington, D.C., July 1, 1976.

individual choice wherever possible. And we should save from destruction important historical and cultural resources. To achieve these goals, a "systematic, interdisciplinary approach which will insure the integrated use of the natural and social sciences and the environmental design arts (NEPA, Section 102(1) (A)" should be implemented as an integral part of the federal planning and decision-making process. Finally, environmental amenities and values should be given appropriate consideration in decision making along with technical and economic considerations.

The Council on Environmental Quality (CEQ), which administers the provisions of NEPA, has issued guidelines that specify policies, concepts, and procedures for federal agencies to follow in order to achieve the purposes of the law. These policies and concepts, in conjunction with the precepts just discussed concerning archaeological resources and the requirements of their professional study, form the basis in later sections of this chapter for a NEPA approach to planning and decision making when federal actions will have potential for affecting these kind of resources. First, however, let us briefly review some highlights of the CEQ's current guidelines.

The guidelines provide that federal agencies should "build into their decision making process, beginning at the earliest possible point, an appropriate and careful consideration of the environmental aspects of proposed actions in order that adverse environmental effects may be avoided or minimized (CEQ Guidelines, Part 1500.1(a), p. 754)." In response to this, many federal agencies have adopted a negative declaration/environmental assessment process as a means to achieve the policy objective. This approach is used in order to identify and evaluate the environmental effects of a proposed action, define and evaluate alternative courses of action (if unresolved resource conflicts exist), document the basis on which a decision has been made to prepare or not to prepare an environmental impact statement (EIS), and provide a mechanism for developing real data needed to complete an EIS if one is required. A negative declaration is usually a document such as a memorandum that briefly records the factual basis on which an agency official has concluded that there are no identifiable environmental issues or conflicts of resource use. An environmental assessment is a documented study or series of studies that establish the substantive basis on which an agency official can determine or has determined that an action, while having environmental effects (even adverse effects), does not reach the threshold necessary to require the preparation of the EIS. Such an assessment may contain a description of the relevant environments affected by a proposed action, an analysis of the environmental issues and effects, identification of beneficial and adverse effects, evaluations of alternatives to the proposed action and their effects on the various classes of environmental resources, and definition of proposals to ameliorate any adverse effects or lessen the adverse impacts of conflicts of resource commitments.

An EIS, however, is required only for those actions which are, first, federal; second, major; and third, have a significant effect on the "quality of the human environment." These are the criteria against which the federal agency official makes a determination whether or not an EIS is required. This determination necessitates the exercise of judgment based on an imprecisely defined if not undefined level of real data about the characteristics of resources affected as well as the characteristics of the effects of a particular action on the resources.

The discussion that follows is aimed at providing some guidance for evaluating the sufficiency of data necessary to address the archaeological aspects of environmental issues framed by these questions: What is a major action? What is a significant effect on the quality of the human environment? What is an adequate level of real data to address the issues of impact on archaeological resources properly, evaluate the effects of alternative proposed actions and propose an appropriate scope and intensity of mitigating action, if the project is to proceed at the expense of significant archaeological resources? CEQ's guidelines address these questions in the following broad terms:

> In considering what constitutes a major action significantly affecting the environment, agencies should bear in mind that the effect of many Federal decisions about a project or a complex of projects can be individually limited but cumulatively considerable. This can occur when one or more agencies over a period of years puts into a project individually minor but collectively major resources, when one decision involving a limited amount of money is a precedent for action in much larger cases or represents a decision in principle about future courses of action, or when several government agencies individually make a decision about partial aspects of a major action [CEQ Guidelines, Part 1500.6(a), pp. 756–757].

From this emerges the concept of not only assessing the direct and obvious impacts but also evaluating the cumulative impact of a series of actions—past, on-going, and those contemplated in the future—in order to determine whether an EIS is required and to calculate the real effect of a proposed action. In order to make such an assessment, some specified level of real data about an action—the action's area of potential environmental impact, the archaeological resources contained in the area, the potential of these resources in studying the human past, the action's effects on the resources, and its effects on the environmental and archaeological context of the entire region—will be necessary.

CEQ's guidelines further state that "adverse significant effects include those that degrade the quality of the environment, curtail the range of beneficial uses of the environment, and serve short-term, to the disadvantage of long term environmental goals [CEQ Guidelines, Part 1500.6(b), p. 757]." Such adverse effects may be directly caused by an action or may be secondary, or indirect. Archaeological resources are among those that must be surveyed and impacts evaluated in any assessment of significant effect, and we are therefore confronted with the need for some guidance on the level of real data needed as a basis for determining whether the adverse effects will reach a threshold of scope and intensity that will constitute a significant effect on the environment or raise the issue of unresolved resource conflicts.

A significant point often overlooked is that the process by which the federal agency makes the determination that an EIS will or will not be required, in most cases demands real knowledge based on adequately documented studies. Properly making the evaluations leading to such a decision will necessitate having sufficient real data about the location, characteristics, and potential of the archaeological resources to allow for a calculation of the scope, intensity, and nature of the proposed action's impact on those resources. This level of real data is necessary whether the ultimate decision is to prepare the EIS or to conclude that an EIS is not required. Regardless of whether an EIS is or is not required, if there are resource conflicts, alternative proposals must be identified and evaluated in terms of their impacts on the resources. In many, many instances the EIS threshold may not be achieved with regard to the archaeological resources, but the resource conflict issue will, and consideration of alternative proposals will be mandatory. This alone will require the application of NEPA's environmental concepts and principles in the project planning and the decision-making process of a federal agency if they are to proceed in accordance with the law.

Keeping in mind the objectives of the anthropological approach to the study of the past, the characteristics of archaeological resources, what it takes to investigate them, and the NEPA concepts just discussed, we turn to a discussion of actions that have potential for adverse effects on archaeological resources. Subsequently, we will discuss the collection and evaluation of real data about archaeological resources within the context of NEPA's environmental approach to planning and decision making.

Any action or series of actions that will result in disturbance or physical change in the landscape or that will lead to an increase in the intensity of use of an area will potentially have a significant adverse impact on archaeological resources. Also it is quite probable that the adverse impact will be cumulative and irreversible. Highway building, mineral exploration, mining, timber harvesting, increases in the intensity of use of parks and recreational areas, expansion of military bases, development of housing projects, managment of natural resources using such practices as controlled burns, gully plugging, or root plowing, float trips on rivers, development of ''jeep'' trails, river channel work, and dam construction are but a few examples of the range of actions that will have both a direct and an indirect potential adverse impact on archaeological resources.

A significant adverse impact may exist if (*1*) an action results in the destruction of the archaeological or environmental context of a single resource, such as a site or a complex of closely related sites that have a potential for providing knowledge not likely to be duplicated elsewhere (for example: circumstances such as large site size, concentrated site density, unusual site situation or combinations of components, exceptional preservation of cultural debris, scarcity of type of site, enigmatic characteristics of a site or a complex of sites, etc.); or (*2*) an action results in the disturbance or destruction of the archaeological or environmental context of an aggregate of resources of a repetitive or apparently pedestrian and duplicative nature but representative of a relevant sample or of significant elements of the pattern or data base of such resources.

The scope of an action does not necessarily correspond to the severity of adverse impact on archaeological resources. It is a truism that large-area, land-modifying programs, such as land leveling, strip-mining, reservoir construction, and construction of utility and transportation corridors, have a high probablity of disturbing or destroying significant archaeological resources. Less obvious, though quite real, is the potential destructive effects of small-scale proposals or a series of related small-scale actions such as occur in upper watershed management projects, channelization projects or opening jeep trails, etc. Development of camping facilities and back-country use of parks, forests, and recreation areas are in this class also. These kinds of actions can have cumulative and seriously adverse impacts on poorly known and inadequately understood archaeological resources that frequently are of a fragile character. Other examples include the disturbance of sites with "horizontal" stratigraphy or of deeply stratified, though small, sites that have the potential for contributing significant knowledge not readily replicated elsewhere.

Actions may set into motion a series of continuous or intermittently repetitive but small-scale, land-modifying activities that, taken in total, have a potential of impacting relatively small archaeological sites possessing a limited and partially redundant content. In these instances the effects may become adverse because of their cumulative nature, which will prevent the study and recovery of a representative sample of the cultural pattern in the area of the proposal's potential environmental impact. This kind of destructive process is apparent in any city or growing metropolitan area, such as the San Francisco Bay area, where the shell middens are all but gone, or the Phoenix metropolitan area, where the Hohokam archaeological record is inexorably being destroyed.

Of considerable importance in assessing the impacts of proposed actions is the scope, depth, and quality of the real data about the archaeological resources within the area of potential environmental impact and the level of that knowledge within the physiographic region that is archaeologically relevant. A basic level of real data is essential to understanding the potential of archaeological resources in order to address relevant and current issues of inquiry about the archaeological record. The lack of real data will, under most circumstances, preclude the development of an adequate and professionally valid assessment of the impact of a proposed action on the archaeological resources. For example, it is generally inadequate to inventory the archaeological resources, identify their culture history, and conclude that the impact is the destruction of "$x$" number of archaeological sites of "Y" culture period. Such an approach merely states the obvious: It enumerates and classifies the archaeological resources, but it provides no meaningful and professionally valid assessment of the effects on archaeological resources impacted or destroyed by a federal action.

Two points directly relevant to the NEPA approach to planning and decision making emerge from this discussion. First, if a proposed action will result in the disturbance of archaeological resources to the extent that there will be potentially significant adverse impacts on these resources, then there is probably a conflict of resources use, and alternatives to a proposed action should be identified and the alternative impacts evaluated. Development of alternatives and analysis of their impacts is specifically required by NEPA when resource conflicts exist, regardless of whether or not the threshold level of impact requiring the preparation of the formal EIS is reached. Second, if the cumulative adverse impacts on the archaeological resources are identified, then there should be an expectation that the threshold level of a major action significantly affecting the human environment will have been breached and the full EIS will be required.

Next we turn to the level of real data that is relevant to assess the impact of a proposed action on the archaeological resources in order to use adequately an environmental approach to the planning and decision making within the context of NEPA and CEQ's guidelines. Identification, analysis, and evaluation of the impacts of a proposed action on archaeological resources should be based (*1*) on knowledge about the archaeological resources and their relationship to the physiography of a region, or to an archaeologically relevant portion of such a region and (*2*) on fairly specific knowledge of the archaeological resources and related environmental factors within a specific geographic boundary defined as the area of potential environmental impact of the proposed action. As a minimum, real data about the physiographic province should be sufficiently specific to allow a competent professional archaeologist to:

1.  Define a physiographic area that is archaeologically relevant to the geographic boundaries of the proposed project's identified area of potential direct and indirect environmental impact;
2.  Describe the ecological zones and microenvironments within the defined physiographic area that are relevant as potential past human habitats or resources exploitation areas;
3.  Describe the culture history of the physiographic area and relate it to cultural ecology and settlement patterns in a generalized predictive model.

In many instances the existing level of knowledge will be insufficient to meet the above criteria. In such cases the adequacy of data available should be assessed in terms of their relevance and usefulness to an effective assessment of the impacts of the proposed action, the requirements for additional data should be identified and justified, and a proposal for the acquisition of needed new data should be formulated. The type, depth, and quality of real data needed and the degrees of specific detail required probably cannot be reduced to any kind of precise and definitive guideline or criteria. However, some parameters and specific suggestions can be provided for those who propose, prepare, or review archaeological studies done in support of the environmental approach to planning and decision making. CEQ's guidelines encourage the development of broad program statements as a basis for assessing the environmental issues of a number of related, generic, or sequential actions within a geographic area. Examples include such items as utility corridors, coal, mineral, or oil lease programs, major lengths of highways, timber sales programs, etc. The requirements for specific data for these kinds of broad program assessments are substantially more general in nature than those appropriate to an action or proposed project with a closely definable and delimited area of potential environmental impact. This programmatic approach is workable at a more general level of knowledge predominantly because CEQ's guidelines require that the environmental assessment–EIS process be undertaken for specific actions or projects that "have significant environmental impacts not adequately evaluated in the program statement."

As a minimum, a programmatic environmental assessment or EIS should deal with the archaeological resources impact issues at a level of knowledge adequate to describe broadly the kinds of information just noted for a physiographic province or region, or appropriate subunit thereof. At this level of environmental analysis the concepts of predictive sampling to provide data on cultural history, on human habitat preferences in relation to land forms, and on general preferred prehistoric settlement patterns would appear to be most useful, both as a basis for a broad approach to environmental planning on a multiagency level and on a programmatic basis and as a means to deal more effectively at the project level with the need for data on the physiographic region as a context for assessing adverse impacts. The ideas and approaches touched upon here are still evolving as archaeologists gain more experience in dealing with the practical realities of evaluating the impact of actions on archaeological resources at the broad program level of environmental assessment EIS.

At the specific action or project level, however, guidance on the collection, analysis, and evaluation of real data can be more specific and can be used to evaluate the adequacy of existing data as well as to formulate a program to acquire needed new data. In order to identify and evaluate the impacts of a proposed action, to determine resource conflicts, to analyze the impacts of alternatives to the proposed action, and to put forth a program for mitigation of adverse effects, it will frequently be necessary to undertake archaeological field surveys to locate, identify, and describe the characteristics and evaluate the potential data content of the archaeological resources that will be affected by the action. The degree of specific detail and the scope of data collected for an inventory that will form an adequate basis for an environmental analysis will depend on (*1*) the existing state of knowledge of the archaeological and environmental resources in the area of potential environmental impact, (*2*) the stage the planning of the project is in, in the agency decision-making process, and (*3*) the characteristics of the impacts that a proposed action has on archaeological resources. A preliminary reconnaissance usually will provide the information necessary for general program studies or for an action in its initial planning stage. Often, an intensive field testing survey will be necessary, however, to obtain data for actions at the feasibility or preauthorization stage of planning and for which the preparation of an environmental assessment or the full EIS is anticipated, or for which an alternatives analysis required by NEPA is deeemed appropriate.

The preliminary reconnaissance, which assumes the available existing data are inadequate, should be an inventory that seeks to define the categories of archaeological resources in the area and the nature of the predictable effects of the proposed action, both direct and indirect, on them. While the exact number of resources and their precise relationship to the action's area of potential environmental impact is not necessary, the inventory should be a realistic and reliable basis for evaluating the known and potential archaeological resources and relevant environmental resources that may be affected by the proposal. The inventory may in some cases be made from existing primary scientific or historical records, such as state survey records; significant information may also be obtained through consultation with competent professional and amateur archaeologists with personal knowledge of the archaeological resources of an area. The degree to which this information represents comprehensive coverage of the area, however, should be described. Significant deficiencies in knowledge should be indicated as background for developing further studies required later in the planning and decision-making process or needed to complete the initial environmental assessment. The inventory should include a definition of the area of potential environmental impact, should identify the indigenous historical and prehistoric cultures of the area, and should state their significance. Resources that are listed on, or appear to qualify for listing on, the National Register of Historic Places should be identified, described, and their significance stated. The expected density of archaeological resources should be estimated, and the settlement patterns should be identified to the extent possible for assessing the effects of an action on these resources. For example, if a particular part of the topography of the area of potential environmental impact is known to have been favored by past peoples, the extent to which the action will affect these locations can be used as one element in predicting the scope of the impact. As a practical matter, the preliminary reconnaissance study should develop a reliable estimate of scope, intensity, cost, and time required for a testing survey (discussed in the next paragraph), which may often be necessary to acquire a sufficient level of real data for the completion of the environmental assessment, preparation of an EIS, or evaluation of the impacts of alternative proposals where resource conflicts exist.

When actions move to the feasibility stage or to a proposal for authorization of funds through the legislative process, a detailed identification and evaluation of the impacts of the proposal on the archaeological resources will usually be necessary. Such an analysis should be based on real data acquired at a level that results from an intensive field testing survey. This kind of survey should involve a comprehensive examination of the project area of potential environmental impact, supplemented by test excavations necessary to accomplish adequately the following:

1. Inventory, identify, and describe the archaeological resources that will be affected by the action.
2. Sample all categories of archaeological resources in all environmental contexts that will be affected directly or indirectly by the action.
3. Develop a reliable statement of the significance of the archaeological resources to be affected.
4. Outline a proposal for research needs in the area of potential environmental impact and develop a research strategy, including cost estimates and implementation priorities, for recovering all significant categories of potential data from the resources to be affected.

5.  Define and describe the range and characteristics of the beneficial and ad-
    verse effects of the action on the archaeological resources.
6.  Develop a program of mitigating the adverse effects of an action on the
    affected archaeological resources.
7.  Identify, describe, and state the significance of sites or districts of sites that
    appear to qualify for listing in the National Register of Historic Places; list
    sites and districts already on the Register.
8.  Develop the basis for recommending alternative dispositions of the ar-
    chaeological resources affected by the action, which may include:

    a.  mitigation through archaeological research;
    b.  relocation of part or all of a project to prevent damage to significant
        archaeological resources;
    c.  development of management programs to preserve and protect the re-
        sources;
    d.  justification that no action is necessary concerning archaeological re-
        sources.

9.  Develop a map of the archaeological resources that clearly and accurately
    shows the distribution of these resources throughout the area of potential
    environmental impact, including areas where indirect effects can be ex-
    pected. The map should clearly delineate the project's actual boundary as
    well as the area of potential environmental impact. And those archaeological
    resources (either sites or districts) in the National Register, pending nomina-
    tion to the Register, or appearing to qualify for listing in the Register should
    be included and distinctively keyed on the map.

The basis for all recommendations and conclusions in the report should be clearly
related to the effects of the action on the archaeological resources.

In order to provide a reliable basis for deciding the effects of an action, the
potential significance of the archaeological resources needs to be defined and
evaluated. Simple description of the physical characteristics, cultural type, or cultural history of these resources will not provide a usable measure of effects. Significance should be evaluated in terms of historical, scientific, and social values. The
historical significance of archaeological resources depends on their potential for the
identification and reconstruction of specific cultures, periods, lifeways, and events.
These resources are historically significant if they provide a typical or well-
preserved example of a prehistoric culture, historical tribe, period of time, or
category of human activity. Archaeological remains are also historically significant
if they can be associated with a specific individual event or aspect of history,
including the history of archaeology.

Scientific significance consists in the potential for using archaeological resources
to establish reliable generalizations concerning past societies and cultures and to
derive explanations for the differences and similarities between them. Much of the
same data are used for scientific purposes as are used in historical studies, but the

treatment and scope of information differ. Generalizations and explanations require controlled comparison of statistically representative samples of all categories of data relevant to past human life. This includes such things as artifacts, settlements, dietary remains, and evidences for past environments. Scientific significance depends on the degree to which archaeological resources in the action's area of potential environmental impact constitute a representative sample of data that can be used in comparative studies. The value of these data should be determined in a regional archaeological context and in terms of known and potential future general anthropological problems of inquiry into and understanding of past human cultural history, cultural processes, and cultural ecology. The importance of the archaeological remains and their scientific potential should be assessed by consideration of (*1*) the relative abundance of the resources to be affected; (*2*) the degree to which specific resources and their contextual-environmental situations are confined to the area of potential environmental impact; (*3*) the cultural and environmental relationships of the archaeology of the impact area to the archaeology of the relevant physiographic province; (*4*) the variety of evidence for human activities and their environmental surroundings that is contained in the impact area; (*5*) the range of research topics to which the resources may contribute, and (*6*) specific deficiencies in current knowledge that the study of the impacted resources may correct. Proper evaluation of these factors will require a reliable and accurate knowledge of the content of archaeological resources; extensive knowledge of culture history; cultural ecology, and cultural processes in the impact area as well as in the relevant physiographic province; and competence in current archaeological theory and method by the persons making such evaluations of scientific significance.

Social significance consists in the direct and the indirect ways by which society at large benefits from the study and preservation of archaeological resources. Factors that should be described and evaluated include: (*1*) the acquisition of knowledge concerning the human past; (*2*) indirect benefits to educational and research institutions from increased opportunities to undertake archaeological studies and enhancement of professional training opportunities; (*3*) the acquisition and preservation of objects and structures from the past for public exhibit, enjoyment, and understanding; (*4*) enhancement of economic benefits that may result from tourism attracted by archaeological exhibits; and (*5*) the practical applications of scientific findings acquired in archaeological research.

The effect of the action on archaeological resources should be clearly stated. All categories of effects—direct, indirect, continuous, permanent or periodic, beneficial and adverse—should be calculated from the archaeological resource locations identified in the inventory report. The effects of land modification action or actions that increase the intensity of use are usually adverse in impact except when the action is planned and executed in a manner that will leave the archaeological resources and their context in an undisturbed condition and protected from human erosion. Provision of an archaeological mitigation program will lessen some the adverse impacts, but it does not eliminate them. It is spurious reasoning to claim that archaeological resources realize their scientific value when excavated, and, therefore, salvage excavations in response to a federal action is an unqualified beneficial effect. Limitations of funds and time impose constraints on the degree to which studies in advance of adverse impacts can mitigate adverse effects. In addition, enforced study of the resources resulting from a proposed action precludes research in the future using more developed theories, alternative hypotheses, varying research strategies, new methodologies, and advanced techniques. Therefore a statement that archaeological studies are planned or scheduled should not be used and construed as a valid basis by itself for either a negative declaration of environmental impact or that the threshold level requiring consideration for preparing an EIS has not been reached; nor should such a statement be the basis for concluding there will be no adverse impacts on the archaeological resources. Archaeological resources that are lost to future study as a consequence of the above limitations in the study and salvage of the resources represent unavoidable adverse effects of a proposed action. Also, the loss of archaeological structures, sites, and districts and the features they contain that may have potential value as public exhibits or public parks demonstrating and interpreting the archaeological past represent unavoidable adverse impact and should be documented in the study.

If archaeological resources are to be adversely affected by an action, the effects can be mitigated by the scientific recovery of the information contained in the resources through the use of archaeological methods and techniques based on professionally appropriate research strategies and designs. An acceptable mitigation program should be put forth when adverse effects are identified. Such a program should provide for the recovery and description of representative categories of data and should make optimum use of the threatened archaeological resources to contribute to the understanding of past human occupation of the region. A proposed program of mitigation should be prepared by a professional archaeologist as part of the archaeological inventory derived from the previously described intensive field survey. The program should be designed to recover a reliable sample of all significant data on archaeological and related environmental resources that will be affected if the project is implemented. The proposed mitigation should be based on current theory, methodology, and techniques. The basis of sampling resources to be studied should be stated. This basis should be the result of a systematically prepared and explicitly stated research design, which should be adequate to contribute to the solution of significant archaeological problems for which the resources are suited. The level of sampling required for an adequate mitigation program will vary depending on the number and significance of archaeological resources affected by the action. In some cases, where only one or a few archaeological localities are affected, study of all resources may be required; in most cases only a portion of the resources will be practicable for study. It is recommended that an estimate of the cost of the mitigation program and the estimated time necessary to implement the program be included in the mitigation proposal.

If a proposed action will result in unresolved resources conflict, which will be the usual situation if significant archaeological resources will be disturbed or destroyed as a result of project implementation, then alternatives to the proposed action should be put forth by a federal agency. In such cases each alternative action should be evaluated in terms of the impact on archaeological resources. The primary criterion for judging the relative impacts of the alternative proposed actions should be the extent to which they permit the preservation of significant archaeological resources and their context for future professional study and public enjoyment. If archaeological resources of major scientific importance will be adversely affected by the action, if the cost of an adequate mitigation program will add markedly to the cost of the action, or if there are considerable and extensive cumulative impacts, then relocating part or all of the proposed project should be evaluated. For each alternative proposed action, the alternative treatments of the archaeological resources affected should be described, the impacts calculated and evaluated, mitigation proposals developed, and the cost of a mitigation program computed. The impact on resources, the significance of resources, the mitigation program's cost, and the cost of long-term, archaeological resources conservation management strategy for all proposed project alternatives should be described and evaluated. In addition, the archaeological inventory report should be of sufficient scope and professional quality to provide the substantive bases for recommendations for preservation of resources indirectly impacted by the proposed action or its proposed alternatives. If the recommended alternative action involves major archaeological loss, the basis for choosing that alternative project proposal should be explicitly stated.

The long-term effects of a proposed action on the archaeological resources should be assessed from the perspective of preserving resources for future generations and providing for their measured investigation under future ideal conditions. Archaeological resources are especially subject to cumulative adverse effects over the long run because of their intrinsic nature and the comparative science approach to their study, which requires the future availability of a representative resource base. Long-term usefulness of this resource to our society is maintained only if a significant and representative sample of the total archaeological resource base in a given physiographic province is preserved for future study. Any disturbance of the cultural debris of the archaeological record reduces the sample and its representativeness; the effects of the disturbance are at best a short-term commitment at the expense of the long term and foreclose future options of succeeding generations to study and enjoy archaeological resources.

Since archaeological remains comprise a limited, finite, already diminished, nonrenewable resource base, any action that further reduces this base will be an irreversible and irretrievable commitment of the affected archaeological resources. For a discussion of irreversible and irretreivable commitments of resources see CEQ's *Preparation of Environmental Impact Statements—Guidelines,* Code of Federal Regulations, Title 40, Chapter V, Part 1500.8(a)(7), p. 761, Washington, D.C., July 1, 1976. The destruction of archaeological resources is irreversible and partially irretrievable; the forced study of archaeological resources as a function of a plan of mitigation is irreversible, and it is an irretrievable commitment of the resources to the extent that appropriate data categories are not studied and opportunities for future research using better or more productive approaches are foregone.

Assuming that an adequate study and evaluation of an appropriate data base has completed, a final task remains to translate the detailed professional studies just described into the language and the format of the environmental assessment, the alternative study, or the EIS. The objective should be to produce a document that communicates in precise, nontechnical language to the varied audiences who will be concerned with the environmental impacts of a proposed action: the federal agency decisionmaker, the agency's environmental planning specialist, the state and federal reviewing agencies (including CEQ), the professional archaeologist, and the public. The content of the environmental document should include as a minimum the following, which may be presented in summary, narrative and graphic form:

1. A descriptive inventory of the cultural resources affected by the proposed action.
2. Maps showing the location, density, and distributional pattern of the resources in relation to relevant natural and environmental factors; and delineation of the areas of potential environmental impact.
3. Evaluation of the potential of the historical, scientific, and social significance of the resources, including identification of resources in, pending nomination to, or considered eligible for, inclusion in the National Register of Historic Places.
4. The predictable adverse and beneficial effects of the proposed action on the resources.
5. A recommended program for lessening the direct, indirect, and/or cumulative adverse effects on the resources.
6. Description and evaluation of unavoidable adverse effects.
7. Description of the relative intensity of impact for each alternative of the proposed action if there are unresolved resources conflicts.
8. An evaluation of the relationship between the short-term commitment of the archaeological resources to mitigation and/or destruction versus their conservation for long-term purposes.
9. A statement concerning the commitment of archaeological resources to impacts that are irreversible and/or irretrievable.

Important conclusions, summary data, judgments, and recommendations should be referenced to the appropriate baseline studies or other professional archaeological reports so that reviewers may independently check out and evaluate their adequacy and the validity of the nontechnical presentation of the environmental document.

## THE INTERFACE OF SECTION 106, THE NATIONAL HISTORIC PRESERVATION ACT WITH NEPA AND THE CEQ GUIDELINES

This chapter has dealt with archaeological resources within the context of NEPA and its mandate to use an environmental approach to planning and decision making.

In addition, the requirements of the National Historic Preservation Act of 1966 (NHPA) buttressed by Executive Order 11593, "Protection and Enhancement of the Cultural Environment," significantly interface with the procedures of NEPA and CEQ's implementing guidelines. We conclude this chapter with a brief overview of this interface.

The Advisory Council on Historic Preservation (ACHP), an independent federal agency established under NHPA, is responsible for commenting on federal, federally assisted, or federally licensed undertakings that affect properties (including archaeological resources) listed in or eligible for listing in the National Register of Historic Places. The council's guidelines (Advisory Council on Historic Preservation, *Procedures for the Protection of Historic and Cultural Properties,* Code of Federal Regulations, Title 36, Chapter VIII, Part 800, pp. 377–384, Washington, D.C., July 1, 1976) establish the policies, criteria, and procedures for federal agencies to follow in meeting the requirements for consultation under section 106, NHPA. The guidelines specifically note that federal agency "obligations pursuant to the National Historic Preservation Act and Executive Order 11593 are independent from NEPA and *must be complied with even when an environmental impact statement is not required* (Part 800.2, p. 378; italics mine)." Studies done to comply with NEPA, in most instances, will identify archaeological resources that will come within the purview of the ACHP's Section 106 commenting authority. When this occurs, the council's guidelines recommend that compliance with their procedures should be "undertaken at the earliest stages of the environmental impact statement process to expedite [the Council's] review of the statement (Part 800.2, p. 378)." The overall objective is "to yield a single document which meets all applicable requirements" of NEPA, NHPA, and EO 11593 (Part 800.2, p. 378).

The identification of properties in the National Register of Historic Places, those pending nomination, and those officially determined eligible for nomination can be ascertained by consulting the National Register and its monthly supplements, which are published in the *Federal Register.* There is, however, an important distinction to be understood as to who does what in the identification of eligible properties versus the determination of eligible properties. It is the responsibility of the federal agency official proposing an action, in consultation with the appropriate state historic preservation officer (SHPO), to *identify* properties eligible (or which appear to be eligible) for entry into the National Register and to seek a *determination of eligibility* for all resources that meet or appear to meet the criteria for nomination. It is the responsibility of the secretary of the interior to *determine* whether a property will be placed in the category "eligible for inclusion" in the National Register. Thus, archaeological studies done in support of NEPA requirements should include the identification of archaeological resources that have potential for being eligible for inclusion in the National Register, and these studies should discuss the substantive basis for such a recommendation. The significance of these seemingly pedantic nuances of bureaucratic procedures is this: If archaeological resources within the area of an action's potential environmental impact are in, pending inclusion in, or determined eligible for inclusion in, the National Register and if the proposed action will have an effect (beneficial or adverse) on these resources, then consultation with the ACHP in accordance with the requirements of their guidelines, ''Procedures for the Protection of Historic and Cultural Properties'' is required.

The preceding discussion only spotlights the requirements of historical preservation law, policy, and guidelines. It is noted here because of the need to understand that there is an important interface between environmental- and historical-preservation laws, even though they are distinctive, possess their own sets of guidelines, and each is administered by independent federal agencies. The criteria for nomination to the National Register (see Advisory Council on Historic Preservation, *Procedures for the Protection of Historic and Cultural Properties,* Code of Federal Regulations, Title 36, Chapter VIII, Part 800.10, p. 383–384. Washington, D.C., July 1, 1976) are broad. Based on the thesis of this chapter, which is that archaeological resources can be expected to possess significant data that are potentially important to the study and understanding of the past, most archaeological resources within the area of a proposed action's potential environmental impact will be found to possess sufficient significance to be eligible or potentially eligible for inclusion in the National Register. Nonetheless, if archaeological studies are carried out as described here, then the basis for meeting both environmental- and historical-preservation requirements, including consultation with the Advisory Council on Historic Preservation and the state historic preservation officer, will have been developed as an integral and cost-effective part of the process of an environmental approach to planning and decision making.

# 3

# Peddle or Perish: Archaeological Marketing from Concept to Product Delivery[1]

### DONALD G. MACLEOD

As a philosopher friend of mine commented when the miniskirt began to show a visible profile in the garment industry, "Goods well displayed are goods half sold." If this is true, then Canadian archaeology is long overdue for a shocking new wardrobe. As a discipline, our scientific art has all the dress appeal of Little Orphan Annie. Deep inside, we realize, is an introspective, sensitive adolescent, full of self-doubt and a yearning to find herself. And in between, her legendary existence already whispered in many public places where the deaf ears of the academician occasionally pass by, is a Raquel Welch ready to burst forth at a moment's notice, with or without any help from the timorous, legitimate archaeological community. We all are privately aware of the lusty fullness of her artifact collections, which are roughly fondled by pot hunting profiteers. We cringe in remorse as she lies naked before resource rapists. We read dirty stories about her on the washroom walls of popular misconception, scrawled by clumsy but fervently mystified seekers of fun and truth. Meanwhile, we huddle in a corner and complain to ourselves.

More accurately, we huddle in three corners: academia, government, and public. If we called our country, for the moment, Archaeologia, these would be the three estates of society in that land. Potentially they form a strong, interlocking tiangle (Figure 3.1). Each corner has its own particular strength: If we consider knowledge for its own sake, the academic salient looms largest, followed by government and the public in sequence. If we consider the power to regulate and coordinate, government overshadows academia and the public sector in that order. But, if we seek the plain, old-fashioned satisfaction that comes from the realization of meaning, and

[1]First published in *Canadian Archaeological Association, Collected Papers, Division of Parks, (Ontario) Historical Sites Branch, Research Report* No. 6.

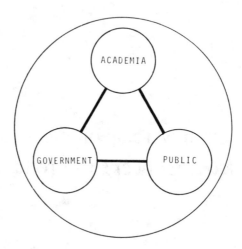

**Figure 3.1.** Triumvirate: The three estates of Archaeologia.

therefore the mandate for an economic base, then we find the public estate wielding the most weight, trailed by government and academia.

Keeping this model in mind as our total community, we confront the two most basic questions about Canadian archaeology in the late twentieth century: (*1*) *Why?* and (*2*) *How?* Why is archaeology worth doing, in a world pressed by many urgent human and resource demands? And, if it *is* worth doing, how do we go about it, how do we get moral and legal support, how do we get money? How do we market our product?

In the world of marketing, two basic scenarios are acted out: Either the salesman presents a prototype to a potential customer, generating a desire for his product by precedent, or else he sounds out the total public by motivational research to identify demands for which he then tailors a product. The methods are complementary. In both cases he has to define his product and all its potential uses—sell it to himself, identify the market, and innovate delivery methods groomed to leap the gap between his offering and his audience. The right parts of his message must be aimed at the right target areas among his buyers. Then he has to keep tight rein on feedback from his product delivery so that his concepts—and therefore his products—stay in style. Peddle the wares, or perish (Figure 3.2).

Today archaeology is in this respect wrestling the same problems as cosmetics, automobiles, or entertainment. We are, in fact, among the leading contenders, as our product is information in an Age of Information. As McLuhan pointed out, AT&T is larger than General Motors. Software has a better future than hardware.

*Why* archaeology? Identify our product and it speaks for itself: Archaeology is knowledge of the human past for its own sake, a source of anthropological data and concepts to apply to contemporary problems, a personal identity in time and space for every individual who is a product of yesterday; archaeology is an environmental awareness in a world beset by environmental crises; it is a detective mystery, an

**Figure 3.2.** Basic sales model: Peddle unperishingly.

artistic adventure, an educational opportunity, a public recreational resource, a focus of thousands of human needs and interests. There's something for everybody, and the entire process for the peculiar few who live it as a career. And, *how* archaeology? We follow through by identifying markets, innovating sales routines, and keeping a close eye on the response. Every estate in the tripartite archaeological community aims at a different market segment but with the same principles.

Government is the youngest and fastest-growing partner in the triumvirate, so let us take our first examples from this arena. To government, things like culture, heritage, resources, and environment are on the same level as Mom and apple pie. Government has responsibilities to people and to resources, often with a "high profile." It needs sound P.R. products. It has dollars. It has power. Major roles affecting archaeology are legislation and its enforcement, land-use planning and management, environmental protection, and the delivery of social and educational programs. Government has a structure that gives official recognition to the functions of planning, development, and management, in that theoretical order, and government has to *look good.* An ideal, integrated program model constructed to sell archaeology to government might take the form illustrated in Figure 3.3. Here we place research in the basal stratum of functions, on the premise that it comes first and lasts longest in the total process. Other functions are phased in, or "come on line" (we must learn the customer's jargon), in sequence, and mutual feedback and audit continue throughout, until an identifiable product is delivered at one or all levels. The jargon is simple. Research encompasses everything from identifying and locating an archaeological resource to completing the most refined scientific and humanistic exercises on the data. Planning means ordering the data in a larger framework: assigning relative values and priorities to the resource in a larger framework in terms of the resource's potential uses. This may vary all the way from total conservation to a concept for interpretative recreational use. Resources have to be rated according to their relative urgency for preservation, intrinsic importance,

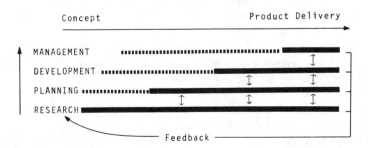

**Figure 3.3.** An integrated program model constructed to sell archaeology to government.

and value in relation to other priorities, such as land development. The development level includes all ways in which a resource in a planning framework might be utilized to create a product. The product could be a simple publication, a media program, a historical reconstruction, a system of parks, or a whole new perceptual mode for an aware public in our contemporary society. Management functions include the actual product delivery as well as conservatorial and administrative activities—law enforcement and maintenance, for instance. It is here, also, that the product-consuming public interacts most frequently with governmental agencies and provides response, which becomes the feedback necessary to keep the program's basic concepts healthy—a further research function. It almost looks like a perpetual motion machine. This sort of model enables a program to audit its own performance in terms of goals and also serves as a sales vehicle when dealing with the decision-making levels of government.

There is great potential within government for meaningful involvement of the archaeologist—potential for the preservation of archaeological sites and for communication with the public—and on a scale much, much greater than has been achieved to date. If we have not realized this potential, perhaps it is because we did not recognize that it was there. But the real, basic problem is that we have been unsure of *how to* realize the potential. *How to* is the important, unsolved problem. When confronted with the ever-changing, many, and complex faces of government, the archaeologist has retreated in confusion and horror to the comfort of his teaching, research, and publication, where, with growing cynicism and frustration, he watches as more and more archaeological resources are destroyed and potential public interest in archaeology remains largely untapped. And all the while, it is within government that programs of land management and resource preservation lie. It is also where widespread recreational programs have contact with members of the public who would seldom, of their own volition, be exposed to archaeology.

An important step in identifying the potential for archaeological programs in government is to think beyond the idea of government support of the study of archaeology for its own sake. Certainly, this intrinsic purpose should be supported by government, but the potential for archaeologists working in or with government is far greater. We must realize that many government departments or ministries have a need, in the implementation of their objectives, to interact with archaeologists. Different groups need the same discipline for different reasons. Each of these ministries has its own planning and management methodologies and processes through which it carries out its objectives.

In order to work effectively with a ministry, the archaeologist must "learn the language." But he is unwise to underestimate the processes involved or merely pay them lip service by using their jargon. Although the processes and methodologies may seem bewildering at first, they were designed to get particular jobs done, and many of them are quite efficient. My own recent experience is in a ministry with recreational, conservational, and land management objectives—all of these serving in some way an urgent archaeological need, and all evoking a stimulating two-way learning experience in dynamic, up-to-the-moment language and paralanguage.

The reason I stress the importance of not merely learning the jargon but also understanding its logic is that the archaeologist is not without allies in government. There are senior administrators and planners who realize that archaeology has a role to play in helping achieve their objectives. Of course, in the past, when a planner has seen an archaeological report, he has had difficulty making sense out of it, and it has been useless for his purposes. This is partially because he knew very little of archaeology, but it is also because the report was in all probability written by one archaeologist for other archaeologists. It is not realistic to expect every senior administrator to become a student of archaeology, although a few do become seduced by the sweet mystery of the art. In the course of his decision-making the senior administrator comes in contact with many disciplines, and he cannot delve into each one of them. Rather, the onus is on the archaeologist to put his information in a form that will be meaningful to the planner or administrator. I should also point out that while the planner sees the worth of having an archaeological component in his program, he is wary of funding for its own sake a program of archaeology that may be only peripherally related to his objectives. Hence the importance of the processes and methodologies.

While the archaeologist is learning, for example, that different levels and types of data are needed for systems planning, master planning, and site planning, the administrator and planner is at the same time tasting the complexities of archaeological research—for example, the high ratio of laboratory time to field time necessary for a successful project. Both planner and archaeologist should learn that it is not a matter of the archaeologist producing a final report on a site and then vanishing from the scene. Rather, the archaeologist must be involved at all levels and stages of the planning and development process, wherever his resource is at stake. A partial measure of the archaeologist's success within government is his ability to work in interdisciplinary contexts with historians, historical architects, biologists, and geomorphologists who are striving to attain similar objectives. While working with and within the methodologies and processes of the government ministry, of course, the archaeologist must insure that his work continues to be of high academic quality. Publication of the results of original research is as essential a component of government archaeology as the egg is to the production of new generations of chickens.

A program is built on its people. We have learned lessons about people who are useful for building a program from scratch. In choosing them, personal vibrations are the most important single factor; in other words, do we subscribe to the same goals and ideals, and can we work together without formal sanctions? Second most important are the practical experiences and down-to-earth capabilities of the people involved. Third, we consider formal paper qualifications. All three are important, but, whereas you can always add to your paper qualifications, you cannot produce a substitute for personal suitability and practical knowhow in the here and now.

This approach leads to a tightly efficient unit operating within the greater government organization. Linked by ideals and professional standards, these people communicate to the greater organization by learning the organization language. Frequent, intense consultation sessions are held. Shared new experience generates effective sales methods. For instance, there is the problem of getting any archaeological ideas whatsoever to the decision-making levels. A busy cabinet minister simply hasn't time for more than 3 pages of quintessential prose, utterly concise and simple. A senior executive or planner wants less than 15 pages that boil down the essence. What, then, of the marvellous 200-page research document that comes out of a research project? Fine, do it. But, for goodness' sake, toss away your academically forged shackles and learn to communicate to the right target! We found a major training problem in orienting academically conditioned people to simple expository communication. By compelling our crew of PhD dropouts and other variously degreed people to use a reporting format that puts the message frontward instead of backward (see Figure 3.4), we have cut across many communication barriers. Recommendations, usually buried at the back of a report by academicians, are displayed prominently at the front. A layman's summary—a difficult job at first for university-trained archaeologists—comes second. This brings us to, perhaps, page 15 out of 200 pages. That is often as far as the decision makers will have time to read. The rest can be published as a technical report or converted to various media for public promulgation. The report can be divided into modular parts (Figure 3.5) to serve specific target functions.

Once we have shown how effectively we can function, we become deluged with requests from land-use planning consultants and from other agencies of government. In response to a request from a housing project we become involved in an economic, long-range plan of environmental inventory to be followed up by sensitive development compatible with resource preservation and eventual educational and community involvement programs. Land Management asks for data on native peoples' resource concerns and we advise them to initiate a program of protection for Indian graveyards in the Far North. Environment requests advice on sensitive areas to be considered in zoning; we give them a set of guidelines on likely site

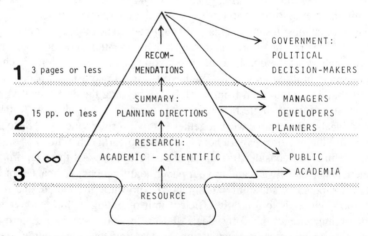

**Figure 3.4.** Where does your projectile point (see Figure 3.5)? Impact-structuring a report to penetrate to the right levels.

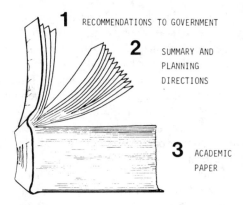

**Figure 3.5.** Cross-section of a report (see Figure 3.4).

areas. The Ontario-wide lakeshore inventory, with a large budget and computerized data system, requests cross-indexable data on cultural values; we write them a field manual for their staff to identify archaeological resources. Education consults with us on input into primary and secondary school programs in environmental awareness, an obvious vehicle for archaeological propaganda. We tell them that if we accomplish nothing other than inculcating the coming generations with an awareness of heritage and concern for the stewardship of the nonrenewable resources in which heritage reposes, then we will have accomplished much. They agree.

In summation, how do we sell archaeology to government? Learn the methodologies and processes of the ministries. Recognize your allies in the executive suites. Learn their language and use it meaningfully, not just as window dressing. Both government and archaeologists have problems to solve—very often the same problems. By coming up with practical solutions at the right time we strengthen the relationship between government and the rest of the archaeological community. A spirit of honest inquiry and "open-line" communication is essential. The benefits are well worth the effort. Hundreds of sites are identified and protected for potential future research. Much pure research is accomplished and published. Coordination of efforts across one province and across Canada is possible through interministerial programs centered on environmental concern. Through exercise of land management responsibilities salvage projects can be carried out, but—more important—the necessity for salvage can be obviated by proper land-use planning. Perhaps most important of all, government offers access to public awareness and reaction on the broadest possible basis.

Compared to the complexities of dealing with government, archaeologists find their relationship to public demands startlingly uncomplicated at first glance. It is very much like standing too close to the nozzle of a huge vacuum cleaner: Rather than learning aggressively forward to infiltrate governmental armour, one has to lean back a bit to avoid being sluiced away by public ardor. The public market for archaeological products in Canada today is so starved for affection that it is almost indecently easy to score points in any sort of casual courtship. The thrust for public archaeological knowledge in Canada in 1975 is stronger than the market for glass beads, muskets, and trade axes at Moose Factory in 1670.

For instance, just before Christmas, 1974, I somehow ended up giving an introductory lecture on archaeology to a local rod and gun club in the metropolitan Toronto area. Having virtually no preparation time, I faced about fifty strange characters in bush jackets and hiking boots, with no interpretive apparatus other than a blackboard and a piece of chalk. Expecting to induce acute group narcolepsy, I was pleasantly amazed by the latter-day hunters and gatherers' immediate, sharp response to my sermon about resource conservation, environmental awareness, and culture history applied to present-day social-environmental problems. They knew all about artifacts and sites, landscapes and ecology. What they sought was a time dimension and humanistic framework for these great mysteries they had all sampled. For over 2 hours they fired questions at me. Several members came forth with data on new site locations. They wanted to follow up the introductory "lecture" with a studio-recorded dialogue session for educational TV. Chatting with a few rod-and-gunners afterward, I noticed on the shoulder of their bush jackets a blue patch with white lettering that read, "I give my pledge as a Canadian to save and faithfully defend from waste, the natural resources of my Country, its soil and its minerals, its waters, forests and wildlife." [2] Aha, I said to myself, potential archaeological wardens, disciples to carry the message across the landscape. Many of these people are financially independent, influential citizens with vast networks of personal contacts across Ontario as well as affiliations with hunters and anglers' and conservation organizations.

This sort of public contact is getting to be the rule. Our archaeological staff, spread thinly across Ontario in regional outposts, are finding that a rapidly increasing chunk of their time is being diverted from what little personal life they have left, to filling the need for this type of personal contact. The immense chain of grass roots communication thus generated is invaluable for resource inventory, conservation, and public education. Virtually all inhabitants of this country have some sort of interest in objects, lore, and ideas from and about the past. But what an immense job to channel this huge people resource toward responsible goals! The fact is that the only chance for a rosy future for Canadian archaeology lives in an aware, concerned, and responsible public. Without their support we might as well crawl back to the ivory tower and write the obituary of our discipline.

The resources are there and the time is now. Never a day goes by but we get a plea from a community college for a special lecture on archaeology; or, a proposition from a conservation authority to provide guidelines, standards, and expertise for an outdoor education project; or, a proposal from a local school board for the same guidance to deliver an archaeological program to primary and secondary schools as part of the environmental studies curriculum; or, a request from a local historical or naturalist organization for a popular publication on the principles of archaeology; or, a phone call from a concerned citizen who has noted with dismay

---

[2] The conservation pledge of the Ontario Federation of Anglers and Hunters.

the activities of pothunters or bulldozers on a site; or, an idea from a TV producer for a half-hour talk show about the sheer adventure of archaeology; or, . . . you name it. Of course, on the same day we will read a newspaper clipping about some country school "doing a dig" without any reference to scientific standards, or we see potsherds for sale in a downtown curio store—"small, 50 cents, large, $1, guaranteed 400 years old."

We have a tremendous duty to grasp this potential and guide it in the right directions. Great caution must be exercised in emphasizing standards and limiting the destructive overenthusiasm that stalks the land. Even sophisticated educators are surprised to learn that about 75% of archaeology is done indoors—with the mind, the emotions, the eyes, and the hands—while digging is only a small part of the total process. But most respond to the idea of responsibility. Most agree that pilot projects have to be carried out with careful controls before big programs can succeed. Most subscribe to the principle that extensive study and interpretation must be done on public demand and response for and to archaeological products.

Make no mistake about it: Their goal, and our goal, is public education. Having admitted this to ourselves as members of the three estates of Archaeologia, we must then insure that the best academic standards are applied to all educational endeavors. We must put the inculcation of public awareness and responsibility first and the digging up of artifacts last. Already the potential of media communication, recreational programs, popular publication, educational programs, museum expansion, and the interplay between public and government have been tested and proved positive. Making best use of the talents of all three estates of Archaeologia— academic knowledge, government coordination, and public quest for meaning—we can orchestrate a total community program with satisfying returns. Satisfaction can come from a realization of purpose and the security of funding generated by public demand (Figure 3.6).

What of the ivory tower to which such disparaging reference has been made? I leave academia to the last for comment because theirs is a very special responsibility. They can be an ivory tower of strength—not an igloo of isolation. As leading members of the national community at large, academicians have a special duty to influence constructively the concepts and activities of government and public. Quite apart from all the ideal tenets of universal scholarship that transcend political boundaries, highly paid and securely ensconced professionals must realize that responsibility, which accrues to the privileged, to the national community of which they are a part. This involves an appreciation of the legal and political traditions and practices of the country, as well as a duty to innovate. Knowledge is power; and power, responsibility. Enough said.

And, what of the sales pitch to academia? This is it! If the marketing exhortations expressed here receive academic applause, we are getting somewhere. Otherwise, back we go to square 1.

Anthropological research could provide the best basis possible for marketing ideas to government and to the public, if enough updated data are developed into an integrated plan of approach. Otherwise, government is liable to regard academia

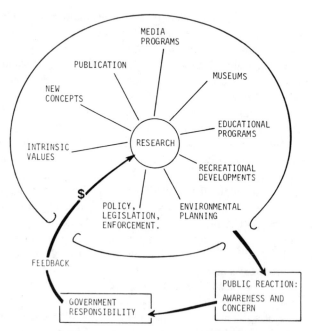

**Figure 3.6.** Satisfaction and $ati$fa°tion. A model of community fulfillment and economic security—"Live better archaeologically."

with the same degree of respect that the Israeli Air Force has for the Arab countries. Furthermore, nothing impresses the public less than squabbling. Again, a plea for a total community program concept for Archaeologia: We, the three estates, can burst forth in an orgasm of mutual support and purposeful activity if we gather and concentrate the tension among us and convert it to a release of energy leading to satisfaction all 'round.

As Pogo said to Walt Kelly, "We have met the Enemy and he is US." We are all in the same boat. Government regulation depends on the exercise of community responsibility by academia through special knowledge. Academia depends on government for funds and resource conservation. Both depend on the public for the mandate and rationale for their existence. Let's pull the oars together and in the same direction.

# 4

# An Ethnologist's Perspective on Cultural Resource Management

DAVID E. STUART

This volume provides an important opportunity for some of us who have been involved, to discuss a variety of practical and theoretical issues that have arisen in contract archaeology as a consequence of the current expansion in cultural resource management. Recently Schiffer (1975b:1–7) has outlined several of these developmental problems in a discussion entitled, "What's Wrong with Contract Archaeology." His concerns focus primarily on a paucity of research results, unrealistic contract specifications, poor information flow, and inflexible organizational structures. I am certain Schiffer's admonitions that we improve in these areas while fulfilling contracts will be met with positive response from archaeological contracting institutions, for I believe that the majority of contract archaeologists are now aware of, and keen to correct, many such problems. The more important concern here is that contract researchers may fail to see these problems as deeply interconnected and, as a consequence, may seek separate solutions for each. As an ethnologist, I contend that these four problems (among others) are but symptoms of a more pervasive one: the curious situation that contract archaeology is often practiced without de facto concern for the purview of general anthropological theory or ethnographic method.

First, let us consider *praecognita*. Many archaeologists have argued on their own behalf that the most productive milieu for their discipline is one in which there is substantial theoretical interplay with broader issues in general anthropology, such as cultural evolution, adaptation, ecology, etc. Most would guess it probable that, as a result of this interface, the school of cultural materialism is more strongly represented today in archaeology than in any other subdiscipline of anthropology. Recall that in 1948 Walter Taylor's conjunctive approach clearly called for a general anthropological perspective in pursuing archaeological research (1967:151, 191), and Binford's (1962) now classic "Archaeology as Anthropology" set forth an even more explicit statement supporting that perspective. Clearly, though their arguments

73

were directed primarily to archaeologists, they were convincing to a wider audience, for there are also ethnologists who have accepted this strategy as valuable. Suffice it to point out that in the course of the last decade many archaeologists and a few ethnologists have actively and productively involved themselves in the notion that archaeology is anthropology (Binford 1968a, 1968b; J. D. Clark 1968; Dozier 1970; Freeman 1968; J. N. Hill 1970b; Longacre 1970b; Renfrew 1969, 1973; Webb 1974).

Enough of precedent. Let us consider a more immediate question: How does an institution that practices contract archaeology realize a practical benefit by focusing on a broader anthropological perspective than is now common? Of interest to those who must have some familiarity with the law, since it provides the basis for their contracts, is McGimsey's (1972a) reminder that both the National Historic Preservation Act of 1966 and the National Environmental Policy Act of 1969 (NEPA) explicitly refer to the preservation of *cultural* heritage (pp. 112, 118; italics mine). Quoting from the former, we see that "the historical and *cultural* foundations of the Nation should be preserved [p. 241; italics mine]," while the purview of NEPA includes the charge that we "preserve important historical, *cultural* and natural aspects of our National heritage [pp. 252–253; italics mine]." There is no doubt that the law intends a broader base of expertise than archaeology to be focused on contemporary cultural resource managment. In modest ways a broader expertise than we ordinarily suppose is brought to bear on cultural resource studies—for example, historians, architects, preservation specialists, sociologists, and, very occasionally, an ethnologist. The curiosity is that the cultural resource (and EIS) studies that have utilized these various kinds of expertise have also generally been conceived and commissioned as if these investigations were somehow unrelated. We are thus left with research projects that are models of insularity, patchworks woven together with the thread of convention rather than of method. I suggest that the comparative and diachronic method of anthropology is *the* only logical solution to our current problems in dealing with cultural phenomena for management purposes.

In addition, the standards and expectations of federal agency reviewers with regard to research methods are becoming more sophisticated. We should not be surprised to find that legal decisions and agency guidelines will as a consequence increasingly amplify the reviewers' interpretation of existing legislation. In this instance, flexible institutions with a well-developed method and the broadest base of expertise will enjoy distinct advantages in pursuing both research objectives and contracts.

We would also be wise to consider the likelihood that the zenith of the mammoth archaeological survey is nearly upon us. If so, what will the future bring? Foreseeably, it will bring more intense pressure from large energy-extraction interests both to litigate and to focus political pressure on the current archaeological handicap. I use the term *handicap* because, at the moment, the land-use contractor who can reduce project time or cost while increasing planning efficiency gains a competitive edge, and archaeology often confounds these efforts. True, one of contract archaeology's major goals is to provide "planning" information to contractors. In reality, though, we often provide information that helps contractors "plan" how best to avoid doing (digging/mitigating) more archaeology. We've all been down this path:

*If we have to "buy" one of these sites to proceed with our project, which one is the cheapest?*
*Well, if it were up to me, I'd go through this one here 'cause that 500-room one to the left is a real hummer.*
*Does that mean this one here is also less* **significant***?*
*Uh, well, uh!*

As I said, litigation and politicking—on both sides.

In the final analysis, legislative safeguards and concerned archaeologists or not, an archaeological site simply cannot vote or retain counsel; living populations potentially impacted by land-use projects can do both. Here, I believe, is one key to the future in cultural resource management. This is most apparent in the West, where land-use projects are often planned on acreage belonging to American Indian populations. In such situations those with the vision to plan on a broad anthropological perspective can shape the future. Here, the extensive archaeological survey can become an extensive "anthropological survey" in which research into prehistoric, historical, and contemporary populations on project lands is developed and proposed as one integrated package. The archaeologist, the ethnohistorian, and the ethnologist are mutually involved. The focus shifts from a singular one on the "archaeological record" and "archaeological heritage" to include "cultural process" and "cultural heritage." No one loses. Archaeological data and impacts are analyzed, but in a broader perspective that also requires attention to data and the analysis of impacts on the contemporary population. Lipe's (1974) goals for conservation archaeology can be pursued; the contemporary population can be provided with information concerning a project's expected consequences on their own cultural and economic lives. Their body politic and their vote become more informed, and the contractor has data on the consequences of his project not only for archaeology but for the contemporary population as well. In contract archaeology we have unwisely tended to overlook this last need, permitting this responsibility to rest elsewhere.

From a day-to-day perspective a well-connected ethnologist can help gain valuable permission for access to project lands, can work through informants to explain the nature of the research project, and can gather information of great value to both local population and contractor. The cultural resource management institution gains by enjoying larger projects with more attractive research payoffs. The contractor also benefits by getting one contract for expanded services, which reduces administrative costs all around and consolidates responsibility for meeting contract goals. The public at large is benefited with far more useful information and a valuably informed local or regional vote to encourage the mandates of its existing legislation.

I believe that the type of project just outlined would be well received by state historic preservation officers and federal agency representatives; let us not forget that they are currently taking the pressure from *all* sides. Recently, one state historic preservation officer in a western state ruled that a number of abandoned habitation sites dating to the 1920s and 1930s did not have to be excavated, since their informational potential could be fulfilled through ethnological and ethnohistorical methods. There is wisdom and flexibility in this decision; the unfortunate aspect resides in the fact that there were no well-developed institutional structures to implement the goal. Schiffer (1975b:2–3) is close to the mark when he suggests that provisions for such eventualities be planned in advance and incorporated into flexible institutional goals.

One must also stand back from contracts, deadlines, and legislation to consider methodological and theoretical aspects of the anthropological survey. As I view it, the everyday management goal of environmental resource studies is to identify and analyze the physiographic, biological, and cultural attributes and complex interactions between them that pertain to a given piece of real estate. This is done so that we may make educated guesses as to the changes that a proposed economic-extractive activity might generate in these attributes and ecological interactions. In terms of the anthropological survey, this invites the use (in the broadest sense) of an ecological-economic-materialist method.

One goal for the anthropologist, then, is to identify in a project area the parameters of human–land relationships that have operated throughout its history of human utilization. This focus on the effects of variables that have dominated human exploitative behavior during succeeding cultural periods permits the identification of a general evolutionary trajectory for such patterns of land use. This trajectory, then, becomes an integral part of developing the "educated guess" as to what will happen to contemporary populations as a consequence of further (proposed) changes in land use. This type of project must not be a patchwork; it must be conceptually unified and truly interdisciplinary. The geologist, hydrologist, paleontologist, zoologist, botanist, and general ecologist set the stage for the anthropological survey with their methods and data. The archaeologist picks up the thread, documenting general patterns of human exploitation and evaluating probable project impacts on archaeological resources. The ethnohistorian focuses even more acutely on social and economic patterns, lending more precision to the identification of developing exploitative patterns. The ethnologist and economic anthropologist focus on the fundamental economic, social, and ideological attributes of the contemporary population and evaluate the probable changes that a given project will induce. The results of this broad research strategy can then be passed on to federal agencies in a form and tone that makes sense to the economists, sociologists (social science program analysts), urban planners, and land managers called in to review and evaluate results and lend their recommendations to the decision-making process. Referring to earlier comments, I also suggest that this anthropological survey approach would in some way lessen the severity of each problem Schiffer has already identified: paucity of research results, unrealistic contract specifications, poor information flow, and inflexible organizational structures.

On the other hand, for the archaeologists who begin to explore implementing and coordinating the type of project I have just suggested, there will still be day-to-day irritations and methodological knots. One that will undoubtedly provide interest value will be encountered when ethnologists are incorporated into archaeological research. I refer specifically to the use of ethnographic analogy. Archaeologists are often quite sensitive about this, and, indeed, the use of such analogy does require considerable care, as Binford (1968b), Freeman (1968), and Webb (1974) have cautioned. However, in spite of potential problems they go on to argue strongly that careful analogy be used. I agree. I also contend that the greatest potential abusers in contract work are not ethnologists, but archaeologists, particularly younger field types still in training. I myself have heard an archaeologist (who cautioned me in the use of ethnographic analogy) announce, while reviewing field notes, that upon finding several discrete food-processing areas he knew he was dealing with mat- rilineal clans. Amazing! This sort of elán is particularly so when one considers the sobering example that in Australia, the last so-called stronghold of the patrilineal band, *no one has ever published a geneology of a patrilineal band occurring in the bush* (Peterson 1970). Such social organizational features are often not so easily documented, even with the advantages of questionnaires and a living population. In short, no worthy anthropologist would ever use analogy as described above; if you've hired one who does (it matters not whether he is an ethnologist or an archaeologist), correct him on the spot!

Let us take another more subtle, and more important, example. In the substantial monograph reporting the large Coal Gasification Project archaeological survey, mentioned elsewhere in this volume (Chapter 25), Reher and Witter (n.d.) de- veloped the hypothesis that the placement of Archaic sites in the study area is a function of vegetative diversity. Their explanation focused on the assumptions that Archaic populations were broad-spectrum hunter-gatheres and generally camped where they had immediate access to both highly diverse and extensive vegetational food resources. The data they bring to bear on their argument are substantial, and subsequent research (Allan, *et al.* 1975) during an adjacent survey did *not* discon- firm the association between site placement and vegetational characteristics. How- ever, a review of literature on ethnographically known arid-lands hunters–gatherers in the American Southwest, Australia, and Africa would have turned up evidence suggesting that such recurring seasonal occupations often create around campsites a wide zone devoid of vegetation. In addition, the literature would also have suggested the availability of water at certain seasons to be a more important factor in site placement. One is thus left with less confidence in the explanation than in the association (site placement and vegetative diversity), which is real and pleasingly documented. The question here is not whether or not the initial work was poorly conceived (which it wasn't), but whether or not every possible clue to explanatory success was pursued. I argue that a broader anthropological perspective could have provided more clues from the outset.

In fact the Coal Gasification survey (Broilo and Reher, Chapter 25) might well have provided a model for the anthropological survey I have proposed. During this survey in excess of 700 archaeological components were recorded. More than 400 of these were Navajo, the majority dating to this century. While Broilo and Reher clearly recognized the potential research value of ethnohistorical and ethnological expertise, their full realization did not come until the project was underway, thus binding them to specific contract obligations. Had they had available a negotiated contract that assumed a priori the necessity for ethnographic and ethnohistorical work with professional and agency guidelines to back them up, a rare opportunity to make even more substantial gains in archaeological and anthropological method might have been achieved. Since the focus of their research was on patterns of settlement and subsistence, an ethnologist–ethnohistorian could have sought out more informants to provide such data with regard to specific abandoned hogan outfits. Think of it! While the archaeologist recorded surficial archaeological data and developed assumptions about population size, subsistence base, and social organizational features, the ethnologist–ethnohistorian could have developed (for many outfits) specific data on population size, family composition, and economic behavior. The archaeologist would then have enjoyed a very solid methodological basis upon which to refine hypotheses about the facts of deposition, and he could also have been able to monitor specific changes in family composition and economics to see how they influenced the archaeological record. This is not quite Gould's "living archaeology" (1968) and not quite his "archeologist as ethnographer" (1971). It is not even ethnographer as archaeologist. It lies somewhere in between. What the hell, let's just call it anthropology. As an ethnologist, I can live with that.

# Part II

# CONSERVATION ARCHAEOLOGY AND RESEARCH ORIENTATIONS

Few investigators need to be convinced of the desirability of carrying out innovative research on contract projects. The problem lies in constructing arguments to demonstrate that the performance of such research is necessary, even to fulfill management information needs, and that it is possible to design projects, including small ones, so that they do yield research dividends. The chapters in Part II and, to varying degrees, the remainder of this volume address the latter two questions.

## THE NEED FOR RESEARCH ORIENTATIONS

An objection often raised against research-oriented conservation archaeology has to do with the investigator's primary responsibility to management interests. That is, if one is under contract to furnish management information to a sponsor, how can the conduct of problem-oriented research be justified? This question, we believe, is based on a naive interpretation of management information needs and the means by which they can be met most efficiently: It is tacitly assumed that the provision of management information requires only the lowest level of archaeological expertise. A corollary of this assumption is that cultural resource management studies may be undertaken by a corps of technical specialists lacking research credentials or commitment to scientific archaeology. This conception, although widespread, is false. In fact, a strong case can be made that the archaeological information that a sponsor must have in order to prepare an environmental impact statement (EIS) is quite formidable, and often it is beyond the capabilities of our most sophisticated method and theory to supply (F. T. Plog 1975). For example, take simply a description of the nature and extent of the resource base. To furnish this information for an overview requires a diligent search and synthesis of extant site records and literature, gaps in which might be filled in with predictive models using ecological, geological, and other archaeological variables. When the same information is needed for a preliminary field study, one is frequently implementing a previously untried sampling program using advanced techniques of statistical inference. Similarly, the forecasting of impacts in field studies may call for the researcher to initiate creative experimental and ethnoarchaeological investigations. All of these research tasks place heavy demands on our expertise and cannot be accomplished by rote application of our simplest techniques.

Moreover, that assessments of significance must be made, especially during intensive field studies, unequivocally establishes by itself the necessity of carrying out innovative research. Arguments supporting this position are developed at length by Schiffer (1975b), Schiffer and House (1977), and by several authors in Part VI. These arguments boil down to the recognition that scientific significance, defined as research potential of several kinds, is a relative quality of the resource base that is not determinable without diligent, problem-oriented research. Although the performance of such research does not insure that all important areas of significance will be identified, one can hardly expect research potential to be revealed by any other means. Needless to say, the consequences of making mitigation recommendations on the basis of faulty assessments of significance can be dire.

In short, the information that the sponsor must obtain in order to make management decisions depends on a very high level of archaeological expertise applied to problem-oriented research. Unless the fulfillment of contract requirements is approached from a research perspective, one runs the serious risk of failing to meet the sponsor's needs. An EIS based on poorly done archaeology can delay a project in court and, at the very least, lead to the loss of good will between the sponsor and archaeologist. Not only may this harm the archaeologist involved, but it reflects badly on the entire field.

Several other convincing arguments can be presented to justify the pursuit of research goals in contract projects. The first of these relates to the exploitative nature of archaeological activity. In order to gain information on the nature, extent, and significance of the resource base it is almost always necessary to remove materials from archaeological context (that is, by surface collecting and testing—see introduction to Part IV). According to the ethical precepts of modern archaeology (Society for American Archaeology 1961; Society of Professional Archaeologists 1976), such exploitative activity can only be undertaken with a research justification. That is, from the standpoint of science the value inherent in archaeological resources lies in their relationship to research questions. Therefore, one cannot justify the exploitation of the archaeological record unless some of that value is realized.

A final argument in support of explicitly research-oriented conservation archaeology concerns the broad areas of public responsibility and the spirit of the legislation relating to archaeological resources. It seems to us that the purpose of spending public money on archaeology (and ultimately it is all public money) is to conserve scarce resources and allow the public to benefit from their justifiable exploitation (see also Miller 1974:152; R. H. Thompson 1974:15–17). If public money is to be considered wisely spent, then our efforts should lead to better management of cultural resources and to greater knowledge about them, the past, and ways to study the past. In the long run, the continued funding of cultural resource management studies and even the position of archaeology as a discipline in the larger society are likely to depend on our ability to obtain research results for every project and to communicate our findings to the public. One suspects that a more convincing argument can be made in support of conservation archaeology when, in addition to preserved sites, we can point to tangible contributions to knowledge.


## ALLEGED HANDICAPS TO RESEARCH IN
## CULTURAL RESOURCE MANAGEMENT STUDIES

If, as we have shown, conservation law, archaeological ethics, and our responsibility to the public mandate that research results be obtained for every dollar spent, then one is entitled to ask if any practical problems hinder this pursuit. Indeed, at least one archaeologist (Reaves 1976:17) has listed several problems in cultural resource management investigations. Not only can the irrelevance of these allegations be easily shown, but we can go on to list the unique advantages that are held by conservation archaeology research. One of the undeniable constraints on contract research is the arbitrary boundary (with respect to archaeological criteria) of the study area. Although this condition does force the archaeologist to seek the research problems that best match the resources instead of vice versa, it should have no effect whatsoever on the actual ability to do high-quality research. One suspects that the proponents of the hypothetico-deductive method in archaeology have made their point that relevant data follow from problem orientation all too well; this has tended to obscure the roles played by tradition, serendipity, climate, and financial resources in the choice of research areas (that only somewhat later come to be justified explicitly by research needs).

Closely related to the arbitrariness problem is the fact that actual sampling designs are a consequence of contract, rather than research, needs. Although there is a grain of truth in this observation, there is also a gram of falsehood. This is so because it is archaeologists who must determine the appropriate sampling design—given sponsor information needs, the nature of the area, and archaeological expertise. A sound survey design compromises many, sometimes conflicting information needs and is always in accord with research needs, taking the latter in the broadest sense (see Schiffer and House, Chapter 14).

Constraints on funding and time are also said to hinder achievement of scientific goals. The financial argument is ludicrous, given the chronic underfunding of academic archaeological research. If anything, contract operations are the only American archaeology undertakings now being supported at anywhere near a reasonable level. Even projects funded generously by traditional sources of grant support, such as the National Science Foundation, usually operate on a shoestring and depend heavily on local institutional contributions and free labor. Admittedly the time constraints on many projects are sometimes debilitating (see Canouts, Chapter 8). But one can expect that as cultural resource management studies move out of the catch-up stage under the National Environmental Policy Act (NEPA), this problem will resolve itself satisfactorily. Certainly, there are already sufficient examples of cultural resource management projects operating on a realistic time frame to indicate that we are in a transition period—and that bodes well for the future.

## SOME ADVANTAGES OF CULTURAL RESOURCE MANAGEMENT RESEARCH

In another sense, of course, the fact that contract projects do have definite deadlines for completion of work and submission of reports can be considered as a substantial positive benefit. Most archaeologists can think of grant-supported projects in their own areas, undertaken more than a decade ago, that still are unreported. In the academic setting, as in the rest of our social system, people perform well (and, often, only) under pressure. That such pressures do exist in cultural resource management studies insures that projects undertaken will be brought to a successful conclusion.

Another clear-cut benefit of cultural resource management studies is the ability to pursue multistage research in an area (Goodyear 1975a). The necessary correspondence between levels of management planning and archaeological activities provides a basic framework for carrying out enlightened multistage research. In many cases, we will be assured for the first time that our explanations and predictions can be tested. We thus have unprecedented opportunities to test general archaeological and anthropological models of site location, sampling and site location techniques, etc.

Cultural resource management projects also make it possible to conduct multidisciplinary investigations. This is so because compliance with NEPA often requires the sponsor to carry out ecological, hydrological, geological, and paleontological surveys. The archaeologist sometimes can make good use of these data, especially if he is interacting with the other specialists at the time the data are gathered. Also, as archaeologists begin rubbing elbows with specialists from other disciplines, as inevitably happens when the archaeologist is employed by a government agency such as the Bureau of Land Management or the Forest Service, they will begin to capitalize on the many opportunities to obtain useful information and plug into advanced technologies.

To this point we have assembled some arguments that suggest the necessity of performing innovative, problem-oriented research on contract projects. We have even argued that cultural resource management studies offer some unique advantages when it comes to multistage, multidisciplinary investigations (Gumerman 1970; Gumerman, Westfall, and Weed 1972). Even so, the reader must suspect that beneath this rosy exterior there must lurk a bed of thorns. Although we tend to emphasize the significant potential for scientific research in conservation archaeology, if only to balance the prevailing academic view to the contrary, we are not unaware of the problems that must be solved to bring research goals to fruition.

## PREREQUISITES TO ACHIEVING RESEARCH RESULTS

The basic prerequisite for achievement of research results is a viable, flexible organizational structure that is capable of matching projects and personnel and supplying the institutional backup for sound research ventures. The variety of organizations that now conduct archaeology have their advantages and disadvantages (see Stephenson n.d. for a thoughtful discussion of these). We mention several types of organization only briefly.

Often conservation archaeology is carried out by an arm of an established anthropology department or museum. While certain obvious advantages inhere in this arrangement (e.g., curatorial capability, ease of access to records and literature, and involvement of students), there are also subtle drawbacks. As an appendage to a larger entity, the cultural resource management division must constantly fight to get its fair share of the overhead money in order to maintain continuity in support personnel and keep the price of their projects competitive (on an equal-quality basis). Furthermore, as the cultural resource management division begins to expand, established interests may feel threatened and attempt directly or indirectly to put the brakes on further growth and cast aspersions on the intellectual content of conservation archaeology. In some anthropology departments, in fact, blocks of nonarchaeologists have even prevented the founding of a cultural resource management program. Despite these problems, many excellent studies will continue to be conducted within this organizational framework.

Insofar as achievement of research results is concerned, the least successful organization is the environmental consulting firm. Such companies suffer from an absence of curatorial capabilities, a lack of records and literature, a dearth of qualified archaeologists, conflicts of interest that may compromise archaeological standards, and an inability to make the kinds of institutional contributions that any university-based research program makes routinely (Stephenson n.d.). The chapter on environmental consulting firms is necessarily far from closed, since they have an uncanny knack for securing contracts, but we remain to be convinced that they can do sound work; the reports that are available do not make us very optimistic.

In his discussion of various organizations Stephenson concludes that a university-based, *independent* research entity, such as the Institute of Archeology and Anthropology at the University of South Carolina and the Arkansas Archeological Survey at the University of Arkansas (and other state-supported institutions), is the optimal solution to the organizational problem for conservation archaeology. We tend to agree with Stephenson's assessment.

A problem common to all organizations is that of matching projects and personnel. Beyond the obvious consideration of trying insofar as possible to place on projects people who have established research interests in study area is the one of insuring the consideration of a broad range of contemporary research problems when structuring a project. Experiments in cooperation on a single project between investigators with different research interests (e.g., Hanson and Schiffer 1975; Schiffer and House 1975b) will need to become commonplace as we recognize that, especially in mitigative excavations, an overly narrow research focus cannot produce an adequate treatment of the archaeological resources. Perhaps a useful model for these endeavors is provided by the NASA space probes. Gero (1976) thoughtfully discusses these points and urges more organizational experimentation (see also Schiffer 1975b). Canouts, in Chapter 8, argues lucidly for an organizational system that encourages the most efficient use of archaeologists and funds to accomplish high-quality research.

A second area requiring urgent attention is that of contract specifications (see also Cunningham 1976). Remarkably, the scope of work in many contracts is drawn up without benefit of any archaeological input. It is nothing short of remarkable that some sponsors presume to know just what kind of a survey and/or testing program is needed to assess the archaeological resources relative to a proposed development—even when they have no archaeologists on their staff. Even more surprising is the fact that archaeologists keep signing—under no apparent duress—contracts with unrealistic terms. Any archaeologist who affirms that he can record all of the sites in an area has simply not thought seriously about the problems of surveying. Any archaeologist who affirms that he can assess the significance of the archaeological resource in a project impact zone (e.g., a transmission line corridor or a drainage channel clear-cut zone) without knowledge of their regional context and archaeological theory can only fall far short of his goal (and thereby fail to meet the sponsor's information needs). In short, it must be archaeologists who determine the research procedures that are appropriate under given circumstances (for more on contract specifications, see introductions to Parts IV and VII).

A third area needing further work is research design. It is difficult to overemphasize the important role that thorough planning plays in archaeological investigation; unfortunately, very little is known generally about the principles of good archaeological research design—in or out of conservation archaeology. For this reason we devote the entire next part of the volume to this topic. In addition, Chapter 7 by Plog, Weide, and Stewart and that by Schiffer and House (Chapter 14) also deal with research design considerations. Our major theme is that research design in conservation archaeology requires the creative, flexible application of modern archaeological method and theory and that cookbook approaches are doomed to failure.

And finally, we list as a fourth problem area the dissemination of information. Since this problem has already attracted a relatively lengthy literature (and a short discussion in the introduction to Part I), we have little to add here. One point, however, does need underscoring. In the long run, work that goes unreported or uncirculated is not really different from work that was never begun. This harsh judgment, an all too appropriate commentary on archaeology in general, finds ample support in the history of science. Ironically, the major barrier to information flow in purely academic archaeology—the lack of analyses and report preparation—does not affect contract work. Thus, one hopes that because the reports usually are written, it will be a fairly simple matter to find ways to reproduce and disseminate them to the appropriate audiences.

## CONCLUSION

Our vigorous plea for a consciously research-oriented conservation archaeology should not be misconstrued as a call to do only new archaeology or analytical archaeology or behavioral archaeology—or any other kind. Just as the discipline of archaeology today recognizes that research contributions come in many forms, lengths, and emphases, we wish to alert the conservation archaeologist to the abundant opportunities for making diverse kinds of research contributions. Not only will such contributions, regardless of scope or theoretical underpinnings, advance the science of archaeology and fulfill the spirit and letter of conservation legislation, but they will doubtless lead to more enlightened management of cultural resources.

# 5

# Resolving a Conflict of Values in American Archaeology

THOMAS F. KING

The rescue of data from the jaws of destruction has been an archaeological preoccupation almost since the birth of the discipline. In North America, at least, a concern with what was to become "salvage" archaeology goes back to the late nineteenth century, with the explorations of the U.S. Geological Survey and the Bureau of American Ethnology. In the 1930s, with the deployment of WPA crews to dig sites in TVA reservoirs, salvage became a major archaeological activity. After World War II the River Basin Salvage Program of the Smithsonian Institution and National Park Service continued and elaborated the development of salvage programs. Salvage as a federal responsibility was canonized in the law by the Reservoir Salvage Act of 1960, the Department of Transportation Act, and other statutes. By the late 1960s most of the archaeology funded in North America was salvage, most professional (i.e., employed) archaeologists did at least some salvage, and archaeology as a set of extractive techniques was very much colored by salvage methodology. At the same time, however, archaeology as a system of thought was increasing in sophistication, and the result was a distinct conflict between the needs and ethic of an explicitly scientific approach to archaeology and the operating assumptions of those governmental agencies that supported archaeological salvage. On the one hand, the "new archaeology" was rising, with its call for an explicitly scientific, problem-oriented approach to research. On the other hand, the salvage support agencies were essentially concerned with the simple recovery of data; the problems to which the data might apply were irrelevant.

In 1969/70, as chief archaeologist at the UCLA Archeological Survey, I was keenly aware of the pragmatic difficulties engendered by this conflict. The Survey was heavily involved in salvage, but the shadow of Louis Binford, who had left UCLA in 1968, lay long across the minds of graduate students, and the remaining faculty members who significantly influenced student thinking were James Hill, James Sackett, and Fred Plog. We at the Survey felt a need to make our operations scientifically relevant, and this need was often hard to square with our equally serious obligations to the agencies for whom we did free or contract salvage. I attempted to generalize and articulate the conflicts we experienced in an article entitled "A Conflict of Values in American Archeology," (*American Antiquity* 1971, *36*(3):225–262), which is updated and republished in part here. I have left the central part of the article intact, with minor editorial changes and updates, but have dropped the rather heavy-handed and now very dated original introduction. More importantly, I have replaced the old concluding section with a new conclusion based on my last 6 years of experience in cultural resource management. The old conclusion presented a tangible example of the conflicts in action and posed a hypothetical solution. Now, because of developments in cultural resource management, I see a *real* solution developing, and it is on this relatively hopeful note that I am able to conclude the article.

## THE BASIS OF CONFLICT

The elements of conflict between an explicitly theoretical approach to archaeology and the organization of the salvage programs that support much of America's archaeological research can be characterized as follows: The central argument of the theory-oriented archaeology of the "new archaeologists" was the call for a deductive approach to research (Binford 1968a:17; Fritz and Plog 1970:405). We were to pursue answers to questions generated out of anthropological (or other) theory via archaeological research, or we were to attempt the explanation of the differences and similarities we saw in the archaeological record through the utilization of general theory. Adherence to a deductive strategy requires generation and testing of hypotheses, a much more specific kind of "problem-orientation"—and one much more definitive of field technique—than most archaeologists had encountered since the days when the problem was where to find the prettiest pot.

The salvage support agency, on the other hand, distributed its funds with occasional recourse, when such justification was called for, to the assumption that archaeology was an inductive "science." It was assumed that the archaeologist worked along the lines suggested by Swartz (1967), through the mechanical (i.e., "objective") acquisition of data and the multilevel study of these data to a point at which complete historical understanding emerged.

In reality, of course, the salvage support agency was seldom under any pressure to justify itself with reference to epistemology, so the assumption of inductive primacy was not well enough articulated to serve as an explicit basis for policy. Presumably, there was nothing to stop the archaeologist from using salvage funds to support hypothetico-deductive research, but this was more easily said than done.

## DEFINING THE CONFLICT

Hypothetico-deductive research, ideally, brings archaeological data to bear on general problems relating to the nature, operation, and evolution of sociocultural

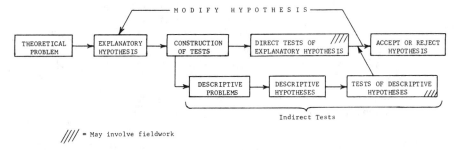

**Figure 5.1.** A deductive strategy (from King, Thomas F., A conflict of values in American archaeology; *American Antiquity* 1971, *36* (No. 3).

systems. On a less general level such an approach can be used to seek explanations for specific regularities and discontinuities in the archaeological record through the application of general propositions. In either case the approach, again ideally, involves the formulation of hypotheses, the recognition of test implications, and the construction and implementation of crucial tests (Hempel 1966; Fritz and Plog 1970:410). These tests may directly reflect on the original hypotheses or, more commonly, comprise complexes of lower-level descriptive statements (e.g., "society X is matrilocal"), the testing of which provides data necessary to the direct test. The strategy employed in this sort of approach is diagrammed in Figure 5.1.

Fieldwork in the context of this approach is a tool employed after the archaeologist has recognized and defined a problem, framed hypotheses relevant to the problem, and designed tests of the hypotheses to which fieldwork is found to relate. The kinds of field techniques employed are determined by the test requirements, within limits of feasibility.

An inductive method is based on the assumption that a valid and worthwhile body of fact will have been attained when enough data have been gathered to permit synthesis and inference. This procedure is diagrammed in Figure 5.2.

According to an inductive ethic, every bit of information can be used in synthesis; presumably, *all* information can be and should be gathered, though this effort is usually thwarted by time, funds, etc. However, as much information as possible should be obtained, and it is quite permissible, indeed preferable, that such data be gathered in a theoretical vacuum to insure objectivity.

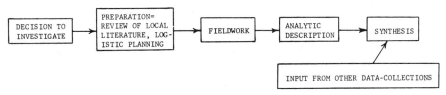

**Figure 5.2.** An inductive strategy (from King, Thomas, F., A conflict of values in American archaeology; *American Antiquity* 1971, *36* (No. 3).

There is a constant and fruitful interplay between induction and deduction in any research program. Objective data gathering is necessary to hypothesis testing and to initial exploration (Caws 1969), and there is no question that data gathered without specific problem orientation can be useful in explanatory research. The possibility of discovering new problems while investigating old ones must always affect one's approach to fieldwork. It can be argued, too, that an inductivist does implicitly deduce, that is, he cannot even decide where to dig without recourse to some kind of general assumption (Fritz and Plog 1970:408). Granting this interplay, however, does not justify the use of induction as an organizing principle in research. Deductive research does not rule out concurrent inductive discovery, but an inductive approach assures that deduction will exist only as uncontrolled bias. Given that it is really impossible to get *all* the information about an archaeological site, this bias will impair the usefulness of data even for inductive synthesis.

This lesson was not lost on many academic archaeologists during the 1960s. An increasing number adhered to a deductive ethic and demanded of themselves, their students, and their research units some kind of hypothetico-deductive approach at the core of research planning.

Meanwhile, the potential for conducting funded research with the support of public agencies increased rapidly during the 1960s. The destruction of archaeological sites was repugnant to the public, and the demand for federal responsibility in preservation and salvage grew steadily. As more and more public and private works came to require federal licensing or assistance, and as the emphasis in land use shifted gradually from piecemeal exploitation toward integrated growth based on regional planning concepts, land-modifying agencies became increasingly receptive to proposals for scientific research stressing the holistic study of regions and systems toward the elucidation of general principles, rather than the particularistic collection of isolated phenomena justified by the satisfaction of public dilettantism. The agencies that distributed salvage funds, however, had developed contract policies and administrative structures based on a vision of archaeology as particularistic and inductive. In the retrospective words of the U.S. National Park Service's Interagency Archeological Services Division (1976):

> Meeting National Park Service report standards had often come to mean an exceptionally low threshold of adequacy. . . . [T]here was little consistent effort to promote professional adequacy in the identification of research needs in development of contract proposals, in generating research designs, and in evaluation of results [p. 15].

Salvage dollars were rarely spent on the development of planned regional programs but were doled out piecemeal for the rescue of individual bits of data that were supposed to contribute, on some final judgment day, to the grand synthesis.

The archaeologist and his research institution dedicated to the strategies of induction could easily handle, and intuitively justify, piecemeal salvage. Such work was justified on the basis of the familiar jigsaw analogy: When we have enough pieces, the picture will become clear. It was not necessary to wonder on what basis we perceived the shape of the pieces, and there was no need to worry about what phenomena we would like to see most clearly pictured when we got through. The central definitive focus of the archaeologist's life, and the measure of one's adequacy in relation to one's professional peers, was fieldwork; the more of it one did, the further one would advance the discipline. Given this bias, a command of excavation technique, and an adequate public-relations capacity, salvage was easy to handle. Further, it was entirely proper for students to spend vast amounts of time in the field doing salvage and in the laboratory doing analyses and writing, toward no other goal than the preparation of "descriptive site reports" that proceeded through standard stages to present the collected data for future reference (Swartz 1967)—another piece added to the puzzle!

The archaeologist and his institution were faced with a dilemma, however, if they opted for deductive research and were faced with salvage exigencies. The sites, or areas, were preselected on the basis of such external factors as danger of destruction and avilability of funds, but a deductive strategy calls for field investigation to take place only when it is required to test an hypothesis. The site should be selected on the basis of the problem, not vice versa. Further, the kind of problem such an archaeologist might be investigating and the hypotheses he might use to investigate it would probably require some specific kinds of excavation, or perhaps very little excavation at all. The problem might require extensive and expensive interdisciplinary or technical studies and relatively little collection of artifacts. It might be necessary to sacrifice artifacts to get at architecture or cemeteries, or vice versa. Descriptive site reports are not always the natural outcome of such research. The necessity to spend money on operations other than the recording and removal of threatened artifacts, the unconcern the archaeologist was likely to feel for the ratio between person-days spent and cubic yards of earth moved, and the likelihood that a standard presentation of observed fact would not constitute an end product of the work were poorly understood by salvage support agencies. Finally, it was logically inconsistent for the hypothetico-deductive archaeologist to encourage or facilitate the conduct of salvage for its own sake by students or research associates. If such work taught only the digging of holes and resulted in the accumulation of nothing but artifacts and notes whose relevance to theory could not be demonstrated—that is, if the work created pedants rather than scientists—what good was it? The student could thus be caught in an excruciating bind. Salvage work tempted him or her with its flavor of conservationist urgency and its monetary rewards, but his or her institution offered no academic rewards for participation in such work and often branded the student as a mere technician unsuitable to the cloisters of academia. The student might starve while getting grades, meanwhile obtaining little practical experience; or he or she could eat, gain experience, feel good about saving something for posterity, and flunk.

## SIMPLE SOLUTIONS

The conflict between deductive-based archaeology and the structure of contract salvage programs was thus simple to define: The suppositions, expectations, and values of deductive archaeologists and salvage support organizations were mutually irrelevant and contradictory. The simple and obvious solution to the conflict was to disengage, and this is precisely what frequently happened in the late 1960s and early 1970s, with sad results.

The salvage support agency's simplest option was to deal only with amenable research bodies; inductively oriented institutions or teams drawn from the agency's own staff. Such a policy, by limiting input from theory-oriented scholars and students, inevitably resulted in increased irrelevance to larger academic and scientific concerns and a diminution of support from the academic community. Lacking these measures of relevance, some salvage support agencies and their dependent bureaucracies began to find it difficult to justify their existence. The following quote, from an environmental planner (E. Barnes 1967) who sought to evaluate archaeological resources from salvage data for integration into regional land-use programs, was typical of the judgment rendered of laissez-faire salvage by thoughtful designers of public policy:

> The scientist has been contracted by the agency on a fee-for-service basis to do limited pieces of work . . . at separated locations, and at different times. The resulting research data has then been entombed in jealously guarded files of rival Departments of Anthropology . . . or lost somewhere in the vaults of the Smithsonian. . . . Among the authors of the thirteen reports resulting from this piecemeal "program" since 1935, only one has made any extensive comparisons with the work or findings of another. That communication between scholars which is essential to scientific progress has been miniscule; the result is scholarly chaos [p. 3].

The deductive scholar and institution had available to them a similarly short-sighted option: to withdraw from, or not cooperate with, salvage programs. While I think it is true that as organized during the 1960s, most salvage programs were more trouble than they were worth to the theory-oriented archaeologist, eschewal of salvage programs by theoretically sophisticated archaeologists was damaging to the interests of the archaeologists themselves, as well as to the data base. Today one might decline to salvage a site because its investigation would be irrelevant to any problem one was concerned with pursuing. Tomorrow one might find a site one needed in relation to a real problem destroyed—by construction one did not know about, by a "salvage archaeologist" digging for his supper who did not collect the data one needed because he did not know it was there, or by local citizens who justified their looting with the argument that "the university doesn't care." The last was a justified argument; if the archaeologist felt no responsibility to his data base, who should?

Moreover, the problems of salvage were not all exclusive to salvage; some were expressions of a larger malady. Struever (1968a) wrote of archaeology in general:

> If a major purpose of archaeology is to elucidate cultural process by *explaining* prehistoric episodes of change or stability, then the strategy of archaeology must shift to long-term programs of field work and analysis. . . . Execution of this design is not feasible within the organizational limitations of archaeology today (p. 133).

> As organized today, archeology lacks the institutional framework within which archeologists, natural scientists, and technicians can work together in a continuing program

> with the facilities and funding necessary to employ the full range of available methods in attacking an explanatory problem. A sharp increase in our capacity to explain culture change will occur if and when we find a way to increase the complexity of archeological research institutions [p. 150].

In short, the problem was not that salvage was intrinsically bad, unscientific, or useless for explanatory research, but that the salvage support agencies' orientation toward the reactive redemption of uncoordinated data, and the organizational structure appropriate to this orientation, operated counter to the needs of explanation.

In the early 1970s an effort was initiated under the leadership of C. R. McGimsey III that eventually reached fruition in the passage of the Archeological and Historic Preservation Act of 1974 (Public Law 93-291). This act makes possible an increase in and regularization of salvage programs. Coming at a time of significant cutbacks in financial support for academic institutions, this act has resulted in a reversal of the trend toward disengagement. At the same time, however, it has resulted in crass mercantilism, struggles for regional hegemony over salvage monies, and practices verging on the piratical by contract archaeologists, while the movement of salvage support agencies toward more responsible management has not always been impressive, despite protestations of vigorous concern for improvement (cf. U.S. National Park Service, Interagency Archeological Services Division 1976). In the contracts game, except to the extent that support agencies are able and willing to exercise intellectually valid quality control, the inductive archaeologist continues to have a selective advantage, and the wages of involvement in salvage (now called by various less odious names) may still be brain death. Although some agencies are attempting to provide for reasonable research designs and attention to scientific problems in their contract programs, this effort is haphazard at best, in the absence of a reasonable effort by the archaeological discipline to get beyond exploitative contracting into responsible planning.

## A COMPLEX SOLUTION

Another solution—or complex of solutions—does exist, however. The 1930s public works programs that spawned reservoir salvage also helped bring architects and historians together in various reconstruction and restoration projects, resulting in a consolidated historic preservation movement. During the 1960s, while archaeologists were salvaging, the historic preservationists promoted a package of planning concepts that became the National Historic Preservation Act of 1966 (Public Law 89-665). Now coming of age, the programs provided by this act offer some real solutions to archaeology's conflict of values.

The Historic Preservation Act is best known for its expansion of the National Register of Historic Places, its creation of the Advisory Council on Historic Preservation, and its provision for state historic preservation officers in all states and territories. A less well-known feature of the act is its requirement that each state develop a historic preservation plan to guide the preservation and use of the state's cultural resources. Most state plans thus far developed have been fluff, but ten years of experience have brought some wisdom, and the secretary of the interior's new regulations for state historic preservation plans call for much more sophisticated efforts. States are now required to undertake systematic statewide surveys for all kinds of cultural resources. These surveys are to be professionally supervised and organized, and the methods and rationale underlying them are to be reported regularly to the secretary. The survey is to result not only in nominations to the National Register but in other inventories of cultural properties and in predictions about where various kinds of such properties may exist. The survey should provide the basis for the state plan, which is to integrate all cultural resource management programs in the state and provide for environmental review and assistance to federal agencies in compliance with historic preservation statutes (U.S. Department of Interior 1976). Federal agencies have been given broad new responsibilities for managing cultural resources not only by the familiar National Environmental Policy Act and Executive Order 11593 but by the implementation of such planning and land-use statutes as the Housing and Community Development Act of 1974, the Water Pollution Control Act of 1973, and the Coastal Zone Management Act of 1973. Procedures now in effect or in circulation call upon the responsible agencies to make their programs of archaeological survey, testing, protection, and salvage consistent with the state historic preservation plans. Taken together, these regulations offer archaeologists a very important opportunity both to preserve a useful sample of the archaeological record and to conduct meaningful deductive research using contract money. This is how it can work.

*First,* the archaeologists of each state (or region) need to organize into credible groups to work with the state historic preservation officer(s). Such groups should be representative of the theoretical, experiential, and professional diversity within the state's or region's archaeological community and should include, if possible, archaeologists interested in all relevant types of archaeology—contemporary, historical, prehistoric, industrial, terrestrial, underwater, etc. Representativeness in the state plan is important; the Department of the Interior reviews these plans and will reject those that ignore real research needs and preservation possibilities.

*Second,* this group should work with the state historic preservation officer in developing and implementing the state plan, including such elements as:

1. Research design formulation: The group should attempt to define legitimate research questions to which the various kinds of archaeological resources in the state may be expected to relate, and to consider what approaches may fruitfully be taken to their study.

2. State survey development: The group should help define strategies and methods for a long-range survey designed to identify ultimately all the state's cultural resources. Presumably, in most cases a sampling approach will be most fruitful, gradually gaining in predictive power as more data are obtained in a systematic fashion.

3. Research prioritization: The group can define research and preservation priorities. Which kinds of sites should be preserved at all costs for future research?

Which kinds should be excavated or otherwise studied to answer immediately important questions? What methods should be employed in different kinds of research?

4. Updating: The group can participate in updating the survey and plan on a regular basis as data accumulate and the state of the art changes.

*Third,* the archaeologists of the state or region should plan their own contract research to fit the plan and encourage agencies with which they work to be consistent.

The upshot of all this would be an end to piecemeal salvage and the rise of regional research and preservation planning and execution. Agencies involved in project funding would benefit because they would have some idea of what to expect when faced with the need to deal with archaeology, but archaeology itself would be the big winner. The conflict would be resolved; salvage (under whatever name) would be placed in the service of research, and the discipline's best thinkers could participate in the preservation and salvage activities of the government. The necessary statutes, policies, and regulations are now in place to bring this resolution to pass, and the logic of the environmental and historic preservation statutes demands it. It only remains for archaeologists to undertake the organizational work that will be necessary for the conflict to be finally resolved.

# 6

# The Reconciliation of Theory and Method in Archaeology[1]

GEORGE J. GUMERMAN

In the past decade archaeological theory has seen considerable change. In this chapter I suggest how present-day theory can be tested using new methods, especially the opportunities provided by contract archaeology.

For years archaeologists have been castigated for their lack of concern about articulating the theoretical basis that underlies their work. Today, however, there is no dearth of theory in American archaeology. The situation of inadequate theory formulation and the virtual nonexistent examination of organizing principles by archaeologists that anthropologists such as Kluckhohn (1940:43–44) deplored decades ago should no longer be an overriding concern. The major archaeological journals seldom have an issue without at least one article devoted to the examination of theoretical concepts, and several excellent volumes expounding archaeological theory and method have been published in recent years (e.g., Clarke 1968; Dunnell 1971; Watson, LeBlanc, Redman 1971). In spite of this flowering of archaeological theory, however, the majority of the published results of archaeological endeavors bear too great a similarity to the survey and site reports of the 1940s and 1950s. The result is that aspects of Kluckhohn's famous 1940 criticism about Middle American archaeologists are still applicable to many archaeologists regardless of their area of specialization.

> I should like to record an overwhelming impression that many students [of Middle American prehistory] are but slightly reformed antiquarians. To one who is a layman in these highly specialized realms there seems a great deal of obsessive wallowing in detail of and for itself. No one can feel more urgently than the writer the imperative obligation of anthropologists to set their descriptions in such a rich context of detail that they can properly be used for comparative purposes. Yet proliferation of minutiae is not its own justification [p. 42].

[1]Adapted from Gumerman, George J., The reconciliation of theory and method in archeology, Redman, Charles (ed.), *Research and theory in current archeology* © 1973, New York, John Wiley & Sons, pp. 287–299. Reprinted by permission of John Wiley & Sons, Inc.

The present contradiction is that in spite of the florescence of archaeological theory much current archaeology is still "on the intellectual level of stamp collecting (p. 45)" that Kluckhohn deplored. Usually articles and monographs either are theoretical in orientation or are description-based culture history. With a few outstanding exceptions, theoretical concepts are usually tested by application to previous excavations that were undertaken for other purposes, or by short surveys and limited test excavations. Rarely are the theoretical articles based on or followed up by major excavation programs. In short, there is too little application of archaeological theory to archaeological method.

In part, this lack of reconciliation is a result of theoretical articles that stress a concern for the formulation and testing of general laws concerning the operation of entire cultural systems in contrast to the problems encountered in single site excavations or in the establishment of phase sequences (Struever 1968b). Hole and Heizer (1969) have expressed in brief form the thrust of current archaeological goals concerning the reconstruction of extinct cultural systems:

> The process of making [archaeological] inferences may become quite complex, but the goal, of course, is to attempt to explain now a cultural system works.
>
> In examining cultural subsystems we focus our attention for the first time on people, not as individuals, but as members of once-living communities. However, we are not able to comprehend people in all of their facets. We can say little about politics or theology, but we can perceive some of the ways to reconstruct how they were organized. All things are made up of organized parts; it is one of our jobs as social scientists to try to discover the principles of organization that make viable societies of collections of people. As archaeologists we must try to reconstruct the organization of the people whose remains we can handle, count, measure, and draw. It is becoming more and more apparent that principles of organization are the basic keys in our understanding of any class of phenomena, including people. This position is taken by general system theorists, and has been echoed in various forms by anthropologists for many years.
>
> It is probably fortunate that organization has emerged as the focal point of behavioral studies, because archaeologists are able to find information in prehistory that relates to organization. The sites, the artifacts in them, and especially the way in which sites and artifacts occur, give clues to the organization of the society that left them [pp. 269–270].

The goals of understanding the organizing principles of extinct cultural systems are, of course, more difficult and time consuming than developing a phase sequence or excavating a single site presumed to be representative of a culture or subculture. Nevertheless, archaeological theorists have suggested a number of ways in which the goals of archaeologists can be met.

It has become quite obvious that to view a culture as a system calls for archaeologists to structure their research within a deductive framework that necessitates an orientation toward the generation and testing of well-formulated theories (Fritz and Plog 1970; Tuggle, Riley, and Townsend 1972). A primarily inductively oriented research strategy does not allow for the necessary control of information and the way it is collected to test general laws concerning the organization of cultural systems. However, the restructuring of research strategy toward a hypothetico-deductive model will not alone ensure the attainment of modern archaeological goals. The concern with the organization of complete cultural systems in Hole and Heizer's statement is obviously a desirable and necessary trend, and yet there has been concern expressed that these goals, no matter how necessary, may not be obtainable. As Struever (1968a:132) has demonstrated, personnel and financial resources are too restricted to devise the means necessary for testing significant laws concerning extinct cultural systems.

Simply, funds are not available to field large research teams to test the many theories that have been advanced concerning the functioning of entire cultural systems. The dichotomy between method and theory lies, in large part, in the financial inability to test current theory; yet, there is no absence of fieldwork. On the contrary, the pace of archaeological survey and excavation has increased greatly in the last decade, and there are many more individuals involved in the profession than in previous years.

The major increase in archaeological activity, however, has been in the realm of cultural resource management, or contract archaeology, while the funding, and consequently the activity, in other types of archaeology has remained static or even declined in the last several years. Without doubt, funds are much more readily available for contract archaeology than for problem-oriented archaeology. It has been estimated that in California there are 100 times more funds available for contract archaeology than for noncontract work (Heizer 1966:58). Because funding is more easily available for the excavation of endangered sites, Heizer predicted that contract archaeology would divert critically needed professional resources from theory-testing investigations to contract archaeology. This has not been the case. Funds used for contract archaeology programs have not been channeled from problem-oriented or theory-testing archaeological projects. Contract programs are usually operated with funds from state and federal agencies and from private industry that does not ordinarily finance archaeological research. Recent products of graduate schools of anthropology are presently having difficulty obtaining professional positions, so that contract-oriented programs do not appear to be diverting needed personnel.

The problem of the reconciliation of archaeological method with theory appears to lie in the utilization of funds from contract projects to formulate and test theoretical concepts, certainly a formidable, but not impossible, task. The conflict between contract archaeology, with its tendency toward fact-gathering inductively oriented research, and problem-oriented, deductive, interdisciplinary team type of archaeology has been adequately detailed by King (1971). While salvage archaeologists continue with fact collection and "filling in the blanks on the archaeological map," other archaeologists are developing sophisticated, and often convoluted, hypotheses for the discovery of laws of the sociocultural process that they have not the time, money, or effort to test by large-scale excavation. It is necessary to meld the majority of the archaeology done today, that is, contract archaeology, with some of the better theory, and to accomplish this requires that contract archaeology be considered as comprising two major types.

The first type of contract archaeology consists of those projects that involve large land masses and in which the archaeologist has at least several months notice before the modification of the land takes place and a number of years in which to do the excavation, analysis, and writing. Most commonly these projects involve the damming of river systems or strip-mining operations. The second type of contract project is the small one, often lasting only a few days. Usually the time between notification of the archaeologist and beginning of construction is short, often nonexistent, and the project covers only a small area and lasts for a short time. Examples of this type include building-site locations, short access roads, and small areas being developed for agriculture. It should be noted that linear contract archaeology—that is, highway, power, and pipeline right-of-way projects—do not necessarily fall under the rubric of small-scale projects, since some construction covers considerable distance and requires years of excavation and analysis.

Obviously, the two types of contract archaeology demand different methodologies to orient them to theory-testing programs, and of course, the large-scale project is the one most easily adaptable to hypothetico-deductive research.

King (1971:260) has suggested that the huge salvage contracts that require large sums and a number of years to accomplish not be awarded without a long-range deductively oriented research program. Currently, large salvage projects are often awarded to a number of different institutions working in the same area with no well-articulated research strategy and little coordination between institutions. Only by orienting integrated aspects of the large-scale contract efforts toward theory testing can the goals of explaining the organization and operation of cultural systems be attempted.

Even more importantly, means currently exist in the American Southwest, and could be developed elsewhere, to bring data from large contract-oriented programs to bear on archaeological theory testing. The means of integrating large-scale contract programs toward hypothetico-deductive research lies in organizations such as the Southwestern Anthropological Research Group (SARG).

In 1971 SARG was formed to assist archaeologists working in the Southwest to aim at least a part of their efforts at developing and testing a common research design (Gumerman 1971). The problem that the SARG associates are attempting to solve involves the explanation of settlement distribution, but this in itself is not of importance here. The significance of the group is that it is attempting to answer basic questions that concern all archaeologists by having all participants contribute to the research design, collect data in a compatible format, and test the design in different areas of the Southwest. No person or institution will abandon individual research interests, but all participants will expend the extra effort and absorb the added expense to collect data that the group requires. A data retrieval system will be established that will allow the collected information to be available to all. The group will meet annually to discuss mutual problems and to modify the research design; it is expected that this will be a long-term project lasting for a number of years.

The importance of SARG is that it enables data collected from large contract projects, as well as from noncontract archaeology, to be programmed for modifying and testing hypotheses generated by the group. Needless to say, each individual contract excavation or survey program may still be primarily inductive, and the reports will probably still be descriptive for the most part. Nevertheless, a part of the project will be directed to the testing of theory related to cultural systems and of concern to most people working in a large region. An example can best illustrate the relationship of a large salvage archaeological project to hypothetico-deductive research and to the testing of research designs of the SARG type.

Archaeological salvage operations have been conducted on Black Mesa in northeastern Arizona since 1967 in areas slated for coal strip-mining. It was apparent that the archaeology program would last for a number of years, and yet the first year was spent in survey and excavation, mostly with an approach directed to the collection of data—that is, with a basically inductive approach—since little was known about the area (Gumerman 1970). Since 1968, however, the direction of the Black Mesa program has changed, with attempts being made to develop well-formulated research strategies and theory testing. This approach is applicable because it is a long-term project and because the study area is not one that covers a narrow right-of-way but instead has an areal expanse of 65,000 acres. The implementation of SARG methodology now means that data collected on Black Mesa will have even greater potential for theory testing. The Black Mesa program will no longer be restricted solely to the testing of theories that can be generated about the prehistoric populations of that area, now the program can be directed to the testing of some of the most recently formulated theories concerning cultural systems. SARG allows the Black Mesa contract effort to be interrelated with comparable contract and noncontract programs throughout the Southwest on a much wider scale than was formerly conceivable.

The large contract project can, like Black Mesa, be oriented to theory testing concerning the operation of cultural systems. The application of small contract projects to a hypothetico-deductive approach, however, is not so easy, and King (1971) feels the single small site excavation on a highway or powerline right-of-way is beyond the scope of such methodology. He states that "any hope that we might be able to develop a set of hypotheses as a bag of tricks from which we could select a guiding proposition whenever we found a site in danger, is probably doomed to disappointment [p.257]." The problem may not be as great as King envisions, and means can be developed to relate archaeological method to theory using funds from salvage archaeology.

The small project, the survey of a 2-mile-long, 50-foot-wide right-of-way or the excavation of a one-room farmhouse, is not easily adaptable to present SARG methodology. SARG is primarily designed for the collection of data regarding settlement patterns and as a result demands a rigorous data collection procedure in a relatively large area, not in a narrow right-of-way selected for the purpose of pipeline or highway construction. In order to direct the small-scale contract job to hypothetico-deductive theory testing, it will be necessary to devise the theories before any work is even contemplated.

Traditionally, small-scale contract methodology has been to develop a set of techniques for an archaeological culture area that can be adapted to most types of sites in the region. Data are collected in similar ways, and information is recorded on general architecture or feature forms, because it is not possible to determine when the necessity for excavation will arise. Because the archaeologist is not certain where, when, or what type of site he will be excavating, preparation for the project has to be made beforehand, and consequently these factors almost dictate an inductively structured research program. Methods are perfected, but theory is usually ignored or inadequately formulated. As a consequence, the contract archaeologist on small projects has worked with the usually poorly stated assumption that the work he will be doing is within the confines of a specific archaeological culture zone and that the planned work will add something, in terms of empirical data, to the general fund of knowledge of that culture zone. The work proceeds with these assumptions in mind, and when the report is completed, if ever, it is primarily descriptive, with a page or two of conclusions. In addition, the descriptions usually record the precise type of data that have traditionally been recorded by previous archaeologists. Interpretations, when they occur, are usually concerned with explaining the degree of variability from the "norm," that is, the material remains and the architecture are compared with those from other sites in the region that have been excavated previously and are considered the "norm" by virtue of their having been excavated earlier. Seldom is an attempt made to explain variability in sites excavated as small contract projects. Often the field archaeologist is well trained in method but knows little about the particular culture zone in which he is working, with the result that the site is excavated mechanically and data are collected "by the book" rather than to test specific theories. The attempt, therefore, to compare the site to nearby excavated sites is done inductively from published reports after the excavations are completed.

Small-scale archaeological excavations can, however, be related to understanding cultural systems if the archaeologists devise research strategies for cultural or subcultural zones prior to the probability of the necessity of contract archaeology. Generally, enough is known about most areas so that specific questions about the regions can be raised other than the usual ones of what are the material remains and who lived in the area and when. It is essential that specific questions be asked about individual areas prior to the announcement of construction possibilities.

In some areas of the United States a framework already exists for devising research strategies about individual culture zones. The Arizona State Museum has divided southern Arizona into 29 different archaeological zones primarily for purposes of administering the National Environmental Policy Act of 1969, that is, for preparing environmental impact statements. The archaeological zone concept will enable the archaeologist to provide the appropriate federal agency and the contracting firms with more accurate information—essentially, about what is known and unknown about the area and about what the general character of the archaeological manifestations are in areas scheduled for construction. In order to orient the small-scale project in a hypothetico-deductive manner, it will be necessary to adopt the concept of the archaeological zone and to devise theories for testing in these individual zones. It should be emphasized that these archaeological zones are not smaller equivalents of the traditional culture area (Kroeber 1947). Instead, they reflect what appear to be regionally distinct variations of archaeological manifestations. In addition, like all classifactory systems, the zones themselves and their boundaries cannot be considered immutable but will probably change as contract archaeology continues. These research designs structured for the zones need not be solely of a culture-historical nature tied only to the archaeological zones themselves, but they should also be concerned with culture process. Again a short example will clarify the scheme.

A north-south highway or powerline being constructed from Phoenix in south central Arizona to Flagstaff in northern Arizona will pass through several major environmental zones and a number of archaeological zones. Theories involving culture history and environment can easily be formulated for testing. For example, instead of simply asking what is the nature of the archaeological manifestations in the different areas, archaeologists may sharpen the questions by devising research strategies for answering such questions as: How did the subsistence base differ in the diverse environmental regions? What was the character of interaction, if any, between zones, and are the cultural manifestations of each zone coterminous with the subenvironmental regions? In this way, by devising a deductively oriented research program to answer these questions prior to the commencement of survey and excavation, archaeologists can collect data in such a manner that the theories are testable within the framework of salvage archaeology.

Theories concerning the organization of cultural systems can also be formulated. The north-south highway will traverse several environmental transition zones between major environments. Ecologists have demonstrated that these transition zones or edge areas contain many of the species of plants and animals found in the contiguous major environmental zones, and often there are a number of organisms found only in the edge area (Odum 1965). There is an excellent possibility that there is a tendency for increased variety in cultural systems as well as in ecosystems in these biological tension zones, or edge areas. The use of the edge area concept to explain cultural variability has been attempted in the Great Lakes region with only partial success because of the difficulty in distinguishing the edge area (Fitting 1966, 1970). Because the edge area is easily definable in central Arizona, Gumerman and Johnson (1971) feel

> that the concept of the [edge area] as a heuristic device is an ideal construct for the study of factors affecting the occurrence and distribution of human habitation in a biological tension zone. The edge area may, in addition, result in and explain what are called sub-cultures, or regional cultural variants. It may also explain other differences between the major environmental zone and the [edge area], such as differences in population density, settlement pattern, and differences and diversity in subsistence patterns. It also may explain site locations in defensive situations due to warfare over the natural resources of the edge area. In other words, the use of the [edge area] concept in archaeology may help anthropologists to understand the zones between culture areas [p. 84].

From these statements a number of hypotheses concerning culture process can be framed for testing. For example, the edge area, as opposed to the surrounding major environmental zones, tends to have increased variety and diversity of plant and animal communities. Because of this diversity, human communities in an edge area will exhibit more diversity in subsistence patterns because of the necessity to develop more varied techniques to exploit the greater variation of plant and animal species.

Certainly, single small-scale efforts will not provide enough information to satisfactorily test broadly framed theories, such as cultural adaptation to an edge area. Nevertheless, data that bear on the questions posed above can be collected. Eventually, enough work may be done in the different archaeological zones so that the theories can be satisfactorily tested. It is doubtful that enough data can be collected to demonstrate laws of cultural process, but it should be possible to suggest the existence of certain principles.

If there are doubts that areas affected by construction, and hence by contract archaeology, are too constricted and isolated to provide answers to specific regional and general questions, the quickening pace of construction in this country should dispel these doubts. I have shown elsewhere (Gumerman 1973) on a map of Arizona the tremendous area of the state covered by contract archaeology projects since 1953. Literally hundreds of smaller projects lasting a day or two have been left off the map. With rare exceptions, these projects have not been oriented toward hypothetico-deductive research. Work in the immense area covered by 25 years of contract archaeology could have answered numerous questions if it had been organized to collect information to test specific theories. The orientation of these contract archaeological projects toward theory testing could have provided an opportunity for integration of archaeological method and theory. Admittedly, the examples I have presented are oversimplified, and the implementation of these programs may be more feasible in the American Southwest because of our vast knowledge about the archaeological manifestations in the region and because it is an area of extremely rapid population growth, necessitating a large amount of contract archaeology. The solutions to the problems discussed above may not be so easily initiated in other portions of the United States, let alone in foreign countries.

It is essential, nevertheless, that attempts be made to apply archaeological methods to theory, not only for the ultimate benefit of archaeological and anthropological goals but also for the optimum utilization of professional archaeologists. The curious dilemma in American archaeology of method unrelated to theory about the organization of cultural systems not only involves the need for the two to be reconciled but also concerns the future employment situations of numerous professionally trained archaeologists. The present reduction in the availability of teaching positions in American universities is common knowledge, and the archaeologist has not been immune to the diminished departmental employment. Recent graduates with higher degrees in anthropology have experienced difficulty obtaining academic positions. On the other hand, it is becoming increasingly difficult to recruit qualified archaeologists for contract archaeological programs. Numerous permanent or semipermanent positions have been filled by poorly qualified archaeologists because those who are qualified have been trained to deal with hypothetico-deductive research problems and disdain, often rightfully so, the primarily inductively structured research of contract archaeology. It is necessary, therefore, that contract archaeology become oriented in a hypothetico-deductive manner, both for the sake of problem solving and for the best utilization of trained professional archaeologists. The solution is not to train more archaeologists for inductively oriented research in contract archaeology, since that would simply widen the already increasing gap between method and theory. The solution is to organize the general research in order most effectively to utilize both contract funds and archaeologists.

The greatest crisis in American archaeology is not, contrary to recent articles, in site destruction wrought by the spreading subdivision and in the increasing numbers of vandalized sites, although these are important problems that must be addressed (H. A. Davis 1972). As archaeologists, we must recognize that we do not need to keep adding to research collections so that so-called representative samples are available for every conceivable type of artifact from every culture area. Nor is it necessary to excavate every endangered site. Rather, we must devise research designs for theory testing and use funds from contract programs to excavate in a manner that will test those theories.

It has often been implied that many of the wrongs of American archaeology, like all other wrongs, could be cured by the infusion of large sums of money. While archaeological research must be funded at a higher level than it is currently, this funding should not be simply to save more sites and artifacts from destruction. Additional funds should go toward the restructuring of archaeological contract research into a hypothetico-deductive framework and should help with analysis and publication of both data and the testing of laws bearing on cultural systems. Funding agencies have to be made aware of the necessity in modern archaeology of preexcavation and postexcavation expenses. No matter how impressive the pictures of archaeologists racing against the bulldozer or the rising waters of a newly constructed dam are, archaeological funds are being misspent if they are not oriented in some degree to theory testing. The crisis in American archaeology is not simply the need to save the endangered site but the necessity to meld method with theory in order to deal with the problems that archaeologists have said are their concern.

# 7

# Research Design in the SUNY-Binghamton Contract Program

FRED PLOG
MARGARET WEIDE
MARILYN STEWART

In recent years a number of archaeologists have advocated the development of more explicit research designs to guide archaeological research. While the specific approaches to this task have varied considerably, the need for the development of such designs has not been questioned. At the same time, there has been considerable casual discussion of the nature of the justification for increased emphasis on research design.

Unfortunately, some have apparently described research designs as if they were close to a guarantee for success in the research to be undertaken. Clearly, research designs provide no such guarantee. But, neither can the vast majority of us count on flashes of insight that will lead to major innovations or discoveries in every piece of research we undertake; we are plodders, and systematic plodding is more likely to lead to insight than is unsystematic plodding.

Archaeologists have for decades been taught that as complete as possible a set of notes on field projects is desirable in order that unanticipated problems may be resolved, unforeseen questions may be answered. In a sense, research design represents no more than the application of this same dictum to the more theoretical and methodological aspects of our research. A complete record of the approach taken to a particular problem, the rationale for this approach, and the changes in approach occurring over the course of a given piece of research are as much a record of the archaeologist's work as are his field notes. Especially through the understanding of the changes of approach that occur in any vital research effort, the investigator is likely to find grounds for the explicit formulation of new concepts, theories, and methodologies.

In a more general sense, it can be argued that learning is most effective, dramatic, and productive when it results from surprises. When phenomena prove to be other than as we have learned to expect them, we will most likely question the knowledge that led us to those expectations and modify or change that knowledge. The more explicitly these expectations are set down in a research design, the greater the likelihood that such surprises will occur and meaningful discoveries result.

A necessary consequence of such statements is the realization that research designs vary in their specificity as the understanding of a given problem increases. Research designs formulated at an early stage in a particular effort may and often do bear little relationship to the final strategy employed. It is a failure to understand this process of designing research that has probably underlain some of the arguments that research designs cannot be done for contract programs where a research problem cannot be identified in advance. Not only do we not believe this argument, but we suggest that the research designs formulated by contract archaeologists in diverse parts of the country provide concrete evidence of its falseness.

Yet, formulating a research design for a project the most immediate focus of which is not research but resource assessment is often quite difficult. This difficulty may sometimes arise from a failure to recognize that research designs are necessarily general at the outset, it is the modification and elaboration of what are often vague beginnings that ultimately come to underlie the research components of contract and noncontract work. As an illustration of this process, we will present an abridged version of a research design written for highway contract work undertaken by the State University of New York (SUNY) at Binghamton in the summer of 1974.

Contract archaeology was first undertaken at SUNY-Binghamton during the summer of 1967. During that and the succeeding 5 years funding from the New York State Department of Transportation was minimal and the work done was principally of a "rescue" nature. This situation changed in 1973 as a result of considerable efforts on the part of archaeologists in the state working through the New York Archaeological Council. During the summer of 1973 over $100,000 was provided for highway archaeology by two universities in the state. In subsequent years this sum grew, and contract work for a variety of other agencies was undertaken.

An initial research design was prepared in the spring of 1973. It differs from the 1974 design, which we will present, only in the relative absence of empirical detail concerning relevant environmental variables. We will present the 1974 design, discuss several of the issues that were of primary importance to us in generating it, and describe some of the newer and different directions that research has taken as a result of both the successes and the failures that we have encountered in attempting to apply this design. While some of the discussion is now relatively out of date, it is our belief that the general and preliminary nature of the design may be of utility to others who are at roughly the same stage in planning research in conjunction with contract programs.

## THE 1974 DESIGN

### Archaeology

Archaeology is a social science that attempts to explicate and explain the behavior of prehistoric populations. In its explicatory efforts the discipline focuses on writing a culture history of a specified area. In its explanatory efforts, it focuses on cultural processes, the linked series of events that account for the patterns that are observable in the archaeological record. Archaeology is, in our view, a science of society, not a science of artifacts.

### Environmental Context

The corridor of the I-88 Expressway trends northeast from the Binghamton area in south-central New York State to the outskirts of Schenectady on the edge of the Hudson–Mohawk Valley. The corridor traverses the Susquehanna Hills, a subregion of the glaciated Appalachian Plateau, but is largely situated within a through valley that drains to the southwest by Schenevus Creek and the Susquehanna River and to the northeast by Cobleskill Creek, a tributary of the Mohawk River. The region is characterized by planed uplands, moderate slopes of 9–18%, and medium local relief, varying from 600 feet to more than 1000 feet from streambed to adjacent upland.

As a zone for archaeological research, the corridor provides only a partial picture of the prehistoric record along its course, for prehistoric populations used both upland and valley foods and localities in the course of their subsistence cycles. Within the corridor, however, the placement of the right-of-way intersects a variety of topographical locations that require particular approaches to assessing their archaeological values. These locations may have played different roles as in the several settlement–subsistence systems (which are explained later) that are projected for the area. The valleys exhibit four internal topographic forms: the current flood plain; depositional terraces, gravel features (including kettle and kame topography), and till remnants; and the valley slopes. The modern floodplain, largely built of silts during the past several thousand years, contains buried occupation layers and requires deep testing to ascertain the presence or absence of evidence of past occupation. Silt terraces occur intermittently along the river's course and appear to be of sufficient antiquity to have served as occupational surfaces well back into the prehistoric period, with Late Archaic and Transitional sites found within their uppermost layers. Occasional deep testing will be needed until a full study of the terrace sequence and dating can be made. The valleys also include gravel features, relics of the glaciated period of the area including kettle and kame topography, dissected tills, moraines, and outwash deposits. We have assumed that these predate the establishment of significant populations in the area and that archaeological remains will be confined to their surficial zone. The course of the expressway is occasionally pressed against one or another side of the valley, benched into the slope. Here the material is largely weathering debris from the valley margins and residues of glacial debris. Our surveys to date show that site density is least along these stretches, but occupation at springs may be expected. Rock-shelters also occur here in the zone of limestones that form escarpments on the norhteastern margins of the Appalachian Plateau. Fan deposits may bury early occupation materials at the base of the valley slopes where smaller streams enter.

### Vegetation

The proportion of the Appalachian Plateau traversed by I-88 is characterized by vegetation of the northern hardwoods zone, but the valleys within it are enough warmer locally that oaks occur in favored localities, and the vegetation falls into the oak–northern hardwoods zone. In the upland we should find beech and sugar maple accompanied by basswood, white ash, black cherry, and white pine. The presence of oak and hickory in the valleys is important in assessing prehistoric subsistence. Here, on the northern edge of their distribution, stands of oak and oak mixed with hickory occur on south- and southwest-facing slopes (J. H. Thompson 1966:95), forming a distinct concentration of collectable resources.

The vegetation of the valley floors has been the most severely disrupted of all zones, as a result of almost 200 years of farming. Defining its plant communities and original riparian vegetation remains an important obligation if we are to understand the productivity of the area for aboriginal populations.

### Water Resources

From the viewpoint of prehistoric populations, the form and distribution of water at the surface is important. Proximity of site locations to springs, marshes, lakes, streams, or rivers may provide important insights into the presence of differing tool types and tool frequencies in assemblages. Unfortunately, the hydrology of the valleys has been much disrupted during the past 200 years by filling of lowlands and other modifications to improve farming and transportation.

### Climate

The area traversed by I-88 is generally characterized by cold, snowy winters and cool, wet summers. It is marginal land for agriculture due to climate, soils, and relief and is presently suffering a high rate of farm abandonment. The upper Susquehanna and the Hudson River valleys have warmer, drier summers than the upland regions. Frost-free periods of 100–150 days can be expected in the area as a whole, with somewhat longer spans in the lower valleys.

### Soils

The soils of the area are acid, mostly thin, and developed on glacial till. Alluvial soils in the valley bottoms are immature, with poorly developed profiles. They too are acid, and as a result, archaeological sites in the area contain little or no bone or other organic materials.

## Prehistoric Period

The primary goal of prior archaeological research in the area has been the understanding of the culture history of the area; the research has met with considerable success in outlining the cultural chronology of the prehistoric period and relating it to adjacent areas of New York State and Pennsylvania. Funk, Rippeteau, and Houck (1973) describe the present state of knowledge for the area in which we are currently working. Continuing research in the area by the state museum, under the direction of Dr. Robert Funk, and the State University College at Oneonta, under Dr. Bruce Rippetau, has had as its primary objectives the completion of the culture-historical record and refinement of the chronologies for the area.

## Objectives

The research goals of the I-88 project, focusing as they do on the settlement subsistence networks of the prehistoric population of the upper Susquehanna, Schenevus, and Schoharie drainages, are complementary to the culture-historical goals of other research in the region in that they provide for examination of cultural processes as expressed in the archaeological record of the area. They are judged most pertinent to the I-88 project because the wide swath of destruction that marks the progress of I-88 will forever distort the remnant archaeological record of the valleys penetrated. Because settlement–subsistence archaeology has as its basic data the distribution and frequencies of different kinds of archaeological sites, the impact of freeway construction of the magnitude of I-88 will destroy significant portions of its data base.

Settlement archaeology has proven to be one of the most productive tools in archaeologists' attempts to understand past human behavior and the cultural processes that have operated over the long run of man's history. Redman (1973:11–16) has commented on how the several kinds of settlement pattern data bear on a wide variety of problems and questions. Results of the application of settlement pattern concepts to New York State archaeology are evident in such work as that of Ritchie and Funk (1973), Tuck (1971 a, b), and the results of the early phases of the I-88 project (Plog and Stewart 1974).

## Procedures of the Research Strategy

The basic kinds of data required for the definition of subsistence–settlement systems include site location, site characteristics, and artifactual variability. These permit the construction of site typologies and in turn the examination of the interrelationship of site types and of the relationship of sites to the environment.

Our primary focus will be on the relationship between prehistoric man and his environment in the Susquehanna Valley and its environs: the effect of the environment on the evolution of cultural systems in the area, the impact of man on his environment, and the interaction between the two. The pivotal concept in our studies will be the *settlement–subsistence system* of local populations. Basically, this concept directs the attention of the archaeologist to (*1*) sites, (2) the kinds and frequencies of artifacts found on specific types of sites, and (3) the environment in which the site occurs and the kinds of resources available in that environment. In short, the archaeologist attempts to understand the relationship between environmental variability and variability in site locations and the kinds of artifacts found on sites.

## Variables

Let us look at the process of defining settlement–subsistence systems in somewhat more detail:

**Site Location:**  Every site has a location in space. So do various resources that might have been used by the inhabitants of the site. Thus, site location can be determined with respect to topographical, hydrological, floral, and faunal resources that might have been important to the inhabitants of the site. In the case of the upper Susquehanna Valley and its environs, there were many resources present that are known to have been used by New York Indians at contact time. Among these are: nuts, berries, herbs, sugar maple; wood, bark, and bast (especially elm bark); flint (nodules), sandstone, basalt, clay, granitic rocks; deer, elk, fish, bear, turtle, mussels, birds, rabbit, squirrel, woodchuck, beaver, and wolf.

**Site Characteristics:**  Every site has characteristics that are independent of the specific artifacts found on the site: site size, artifact density, etc.

**Artifact Variability:**  Artifacts were used by prehistoric populations in specific extractive and maintenance activities at the sites where they are found. Archaeologists can reconstruct with some accuracy the kinds of activities with which specific artifacts were associated. For example, we can use the edge angle, edge length, edge configuration, and edge orientation of chipped stone artifacts to create a functional typology of these tools. (One could easily do a similar analysis of tools from our own society.) More refined information concerning the use of tools may be obtained by examining minute patterns of wear and organic residues on the edges of tools. Different frequencies of tool types are found on different sites. The variability in these frequencies reflects the differential importance of tools and, thus, the activities with which the tools are associated at different sites. Similarly, one can study variability in the style of manufacture of the tools from site to site.

**Site Types:**  On the basis of site locations, site characteristics, and the kinds of activities that were carried on at sites as reflected in artifactual variability, one can define site types. Each of these types represents a locus at which particular sets of activities were carried out at some particular time following some organizational pattern. The site types associated with a particular population reflect the fashion in which that population organized its subsistence and maintenance activities. This organization is the settlement–subsistence system.

Known site types in the upper Susquehanna Valley include camps, hamlets, villages, workshops, and burial sites. Kill sites are also probably represented. What we do not know, and will be trying to find out, is how many (relatively) of each of these site types there are and how they were interrelated.

**Interrelationships of Site Types:**  Having defined a typology of sites, the archaeologist can examine the relationship between them. Do sites of the same type tend to occur together, or is there a regular articulation of sites of different types? Are different types of sites associated with different time periods or are they contemporaneous? What set of types of sites can we associate with a single time period, a single population? Is there evidence that a population was inhabiting different types of sites during different seasons of the year? In short, patterns of stylistic variability will be used to establish the contemporaneity of sites and cultural boundaries; and patterns of functional variability will be used in inferring the way that particular populations organized their subsistence and maintenance activities.

Ethnographic data on the Iroquois and other New York Indians suggests, for example, that settlement–subsistence systems in the area were fairly complex. We know that the Seneca, for example, had a two-village system, perhaps with additional satellite villages. The eighteenth-century Onaquaga Indians lived in three villages that functioned as a single community. In addition we have to consider that even the most sedentary Iroquois villages were occupied by only a small proportion of the aggregate of inhabitants during certain seasons and that males were seldom living in the villages. It was typical for a family to be away from a village fishing or hunting (and, therefore, occupying a fishing or hunting camp) and for men to be away at war, or at trade, leaving women, children, and the old in the villages. Among at least the Hurons, women left the village to live in their fields (field camps) during peaks of agricultural activity. In short, our efforts will be to determine which of these as well as other organizational patterns existed in the prehistoric past.

**Relationship of Sites to the Environment:**  Once the socioeconomic organization of an adaptation has been defined, one can examine the effect of the environment on that organization and changes in it, as well as the probable impact of the population on the environment. The upper Susquehanna Valley includes several environmental zones, each with potential site situations. Major environmental zones are: floodplain-riverine, floodplain-inland, terraces, valley slopes, and upland. All of the zones, except the last, appear to be represented within the I-88 right-of-way. Crosscutting these zones are local features such as gravel knolls, swamps, springs, rock cliffs, and smaller streams. Thus, there is a maximum of environmental diversity providing a significant opportunity for the study of settlement–subsistence systems.

## Methods

An explicit set of field techniques was developed, designed to meet the differing needs of corridor and right-of-way survey. The methods produce information appropriate to the several stages of expressway planning in order to permit avoidance and other forms of conservation of archaeological sites. They also yield data pertinent to the research design.

**Corridor Survey:**  The specific sampling strategy that we employed was sensitive to both past archaeological knowledge and statistical sampling. Both are necessary to the success of any effort. Not to look for sites in locations that past research has indicated were often selected as site locations by prehistoric peoples is to ignore the assembled knowledge of archaeology. To rely exclusively on this knowledge is to assume that it is complete and thereby limit the growth of knowledge. For these reasons our sampling strategy was a mixed one. It proceeded essentially as follows:

1. Transects as long as the corridor was wide were defined on a map every 300 m or 900 m. Each transect was 20-m wide.
2. Of necessity (because, for example, permission of the landowner could not be obtained), not all of these transects were surveyed. However, an average of 3½ transects in each linear mile of corridor was surveyed by a crew of four people, placing shovel test pits at regular intervals.
3. Crews were also responsible for identifying likely site locations that fell between the transects, which they then surveyed.

**Right-of-Way Survey:**    The need for a consistent, systematic set of methods for surveying the right-of-way was recognized in the 1974 season. The methods developed and employed were based on the following premises:

1. The expressway segments to be surveyed were characterized by extensive vegetation cover, including pasture, brush, and woodlands. Therefore, some form of excavation at intervals would be the only way to assess the amount of prehistoric and historical resources endangered by the right-of-way.
2. Given the imminence of the scheduled construction in these segments, it was necessary to complete the survey in a single season.
3. The rate of excavation of shovel test pits per crew was estimated from ongoing corridor survey and found to average in the order of 50–100 shovel test pits per crew day.

A minimum, systematic coverage of 1 shovel test pit per 20-m interval down the center line of the right-of-way was the resulting standard. Crews were required to maintain a pace of .5- to 1-km linear coverage of right-of-way per day, and additional shovel test pits were placed in the right-of-way at the discretion of the crew chief, who had the responsibility for maintaining the desired pace of right-of-way survey. When the center line could not be approximated, crews used the surveyed base line of the right-of-way as a guide to its course and aligned their test pits along it.

The dictated pace permitted some additional testing in the course of right-of-way survey, particularly because some segments remained unsurveyed due to standing crops or permission refusals. The available field time that resulted was applied to additional testing in localities to determine the extent of sites that had been discovered. The schedule was also designed to bring the survey to completion a week before the end of the field season in order to allow for contingencies. The remaining field time at the close of the season was also devoted to determining the extent of some of the sites that had been discovered.

**Site Examination and Excavation:**    The I-88 Archaeological Project is committed to the application of statistical sampling to appropriate stages of archaeological investigation. While no standard form of sampling was applied to the sites tested in the 1974 season, experiments in statistical sampling were undertaken at the Hendrick sites and the Sidney Airport site. Results of the sampling designs applied to these sites were analyzed, and as a result, statistical sampling was more broadly employed in the 1975 season.


## ISSUES UNDERLYING THE 1974 DESIGN

The approach taken to research during the summer of 1974 represented reactions to a variety of different issues directly and tangentially related to the specific requirements of contract work. Sampling, survey strategy, and excavation strategy were of primary concern.


### Sampling

Any archaeologist who does not dig every square meter of a site is sampling that site. Any archaeologist who does not survey every square meter of a study region is sampling that region. Unfortunately, too many pieces of archaeological research in the past have been based on the assumption that any sample is a valid sample. Increasingly, we are accumulating evidence suggesting that unless samples of sites and regions are carefully, usually statistically, chosen, the results of excavations are likely to be misleading or wrong. Recent analyses of survey data from the Southwestern United States that one of us (Plog) has undertaken have shown that traditional site surveys have tended to underestimate the number of sites in a survey area by a factor of 5 to 10 and to overestimate the average size of sites by a similar factor. Clearly, inferences based on such data are going to be very misleading. Let us briefly mention why such a difficulty arises.

In the context of survey archaeology certain kinds of sites—sites of particular cultures, time periods, or activities—are more likely to be found by a survey than others because of their size, location, or other factors that affect "visibility." In order to insure that sites of all cultures, types, and time periods are found, an intensive study of a statistically selected sample of locations in a survey region is required.

Similarly, archaeologists too frequently respond to the satisfaction of finding large numbers of sites by concentrating survey work in areas where sites are abundant. Such tendencies ignore the fact that the differential distribution or density of sites in a region, including information on areas where there are no sites at all, is a powerful source of evidence of the way in which prehistoric populations adapted to their environments. Rich areas do often reflect organizationally or exploitatively important locations within a region, but a failure to explore areas with low site density often leads to a failure to understand significant organizational or exploitative components of a settlement–subsistence system that did not involve large sites, large numbers of sites, or highly visible sites.

These same problems are important in excavation. If sites are not selected for excavation on the basis of some sampling procedure, particular cultures, time periods, or site types are likely to be systematically underrepresented. Similarly, excavations that concentrate on rich areas within sites are systematically failing to record areas where activities that involved limited numbers of artifacts and left low artifact densities were carried out.

Not all of the justifications for statistical sampling are negative ones—problems that will occur if a sample is not a statistical one. When a statistical sample is employed, a far smaller percentage of a site can be excavated or a region surveyed in order to achieve a high probability of accurately characterizing activities carried out at the site or in the region. Moreover, knowing the prehistory of an area on the basis of a small sample means that a higher percentage of the archaeological evidence at the locus will be available for subsequent archaeological research.

## Survey Strategy

Our survey has been the corridor within which the right-of-way for I-88 between Binghamton and Schenectady, New York, is being located. A part of this work during the summer of 1973 involved surveying already chosen right-of-way segments. But the survey strategies employed in the reconnaissance of a highway right-of-way and those employed in the reconnaissance of a corridor are markedly different. In the case of the former, the territory that the archaeologists must cover is limited and can be surveyed in great detail. Similar detail is not possible in the case of a corridor survey; the amount of territory to be covered and the need to obtain permission from landowners (sometimes not granted) prohibit it. During the summer of 1973, for example, we contracted to survey 33.8 linear miles, or approximately 20.4 square miles, from Oneonta and Cobbleskill, New York. Normally an archaeologist might spend as many as 2000 man-days in such an effort in areas where conditions for survey research are ideal. In an area such as the I-88 corridor, where due to multiple landowners and the vegetation cover, conditions are not ideal, 4000 to 5000 man-days would be required to survey the corridor in the same detail as a right-of-way.

Manpower in such quantities is rarely available. Fortunately, at this stage in contract research it is not necessary to examine the entire land surface in such detail. By a judicious sampling of the relevant territory the archaeologist can accomplish the primary goal of his task—providing information that will assist the agency in selecting a right-of-way. Specifically, what is required is a body of data that will characterize the relative density of sites in different geographical locations. With such information the archaeologist can identify within both broad and limited parameters which alternative locations of a right-of-way will necessitate considerable or limited further expenditure of funds for mitigation. Such data can be obtained from a relatively small sample.

The specific sampling strategy that we employed was sensitive to both past archaeological knowledge and statistical sampling.

This effort generated three sets of information that allowed us to evaluate the impact of alternative right-of-way locations on archaeological resources:

1. A map of known site locations. To the extent that a right-of-way is chosen that passes through these locations, provisions for mitigation must be discussed.

2. A map of relative site densities. Since it is clearly the case that many sites in the corridor have not yet been identified, we have used the map of known site locations (a) to identify localities where there are sites and (b) to project the relative density of sites in these localities. To the extent that the right-of-way passes through high-density localities, the need for funds for archaeological survey and testing will be greater. Moreover, these maps will guide future work in testing sites once the right-of-way is defined.

3. Locational conclusions within localities. Within each locality somewhat finer discriminations can be made on the basis of topographical situations in which sites most typically occur.

Thus, we feel that given the financial and manpower constraints under which we were operating, the use of the sampling technique just described has permitted us to obtain the information needed by the New York State Department of Transportation in its preliminary planning. In particular, projecting relative site densitites would have been impossible without the statistical sample. Finally, we believe that the sites we have found are likely to reflect the different cultures, time periods, and activity loci represented.

## Excavation Strategy

Too frequently, approaches to site excavation are based on the assumption that sensitivity to space–time criteria will produce excavated materials sufficient for any analytical task. It can be shown that a concern for settlement–subsistence information and sampling result in different decisions at a number of points in the excavation process.

Let us look first at the task of selecting sites for excavation. If one is interested in reconstructing prehistoric settlement–subsistence systems, sites cannot be selected for excavation solely on the basis of their size or the cultural tradition or time period that they are believed to represent. Equal attention must be paid to smaller sites that, because of the initial artifactual material collected from them or because of their location, seem to represent functionally different site types. Without excavating the known range of functionally different site types it will be impossible to accurately describe the settlement–subsistence systems of the prehistoric populations in question. In the absence of a clear initial understanding of these functional differences randomly selecting sites for excavation is more likely to produce an understanding of local settlement–subsistence systems than excavations focused on large sites.

Similarly, archaeologists interested in settlement–subsistence systems cannot afford to ignore disturbed or plow zone sites. While such sites do not require the same careful excavation techniques as a stratified site, the possibility that they represent functionally different activities from those carried out at the larger and stratified sites must be investigated. While disturbance of sites by plowing may render an analysis of activity areas within the sites difficult or impossible, it in no way hinders comparison with artifacts from other sites. The mixing of different time periods and/or different cultural traditions at such sites is nonproblematical if populations returned to the location to carry out the same or similar activities. For example, analyses were undertaken of materials from four plow zone sites during the fall of 1973. A 25% sample of the sites was taken primarily from the surface of the sites, and important intersite differences were identified. It was possible to distinguish some functionally different areas within the sites despite the disturbance by plowing.

A concern with the reconstruction of settlement–subsistence systems also has important consequences for the way in which excavations are carried out. Sampling of sites is necessary in order to insure an understanding of the distribution of activities within individual sites. Sampling also saves time in excavation. Screening and flotation are mandatory if faunal and floral data are to be recovered. Experiments carried out at the four sites mentioned earlier suggested that in the absence of screening waste flakes and other small artifacts will almost necessarily be missed. Thus, the varying importance of tool-making activities at different sites is likely to be missed when screens are not employed.

## Analysis

When the concern of a research effort is principally a culture-historical one, the "diagnostic" artifacts found at a site are typically seen as more important than artifacts in general. As a result, archaeologists operating in this tradition have thrown out nondiagnostic artifacts, such as waste flakes, or have failed to use excavation procedures that would be likely to recover them. A settlement–subsistence approach necessitates a concern for all artifacts and classes of artifacts. Understanding the nature of the activities carried out at a given site or understanding the differences between two sites may rest as heavily, or more heavily, on knowing the pattern of variation in unutilized or slightly utilized flakes as on diagnostic artifacts. The former provides a key to the activities carried out at the site, while the latter do not.

The bulk of the information collected to this date in the I-88 contract program is survey information. Thus, our efforts have only partially been directed toward the reconstruction of prehistoric settlement–subsistence systems. An equal importance has been attached to generating a preliminary definition of site types that will guide us in excavation during the coming summers. Basically, we have proceeded as follows:

1. We have used the variability in site density to identify spatially distinguishable settlement clusters.
2. We have used diagnostic artifacts to identify the time periods during which individual sites were occupied.
3. We have used variation between sites in the ratios of different patterns of edge wear and in the ratios of different types of retouched artifacts, as well as the variable size, location, and content of sites, to define functionally specific site types.

## RETROSPECTIVE COMMENTS ON THE 1974 RESEARCH DESIGN

A retrospective examination of the I-88 research design as it stood in 1974 requires comments in three areas: research strategy, problem formulations, and methods. While as of this writing no segments of I-88 have been advanced into final excavation since 1974, an additional field season and two seasons of analysis have tested the utility and fertility of the ideas that have guided the project.

The concept of site type was central to the research strategy. It was anticipated that site types would be defined from the variables of site location, site characteristics, and artifact variability or assemblage composition. We have not made much progress toward that goal. Rather, we have found that each of the variables is a productive and complex subject of investigation. While it may prove possible to define site types on the basis of statistical associations of attributes of these variables, it does not now appear that site types will be as sensitive indicators of the relationships between prehistoric communities and their environments as will be the explicit study of each variable and its relationship to the others and to the environment. The difficulties encountered in attempting to work with the site type concept was a factor that led one of us (F. Plog 1975) to question the feasibility of the settlement–subsistence system concept.

We also find that sites as commonly defined are not the most suitable units for analysis. We encounter very few situations in which we are dealing with either a well-defined, single-component site or a well-stratified, multicomponent site. Most of the sites that we are dealing with are the result of multiple occupations of a general locality over a period of time, with most of the archaeological record in surficial deposits that have been plowed. Except for pits and other features that extend below the plow zone and may or may not represent sealed deposit from a particular time and activity, we must primarily rely on spatial distributions to identify units within sites that may represent specific activities at a point in time. Such loci, once defined, form a more suitable basic unit for comparison.

Site location relative to resource availability has proven to be a more subtle variable than anticipated. The glaciofluvial trough in which I-88 is routed is a mosaic of microenvironments, and site locations generally have access to floodplain, hillside, and upland vegetation zones, and to riverine and/or marsh resources. This is only to say that if we are to discern significant differences in site locations, we will have to examine carefully hydrology, exposure, slope, and edaphic conditions as well as come to control the changes that have occurred during the Euramerican period.

Methodological studies have dominated the research that has been completed. The research design has stimulated lithic analyses directed toward procurement of raw materials, technology, and function, as we have sought to understand assemblage composition. The need to design recovery strategies for endangered sites has led us to investigate and experiment with sampling fraction and sample unit size to be used in the site examination phase of highway work. Statistical methods for defining spatial clusters and characterizing their composition from surface collections have advanced our ability to extract information from plow zone site samples.

The research design did not sufficiently specify a problem or series of problems to which the I-88 research was directed. We have, however, developed a series of midrange questions, regional in scale, that can be addressed in part with information from I-88, which we will not detail here. In addition, we have used a populations dynamics perspective from which to pose a series of more general questions of the archaeological record (Weide 1975).

The Northeast, like other areas, has had its prehistoric record subjected to the assumptions of population growth as inherent in human populations, providing a convenient causal factor in attempts to describe or explain change (e.g., Ford 1974; Kinsey 1975). Krober's (1939) observation to the contrary that the apparent population densities of the eastern United States at contact did not exceed levels that might be expected of hunters and gathers leads us to take something of the devil's advocate role and to propose the following hypotheses:

1. The low rate of discovery of early Archaic occupations results from natural processes that have obscured and partially destroyed the archaeological record of this period. It is not due to lowered population levels resulting from the lowered productivity of the early postglacial forests, as Ritchie and Funk (1973) prematurely explained.

2. Accepting the qualitative observation of significant population increase in the Late Archaic, we predict that Late Archaic population densitites were essentially as high as those of the Late Woodland. We further predict that the major difference will be found in the distribution of population rather than the overall density.

4. The dominant population dynamic of the Late Woodland were not population increase, but rather increasing nucleation into fewer, larger communities.

# 8

# Management Strategies for Effective Research[1]

VELETTA CANOUTS

American archaeologists increasingly find themselves in the company of environmentalists because of a growing awareness of a diminishing resource and research base. Recent evaluations of the current status of archaeological resources have fostered the development of a conservation philosophy (Lipe 1974), whose implementation requires a management approach. A realistic and comprehensive appraisal of adverse effects on archaeological resources recognizes that construction, vandalism, and even research will continue their roles of attrition, rendering an exclusive protection position untenable. Management insures that this exploitation will occur only when all other protection options have been explored and that this exploitation is a form of data preservation that conforms to the highest research standards in the discipline.

The subject of this chapter concerns management strategies for effecting research in a cultural resource management framework. These strategies are not related to fiscal or administrative management aspects of contract projects. Instead, they concern the implementation of theoretical, methodological, and technical strategies by the archaeologists. For the purpose of this discussion, time is considered to be the most important variable affecting the implementation of these strategies. Time is one factor in contract projects over which archaeologists have had the least control. "Salvage archaeologists working against time," a commonly heard utterance, implies that pressure of time means the inability to perform good or innovative research in the context of contract projects. This concept of salvage and time and their relationship to research needs to be examined from a current contract perspective.

Contract archaeologists have been successful in extending planning time and work schedules beyond previous limits. However, this does not necessarily mean that archaeologists have as much time as they want or need to plan and conduct

[1]Adapted from a paper presented at a meeting of the Society for American Archaeology, Dallas, Texas, May 1975.

121

research. How can projects be operationalized to maximize research potential, and thus resource potential, through a more efficient use of time?

Research, as conducted in a conservation model, should be problem-oriented and result in a representative preservation of the data base (Lipe 1974). To accomplish this end in a time–research framework, archaeological strategies may be seen to relate to the following three management principles:

1. Each stage of a project's research program must be a refinement of the preceding stage.
2. Research continuity must insure that a project is independent of a single researcher's commitment.
3. Project research should be utilized as a cumulative base upon which subsequent contract projects can build.

## EACH STAGE OF A PROJECT'S RESEARCH PROGRAM MUST BE A REFINEMENT OF THE PRECEDING STAGE

Working from an integrated information base, one that is continually updated and synthesized, is more efficient than working with unconnected data bits. Such integration allows research problems to be more easily developed and scaled to fit the resource potential. One of the biggest problems or greatest challenges facing archaeologists in contract research lies in defining problems that correspond to the impacted portion of the archaeological record. Archaeologists have usually selected sites to fit their research interests. Where the data base is arbitrarily defined by project boundaries, a 180° reversal of this procedure is necessary. Forcing a data base to fit predetermined and narrow research interests is liable to be nonproductive (cf. Reid 1975).

Very broadly, the research stages in contract archaeology involve an information search, survey, and mitigation. A check of site survey files, a review of the literature, and communication with relevant informants, such as outside specialists, amateurs, and other archaeologists, furnish information about probable site types, allow projections about site densities, and identify critical problems that may be encountered in a project area. A research orientation can generally be outlined upon the completion of the information search.

To make this search and identification process more effective, documentary information must be kept up to date. One of the faster techniques now being explored for storing data and updating site survey files is the use of the computer. Quick dissemination of research results is also needed, especially to utilize the information generated by the volume of contract projects (Schiffer 1975b). Thus far, area institutions and regional meetings continue to be the primary sources for this information.

Ideally, background research precedes any fieldwork. Where projects proceed at a rapid rate, institutionally based research teams and field teams may engage in a cooperative research exchange. The Arizona State Museum has found that it maximizes research time by consistently using an in-house research team to prepare background information on archaeological and environmental variables encountered in the field and to review problems with the incoming field data while the fieldwork is still in progress (Kemrer, Shultz and Dodge 1972).

Surveys, whether sampling surveys or intensive surveys, should be guided by a problem orientation, preferably generated from a background review. Surveys that do not assess resource potential or recover data in a problem context are not maximizing the survey methodology. Research problems should be refined through survey, variables and their measuring criteria should be defined, and survey information should be applied toward answering specific questions about the archaeological record and/or questions about human behavior.

This aspect of survey research is increasingly important in contract projects. Survey management recommendations that are phrased in a conservation format primarily reflect a protection orientation. Sponsors, realizing the temporal and monetary benefits of site avoidance, are increasingly amenable to protecting sites whenever possible. Unless surveys are viewed with this in mind, information obtainable through survey may not be sought, and there may even be a predilection to continue a project into an unwarrantable excavation phase.

When a mitigative program for data recovery must be developed, the survey research framework should provide the impetus for a specific research design. Implementing mitigative programs is one of the most critical pressure points in contract projects. The public and sponsors often assume that, once a site is located and recorded, mitigative action can begin immediately. While educating the sponsors that sites are investigated using research guidelines, that problems determine data recovery methods, researchers can maximize the planning time allowed them by building upon the survey research recommendations.

Use of a research design to focus research testing priorities and statistical sampling are important time-saving methodologies in effecting one of the more important strategies for data recovery programs. This strategy is the ability to formulate and conduct excavation and analysis in evaluative stages (cf. Redman 1973). An evaluative stage is that increment of research where data can be synthesized in a manner that suggests future research directions while answering some research questions. Evaluative stages are very important for reasons that apply specifically to contract projects. Contract projects, more than any other research project, are subject to sudden stops and starts. Spreading investigations too thin in the initial stages may contribute to a research hiatus for a period of time if project plans change. Evaluative stages maximize research returns and minimize the effects of project uncertainties. Working in a format that has evaluative stages need not necessarily mean that an archaeologist should interrupt fieldwork flow if the project is continuous. But the archaeologist should have evaluative points available for assessing temporal and other logistic needs during the research season.

Proceeding in evaluative stages during data recovery also aids in reviewing and modifying the research design. The argument that data recovered after design changes will not be comparable with data recovered before is spurious. If research is directed toward the understanding of human behavior, comparisons at that level of interpretation are the most important. Comparisons of interpretations based on different data bases are still valid if the interpretations are valid. As data recovery programs in contract projects usually correspond to partial or whole destruction of sites, waiting until the end of the fieldwork to incorporate field feedback may mean discovering that modifications that can no longer be realized would have profited the research. The next principle reinforces and complements the strategy of developing research programs in evaluative stages.


## RESEARCH CONTINUITY MUST INSURE THAT A PROJECT IS INDEPENDENT OF A SINGLE RESEARCHER'S COMMITMENT

The relationship between this principle and maximizing research time may not be obvious, as it issues primarily from a cultural resource management framework. Contract projects are numerous, and many operations are sizeable, complex, and long-term. Implementing a large number of programs either within or outside of institutions would quickly overwhelm a single individual. Besides, research directions totally supplied by a single individual may be undesirable. One of the most challenging aspects of contract research discussed earlier is the need to fit research problems to the resource base. Most individuals, alone, do not have the adaptability through training or inclination to pursue different research objectives.

At this stage one management strategy might be to place an individual in charge of fewer projects, but that solution suffers from other project constraints. Due to the success of management archaeologists' attempts to involve archaeology in early project planning stages, research time is expanding. This time expansion, however, stems primarily from interim halts between project stages. Since, to date, most cultural resource management programs in the country operate on funding that is project specific, there is the problem of employing permanent personnel. A core of permanent personnel can guide a large variety and number of projects, but most follow-through research will have to be performed by a temporary, mobile pool of archaeologists. Therefore, a number of archaeologists are apt to be involved on any one project.

If archaeologists are not to be caught up in *informant archaeology*—that is, interviewing various individuals to find out why they initiated certain actions and what interpretations they made about the resource base—projects must be conducted in stages that are conducive to research interests and syntheses, ideally comparable to the evaluative research stages just discussed. One of the principal strategies for insuring project continuity is adequate documentation. The documentary form offering the greatest contribution is an evaluative report that includes a presentation of research goals, methodologies, results, and recommendations. Several types of reports, such as progress reports or preliminary reports, have traditionally been more limited in scope. These reports plus research designs, research appraisals, background research, and research findings can be assembled into a set of working papers forming an evaluative project report. These working papers are extremely useful in initiating new project personnel.

In order to retain project continuity and complete contract projects within a reasonable amount of time, archaeologists must begin to work together at all levels of research responsibility. Archaeologists may find themselves working together in teams where research exchange is immediate and constant. A number of archaeologists with different archaeological skills may be needed to realize a project's research potential (cf. Reid 1973; Schiffer 1975b). For example, expertise in terms of ecological models, typological definitions, quantitative methods, or field interpretations may be elicited from a number of individuals. In addition, archaeologists with management training will have to provide the decision-making information and recommendations for legal, sponsor, and administrative requirements.

Project stages also involve archaeologists in a progressive work pattern where guidance is provided by the evaluative report. The major problem confronting this work pattern is that of adapting a new researcher's interests to a project's research framework. If new researchers are introduced at project stages that conform to archaeological research stages, these problems should be minimal. The researcher would only have to contend with previous research recommendations. Even if researchers enter an on-going project stage, research designs are usually not so detailed as to disallow additions or modifications. Such innovations challenge the archaeologists' ingenuity.

Because archaeologists are building upon or supplying the basis for their colleagues' performances, another problem involving research ethics arises. There are two immediate reasons why researchers cannot ignore previous work: time and money. While understanding that growth in a discipline stems from disagreement, duplication of work at the sponsor's expense is unethical, as well as confusing to the public, who must often weigh a number of contradictory opinions. Research must be reviewed fairly, critically but without bias, and this research must be conducted in a manner that conforms to the standards now professed by the discipline.

The foregoing emphasis on individual cooperation may suggest that all research stages of a single project are conducted by individuals at the same institution. This is not always the case. Due to institutional capacities and scheduling problems, different institutions may well be involved at different stages of the same project. Problems of logistics and communication between institutions increase the problems already hindering research continuity. Institutions will need to operate on a cooperative basis, like researchers, with respect for research goals and a follow-through response on research recommendations. Institutions working in the same geographic area should benefit from the application of the last management principle to be discussed.

## PROJECT RESEARCH SHOULD BE UTILIZED AS A
## CUMULATIVE BASE ON WHICH SUBSEQUENT
## PROJECTS CAN BUILD

The cumulative process is the assimilation of the research results of a number of projects into an integrated whole. As the efforts of the entire discipline are directed toward this goal, the following remarks are addressed to a cumulative research base that is regional or institutional in scope.

Contract archaeology, to effect good research in a limited amount of time, must operate from a cumulative research base for several reasons. In the first place, a number of contract projects do not provide enough resources to permit the development of a full-fledged research program, yet a certain expenditure of time and money for research is necessary whether archaeological resources number 1 or 100. There are at least two strategies that may alleviate this problem. The use of regional research designs, which are now in their formative stages, is one. Building upon research designs already generated for other projects is another. When using other research designs, archaeologists should not simply extend a sample size or test previous studies. True, these are aspects of accumulation, but increasing a sample size does not maximize the potential of the resources. Testing previous data interpretations can be incorporated into investigations that will also further refine methodological considerations or add to an explanatory model.

Building and utilizing a cumulative research base maximize time because of the use of a common communication base. This is especially important on the institutional level. In dealing with numerous contract projects institutions or special institutional programs may establish major research orientations to realize minimal comparability in data synthesis (cf. Goodyear 1975a). Institutions working in the same area will be better able to generate research recommendations if the full range of problem orientations and needs of cooperating institutions are known, and new researchers in such programs can more quickly assimilate background information.

Perhaps one of the more important reasons for building and utilizing a cumulative research base is to answer the questions, What did or did not work and why? Contract research of a relatively short-term nature wastes time in finding out the answers to these questions the hard way. Rather than repetitious effort, evaluation and recommendation sections of research reports should be expanded and strengthened. Recommendations are ways of adding to a cumulative base, since researchers cannot develop all lines of inquiry equally. Recommendations in view of the dynamic research stages advocated here are extremely important; just how important may be illustrated historically. Many cultural resource programs are in the process of evaluating archaeological sites affected by projects constructed in the 1950s and 1960s that are now being redesigned or elaborated. Archaeologists are often unable to predict the impact of the redesigned project on possibly remaining site potential because they are unable to evaluate the initial impact upon the resources.

Finally, the dynamics of a cumulative research base allow results to build on results and not data bits. This point raises a question about representative sampling in data recovery programs. The idea of obtaining a representative sample, again, arises from the special nature of contract projects, in which a large number of sites can be irrevocably damaged. There is a feeling of commitment in recovering a representative data base for colleagues and future generations (Lipe 1974). Although the commitment is laudable, effecting it raises some problems. For example, is a representative sample a class of data, a site, a geographic area, an area's environmental resources that contribute to the understanding of certain models of human behavior? Archaeologists are continuously redefining and establishing data classes for interpreting problems of human behavior. As paradigm shifts occur, the problems themselves have to be reexamined.

Perhaps representative data could, in part, be realized as explanations of human behavior that point to new problems and data classes. This would constitute sequential, multistage research in adjacent geographic areas. Within this building-block concept it should be possible for a research team to answer a comprehensive set of research questions, but the project should be relieved of the burden of recovering a *total* representative sample that is beyond the capabilities of many institutions, let alone archaeologists, to process, interpret, and evaluate.

Additional support of this position may be cited from evidence of archaeological tendencies to parcel out sections on project findings. Evaluative and even descriptive sections suffer from a tendency to collect everything from the field now and to store much of it for later analyses that somehow never occur. These data do not participate in the cumulative growth of the research base; it is as if they were never collected.

Furthermore, field collections may not be readily available. Cultural resource management programs are increasing the pressure on storage facilities. Museums may have to resort to underground and warehouse storage that is relatively inaccessible. The public, responding to educational programs, wants to see materials displayed and explained. Some special interest groups are demanding title and possession of cultural collections. Until storage, educational, and ownership demands are resolved, data collections may be temporary things in the hands of the archaeologists.

In summary, these management strategies are not new. Archaeologists have generally employed a number of them. What has been presented is the conceptualization of these strategies into a time–research framework. The principles incorporating the various strategies are abstracted from an interdependent set of relationships. Contract research, or for that matter, any research endeavor that must maximize time, must, therefore, operationalize all three of these principles—not intermittently for specific projects, but consistently for every project.

# Part III

# RESEARCH DESIGN

An appraisal of modern archaeology to which we come reluctantly is that precious little is known about how to design the kinds of projects that address timely research questions in a realistic manner. Far too often, research is characterized by a poor fit between questions and resources, the use of techniques of recovery and analysis without adequate justification, and a failure to achieve sufficiently credible results to serve as a foundation for future research or as a basis for management recommendations. The shortcomings in many investigations (cultural resource management and others) highlight the need to accord the study of research design a high priority.

The archaeological literature specifically dealing with the topic of research design consists of few titles. Binford (1964) was one of the first to raise some of the issues surrounding design of regional projects of the type that now are frequently carried out in conservation archaeology (see also Struever 1968a, 1971). Fritz and Plog (1970) urged the use of a rigorous hypothetico-deductive approach in all studies (see also J. N. Hill 1972; F. T. Plog 1974b; Watson, LeBlanc, and Redman 1971), as a counterpoint to the inductive strategy outlined by Swartz (1967). Redman (1973) lucidly treated multistage research, a subject that has obvious implications for conservation archaeology. In a paper that deserves to be read often, Daniels (1972) examined archaeological research design from the standpoint of how to improve the quality of archaeological data. Goodyear (1976) contributed a general discussion on the importance and benefits of careful research design in conservation archaeology. And finally, the Airlie House seminar on archaeological reports set forth guidelines for research designs and research proposals (Vivian *et al.* 1977). In Chapter 13 Raab adds to this literature with his insights into the research design process.

One should not conclude, simply because the general literature on research design in archaeology is small, that few works need to be consulted when designing research. On the contrary, a little reflection will reveal that the successful research design is an outgrowth of the creative application of archaeological expertise to the problem at hand. This endeavor requires on the part of the investigator nothing less than a exhaustive knowledge of archaeological method and theory, a close familiarity with previous research on the problem, and an intimate acquaintance with available information on the archaeological resources. As often happens, a single individual does not command all of these areas of expertise; as a result, the research design process becomes a cooperative activity. We do not presume in this volume to be able to teach method and theory; we do assume, however, that the conservation archaeologist will obtain such knowledge *and keep it current*. Becoming familiar with the resources and research problems is, of course, a project-specific task—about which we say no more.

Before we outline the uses to which research designs are put in conservation archaeology, it is perhaps necessary to discuss what a research design is not. A research design does not resemble a procrustean bed in which all data are forced to lie. A research design does not preclude alternative courses of action, especially when something new or unexpected turns up. And a research design does not force one to ignore or destroy important data. Curiously, all of these charges (and others) have been leveled against the proponents of explicit research design—when they should have been aimed at specific examples of poorly planned research. It is fair to deplore poor research planning, but one can hardly defend the position that planning per se is unnecessary (see also Reher n.d.; Goodyear 1976).

As Goodyear (1976) points out, explicit research designs offer the investigator and the archaeological community at least four distinct advantages over implicit approaches. First of all, if the problems and hypotheses are set forth at the outset of research, the archaeologist is much more likely to specify and gather the relevant data. Second, an explicit research plan allows for public monitoring of research biases. Third, the progress and efficiency of an undertaking is more readily evaluated. And fourth, explicit research designs allow for better integration of the conceptual and empirical components of investigations. Hopefully, it will not be necessary much longer to justify the development of explicit research designs in archaeology. Certainly, the need to conduct research efficiently and in several stages is already leading to widespread formulation and implementation of research designs in conservation archaeology.

## PROBLEM DOMAINS

The process of research design starts with the identification of problems that need to be solved. In conservation archaeology the search for timely research problems in addition to those specified in the contract begins at the overview and assessment stages. Sometimes during these early-stage projects, and especially in field studies, it becomes possible not only to pinpoint research questions but also to suggest tentative avenues for answering them. When the process of research design has progressed to the latter stage, one begins to formulate *problem domains*. The latter may be thought of as incipient research designs. Canouts in Chapter 9 illustrates their construction and use (see also Fuller, Rogge, and Gregonis 1976; Stewart and Teague 1974).

## REGIONAL RESEARCH DESIGNS

The process of designing projects can be considerably enhanced at all stages if a regional research design is available that encompasses the study area. Regional research designs vary greatly in their degree of specificity and elaboration; some, like the pioneering effort of the archaeologists working in the Mississippi Valley, consist primarily of a listing of then current research questions (McGimsey, Davis, and Griffin 1968), while others contain a narrower problem focus with some plans for implementing the research (e.g., Grady 1976; Plog and Hill 1971; King and King 1973). Goodyear's research design for highway archaeology in South Carolina (Chapter 12) furnishes a tidy example of a specialized regional research design, as does Trubowitz's plan for highway work in New York State (Chapter 10). When using a regional research design, one should keep in mind at all times that additional research problems, specific to the study area, may be investigated. Furthermore, project-specific considerations usually dictate modifications to the regional research design. To be most effective, regional research designs should serve to stimulate thought (not substitute for it) and provide some of the information needed to erect a project-specific research design; never should they be used as a crutch or in place of adequate background studies.

## FIELD STUDIES—CONSIDERATIONS FOR RESEARCH DESIGN

The absence of problem domains and regional research designs complicates only slightly the process of designing field studies. It means that the investigator must do additional studies in order to reach the point of identifying problems amenable to treatment at that particular stage. Research designs for field studies must be carefully formulated in order that research questions and management information needs are taken into account. The chapters in the remainder of this volume indicate some of the research procedures by which management information (i.e., nature and extent of the resource base, assessment of significance, project impacts, mitigation recommendations) may be obtained. It is hoped that these considerations will be joined with purely research concerns to form creative and realistic research designs. Raab in Chapter 13 illustrates such a program, with emphasis on archaeological needs. Beyond urging that research designs for field studies make use of up-to-date knowledge of the area, incorporate modern archaeological theory and method, and involve a clear sense of problem(s), we offer no advice; in fact, we strongly caution the investigator, in research design as well as other aspects of conservation archaeology projects, to avoid relying on neat, prepackaged approaches.

## RESEARCH DESIGNS AND ASSESSMENTS OF SIGNIFICANCE

Research designs not only give direction to field studies (and other types of projects), but they also may be derived from them (or even early-stage projects—e.g., Stacy and Hayden 1975). Especially in intensive field studies, research designs may be included in a report to help justify assessments of significance and to provide recommendations for future research. Raab and Klinger (n.d.) cogently argue that explicit research designs should play a prominent role in assessing significance. Research designs included as part of a field study report are generally developed considerably beyond the problem domain stage but often lack refinement and details for implementation. The report of the Cache River Archaeological Project contains 10 such research designs, none of which could be applied directly without further work, but all of which nudge the frontiers of knowledge in sometimes exciting ways (Schiffer and House 1975b:187–269). They range widely over substantive, technical, methodological, and theoretical questions. The assessments of significance in the report of the Village Creek project are also buttressed by research designs (Klinger n.d.b). Chapter 11, by Garrison, is an excellent example of a partially developed research design, concerned with technical and methodological questions, that easily could be the product of an intensive field study and could give direction to future research.

## RESEARCH PROPOSALS

Vivian et al. (1977) draw a useful distinction between a research design and a research proposal. The latter is a document that, although it does contain plans for future research, is written primarily with the audience of the sponsor in mind. In some instances a research proposal is simply a research design with an attached budget; other sponsors may require the inclusion of only simplified discussions of the proposed research but will expect a vastly more detailed budget. Vivian *et al.* (1977) delineate the elements of a typical research proposal; they should be consulted for guidance.

## CONCLUSION

The diversity of research designs that follow in Part III should by themselves suffice to disabuse the casual reader of the notion that research design in conservation archaeology is anything but the product of creativity and archaeological expertise in the context of particular circumstances (see Grady and Lipe 1976). Let no one expect a research design to conform to a preordained formula. We should, however, expect all research designs to isolate cogent problems worthy of study and to propose up-to-date and realistic procedures for solving them.

# 9

# Problem Domains in the Santa Rosa Wash Project, Arizona

VELETTA CANOUTS

To evaluate the research potential of archaeological resources affected by the Santa Rosa Wash project, the archaeological record was stratified by site into five problem domains. Their formulation appears to have been effective in staging and anticipating the coordination necessary to solve research and management problems encountered during the course of the project.

The Santa Rosa Wash project area lies within the northernmost extension of the Papago Indian Reservation in southern Arizona. There, in 1970, the United States Army Corps of Engineers was in the process of planning Tat Momolikot Dam. This earthen dam was intended to impound water in the upper Santa Rosa Wash, which is a major north-flowing ephemeral drainage of the northern Papaguerian desert. Under the Reservoir Salvage Act of 1960, an archaeological survey funded by the National Park Service was conducted specifically within the proposed construction zones. The number and nature of the archaeological resources encountered (Stacy and Palm 1970) led to a proposal for further survey and testing in the project area. The provisions of the proposal by the Arizona State Museum involved surveying, intensively, all lands within the conservation pool, surveying the flood zone with particular attention to immediate construction activity areas, and testing three archaeological sites recorded in 1970 to determine the area's subsurface historical and structural potential.

When the survey began in the summer of 1972, the Arizona State Museum was developing an expanded archaeological program to implement the evaluative requirements of the National Environmental Policy Act (NEPA). In line with the guidelines prepared by Scovill, Gordon, and Anderson (1972), the museum composed a set of evaluative criteria for site survey, which included assessments of cultural and temporal affiliations, nature and extent of archaeological deposits, disturbance factors, and site interrelationships and intrarelationships as well as National Register eligibility and statements of significance on which recommended

135

protection and mitigative programs would be based. The fulfillment of these criteria provided a comprehensive review for any project. Although the Santa Rosa Wash project was not initiated through NEPA legislation, the survey was implemented through the museum's reorganized efforts to discharge all the legislative mandates.

In addition, the museum's revised survey format stressed an analysis of environmental as well as archaeological variables. The recording of environmental variables is extremely well suited to the Lower Sonoran desert region of southern Arizona, where desert limitations relate directly to the natural and cultural transformation processes affecting the archaeological record (cf. Schiffer and Rathje 1973). Cultural-environmental data also contribute to a major interest in settlement–subsistence research. Because of their visible associations and because land alteration affects these associations, consideration of cultural and environmental variables at even standardized levels of survey recording are useful in framing immediate survey assessments of site data potential as well as in framing research problems for mitigative studies.

Guided by these dual aims within the museum's survey program, the fieldwork itself was essentially inductive. Use of this term conforms to Judge's (1972) discussion of a survey methodology. While no specific questions concerning human behavior were generated, more than a site inventory was expected. Aside from the culture-historical sequence from Ventana Cave (Haury 1975), the prehistoric archaeological literature for the Arizonan Papagueria was almost a blank page. Therefore, information was to be gathered in a manner that would facilitate the identification of problem areas for future archaeological work. The survey's major purpose was to determine the data potential of the area—the variability in archaeological resources, their density, state of preservation, and contextual associations for which suitable research questions could be framed.

A total of 38 sites were recorded. All were incorporated into problem domains that appeared representative of research interests for the regional area. This approach follows Lipe's (1974) charge to archaeologists in contract salvage situations to consider "representative samples of all types of data [p. 234]." Separately referencing the research potential of each site might have influenced a fragmentary, piecemeal mitigative program. Completion of a more detailed research design, requiring more time and effort, could have alleviated this problem, but it was deemed inappropriate at this stage due to uncertainties about project scheduling, funding levels, excavation permission, and supervisory personnel whose research interests and skills should be considered. An intermediate synthesis was imperative, however, in order to present an integrated account of the research potential on which requests for mitigative studies and funding could be based. The problem domains became a research framework in which to accomplish these ends.

The problem domains were constructed on the basis of geographic, chronological, and material cultural relationships in the archaeological record. Whether or not behavioral activities were isomorphic with these domains was questionable (cf. Reid 1973; Schiffer 1976). In order to convey possible interaction spheres examination of each of the following domains and their interrelationships was essential.

## PROBLEM DOMAIN I: TRAILS

Fragmentary evidence of trails too numerous to be recorded individually, occurred in the project area where there was little erosion, especially in areas of desert pavement. Trails indicate movement and, if human in origin, should ultimately connect areas of human activity. If we assume their status as human manifestations, a number of statements about mobility and communication may be advanced, for example:

1. Trails are purposively oriented.
    a. Long-distance linear routes may suggest long-range travel or trade.
    b. Nonlinear patterns may contrast as a desert transhumance pattern of exploitation.
2. Trails connect areas that have different biotic or abiotic resources.
3. Trails connect areas of specific-task sites with multicomponent base camps.

It is obvious from these few statements that in order to evaluate the exploitation and communication processes that may have occurred, the trails need to be mapped.

Because of the fragmentary and eroded aspect of these features and general inaccessibility within the project area, aerial mapping is proposed. From an elevated position, an archaeologist, using different types of photographic film and filters, may be able to trace trails and discover trails in areas other than higher desert pavement, where their observation may be a reflection of natural preservation rather than of behavioral preferences. After the spatial location of these trails is established, a further attempt should be made to place them temporally. Besides discarded artifacts or "trail breaks," the most important temporal resource is in the trails' association with sites at stopping points.

## PROBLEM DOMAIN II: AREAS OF LITHIC ACTIVITY

Thirteen sites recorded in the project area are essentially comprised of lithic materials: Assemblages at eight sites in the upper reaches of the Tat Momoli Valley primarily consist of chipping debris; assemblages at five sites in the Tat Momoli Mountains feature rock circles. Both of the lithic areas appear at higher elevations, usually in desert pavement areas, which may have aided site recognition. The difference in site composition, however, between two distinct geographic areas may indicate meaningful exploitation differences despite the vagaries of archaeological preservation. Since the lithic assemblages appear culturally and temporally undiagnostic, subdividing the domain on the basis of technological and topographical associations should lead to more definitive research questions.

Sites in the upper Tat Momoli Valley, which arc around a quasi-playa area, need to be examined from the standpoint of geological and biological resources. Stone resources in the area need to be mapped and matched with chipping debitage. Since the sites' inventories include mainly cores and flakes, the assemblages appear to reflect stone resource procurement or manufacturing sites. Site mapping and lithic analysis may indicate the following:

1. The quality of the source material
   a. Preference
   b. Efficiency of this material for manufacturing observed forms
2. Manufacturing techniques
   a. Percussion
   b. Pressure
   c. Special preparation of cores
3. Number of stages of manufacture from quarrying to final retouch
4. Estimated quantity of material struck but not present, size of removed flakes
5. Number of chipping events

If tool forms are present or flakes exhibit use scars, further resource procurement and processing may be postulated. Wear patterns on flakes may indicate plant or animal exploitation. Today, floral species preferring wetter locations grow one mile away in the playa, and the area may once have drawn wild animals to a water source. Botanical and hydrological studies are necessary to reconstruct microenvironmental conditions.

Two of the sites exhibit additional features that may augment the interpretation of animal or plant exploitation. One site with a hearth and the other with a ceramic assemblage suggest either specialized-exploitation sites or perhaps the occupation of a base camp around which specialized-task areas occurred. These possibilities raise the problem of establishing the contemporaneity of the sites. Chipped lithics are a basic aspect of prehistoric man's tool kit. Determining singular events, reuse, or reoccupation of a lithic resource area is difficult. Establishing patterns in the following may be helpful: (*1*) similar patterns of resource procurement; (*2*) similar patterns of distribution; and (*3*) similar degree of patination.

Sites in the Tat Momoli Mountains, spread over a slightly wider geographical area, appear to be related because they feature rock circles. These features occur either in outline form or, in the case of one site, consist of filled-in circles. Their function, if they are indeed functionally alike, is unknown. The environment of the area should be examined for natural resources that require specialized extractive techniques. An analysis of associated chipping debris may aid in this identification. Their mountainous setting may also suggest that these sites are positioned along natural travel or communication routes or are excellent observation or defensive positions.

One remaining isolated site is located in eroding alluvial soils adjacent to a Papago settlement. If the site is not associated with the village, it is the only example of a nonceramic-associated activity in the valley proper. If associated, the lithic assemblage may reflect a specialized task area used by the villagers. In either case, a full examination of the site area should be undertaken in order to determine the site's integrity.

## PROBLEM DOMAIN III: SHARD AND LITHIC
## SCATTERS ON THE SANTA ROSA WASH
## FLOODPLAIN

Sites in the third problem domain are located adjacent to the upper Santa Rosa Wash. With one exception, these sites lie west of the main drainage channel on the alluvial floodplain. At least one site (Arizona AA:5:43) has an extensive spatial distribution and evidence of a feature. A small circular mound covered with gravel and shards and exhibiting a depressed sandy center appears to be a cultural structure. Although other gravel bars occur on the floodplain, this one does not align with any local drainage pattern. The cultural debris and vague literary references to similar features in the Papagueria make its exact origin and character important to establish. Collections from the site include Hohokam ceramics, and this site should offer data on problems relating to intersite as well as intrasite development in an area marginal to the Hohokam cultural sphere of influence. A nearby site (Arizona AA:5:30), a fairly concentrated area of cultural debris located on the eastern side of the channel, should be tested because of its proximity and similarity to the material culture present at AA:5:43. Heavy earth-moving equipment will probably be necessary to test for subsurface structures in both of these relatively extensive areas.

The remaining seven sites are less diagnostic. Seemingly surficial, especially in view of the survey testing results (Canouts 1972), these sites are affected by a number of erosional and depositional processes that bear investigation. A geological analysis should be undertaken to elucidate information about the natural processes of site formation:

1.  What is the velocity of the floodwater?
2.  Has arroyo cutting continued laterally or vertically?
3.  Are the elevated areas on which the artifacts rest depositional or remnants remaining after downcutting has occurred?
4.  Are the sites primary or secondary deposits?
5.  Where are the projected channels of erosion and sources if the material is redeposited?

In conjunction with the geological study, questions about artifact distributions need to be raised:

1.  Do differences in weight and size of artifacts rule out water suspension and transport?
2.  Does the assemblage make sense as either a specific-task site or a multicomponent site with a fair representation of artifacts?
3.  Does an evaluation of the subsistence base or a locational analysis illuminate the site setting?

Once the character of these alluvial sites is established, further inferences concerning the spatial and temporal relationships to more substantive sites, such as AA:5:30 and AA:5:43, may be advanced. If these sites are surficial, they may represent areas of limited or specialized activities associated with larger settlements. Or they may form an interaction network, a dispersed village network, operating through subsistence exchange.

## PROBLEM DOMAIN IV: TAT MOMOLIKOT SERIES

Seven sites and the present Papago community of Tat Momolikot are included in the Tat Momolikot series, a study of community development through time. Historically, the Papago settled in large, defensive "well" villages adjacent to major north–south drainages in the Papagueria. Smaller units that spread along these drainage axes for floodwater farming depended upon these village locations for permanent water and a concentrated defense against the Apache. After the Apachean menace lessened in the mid 1800s, deep-well technology permitted the growth of these smaller units. The settlement patterns described by the early ethnographers were influenced by Apachean warfare and new technoeconomic introductions. Village structure and growth in the project area are still unclear prior to and at European contact.

Kohatk, a large permanent settlement to the west of the project area, is referenced in the early literature, ca. A.D. 1700. Tat Momolikot, located within the project area, is supposedly more recent, founded in the late 1800s near the Jackrabbit mining area. A number of historic Papago sites in the project area suggest that aboriginal settlements were not limited to these two sites. Concentrating on these two village units to study population densities may not reveal the true complexity of the habitation pattern.

One site in the series contains aboriginal and European materials and, together with another nearby site, containing no historical materials, could represent settlement evolving north of the present-day Tat Momolikot area. A series of three sites, identified as early Tat Momolikot sites and inhabited consecutively since the late 1800s, provides a unique opportunity to study the settlement–abandonment cycle of a single Papago community.

The Tat Momolikot series presents manageable units of study for gathering information in the following areas: (*1*) demography; (*2*) cultural acquisitions and preference patterns; (*3*) dietary analysis and preferences; (*4*) mobility; (*5*) use of new techniques or tools to perform aboriginal tasks; and (*6*) reuse of cultural materials. Extraction of these data will depend on the skills of both ethnographers and ethnoarchaeologists. By using two independent lines of evidence, informants and studies in modern material culture, behavioral models dealing with more contemporary phenomena may be proposed and tested.

## PROBLEM DOMAIN V: HISTORICAL MINING AND RELATED ACTIVITIES

Historical mining activity in the Slate Mountains directly influenced community settlement in the project area. It has been cited as the impetus for Tat Momolikot's development and growth. Requiring specialized knowledge in ethnography, history, and historical archaeology, an anthropological study of this domain might treat the following:

1. Subsistence activities
   a. Degree of direct exploitation
   b. Degree of market exchange
2. Patterns of competition or acculturation effected through material change
3. Social or economic stress in relation to population density
4. Spatial distribution of different ethnic groups
5. Special technologies and their influence on traditional structure of the work force

Evidence at the Turning Point Mine, the Desert Queen Mine, and Jackrabbit Mine should provide information about early mining technology, specialized-task areas, and socioeconomic relationships to the Papago villages; to Jackrabbit House, a historical general store at Jackrabbit Mine; and to an isolated historical habitation structure whose cultural affiliation has yet to be determined.

## CONCLUSIONS

Several research and management advantages emerged from the formation of these problem domains. One advantage became immediately clear in planning the mitigative proposal. It was assumed that a sampling of sites would produce the pattern recognition necessary for the investigation of these problem domains. Future sampling procedures for each domain could be applied to each site or to a selected few, depending upon the specific research design, as each site had already been stratified. However, sites of particular research interest were noted.

Sampling percentages (Canouts 1972:44–45) were calculated from the total cost recovery estimates and reflected pragmatic considerations of site number, size, location, and accessibility, as well as research interest. The sampling level for each domain ranged from 27% to 73%. Although the percentage of recoverable information cannot be considered identical to these cost recovery percentages, such estimates did afford guidelines for operationalizing relative, and perhaps realistic, research potential.

Another advantage of the domains was that they could accommodate a number of specific research interests. The development of a specific research design had been recommended as part of the mitigative studies. The summaries of all the problem domains indicate the total range of archaeological resources affected by the project. Even though the sites could have been stratified on other criteria that crosscut these domains, this set could and was used as a guide for evaluating mitigative activities.

Recognizing that a great many research designs could be educed and might even be required before the research potential of all five areas was significantly tapped, the National Park Service contract specifications requested the preliminary preparation and review of a specific research design for the Phase I fieldwork. Supervisory archaeologist L. Mark Raab (1973a) prepared a set of hypothesized settlement–subsistence relationships structured around the problem domains. Due to project clearance needs for sites found in four of the five domains, and in the event that unforeseen areas had to be investigated during Phase I, it was desirable to incorporate aspects of all the domains into a comprehensive research design. This action was taken with the understanding that the design should be reviewed and modified in subsequent phases.

The primary research efforts in Phase I focused on the problem of the shard and lithic scatters in the Santa Rosa Wash floodplain. Ongoing archaeological investigations for the Hecla mining project (Goodyear and Dittert 1973) in which Raab (1973b) had participated was providing information about exploitation patterns in the adjoining Slate Mountains. Research into exploitation patterns in the environmentally distinctive riverine area was a logical extension of this work. Through quadrat and transect vegetational sampling, soil analysis, and palynological analysis, which would quantify environmental indices, and through the statistical sampling of the material culture, Raab planned to test quantitatively his hypotheses about patterned human behavior. The results of his work from the Santa Rosa Wash project (Raab 1974a, 1976e), together with Goodyear's (1975b) results from the Hecla project, form one of the most complete ecological models yet proposed for prehistoric adaptation in southern Arizona.

Data from the floodplain sites, as well as data from trails, lithic resources, and Jackrabbit Mine (Raab 1974a; Reynolds, Sobelman, McCarthy, and Kinkade 1974), have answered some research questions and posed others pointing in new research directions. For example, the identification of the circular mound at AA:5:43 as a reservoir (Raab 1975) indicates more complexity in the floodplain's demographic and land-use patterns than ever before realized. All of these studies have caused the substance of the original domains to be of little more than historical interest, although areas that have not yet been investigated may continue to be referenced by the domains.

This last point raises one final advantage pertaining to the form of these domains: their formal, intermediate position between a site-by-site evaluation in a regional survey and a specific mitigative research design. Using the Santa Rosa Wash and Hecla results, another Arizona State Museum project constructed more specific but complementary problem domains for an ethnoarchaeological study in the Vekol Mountains, an area bordering on the western edge of the Santa Rosa Wash project area (Stewart and Teague 1974). Administrative and procedural problems outside of the museum's influence have held both the Vekol project and Phases II and III of the Santa Rosa project in abeyance. The synthesis of information into problem domains has refined the data base, placed it in a usable format, and furnished a framework to which data from other projects can be applied. Specific research designs, therefore, can await protective or mitigative decision making and the availability of planning resources, and they should thus benefit from the acquisition of further research in adjacent areas and from theoretical and methodological advances in the discipline.

# 10

# Archaeological Research Design for the Genesee Expressway

NEAL L. TRUBOWITZ

Archaeological investigations of highways are structured by the various state and federal laws and regulations that apply to the work; this affects the way in which archaeological research is carried out and sets limitations on what kinds of research can be undertaken within the program. Long-range goals are difficult to pursue when the highway projects are small and widely separated geographically. Reconnaissance on short highway rights-of-way can provide data on survey methodology and scattered site location information. However, the survey of major routes passing through a naturally bounded region provides an opportunity for large-scale, long-term investigations. The Archaeological Survey of the State University of New York (SUNY) at Buffalo is attempting such research whenever contiguous projects make it possible. The primary example of this has been on the Genesee Expressway, which passes through the Genesee Valley in Livingston and Monroe Counties, New York.

The SUNY-Buffalo Highway Archaeology Program in the Genesee Valley is designed to apply research goals within the structure of a highway archaeological investigation. Besides the identification and definition of sites threatened by the expressway in order to provide site eligibility determinations for the National Register of Historic Places (required by law for assessing the impact of the project on cultural resources), the research design focuses on settlement systems and survey methodology. The survey provides data suitable for investigating the criteria used by prehistoric and early historic cultures to select their living and working sites. The long-range research goals are (1) to seek information on culture history, paleoecology, and archaeological site location, (2) to determine the relationship between culture and environment (settlement systems), and (3) to assess the research techniques used in the project in order to standardize and refine them. For example, watching the construction of the highway may ultimately provide a check on the predictive powers of survey technology and on current ideas of sampling.

It is assumed that the biophysical environment is structured and that human groups utilize the environment within a framework of potentialities and limitations defined by their culture. Using a systemic definition, culture is seen as consisting of structurally different components that are articulated with one another and the environment within an overall system. The study of cultural systems requires investigation on a regional basis with a work program aimed at identifying functional types of archaeological sites as they are distributed about the geographic area occupied by a culture or cultures.

The study area must be understood as a region that is composed of (1) minor physiographic units, such as floodplain, upland, etc., and (2) still smaller microenvironments that have sites located on them, for example, a small rise near a swamp on the floodplain. Natural conditions that are to be considered include the following general categories: (1) geological factors (topography, subsurface geology and rock outcrops, soils, etc.); (2) hydrological factors (drainage patterns, water sources, etc.); (3) floral distribution; (4) faunal distribution, and (5) climatic factors (rainfall, snowfall, temperature, length of growing season, etc.). These biophysical factors have variable distributions, and cultural activities will vary in response to them. This depends on the importance of particular environmental factors or combinations of them to each cultural group, based on its scheduling choices. Cultural groups may adapt to specific ecological situations (one or many) or to a series of ecological factors, such as plant and animal genera whose ranges cut across several local ecological units or microenvironments within the region.

Among the minimum biophysical data that will be available through highway investigations are landform, soil type, distance from and type of water source, and flotation, faunal, and current plant community data. These data are considered in terms of their presence or absence, spatial distribution, amount or density, and accessibility to human groups.

The study of the cultural data is arranged in a hierarchical framework. The regional unit of investigation is the settlement system. A settlement system includes all the sites of a cultural group. Sites are the local units, and settlement pattern is the smallest unit of investigation.

> A site is an occupation of a particular geographic locus by one or more individuals for any amount of time that alteration of the natural environment results. Campbell (1968:15) would add that the occupation should fall within the "ordinary, expected and predictable round of activities of the society in question." A settlement may be the locus of human activity resulting in archaeological remains, and for practical purposes this usually means a dwelling area or a functionally specific activity area, such as a manufacturing workshop, a kill site, or a quarry [Fitzhugh 1972:7].

Size is not a factor in defining a site or settlement. Sites that are small in terms of size and quantity of cultural material are as much settlements as "large" sites because they represent certain human activities that are an integral part of a settlement system. Even stray finds must be recorded as sites because they provide information on dispersed activities. Settlement pattern is the arrangement of activity areas within a site.

Every site has characteristics that are revealed at different levels of archaeological investigation. Site locations are determined through reconnaissance of the corridors and rights-of-way. Systematic surface collection provides information on site size (horizontal) and activity patterns. Limited site testing, which is part of the highway program, will provide further data on site size, artifact density and distribution, cultural affiliation, etc. Floral, faunal, and feature data in addition to artifactual material may be gathered depending on the extent of testing, size of excavations, and success in locating cultural remains within a site. Only large-scale excavations will reveal full details of settlement pattern within sites. (Large-scale excavations are not expected to take place on the highway projects unless impacted sites cannot be avoided; as of 1976, after 4 years of investigation, no such excavations have been undertaken.) Analysis of the manufacturing techniques and wear patterns of recovered tools provides data on their function, while study of artifactual variability provides further information on the kinds of activities that were taking place on a site.

Site types are then defined on the basis of their location, internal characteristics, artifact content, and any floral and faunal remains. These types represent particular activity sets that were carried out at some interval in time by particular human groups who were following an overall organizational settlement system. The relative cultural affiliations of the sites are determined through comparison of patterns of stylistic variability of artifacts and settlement pattern with previous archaeological investigations in the Northeast that have produced cultural-chronological definitions. Radiocarbon dating when available will also fit sites into chronological frameworks. Following the reconnaissance and site-testing phases of highway investigation, sufficient data will have been gathered to outline culture history, site distribution, and paleoecology, which was the first of the goals.

After the background data have been collected, sites are correlated with biophysical factors to outline the interface of culture and environment. The details of each site's environmental situation can be taken and compared with the region as a whole. Percentage differences are computed and $\chi^2$ and other tests of significance can be made to determine whether the variables in question were a factor in site selection. The variables will be tested alone and in combinations, possibly revealing the ranking of biophysical factors or combinations of them in site selection.

Settlement systems, that is, the types of sites and environment associated with individual populations or time periods, may be isolated by these means. Depending on the settlement system in use by a culture, similar type sites may occur together and/or there may be connections between different types of sites. The Genesee Valley offered various combinations of plant and animal food sources to prehistoric and early historical populations. It is assumed that no one food resource at any time has accounted for all the food energy that the various cultural groups required for existence. Therefore, it is expected that over time there were mixed strategies of biophysical adaptation designed to take advantage of both stable and mobile foods, with a balance struck between the efficiency of procuring each type of food as it was available. As large-scale excavations are limited in the program, it is not expected that sufficient data will be available to link social groups to specific territories or to specify the interaction between groups.

The Genesee River Valley basin lies in the eastern portion of the Great Lakes region of North America. The basin is roughly elliptical in shape, with a north–south major axis of approximately 100 miles and a maximum width of about 40 miles.

The portion of the valley crossed by the proposed Genesee Expressway runs from the village of Dansville at its southern limits northward to the outskirts of the city of Rochester, a linear distance of 49 miles. This path corresponds to the lower half of the Genesee Valley, and the expressway corridor (1-mile wide at maximum) provides a nonstatistically drawn, disproportionally stratified sample of Genesee Valley landforms. Its linear path is composed of four physiographic units, as follows: upland, valley slope, lake plain, and floodplain. After a calculation of the total areas of each type of physiographic unit in the valley as a whole, the corridor can be used statistically by comparing its relationship with the valley, both in terms of environment and the archaeology that corresponds to it.

It is generally assumed that the linear nature of highway archaeological surveys will introduce a bias into the overall distributional picture of prehistoric settlement systems but that it should not significantly distort the sample of the types of sites that are to be found. When plotted on maps, concentrations of reported sites reflect the parts of the highway that have already been subjected to systematic archaeological investigation, as contrasted with the hodgepodge of scattered sites around the study area that have been recorded through checking literature and institutional records or private collections.

There has recently been a suggestion that assumptions of the biased nature of corridor and right-of-way surveys may *not* be correct. James W. Mueller conducted an experiment on the use of sampling in archaeological survey in which 326 simulated, sampling-based surveys were compared with an empirically derived population of 488 sites surveyed in or near the Paria Plateau in north central Arizona. The $\chi^2$ tests at the .05 level of accuracy indicated that while the right-of-way sampling method is certainly biased, the five test results run on the method suggest that the scheme is an accurate population predictor. However, more tests are needed to challenge seriously the assumption of bias (Mueller 1974:66). Even if the highway investigations by themselves do not provide statistically valid predictors for delineating settlement systems within the study region, they are the most exhaustive and systematic reconnaissance project ever undertaken in this area and will provide more extensive data than have previously existed.

The minimum benefit to archaeology expected from the highway program is the documentation of previously unknown archaeological sites, providing basic culture-historical and site location data for the region. In this regard the program has already been successful, as a total of 233 sites have been added to the SUNY-Buffalo site files since 1972 due to the highway survey in the Genesee Valley. Evidence for the existence of cultural groups thought to have been only peripheral to the area has been found indicating that these groups had actually made extensive use of the area (Trubowitz and Snethkamp 1975). Due to the alignment of the highway, areas that previously were thought to have been lightly utilized by prehistoric groups were investigated systematically for the first time, revealing that areas such as upland were utilized frequently and for long periods of time. Test excavations have recovered floral remains that have provided new information on subsistence, paleoenvironments, and plant succession in the valley (Ford 1976).

Within the highway program there has been the opportunity to assess various instrumental and chemical methods of site survey, including low-level aerial photography, magnetometry, and phosphate testing (Trubowitz 1974). Different kinds of surface collection techniques and the effects of plowing on archaeological remains are also being studied (Trubowitz n.d.).

Thus, the highway program is providing a viable research opportunity for the study of culture history, paleoecology, settlement systems, and archaeological field techniques. The isolation of the criteria used in settlement and the determination of the density of sites on different microenvironments within the valley improve our predictive capabilities for assessing the impact of construction projects on archaeological resources and contribute to better cultural resource management. Settlement system research within highway archaeological programs is an appropriate research orientation because it benefits the highway planners and helps meet legal requirements of mitigation of effect on cultural resources. The study of archaeological methodology improves the efficiency of the survey and brings costs down.

The Highway Archaeology Program provides a major starting point for regional investigation of settlement systems. These systems reflect the ways in which human groups are organized to deal with their natural and social surroundings. Once these data have been gathered from many preservation projects such as the highway survey, it will be possible to construct and test models of human behavior and perhaps to explain that behavior and the changes that have taken place over time.

# 11

# Modeling Inundation Effects for Planning and Prediction

ERVAN G. GARRISON

Water impoundment projects in all areas of the United States represent the princi-pal segment of land modification projects that by their scope involve the major portion of cultural resources threatened today. The advent of legislation such as the National Environmental Policy Act (NEPA) and the Archaeological Conservation Act (1974) has found the body of archaeological method and theory ill equipped to assess and mitigate the effects of such projects, either short or long term. The guidelines of the Council of Environmental Quality require that the *long-range* effects of destruction or *alteration* of the present state of archaeological resources be assessed. A systematic body of method, theory, or data on which logical, scientific conservation measures for inundated resources can be based simply does not exist.

The assumptions from which today's mitigative procedures derive are at best simplistic generalizations based on little empirical data or just patent misconcep-tions. The sheer magnitude of the conservation management problem makes these assumptions even that much more inadequate and research designs predicated on them less than scientific. The two principal misconceptions relative to the study of the inundation effects on archaeological resources are directly contrapositive. The first misconception proceeds from the basic assumption that sites that are inundated are preserved. Needless to say the logical management step required by the ac-ceptance of this misconception is frighteningly simple and direct. Flood the sites for posterity. The second guiding misconception is that all sites will be so altered by inundation as to be useless sources of knowledge. In the case of some sites this is too true, but it does *not* apply to the majority of threatened sites. Again, conserva-tion measures structured on such an assumption are reactive and do more disservice than service to scientific research.

Archaeologists today have generally adopted mitigative procedures based on a rationale that requires that all that is deemed significant must be recovered. If we accept Schiffer and House's (1975b) statement that "archaeological resources ac-

151

quire scientific or historical significance only as they relate to specific research questions is substantive, technical, methodological and theoretical contexts [p. 163]" then it follows that archaeologists should desist from their attempts to dig every site in every reservoir. Given this admonition, we are still left without guidance as to *which* significant sites are most threatened by inundation. Research on inundation effects is the only way a truly integrative framework can be evoked wherein specific research questions and their priorities can be evaluated relative to the short- and long-term effects of inundation processes. With such a framework archaeologists can avoid the mistakes engendered by applying conservation measures based on the misconceptions just discussed.

Methodology and problem orientation in scientific endeavor shift in relation to changes in the theoretical positions that are current to a specific time. Whether we adopt a "salvage-oriented philosophy" or a "policy of disregard" relative to inundated sites, we do current as well as future science and society a disservice. Longitudinal scientific research, such as the study of past and extant cultures, is an ongoing study. In scientific research no final truth is ever possible, only better and better approximations of accepted theories. Hence, our conservation measures must include these truisms as touchstones if they are to be conservative in the truest sense and not stopgap, short-term responses pursuant only to a well-meaning but misinformed group of managers. What is clear from the foregoing discussion is that archaeologists as scientists *and* cultural resource managers must develop a systematic body of knowledge for the effects of inundation on archaeological resources before any rational decisions can be made concerning their fate.

A growing list of investigators have addressed the problem of inundation of archaeological sites (B. A. Anderson 1974; Carrell 1974; Lenihan *et al.* 1975; Garrison 1975; Jewell 1961; Lenihan 1974; Prewitt 1972; Prewitt and Dibble 1974; Ruppé and Green 1975). A central theme in all these writings has been the recognition of the lack of knowledge relative to inundation processes. Research specifically directed at the effects of inundation on archaeological sites has not been undertaken on a large scale. Reasons for this lack of emphasis are varied but can be traced to (*1*) an absence, until now, of a pressing archaeological need for these studies, and (2) technological inadequacies. Jewell (1961) was the first to point out the need for such research; he was also one of the first archaeologists to take advantage of a newly developed diving apparatus that made inundated sites accessible for research at times other than fortuitous low-water periods.

Generally, observations of inundation effects have been ancillary to the other research goals of investigations. More specifically, the observations have come from investigators involved in a survey or resurvey of an affected area. Examples of these kinds of studies are more numerous than specific inundation studies but are still few in number (Brauner, Hammet, and Hartman 1975; Dragoo and Lantz 1969, 1971; Livesay 1974; Neal and May 1974; Prewitt 1972; Witty 1973). The information derived from these studies is important to our understanding of inundation processes but is unstructured in the sense that it was collected in an unsystematic manner. Further, an integrative framework did not exist within which the collected data could be utilized to evaluate specific problem areas relating to inundation effects.

I have proposed a model, admittedly tentative, with which such data can be structured relative to problem-oriented research (Garrison 1975); the model is outlined in Table 11.1. Its merit lies in the recognition that it can be modified where necessary in order to be responsive to the needs of the researchers. Such a model represents a first step toward the more refined, quantitative models that will guide the elaborate research needed in the study of inundation effects, both natural and man-made. Several inundation processes and their postulated effects are listed in Table 11.1.

It should be noted that the distinction between natural and man-made effects is real. Mechanical effects are as much the product of the control devices of dams, such as floodgates and power generation facilities, as of the more familiar natural forces, such as precipitation, stream inflow, erosion, etc. Marked changes in these control parameters, man-made or natural, produce, fundamentally, the same mechanical effects; the chemical effects, on the other hand, are less predictable,

**TABLE 11.1**

| Inundation processes | Inundation effects |
|---|---|
| | Loss or Alteration of: |
| 1. Mechanical (natural) | |
|   a. Waves—wind, subsurface | 1. Geological and cultural strata |
|   b. Currents—surface, subsurface | |
|   c. Erosion—result of (a, b) and runoff | 2. Geomorphological features |
| 2. Mechanical (manmade) | 3. Structures, middens, and cultural |
|   a. Waves—boats |    features |
|   b. Currents—floodgates and power generation structures | 4. Distributional patterns of artifacts and cultural features |
|   c. Erosion—improper land management practices | 5. Soil structure |
| 3. Chemical (natural) | 6. Artifacts |
|   a. pH and temperature related—reduction/oxidation, complextion, precipitation/solublization | 7. Faunal and floral material; artifacts produced from such resources |
|   b. Biologically related—euphotic zone and bottom sediments; same as (a) but influenced by aerobic and anerobic microorganisms | 8. Soil chemistry |
| 4. Chemical (manmade) | 9. Archaeometric data; hydration rates, radiocarbon content, trace element concentrations, and thermoluminescence |
|   a. pH and temperature related—same as (3a), but produced by industrial waste, effluents from power generation facilities, etc. | |
|   b. Biologically related—organic enrichment of waters by processes in (4a) increases effects of microorganisms | |

though they are highly contingent on other man-made or natural alteration in the chemical environment of the reservoirs. The most indeterminate factor is that of man-made pollution. This factor should become significantly more critical as the impoundments become more and more utilized for recreational purposes as well as more settled by lakeshore populations on a permanent or semipermanent basis.

Specific classes or indices within archaeological contexts, cultural and noncultural, are the parameters with which to analyze the effects of inundation on a specific site or a large sample of sites. Research strategies that suggest themselves for such intrasite and intersite studies are twofold:

*Strategies*

1. Control (noninundated)—Test (inundated)
2. Control (inundated)—Test (inundated)

*Indices*

1. Weight ratios
   Example:    Heavy tools/light tools
   Rationale:  Lithic items, such as stone tools (mauls, hoes, blades), will be differentially affected by water movement and silting. Large items will be less subject to lateral and/or vertical displacement in deposits.
2. Distributional patterns
   Example:    Activity areas/refuse areas
   Rationale:  Lateral displacement of material will alter the nonrandom distribution of artifacts and refuse. Inundated sites will appear more "random" in distributional characteristics.
3. Material ratios
   Example:    Metal artifacts/wood artifacts
   Rationale:  Differential chemical factors (pH variation, reactivity, solubility) will alter ratios of specific materials. Wood may be preserved, whereas metal will be corroded or destroyed altogether.
4. Fauna/flora ratios
   Example:    Pollen/plant or wood/bone remains, etc.
   Rationale:  Again, cellulose materials may be preserved in some situations; pollen will be lost or scattered; pH shifts in acid or alkaline solutions may either preserve or speed deterioration of bone and/or protein materials.
5. Attribute ratios
   Example:    Technofunctional attributes of stone tools
   Rationale:  Displacement and abrasion of stone artifacts in saturated deposits can produce damage and striations on worked edges that skew reasonable or nonrandom proportions of functional categories defined in these bases (see Neal and Mayo 1974; Tringham *et al.* 1974:189).
6. Artifacts/biological remains ratios
   Example:    Ceramics or groundstone/plant remains or pollen
   Rationale:  Differentiated effects of water chemistry and mechanical movements will produce unreasonable ratios of specific classes—for example, many shards or vessel remains and little or no plant or pollen remains.
7. Archaeometric data
   Examples:   Chronological information; trace element distribution; soil chemistry–composition alteration
   Rationale:  Displacement of fired clay, such as in hearths or house floors, can skew archaeometric results; differential leaching of trace elements and minerals can alter results of

neutron activation, X-ray fluorescence, or other instrumental analyses of geological–cultural deposits and biological remains. Bone, wood, and charcoal as sources of chronological data are subject to demineralization and other alteration by water chemistry effects.

The indices enumerated are just a few of the more obvious indications of inundation effects on archaeological assemblages. It has been pointed out that the detection of inundation effects utilizing the suggested strategies may suffer from more than just the usual criticisms leveled at such methods (see Brim and Spain 1974:9–30). Colleagues have pointed out that the variation in sites and their contituent assemblages is so great within all categories of noninundated sites that comparison with inundated sites is almost meaningless. Variation is a problem, but archaeologists have abandoned the type of archaeological investigation limited to descriptions of certain, imperishable artifact categories. This view of archaeology disappeared with the development of a holistic or systems-oriented research designs with data recovery techniques including coprolite analysis, pollen analysis, seed flotation, soil analysis, trend and spatial analysis of the distribution of structures and remains, etc. Furthermore, we as investigators have derived reasonable expectations of site location and content based on these thorough analyses of the broad spectrum of archaeological sites. The point is that our analyses have given us more than an intuitive feeling for what to expect at various locales and sites within these locations. When inundated sites are studied with the same rigor and philosophy guiding the analyses, then obvious and even fine-grained variations should be evident when compared with our control cases or with our theoretical expectations. Objections to the study of inundation effects based on narrow methodological views are facile and out of place. Inundation studies will be conducted with research designs pursuant to the concepts of systems, ecology, and the interrelationship of multiple variables.

Mitigative measures to ameliorate the effects of inundation are few in number and their effectiveness unknown. Proposed mitigation (Garrison 1975; Lenihan 1974; Lenihan *et al.* 1975) includes the use of:

1.  Capping: Riprap, Gunnite, sandbags, earth and gravel fill have been suggested for near and long-term protection of effected sites.
2.  "Landscaping": Differential clearing, cofferdams, breakwaters, and the planting of protective vegetation can reduce the effects of both mechanical and chemical processes.
3.  Recreational facility planning: Location of launch areas, boat docks, campgrounds, and swimming beaches away from archaeological resources is essential to the preservation of these materials.
4.  Excavation: Complete excavation of significant sites within high-risk zones is a logical mitigative step. Revisitation resurvey and excavation of newly discovered or nonexcavated sites are management steps that best serve the changing needs and priorities of archaeological science. Certainly the revolutionary advances in underwater technology and the signal contributions of archaeological pioneers in the often demeaned subfield of underwater archaeology now permit us rigorously to investigate and recover data from sites that economic or other considerations prevented study before inundation. This should be a necessary step in the long-term study of inundated cultural resources.

In summary, the pressing need for data on inundation effects relative to archaeological sites is further accentuated by the policy vacuum that exists for the management of this portion of the cultural resource base. Awareness has dawned, but too late for projects now underway. Unless management decisions based on a thorough scientific evluation of inundation such as that being conducted in recent studies by the National Park Service (Lenihan *et al.* 1977) are applied retroactively, where possible, the lag between the making of policy and its acceptance will be such as to exclude thousands of archaeological sites from the beneficial effects of this policy. Until the research is conducted and the results effectively utilized, it is incumbent on archaeologists and managers to recognize that inundation of archaeological resources is a crucial and complex issue. The fragmentary data and elementary models relevant to inundation effects must be available and studied by all concerned with cultural resource management. Thus informed (though imperfectly), they can slow and even reverse the nonproductive and negligent trend in the study and mitigation of inundation effects.

# 12

# Research Design in Highway Archaeology: An Example from South Carolina

ALBERT C. GOODYEAR

This chapter represents a summary and preliminary progress report of a general research design written during 1974 for the highway archaeology program of the Institute of Archeology and Anthropology (IAA), University of South Carolina. This design was published during the first year of operation (Goodyear 1975a) and is currently being operationalized. This design is referred to as the general research design (GRD) and was written before any fieldwork was undertaken. The GRD performed, and continues to provide, two main functions. First, it examined and identified early in the program inherent strengths and weaknesses of doing research in a highway context. Second, based upon these considerations and the primary goal of the program—the systematic reconstruction and explanation of activities represented by highway-intercepted sites—four major problem domains are provided. The anticipated interrelationships are considered between environmental impact statements (EIS), project-specific research designs, mitigation-phase research, research results, and the GRD conceived as a multistage enterprise.

## THE NEED FOR RESEARCH DESIGN

Perhaps no other area of archaeology has remained so underdeveloped in terms of taking advantage of modern scientific procedures as that of highway archaeology. In this regard, highway archaeology has shared with traditional salvage archaeology a somewhat less than respected reputation, as imposed by communities of archaeologists involved in "pure research." In recent years, in an effort at self-criticism and improvement, contract archaeology has been attempting to upgrade the theory and method of its operations and to take a broad, socially scientific

157

approach toward the management of its nonrenewable resource base (Canouts 1972, 1975; Goodyear 1975b; Gumerman 1973; Lipe 1974; McGimsey 1972a; Schiffer and House 1975b; South 1974b).

Explicitly written and published research designs are an extremely useful means by which contract research, even small-scale projects, can more effectively manage and learn from the archaeological data base. The use of research designs in other scientific disciplines is commonplace, and within archaeology Binford (1964) was an early advocate. Currently in archaeology, there still seems to be some confusion regarding the nature of research design. A design does not consist solely of a budget for operations or a projection of person-days and equipment costs to dig sites. It is true that a well-constructed research design will make careful provisions for the logistical operations of research. But the sine qua non of a research design must be the questions, problems, or hypotheses that are being formulated and tested, which can also be linked to methods and techniques adequate to their evaluation (cf. Phillips 1966).

## ARCHAEOLOGY IN THE HIGHWAY CONTEXT

There are two primary limitations in highway research. The first relates to the linear or transectlike sampling spaces imposed by the highway corridor. Whereas in many types of contract projects the impact area may be coterminous with complete or significant portions of prehistoric territories (e.g., river basins, floodplains, mountain slopes), it can hardly be said that narrow transects effectively cover any one region or a major aspect of an exploitative territory. The second constraint on regional sampling within highway corridors relates to the obvious source of bias pertaining to the geographic placement of highways by planners and engineers.

These limitations, however, are not as imposing as they might seem. While highway transects lack the dispersion of sampling units located throughout all relevant parts of a region with proportional coverage (cf. Mueller 1974), due to their length they often crosscut several types of environments and are thus capable of elucidating variability in types of archaeological sites (cf. Gumerman 1973). While the proportions and ratios of site types are probably unrepresentative statistically, a close examination of environmental variables in conjunction with technofunctional studies is a powerful method of identifying intersite functional variability (cf. Binford 1973). Thus, highway corridors, especially long ones, are an excellent means of generating large *varieties* of sites.

The problem of human bias in the placement of highway paths, although always present, is not beyond human scrutiny in evaluating its nonrandom characteristics. In some ultimate sense the placement of all highway paths are decisions based on economic, demographic, political, and geographic factors. Nevertheless, for certain types of environmental variables a highway prism may be effectively "random." For example, in our work in the South Carolina Piedmont, an environment that can be described as relatively homogenous due to repetitive mosaics of identical microenvironments, we are placing random vectors on U.S. geological survey maps in regions around the highway corridor in order to compare them with the highway "vector." Searching for differences using $\chi^2$-square and Kolmogorov-Smirnov tests for such variables as drainage ranks, drainages to miles, mean elevation, percentage slope, degree of facing, etc., we have found our highway path differs very little *environmentally* from a completely random vector (Goodyear, Ackerly, and House 1977). While such results are encouraging, they cannot necessarily be transposed to an ability to sample regional settlement systems. The results do give confidence, however, to the assumption that the highway corridor *in this case* is cutting in a representative fashion environmental features of probable cultural significance, and they accordingly inspire some confidence that we are likely to contact accurate varieties of site types if not their proportions.

There are certain positive features related to highway archaeology that are shared with any form of archaeological research regardless of source of funding or project scale. These are briefly discussed in relation to the highway program.

## Single-Site Studies

Although there are inherent problems with regional sampling using highway corridors, sampling difficulties disappear at the level of individual sites, since we presumably have complete access to their contents and internal organizations. Basic kinds of archaeological information are only available through intensive analyses of individual sites, and such studies form the basic building blocks of more abstract settlement models. Intensive intrasite analyses with reliable behavioral reconstructions are still noticeably absent in North American archaeology. Given the rich behavioral data within individual sites available to the investigator with well-conceived hypotheses and excavation strategies, criticisms regarding the small information return from single sites are groundless. This is *not* an advocation that we return to a focus only upon large, well-preserved stratified sites; rather, it is a reaffirmation of Schiffer's (1975e) claim that "there is *no* site that cannot provide relevant information for some substantive, technical, methodological, or theoretical problem of interest in archeology [p. 1]." This *does* necessitate, however, that we have some problem in mind.

## Culture-Ecological Analysis

As mentioned, highways tend to intersect numerous environmental zones. In low-energy societies the articulation between activities and the immediate biophysical environment is rather direct. Intensive studies of individual sites cannot be effectively realized without some examination of their ecological position. In South Carolina there is great environmental diversity compacted in a relatively short distance, which includes the Piedmont Upland, the fall line, the Atlantic Coastal Plain, and the littoral of the Atlantic Ocean.

## Geographically Extensive Investigations

Since highways are being planned and built in virtually every part of the state, the highway program has an opportunity to reconnaissance and survey extensively diverse areas. Rather than being restricted to one particular area or region of the state on a long-term basis, highway-related research allows an extensive and rapid accumulation of site information throughout South Carolina. This is valuable to an archaeological program of South Carolina, since very little professional research had been conducted here prior to the establishment of the Institute of Archaeology and Anthropology (Stephenson 1975). The highway program provides an information balance to other projects within the Institute of Archaeology and Anthropology, since its wide-ranging path of investigation provides a complementary relationship with more intensive and geographically circumscribed projects. The reverse is obviously true as well.

## Multistage Research

Since highway corridors only affect minor areas of any region (400 feet $\times$ $n$ miles), only a small portion of the total data base is contacted and destroyed with investigations. This means that subsequent projects, highway related or otherwise, that operate in these previously contacted regions can take advantage of highway studies. Highway studies, of course, can do the same. Since there are at least three phases in our current program (1: Reconnaissance; 2: Survey; 3:Mitigation), there are different phases with which to achieve the effects of multistage research (Redman 1973). In order to maximize the information feedback of early phase research to that occurring in later phases, several problems and hypotheses must be identified *prior* to final mitigation. The EIS phase involving reconnaissance and intensive survey must perform this function. This is the basic function of the EIS anyway, and agencies including archaeologists should purposefully allow preliminary studies systematically to feed information into later phases.

## Theoretical and Methodological Contributions

While the limitations on regional sampling have been recognized, this does not preclude the construction and testing of interesting hypotheses and models of various scales. Perhaps intersite and interregional models of settlement may require subsequent projects of nonhighway-related organization for their decisive confirmation, but much of this testing must take place within theoretically specified single sites. This certainly is within the investigative powers of highway archaeology. New statistical methods of analysis and models of interpretation are rapidly accumulating regarding intrasite spatial analysis and offer a productive area for model building and methodological experimentation.

# A GENERAL DESIGN FOR THE HIGHWAY ARCHAEOLOGY PROGRAM

It is generally accurate to say that contemporary archaeology is striving to make scientific explanations at two levels. First, at the most abstract level, archaeology must explain through the use of theories and laws the origins, functions, and extinctions of cultural systems. This goal links archaeology securely to social science. At another level archaeology must reconstruct and explain specific properties of individual cultural systems by their material remains within the archaeological record. This latter form of study, which necessarily includes the modeling of site formation processes (Binford 1972, n.d.a; Schiffer 1972a; Schiffer and Rathje 1973), makes archaeology unique within diachronically oriented scientific disciplines. In the past these goals and the actual practice of highway archaeology have seemed rather disparate. In designing archaeological research, however, goals of this nature must be kept in mind at all phases in order to achieve a mutual interdependence of theory and practice.

## Goals and Problem Domains

The primary goal of the GRD is "to systematically explore and reconstruct past activities represented by highway intercepted sites [Goodyear 1975a:15]." Focus at the site level relates to the problem of regional sampling in corridors. This does not necessarily entail a fragmented or particularistic approach to site analysis. In order to adequately elucidate its full information value, every site must be examined from several perspectives. Every site must be studied for its own individual properties and then related to its functional position in a wider cultural system.

In order to bring to each site a common set of analytic perspectives, four problem domains were constructed. These domains and their relevance to systematic behavioral reconstruction are discussed.

### *Cultural Identification*

By using archaeological methods, it is possible to isolate certain indicators that allowed prehistoric groups or "societies" to identify and distinguish themselves internally and externally from other, contemporaneous societies. Society can be thought of in a behavioral and adaptive sense as Harris (1975) has defined it: "A group of people who share a common habitat and who are dependent on each other for their survival and well-being [p. 145]." While the emphasis on a behavioral, as opposed to a cognitive, definition is more operable for archaeological analysis, the behavioral aspects of social integrity are nevertheless as important as the psychological aspects, and short of mental telepathy, the latter are always transmitted through the former. In this behavioral transmission of social information several material items are often used to aid in nonverbal communication (Knapp 1972:25–90). Where material culture—such as a dress, ornaments, architecture, decoration on tools and weapons, mode of burial, etc.—is regularly employed to communicate and maintain social structure, archaeology begins its analysis. Archaeology's most obvious successes in cultural identification and differentiation have thus far been with ceramic attribute analysis (J. N. Hill 1970a; Longacre 1968; Woodall 1972) and mortuary studies (Brown 1971), although archaeologists are beginning to explore social dimensions of stone tools as well (Gorman 1972; Knudson 1973; Morse 1975a; White and Thomas 1972; Wilmsen 1974).

### Activity Analysis

As just discussed, reconstruction and explanation of site activities is the fundamental goal of the GRD. It is useful to think of archaeological records as having three basic properties: content, form, and structure (Schiffer 1972a:156). These must be accounted for in thorough reconstructions with arguments of site information. In order to more accurately sample for these three elements, we have been experimenting with statistical intrasite sampling designs for both surface and subsurface remains. Computer-mapping programs such as SYMAP (Synagraphic Computer Mapping) and statistical methods are currently being applied to these data (Goodyear 1975a:18–20). Archaic stage sites of low artifact density, which have generally been regarded as internally random in spatial organization, are being examined by SYMAP with interesting results. Through the mapping of debitage variables related to biface reduction by stage and raw material, utilized flakes, and firecracked rock, subtle and unsuspected intrasite patterning is being revealed. These data are being collected during EIS-phase research and provide interesting patterns from which hypotheses can be derived and site significance can be better assessed.

### Subsystem Reconstruction

This problem domain serves to tie individual sites and their specific characteristics to their parent cultural system. A site will often reflect not only the subsystem in which it spatially functioned (e.g., agricultural, quarry, cemetery) but may indirectly reflect or implicate other subsystems as well. For example, in South Carolina siliceous raw materials such as chert and slate used for chipped stone tools have a rather limited natural geological distribution. Some of these materials, especially Coastal Plain cherts, were prehistorically transported by varying mechanisms. Studies of raw material diversity and reduction stage of biface-related debitage have been especially productive for the Piedmont, which seems to have no natural chert outcrops, but yet the sites of which exhibit a variable distribution in the presence of exotic cherts (Goodyear et al. 1977; House and Ballenger 1976). Subsystem identification is basic to the pursuit of settlement functional variability and offers almost limitless avenues of research.

### Ecological Analysis

Human societies of all organizational scales are directly and indirectly articulated with their biophysical and social environments. Broadly conceived, our research is intended to inform on the patterned adaptive responses of past societies with varying physical, biological, and social parameters. At the moment we are experimenting with ecologically relevant variables relating to the environmental context of individual sites and sets of sites and examining through the use of maps environmental data outside the perimeter of highway impact. Using U.S. Geological Survey quad maps, soil maps, and aerial photographs, we can analyze each site for its proximity to a variety of natural resources, such as topographical setting, elevation, soil association, distance to permanent water source, drainage rank, etc. (cf. Plog and Hill 1971). These data cost virtually nothing to obtain and usually require little extra fieldwork, if any. We are also experimenting with site catchment analysis (House and Ballenger 1976) and random vectors drawn from comparable adjacent environments (Goodyear *et al.* 1977) in order to obtain comparative regional data for ecological analysis.

### Summary of General Problem Domains

The four problem domains just described are intended to give some theoretical orientation at a general level for any site or set of sites regardless of the extent of our prior knowledge. These categories are necessarily broad and their data types per any set of remains are flexible in order to best accommodate site variability along several different dimensions. In time, through several repeated studies of different cultural systems in their regional contexts, it should be possible to increase the number, specificity, and relevance of variables by regions. The presence of the four problem domains in the GRD is intended to insure their recognition before, during, and after field studies regardless of phase and to guarantee the systematic investigation of additional subproblems related to each domain. The most efficient use of the problem domains is through the construction of models that draw on them for information.

## RELATIONSHIPS BETWEEN THE GENERAL RESEARCH DESIGN, ENVIRONMENTAL IMPACT STATEMENTS, AND SPECIFIC RESEARCH DESIGNS

It is important that all phases of field and laboratory research have some information input toward the general design and toward one another. This is necessary in order to achieve a multistage effect, and it is further desirable because each phase of field research differs in terms of intensity of data collected and consequently, data reliability.

That phase with the weakest observation powers, the EIS, in particular needs serious review and evaluation. These limitations refer to difficulties in intersite and intrasite sampling and the low reliability of surface and subsurface resource estimates, especially in the forested southeastern United States. Even surveys undertaken in EIS studies provide data that can be fed into subsequent phases (see Figure 12.1), although the reliability of EIS-phase data should be monitored and verified in many cases by the utilization of more intensive sampling strategies in subsequent

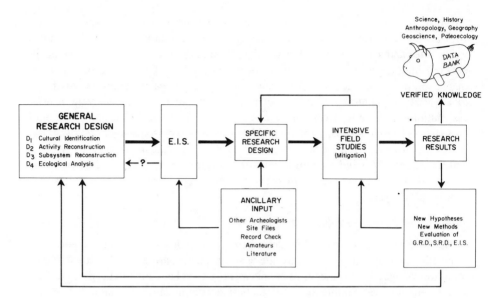

**Figure 12.1.** Flow model of multistage research and role of the general research design.

phases. The need for confirming EIS-phase research can be underscored by the fact that much contract research never goes beyond the EIS phase, and we would like to have confidence limits on the general usefulness of such data. The EIS phase occupies a critical role in multistage research, since it is usually the first phase of field studies (Figure 12.1). The data collecting activities of the EIS are generally guided by the problem domains of the GRD. The EIS must then begin to examine the particular impact area in terms of site-specific characteristics and potential regional patterns. The latter function is necessary for the creation of a relevant specific research design (SRD), which must be formulated *prior* to performing mitigation-phase fieldwork.

If the EIS is very thorough, the SRD may be in hand upon its completion. If much time has passed between the EIS and the mitigation phase, it might be well to prepare a new SRD based on additional survey data, if needed, and certainly in light of recent advances in theory, method, and substantive new knowledge of the project area. A well-done SRD should consider problems related to the particular attributes of the data base at hand, the position of the sites in their regional context, and their relationships to wider problems of a general nature in anthropological archaeology (see House and Schiffer 1975b).

In addition to data collected during the EIS phase, other ancillary sources should also be incorporated where appropriate. Regional symposia, site files, amateur collections and site leads, plus the published literature, are all important sources of information (Figure 12.1).

The outcome of a field-operationalized SRD will be evaluated in many ways (Figure 12.1). In a substantive way the field and laboratory analysis will increase and refine our knowledge about regional manifestations. Such information will have been accumulating since the EIS phase. Much of this information of a factual nature will be of interest and value to other disciplines as well, *provided* such data are adequately disseminated. The utility and relevance of the GRD will also be examined, based on the results of various operationalized SRD's, and through time the GRD will be revised and ultimately replaced. This feedback relationship to the GRD is illustrated in Figure 12.1.

## CONCLUSIONS

This chapter has attempted to deal with problems basic to a specialized contract program, highway archaeology, by constructing a general research design to effect methodological and theoretical continuity in research. The general goal of activity reconstructions for individual sites was justified in terms of limitation in regional sampling, although this was qualified by the suggestion that regionally based patterns of cultural systems could be elucidated and partially confirmed by highway research. The four problem domains were provided as a means of promoting this goal by encouraging research in predetermined areas or topics. The flow of research from Phase 1 EIS studies to final mitigation was outlined in terms of mutually beneficial interrelationships. The main function of the GRD is considered to be not so much one of *theory using,* although at a general level various useful concepts of archaeological theory are exerting influence on the direction of research. Rather, the design is viewed as a means of systematically and explicitly generating theory.

## ACKNOWLEDGMENTS

This chapter has benefited from the readings of several generous persons. I would like to thank Robert L. Stephenson, John D. Combes, Stanley A. South, and Leland G. Ferguson for their comments. Michael B. Schiffer made valuable criticisms of the design in its formative phases and inspired the flow chart, although he is in no way to blame for the piggy bank. Kenneth E. Lewis, Richard F. Carrillo, David G. Anderson, and John House also provided useful suggestions.

# 13

# The Santa Rosa Wash Project:
# Notes on Archaeological Research Design under Contract

L. MARK RAAB

## THE NATURE OF AN ARCHAEOLOGICAL RESEARCH DESIGN

### Misconceptions about Research Design

There are a number of widespread misconceptions about what an archaeological research design is. It may be helpful in this regard to point out first what an archaeological research design is *not*.

At its best, a research design is not a *rote, pedestrian exercise*. Some archaeologists seem to regard a formal research design as a set of simplistic procedures (somewhat like the steps in "The Scientific Method" from high school biology, perhaps) that are, after all, a caricature of how things are "really" done and a waste of time. A corollary of this view is the notion that perfectly good research can be done with one's research design "in one's head," it being unnecessary to compose formally one's ideas on paper.

There are a number of problems with these conceptions of research design. First, research designs need be no more rote or simplistic than researchers allow them to be. Formal research designs can and should accommodate an unlimited range of creative archaeological research. The second notion, that implicit "research designs" are an acceptable approach, is a more serious problem. Without formal research designs much of the archaeological research done in this country will remain beyond adequate assessment. The health of archaeology as a scientific discipline, both under contract and otherwise, depends on critical assessment of the total research process by a community of scholars. I cannot see how this critical process can be sustained without explicit mechanisms for communicating our ideas to one another. Here I do not mean the traditional archaeological report that relates the results of research after the fact, but an assessment of the total research process from its inception to its conclusion. The importance of this point is underscored by the expanding scope and intensity of archaeological research in this country.

A research design can also be misconceived as a *list of unresolved research questions*. For example, upon being asked to produce a "research design," an archaeologist may indicate that it should be determined whether ceramic type X or ceramic type Y is the earlier in the local stratigraphic sequence or whether there was a Paleo-Indian occupation of a particular river basin. A mere list of possible research questions has relatively little utility, however. Among other problems, such a list provides little insight into why the listed research questions, as opposed to others, are particularly worth investigating. Faced with a rapidly disappearing resource base, we should have some sense of strategy in the selection of research questions. Moreover, selection of research questions should be an open process in which, again, a community of scholars participates. This does not mean that the research that a particular archaeologist wants to undertake should be decided by committee. It does mean that selection of research strategies can benefit from open discussion and comment. Again, this process will require a more formal and rapid means of communicating ideas than was true when archaeology was a smaller, more informal discipline. Explicit, problem-oriented research designs seem an ideal answer to this need.

Another misconception is the equation of a "research design" with a *logistics plan*. The difficulties with this approach are obvious. A research proposal that dwells largely on matters of budgets, equipment, work schedules, and personnel really begs the question of what the proposed research is all about in the first place. Certainly, logistic factors must be considered in well-planned research, but these concerns are properly considered in addition to the goals and methods of the research and after these goals and methods have been clearly identified.

## Essential Elements of a Research Design

I have just tried to emphasize that a research design should not be a superficial exercise, rote and unimaginative; nor should it be equated with enumeration of possible research questions and logistics plans. Nevertheless, for a research design to serve as an efficient guide to the conduct of research, it should contain at least five essential elements. The following brief discussion touches on each of these elements.

### The Theoretical Basis of the Proposed Research

A research design should discuss the theoretical basis of the proposed research in sufficient detail to indicate the specific theoretical concepts to be employed. In this discussion it would also be helpful to indicate the anticipated gains in archaeological knowledge that will result from adopting the indicated theoretical concepts.

### Implications of Previous Research

A discussion relating the proposed research to previous archaeological research, topically and/or regionally, should be useful in clarifying research goals. The strategic importance of the proposed research goals may also be indicated in relation to previous research results. This discussion may overlap the discussion of the theoretical basis of the research, though it need not necessarily do so.

### Specific Hypothesis(es) to be Tested

There appears to be a growing consensus that formulation and testing of explicit hypotheses ought to be an integral part of scientific archaeology. Excellent archaeological examples of this view are presented by Gorman (1972), J. N. Hill (1966, 1970b, 1972), Longacre (1970a), F. T. Plog (1974b), Thomas (1973), and Vivian (1970). The position taken here is that deduction of hypotheses from significant theoretical domains is a highly useful way to begin the process of archaeological research.

Discussion of theoretical goals has little meaning unless these goals are implemented in the proposed research. Implementation of the theoretical goals can be achieved through testing one or more specific derivative hypotheses. For example, it might be argued that the appearance of social ranking in any society is a predictable result of population growth (according to a set of theoretical arguments). Moreover, it could be contended that an understanding of the conditions that bring about social ranking would offer substantial insight into the evolution of human society generally. Given the elucidation of the social ranking–population growth relationship as a major theoretical goal, it might be appropriate to derive the following specific hypothesis: If degree of social ranking is determined by the magnitude of population growth, then degree of social ranking as determined by burial practices should be closely covariant with the magnitude of population growth.

Ignoring the merits of this particular theoretical problem and hypothesis, we will note that the derivation of a specific hypothesis takes us one step closer to a concrete research situation. Once a hypothesis has been framed, we are no longer talking about a theoretical problem (the cause of social ranking) with the same degree of generality. The equation of the variable social ranking with differences in mortuary treatment introduces a specific material referent, which is potentially amenable to archaeological study. Similarly, specification of a material referent for the variable magnitude of population growth would also introduce a more specific potential for archaeological investigation. The hypothesis, which relates mortuary data and data on population growth rates, is also a specific logical derivative of the general theoretical proposition that social ranking is determined by magnitude of population growth. This derivative quality of a hypothesis is an important part of the logic of research design, which we shall return to shortly in the discussion of the *hierarchical structure* of research design.

### Test Implications

Once a specific hypothesis(es) has been proposed, an effective research design should also provide a related set of test implications. Test implications of a hypothesis are the empirical consequences one would expect if the hypothesis were true. In our hypothesis above, for example, if growth in population were related to an increase in social ranking, we might predict that we would find an increase in the occurrence of "luxury" ceramics in the graves of a few individuals as population expanded. Test implications have an important function of acting as a bridge between the abstract language of the hypothesis and the facts of the empirical world.

### Data Collection and Data Analysis Techniques

Once we have taken a particular theoretical position and derived one or more hypotheses and test implications, it then becomes relatively easy to select appropriate data collection and analysis techniques. It is important that data collection and data analysis methods be made explicit because the manner in which data are to be collected and analyzed will determine whether a hypothesis can be meaningfully tested. The growing concern with sampling methods in archaeology, for example, reflects an increased awareness of the effects of data collection methods on the validity of hypothesis testing.

Notice that we have now come from a very generalized theoretical position to a concrete entity that one could expect to encounter in an archaeological site. At the same time, however, all parts of our make-believe research design form an integrated logico-empirical structure.

### The Hierarchical Structure of Research Design

It should be apparent that the five elements of research design just presented form a structure composed of levels that are successively more abstract or concrete, depending on which end one begins. In this sense the structure of the research design is *hierarchical*. The structure has another important property as well: It is a *logico-empirical* structure. By "logico-empirical," I mean that the structure combines both theoretical and empirical domains. In combination, the hierarchical and logico-empirical properties of the research design allow it to test general theoretical concepts and at the same time to deal with concrete empirical entities. The ability to

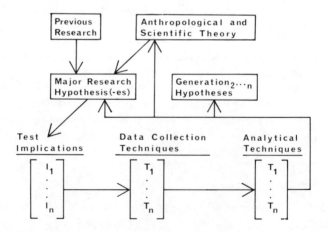

**Figure 13.1.** Schematic representation of an integrated research design.

derive (or deduce, if you prefer) increasingly specific derivatives of a theory through successive logico-empirical levels allows the researcher to deal successfully with a perennial problem in archaeology: relating particular archaeological resources to general theoretical concepts in a scientifically productive way. Figure 13.1 is a schematic representation of this process.

There are other possibilities. One can begin an investigation in the hope that if enough "data" are collected, they can eventually be assembled into some kind of general principle. More often than not, however, this passively inductive approach ends up with description rather than tested knowledge, and site-specific "interpretations" rather than general principles. I prefer to *begin* research, insofar as it is possible, with general theoretical concepts or principles (some would use the term *law* here, perhaps) because this approach helps to assure that research will have some sort of nomothetic importance and effective integration of theory and method.

The research at Santa Rosa Wash project was an experiment in this conception of archaeological research design.


## THE SANTA ROSA WASH PROJECT

Between June and November 1973 the Arizona State Museum conducted the first phase of archaeological field investigations at Santa Rosa Wash, Papago Indian Reservation, approximately 25 miles south of Casa Grande, Arizona. Construction of Tat Momolikot Dam across Santa Rosa Wash and subsequent regional development will adversely affect archaeological resources in an area of about 33 square miles along the upper wash. Phase I of the Santa Rosa Wash project, under my field supervision, was intended to mitigate unavoidable destruction of these resources.

At the completion of fieldwork 197 prehistoric and historic sites had been recorded and investigated. Some of the sites were rediscovered from two previous site surveys (Canouts 1972; Stacy and Palm 1970); others were located by additional survey during Phase I. Prehistoric sites ranged from isolated stone tools and small sherd scatters collected from the surface, to buried house floors, occupation surfaces, trash deposits, storage pits, and a large water reservoir (Raab 1975) uncovered by excavation. A complete description of sites investigated during Phase I is available in Raab (1974a, 1976e).

The project area is located within the Lower Sonoran desert life zone, with its characteristic physiography, climate, and plant and animal communities. Physiographically, the project area is part of the Basin and Range province of the western United States, where small but rugged mountain chains rise abruptly above broad alluvial plains. Steep arroyos drain the flanks of the mountains onto the floodplains, where runoff from summer thunderstorms floods the major wash channels. Within the project area the Santa Rosa Wash is the major stream channel. The Slate Mountains, a linear chain of mountains about 6 miles in length, parallel the eastern floodplains of the Santa Rosa Wash. Together, the wash and mountains form a physiographic system that is typical of much of southern Arizona.

The climate of the project area is characterized by high annual temperatures and aridity (<10 inches of rain annually). The climate and physiography, as well as other factors, support a series of distinct plant and animal communities with relatively discrete spatial distributions.

The research design discussed in the following pages, insofar as the major hypothesis and test implications are concerned, derived from a research design I prepared for the National Park Service and the Arizona State Museum (Raab (1973a). This research design was written *before* the beginning of archaeological mitigation studies at Santa Rosa Wash. This point is crucial to certain arguments regarding the efficient management of archaeological research. The research design also served as the basis of an extended analysis of archaeological resources at Santa Rosa Wash (Raab 1976e).

## THE SANTA ROSA WASH RESEARCH DESIGN

### The Theory of Behavioral Ecology

The metatheoretical, or logically fundamental, premise of the research design is a conception of *behavioral ecology*. It should be understood at the outset, however, that this concept is not isomorphic with certain anthropological interpretations of human "ecological" studies. Indeed, cultural anthropology seems to have difficulty coming to grips with the concept of ecology because of a tendency to dichotomize human existence into "material" and "superorganic" realms. Harris's (1968: 580–604) "emic"–"etic" distinction would be another way to conceptualize this dichotomy in the sense that *etic* refers to phenomena verified by a community of scientific observers and *emic* refers to phenomena verified by an informant's subjective notion of "meaning" or "appropriateness." This dichotomy runs the risk of facile generalization but nevertheless illustrates a characteristic of anthropological theory from its inception.

The difficulty with this tradition, insofar as ecological studies are concerned, is that anthropologists have not been able to develop an effective theoretical position because of their proclivity for parceling human existence into disparate ideological pigeonholes.

The present discussion rejects any dichotomy between "animal" and "human" ecology and between "organic organization" and "superorganic organization" (cf. Helm 1962) on the ground that this distinction is neither scientific nor necessary. This distinction is, first of all, nonscientific because it establishes a category of entitites, the "superorganic," which is by definition removed from physical reality. All genuine science is founded on phenomenal events. Suffice it to say that any conception of human experience that is held to exist "beyond" the scope of physical or biological reality is also well beyond the scope of science (a circumstance that has provided great relief to some). This is not intended as a polemic against nonscientific knowledge but, rather, as a recognition of the fact that there are many kinds of knowledge, only some of which are apparently amenable to investigation by science.

The basis of the second objection, that the dicotomy between material and cultural entities is unnecessary in ecological studies, is somewhat more complex. In its basic form this notion simply suggests that any aspect of human existence that is *behavioral*—that is, subject to direct or (in the case of archaeology) indirect *observation*—is the fit subject of ecological analysis. Vayda and Rappaport (1968) make an excellent argument for this case by suggesting that *all* aspects of human behavior may play a role in the functioning of the biophysical system that constitutes human society.

The conclusion to be drawn from this line of reasoning is clear: There is nothing inherent to an ecological approach to human behavior that limits it to any particular subject matter. The key word here is *behavior;* any behavioral, or empirical, aspect of human existence is susceptible to ecological analysis. In this sense it is unnecessary to distinguish between a "cultural," or (as we have called it) a "superorganic," realm and an "organic," or material, realm of human existence. All of the traditional concerns of anthropology, including art, religion, and social organization, may be treated as ecological variables.

## Biophysical and Social Ecology

The preceding discussion suggested that ecological studies are or can be applicable to a wide range of human behavior; it will now be argued that these studies can be classified along a typological continuum. This continuum is a theoretical construct that allows us to organize and describe the various possible applications of ecological analysis. This construct is best conceived as a continuum because it allows us to classify an infinite number of ecological analyses between *ideal* types.

At one end of the continuum we have what might be called *biophysical ecology.* The distinguishing characteristic of this type is that it specifies some aspect of human behavior as its *dependent variable* (the dependent variable is that part of a scientific hypothesis that is to be explained), and some aspect(s) of the biophysical environment as the *independent variable(s)* (the independent variable is that part of a scientific hypothesis that is supposed to explain the dependent variable). Put more simply, this approach attempts to show that some aspect of the natural environment is responsible for *causing* some type of human behavior. It seems fairly obvious that this type is best suited for the study of technologically primitive societies, where much of the society's behavioral repertoire articulates directly with the biophysical environment. Human behavior is the dependent variable and the biophysical environment is the independent variable that in some sense causes people to behave as they do.

At the other end of our theoretical continuum we find *social ecology.* The distinguishing characteristic of this type of analysis is that it specifies human behavior as both the dependent and the independent variable. Flannery (1972a) has made a pioneering effort in this type of analysis in archaeology in the sense that he attempted to relate change in complex social organizations to changes in mechanisms

of social control. The important point for the present discussion is that both dependent and independent variables are behavioral (i.e., subject to observation).

It should be noted, too, that both these types are not mutually exclusive, but grade
into each other in actual research situations. In fact, investigation of one type should
lead to insight into the other.

## The Method of Behavioral Ecology

As is often the case in research, it is usually easier to indicate how research might
be done than actually to carry it out. Nevertheless, I believe that certain procedures
are fundamental to any ecological study. The enumeration of these may help give a
clearer picture of the goals of ecological research as well as its procedures:

1. *Behaviorism.* The ecological approach is based on the study of behavior, a
category of events that has phenomenal (observable) referents. It is therefore subject
to objective scrutiny through the use of explicit hypothesis testing and may be
accompanied by quantification of data. In the case of biophysical ecology the
research should demonstrate an empirical relationship between human behavior and
parameters of the biophysical environment. In social ecology the research seeks to
show an empirical relationship between organizational characteristics of human
behavior.

2. *Reciprocity of cause.* Ecological research attempts to relate human behavior
and environment (social or physical) in a mutual causal system. This notion simply
posits that human behavior is caused by and in turn causes behavior in a system
(ecosystem). This truism can be given explanatory power if we specify a series of
testable hypotheses about the nature of the behavior–environment relationship. The
behavior–environment relationship can be approached on a primitive level by the
verification of correlations between behavior and environment. At a more sophisticated level the behavior–environment relationship can be specified in terms of
systematic, or processual, models. The latter, in practice, are far more difficult to
achieve.

3. *Selective advantages of behavior.* If we concede that behavior is just as
important to the functioning of an animal as are its physical attributes, we must also
concede that behavior has selective advantages according to the conditions of the
animal's ecosystem. There is an obvious analogy here between human behavior and
biological adaptation, but it is not necessarily generally valid. In the case of
biophysical ecology, for example, it may have some application to human populations, but it is probably less important to social ecology.

## Implications of Previous Archaeology in the Papagueria

The previous sections of this chapter presented arguments in support of the
concept of behavioral ecology. This concept emphasizes the need to cast archaeological research in terms of behavioral variables and explain the relationship
between these variables in terms of systemic, or "ecological," interrelationships.

This approach also contains a substantial evolutionary component concerned with processes that cause change in systems of variables through time.

The present discussion attempts to provide a background for the hypothesis and test implications that follow by indicating in a general way the continuities and differences between past work and the behavioral ecology approach. In this way an attempt is made to show how the Santa Rosa Wash research incorporates past work but also seeks to expand on this previous work within the theoretical position of behavioral ecology.

## The Early Investigations: Culture History and Behavioral Ecology

Compared with other regions in Arizona, the Papagueria has received relatively little attention from archaeologists. Remoteness and summer heat have not made it a favored locality for field operations, and few excavation reports have resulted. Nonetheless, a regional synthesis is presented in the Ventana Cave monograph by Haury, Bryan, Buerer, Colbert, Gabel, and Tanner (1950). The synthesis of these and other investigations produced the outline of a behavioral chronology that extends from perhaps the seventh millennium B.C. to about A.D. 1400.

Apart from an obvious concern with time–space schemes and artifact-centered problems, the theoretical basis of this earlier work often remains implicit. When there is an explicit concern with theory, it is often of a type that may be called the "normative," or "culture historical framework [Flannery 1967]."

Critics of the culture-historical school (Binford 1968a; Flannery 1967) argue that a normative approach to prehistory yields a historical, that is ideographic or particularizing, form of knowledge. These same critics emphasize the need for commitment to scientific explanation of the *processes* that make for behavioral change or stability, rather than particularistic description. Binford (1964) phrases this difference as a concern with the "how" and "why" questions of process, in addition to the "what, where and when questions so characteristically asked by archaeologists [p. 425]."

Concomitant with the emphasis on explaining the mechanisms of behavioral change, there has developed an increasing recognition that in order to understand the functioning of social *systems,* we must have a better understanding of the environments in which these systems participate (e.g., Binford 1964:426). Both of these notions, that is, the idea of a *behavioral system* and the study of social systems in their *adaptive context,* are integral to the conception of human ecology presented earlier and a departure from the aims of normative archaeology.

The distinction between culture history and behavioral process was not introduced for the sake of generating an abstract, academic debate. Implementation of one or the other strategy produces tangible differences in the results of archaeological research.

Unquestionably, the early investigations in the Papagueria are highly significant achievements that provide a starting point and frame of reference for later studies. Without the ability to order archaeological behavior in time and space it would be

very difficult, if not impossible, to formulate and test meaningful hypotheses regarding behavioral process. The early culture-historical studies in the Papagueria
(and elsewhere in southern Arizona) provide the necessary framework for processual studies.

Building on the culture-historical precedents, we may expand our concerns to
include a broader range of artifact–environment relationships such as:

1. Determination of time–space relationships that can serve as a matrix for
   *testing* increasingly precise hypotheses about past human behavior
2. Typing and study of artifacts in terms of *function* as well as stylistic variability, which would allow maximum utility in testing hypotheses about
   behavior as well as provide time–space markers
3. Collection of detailed environmental data for correlation with artifacts and
   with sites in order to test relationships between behavior and environment

### The Major Hypothesis

The research design was calculated to test the *major hypothesis* that: *Given a
low-energy prehistoric technology and the parameters of the Sonoran Desert
ecosystem, the type of prehistoric settlement at Santa Rosa Wash will vary significantly in function and distribution in relation to variable biophysical factors.* In
effect, the hypothesis suggests that prehistoric settlement at Santa Rosa Wash was a
form of behavioral organization that functioned to secure subsistence (food, water,
and shelter) from the physical environment. This general type of hypothesis is, of
course, not new in anthropological research. Indeed, Helm (1962) traces an interest
in settlement–subsistence relationships to an older and more encompassing tradition
in geography and social anthropology. It might be argued, however, that archaeology is in a unique position to test relationships between settlement and subsistence. In the first place, archaeology has the potential to observe the interaction of
subsistence and settlement in relatively simple behavioral systems under a wide
variety of environmental conditions. This does not preclude study of more complicated behavioral systems, but it does allow the initial development of theory and
technique in the study of relatively simple societies. It should not be overlooked,
too, that most of human history has been spent in relatively simple behavioral
systems. Second, the archaeologist can observe settlement–subsistence change over
time. Access to behavioral time depth is not to be underestimated in the process of
theory testing. These circumstances provide a unique opportunity to study the
mechanisms of human ecology as they relate to settlement–subsistence. Moreover,
knowledge of settlement–subsistence systems yields a wide range of information
about extinct societies. When we understand subsistence practice, we also know a
great deal about the form and function of technology. On the other hand, an
understanding of settlement patterns is likely to provide useful indicators of prehistoric social organization (Chang 1967, 1968). An understanding of these and other
variables may place us in a position to explain, as well as to describe, the evolution
of human society.

*Hypothesis Testing*

We might wonder what it is that constitutes hypothesis testing. In the widest sense it means confronting a hypothesis with relevant empirical data to see if the phenomena entailed in the hypothesis behave as predicted. This "confrontation" between the hypothesis and the empirical data takes place through intermediate propositions, or test implications. Test implications may be thought of as the empirical consequences of a theoretical statement (Watson, *et al.* 1971:8).

## Quantitative Assessment of Environmental Parameters

In relation to the settlement/subsistence hypothesis, which forms the gist of the research design, environmental data should allow the archaeologist to compare the distribution of human behavioral indicators (sites, artifacts, etc.) with biophysical gradients. In order for this procedure to have maximum value, however, environmental data must be collected in a quantitative format whenever possible.

The major part of environmental sampling at Santa Rosa Wash involved collection of detailed information on vegetation. Vegetation is an extremely sensitive indicator of total environmental conditions (Billings 1970:41; Oosting 1956:17–29). Plant communities provide information about moisture, temperature, and soil conditions as well as sources of food and raw materials for man and other animals. Based on paleoclimatological work in southern Arizona (Bryan 1925:65; Martin 1963:61), it appears that the region has been characterized by an arid environment similar to that of the present for perhaps the last 10,000 years. If this is the case, modern studies of vegetation may reveal man–plant relationships in the prehistoric past.

Field sampling was implemented by two techniques: *quadrat* and *transect* sampling (Greig-Smith 1964; Oosting 1956:30–55). Quadrat sampling refers to a procedure in which all relevant species are enumerated and recorded by estimated biomass (cover value) within a sample square of designated size. A transect sample is a linear sample space composed of continuous quadrats. Quadrat sampling is useful for characterizing vegetation within a small sample space; transect sampling is useful for detecting shifts in plant communities along environmental gradients. Both of these methods can be implemented with quantitative measures (Curtis and McIntosh 1950), which allow statistical analysis.

## Initial Research Schedule of Problem Domains

It should be noted that a 1972 field survey report from Santa Rosa Wash (Canouts 1972:46–51) organized the sites found during this survey into five "problem domains." These were simply convenient categories that classified sites according to site type. *Three of the five problem domains* were investigated during Phase I at Santa Rosa Wash: *trails, areas of lithic activity, sherd and lithic scatters on the Santa Rosa Wash floodplain.* The outline that follows is an initial schedule of investigations that specifies *test implications* and *data collection methods* relevant to the major hypothesis. Test implications, it will be recalled, are directed at testing the major hypothesis. In this sense, test implications specify how one plans to measure variables set out in the major hypothesis; as such, they represent a bridge between the theoretical terms of the hypothesis and the empirical events of the real world. Data collection methods are field procedures designed to recover data necessary to verification (or nonverification) of the test implications.

I. *Problem domain I: trails*
   A. *Test implications* (modified from Canouts 1972:46)
      1. Trails connect different abiotic and biotic resources areas
      2. Trails connect specific-task sites with multicomponent "base" camps
      3. Trails connect areas of differential natural and behavioral advantage
   B. *Data collection methods*
      1. Aerial photographs of the project area
      2. Ground recording and mapping
II. *Problem domain II: lithic activity areas*
   A. *Test implications*
      1. Sites that are internally organized in demonstrable patterns
      2. Sites that are functionally specific, that is, specific in terms of manufacturing, processing, or extractive activities
      3. Sites that are significantly related to demonstrable biotic or abiotic resources
         a. Sites found on ecotones between resource zones
         b. Sites found within resource zones
         c. Sites located adjacent to resource zones
   B. *Data collection methods*
      1. Site mapping by artifact clusters
      2. Site mapping in relation to environmental resources, that is, vegetation, topography, and abiotic resources
      3. Collection of artifacts in all stages of manufacture and use, as well as waste products from manufacture and use
III. *Problem domain III: lithic and shard scatters on the Santa Rosa Wash floodplain*
   A. *Test implications*
      1. Sites that are internally organized in demonstrable patterns
      2. Sites that are functionally specific in terms of manufacturing, processing, extractive, domiciliary, or other activities
      3. Sites that are significantly related to demonstrable biotic and abiotic resources
         a. Sites found in ecotones between resource zones
         b. Sites found within resource zones
         c. Sites located adjacent to resource zones

    4.  Sites that are significantly related to one another spatially or functionally

    5.  Domiciliary sites that are occupied seasonally

B.  *Data collection methods*

    1.  Site mapping by artifact clusters, or detectable activity loci

    2.  Site mapping in relation to environmental resources, that is, vegetation, topography, and abiotic resources

    3.  Collection of artifacts in all stages of manufacture and use

    4.  Soil sampling from sites and site areas

    5.  Flotation samples taken from stratified activity areas, especially habitations

    6.  Pollen samples taken from stratified sites

    7.  Hydrological evaluation of project area

## EVALUATION OF THE RESEARCH DESIGN CONCEPT

In the research design we are told what problems the research seeks to solve and how it plans to go about it. Significantly, however, the research design cannot provide an answer to a more fundamental question: Why include an explicit research design in archaeological research at all? Yet an answer to this question is critical to an evaluation of the successes and failures of the Santa Rosa Wash research. The answer is critical because the particular conception of research design employed at Santa Rosa Wash had a powerful impact in the kind and quality of research results that were obtained (Raab 1976e). No doubt serendipity often does play a part in research, but the findings of the Santa Rosa Wash project, both in terms of its strengths and weaknesses, are much more nearly the result of the kinds of questions asked and the process of seeking answers.

A number of arguments could be made in support of the scientific and management benefits of explicit research designs (see, for example, the excellent discussion by J. N. Hill 1972), but it seems to me that they all relate to a single benefit: *increased research efficiency.* In general, research undertaken without specific, testable hypotheses results in relatively inefficient use of archaeological resources.

A research design is preferable to a more unstructured initial approach because the former allows more efficient achievement of research goals. An explicit research design specifies the problems to be attacked and directs attention to appropriate kinds of data, data collection methods, and analytic techniques. Special emphasis is given here to the role that the research design played in ordering research priorities at Santa Rosa Wash. The Phase I site survey (Raab 1976e:126–130) is an excellent illustration. During the course of field research it became apparent that we did not have an adequate picture of the range of variability in prehistoric settlement, even though this information was essential to testing the major hypothesis. This realization raised a number of questions and problems that had not been anticipated prior to fieldwork.

At Santa Rosa Wash the research design was concerned with explaining variability in prehistoric settlement. When, therefore, it became apparent that we did not have an adequate understanding of certain kinds of sites located on the slopes of the Slate Mountains and on the western floodplain of the Santa Rosa Wash, we were faced with a conflict in priorities. Should we use our resources to continue investigation of the relatively large and complex sites along the Wash? Alternatively, should we turn our resources to the investigations of smaller, more ephemeral sites that had accidentally been discovered during vegetation mapping? A number of approaches could have been justified. From a culture-historical point of view the large sites on the wash, with painted ceramics and buried architectural features, could have been the major focus of attention. If we had been primarily interested in prehistoric utilization of the paloverde–saguaro plant community in the Slate Mountains, as was another investigator (Goodyear 1975b), we could have largely ignored the floodplain settlements. As it turned out, however, we were interested in settlement variability, and that fact suggested that we should attempt to account for all types of sites. On this basis we undertook a survey of small sites in the Slate Mountains. *It is important to note that sites were treated according to criteria set forth in the research design and not according to characteristics of the sites themselves.* In this way the progression of research was subordinate to explicit research goals and not the vagaries of data collection.

Discovery of new data is a normal and expectable event that often requires the archaeologist to reevaluate existing research goals in light of the new information. In the absence of explicit, well-conceived research designs, however, the probability is increased that the archaeologist will deal with this new information in a relatively inefficient way. "Inefficient" in this sense does not mean that nothing new is learned; rather it means that research undertaken without the aid of an explicit research design often yields less information than might have been the case if there had been more effective guidance from specific hypotheses. The efficiency of explicit research design resides, then, in its ability to coordinate research goals and data collection derived from specific hypothesis. This conception of research efficiency is especially important to large-scale archaeological projects, which require greater planning and organization. And, of course, this idea is fully compatible with multiphase projects of the kind proposed by Redman (1973).

Explicit research designs contribute to research efficiency in another way as well: They serve as a *systemic basis for generating new, more specific hypotheses.* This is an extremely important consequence of research design and one that demonstrates great superiority over more passively inductive methods.

In one sense a research design should be considered a *process of investigation.* Although a research design begins with research questions in the form of one or more specific hypotheses, it also serves as a means of generating new research questions. This characteristic of research designs is a property of their analytic structure. Evaluation of specific hypotheses requires systematic examination of patterns of evidence, and this process often produces new, more specific insights. Frequently, new hypotheses can be proposed and tested within the framework of an initial research design. These new hypotheses and the logical steps leading to their formulation and testing have been referred to as *second-generation hypotheses*. In the Santa Rosa Wash research (Raab 1976e:205–224) it was possible to develop and test three second-generation hypotheses concerning prehistoric cactus fruit-gathering camps in the Slate Mountains, population increase in the project area during the prehistoric era, and the use of certain environments on the Santa Rosa Wash floodplain for prehistoric farming. Significantly, these hypotheses inform on behavioral systems far more complex and detailed than those outlined in the test implications of the problem domains. Yet it was the major hypothesis and initial schedule of test implications that served as a beginning point for an investigative process that generated these hypotheses. In this sense it is less important if an initial research design is somewhat generalized because it should be the beginning of an efficient process of investigation. What is more important is that the process *begin*.

Again, the settlement hypothesis represented a specific instance of the generalized theoretical position outlined in the discussion of behavioral ecology. More precisely, the settlement hypothesis, to the extent that it was supported or rejected by testing, reflected on the adequacy of theory at higher levels of abstraction. This conception of theory rests on the hierarchical organization of logico-empirical levels schematically represented in Figure 13.1.

The great bulk of past archaeological work, both in the Papagueria and elsewhere, was directed towards defining sets of temporal and spatial units based primarily on *stylistic traits of artifact classes*. The difficulty that artifact-centered studies have in relating to specific patterns of past human behavior resides in part in the process of inference that these studies rely on. If one approaches the study of archaeological materials with the assumption that one must *first* define a series of artifact types, one must ultimately make inferences about specific forms of past human behavior from these types. Unfortunately, without specific notions about what kinds of human behavior the artifacts might reflect (theories) or rules for making inferences from artifacts to behavior (hypotheses and test implications), artifact types tend to be frustratingly vague about the specifics of past human life.

On the other hand, if one begins an archaeological investigation with specific questions about human behavior and a set of rules to govern inferences from archaeological data to behavior, artifacts assume a relatively definite place in the scheme of scientific explanation. In this type of approach the phenomena to be explained and the role of various kinds of evidence in explanations are relatively explicit and, therefore, subject to conscious control. This is an important utility of an explicit, a priori research design.

In the case of the Santa Rosa Wash research, settlement patterns were conceived as behavioral variables in processes of adaptation to the Sonoran Desert ecosystem. Not only was it possible to establish a reasonably detailed picture of prehistoric settlement in the project area, based on the original research design, but it was also possible to propose and test three second-generation hypotheses related to settlement behaviors. Since this research took the explanation of human behavior as its immediate and primary goal, we now have a much more detailed picture of prehistoric human behavior in the project area and a body of information that can systematically be evaluated as to its validity and applicability to future research.

In its substantive findings the Santa Rosa Wash research also extends the usefulness of culture-historical analyses. The ecological frame of analysis places human behavior in a context that is amenable to study with the methods and theories of the biological and physical sciences. This move cannot but increase the quantity and quality of information on prehistoric human behavior. In this expanded context, studies of artifact-style chronology become more useful means toward explanation of human behavior, not as ends in themselves as they have too often tended to be.

From the results of the last 50 years of archaeological research it seems clear that the only way archaeology will become a science of human behavior is for it to seek explanations for human behavior as the immediate and primary goal of its researches. Archaeologists cannot put off the task of explicitly developing theories of human behavior in the hope that theories will spontaneously generate from inductively derived schemes of description and classification. Such a hope places expectations on the methods of description and classification that cannot be met in the absence of consciously developed theory and explicit research designs.

## ACKNOWLEDGMENTS

Gwinn Vivian, Mark Grady, and Val Canouts of the Arizona State Museum deserve special thanks for their support of the Santa Rosa Wash research. My field and lab crew also have my gratitude for their willingness to endure the Arizona desert in the summertime. Any errors in fact or interpretation are the author's alone.

# Part IV

---

# ACQUISITION OF SURVEY DATA

---

The emergence of conservation archaeology, with its singular dependence on survey data, has fortunately been able to capitalize on the advances in survey techniques ushered in by the new archaeology (F. T. Plog 1975). Despite this recent progress, however, it has become apparent that conservation archaeologists cannot expect to find an extant survey design exactly appropriate for most projects. Indeed, it has already been discovered that current survey methodology can take the conservation archaeologists only so far, and that distance in some cases is somewhat short of the sponsor's needs. In view of this situation it is not surprising to find that conservation archaeologists themselves are beginning to contribute to the development of survey methods, to define new topics for investigation, and to clarify concepts long in need of systematization. We briefly review several basic concepts, recent developments, and pressing issues in archaeological survey. The subjects we treat are only some of those that must be considered when surveys are designed and also when completed surveys are reported.

## WHAT IS A SITE?

The first task at hand is to decide what a site is. This decision has two interrelated and problematical components: a definitional component and an operational component. Sites have been defined as (*1*) a locus of past human behavior, or (*2*) a locus of cultural materials. If the former definition is chosen, then areas of secondary deposition (i.e., materials redeposited by noncultural processes) are excluded, even though they still may contain potentially useful data. The latter definition is to be preferred because, even if one desired deliberately to exclude loci of secondary deposition, the determination of which deposits are primary and which are secondary is an analytic task of sometimes great difficulty; such determinations often can be made only after survey and testing activities have been completed. It is wise, we believe, to record all deposits. For various *analytic* purposes, of course, the archaeologist may need to deal only with areas of primary deposition. It is therefore important to record in the field as much information as possible on depositional conditions so that intelligent decisions can be made about specific deposits.

The operational problem is one of specifying the empirical criteria that must be met in the field in order to designate a phenomenon as a "site." The Southwestern Anthropological Research Group has defined a site as any cultural manifestation having a density of five or more artifacts per square meter (Plog and Hill 1971:25). Other definitions based on similar arbitrary criteria are in widespread use. This approach assumes that sites are artifact clusters that generally exceed a specified level of object density. There is little alternative but to employ arbitrary definitions of this threshold value; we expect, however, that local conditions, prior knowledge of the area, and specific research problems will have some influence on this definition.

Explicit criteria for defining a site solve only part of the operational problem; one must also contend with the archaeological phenomena that fall below the threshold value—the nonsites (Thoms 1975). Techniques of nonsite survey have assumed some importance because of the repeated demonstration (in western North America, and especially in conservation archaeology projects) that isolated artifacts and diffuse scatters exhibit considerable patterning in space and provide information about past human behavior available from no other source (e.g., Dancy 1974; Doelle 1976; Goodyear 1975b; Morenon, Nielsen, and Henderson 1976; Rodgers 1974; Thomas 1972, 1973, 1975; Wait 1976). Doelle in Chapter 15 discusses some of the problems in integrating site and nonsite survey into a single project. Techniques of nonsite survey need to be tested outside of the Southwest and Great Basin; the existence of nonsite phenomena elsewhere is not in question, only the resultant payoff in new information in relation to the effort expended.

## COVERAGE AND INTENSITY

In addition to furnishing information on how sites are defined, conservation archaeologists need to consider two other characteristics of archaeological survey: *coverage* and *intensity*. Coverage is a straightforward description of the localitites to which archaeological survey techniques were applied in the study area. For example, if a 25% simple random sample was employed, one can then report a coverage of 25%, in addition to delineating the sample units covered. Intensity, or *intensiveness* (Plog and Hill 1971:20), is a measure of the amount of effort actually spent in surveying the covered areas. Usually intensity is expressed in person-days per square mile (or km²); this figure may or may not include the travel time spent getting to and from the survey units.

The question of coverage has been hotly debated, if not in the literature, then at least in the oral tradition of conservation archaeology. As we mentioned previously (introduction to Part I), the laws are in conflict on the need for total coverage, and total coverage per se is often difficult to justify in terms of research and management needs. We shall follow the lead of several federal agencies now implementing surveys for compliance with Executive Order 11593 (like the U.S. Forest Service, the Bureau of Land Management, and the National Park Service), which have in most cases opted for the use of modern sampling methods (Donaldson 1975; D. F. Green 1975b; Raab 1976a; Ritter and Hanks 1976; Rock 1975). We also urge the flexible application of these approaches in a multistage framework according to the specific information needs of each project. We caution, however, that one cannot simply apply uncritically the sampling design from one area to another. The actual design of a sampling program will depend on a variety of project-specific factors, including the research and management problems being addressed, stage of the investigation, initial estimates of the parameters of the archaeological resource base, and the other kinds of data being gathered.

The sampling literature in archaeology is now burgeoning, although some of it is quite unsound. The collection of partially redundant essays in *Sampling in Archaeology* (Mueller 1975b) is an excellent place to begin, especially the fine chapter by Cowgill (1975), as is Redman's (1974) introductory module on sampling. The results reported by Mueller (1974) in his lengthy monograph on sampling have been frequently used to orient the design of other projects. Given the problems that S. Plog (n.d.) has uncovered in Mueller's statistics and the vanishingly small probability that the parameters of his resource base are closely approximated elsewhere, this is indeed a risky procedure. While we acknowledge the need for and even encourage the application of rigorous sampling approaches in conservation archaeology, we also urge investigators to resist the temptation to apply extant methods uncritically. Appropriate sampling designs derive from the creative interplay between general sampling expertise, the nature of the study area, and project-specific research and management needs. In Chapter 14, Schiffer and House use the Cache River Archaeological Project of northeastern Arkansas to illustrate how a consideration of these factors goes into forming a viable sampling program.

The intensity with which archaeological surveys should be pursued is a matter for considerable discussion (see Klinger n.d.a). It is quite clear that in some sense intensity should relate to the parameters of the resource base the archaeologist is interested in measuring and the level of precision that is deemed acceptable. For example, if one were interested in estimating the number of very large sites in a region, then perhaps surveyors spaced 100 m apart would suffice. An estimation of nonsite parameters, on the other hand, may well call for an interval of 5 m or less between crew members. In order to provide some information on the parameters of small sites, most recent surveys have employed compromise intervals that lie between 10 m and 150 m. In Chapter 15 Doelle provides important insight into what may become a far more reliable and efficient compromise strategy. He suggests that an area in effect be surveyed several times, with each survey closely tailored to estimating a segment of the resource base. Used in conjunction with appropriate sampling techniques, Doelle's recommendations could lead to significant improvements in survey methodology. Needless to say, most techniques one might consider using in conservation archaeology are fairly intensive, at least when they are compared to traditional types of archaeological survey (see House and Schiffer 1975a:40–41; Ruppé 1966).

The increased use of highly intensive techniques, spurred in part by the modern archaeological emphasis on settlement–subsistence questions, has begun to provide some quantitative data that may be useful in designing projects. Time–labor data in the literature suggest that intensive survey requires between 10 and 60 person-days per square mile (Dancey 1974:107–108; Fehon and Viscito 1974:70–72; Lipe 1974:225; Martin and Plog 1973:8; Redman 1974:23; Wait 1976). The actual amount of effort (within the above range) needed to cover a particular area depends on a variety of project-specific factors, including the spacing interval between crew members, accessibility, logistics, vegetation, weather, capabilities of the personnel, ruggedness of the terrain, and the nature of the observations being recorded (including collections). Unfortunately, available data do not yet permit time–labor expenditures to be related to these factors quantitatively, although one can readily perceive the general influence of each factor. One may expect that as more careful records are kept of survey activities, we shall eventually have available a fairly precise basis for designing archaeological surveys.

## ACCESSIBILITY AND VISIBILITY

It is no secret that many factors in a study area affect the archaeologist's ability to find and record sites and nonsites. Therefore, two additional characteristics of any study area, *visibility* and *accessibility,* need to be treated explicitly when designing and reporting upon archaeological surveys. Visibility is simply a measure of the degree to which water, ground cover, soil and sediments, and subsequent occupations obscure the ground and, thereby, the surface of sites. Visibility problems are most severe, of course, in planted fields, swamps, forests, areas of recent alluvial deposition, and in modern settlements; the problems are least in deserts and some fallow fields. It is certain, however, that in no area is visibility 100%. The investigator needs to attempt to overcome visibility handicaps, using available techniques and experimenting with new ones (e.g., shovel testing, resurvey under more favorable conditions, soil phosphate analysis; magnetometry, radar, and acoustic holography—see, for example, Birk and George 1976; Claassen and Spears 1975; Lovis 1976; Rothschild 1976; K. R. Williams 1976), and to document the extent of the problem and assess its likely effect on estimating the parameters of the resource base (see Fehon and Viscito 1974; Price, Price, and Harris 1976; Schiffer and House 1975d).

Even when the surface of the ground is visible, the investigator may not be able to get to it. This can happen when landowners refuse to permit surveys, when landowners or tenants are repeatedly unavailable to grant permission, or when the terrain is so hazardous that it precludes access of safe walking. Accessibility limitations (which, of course, also may affect visibility—for example, swamps and dense forests) also need to be treated explicitly and, whenever possible, reduced by the use of modern technology and ingenuity (e.g., remote sensing—Lyons 1976).

It is crucial that headway be made in solving problems of visibility and accessibility, for, unlike most previous investigators, conservation archaeologists do not have the luxury of being able to refuse to work under less than ideal field conditions.

## WHERE TO SURVEY

The question of *where* to survey is one that seemingly need not be treated; after all, the study area is specified in the contract. Unfortunately, sponsors often present a scope of work that fails to consider all relevant factors. For example, it is not uncommon to find study areas defined exclusively on the basis of only the major zones of direct impact. However, in order for a field study to supply information adequate for compliance with the National Environmental Policy Act (NEPA), all areas of potential impact need to be treated. In the introduction to Part VII we discuss how preliminary forecasts of project effects can aid in the formulation of a realistic scope of work. Here we wish only to emphasize that the proper designation of the study area depends on close cooperation between the sponsor and archaeologist. Unless archaeological expertise influences this decision at the outset, it will be discovered (frequently after it is too late) that additional survey work is required—at great expense and with resultant delays to the sponsor.

## MULTISTAGE INVESTIGATIONS

The structuring of survey work within a multistage program of diversified research activities should provide the investigator with the occasion to make full use of his organizational and creative faculties. In recognition of the varied project-specific factors that go into designing archaeological surveys, we shall limit ourselves to offering only the most general advice. Although it is seemingly obvious, we suggest that one should never design a sizeable field study without some firsthand information on the nature and density of resources and on the local factors that affect the conduct of fieldwork. This kind of data may be acquired by means of a *reconnaissance survey* (not to be confused with the synonym for preliminary field study), as described by Grady (1975):

> The object . . . is to determine archaeological and logistic factors which relate to the implementation of more in-depth kinds of field work. Observations such as archaeological site distribution indicators, access problems, manpower needs, terrain coverage estimates, and support facility availability are documented [p. 4].

The rather informal technique of reconnaissance survey may be used profitably during overview and assessment projects. Such relatively inexpensive forays into the study area will appreciably increase the reliability of budgets proposed for field studies and perhaps, along with other data, make it possible to produce initial estimates of archaeological variability that can influence the first stage of a sampling program (see S. Plog 1976:279).

Preliminary field studies provide the archaeological information that can affect decisions regarding the placement of such projects as highways, powerlines, and pipelines. When actual alternate versions of a project are under consideration, the emphasis is less on precise estimation of the parameters of the entire resource base than on determining project-specific impacts. Proper design of this type of field study depends upon consideration of the anticipated range and severity of the direct and indirect effects of the various projects (see introduction to Part VII for elucidation of this point). If the areas of potential impact are sizable, probability sampling in one form or another is ordinarily advisable (e.g., Fehon and Viscito 1974). Once the sponsor adopts a final plan, then an intensive field study, often of complete coverage, is necessitated.

The factors influencing the design of intensive field studies are varied and may be related to one another in a complex fashion, as Schiffer and House point out in Chapter 14. Nevertheless, all such studies must endeavor to allow the sponsor to fulfill the requirements of NEPA with high-quality information. Although *preliminary* estimates of the resource base, forecasts of impacts, assessments of significance, and recommendations for mitigation are offered in assessments and preliminary field studies (and even overviews), it is only after an intensive survey of adequate coverage, in conjunction with ancillary reseach activities, that one can furnish compliance-level information on the former subjects (see King 1975a; McMillan *et al.* 1977). A major theme that runs through Chapter 14 is that in an intensive field study one is inevitably operationalizing a complex research design involving many activities in addition to field survey. Careful provision for the entire range of research efforts accomplished early will lead to a better integrated project that is far more likely to provide the sponsor with useful management information and lead to fruitful research results.

We also note that surveys on the scale of intensive field studies may be conducted by land-holding federal agencies in order to begin compliance with EO 11593 (e.g., Donaldson 1975; Weide 1973). Such studies should be designed with the same research considerations as any field study, but without concern for particular land modification activities.

## SURFACE COLLECTING AND TESTING

An important issue in conservation archaeology is the extent that the archaeological record may be exploited (that is, surface collected and tested) during field studies. Morenon *et al.* (1976) list several arguments in favor of leaving surface materials as they were found (see also Fuller, Rogge, and Gregonis 1976:68). They point out that analysis in the field facilitates better integration of sampling and analysis; eliminates future costs for collecting, processing, analysis, and storage of collections; and leaves more information intact for subsequent investigators. On the other side of the argument, we note that many research designs require detailed analysis of materials that simply cannot be performed in the field. One suspects that the range of innovative research problems that depend upon only the simplest analysis using extant data categories is quite small. In addition, ground cover, weather, and increased time spent recording in the field all must be weighed in the decision to collect or not to collect. Ultimately, the decision needs to be based on archaeological expertise applied to project-specific considerations. We note, however, that unless one actually intends to analyze the materials, there is little justification for making surface collections (see also Morenon *et al.* 1976). S. Plog (1976) describes an efficient technique for making surface collections that preserves some intrasite provenience relationships (see also Rodgers 1974).

Surprisingly, the use of test excavations (sondage) is a far less controversial procedure in conservation archaeology than surface collecting. There seems to be a near universal appreciation for the need to test sites in order to learn about characteristics of the resource base obtainable (usually) by no other method. It is especially important in an intensive field study, for instance, to be able to test some of the inferences one makes about a site's contents on the basis of surface observations (e.g., depth of deposit and extent of multiple occupations—see House 1975e). Thus, the findings of a testing program have an important role to play in describing the nature and extent of the archaeological resource base. Testing also permits one to determine conditions of artifact, ecofact, and feature preservation, especially as they relate to assessing significance (see D. E. Fox *et al.* 1974; House 1975e). Moreover, testing enables the investigator to furnish realistic cost estimates for full-scale excavations (see Skinner and Gallagher 1974). Some researchers are now experimenting with augers and other probing tools (e.g., Schoenwetter, Gaines, and Weaver 1973), which may be useful for determining stratigraphic patterns and establishing conditions of artifact and ecofact preservation, but one should not expect them to retrieve much in the way of an artifact sample.


## CONCLUSION

Field studies provide conservation archaeologists with almost boundless opportunities for integrating research and management goals into a single project. In addition, because techniques of archaeological survey and sampling are still in their infancy, field studies can also be used for testing and refining those techniques now in use and for devising others more appropriate for the demands of cultural resource management work. We recommend that the conservation archaeologist become thoroughly familiar with present survey methodology in order to move well beyond current capabilities and to create appropriate project-specific survey designs. We cannot stress strongly enough the necessity of avoiding cookbook approaches in the design of field studies (see also Grady and Lipe 1976). The chapters in this section emphasize the need for adequate research designs for survey work. The implementation of research designs for excavation programs has been well argued. Archaeologists of all stripes have to follow the lead of the articles in this section in demanding research designs for surveys as well.

# 14

# The Cache Project Survey Design

MICHAEL B. SCHIFFER
JOHN H. HOUSE

Effective research design, like successful diplomacy, involves compromise. Just as the diplomatic process effects concessions among competing interests, the process of research design strives to strike a balance between conflicting information needs. Like the negotiation process, which leaves no one completely satisfied, the compromises reached in research design inevitably leave room for grousing and regrets. While diplomacy is considered an art, archaeological research design aspires to be scientific. That compromises are needed in itself makes research design no less scientific, although it does place a considerable burden on the investigator to outline the information needs, assign priorities to them, and justify the resultant general research design explicitly.

The basic dilemma presented by archaeological research design is that, for a given level of financial support, there is a theoretical limit (seldom specifiable, however) to the accuracy achievable in estimating any one population parameter (e.g., site density, average site size). Multistage designs and those making use of ancillary techniques and stratification (i.e., division of the study area into arbitrary or natural subunits) may lead to significant improvements, but in the final analysis, they simply approximate more closely the ultimate limits of accuracy in parameter estimation. It follows that in multiparameter problems (the usual situation in archaeology), there are inverse relationships between the accuracy of various parameter estimates. For example, it has long been known that the size of excavation units must be scaled according to the size of the items in the target population (Binford 1964; Cowgill 1975; Hanson and Schiffer 1975). Using different mixes of 1-m pits to sample artifacts and 4-m pits to sample features, one can devise numerous sampling programs. If the overall effort expended must remain constant, however, then any gain in the accuracy of estimating the artifact population is offset by reduced accuracy in estimating the feature population (and vice versa). This characteristic of multiparameter problems requires that compromise play a large role in research design—that is, we must concern ourselves explicitly with the tradeoffs in accuracy that obtain among parameter estimates when various strategies of data acquisition are employed.

The necessity of compromise in archaeological research design is superbly illustrated in cultural resource management studies, where, for the first time, several information needs—some clearcut, some less so—are imposed upon the investigator and must be met. The National Environmental Policy Act (NEPA), for example, requires in an environmental impact statement (EIS) information on the nature of archaeological resources, their extent, their significance, and forecasts of the probable direct and indirect impacts of a project and alternatives on those resources (Scovill, Gordon, and Anderson 1972). The first two items seem to be unambiguous parameters of the archaeological resource base and could be met in part by a delineation of types of sites and their quantitative and spatial distributions. Only complete survey coverage of an area, however, could provide information for both requirements without compromise. In the more usual situation some type of probability sampling along with other sources of data will provide usable estimates about the nature and extent of sites, but these estimates of multiple parameters always will be less accurate than if one parameter alone were the object of investigation. This is so because techniques of data acquisition that are adjusted to measuring one parameter (such as quantity of sites) may not be as well suited for determining others (e.g., range of site types). Furthermore, as C. L. Benson (1976) has so clearly shown, because types of sites in one area may have varying distributions (in a statistical sense), the estimates of even a single parameter may themselves be made up of diverse sorts of nonequivalent information.

If the straightforward information needs of cultural resource management lead to no cut and dried data-gathering techniques, what happens when significance and impacts reenter the picture? Understandably it becomes even more complex, as sometimes conflicting information needs must be reconciled in a general research design. The remainder of this paper illustrates the process of designing cultural resource management surveys and outlining the kinds of compromises that they require in order to fulfill information needs generated by law and by the archaeological framework of question asking. Our example is drawn from the Cache River Archeological Project, an intensive field study carried out in northeastern Arkansas by the Arkansas Archeological Survey for the Army Corps of Engineers in 1973–74 (Schiffer and House 1975b; this volume, Chapters 18 and 23). Certain liberties have been taken with the details and history of the Cache project design in order to present its essentials in the allotted space.


## THE CACHE PROJECT

The Cache River basin is a banana-shaped area, 2018 square miles in extent, located mostly in northeastern Arkansas with a tiny projection of land in southeastern Missouri. The basin lies within the lower Mississippi alluvial valley, mostly in the region known as the Western Lowlands. Within the basin, 90% of the area is lowland and includes late Pleistocene braided Mississippi terraces and modern floodplains. Major streams are the Cache River and its tributary, Bayou de View. About 10% of the basin is on Crowley's Ridge, an insular area of eroded and dissected terraces and loess deposits that is elevated 50–250 feet above the alluvial valley (Saucier 1974).

Formerly, extensive woodlands were present throughout the basin, but in the lowland areas they have been largely cleared for cultivation of row crops. Some areas of bottomland forest and swamp, however, do remain—primarily in the southern portion of the basin (Holder 1970; U.S. Department of the Army 1974). Much of Crowley's Ridge was cultivated during the late nineteenth and early twentieth centuries, resulting in widespread erosion and gullying; at present it is mostly woods and pasture.

With new crops and the advent of modern mechanized farming techniques, the lowland portion of the basin became exceedingly productive agricultural land. The clearing of forests there in the last few decades is part of the headlong expansion of agriculture that is occurring throughout the Mississippi Valley. This trend of land conversion has intensified in recent years, with the result that more and more marginal acres—those subject to frequent flooding—have come under cultivation. Not unexpectedly, the Army Corps of Engineers was authorized by the United States Congress to implement over a 20-year period a major drainage project consisting of realignment, clearing, and enlargement of 232 miles of the Cache River and its tributaries. The corps filed a 17-page EIS for this project (U.S. Department of the Army 1972). Inadequacies in this statement provided ample ground for a successful suit by the Environmental Defense Fund, and in the spring of 1973, after 5 miles of channelization had already been completed, the corps was ordered to cease work and prepare a new EIS, one that would meet the provisions of NEPA.

In July of 1973 the corps negotiated a 1-year contract with the Arkansas Archeological Survey to carry out a study of the archaeological resources in the Cache Basin for $48,000. This study was supposed to provide sufficient information for inclusion in their revised EIS and for long-term management needs. The contract specifically required an inventory and assessment of the significance of the archaeological resources, an evaluation of the direct and indirect impacts of the authorized channelization project and alternatives, and recommendations for mitigation of adverse impacts. The contract also specified three "levels of effort": use of secondary source data, reconnaissance of the entire alluvial portion of the basin, and a comprehensive inventory of the direct impact zone of the authorized channel (the area subject to construction-related activities).

In the early stages of the Cache project it became possible to outline a series of specific research designs, each with its own problem focus and appropriate strategies for data collection, geared to provide the Corps with the information specified in the contract. The specific research designs, seemingly independent, were related to one another in having overlapping and complementary data requirements and were in all cases pertinent to fulfilling the contract specifications (House 1975a; House and Schiffer 1975a). The difficult task was melding them into a general research design. We now present capsule summaries of these initial, single-purpose research designs, emphasizing how they would have been operationalized had each alone served as the principal focus of the research. This enumeration provides the background for illustrating the process of compromise out of which the Cache project general design evolved.

## Estimation of the Resource Base

The corps required an "inventory" of the archaeological resources, which we took to be an estimate of the total number and kinds of sites that were or might be present, as well as a listing of other resources important for archaeological research. To obtain this information, it would have been desirable to administer, in several stages, a stratified random sampling design to the entire basin, perhaps incorporating nonrandom elements in the final stage. The appropriate sample size, and the shape and size of sampling units in the first stage survey, would be determined by results of sampling a simulated basin stocked with sites according to initial parameter estimates based on available data, and by logistic factors (cf. Mueller 1974). Extrapolation of these survey data would serve to represent the entire resource base, at least with respect to its most frequently occurring elements. Perusal of site records in the files of the Arkansas Archeological Survey, reconnaissance, and consultation with amateur and professional archaeologists who know the area would provide the all-important information on types of sites, such as Mississippian villages, that occur infrequently. These lines of evidence as well as literature searches would also provide some indications of other archaeological resources that might be present (pristine examples of particular environments, paleontological resources, etc.).

## Direct Impacts

The corps also required information on the direct impacts of the channelization project (and alternatives). In fact it was spelled out in the contract that a comprehensive inventory of sites was to be made in the direct impact zone of the proposed channel. Seemingly the only way to provide this information was to implement an intensive survey of the entire 65-square-mile direct impact zone. Surveys for the direct impact zones of alternative projects also would be required—in one instance covering at least 150 square miles.

## Indirect Impacts

In addition to sites that might be damaged by construction activities, sites in much of the remainder of the alluvial portion of the basin were expected to be adversely affected by the authorized project and several alternatives by accelerating destructive processes, especially the clearing of woodland and the intensification of agriculture. We therefore required information on (1) the number and kinds of sites that would be exposed to destructive forces by induced land clearing, (2) the number and kinds of sites that would be affected by other land-use intensification activities, and (3) the nature and extent of destructive processes presently acting on the archaeological resources. Since much of the alluvial portion of the basin would be affected by indirect impacts, data were required on the nature of the entire resource base, as also specified in the first research design. Additionally, information on pot-hunting, erosion, and other destructive uses of the land would have to be obtained from a sizable sample of sites and from ethnoarchaeological observations.

## Site File Evaluation

Because sponsor agencies placed increasing demands on state files for data on site locations and density, we thought it was high time to evaluate the biases inherent in the haphazardly accumulated site files. This information would also permit us to assess the data recorded previously on 543 sites in the Cache Basin. In order for this research to be carried out, a sizable, representative sample of sites would be needed from the entire basin to compare in various ways with the already recorded sites.

## Dalton Settlement Pattern

Because most of the known sites were shallow, multicomponent, and in cultivation and because they had been assiduously picked over by relic hunters, amateurs, and professional archaeologists, there was some doubt about whether or not such sites, and especially surface collections made from them, could contribute to settlement pattern studies. An attempt would be made to determine this potential through a provisional test of Morse's (1971) Dalton culture settlement hypothesis, which postulated two kinds of sites with varying artifact content (base camps and hunting–butchering camps). A full-scale test requires that rigorously controlled surface collections be made from a sizable, representative sample of Dalton components. A large sample was needed in order to insure that representatives were present of the infrequent settlement type (base camps) postulated in Morse's model. These data could be readily procured by the research design concerning estimation of the resource base, provided that the sample size was large enough to produce at least 100 Dalton components. It would be necessary perhaps to revisit and re-collect materials from previously discovered sites that had yielded Dalton remains.

## Lithic Resource Distribution and Utilization

In order to investigate the potential of Cache Basin sites to contribute to research on models of lithic procurement, manufacture, use, and recycling (important problems, since chippable stone is absent from most of the basin), several prerequisites had to be met. To carry out such investigations requires that raw materials from different sources be consistently identifiable, that technological studies of tool making with different raw materials be conducted, and that loci of raw material procurement be identified and sampled. Achievement of these research goals involves locating known and expected quarry and workshop sites on Crowley's Ridge and outside of the basin on the Ozark Plateau. Collections were also required from a sizable, representative sample of Cache Basin sites. In addition, the study would be immeasurably improved if experimental lithic research were carried out on the same raw materials as those used prehistorically in the Cache Basin.

## Functional Classification of Lithic Artifacts

The last research design deals with construction of a comprehensive, functional typology for chipped and ground lithic artifacts to facilitate implementation of the previous two research designs. The construction of such a typology requires, of course, a large, diverse sample of archaeological materials such as might be obtained in operationalizing several of the other research designs. Complete success at constructing a functional typology also depends on experimentally produced data on technology and use-wear. To operationalize fully this research design, one would perform an extensive series of experimental studies to establish qualitative and quantitative correlates between human behavior and attributes of lithic artifacts.

## THE GENERAL RESEARCH DESIGN

Even the casual reader should have noticed that, with only 1 year and $48,000 available for the Cache project, it would be impossible to implement all of these research designs in their entirety. It should also be noted that the two research designs directed primarily at assessing significance (the Dalton and lithic resource research) only begin to scratch the surface of possible areas of significance that need to be documented. In the extreme, one can probably argue that there are no inherent conflicts among the information requirements of the various research designs that couldn't be resolved with 5 years and several million dollars. That line of argument, however, really misses the point. The Cache project, and all archaeological investigations, *do* labor under time–money constraints; and even projects that seemingly are well funded cannot begin to exhaust the lines of important research that might be pursued. Thus, projects with insufficient resources and projects with generous resources must, if they are to obtain more than one kind of information, compromise the various problem-specific research designs and erect a general plan for investigation. To see how these problems were handled by the Cache project, we now turn to the general research design.

The Cache project research design and the specific methods and techniques used to operationalize it were developed over a period of months during the early stages of the research. The results of earlier stages of the fieldwork were used in designing the later stages.

From the outset we placed a high priority on acquiring information about direct impacts. The fieldwork began with an intensive survey of the direct impact zone in

the lower end of the basin, where imminent resumption of construction was anticipated and the need for cultural resource management decisions was most urgent.
The analysis of the data from this initial survey provided a basis for standardizing a
set of field methods and identifying problem domains. Also at this time the data
requirements of specific research designs were embodied in a detailed site survey
form devised especially for the Cache project (House and Schiffer 1975a:43–44).

The second stage of the fieldwork began with an intensive survey of a portion of
the direct impact zone at the extreme upper end of the channelization project. This
brief foray revealed that the site density in the upper part of the basin was significantly greater than that encountered in the lower portion during the initial stage of
fieldwork. With this information we were able to project time–labor costs for
completing the remaining 90% of the direct impact zone. Using conservative site
density estimates, we determined that our entire budget would be spent merely in
*locating*—in the sense of putting dots on a map—all the sites in the 65-square mile
direct impact zone. That would leave us with no resources for investigating direct
impacts of alternative projects, let alone fulfilling other information needs. Naturally we opted for a sampling approach to the direct impact zone and devised an
indirect method for assessing impacts of alternative projects. Because construction
of the channelization project was to take place during a 20-year period, we felt that
detailed site location information on the remainder of the direct impact zone could
be obtained in the future; additionally, the Corps displayed a willingness to fund
such studies. Using a simulated direct impact zone stocked with sites according to
the north–south density gradient known from previous records, we determined that a
10% stratified random sample would provide a usable estimate of the total number
of sites. A 12½% stratified random design was implemented, which, because of
problems in aligning the arbitrary strata with areas of channel modification, was
actually an 11% sample.

The research design on indirect impacts received second priority. A stratified
random sample was designed for the basin as a whole consisting of ¼-mile-wide
transects, running east–west, placed randomly within the same arbitrary strata that
defined the direct impact zone sample for the main Cache channel. Unfortunately,
owing to lack of time, only two of six projected transects were completed. The use
of transects ¼ mile wide was itself an unhappy compromise; better coverage of the
entire basin could have been obtained from placing many more transects of 100
yards in width. Our reason for choosing the ¼-mile unit was based on the consideration that narrower transects involve considerable logistical hassles in obtaining
permission to visit the often small, privately owned areas in the sample units.
Despite our inability to complete the transect survey, the data from the two transects
and careful treatment of site file records allowed us to make reasonable (but hardly
accurate) estimates of the number of sites that would indirectly be affected by the
channelization project.

A third major data-gathering strategy was also implemented to meet some of the
data requirements not fulfilled by the probabilistic sampling. Rarer kinds of sites are
easily missed by probabilistic sampling but may nonetheless be quite important in

understanding past human behavior and in assessing project impacts. Therefore, some reconnaissance was carried out, following leads from collectors and other local residents, to obtain information on mound groups, large Mississippian villages, and other kinds of rare sites that were considered to be of potential importance. To recapitulate, three major data-gathering strategies were employed for most of the fieldwork on the Cache project: (1) a 12½% stratified random sample of the direct impact zones; (2) a stratified random sample of transects across the basin as a whole; and (3) reconnaissance of selected areas.

We obtained information on ongoing destructive processes by recording the condition of all surveyed sites and the use(s) that they were experiencing. Dan Morse, survey archaeologist with Arkansas Archeological Survey for northeastern Arkansas, provided us with invaluable information on pot-hunting and collecting activities. We were unable, however, to conduct systematic ethnoarchaeological studies of collecting and pot-hunting, although some private collections were examined. Several studies of agricultural practices and site destruction in the Mississippi Valley had recently been carried out, and these were put to good use (see this volume, Chapter 23).

To evaluate the direct and indirect impacts of alternative projects, we contrived a simple strategy to gain information on patterns of site location. Data on the topographical position of sites and their surrounding environment were recorded on the project site form. Analyses of the locational data from sites in the two probability samples allowed us to uncover patterns in the distribution of various kinds of sites by landform and differential site densities by landform—even though the samples were small and weighted toward landforms in the immediate vicinity of the Cache River and Bayou de View. The analyses tended to confirm our judgments that sites are generally located on terrace edges overlooking floodplains. Also, because of the intensive coverage of areas of the direct impact zone, we were able to show, somewhat surprisingly, that there was at some times considerable occupation of the Cache floodplain itself. These findings allowed us to rank alternative projects on the basis of potential impacts.

The research designs for estimating direct and indirect impacts were the major determinants of the site survey strategy. Even so, both research designs were compromised substantially, with the result that impacts could be forecast reliably only within an order of magnitude. The data generated by these designs formed the basic data set used for investigating the additional problems chosen by the Cache project. Needless to say, if the general research design provided somewhat less than ideal data for estimating project impacts, then it probably had more drastic effects on the other research results.

The lack of a good probability sample for the entire basin required that indirect methods be employed for estimating the resource base. With 543 previously recorded sites and 198 new ones, it was possible to use indices of previously discovered to newly discovered sites in the sample units to extrapolate site totals for the whole resource base. In this way we arrived at an estimate of 13,287 sites in the entire basin. A second estimate of 16,870 sites was made by extrapolating the site density observed in the sample units to the basin as a whole. Remarkably, the two figures are within 25%, and their mean of 15,074 sites was considered a usable (but far from ideal) estimate of the resource base.

The newly recorded sites also provided satisfactory information for evaluating site records in the files of the Arkansas Archeological Survey. For instance, a comparison of the occupational history of the basin and gross site distributions and characteristics from the two samples gave consistent indications of a gradient of decreasing site density from north to south and suggested similar hiatuses in the occupational sequence. These findings, based on the slim number of 198 new sites, allowed us to make generalizations from the site file data with some confidence. In other respects, of course, the site file data proved to be biased: Larger sites and those with mounds were overrepresented (inexplicably, we neglected to point this out in the Cache volume).

The general research design took its greatest toll on the Dalton study. We were able to locate and make collections from only 22 Dalton components, and time did not permit us to revisit already known sites. As a result of the inadequate sample size (and other causes) the test of Morse's Dalton settlement hypothesis was inconclusive (House, Klinger, and Schiffer 1975). Even so, the test did indicate that the damaged resource base of the Cache Basin may contain information usable in settlement studies.

Success of the lithic resource study was also dependent on the availability of a large, representative sample of sites and excursions to some sites outside the basin. Once again the small site sample of unknown representativeness provided a usable set of collections from which hypotheses, largely in accord with previously suspected patterns, could be framed. Some quarry and workshop sites on Crowley's Ridge and the Ozark escarpment were visited and provided important data on lithic resource distribution and workshop activities. Unfortunately, no experimental studies were carried out. Nevertheless, the results of this investigation (reported by House in Chapter 27, this volume) were far more successful than we had any right to expect on the basis of our sample. Some areas of significance were pinpointed, and numerous hypotheses were suggested for future research.

The construction of an adequate functional typology for lithic artifacts could be carried out on collections from any large, diverse sample of sites. In this respect the Cache project sample does probably represent the range of artifact variability in the basin, although we cannot demonstrate it. House, in formulating the typology, also had access to Morse's comparative lithic collections, many of which were also from the Cache Basin, and Goodyear's (1974) analysis of the Brand site lithics. In conjunction with this study, an experimental investigation of fire-cracked rock was conducted in order to clarify distinctions among certain items of debitage and fire-cracked rock. Since this was the only experimentation completed, the bulk of the typology rests on hypothesized behavioral–material relationships that remain to be tested.

A final component of the general research design, operationalized during a testing program, was devised to permit certain areas of significance to be assessed and also to facilitate evaluation of the inferences made about site contents from collections and observations made during surface survey. In order to test the posited principles of surface–subsurface site relationships and determine the extent of intact occupation surfaces, features, bone, macrofloral remains, and pollen from a diverse sample of sites would have to be observed. Needless to say, the criteria for selecting sites were influenced heavily by considerations of logistics (the testing was carried out with the aid of Arkansas State University student volunteers during a rainy, 1-week spring vacation) and our ability to get permission from landowners. In addition, at some sites we were able to excavate only one test pit. Despite these limitations, we did manage to test at least one Archaic, one Woodland, and one Mississippian site and gain some idea of variability in conditions of preservation in the basin. To achieve fully the aims of the testing program would have required examination of a much larger sample of sites in varied situations and more extensive excavations at each of them.

## CONCLUSION

Research design in cultural resource management does not differ substantially from traditional academic investigations in its necessity for effecting sometimes painful compromises. Where it does differ, however, is in the necessity of spotlighting the process of assigning priorities to research needs and designing justifiable compromise strategies. The importance of this evolution in research design is that we not only evaluate the particular methods that comprise a data-gathering program, but we may also initiate discussion on the seldom-broached subject of the investigator's ordering of priorities. In purely academic research such evaluations are often deferred (for whatever reason) until some distant time when they lose all practical import—or they are not made at all. In cultural resource management, on the other hand, there must be immediate feedback on the success of one's strategies—for surely the next project awaits immediate attention and demands a higher level of methodological awareness and substantive achievement.

The Cache project illustrates well the general problem of assigning research priorities and designing compromise strategies for data retrieval. Although highest priority was placed on questions about the direct and indirect impacts of the authorized channelization project, even those research designs were modified in order to obtain some data relative to the other information needs. For all of the research questions the data gathered were always useful, sometimes quite appropriate, but never ideal. The unevenness in fulfilling information needs is inevitable, even if the priorities are ordered differently. It is true that the Cache project is not typical of cultural resource management studies in all respects, because of unrealistic funding and contract specifications; this does not, we feel, detract from its usefulness as an example of the research design process. For, even if one has obtained an enlightened contract and ample funding, archaeological research will always involve multiple information needs that must be compromised.

# 15

# A Multiple Survey Strategy for Cultural Resource Management Studies

WILLIAM HARPER DOELLE

The Conoco Project, a study recently completed by the Arizona State Museum, employed a data recovery strategy that involved two separate surveys of the same area. The methods employed in each survey were very different, a situation made necessary by the nature of the archaeological resources of the study area. A description of how this multiple survey approach was used by the Conoco Project and an argument for its more general applicability are considered in the following discussion.

The Conoco Project area was located north of the Gila River, near Florence, Arizona, in the heartland of the prehistoric Hohokam culture area. The Hohokam adapted to the arid climate of southern Arizona by means of a sophisticated irrigation technology and were able to maintain permanent settlements along such major watercourses as the Salt and Gila rivers. Away from these rivers, however, occupation tended to be seasonal. The Conoco Project adjoined an area of dense prehistoric settlement along the Gila River. The study area covered over 12 square miles and included two distinct environmental divisions. Over half of the Conoco area consisted of gravel terraces that support a paloverde–saguaro community. The other major environmental unit was an area of deep alluvial soils vegetated by creosote bush and bursage. A single major wash runs through the creosote bush–bursage community and supports a dense growth of mesquite. While the Conoco area was not suitable for irrigation agriculture using aboriginal technology, it hosts a number of wild resources that are known to have been exploited by the historic and prehistoric human groups along the Gila River. Therefore it was hypothesized that the Conoco area had served as a source for a variety of edible wild plants and animals (Doelle 1975:78).

An important goal of the survey of the Conoco area was to develop an inventory of the archaeological resources. A second goal was to gather the kinds of data specified in the project research design (Doelle 1975:Appendix II), which focused on the identification of resource-processing sites within the study area. Both of these goals were to be met through the use of intensive survey techniques. Therefore, field personnel systematically walked the entire area, varying the spacing interval between crew members from 20 to 50 m depending on conditions of terrain and vegetation density. An archaeological site was defined in the field according to the following criteria:

1. It must exhibit definable limits.
2. It must contain evidence of more than a single occurrence of human activity.
3. If no other criteria exist for defining a site, then artifact density must be greater than five artifacts per square meter.

While only eight sites were encountered during the 8 weeks of fieldwork, many isolated artifacts and artifact clusters that did not meet this site definition were located and recorded.

The low frequency of sites in the Conoco area, and the fact that resource-processing tools and facilities were found at only a few of these sites, strongly suggested that resource processing was not the primary activity carried out in the study area. However, the widespread occurrence of cultural materials at densities too low to qualify as sites was definite evidence of prehistoric activities. Therefore it was hypothesized that these remains resulted from resource gathering in the study area, with processing most likely taking place in the permanent villages located nearby. While many isolated artifacts and artifact clusters were described and plotted as they were encountered during the original survey operations, this method of data collection did not provide enough information, nor was it sufficiently systematic, to allow an objective evaluation of hypotheses about wild resource gathering. At this point, then, the research design was modified to focus on gathering, and new field methods were instituted.

Field techniques employed by archaeologists working in other areas of low artifact density were found to be especially helpful. In much of western North America conditions are favorable for the recovery of detailed archaeological information by means of surface survey. Often conditions of geological stability, or perhaps slight deflation, result in past material remains occurring on or very near the surface, while sparse vegetation insures rather high visibility of artifacts and features. Under such conditions it has been both possible and rewarding to develop survey techniques that consider the patterned distribution of even single artifacts. Thomas (1975) calls such an approach nonsite archaeology. He states that nonsite archaeology takes

> the cultural item (the artifact, feature, manuport, individual flake, or whatever) as the minimal unit, and ignore[s] traditional sites altogether. . . . This is not to deny that artifacts generally occur in well-defined sites . . . but rather to assert that in some instances, under special research circumstances, discrete clumpings of artifacts (a) either do not occur or (b) are not relevant to the problems immediately at hand [p. 62].

Some recent studies have included a nonsite approach as a secondary aspect of the survey strategy (e.g., Debowski, George, Goddard, and Mullen 1976; Grady,

Dodge, Kemrer, and Schultz 1973), while others have developed a nonsite approach as a central focus of their survey work (e.g., Doelle 1975, 1976; Goodyear 1975b; Morenon, Henderson, and Nielsen 1976; Rodgers 1974; Thomas 1975).

The nonsite study of the Conoco area utilized 193 sample units measuring 100 m on a side that were randomly selected and represented 9% of the total study area. Within these sample units all artifacts were located, mapped, and collected separately. Since each of the four field recorders worked in only one quadrant (area = 50 m × 50 m) of the sample unit, and since that area was walked from two to four times, close to 100% recovery of surface artifacts was assured. In addition, detailed information on environmental conditions within and adjacent to each sample unit was recorded. The result was a statistical sample of the distribution of prehistoric material remains that could be directly related to variation in environmental conditions within the survey area.

The archaeological information gathered by both of the survey techniques just described was complementary and necessary for a full understanding of the prehistoric utilization of the Conoco area. Data from the nonsite study were found to support hypotheses of cactus fruit and mesquite pod gathering, dry farming, and hunting (Doelle 1976). Five of the eight sites recorded were not anticipated by the original research design and served to broaden our knowledge of the kinds of archaeological manifestations that may occur in nonriverine areas of the southern Arizona desert. These included three sites where rock alignments were the central features, an extensive lithic manufacturing site, and a Hohokam site whose function remains enigmatic.

With hindsight, a serious drawback to the way the Conoco survey strategies were implemented can be seen. The problem was that the original survey attempted to record *both* site and nonsite data simultaneously. Information on both levels was essential for the adequate assessment of the nature of the archaeological resource base as well as for the evaluation of specific hypotheses on prehistoric resource use. But while the nonsite data collected during the first survey served to document that low-density scatters of material remains were common in the study area, the lack of systematic sampling and data-recording methods resulted in this information being insufficient for research purposes. A more efficient approach to data collection would have been to consider only site-level manifestations during the first phase of survey. Relatively wide spacing and a rapid pace would have quickly produced a reliable site inventory of the area, since the site-level features were generally large and highly visible. This would have made more time available for the nonsite study and would have allowed a slightly higher nonsite sampling fraction.

## THE MULTIPLE SURVEY METHOD IN CONTRACT ARCHAEOLOGY

The method of multiple surveys of the same study area seems to have wider applicability than to just the Conoco Project. An important goal of cultural resource management studies is to assess the nature of the archaeological resource base within an area. This should involve consideration of the entire range of archaeological remains, which can include large, multiphase habitation sites on one end of the continuum to isolated artifacts at the other end. A discussion of both intensive survey techniques and some general characteristics of the archaeological record will help to show the utility of multiple surveys in assessing the archaeological resource base.

## Intensive Surveys and Survey Intensity

Ruppé (1966) defines a Type IV survey as "an intensive study of a local area designed to extract all possible information from the surface of every site that can be found [p. 315]." While House and Schiffer (1975a:41) have legitimately questioned the ability of archaeologists ever to obtain a *complete* inventory, there seems to be little doubt that intensive survey methods are a necessity for gathering data with which to make estimates of the archaeological resource base. But intensive surveys can vary in their degree of intensity. This concept of survey intensity is important to an understanding of the multiple survey approach. The best general indicator of survey intensity seems to be the spacing interval between field crew members. While vegetation conditions and terrain affect the results obtained by different spacing intervals, the interval remains a useful measure of intensity because it can be expressed quantitatively and because it relates directly to the size of the archaeological remains that can be expected to be encountered. The multiple survey method provides a means to vary survey intensity in a controlled manner depending on the nature of the archaeological data that are required.

## The Size and Frequency of Archaeological Remains

The effectiveness of a particular survey intensity as a discovery technique greatly depends on the size and visibility of the things being sought. Therefore a brief consideration of the frequency distribution of archaeological remains according to their size will provide some insight into how survey intensity should be varied.

Intuitively it can be suggested that the largest sites will be the most infrequent, with medium sites, small sites, and isolated artifacts increasing in frequency respectively. The results of the Orme Alternatives Project (Fuller, Rogge, and Gregonis 1976) serve to support this generalization for site-level manifestations (Figure 15.1). Data on the number of sherds from each spatially isolated artifact cluster, or locus, identified during the nonsite study of the Conoco Project also support this statement (Figure 15.2). It seems very likely that consideration of more data from other intensive surveys would serve to confirm this pattern even more conclusively.

Explicit recognition of this general patterning of the archaeological record allows survey intensity to be varied so as to insure field location of a representative sample of archaeological remains within particular size categories. For example, a large area could be covered rapidly by spacing crew members at 100-m intervals. This would insure that all sites whose shortest dimension measured 100 m or more would

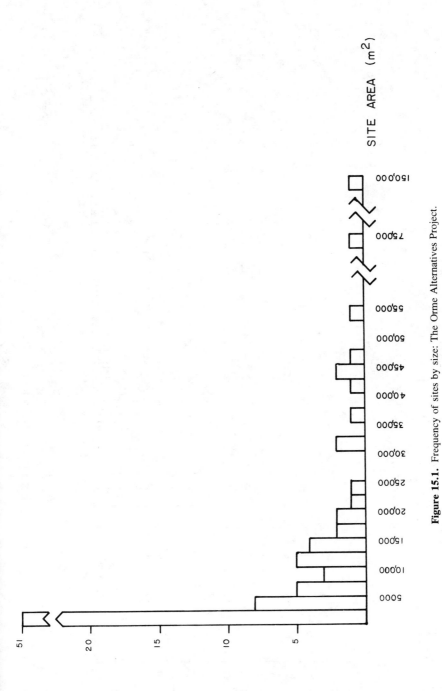

**Figure 15.1.** Frequency of sites by size: The Orme Alternatives Project.

205

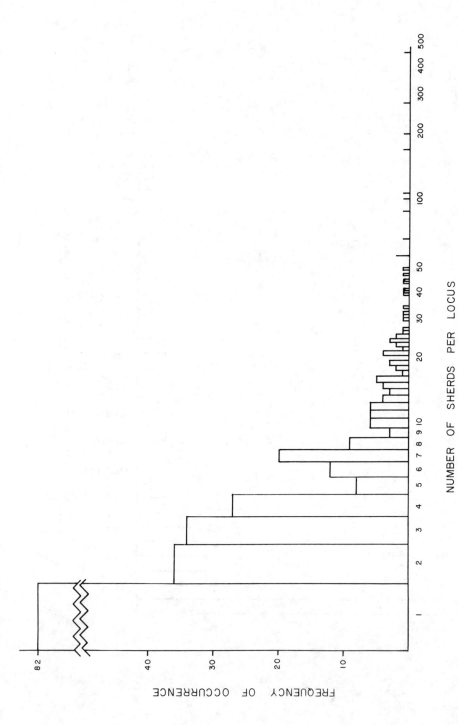

**Figure 15.2.** Frequency distribution of sherds: The Conoco nonsite study.

be located. Then, a portion of the area surveyed could be chosen by statistical sampling techniques for further survey. The sample units for the second phase should be surveyed with a much greater degree of intensity. For example, if every square meter of the sample units was examined at least once, then the two surveys in combination would insure a statistical sample of the full range of archaeological remains—from the largest sites through single isolated artifacts.

There are at least two strong reasons for using sampling techniques when considering small sites and isolated artifacts. First of all, their higher frequency makes them much more amenable to sampling. High frequency increases the probability of their being included within sample units and therefore helps insure that the range of variability is measured by the sample. The second factor is cost. A great deal of time is expended maintaining the level of survey intensity that is necessary in order to identify small sites and isolated artifacts in the field. To illustrate this point, the average daily coverage rates for the Orme Alternatives and Conoco projects are compared in Table 15.1:

**TABLE 15.1.**
**Acreage Surveyed per Person-Day during the Orme**
**Alternatives and Conoco Projects**

| Orme Alternatives | | Conoco |
|---|---|---|
| Roosevelt Lake | Horseshoe Reservoir | |
| 26.5 acres/day | 16.8 acres/day | 2.6 acres/day |

The research orientation and the field-recording techniques of the Orme Alternatives Project focused on site-level manifestations; they made no attempt to employ a nonsite method of data recovery. The figures cited for the Conoco Project include only field time spent on the nonsite study. On the average the Orme Alternatives crewperson covered from 6.5 to 10 times more area per day than the Conoco crewperson. Since the time-consuming data collection methods used by the Conoco nonsite study were found to be necessary in order to obtain adequate contextual information for interpreting artifact distribution, the essential role of sampling is strongly underscored. Costs of "100%" recovery using a nonsite method would clearly be prohibitive.

While the examples just discussed are from areas of relatively sparse vegetation cover and high surface visibility, these should not be viewed as the only conditions suitable for a multiple survey strategy. For example, Lovis (1976) recently surveyed a densely wooded area in northern Michigan. He employed transects spaced at 100-yard intervals, and small 1-foot × 1-foot test pits were cut into the forest floor every 100 yards along these transects. After assessing his survey results and finding that the minimum dimension of most of the sites was significantly smaller than 100 yards, he concluded that "a transect interval of 25 yards would yield a much more reliable sample [p. 371]." But he notes that "if 25 yard transect and test pit intervals were utilized . . . the number of test pits [per quarter section] would rise from 64 to 1225 [p. 371].'' This would appear to be a case where a multiple survey strategy could be effectively employed. To lessen the tremendous increase in time–labor investment that would be necessary to insure that small sites were located, a survey such as Lovis completed could be implemented. This could be followed by a second survey that reexamined a sample of the original study area using more intensive methods—such as the 25-yard transect and test-pit intervals mentioned by Lovis. It would appear, then, that a multiple survey strategy can be effective under a variety of conditions.

## The Role of the Reconnaissance

The concept of multistage research is not new to archaeology (Redman 1973; Canouts, Chapter 9, this volume), but there has been an underemphasis of the value of a reconnaissance phase in multistage contract research. A field reconnaissance is essential to the effective implementation of the multiple survey strategy outlined here. A reconnaissance should meet the following goals:

1. Sufficient fieldwork should be completed to enable assessment of the general nature of environmental and archaeological variability in a study area. The time required and the data collection techniques employed will vary from project to project.
2. Based upon the knowledge gained from the reconnaissance, plus the existing literature, *appropriate* research problems should be developed. Use of the word *appropriate* is meant to emphasize the necessity to choose problems that can be answered by study of the available archaeological resources.
3. Based upon Items 1 and 2, effective and efficient data collection techniques should be developed. For example, decisions must be made as to the appropriate level of survey intensity, whether or not a multiple survey strategy is to be employed, and the necessary sampling fractions for the various survey stages. Only a field reconnaissance can provide sufficient information upon which to make intelligent decisions on these questions.
4. Finally, an adequate time frame and budget should be developed to meet the above needs.

## SUMMARY

The Conoco Project has shown that multiple surveys—a 100% survey and a nonsite sampling program—can be made to work in complementary fashion in order to meet both research and management goals in contract archaeology. A field reconnaissance prior to full-scale implementation of fieldwork probably would have resulted in greater efficiency of information recovery, however. A reconnaissance would have provided the necessary information for making decisions about the survey intensity necessary during the 100% survey and about the appropriate sampling fraction for the nonsite study. A field reconnaissance prior to developing detailed research designs and funding proposals is highly recommended for all large contract projects and is a necessity if a multiple survey approach is to be used. The multiple survey strategy outlined here should serve to maintain flexibility in research problems and methods—an essential element if contract archaeology is to produce quality research.

# Part V

---

# ESTIMATING THE NATURE AND EXTENT OF THE RESOURCE BASE

---

If the archaeological record of a project area were entirely visible and accessible to pedestrian surface survey, and if it could be covered completely with great intensity using the time and money available, there would be no need to *estimate* the nature and extent of the resource base; it could merely be *described*. That these conditions are never encountered dictates that conservation archaeologists devise appropriate inferential procedures for characterizing the resource base of study areas.

Let us first examine what is meant by the phrase *nature and extent of the resource base*. Generally, conservation and other archaeologists attempt to infer the *kinds* and *quantities* of sites and other resources with the supposition that more might be present. For making these estimates, "types" of sites would ordinarily be defined in terms of gross culture-historical and functional categories (e.g., 15 Archaic campsites, 39 Archaic hunting–butchering stations, 12 Mississippian hamlets). These inferential categories would, of course, be provisional, owing to the difficulties of making chronological and functional inferences primarily on the basis of survey data (cf. Sullivan and Schiffer n.d.). The spatial distribution of site types in the project area, usually with respect to features of the natural environment (e.g., landforms, soil types, vegetation communities), is another parameter of the resource base that is sometimes estimated. And finally, no characterization of archaeological resources would be complete without some statement about their present condition—that is, the degree to which they have been affected by recent and ongoing destructive processes (e.g., agriculture, pot-hunting, construction). The topic of ongoing processes receives attention in the introduction to Part VI.

The parameters just enumerated comprise the minimal level of descriptive information about the resource base required for management purposes. It should be apparent that other variables—pertaining to the present nature and distribution of resources and also to prehistoric events and processes—will necessarily also be of concern, depending on the specific research problems being addressed. Since the latter requirements cannot be generalized readily and are more properly the province of individual investigations, we shall deal here only with ways to obtain the minimal level of information on the nature and extent of the archaeological resources. It should always be remembered, however, that provision of the latter information represents the starting, not stopping, point for any study.

## ESTIMATES FOR OVERVIEWS AND ASSESSMENTS

At the overview and assessment levels, the archaeologist usually is at the mercy of available site records and literature. The information gleaned from existing survey records will not, except under unusual circumstances, furnish *by itself* adequate data for management purposes. Wherever intensive survey data have been compared with information available previously for the same area, it has been discovered that site density is underestimated by at least one order of magnitude (a factor of 20–40 is not unusual) and that known sites are biased toward larger size, association with prominent features (e.g., architecture, mounds), and occurrence on a restricted range of landforms (e.g., terrace edges) (Fehon and Viscito 1974:28–29; Schiffer and House 1975d and this volume, Chapter 14). Thus, a "records check" per se is neither a recognized type of cultural resource management report (Vivian *et al.* 1977) nor a recognized portion of an overview of assessment. In most instances the use of a records check for any management purposes would be inappropriate. In the future, however, it should be possible to devise corrections for the skewed sample of known sites, either by reference to adjacent areas or by use of general statistical properties of archaeological data (Charles M. Baker, personal communication, 1976). These avenues of estimation await exploration.

There are, of course, situations when existing site records can be combined with archaeological and anthropological expertise to create a somewhat closer approximation to the parameters of the resource base than the records alone provide. In Chapter 16 Bettinger shows how ethnographic information and some knowledge of adjacent areas can be used to formulate expectations of the sites that might be present in a study area. Lack of suitable ethnographic data, and rather more dynamic cultural developments, may preclude the application of Bettinger's technique to many other areas; even so, there is no good reason why theoretical models, incorporating likely patterns of cultural change, cannot be employed instead. In that situation the investigator might use theoretical models to predict the way in

which an area containing specific landforms and biotic and abiotic resources could have been adapted to with various technologies, and the
resultant archaeological patterns that such adaptations (and other variables)
might produce. When it is available, data on cultural adaptations in adjacent areas can influence (but not determine) the construction of the models.
Because subsequent projects may allow these predictions to be tested with
little effort, such procedures lend themselves admirably to evaluating
cultural-ecological formulations (Charles M. Baker, personal communication, 1976).

Another approach that has some merits is the extrapolation of patterns
discerned in adjacent areas. The assumption that underlies this method is
that cultural variability and variability in archaeological remains exhibit
patterns of gradual change over space. Thus one can extrapolate and inter-
polate to unknown areas with relative ease. There is little doubt that at the
most general level this assumption is true; use of it to generate expectations
of a resource base is bound to yield some helpful insights. Nevertheless,
one must be sensitive to the possibility that abrupt spatial boundaries do
exist in archaeological phenomena and that the probability of their existence varies inversely with the size of the study area. As one deals with
smaller and smaller study areas, there is a considerable chance for making
large errors. Price, Price, and Harris (1976) go so far as to caution that
"each watershed must be considered unique in its physiographic setting
and cultural resource content [p. 41]." Although they overstate the case for
uniqueness, their warning against uncritical extrapolation from adjacent
areas is well taken.

When all is said and done, the precision with which parameters of the
archaeological resource base can be estimated at the present time without
high-quality field data is generally quite low; we should heed Wildesen's
(1974) caution against making exaggerated claims for our predictive
models. Although we should strive to experiment further with the techniques of estimation mentioned, devise other techniques, and refine them
insofar as it is possible, we would do well to encourage the sponsor to
initiate field investigations as soon as practicable—even at the assessment
stage.

## FIELD STUDIES

Ideally the field study should provide data from an intensive survey of the
study area or a representative sample of it. Schiffer and House (Chapter 14)
describe two such techniques:

1. Constructing for intensively surveyed units indices of previously discovered to newly discovered sites. The composite indices can then be

used for extrapolating previously known sites in the project area to the entire resource base (or its subpopulations).

2. Calculating site density values for intensively surveyed units and extrapolating these to the resource base as a whole (or its subpopulations).

Both techniques have obvious drawbacks and should be used judiciously.

When surveys based on probability samples have been conducted in the study area, difficulties in estimating the resource base are reduced somewhat, but problems still remain. Rogge and Fuller in Chapter 17 provide an incisive discussion of the use of probability samples for estimating parameters of the resource base (see also Doelle, Chapter 15).

The availability of adequate probability samples for an area insures only that one can offer reasonably precise estimates for common elements of the resource base. Estimates for rare types of sites (and other archaeological resources) will still depend on information obtained from judgmental sampling, reconnaissance, and interviews with informants. Unfortunately, statistically rigorous methods for making parameter estimates from such motley assortments of data do not exist, and the investigator should be wise enough to admit it to the sponsor. We say this, not to discourage experimentation with techniques for estimating rare elements, but to encourage candor in cultural resource management studies about the present limitations of our expertise.

Even when survey coverage of an area has been complete, the investigator's job of estimation is not over when he provides an inventory of the sites discovered. It is a common feature of surveys that because of problems in accessibility and visibility coverage is usually somewhat less than total. If one has kept careful records of areas not visited, then some estimates of what was missed may be offered. In making such estimates, it is unwise for the archaeologist to assume that inaccessible areas are in all respects similar to accessible ones, or that areas of low visibility resemble areas of high visibility in terms of the archaeology. Modern land-use patterns, for example, are sometimes remarkably similar to those in the past; thus, depending on the particular case, one could systematically miss areas of high or low site density. Ways to deal satisfactorily with these problems remain to be solved and applied to all estimates based on field data.

The possibility of buried sites also requires consideration. Naturally, if the investigator discovers a site eroding out of an arroyo wall or stream bank, we will suggest that other buried sites probably remain unexposed to indicate the existence of buried sites; sites become buried because of the operation of predictable natural processes. Therefore, the knowledge that sediments have been deposited on certain areas during a relevant span of recent time indicate some probability for the occurrence of buried sites. The probabilities are increased considerably if it can also be shown that the same localities would likely have been occupied prehistorically or historically. A number of investigators already have begun to take buried resources into account. Evans and Ives (1976), for example, report that the Meramec Basin project of east central Missouri, a large scale, interdisciplinary undertaking, includes "initiation of a geomorphological study to determine the potential for the occurrence of Archaic and earlier sites on buried terraces [p. 2]" (see also Taylor 1975; Skinner and Humphreys 1973).

As we shall note frequently in the remainder of this volume, a consideration of sites provides only a partial picture of the archaeological resource base. The study of biotic communities and living human groups, for example, may also provide the archaeologist with important information. The identification of such resources and estimation of the total populations are a task that is best handled on a case-by-case basis.


## CONCLUSION

If anything is certain, it is that estimating the parameters of the archaeological resource base is indeed a problematic process. Although advances in theoretical modeling and sampling methods will continue to provide ways for increasing the precision of parameter estimates, conservation archaeologists need to remain flexible in their approaches and accept and discuss openly the inevitable uncertainties that are inherent in their conclusions.

# 16

# Predicting the Archaeological Potential of the Inyo–Mono Region of Eastern California[1]

ROBERT L. BETTINGER

If there is a dominant trend in contract archaeology today, it is the increasing government and industry demand for competent archaeological research and the increasing inability of the archaeological community to meet this demand. There are no simple solutions to the problem, but the gap between archaeological supply and demand can be at least partly closed if institutions with similar regional interests maximize their research potential by allocating contracts among themselves according to their individual problem orientation and research capabilities. In turn, the success of such a procedure depends on a reliable initial estimate of the quantity and nature of archaeological resources encompassed by each project under consideration. Such estimates can be obtained during the preliminary literature assessment that is often funded by contracting agencies both to initiate the conservation archaeology cycle and to obtain information essential to their project plans.

The literature search is typically used to compile a working set of reference materials for use during the remainder of the project and to establish whether previously located archaeological sites will be impacted. It is rarely used to estimate the density and diversity of archaeological resources that might be encountered; yet it is clear that without quantitative estimates decisions regarding the disposition of archaeological contracts among cooperating institutions will remain guesswork. Beyond these purely practical applications, resource estimates based on reasoning that is both sound and explicit are perfectly valid archaeological hypotheses that can be tested by subsequent project fieldwork. The following example illustrates one approach to the quantitative assessment of archaeological resources during the preliminary phases of a contract project.

[1]This chapter is a revised version of a manuscript submitted to the Southern California Edison Company.

## BACKGROUND

In early 1973, the Archaeological Research Unit (ARU) of the University of California, Riverside, was granted a small contract to make a preliminary assessment of archaeological resources along the 53-mile route of a proposed powerline in Inyo and Mono counties, eastern California. The contracting agency, the Southern California Edison Company, was interested in the assessment as a source of planning information. As the logical choice to conduct eventual survey and mitigation phases of the contract, the ARU needed a similar assessment to decide whether the mitigation phase would be within its technical capabilities and relevant to its research interests.

### Approach

The estimation of archaeological resources was based on an approach similar to that described by O'Connell (1976) and Struever (1968b). First, it was assumed that potential subsistence resources in any region are unevenly distributed across the landscape and that this distribution is regularly patterned. It was further assumed that culture systems are adaptations to their environments, and, as such, their subsistence and settlement patterns are structured to fit the existing patterns of regional resource distribution. The pattern of resource distribution in the Inyo–Mono region was described as a series of biotic communities, each comprising a characteristic set of potential plant and animal resources (Odum 1959). The basic units for interpreting the regional settlement–subsistence system were its constituent settlement categories, which occupy discrete segments of the annual settlement pattern and comprise distinct sets of extractive and maintenance activities, occupying groups, and biotic settings.

A third assumption was that settlement–subsistence patterns of the Inyo-Mono region had remained relatively stable during the period of prehistoric occupation and were essentially comparable to the historic patterns described by ethnographers (Chalfant 1933; Parcher 1930; Steward 1933, 1934, 1938, 1955). Previous archaeological investigations in the Desert West have amply demonstrated the utility of ethnographic models as a source for archaeological hypotheses in those areas where relatively little is known about prehistoric settlement–subsistence systems (Jennings 1957; O'Connell 1976; Thomas 1973). As a corollary of this assumption, the diversity in archaeological assemblages was interpreted as representing different functional aspects of the same settlement–subsistence system rather than a succession of such systems (cf. E. L. Davis 1963:204).

Given these assumptions and definitions, the procedure for estimating the archaeological resource base was relatively straightforward. Ethnographic accounts were used to derive a model of the prehistoric settlement–subsistence system and its component settlement categories; a combination of environmental, demographic, and archaeological data were then marshaled to estimate the density and distribution of archaeological resources that would be produced by this system.

## Environment

The study area comprises the upper Owens River drainage, a northwest–southeast trending troughlike complex of mountains and valleys in central eastern California. The northern two-thirds of the trough is dominated by Long Valley, an east–west oriented volcanic caldera measuring 9 miles × 19 miles; the southern third is formed by Owens Valley, a block-faulted graben less than 10 miles wide in this area. The western boundary of the trough is sharply demarcated by the Sierra Nevada range, which reaches maximum elevations in excess of 13,000 feet throughout this section. The eastern boundary is less well defined, consisting of the White Mountains in the south and the low-lying Benton Range and Glass Mountain in the north. The floor of the trough drops abruptly from an elevation of 7000 feet in Long Valley to less than 5000 feet in northern Owens Valley.

The natural environment of the trough can be divided into a series of biotic communities, each distinguished by a characteristic set of plants and animals. Four of these were particularly important to aboriginal subsistence.

First of these is the riverine community, which occurs along the margins of the Owens River in the center of the trough. The vegetation in these well-watered areas comprises stands of tule (*Scirpus* spp.), cattail (*Typha* spp.), and other hydrophytic plants. The more important fauna are mollusks, fish, and migrant and resident waterfowl.

In Owens Valley the zone between the riverine community and coniferous woodland in foothills on either side of the trough is characterized by a desert scrub community, an arid association dominated by low shrubs and seed-bearing grasses. The resident fauna are chiefly small rodents, but antelope (*Antilocapra americana*) occupy the zone year round, and deer (*Odocoileus hemionus*) and mountain sheep (*Ovis canadensis*) use it as winter rangeland.

The third important community, the piñon woodland, is largely restricted to elevations above 6500 feet in the White Mountains, Benton Range, and Glass Mountain east of the trough. The zone is dominated by open forests of piñon pine (*Pinus monophylla*), which produce annual crops of edible nuts. Large ungulates use the community as summer rangeland.

The final community relevant to aboriginal settlement and subsistence patterns is the zone of upper sagebrush, which blankets the floor of Long Valley but also dominates open meadows and depressions within the piñon woodland communities east of the trough. The edible plant resources of this community are sparse; its major potential food sources are the large ungulates—principally deer, mountain sheep, and antelope—that use the upper sagebrush zone as summer rangeland and as a migration route in early fall.

Three other communities—the limber pine and bristlecone pine forest in the White Mountains, and the sierra meadowland and sierra conifer zone in the Sierra Nevada—contain relatively few subsistence resources and were largely ignored by aboriginal groups (Steward 1933:253, Map 2). As a minor exception to this, the sierra conifer zone in northeastern Long Valley was occasionally exploited for ungulates and pandora moth caterpillars (*Coloradia pandora*).

## Ethnography

In historic times the upper Owens River drainage was occupied by Western Numic speakers. Owens Valley was inhabited year round; Long Valley was apparently occupied only in the summer and early fall (but see Merriam 1955:227–229). The ethnographic accounts of Steward (1933, 1934, 1938) and others (Chalfant 1933; Parcher 1930) permit reconstruction of the historical settlement–subsistence system as follows: Throughout the spring, summer, and early fall the aboriginal population was centered at several lowland occupation sites situated in desert scrub communities in Owens Valley. Major activities in this interval included procurement, processing, and storage of a variety of desert scrub seeds and roots, and to a lesser degree, riverine roots and seeds, both of which could be obtained in large quantities within a 2-hour walk of the lowland occupation sites; the growth of some root crops was encouraged by artificial irrigation in plots near these base camps. Trips for plant resources available at some distance from occupation sites involved the use of temporary camps in the riverine and desert scrub communities as collecting stations by family-sized groups. Riverine temporary camps were also established for communal fishing in the spring and for communal antelope and rabbit drives in the fall. In the summer and early fall months, small hunting parties pursued large game in upland communities, where they occupied temporary camps.

In the fall, when a nut crop was present, small groups of from one to three families occupied mountain piñon camps while harvesting this resource. In years with unusually large harvests, habitation at piñon camps might last throughout the winter, but these settlements were usually abandoned immediately after the harvest was complete, and the winter was spent at lowland occupation sites.

## A PREDICTIVE MODEL

Archaeological and ethnographic data may be incorporated in a model predicting the distribution, function, and density of archaeological materials in the Inyo–Mono region. Six important settlement categories are postulated as follows: *base camps, piñon camps, temporary seed-collecting camps, riverine communal sites, temporary hunting camps,* and *special-use sites.* These are distributed among five biotic communities, including the desert scrub, riparian, piñon woodland, upper sagebrush, and sierra conifer.

### Base Camps

Base camps were the center of nearly every economic and social activity. Archaeological materials expected at these sites are house rings, storage pits, cooking hearths, a wide range of tools, scattered pottery sherds, and moderate to heavy amounts of chipping waste—in short, practically the full range of aboriginal products. When such sites are endangered by development, excavation is usually recommended. Archaeological and ethnographic information indicates base camps were almost exclusively located in desert scrub communities, where a wide range of plant resources were available within a relatively small area.

## Piñon Camps

Piñon camps were occupied during the winter months in years when nut crops were exceptionally abundant, about 1 year in 7 (Thomas 1973). Artifacts and features found at such camps are comparable to those from base camps; but given the absence of subsistence activities during winter, piñon camps can be expected to produce relatively higher proportions of manufacturing tools than can base camps. Because these localities were used infrequently, usually by groups numbering no more than 20 people, they generally lack middens and, hence, do not require excavation. On the other hand, they are susceptible to a wide range of surface sampling techniques. Piñon camps are nearly always situated within the piñon woodland zone and are most frequent near the lower piñon ecotone.

## Temporary Seed-Collecting Camps

These localities were used by groups of from one to three families during short collecting forays. The principal factor controlling the distribution of these sites was the availability of plant resources. On the average, families might establish two such camps during the brief interval when summer seed crops ripened. Although men hunted during these gathering trips, this was clearly a minor activity; the majority of artifacts recovered from such camps are seed-grinding tools. The brevity of occupation is reflected by the absence of middens and habitation structures such as house rings. Like piñon camps, temporary seed-collecting camps can be effectively studied by means of surface sampling. These sites occur in great numbers within the desert scrub community but are rare in other zones.

## Temporary Hunting Camps

These camps were established by hunting parties on exceptionally long trips or when a kill late in the day precluded returning to a base camp. In general, hunting camps lack structures and middens, consisting almost entirely of stone chippage, broken knives, and projectile points. Game animals were particularly abundant in upland areas including piñon woodland, upper sagebrush, and sierra conifer communities. Within these areas, hunters favored springs, narrow canyons, saddles, and cliffs as ambush locations and temporary campsites.

## Riverine Communal Sites

Communal activities centered in the riverine community along the Owens River. Here, antelope and jackrabbits attracted by lush plant growths could be cooperatively driven, and the deep water was used as a barrier to prevent their escape. Communal fishing was an equally productive activity. Most of the equipment employed in these tasks, including sagebrush fish dams and antelope corrals, and fiber nets for rabbits and fish, is seldom preserved; imperishable butchering tools in the form of flake knives and fleshers comprise the majority of artifacts at these sites. The relatively large number of individuals involved in these activities is commonly reflected by unusually dense scatters, consisting of tools and chipping waste. The changing river bottom and shifting animal and fish populations make it unlikely that communal hunting and fishing were restricted to any single area; rather, it is likely that these settlements will be represented as extensive artifact scatters on the margins of Owens River along its entire length.

## Special-Use Sites: Rock Art and Quarries

Great Basin rock art sites are generally associated with ambush locations or hunting camps, suggesting use as "hunting magic." They are particularly common near natural traps, such as box canyons, which could serve as game corrals. These sites are clearly a special class of hunting camp and should exhibit distributions similar to that settlement type.

Quarries are locations where stone used for tools was collected and chipped into rough blanks; their distribution is naturally limited to outcrops that produce usable raw material.

## A Site Density Model

Predicting the density of archaeological sites is a difficult proposition at best. Frequently the information necessary for the proper computations is unavailable, requiring more assumptions than are desirable. The archaeology and ethnography of the Inyo–Mono region, however, is known in sufficient detail to permit reasonably reliable estimates of site frequencies.

As the initial step in the analysis, I estimated the ratio between the densities of major settlement categories within their usual biotic communities—for example, the ratio between the density of seed camps in the desert scrub community to that of piñon camps in the piñon woodland. Published archaeological survey data were then used to estimate the actual site densities, using the density ratios as a cross-check. Base camps, temporary seed-collecting camps, and piñon camps were treated in this fashion; hunting camps, riverine communal sites, and special-use sites present unique problems and are discussed separately.

The predicted ratio between seed camp density and piñon camp density is 1:2. This figure is based on the assumption that local abundance of subsistence resources dictates the density of temporary camps used to procure those resources. Data from the Southwest show that piñon groves will yield a maximum of about 4.6 lb of pine nuts per acre (U.S. Department of Agriculture, Forest Service 1941:40); seed plants such as *Elymus, Panicum,* and *Eragrostis* yield as much as 200 lb per acre in pure stands under optimum conditions (Hoover *et al.* 1948:641–648, 669–671, 679, 698) but are minor constituents of the desert scrub community, covering perhaps 1.2% of its surface (Mooney 1973:Table II). Thus, the potential seed yield of the desert scrub community is 2.4 lb per acre, roughly one-half that of the piñon woodland.

The predicted ratio of base camps to seed camps is 1:25, a crude estimate computed by assuming that an average village (base camp) population of 150 people (Steward 1933:237), or 23 families, would occupy 20 different seed camps per year.

TABLE 16.1.
Predicted Density of Base Camps, Seed Camps, and Piñon
Camps

| Settlement type | Community | Density/square mile |
|---|---|---|
| Base camp | Desert scrub | .16 |
| Seed camp | Desert scrub | 4.80 |
| Piñon camp | Piñon woodland | 9.00 |

This permits 10 groups consisting of 2 families each to establish 2 such camps a year. An additional 5 camps allow a 25% gross increase in the number of these settlements within the village exploitation area, after which the existing seed camp locations are repeatedly reoccupied. Beyond this, any substantial increase in the number of seed camps would probably require a major population movement accompanied by relocation of the base camp, thus initiating a new cycle in which a series of seed camps are established around a base camp and maintaining the ratio of 1 base camp to 25 seed camps. In sum, then, the ratio between base camps, seed camps, and piñon camps is 1:25:50.

Actual densities of archaeological sites can only be reliably estimated on the basis of empirical evidence. Meighan (1955) provides the only quantitative data regarding site densities in the study area. His research disclosed an average of 4.8 sites per square mile in the desert scrub communities of Chidago Canyon, Mono County, and about 9 sites per square mile in the piñon woodland of the Benton Range. The former can be classified as seed camps; the latter are clearly piñon camps. It is reassuring to note that the observed ratio between seed camps and piñon camps, 1:1.9, agrees remarkably well with the expected ratio of 1:2.

Unfortunately, comparable data are unavailable for base camps; their density is estimated as .16 per square mile based on the expected site ratios and the observed density of seed camps and piñon camps. These data are summarized in Table 16.1.

## Hunting Camps, Riverine Sites, and Quarries

The distribution of hunting camps and rock art sites associated with hunting camps is not easily described in terms of a few simple principles. A review of the evidence, however, indicates some regularities. Hunting parties frequently used locations of steep vertical relief that afforded concealment or detoured animals within target range: Cliffs and arroyos are typical examples. In addition, herbivores were also ambushed near seeps and springs, which are particularly common near fault zones, where the slope aspect is similarly severe. Since game animals and hunters alike are drawn to steep terrain, hunting camps and rock art associated with hunting camps should be more common in areas of marked vertical relief than in areas lacking this characteristic. Detailed consideration of this problem is beyond the scope of this discussion, but I would tentatively suggest that the density of hunting camps ($D$) might be roughly estimated by the product of a slope function ($S$) and an empirically determined constant (c), or $D = cS$.

Riverine communal sites and quarries present no problems of prediction. The first category occurs as a single linear scatter distributed along the entire length of the Owens River. Quarries are confined to outcrops that produce stone suitable for tools. If we can assume the geology of the Inyo–Mono region to be reasonably well documented, quarries should be restricted to known obsidian sources within the study area.

## PREDICTIONS

Final site predictions were calculated for the proposed Southern California Edison power line route, which was 53 miles long and .25 miles wide, covering an area of 13.25 square miles. Topographical maps were used to divide the survey area into biotic communities, and the expected numbers of base camps, piñon camps, and seed camps were computed from the community areas and predicted site densities as summarized in Table 16.2.

The calculations for riverine communal sites and quarries were less elegant: The route crossed Owens River at two points, and passed near two obsidian sources; a riverine communal site was expected at each of the former, a quarry site at each of the latter. The density and distribution of hunting camps were not estimated in actual numbers.

### Prediction Accuracy

Between 1973 and 1974 ARU field teams surveyed the power line route and conducted excavations and surface samplings at several sites as summarized by Cowan and Wallof (1974). These investigations disclosed 1 base camp, 5 piñon camps, 8 hunting camps, 1 quarry site, and 4 untyped sites. Cowan and Wallof report no examples of seed-collecting camps, but examination of their data reveals

**TABLE 16.2.**
**Biotic Composition of Powerline Route and Expected Numbers of Base Camps, Seed Camps, and Piñon Camps**

|                    | Riverine | Desert scrub | Piñon woodland | Upper sage | Conifer | Total |
|--------------------|----------|--------------|----------------|------------|---------|-------|
| Area               | .24      | 6.61[a]      | .97            | 3.61       | 1.75    | 13.18[b] |
| Base camps expected | —        | 1.06         | —              | —          | —       | 1.06  |
| Seed camps expected | —        | 31.70        | —              | —          | —       | 31.70 |
| Piñon camps expected | —       | —            | 8.65           | —          | —       | 8.65  |

[a]In an earlier draft of this chapter, the desert scrub area was erroneously computed as 7.71, producing inflated expected values for base camps and seed camps.

[b]The discrepancy between this figure and the theoretical value of 13.25 reflects rounding error.

that 3 hunting camps, 1 quarry site, and 2 untyped sites produced groundstone tools, suggesting use of the sites as seed-collecting and -processing stations (Cowan and Wallof 1974:Table 6). There were 2 additional sites identified as hunting camps that lacked both grinding tools and projectile points; they contained a few tools and flakes that might easily have been used in connection with basketry repair—a maintenance activity common at seed camps. Similar tool kits representing seed procurement may have gone unrecognized in the assemblages recovered from other hunting camps. Thus, the 6 sites I have identified as seed camps probably represent the minimum number for that category.

Overall, the predicted numbers of base camps, seed camps, and piñon camps were reasonably close to the observed numbers (Table 16.3):

**TABLE 16.3.**
**Expected and Observed Numbers of Base Camps, Seed Camps, and Piñon Camps[a]**

|  | Base camps | Seed camps | Piñon camps |
|---|---|---|---|
| Expected | 1 | 32 | 9 |
| Observed | 1 | 6 | 5 |

[a]Observed data modified from Cowan and Wallof (1974).

As expected, one base camp was found; its location was anomalous, however, being within the piñon woodland rather than the desert scrub as predicted. Greater discrepancies characterized seed camps, which were only one-fifth as numerous as expected, and piñon camps, which were about three-fifths as numerous as expected. Unexpected deviations in the final powerline route precludes comparison between the expected and observed numbers of riverine communal sites and quarries.

Failure to predict site numbers more accurately can be at least partially attributed to differences between the size of the proposed survey area and the area actually surveyed. Similarly, recent vandalism has undoubtedly altered or entirely erased archaeological assemblages at many fragile-pattern sites, changing the relative frequencies of settlement categories and reducing the overall site densities. Despite these and other practical problems, the differences between the expected and observed site numbers compare remarkably well with experimental results obtained under far better controlled circumstances (cf. Judge, Ebert, and Hitchcock 1975:Table 6). This suggests that the procedure used to predict site densities has merit for future archaeological contract projects in eastern California; investigators may find the method applicable to similar projects in other areas as well.

## ACKNOWLEDGMENTS

Thanks are due to James Stuart, Patrick Barker, Sylvia Broadbent, Phillip Wilke, Don Miller, and Rocky Rockwell, who read and made comments on various drafts of this manuscript. The Southern California Edison Company provided financial support for this research.

# 17

# Probabilistic Survey Sampling: Making Parameter Estimates

A. E. ROGGE
STEVEN L. FULLER

Archaeological research done under the rubric of cultural resource management has the potential to contribute to the broader field of general research archaeology in many ways, but the potential is particularly promising in the realm of developing and refining methods and techniques (F. T. Plog 1975). Conversely, it is also imperative that cultural resource management studies productively employ the methods and techniques that have been developed in association with noncontract research endeavors. This chapter examines the use of probabilistic sampling within this framework.

Probabilistic samples are those samples in which every element in the population has been assigned, by means of some mechanical operation of randomization, a *calculable,* nonzero probability of being selected (Kish 1965:20). Because the laws of probability are used to avoid human bias, probabilistic sampling allows the archaeologist to make quantifiable predictions about entire populations of items on the basis of observations of only a sample of the population (Mueller 1975b:2). Statisticians have developed many types of probabilistic sampling designs (cf. Cochran 1963; Hansen, Hurwitz, and Madow 1953; Kish 1965), but archaeologists have just begun to test the efficacy of different designs for various archaeological problems and contexts (DeBlois 1975; Judge, Ebert, and Hitchcock 1975; Mueller 1974, 1975b; S. Plog 1976a).

From a historical perspective archaeologists have always sampled, but until recently all sampling had been nonprobabilistic "probing" or "purposive selection" (Cowgill 1975). Only in the past 15 years have archaeologists begun to recognize that the intuitive "grab" or judgment sampling techniques, often mistakenly called random samples (Mueller 1974:26–27, 1975b:2), are in many cases neither the most appropriate nor the most efficient for archaeological research (Redman 1974:5).

The major thrust of many pioneering archaeological applications of probabilistic techniques was to insure that some form of randomization was incorporated into sample selection procedures. This laudable goal was soon modified, at least implicitly, by the assumption that the quality of sample data was proportional to the complexity of sampling designs. Evaluation of such designs was, however, largely intuitive. The major advantage of probabilistic sampling is that the data gathered by such techniques need not simply be assumed to be representative but can be quantitatively evaluated. This was largely ignored in many of the early archaeological applications, probably because the goal of these studies was not to use sample data to estimate such population parameters as means, percentages, ratios, and totals. Instead, these studies were oriented toward investigating the spatial structure of archaeological materials, a purpose for which probabilistic sampling techniques were not specifically designed (cf. Asch 1975:181–182).

In this chapter we describe an attempt to use probabilistic sampling for a more appropriate purpose. On the basis of a sample survey the number and nature of sites in a complete study area are estimated. An evaluation of the adequacy of our sample design is summarized, and the implications of our evaluation for designing future sample surveys are briefly discussed.

## ORME ALTERNATIVES: THE SAMPLE SURVEYS OF ROOSEVELT LAKE AND HORSESHOE RESERVOIR

The Bureau of Reclamation, Arizona Projects Office, contracted the Cultural Resource Management Section of the Arizona State Museum to conduct an ar-

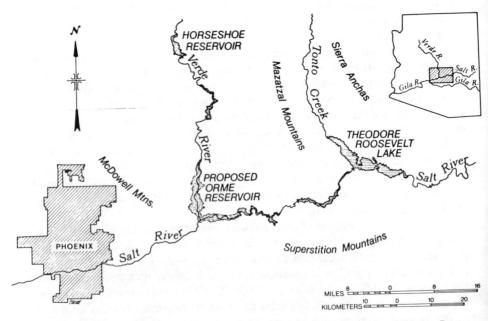

**Map 17.1.** The areas studied by the Orme Alternatives Project were the perimeters of Theodore Roosevelt Lake and Horseshoe Reservoir. The location of the proposed Orme Reservoir is also indicated.

chaeological sample survey of areas to be flooded by the proposed enlargement of two existing reservoirs in central Arizona. Map 17.1 shows the areas studied. At Theodore Roosevelt Lake on the Salt River, approximately 12.7 square miles (32.9 km²) would be inundated by raising Roosevelt Dam 30 feet (9.1 m). At Horseshoe Reservoir on the Verde River, approximately 7.8 square miles (20.2 km²) would be inundated by raising Horseshoe Dam 140 feet (42.7 m). As stipulated in the contract between the Arizona State Museum and the Bureau of Reclamation, the purpose of the sample survey was to provide data that could be used to predict the quantity, nature, and significance of the archaeological resources within the entire direct impact zones of both reservoirs. These resources were to be compared with those recorded by a complete survey of the proposed Orme Reservoir Project area (Canouts 1975), which is located just northeast of Phoenix, Arizona. The overall purpose of this comparison was to determine the relative impacts upon archaeological resources that would be caused by constructing or altering any of these three reservoirs (Fuller, Rogge, and Gregonis 1976).

## The Sample Design

The design of any probabilistic sampling plan requires decisions in four option domains, which, to use Mueller's (1974:28–30) terminology, are (*1*) sampling technique; (*2*) sampling scheme; (*3*) sampling fraction; and (*4*) sampling units.

With regard to *sampling technique,* two choices are available: *element sampling* or *cluster sampling.* In element sampling the items or events that are the focus of research are individually selected for incorporation into the sample. This requires that the *frame,* which is the list of items or events to be sampled, consist of all individual elements. In cluster sampling the elements are incorporated into the sample by groups or clusters, and the frame consists of a complete list of clusters. It is not necessary to be able to list each element. Some of those who first argued for the use of probabilistic sampling realized that archaeological surveyors are often forced to use a cluster technique, since a complete list of all sites is not available (Rootenberg 1964; Vescelius 1960). Cluster sampling is associated with more complex statistics and usually results in less precise parameter estimates (Asch 1975:179–180; Blalock 1972:527; Judge *et al.* 1975:86–88; Kish 1965:149–150; Matson and Lipe 1975:128–134; Mueller 1974:62–63, 1975a; Read 1975:54–58; Thomas 1975:77–81). Fortunately, we were able to follow the approach used by Thomas (1975) in his Reese River Ecological Project and consider our sampling problem as one of determining site density. This allowed us to use areal units rather than sites per se as sampling elements. We were therefore able to use an element sampling technique.

The choice of *sampling schemes* that can be combined with the element sampling technique are *simple random, systematic, stratified random,* or various combinations of these schemes. We opted for a stratified random scheme, as it tends to insure more uniform coverage than simple random schemes, and it also allowed us to incorporate what previous research had indicated would be relevant prior knowledge about the distribution of sites. The sample units were stratified into three physiographic categories. The first of these microenvironmental categories consisted of floodplain and river terrace settings, the second of gently sloping ( < 10% slope) pediment terraces, and the third of steeply sloping (> 10% slope) zones.

The determination of an adequate *sampling fraction* for any given problem is difficult, but in this case the choice was made for us. After consulting with U.S. Forest Service, National Park Service, and Arizona State Museum archaeologists, the Bureau of Reclamation decided to fund a 20% sample.

The last decision to make in designing a sampling plan is what size and shape of *sampling units* to use. For regional site surveys archaeologists have often used arbitrary units of one form or another (e.g., quadrats, transects, or circles), which commonly vary in size from 25 to 160 acres (10.1 to 64.8 ha). Because the two areas we had to survey were very narrow, irregular strips surrounding existing reservoirs, using any form of arbitrary unit would have been difficult. We realized that intermittent streams plotted on 7.5′ U.S. Geological Survey quadrangle sheets could be used as natural boundaries to divide the study areas into a series of roughly similar sized sample units. The study area at Roosevelt Lake was divided into 122 sample units, each averaging about 67 acres (27.1 ha) in size. The study area at Horseshoe Reservoir was divided into 54 sample units, averaging approximately 93 acres (37.6 ha) each.

With a table of random numbers, enough units were selected from each stratum at each reservoir to include at least 20% of the area of each stratum. Because the sample units were irregularly shaped and of unequal size, the same proportion of sample units was not selected from each stratum. Such a design is technically labeled a *disproportionate stratified random sample*.

## The Sample Survey Data

At Roosevelt Lake a total of 1801 acres (728.8 ha) were surveyed during 68 person-days of fieldwork, revealing a total of 29 archaeological sites. It was estimated that 10,820 "total data recovery days" would be required to excavate these sites completely.

At Horseshoe Reservoir 64 sites were recorded during 66 person-days spent surveying 1108 acres (448.4 ha). It was estimated that about 13,740 "total data recovery days" would be required to excavate these sites.

## Parameter Estimation

Once the sample data were collected, they were used to estimate the total number of sites. In order to estimate and compare mitigation costs according to survey procedures developed for the Orme Reservoir Project (Canouts 1975), we also had to estimate the number of *total data recovery days,* which is the number of working days that are required to thoroughly excavate every site. Practically, of course, we recognize that recovery of all data is impossible. We also made a preliminary settlement pattern analysis of the Roosevelt Lake and Horseshoe Reservoir study areas, which required estimating such values as total number of habitation and nonhabitation components. In order to estimate these totals, we first calculated the ratio of elements per acre per sample unit, which compensated for the unequal sizes of our sample units. Additionally, such a ratio estimation procedure increases the precision of the estimated totals in proportion to the degree of correlation between the variables used to construct the ratio.

The formula used to estimate the total number of elements is:

$$\hat{X}_c = r_c Y = \frac{\hat{X}_{st}}{\hat{Y}_{st}} Y = \frac{\sum\limits_{}^{L} (N_h/n_h) \sum\limits_{}^{n_h} x_{hi}}{\sum (N_h/n_h) \sum y_{hi}} Y,$$

where

$\hat{X}_c$ = estimated total number of elements by the combined ratio estimate,
$r_c$ = the combined ratio estimate of the number of elements per acre,
$Y$ = total number of acres,
$\hat{X}_{st}$ = total number of elements as estimated by stratified random sampling,
$\hat{Y}_{st}$ = total number of acres as estimated by stratified random sampling,
$L$ = number of strata,
$N_h$ = the number of sample units in stratum $h$,
$n_h$ = number of sample units surveyed in stratum $h$,
$x_{hi}$ = number of elements in sample unit $i$ in stratum $h$, and
$y_{hi}$ = number of acres in sample unit $i$ in stratum $h$        [Modified after Yamane 1967:350–353].

When using ratio estimation with a stratified sampling scheme, it is possible to calculate a separate ratio for each stratum, which is more precise if the ratios vary much from stratum to stratum. However, we chose to use the combined rather than the separate ratio method because when the number of surveyed sampled units per stratum ($n_h$) is small, as it was in both of the study areas, the separate ratio method tends to be more biased, and estimates of parameter precision are not valid (Cochran 1963:171; Hansen *et al.* 1953:194–196; Kish 1965:206; Yamane 1967:359–360).

Once estimates of totals have been calculated, it is necessary to evaluate their reliability. Two factors must be considered—*precision* and *accuracy* (cf. Cochran 1963:12–16; Lazerwitz 1968). Precision refers to the nature of the sampling distribution of an estimating method. For example, one estimating method is more precise than another if its distribution of estimates of the total, based upon all possible samples of a given population, deviates less from the mean. Accuracy refers to the relationship between the mean of the sampling distribution and the actual population value of the variable being estimated. If the mean of the sampling distribution of the estimate is not the same as the actual population value, the estimating procedure is said to be *biased*. The magnitude of this bias can usually be calculated. A second type of bias, which is difficult to estimate quantitatively, can enter into sample survey data because of measurement and data collection errors. Unbiased and precise estimating procedures are ideal. Often in practice, unbiased estimates are imprecise. If a more precise but biased estimating procedure is available, it is often used if the bias is relatively small. Ratio estimation usually falls into this category.

The formula used to estimate the bias of the combined ratio estimate of the total is:

$$\text{Bias } (\hat{X}_c) = (Y)E(r_c - R_c) \cong Y \sum^{L} \left[\frac{N_h - n_h}{N_h n_h}\right]\left[\frac{1}{\bar{y}_h^2}\right] (r_c s_{yh}^2 - \rho_h s_{xh} s_{yh}),$$

where

$E(r_c - R_c) = $ expected difference between $r_c$ and $R_c$,

$R_c = $ population ratio of the number of elements per acre,

$\bar{y}_h = $ average number of acres per sample unit in stratum $h$

$\qquad = \sum^{n_h} y_{hi}/n_h$,

$s_{yh}^2 = $ variance of acres per sample unit

$\qquad = \sum^{n_h} (y_{hi} - \bar{y}_h)^2/(n_h - 1)$,

$\rho_h = $ coefficient of correlation between the number of elements and number of acres per sample unit in stratum $h$

$$= \frac{s_{xyh}}{s_{xh} s_{yh}} = \frac{\sum^{n_h} (x_{hi} - \bar{x}_h)(y_{hi} - \bar{y}_h)/(n_h - 1)}{\left[\sum (x_{hi} - \bar{x}_h)^2/(n_h - 1)\right]^{\frac{1}{2}} \left[\sum (y_{hi} - \bar{y}_h)^2/(n_h - 1)\right]^{\frac{1}{2}}},$$

$s_{xh}^2 = $ variance of elements per sample unit

$\qquad = \sum^{n_h} (x_{hi} - \bar{x}_h)^2/(n_h - 1)$, and

$\bar{x}_h = $ average number of elements per sample unit in stratum $h$

$\qquad = \sum^{n_h} x_{hi}/n_h$                    [Modified after Yamane 1967:334–336;351].

The precision of an estimate is commonly measured by calculating the standard error, which can be used to calculate confidence intervals for an estimate. By the empirical rule, a confidence interval of $\pm 1$ standard error has a confidence coefficient of 68% (Mendenhall, Ott, and Scheaffer 1971:7). This means that there is a 68% probability that the actual parameter value is within $\pm 1$ standard error of its estimated value. If the confidence interval is increased to $\pm 1.96$ standard errors, the confidence coefficient increases to 95%. The value 1.96 is known as the $z$ score. If $z$ is increased to 2.58, the confidence coefficient increases to 99%. The coefficients are based upon the assumption that the estimating statistic is distributed normally in a bell-shaped curve and that the sample size is large. When sample size is small ($<30$ sample units), $t$ values can be subsituted for $z$ scores to compensate for the nonnormal distributions of small sample estimates (Parl 1967:150–153), although if the population being sampled is highly skewed, the distribution of estimating statistics also tends to be skewed. The sampling distribution of most statistics approaches normality as the sample size becomes large, regardless of the distribution of the elements being sampled. The problem of estimating confidence intervals with small samples from highly skewed populations, which is increasingly being recognized as a common archaeological problem, will be discussed in more detail in the next section.

The formula used to estimate the size of the standard error of the total number of elements is:

$$SE(\hat{X}_c) = [\hat{V}(\hat{X}_c)]^{\frac{1}{2}} = [(Y^2)\hat{V}(r_c)]^{\frac{1}{2}} = \left[\frac{Y^2}{\hat{Y}_{st}^2} \sum^{L} (N_h^2)\left(\frac{N_h - n_h}{N_h n_h}\right)(s_{ch}^2)\right]^{\frac{1}{2}},$$

where

$SE(\hat{X}_c)$ = standard error of the total number of elements as estimated by the combined ratio estimate,
$\hat{V}$ = estimated variance, and
$s_{ch}^2$ = variance of the sample ratio of elements per acre
$\quad = s_{xh}^2 + r_c^2 s_{yh}^2 - 2r_c \rho_h s_{xh} s_{yh}$ [Modified after Yamane 1967:351–353].

The parameter estimates calculated with these formulas for the two study areas are summarized in Table 17.1. A brief glance at this table will indicate that the calculated parameter estimates are not very precise. What kind of reaction can be expected from a sponsoring agency when we report that, with only a 7-out-of-10 chance of being correct, there are somewhere between 43 and 139 sites in the Roosevelt Lake study area? The Horseshoe Reservoir parameter estimates are considerably more precise, and a comparison of the two sets of data does indicate ways to improve sample designs. In the following section we evaluate each of the decisions made in the four option domains of sample design.

TABLE 17.1.
A Summary of Parameter Estimates for Various Data Categories at Roosevelt Lake and Horseshoe Reservoir Survey Areas[a]

| Data category | Roosevelt Lake | Horseshoe Reservoir |
|---|---|---|
| Sites | 91 ± 48 | 283 ± 39 |
| "Total data recovery days" | 44,200 + 41,300 − 33,400 | 79,500 ± 10,400 |
| All prehistoric components | 107 ± 63 | 338 ± 48 |
| Nonhabitation prehistoric components | 49 ± 19 | 215 ± 24 |
| Habitation components: Period 1 (A.D. 700–1100) | 2 + 3 − 1 | 42 ± 10 |
| Habitation components: Period 2 (A.D. 1000–1300) | 70 ± 39 | 65 ± 22 |
| Habitation components: Period 3 (A.D. 1200–1450) | 9 + 9 − 7 | 5 + 8 − 2 |

[a] The 70% confidence intervals listed were calculated by multiplying the estimated standard errors by the appropriate $t$ values. The asymmetrical confidence intervals result from the fact that the actual sample data sometimes exceeded the minimum estimates.

## AN EVALUATION OF THE SAMPLE DESIGN

A cluster sampling technique can be expected to result in more imprecise estimates than an element sampling technique if the data being sampled are arranged in a clustered manner. Figure 17.1 indicates that the frequency distribution of site densities per sample unit is not normally distributed in either survey area, but the spatial arrangement of sites is not intuitively obvious on the basis of such data. Morisita's index of dispersion is a statistic that can be calculated using such sample frequency distribution data in order to make inferences about the arrangement of sites (Greig-Smith 1964:67; Poole 1974:116–117; Southwood 1966:37; Pielou 1969:102–104). The formula for the index is:

$$I_\delta = N \frac{\sum\limits_{}^{N} x_i \, (x_i - 1)}{(\sum x_i)(\sum x_i - 1)} = N \frac{\sum\limits_{}^{N} x_i^2 - \sum\limits_{}^{N} x_i}{(\sum x_i)^2 - \sum x_i},$$

where

$N$ = total number of sample units, and
$x_i$ = number of elements in the $i^{\text{th}}$ sample unit.

The statistic is based upon the fact that the frequency distribution of element densities per sample unit will fit a Poisson curve when the elements being sampled are relatively rare and randomly arranged (Collier, Cox, Johnson, and Miller 1973:167–168; Greig-Smith 1964:12–14; Kershaw 1964:96–106; Odum 1971:206;

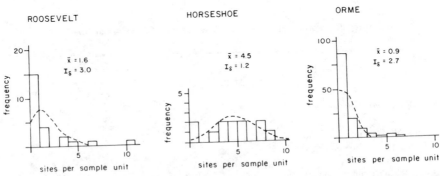

**Figure 17.1.** Frequency distribution of the adjusted site densities per sample unit for the Roosevelt Lake and Horseshoe Reservoir surveys and the Orme Reservoir area simulation data. The raw data were adjusted because the sample units were not of equal size. The adjustment was made by multiplying the actual number of sites by a weighting factor that compensated for deviations from the average acreage per sample unit. The weighting factor was the quotient of the average sample unit size of each sample divided by the actual acreage of each sample unit surveyed. This assumes that the ratio of sites per acre would remain constant if each sample unit were adjusted to the average size. Since in reality this ratio would undoubtedly change, these graphs are only approximations. Dashed lines depict Poisson distributions (randomly dispersed sites).

Pielou 1969:79–110; Southwood 1966:23–43). In such cases Morisita's index is equal to 1. When elements are uniformly dispersed, the index will be less than 1. Values greater than 1 indicate a clustered arrangement of elements.

The value of Morisita's index for all sites is 3.0 at Roosevelt Lake, and 1.2 at Horseshoe Reservoir. Thus the arrangement of sites is clustered in both areas, but especially at Roosevelt Lake. These values are respresentative of the values of Morisita's index calculated for the various categories listed in Table 17.1. Because all of these data classes are dispersed across the sample units in a clustered manner, any cluster sampling technique would have resulted in larger standard errors than the element sampling technique we used.

The efficiency of the combined-ratio estimation procedure, which was used in conjunction with the element sampling technique, varies with the degree of correlation between the variables used in the ratio. At Horseshoe Reservoir the number of sites per sample unit was highly correlated with the number of acres per sample unit. As a result, ratio estimation reduced the size of the standard error of the estimate of the total number of sites by about one-half what it would have been without ratio estimation. At Roosevelt Lake the number of sites per sample unit was not closely related to the size of sample units, and ratio estimation resulted in no increase in the precision of parameter estimates.

In order to investigate the nature of the sampling distribution of this estimation procedure, we made a simulation sampling study using some of the 100% sampling data that had been gathered during the study of the proposed Orme Dam and Reservoir area (Canouts 1975). To duplicate the Roosevelt Lake and Horseshoe Reservoir sampling problem as much as possible in the experiment, we simulated an existing reservoir in the Orme area with a high water level that was to be raised 80 vertical feet (24.4 m). The study area defined in this manner encompassed about 15,400 acres (6232.3 ha). We defined a total of 124 "naturally bounded" sample units and assigned them to three microenvironmental strata, following the procedures used in designing the Roosevelt Lake and Horseshoe Reservoir surveys. The sample unit size averaged 124 acres (50.2 ha) and was therefore larger than in either of the Orme Alternatives Project surveys, although site density was considerably lower. As a result, the average adjusted number of sites per sample unit was about 0.9, less than both Roosevelt Lake and Horseshoe Reservoir. Morisita's index for the Orme simulation site data was 2.8, indicating that sites were dispersed in a clustered manner similar to that in the Roosevelt Lake area. The simulated sampling situation was therefore as severe a test for the combined-ratio-estimate-of-the-total statistic as either of the sample surveys.

An interactive FORTRAN IV program was written to select stratified random samples just as they had been for the Roosevelt Lake and Horseshoe Reservoir surveys. The program allowed us to designate the number of simulated samples to be drawn at any given sampling fraction. It then calculated the combined ratio estimate of the total number of sites and "total data recovery days" for each sample, plotted the estimates in a histogram, and printed the low, high, and mean estimates and standard deviation of the estimates. Estimated sampling distributions of combined ratio estimate of the total number of sites and "total data recovery days", as based on 300 simulated samples at various sampling fractions, indicate that the skewness and bias of the distributions at low sampling fractions cannot be ignored.

Ideally, our stratified random sampling scheme should have grouped sample units with similar site densitites into the same strata. A simple inspection of the sample data indicated that our stratification criteria were not particularly successful in accomplishing this. The simulation sampling program was written so that simple random and systematic samples could be selected as well as stratified random samples. A comparison of the results indicates that stratification resulted in no decrease of bias or imprecision as compared with simple random sampling (Figure 17.2), but systematic sampling was more biased and precision increased erratically with increasing sample size. This may be due in part to periodicities in the distribution of site densities, which may have been amplified by using intermittent streams as natural boundaries.

The lack of success of our stratification was probably not due to the irrelevancy of the criteria used but to their crudeness. Field inspection indicated that most sample units did not fall neatly into any of the microenvironmental categories that we had defined on the basis of available mapped information but were actually complex mosaics of several microenvironments. Better documentation of microenvironments would have been useful, but improving the success of stratification will, in general, depend upon the success of research aimed at improving our ability to predict site locations (e.g., Gumerman 1971). Multistage samples are probably the best type of design to use for insuring effective stratification. It should be noted that the advantages of successful stratification will be vitiated by the necessity of using a

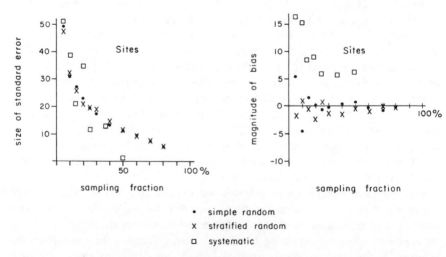

**Figure 17.2.** Rate of decrease of standard error and bias of combined ratio estimates of the total number of sites with increasing sampling fraction based upon 300 simulated simple random, stratified random, and systematic samples of Orme Reservoir survey data.

combined-ratio estimation procedure rather than a separate ratio when sample sizes are small.

The adequacy of our 20% sampling fraction depends upon whether it yields precise enough estimates to answer the questions being asked. Even though our estimates of mitigation costs were very imprecise, they were good enough to allow us to conclude that they were higher than the estimated costs of mitigating the effects of the construction of the proposed Orme Reservoir. Thus the sampling fraction was adequate.

Our simulation study did allow us to investigate, in a more general way, how bias and imprecision decrease with increasing sampling fractions. This analysis indicated that initial increases in the size of the sampling fraction lead to substantial increases in precision, but the rate of improvement declines as the sampling fraction becomes larger (Figure 17.2). The bias of the combined ratio estimate was negligible compared to the standard error under the conditions of the simulation study.

For many archaeological sampling problems, absolute sample size is more important than the sampling fraction. The Roosevelt Lake sample consisted of 24 sample units, and the Horseshoe Reservoir sample had only 12—both less than the magic number 30, which statisticians commonly use as the upper limit of small sample sizes. The fact that the Horseshoe sample was only half the size of the Roosevelt sample was obviously compensated for by other factors. Perhaps it is appropriate to note at this point that a 20% sample of a 20-square-mile (51.8-km²) study area in 80-acre (32.4-ha) sample units would be only a sample of 32 units. Since this would be a fairly "large" project by archaeological standards, many site survey samples can typically be expected to be "small" by statistical standards.

The last aspect of the sample design to evaluate is the size and shape of the sample units that were selected. The fact that the sample units were of unequal size and irregular in shape created no problems. Because each of the sample units was naturally bounded on three sides, all were easy to locate, and this resulted in a substantial savings of field time.

The average size of the sample units did differ considerably between the two survey areas. Sample units at Horseshoe were on the average almost 40% larger in terms of area than those at Roosevelt Lake. More importantly, the sample units at Horseshoe were almost 3 times larger than those at Roosevelt Lake in terms of the adjusted average number of sites. Although it is not immediately obvious, this may well be a major reason for the relatively greater precision of the Horseshoe Reservoir parameter estimates.

As pointed out above, frequency distributions of element densities per sample unit will approximate Poisson curves when the elements being sampled are arranged randomly. Poisson curves are markedly skewed when the mean number of elements per sample unit is small, but they approach bell-shaped normal curves with increasing mean size. Sites commonly tend to be arranged in a clustered rather than random pattern. Therefore, frequency distributions of densities per sample unit will be even more skewed than Poisson curves. However, an increase from 1.6 sites per sample unit at Roosevelt to 4.5 sites per sample unit at Horseshoe resulted in a substantial decrease of skewness as shown in Figure 17.1, although part of this decrease was due to the more random arrangement of sites in the Horseshoe Reservoir area. It seems wise to define sample units large enough to contain at least several sites on the average. As increasing sample unit size often means reducing the number of sample units that can be surveyed, compromises must be made between these conflicting design goals.

## SUMMARY AND CONCLUSION

As probabilistic sampling techniques are increasingly applied in archaeological research, it is becoming clear that the discipline faces special sampling problems. Contract archaeological projects often provide ideal opportunities to experiment with sampling techniques. If the sample designs used in each of these situations are critically evaluated, the resulting analysis will provide a basis for formulating generalizations that relate sample design efficacy to different archaeological situations and problems. On the other hand, the use of probabilistic sampling techniques can also provide the hard data needed by the land-use manager for assessing project environmental impacts.

The Orme Alternatives Project, which was used as the case study for this chapter, sought to fulfill both of these goals. First, relatively inexpensive 20% probabilistic sample surveys were made at Roosevelt Lake and Horseshoe Reservoir. Although problems associated with sampling skewed populations resulted in fairly high ranges of error, it was possible to predict quantitatively the number of sites and number of person-days needed for "total data recovery." These parameter estimates were then compared to survey data from the proposed Orme Reservoir area and were found to be significantly greater. These predictions have been of subsequent use to land-use and cultural resource managers.

An evaluation of the sample design was made by comparing the results of the two surveys and by a simulation sampling experiment that applied the Orme Alternatives sampling design to 100% survey data collected in the nearby Orme Reservoir Project area. Although we make no claims for providing generalizations or recipes useful for other sample surveys, the evaluation did illustrate both problems to be avoided and suggestions for alleviating large standard errors.

## ACKNOWLEDGMENTS

The authors would like to thank all of the members of the Cultural Resource Management Section of the Arizona State Museum for various contributions at different stages of the Orme Alternatives Project. We especially acknowledge assistance provided by Lynn S. Teague, head of the Section; Linda Mayro, project director for the Orme Alternatives Project; Linda M. Gregonis, who worked as a researcher and co-author on the Orme Alternatives Project; and Larry Manire who wrote the simulation program.

# Part VI

---

# ASSESSING SIGNIFICANCE

---

The concept of significance, like no other in conservation archaeology, is a constant source of frustration and inspiration. We are frustrated because we wish that significance could be ignored; indeed, most archaeologists suffer considerable anguish in making the kind of evaluations that may result in some sites being preserved at the expense of those condemned to the oblivion meted out by the bulldozer. Nevertheless, the many kinds of significance that need to be taken into account when assessing resources often immerses the investigator deeply in the most fundamental, intriguing problems of the discipline: the nature of archaeological data and the relationships between archaeology and society. The alternating repulsion and attraction that the concept of significance exerts on archaeologists, and its central place in cultural resource management law, has led in a short time to the growth of a fairly large literature.

The concept was first treated in a discerning manner by Scovill, Gordon, and Anderson (1972). It is their discussion, as skillfully expanded by Moratto (1975b) that forms the framework for the present treatment. Somewhat later, several types of scientific significance were defined by House and Schiffer (1975b; Schiffer and House 1977). Ideas from the latter works, and the brief review of approaches to assessing scientific significance by Raab and Klinger (n.d.), will be used to embellish our survey of the varieties of significance that concern the conservation archaeologist.

The outstanding quality of the concept of significance is its relativity: The significance of something can only be interpreted relative to some frame of reference. For ease of discussion we shall designate each frame of reference as a *type* of significance. It is true, of course, that properties of the

resource base play a part in *determinations* of significance, but those properties in no way define the relevant types of significance. Identifying the
latter is the task of conservation archaeologists and the society in which
they function.

In principle, the process of assessing significance is relatively straightforward once there is agreement on the types of significance that need to be
considered. One first specifies explicit criteria for judging resources in
relation to each type of significance. Then the fit between the criteria and
the resources is evaluated. And finally, it may be desirable to arrive at an
overall judgment based on a weighting of the types of significance that
have been considered.

As an example, let us take "newsworthiness" as a type of significance.
Several criteria for newsworthiness come to mind for evaluating individual
sites: size (the greater the size, the greater the newsworthiness), age (the
older the better), richness (newsworthiness varies directly with the number
and variety of "goodies"), and the exotic factor (that which is unusual or
unexpected is newsworthy). In this instance, scaling a site according to
each criterion would be an easy task. The individual rankings could then be
given weights, and a composite judgment on a site's newsworthiness could
then emerge. And finally, assuming the investigator was conscientious, he
could devise a way to consider other types of significance and furnish an
overall assessment.

Although the process is simple in principle, assessing significance has
proven to be one of the most difficult chores facing the conservation
archaeologist. Seemingly there are as many approaches as there are conservation archaeologists. The most common flaw in assessments of significance is a failure to treat all relevant types of significance. This situation is
beginning to improve as agreement converges on several major types.
Serious problems remain, however, in determining the appropriate criteria
for measuring each kind of significance, and only now are methods for
operationalizing the criteria, weighting the criteria, and weighting the various types of significance becoming recognized as problems. These differences are readily apparent in the papers in Part VI. Dixon (Chapter 21),
for example, would probably argue that social significance should be
weighted heavily, while Schiffer and House (Chapter 18) would tend to lay
more emphasis on scientific significance. In both cases, we have only the
faintest inkling of how to construct and operationalize appropriate criteria.

In the remainder of this introduction we set forth the major types of significance that are generally recognized, and, to the extent possible, we list
various criteria used to measure them. The types of significance we list are
probably not exhaustive, and they do contain some overlaps.

## SCIENTIFIC SIGNIFICANCE

A site or resource is said to be scientifically significant when its further study may be expected to help answer current research questions. That is, scientific significance is defined as research potential.

Schiffer and House in Chapter 18 identify several varieties of scientific significance relating to archaeological, anthropological, and other social science questions. They also argue that vague impressions of significance and overly mechanistic evaluations are not a stable foundation upon which to erect adequate assessments of significance. They propose on the contrary that significance in relation to timely and specific research questions can only be documented by a creative process of problem-oriented research that in effect probes the research potential. Research potential may be probed in a variety of ways, including analysis of surface collections and test excavations (see Fox *et al.* 1974; House 1975e; Rothschild 1976; Skinner and Gallagher 1974). Needless to say, at the levels of overview and assessment, one can but offer the most preliminary treatments of significance. Some investigators may find these requirements for assessing scientific significance to be disquieting (e.g., Aten 1972), for it involves one in an open-ended procedure that permits no shortcuts. Despite its rigid avoidance of easily applied formulistic criteria for judging scientific significance, the Schiffer-House approach and independently developed analogs seem well on their way to universal adoption (e.g., Canouts 1975; Debowski *et al.* 1976; Goodyear 1975a; Grady and Lipe 1976; McMillan *et al.* 1977; Moratto 1975b; Price *et al.* 1975; Raab 1976c; Raab and Klinger n.d.).

Raab and Klinger (n.d.) embrace the basic premise that scientific significance is assessed in terms of research potential for timely and specific questions. They go on to suggest that the assessment process would be streamlined considerably by the availability of regional research designs. We are not convinced that regional research designs will be a panacea, for they are bound to be oriented primarily toward what Schiffer and House (Chapter 18) call "substantive" significance and omit much else that is important; even so, we acknowledge that they cannot but help to improve the present situation. We urge those who intend to contrive such documents to include a broad range of current research interests and update them frequently. Furthermore, even with a regional research design in hand the investigator is not relieved of the need to probe the research potential in order to find out the degree of fit between the current questions and the resources being studied. In the absence of a regional research design, which is presently the situation in most areas, some investigators have evaluated resources with the aid of models and research designs erected especially for that purpose (e.g., Raab 1976d; Windmiller 1975). Additional creative attempts along those lines are to be expected.

Some conservation archaeologists have adopted several rather more concrete criteria of scientific significance that, despite some problems, may be useful under certain circumstances. Bell and Gettys (n.d.) identify more than a dozen "factors" (criteria) for assessment of (primarily scientific) significance. *Size,* or *area of occupation,* they suggest, is an indication of the general amount of potential information in a site. Although this criterion is also employed by other investigators (e.g., T. R. Hester, Bass, and Kelly 1975; Pilles and Haas 1973), there is little to commend it. In the first place, one can justifiably question the need for a unidimensional concept, "total information potential," by which sites are expected to vary. Even if there were reason to invent such a quantity, there is no a priori reason to think that it would correlate directly with site size. Secondly, with the advent of settlement system analysis and other approaches in modern archaeology, the smallest site in a region may be as important or more so than the largest for furnishing important information (see F. T. Plog 1974b; Moseley and Mackey 1972). *Depth* of a site, like size, is an unsatisfactory criterion unless it is used merely to signify the probability that stratified or undisturbed deposits are present. Degree of *multicomponency* might, in some very few instances, also be an index to stratification. Bell and Gettys (n.d.) also list *range of activities* and *ecological setting;* neither of these criteria seem capable of reflecting research potential unless they are coupled to specific problems.

Two other criteria, *preservation* and *condition of deposits,* are widely used and demonstrably related to research potential (Bell and Gettys n.d.). Clearly, when floral and/or faunal remains, architecture, or even pottery are not preserved, one is decisively precluded from handling certain research questions. In addition, the degree to which deposits are disturbed, such as by plowing or vandalism, affects some kinds of research potential. However, there has been a tendency by some workers to dismiss damaged sites too hastily without adequate demonstration that all research potential is lost; indeed, many damaged sites are still quite suitable for certain kinds of studies. This point is dealt with by Schiffer and House in Chapter 18 and by Henderson (1976).

Four other interrelated criteria advanced by Bell and Gettys (n.d.) bear upon research potential: *previous knowledge; uniqueness; period of occupation; and regional, state,* or *national interest.* In terms of previous knowledge, sites that may yield new rather than redundant information for most problems are safely considered more significant, though this is a tricky criterion to apply. Unique or rare sites are reasonably judged to contain research potential shared with few or no other sites. Period of occupation is related both to previous knowledge and uniqueness, and it merits no special attention. And finally, sites that hold information for questions of national or even international import are considered to be more significant than those with only local or regional research potential.

Taken one at a time, these and similar criteria relating to research potential may easily be misused. We present them tentatively in the hope that they will merely alert the reader to some of the criteria that might assist one in the process of evaluating scientific significance.

One must also remember, when assessing cultural resources, that the latter include more than archaeological sites. For example, in many areas the study of living peoples can provide important scientific information for archaeology; several investigators already have recognized such research potential among contemporary Anglo (Henderson 1976; Price et al. 1975), black (G. Fritz 1975), and Indian (Doelle 1976) groups. The uses of living groups, especially in historical sites research, is discussed and exemplified by Hickman in Chapter 20. In Chapter 19 Grady also illustrates the scientific values obtainable from study of contemporary communities. In addition, examples of undisturbed environments, paleontological deposits, and other environmental resources may in some cases contain information of considerable importance to archaeology.

Finally, we point out that sometimes the materials in archaeological sites, because of content or location, furnish valuable data to fields beyond archaeology and anthropology. In the lower Mississippi Valley, for example, Paleo-Indian and Archaic deposits have helped geologists to establish minimal ages for the formation of alluvial surfaces (e.g., Saucier 1974). The significance of archaeological resources to other sciences is ably discussed by Dixon in Chapter 21.

Undeniably, when the broadest conception of research potential is applied to archaeological sites, none would fail to be significant (Moratto 1975b; Schiffer and House 1977). After all, as we have argued elsewhere (introduction to Part II), all sites have some research potential. Furthermore, given our inability to predict the questions that will captivate the archaeologists of the future, we are again forced to conclude that all sites may be significant, and equally so. It is true that all sites are significant in both of these senses; but the stubborn fact remains that as a result of our recommendations some sites may be preserved, others excavated, and still others destroyed. While we can recommend that a representative sample of sites be preserved for the future (Lipe 1974), we had better provide alternatives for the many situations when that preferred option is not feasible. In short, there is no escape from the certainty that in a management framework some sites are more significant than others. If we, as archaeologists, fail to find ways of evaluating research potential and translating it, along with other types of significance, into sound recommendations, then decisions affecting the destiny of sites will assuredly be made on other, less satisfactory grounds.

## HISTORICAL SIGNIFICANCE

According to Scovill, Gordon, and Anderson (1972) and Moratto (1975b), archaeological resources are said to be historically significant if

> they provide a typical or well-preserved example of a prehistoric culture, historic tribe, period of time, or category of human activity... [or] if they can be associated with a specific individual event or aspect of history [or prehistory] [Scovill, Gordon, and Anderson 1972:19–20].

This definition is necessarily broad and, in some respects, overlaps with scientific and public significance (the latter to be presented shortly). Nevertheless, one can certainly think of many sites that could be considered historically significant by one of the above criteria but that might have little research potential. Hickman in Chapter 20 illustrates the criterion of representatives as applied to historical sites.

Schoenwetter, Gaines, and Weaver (1973) add another criterion for evaluating historical significance. They suggest that a site may attain significance, at least with respect to the history of archaeology, if many prominent investigators have worked there. It is worthwhile keeping this criterion in mind, even though it is likely to be invoked infrequently.

## ETHNIC SIGNIFICANCE

According to Moratto (1975b), "An archaeological entity which has religious, mythological, social or other special importance for a discrete population is said to be ethnically significant [p. 5]." By this definition, of course, ethnic significance overlaps somewhat with historical significance, but that is of little concern. Ethnic significance has been overlooked in much of previous conservation archaeology; today, however, with the heightened awareness of many groups to their cultural heritage as revealed in archaeological sites, the investigator ignores ethnic significance only at great peril. Determination of ethnic significance requires consultation with groups who occupied a site, descendants of such groups, and also groups who presently own or live near the sites under consideration. The latter criterion should be taken seriously; sometimes an archaeological site is an appreciable source of pride for a nearby community (Bell and Gettys n.d.). A potential problem is that archaeologists might not have the ability to define what is ethnically significant, and the suggestion they do smacks of some ethnocentrism. The problem of ethnic significance must therefore be addressed cautiously. Grady in Chapter 19 furnishes a nice example of how ethnic significance may be recognized (see also Rohn and Smith 1972).

## PUBLIC SIGNIFICANCE

The area of public significance includes, but is not limited to, the use of archaeological sites to educate the public about the past and the ways it is studied; the use of research findings to enrich our present existence; the use of archaeological information by industry for practical applications; the use of objects, ruins, and stabilized or restored structures for public exhibit and enjoyment; and benefits to the local economy that result from tourism attracted by archaeological exhibits (Moratto 1975:6–7). The concept of public significance strikes close to the ultimate purposes for doing archaeology; we would do well to consider these criteria more often if we expect society to continue to support our purely scientific efforts. Grady (Chapter 19) and especially Dixon (Chapter 21) have more thoughts on public significance.

## LEGAL SIGNIFICANCE

The Federal government has kindly set forth criteria by which legal significance pursuant to the Historic Site Preservation Act of 1966 may be determined. Moratto (1975b:2) has exerpted the relevant statements from the *Federal Register* (January 25, 1974):

> The quality of significance in American history, architecture, archaeology, and culture is present in districts, sites, buildings, structures, and objects of State and local importance that possess integrity of location, design, setting, materials, workmanship, feeling and association and:
>
> (1)   That are associated with events that have made a significant contribution to the broad patterns of our history; or
>
> (2)   That are associated with the lives of persons significant in our past; or
>
> (3)   That embody the distinctive characteristics of a type, period, method of construction, or that represent the work of a master, or that possess high artistic values, or that represent a significant and distinguishable entity whose components may lack individual distinction; or
>
> (4)   *That have yielded, or may be likely to yield, information important in prehistory or history* [p. 3369; emphasis added].

These paragraphs define the criteria used to assess legal significance in compliance with Executive Order 11593, the National Environmental Policy Act (NEPA), and the Archaeological and Historic Conservation Act of 1974 (Moratto 1975b), and to determine the eligibility of sites for nomination to the National Register of Historic Places.

The criteria for establishing legal significance are not without difficulties or controversy. As can be readily noted, for example, Item 4 is so broad that it excludes no site, while Items 1, 2, and 3 bear only on historical or public significance. It is no wonder that recent attempts by some federal agencies to turn the National Register into a planning tool (see King, this volume, Chapter 5), contrary to its obvious preservationist design, are meeting with considerable resistance from the many thoughtful archaeologists who note that the eligibility criteria are simply unworkable in an enlightened research and management context (see Grady and Lipe 1976; McGimsey 1972a; Raab and Klinger n.d.). At the time of this writing, the relationships between legal and other kinds of significance and the function of the National Register are among the most hotly debated topics in conservation archaeology, with no apparent resolutions anywhere in sight (see McMillan *et al.* 1977).

## MONETARY SIGNIFICANCE

In their otherwise exemplary guidelines for implementing NEPA with respect to archaeological resources Scovill, Gordon, and Anderson (1972) included as one kind of significance the monetary value of archaeological resources. The monetary value

> should be calculated by a competent professional archaeologist, as the amount of funds required to cover all significant archaeological data (cultural and environmental) using the most current methodology, technology, and theory available. This cultural inventory should provide the factual basis for this estimate [p. 22].

Because it is impossible for any site to be excavated in such a manner that all modern techniques, methods, and theories are applied to retrieve all significant information, this measure of significance is untenable. For this reason and others the concept of monetary significance is now discredited (House and Schiffer 1975b; Moratto 1975b; Raab and Klinger n.d.). Unfortunately, in many cases monetary significance is given primacy by those submitting proposals, and those awarding contracts. Such estimates are falling into disuse—though they still have some limited utility in formulating mitigation proposals (see Grady, Chapter 19). We mention the concept strictly as a historical curiosity.

## CONCLUSION

As of 1976 we are still some distance away from reaching total agreement on the major varieties of archaeological significance and the criteria for use in evaluating specific resources. Even so, the basis of a sound framework for assessing scientific significance is in the making. Unless its development is compromised by overzealous archaeobureaucrats or lazy archaeologists seeking simplistic means for evaluating sites, one can expect that the concept of scientific significance will continue to provoke creative research and deep reflections on the nature of archaeological data. Other types of significance are perhaps a bit easier to assess, but nowhere do we see a place for cookbook approaches. Public significance, above all, requires that we grapple with the value of our work to the society that supports it. Because our assessments may lead to practical actions, the handling of significance will sometimes give us pleasure, sometimes give us pain. We suspect, however, that it will seldom be boring.

# 18

# An Approach to Assessing Scientific Significance

MICHAEL B. SCHIFFER
JOHN H. HOUSE

Although few investigators realize it, the practice of archaeology has always involved a concept of significance. That only some regions are investigated, only some sites excavated, and only some classes of data recovered implies that criteria of significance are being employed. Seldom, however, are those criteria made explicit. The passage of the National Environmental Policy Act (NEPA) and other legislation affecting cultural resources necessitates that archaeologists now take a less casual approach to defining and assessing scientific significance. Only by developing a consistent framework for evaluating the research potential of sites and areas will it become possible to formulate responsible management recommendations.

Not surprisingly, it is in the context of cultural resource management studies that the complex topic of significance is for the first time receiving serious attention. Although we are still a respectable distance away from resolving the many issues surrounding the concept of significance and its applications, some progress is evident. In this chapter we shall report on how scientific significance was defined and assessed by the Cache River Archeological Project, an intensive field study performed by the Arkansas Archeological Survey in northeastern Arkansas for the Army Corps of Engineers (Schiffer and House 1975b; this volume, Chapters 14 and 23).

It is now generally agreed that archaeological resources acquire scientific significance when their systematic study may be expected to help resolve current research problems (Goodyear 1975a; House and Schiffer 1975b; McMillan *et al.* n.d.; Moratto 1975b; Raab 1976c; Raab and Klinger n.d.; Scovill, Gordon, and Anderson 1972; Schiffer and House n.d.). In this framework the significance of resources is evaluated with respect to *timely* and *specific* research questions. Although this definition forms the foundation for handling scientific significance, in itself it provides little insight into the *process* of effecting a match between specific questions and specific resources—and this is the central problem in cultural resource management studies at all levels (Lipe 1974; Reid 1973, 1975).

The "new archaeology" of the 1960s recognized the shortcomings of implicit approaches to handling significance and recommended more candor in describing research procedures and selection of relevant data (e.g., J. N. Hill 1972; Watson, LeBlanc, and Redman 1971). Their solution, which inexplicably failed to recognize the need to justify choice of the problem itself, fosters the curious belief that data from any site—if sufficiently coaxed with sophisticated analytic techniques—can reveal their secrets on any question. This formulation is unsatisfactory, from a practical as well as a methodological standpoint. For, if all sites are equivalent, then there can be no basis for assessing relative significance. Without such assessments, one cannot generate viable management recommendations. While the new archaeologists can be applauded for their desire to promote long-needed intersubjective verifiability in archaeology, they must be faulted for not going far enough and especially for obscuring the fact that, with respect to specific questions, not all sites are equal in research potential (Sullivan 1976).

It would be desirable to begin the assessment process with a list of outstanding research questions and priorities for an area, framed within an explicit regional research design (Raab and Klinger n.d.). One could then pursue various investigations to determine the applicability of specific questions to the resources being considered. The availability of up-to-date regional research designs can indeed enhance the assessment process. Unfortunately, very few have been written—although that is beginning to change (e.g., Goodyear 1975a; Grady 1976). In the near future, however, most projects will continue to labor without benefit of a regional research design. This handicap may be partially overcome if previous contract investigations or other work have succeeded in outlining research domains (see Canouts, this volume, Chapter 9). Where earlier contract work has not been done or was done inadequately, the investigator will ordinarily draw upon a variety of available lines of information for identifying research questions, including literature searches and discussions with other archaeologists interested in the area. In the Cache project, for example, 7 years of previous work by Dan Morse in the northeastern Arkansas region provided an extensive backlog of research questions of many sorts.

We begin our presentation by defining four major types of archaeological research questions—thus delimiting major kinds of scientific significance. Although the present rendering of question types differs slightly from the treatment in the Cache project report (see also Schiffer and House n.d.), the ideas and arguments are similar.

## SUBSTANTIVE SIGNIFICANCE

In all parts of the globe archaeologists strive to describe and explain the events and processes that occurred in the past. The questions that orient those inquiries are substantive questions; they relate to particular times and places and are known as ideographic. For example, why was agriculture adopted in the southeastern United States? What kind of social organization characterized Dalton adaptations in eastern Arkansas? Why was northeastern Arkansas apparently abandoned during the middle Archaic? Substantive questions encompass a vast array of topics and crosscut both culture-historical and most processual research interests.

As conservation archaeologists, our problem is to provide a framework for assessing the degree of fit between questions and resources. Although it may come as a surprise to some investigators, especially those seemingly intent on inferring marital residence patterns wherever there are archaeological remains, not all sites yield information for answering all substantive questions. The sooner we find ways of predicting when we can and cannot reasonably expect research effort to be rewarded with substantive results, the sooner we will have a responsible basis for assigning priorities to research problems and therefore assessing significance.

By illuminating the process of matching questions and resources, the concept of *analytic unit* from behavioral archaeology (Reid 1973; Reid, Schiffer, and Neff 1975; Schiffer 1976) provides the key to measuring substantive research potential. Analytic units are deposits or sets of deposits of archaeological materials produced by specified cultural and noncultural formation processes. In the present framework, a substantive question can be answered if the analytic units it requires (or acceptable approximations) can be operationalized on the given archaeological resources. When such units cannot be identified, or are very difficult to identify, substantive research potential with respect to a particular question or class of questions is diminished (though it can rarely be said to be totally absent).

The flexibility and usefulness of this definition of substantive significance is easily illustrated. Suppose that an investigator wishes to study the development of chiefdom societies in an area. The major analytic unit that must be operationalized is *refuse produced by the settlements organized at a chiefdom level*. A more exact statement of the problem would lead to a more precise delineation of the relevant analytic units. An example of a more fine-grained problem is whether or not middle Mississippian villages in the Western Lowlands of northeastern Arkansas were abandoned suddenly, under violent conditions. A test of the alternative abandonment hypotheses requires in part the examination of *de facto refuse produced by the last occupants of these villages*. In the latter case, if sites had been badly pothunted, plowed deeply, or farmed erosively, one might suspect that it would be difficult to identify and analyze deposits of de facto refuse. Under such circumstances one might justifiably predict that there is a diminished potential to answer questions about abandonment conditions.

Unfortunately, archaeologists with a research problem in hand are rarely able to specify exactly what analytic units they need operationalized in order to solve it, and others with resources to evaluate are seldom able to provide a catalogue of readily available analytic units. Furthermore, in few instances does it boil down to a clear-cut presence or absence of research potential. Given the presently undeveloped state of archaeological theory and method and the chronic dearth of information about resources in most study areas, we must work with varying degrees of certainty as to whether or not particular analytic units can be operationalized. Determining these probabilities usually requires the expenditure of considerable research effort, examining and probing the resources to discover minimally just what materials are present and in what sorts of deposits. Rarely is it possible to make these determinations without research effort (Schiffer and House n.d.). Examples from the Cache project illustrate how the process of problem-oriented research aids in assessing substantive research potential.

An important area of current research in northeastern Arkansas concerns the nature of early Archaic, or Dalton, settlement patterns (Goodyear 1974; Morse 1973a). Given this regional research context, it was important for the Cache project to learn if the surface collections obtained from early Archaic sites could provide information relevant to the ongoing settlement studies. In order to answer settlement pattern questions, one needs to operationalize the analytic unit *undisturbed deposits made by the same group in different locations in the environment*. At the outset of fieldwork it was apparent that plowing, collecting behavior (by relic hunters, amateurs, and professional archaeologists), and subsequent occupations had modified the archaeological record of Dalton systems. Thus it was not known if the available analytic unit *Dalton plus other deposits that have been plowed and collected* could still be used to answer settlement pattern questions.

In order to assess the potential of Cache Basin sites to contribute to settlement studies, we had to learn if the available analytic units could serve as acceptable approximations of the more suitable ones. This was accomplished by a provisional test of Morse's (1971) Dalton settlement pattern hypothesis. Surface collections were obtained from 22 Dalton-bearing sites. The chipped- and ground-stone artifacts were classified using House's (1975b) functional typology, and the more frequently occurring types were factor-analyzed (House, Klinger, and Schiffer 1975). Eight factors were produced, some of which seemed interpretable behaviorally. The results, while not completely compatible with the Morse hypothesis (which had postulated two kinds of sites with simple patterns of artifact differentiation), were not definitive enough to allow for its rejection; nevertheless, on the basis of our findings Schiffer (1975h) offered an alternative settlement model and reinterpreted major site evidence bearing on Dalton lifeways in northeastern Arkansas. Despite the inconclusiveness of the test, sufficient intersite variability of the commonly occurring Dalton artifacts was disclosed to suggest that some further potential is present in the Cache Basin for investigating the nature of early Archaic settlement and perhaps later systems as well.

Other research designs implemented by the Cache project were directly related to assessing substantive research potential. The testing program in particular was geared to determine the presence or absence of intact occupation surfaces and the degree to which pollen and other organic materials were preserved.

The Cache project demonstrates that we cannot now, or perhaps ever, assess the substantive significance of archaeological resources mechanically. Matching operationalizable analytic units to appropriate research questions is itself dependent upon the conduct of innovative, problem-oriented research. Thus, while the framework of behavioral archaeology, and particularly the concept of analytic unit defined in terms of formation processes, provides a way for conceptualizing and attacking the problem of relating resources to research questions, it does not relieve the investigator of the need to probe the research potential (see Schiffer and House n.d.).

## ANTHROPOLOGICAL SIGNIFICANCE

Another major area of significance, closely tied to some processual research questions, may be termed anthropological significance. Here investigators must discern the extent to which study of specific resources might be expected to contribute to testing general anthropological principles, especially those relating to processes of long-term culture change and ecological adaptation (e.g., F. T. Plog 1974b; Zubrow 1975). Assessment of anthropological significance requires familiarity with a range of nomothetic questions originating beyond the regional context of research. The questions that illustrate the anthropological domain include: Why is there variability in degrees of sedentism among communities? What are the conditions that favor development of ascribed status? What are the relationships between seasonality of resources, procurement subsystems, and technology? Under what circumstances will a band become a tribe; or a tribe a chiefdom; or a chiefdom a state?

One area of anthropological research potential that was tentatively identified in the Cache Basin concerns abandonment phenomena. The general causes of regional abandonment are poorly understood at present (e.g., Culbert 1973), and the Cache Basin, with its several major hiatuses in occupation (e.g., middle Archaic, late Mississippian), seems to provide a setting where they could be studied profitably. To *demonstrate* this research potential, however, would require assembly of relevant abandonment models and testing to determine if the requisite analytic units could be identified. Unfortunately, we were unable to complete the assessment process.

## SOCIAL SCIENTIFIC SIGNIFICANCE

Closely related to, and perhaps not distinct from, anthropological significance is social scientific significance. The latter category of nomothetic questions is found in the context of social science generally and thus may also include specifically anthropological questions. In the Cache Basin it was learned that chippable stone resources were generally procured from adjacent areas of the Ozark Plateau on the west and from Crowley's Ridge on the east. Perhaps because lithic resources were scarce, they were often reused in complex ways. The topic of reuse processes, specifically recycling, is one of current interest in economics and environmental studies (e.g., Smith 1972). Because various reuse processes occurred over a long span of time in the Cache Basin (and continue today), it is conceivable that general principles could be illuminated by careful analysis of lithic artifacts in the light of available recycling models. Although we did not attempt to ferret out those models, or to specify relevant analytic units, we did call attention to this area of inquiry and alerted future investigators to the need for probing this potential.

## TECHNICAL, METHODOLOGICAL, AND THEORETICAL SIGNIFICANCE

Not only must assessments of significance use as a frame of reference substantive archaeological questions and general questions derived from broad disciplinary contexts, but they must treat general questions relating to archaeological theory, method, and technique. The conduct of archaeological inquiry, like that in all sciences, is a ramifying activity. When an investigator raises a substantive question and designs research to answer it, certain analytic units and data within them will be specified as relevant. Unfortunately, few substantive problems of a nontrivial nature can be raised for which an already available set of recovery, analytic, and interpretive tools exist. Thus, in acquiring, analyzing, and interpreting the relevant data, new problems, requiring other research designs, are often discovered. The perceptive investigator will anticipate or rapidly become aware of these additional problems and carry out subsidiary research activities to solve them. These adjunct research designs may involve experimentation, computer simulation, literature searches in nonarchaeological fields, ethnoarchaeology, and a variety of other activities that superficially bear little relationship to the original substantive problem. Nevertheless, these subsidiary research projects are of considerable importance, for they increase the probability that the substantive research can be brought to fruition.

The tension zone in substantive research between the known and the unknown in general archaeological theory, method, and technique is the fertile ground for innovation. The archaeological literature documents time and again the process of significant contributions to general topics arising from an ostensibly substantive investigation. Archaeologists should not be surprised that, even in their own field, necessity is often the mother of invention. From the perspective of having to assess this kind of research potential, it is noteworthy that certain kinds of questions and innovations are more likely to arise when some archaeological resources rather than others are being studied. We believe that it is possible and necessary to assess the probabilities that various technical, methodological, and theoretical advances are likely to occur during investigations of a specific body of archaeological resources. This formulation adds to the concept of scientific significance a long-overdue component and leads to a better appreciation for the integrity of the diverse strands of archaeological inquiry (see also Reid, Schiffer, and Rathje 1975).

One broad area of technical and methodological significance documented in the Cache Basin deals with archaeological survey and the nature of surface artifact collections. Because some parts of the basin are still in woodland, there is considerable potential for developing and applying new techniques of finding sites where, for all practical purposes, the ground is obscured. Similarly, because most sites are under cultivation and also have been repeatedly picked over by artifact collectors, considerable incentive exists to study the effects of plowing and collecting behavior in order to provide a sound base for interpreting material distributions and intersite variability. These studies could easily involve both ethnoarchaeological and experimental research. Although none of these survey problems is unique to the Cache Basin, the success of future work there does depend in part on solving them, and thus the research potential is demonstrable.

Relative temporal ordering of sites is a methodological problem of long-standing concern in the eastern United States. It is not surprising that until very recently it was in the Mississippi Valley, and not in the American Southwest with its tree-ring dating, that major innovations and applications of seriation methods have taken place (e.g., Philips, Ford, and Griffin 1951). Unfortunately, in the Cache Basin (and probably elsewhere in the Southeast) most sites are the product of multiple occupations and cannot be reliably seriated by standard techniques. There is, therefore, considerable potential for evolving more sophisticated methods for establishing relative temporal control. Recognition of this research potential during the initial stages of the Cache project led to the development of one possible technique, called *arrangement,* to accomplish this task (Schiffer 1975c).

Other features of the Cache Basin archaeological resource base yield ample opportunities for developing a variety of theoretical models, particularly those concerned with cultural formation processes (cf. Schiffer 1976). Schiffer (1975d) has pointed out, for example, that, theoretically, differences in duration of site occupation could lead to important quantitative and *qualitative* differences in assemblages—even when the activities carried out were the same. There are many small sites in the Cache Basin of presumed short occupation, where the postulated effects of occupation span could substantially contribute to assemblage variability. In any intersite comparisons, such as would be required for settlement–subsistence analysis, one would have to control for these factors. Investigation of this and related theoretical questions would lead to development of quantitative models and to experimental simulation of formation processes. In short, because of the nature of the deposits in the Cache Basin, and the range of substantive problems that one is likely to attempt solving there, certain theoretical problems will have to be solved relating to the explanation of interassemblage variability.

Although it is fruitful to view technical, methodological, and theoretical questions as adjuncts or ancillary studies in the pursuit of substantive results, it is evident in the recent history of archaeology that these studies form bodies of knowledge that are developing in their own right, not wholly subservient to substantive goals. For the first time archaeology is beginning to witness the sustained emergence of essentially full-time methodological, theoretical, and technical specialists and the cumulative growth of general principles. As a result, it is now possible in many cases to pinpoint significance for these kinds of questions independently of the substantive potential of the resources. For example, in a small project carried out in the Ozarks near Batesville, Arkansas, the investigators were able to take several surficial Archaic lithic scatters, judged deficient in potential for contributing directly to most substantive questions, and pursue promising experimental studies in lithic technology (Spears 1975) and site survey techniques (Baker 1975; Claassen and Spears 1975). We should not eschew recognition of these types of significance just because they often lack the flash of many substantive topics. Not only can such methodological, theoretical, and technical investigations make widely applicable general contributions, but ultimately the existence of those research questions makes it possible for every project to advance the state of the discipline.

This brief treatment we hope illustrates the nature of technical, methodological, and theoretical significance and will perhaps lead other investigators to devise rigorous ways to assess it. Although the Cache project was somewhat successful in outlining areas of research potential with regard to these questions, we are not satisfied that we can yet formulate a general process for making these assessments. Although sites doubtless vary in their potential to lead to technical, methodological, and theoretical breakthroughs, it is far from easy to evaluate this potential; this is an area that needs further exploration.

## DISCUSSION

At this point the critical reader may wonder if perhaps our treatment of scientific significance has really gone beyond the practical implications of the new archaeologists' formulations. For, if a site decisively lacks substantive research potential, its study may still lead to innovations in technique, method, and theory. If that is so, then all sites are significant—because their scientific study may help resolve some research problem. It is true that we have returned, albeit circuitously, to the unsatisfying realization that all sites are significant; yet we have also provided a way to dismount uninjured from the horns of this dilemma. To get beyond this practical impasse, our approach to significance assessment requires that we assign relative priorities to research questions and, by extension, evaluate the sites where these questions may be tackled. This is achieved first by identifying for all resources the range of research questions in the substantive, anthropological, social scientific, technical, methodological, and theoretical domains that can be answered. Then, by considering where else these same questions may be answerable, one determines relative priorities and significance. If, for example, it turns out that studies at a particular site are likely to lead only to experiments in lithic technology, which could also be pursued in relation to a host of other sites, then the conclusion is justified that the relative significance of the site in question is small. By this process one can place relative values on resources and go beyond the rudimentary insight that all sites are significant. To be sure, this approach for determining scientific significance is far from streamlined, but why should we expect significance assessments to be somehow easier than other archaeological research activities?

As cultural resource managers refine and apply various approaches to measuring research potential, especially substantive significance, there is a considerable danger that the research actually undertaken, for environmental impact statement work and mitigation, will come to deal with only those questions that have a high probability of being answered. If this occurs, and the beginnings of this process already are painfully evident, then we shall certainly cut off great sources of intellectual variety and innovation as pedestrian and safe research proliferates. The important role played by serendipity in all sciences and our limited ability to predict success in research efforts should make us somewhat reticent to push our applications of the concept of significance too far. While we do need to evaluate research potential and sometimes play it safe, we also need to take calculated risks for the vitality of archaeology. To the extent that we can predict research potential we should do so. But let us not forget that the true frontiers of knowledge in science are likely to lie considerably beyond current standards of what is feasible.

The concept of scientific significance perhaps has no rivals in cultural resource management for creating knotty practical problems. In cultural resource management work as a whole, then, one can document the potential to investigate more fully the nature of scientific significance and ways to assess it. The Cache project, as an example of such research, allowed us to experiment with ways to identify substantive significance and to define formerly unrecognized research domains relating to technical, methodological, and theoretical questions. We expect that continued refinement of the concept of scientific significance through specific investigations will lead not only to more enlightened management of the archaeological resource base, because of the more informed recommendations for mitigation that reliable significance assessment makes possible, but also to considerable advances in archaeological method and theory as we grapple with the nature of our data and our imperfect ways of reconstructing the past.

## ACKNOWLEDGEMENTS

We thank Albert C. Goodyear, Mark Grady, and David R. Wilcox for helpful ideas and suggestions.

# Significance Evaluation and the Orme Reservoir Project

MARK A. GRADY

The proposed Orme Reservoir is one part of a Bureau of Reclamation program to divert and distribute water from the Colorado River to central and southern Arizona. The dam is to be located at the confluence of the Salt and Verde rivers and will flood approximately 24,000 acres of bottomland along both rivers (Map 19.1). In order to fulfill bureau responsibilities under the National Historic Preservation Act of 1966, the National Environmental Policy Act of 1969, Executive Order 11593, and attendant regulations, the Cultural Resource Management Section of the Arizona State Museum was contracted to conduct an intensive archaeological survey of the project area. Completed in 1972, this survey located 204 archaeological features representing 178 sites. The cultural resources ranged from prehistoric Hohokam–Salado manifestation dating as early as A.D. 100 to contemporary Anglo and Indian farming and ranching sites.

The final report on the archaeology of the study area (Canouts 1975) was accepted by the Bureau of Reclamation several years after completion of the fieldwork. The chapter on cultural resource significance in the Orme Reservoir report was originally written by me and was subsequently partly revised by others in the Cultural Resource Management Section to comply with later changes in contract requirements. This chapter is a synthesis and update of the significance evaluation developed for that report.

## THE CONCEPT OF SIGNIFICANCE

It should be self-evident that the significance of cultural remains may be evaluated using many different frames of reference. Because of the varied interests of archaeological researchers, the developing nature of the discipline, and the project-specific problems related to responsible management planning, significance

259

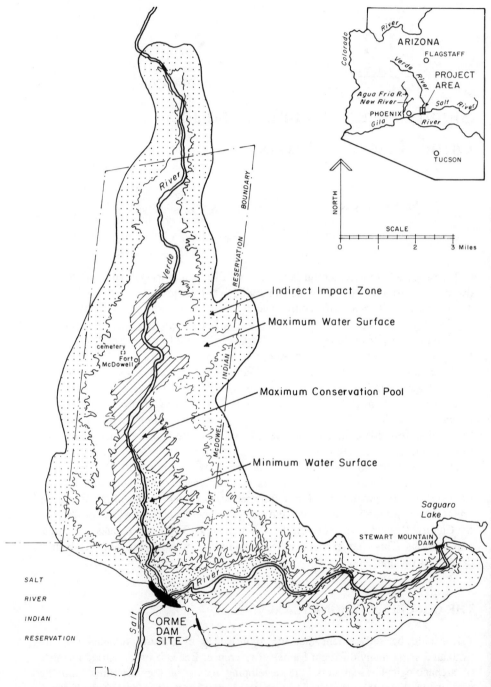

**Map 19.1.** Proposed Orme Reservoir project, areas of archaeological impact.

cannot be viewed as a static property inherent within archaeological resources. There is no universally applicable set of significance criteria that can be used in the same way that determinations of such factors as site type, cultural affinity, or temporal period are made. This point has been emphasized in a number of recent sources (Lipe 1974; McMillan, Anderson, Davis, Grady, Lipe, Pierson, and Weide n.d.; Moratto 1975b; Schiffer and House 1975a, 1975c). The Orme statement, however, was developed with reference to the Scovill, Gordon, and Anderson guidelines for writing archaeological impact reports (1972). Although the authors of these latter guidelines recognized the need for retaining flexibility in defining archaeological significance, they proposed four general categories under which significance should be considered: historical, scientific, social, and monetary.

## SIGNIFICANCE OF THE ORME RESERVOIR
## EXTINCT CULTURAL RESOURCES

The proposed dam runoff structures and reservoir are slated to affect over 40 square miles of the drainage basins formed by the lower Verde and Salt rivers. These drainages represent in microcosm essentially the full range of environmental and sedentary prehistoric cultural phenomena found in this region and are particularly important because they provide a geographically definable area within which the relationships among these phenomena can be studied. Prehistoric Hohokam–Salado cultural remains include a variety of natural resource exploitation areas, habitation localities, water control features, and other manifestations. Protohistoric Apachean, Piman, and Yavapai use of the impact area is known. The drainages were important foci for early American military activities as well as Anglo and Mexican mining, farming, and ranching. In the early twentieth century the Fort McDowell Indian Reservation was established, and it serves as a home for the Yavapai and Maricopa today. In addition, other parts of the study area are still being used for Anglo farming and ranching, as well as for recreational purposes.

### Historical Significance

Historical significance is equated with particular cultures, periods, lifeways, and events that transpired in the study area (Scovill *et al.* 1972:13). As will be seen, this definition is closely related to scientific significance, and the discussions under these two categories overlap somewhat.

The Orme data are relevant to a great range of historical questions, only a representative sample of which was discussed in the report. With respect to prehistoric cultural resources, emphasis was placed on filling in the gaps in regional culture history. The problems associated with a possible Hohokam expansion between A.D. 1 to 700 and contraction between A.D. 900 to 1100 were posed as viable considerations. The changes in lifeways reputed to have resulted from intrusion of the Salado at approximately A.D. 1100 were also suggested as worthy of evaluation.

One of the most important protohistoric lines of inquiry has to do with the question of whether a Hohokam–Pima continuum can be documented. A great deal of unverified speculation has centered around the proposition that the Pima Indians, who occupied the Salt and Gila basins of Arizona at the time of European contact, were direct descendants of the prehistoric Hohokam, who had inhabited the region several hundred years previously. This is of considerable consequence to the Pima tribe as well as to anthropologists. Knowledge of the existence of such a continuum would explain many phenomena present in contemporary Pima culture previously attributed to historical parallelism or proposed continuity. It would place in proper perspective the caliber of overall aboriginal heritage present within the study area, as well as elsewhere in the Pima cultural area. Such study could at the same time define the relationship between the Pima and the later introduced Apache, Yavapai, and Maricopa. The early history of these latter peoples in the area is poorly documented, and the amount of influence nonindigenous aboriginal adaptive strategies have had on the Pima groups is a relevant problem.

Considerable historical significance is also attached to the Fort McDowell cemetery. The cemetery area, slated for inundation, is still being used by the Fort McDowell Indians. Among the interments is Carlos Montezuma, an Indian doctor highly revered by the local inhabitants.

Other locales of considerable historical significance include the Fort McDowell site complex, Reno Road (a throughway from Fort McDowell to the Tonto Basin to the north), a set of nineteenth-century limekilns, Jones' Ditch (an extensive water control system built in the 1880s), the two extant Indian communities, and more recent Euramerican manifestations. Many of these sites, although of considerable historical value, relate to other factors of significance as well. For example, investigation of the Fort McDowell complex or Reno Road would integrate the concepts of scientific and historical significance. Study of the Indian communities would be a similar situation. The contemporary cultural manifestation on both reservations not only are historically significant entities but also characterize the latest in the development of aboriginal human–land relationships. Thus, the reservations themselves are of importance as they relate to local heritage. They also represent anthropologically relevant phenomena as the end product of changing adaptation to the environment through time.

## Scientific Significance

This category includes a broad set of values characterized by the overall goal of making generalized statements about cultural processes. The majority of the report was devoted to elaborating upon scientific research concerns. The survey data were discussed within a framework that emphasized the community as an integrative mechanism within the study area. This was the main thrust for generating mitigative research questions. However, other areas of research potential were also recognized in the data, and these were included as viable avenues of inquiry. A general cultural-ecological perspective was outlined, as were a settlement–subsistence orientation and a diachronic approach emphasizing culture change. Specific research recommendations included considerations of Hohokam–Salado growth and development with respect to a number of models applicable to regional adaptation. These models considered such variables as: environmental resources, subsistence, and carrying capacity; social, political, and economic organization; and the changes in these variables through time. A case was developed for the impact area being of more scientific significance than the sum of its individual archaeological resources because it contained all of the cultural and environmental factors required for implementing such studies. This case was supported by comparing the resources of the Orme project area with other known regions in southern and central Arizona where comprehensive information on the archaeological resource base was available. Comparisons were made with the cultural inventory of the Santa Rosa Wash area, south of the proposed Orme Reservoir (Canouts 1972); the Painted Rocks Reservoir survey, southwest of the project area (Wasley and Johnson 1965); a partial survey of the Gila River Indian Reservation, also located south of the Orme impact zone (Wood 1971, 1972a, 1972b); a recent study of the lower New River and middle Agua Fria River drainages, both northwest of the damsite (Dittert 1975); a discussion of the archaeology of the upper Agua Fria River (Gumerman and Johnson 1971), due north of the reservoir area; and data from an Arizona State University cultural inventory of the Salt River Indian Reservation, which is partially included in the project area (Dittert and Laughlin n.d.). The results of these comparisons suggested that the proposed Orme Reservoir locality represented one of the few remaining regions where almost the full range of known Hohokam–Salado cultural manifestations still existed in a relatively undisturbed environmental context. Although the information potential of the Orme area resources may be equaled or surpassed with regard to the study of specific problems, there is no location or combination of locations that could provide the quality of data applicable to the range of problems discussed in the report. Thus the lower Verde and Salt drainages are particularly significant in containing regional-level information that is essentially unavailable elsewhere in the Hohokam–Salado cultural area.

Similarly the protohistoric and historical cultural remains are important to the comprehensive understanding of regional adaptation, given changing cultural values. The Fort McDowell complex in particular represents a unique opportunity to study a well-documented military establishment from the perspective of introduced social and technological change and its impact on local behavior through time.

## Social Significance

Social significance refers to the benefits that the public as a whole would derive from the detailed study and conservation of the potentially affected archaeological resources. This is an important factor, and one which has been slighted by archaeologists in the past. Archaeology, by its very nature, includes a commitment to disseminate archaeological data to the public. Conversely, it is only when the public can be made fully aware of the importance and potential of archaeological resources that responsible management of these resources can be formulated and implemented.

More intensive long-term study of the cultural manifestations documented by this survey could at the very least provide a more accurate picture for the public of past behavioral patterns. The preserving, developing, and managing for public use of a core of representative sites would not only be one provision for permanently protecting these sites against future disturbance but would at the same time provide an educational facility informing visitors of the history of the area. Such facilities, properly organized, could make residents aware of their place in the legacy of the region and could indicate the value of surrounding natural and cultural resources. Perhaps most importantly, such displays could explain how archaeology provides the means by which cultural-environmental adaptations found to be successful in the past can be applied to current situations. The potential economic assets of these endeavors should be kept in mind as well.

One of the most economically, socially, and educationally visible locations to preserve and develop is Fort McDowell. With so few examples of authentic military establishments in the Southwest readily accessible to the public, the reconstruction, stabilization, and commercial development of the fort and its immediate cultural surroundings would be a unique opportunity for the Fort McDowell Indian Reservation to capitalize on its cultural resources. No fort complex in the state has been systematically studied with a comprehensive problem orientation, and the long-range research potential at Fort McDowell represents one of the few remaining possibilities.

In addition to the fort proper, a series of adjacent historical and prehistoric remains provides an opportunity to excavate and develop a range of Euramerican and aboriginal sites. Such sites could collectively encompass the remains of much of the past human activity that took place in the proposed Orme Reservoir region. They might be studied and maintained as an example to the public of differential adaptive measures through time. Development would provide unique research opportunities while also involving tribal personnel in the examination, commercialization, and continued interpretation of the resources. The results could represent a long-term source of income for the Fort McDowell tribe while at the same time acquainting the Indians and other visitors with the importance of Fort McDowell and other nearby archaeological features.

The public could benefit from other aspects of the study of the past in the Orme Reservoir region as well. More intensive and long-term archaeological examination of the archaeological resources would provide a training ground for future professionals. In addition, such research could include active participation by the non-professional. The results of these endeavors, following analysis and publication, could become a part of museum displays and exhibits. Undoubtedly the exhibitions could be integrated with commercial plans to enhance the educational value and public attraction of any ancillary development.

## Monetary Significance

The Scovill *et al.* guidelines indicate that this value should be expressed as the estimated cost of responsible study of the potentially impacted resource base (1972:14). A number of professionals have taken issue with this view, claiming that financial worth cannot be used as a measure of resource significance (McMillan *et al.* n.d.; Moratto 1975b; Schiffer and House 1975b). Such a position has considerable merit. There is no way that the full range of significance associated with cultural resources can be converted into monetary figures. Not only are the intangible values associated with the aesthetics of cultural resources in their natural settings beyond quantification, but the same problems are recognized as applying to the monetary significance category as apply to any attempt to standardize other significance criteria. In other words, monetary significance is a reflection of the evolutionary state of the discipline and the research interests exhibited by those dealing with the resource base.

Although cost is thus a severely limited indicator of resource significance, an estimate of the funding required to conduct data study within a range of applicable research strategies is one quantifiable measure of the value of the resource base. Current trends seem to be moving away from an emphasis on cost–benefit ratios as the primary means of evaluating the worth of a land modification scheme (*Harvard Law Review* 1975), but decision makers are still considering cost as one aspect of the evaluation process, and no pragmatic cultural resource manager can ignore that fact. Archaeologists in specific, and environmentalists in general, are engaged in no more speculative an endeavor in attempting to quantify important aspects of environmental resources than are land alteration promoters, who use similar approaches to support the value of their projects.

Monetary considerations are particularly important with respect to the implementation of management activities, for even the most currently enlightened management policies require funding. Any decision made about managing cultural resources must take into account responsible estimates of the cost of that management activity. Thus, although monetary values must be related to legitimate archaeological needs in order to be meaningful, they are nonetheless necessary for all management procedures.

In the Orme report, monetary significance was computed by estimating the cost of total data study, given the range of potentially applicable research strategies outlined previously. This figure represented an idealized evaluation based on professional projection from the survey data. The cost of minimally acceptable mitigation of the potentially affected archaeological resources, in this case, was then derived from the former figure.

In order to insure that the evaluation process would be as explicit as possible, unit cost figures were developed on the basis of site categories and then applied to the complete data base. Efforts were made to compensate for the fact that the nature of archaeology and the archaeological record do not permit precise cost estimates to be made. The funding figures were therefore generated in order to allow for maximization of the data base information potential as recognized by the authors of the report. These procedures are detailed in Chapter 24.

## SIGNIFICANCE OF THE ORME RESERVOIR EXTANT CULTURAL RESOURCES

The discipline of archaeology is not solely concerned with the study of past cultural remains. Equally as relevant are studies of modern groups, particularly nonindustrial societies. Research of this caliber can be used to gather contemporary cultural data relevant to archaeological inquiry. As anthropologists, archaeologists look to extant communities to provide data for the generation of hypotheses and propositions related to the material correlates of extinct human behavior. Thus, the physical remains of indigenous populations represent an extremely important cultural resource base.

Any consideration of contemporary cultural manifestations as archaeological resources is ineluctably related to the people themselves. Cultural resource management studies, while explicitly directed toward assessment of the importance of threatened cultural remains, seldom take into account the adverse effect that major federal actions will have on the indigenous population. This is a failing that is particularly important in the West, where many land modification projects directly or indirectly influence the life-styles on Indian reservations. In situations like this, where Anglo attitudes toward technological development must be compromised with non-Anglo views concerning land management policies, accurate and responsible evaluations of the effects of land modification actions in terms of the indigenous groups should be obtained.

Both the Fort McDowell and the Salt River Indian reservations as cultural entities in themselves can be construed as important from this perspective. Fort McDowell in particular represents a situation in which a group of people are implementing their own land management practices and relating socially and economically, albeit peripherally, to more metropolitan areas of the Southwest. The importance of this interaction has not been assessed, but it can hardly be construed as unquantifiable. Tribal attitudes, standards, and concepts of change are only a few aspects of the Indian world view that could be elicited through proper anthropological-sociological analysis of reservation feeling about reservoir construction. As the building of Orme Dam will directly and indirectly affect both the Salt River and the Fort McDowell Indian reservations, an unbiased cultural impact study should be conducted that would document the positions and desires of involved parties. As suggested by Fawcett and Cleveland (1973:39) and implemented by McCall (1972), such studies could also provide guidelines for evaluating the trauma of forced change, thus indicating the most viable procedures for carrying out population relocation, should that become necessary.

As archaeologists, members of the Cultural Resource Management Section of the Arizona State Museum can evaluate the significance of the contemporary Fort

McDowell Reservation cultural manifestations and have even observed that current inhabitants are protecting these and older archaeological resources in the immediate area. As anthropologists, these same archaeologists have the expertise required to recognize that more detailed assessment of Indian attitudes toward the Orme Reservoir should be obtained. Such assessment, however, should be made by anthropological–sociological experts capable of properly eliciting this information.

## SUMMARY

This discussion has provided a partial synopsis of the historical, scientific, social, and monetary significance of the Orme Reservoir cultural resources. These resources have great potential for providing information pertinent to a variety of anthropological problems as well as more general public concerns. No attempt has been made to consider all factors for which the Orme data might be significant. Instead, a broad framework has been developed within which the cultural resources are demonstrated to be of major importance. As was emphasized in other parts of the report, however, the greatest significance of these resources is in their potential for future research and public use. There is no doubt that the Orme Reservoir cultural manifestations as a whole are irreplaceable, and the data available in the area simply no longer exist elsewhere in as complete a form.

## ACKNOWLEDGMENTS

Veletta Canouts and Lynn Teague are responsible for much of the quality of the original report, which is manifested in this chapter. Shortcomings, however, are a reflection of my biases alone.

# 20

# Problems of Significance: Two Case Studies of Historical Sites

PATRICIA PARKER HICKMAN

As contractors on environmental and historic preservation projects, archaeologists are sometimes asked to consider the research significance of historical sites. Two anthropologically based evaluations of historical sites are discussed here. In one study written records and oral testimony were used as the basis for a projection of the kinds of historical sites that could be expected in a California agricultural valley. This study emphasized preserving a sample of historical sites representative of all the ethnic and occupational groups who had contributed to the valley's history. The research significance of individual sites was to be considered in terms of each site's relationship to the sample. In the second example the history of a single ranch site in the southern California desert was studied within the social context of the region. Historical records were used to identify social and economic interactions that took place at the ranch and in the surrounding region. The analytic concept of social network was used in conjunction with a model taken from exchange theory in order to predict how developments in the surrounding region could have affected behavior at the ranch. This provided a basis for evaluating how the ranch could be used to test theory-based assumptions about relationships between regional and local sociocultural change.

## SIGNIFICANCE AS REPRESENTATIVENESS: SAN FELIPE

As part of the San Felipe Archaeological Study (see King and Hickman 1973; this volume, Chapter 26), I was responsible for dealing with the historical resources of the southern Santa Clara Valley, an area of about 60,000 acres, subject to indirect impacts as a result of a proposed water project. I was asked to ascertain what types of cultural resources from the historical period might exist in the area, how they

269

might be distributed, and what sorts of information contained in such resources might be pertinent to future research. I planned my study to include a survey of published and unpublished literature and interviews with people who knew about local history or who had been connected with key historic events, groups, or personalities. I was also concerned with the activities of local historical groups, planning agencies, and service organizations interested in historic preservation; I wanted to develop a mitigation plan that would integrate their concerns with those of the academic community.

A variety of interest groups were interested in historical properties in the Santa Clara Valley, and each group had its own perception of what historical properties were and why they were—or were not—significant. Predictably, the interests of various groups sometimes conflicted with one another and with what I, as an anthropologist, saw as important. What is important to members of a local historical society is not always relevant to an archaeologist, and vice versa. The interests of an architectural historian may work at cross-purposes to those of an anthropologist or historian. What is important to a project or program planner often hinges on what precisely is demanded of him or her by law and how much it will cost. In this welter of conflicting views it is possible to lose sight of one's own expertise and responsibility as an anthropologist and fall into a narrow historicity that attaches "significance" to historical properties only if they are the first, biggest, smallest, or best recorded of local historical phenomena.

During the summer of 1973 several groups in the Santa Clara Valley were in the process of making inventories of historical properties. Thus it was possible to describe the range of property types that they found interesting and worthy of preservation. I found, understandably enough, that the local programs emphasized the preservation of attractive, famous, locally unique, and visually outstanding properties. Some groups were using criteria recommended by local historical commissions. These criteria were both specific—for example, association with an architectural style, person, event, etc.—and general—for example, exemplification of "broad aspects of local history" or reflection of "larger patterns of California history." The specific criteria were overwhelmingly emphasized in the inventories. Choices were being made that (1) emphasized standing structures over sites, districts, and other less obvious entities, and (2) selected structures reflective of the more flattering aspects of local history, as construed by modern concerned groups. The homes, mills, schoolhouses, and public buildings selected tended to be those constructed and maintained with large amounts of money, and although these structures are of undoubted value to the community, they represent only a small segment of past human behavior—the behavior of the wealthy, successful segments of the community during various time periods. The record of less successful groups—migrant workers, tenant farmers, postmissionization Indians—might be lost if this bias continued. This loss would be unusually significant because it was just these groups that typically had not left extensive written documents. In such a situation an anthropologist has a special responsibility to identify and point out for preservation those historical properties that are "invisible" to the general public.

Some groups were working within the context of state standards. The California Environmental Quality Act, for example, mandates the preservation of historical resources representing the major periods of California history. This requirement was easily met in the general sense: A Victorian mansion is a property representative of the southern Santa Clara Valley in the 1880s. However, such a property does not by itself represent all major aspects of local history. The remains of a labor camp that housed orchard workers is also representative of the period, regardless of the facts that it may be unrecognizable to the general public and that it may be considered unimportant by local historical societies or even by the descendents of the workers themselves.

My review of current work, then, pointed out an important role for the anthropologist in identifying historical properties that were not otherwise being considered; it also revealed the need to assign significance to properties in terms that would be meaningful both to local government and to scholars interested in studying the area.

My data were obtained from standard library sources, local museums and archives, and interviews with descendents of pioneers and representatives of the various racial and ethnic groups of the area. I sought information about the life style of each social group that had lived or worked in the valley and about the potential distribution and nature of the archaeological sites left by such groups. This material was synthesized into a historical synopsis in order to distill the large body of data into a comprehensible form and to provide a basis for constructing a taxonomy of historical resources that might be found in the valley. The taxonomy was meant to include the whole range of local historical resources and to provide guidance to future inventory efforts toward greater representativeness.

I observed that the history of the area had been shaped in large part by the economic interplay of two factors: land use and systems of land ownership and control. Different social and economic groups, each with a special type of occupation, appeared as changes took place in land use and control. I saw economic occupation as a key variable defining subpopulations within the cultural system. Concentrated land ownership in the valley, continuing a division into large single-family ranches established in Spanish–Mexican times, resulted in a small landed aristocracy and a large class of landless tenants and homeless farm laborers. Laborers worked on land owned and controlled by others, and the rhythm of their lives responded to the demands of particular farm and ranch products. Occupation was often associated with racial and ethnic background.

My method of analysis was to identify time units according to major changes in land use and control and to discuss the occupational patterns of each subpopulation within each time unit. I assumed that each subpopulation left recognizably distinct sites and that, potentially, each of these kinds of sites would contain data that, if studied, would tell us about human behavior within a complex cultural system. This thinking provided a crude basis for establishing a classificatory system in which significance is assigned on the basis of a property's representativeness of a particular occupational pattern during a particular time period. I recommended that a representative sample of historic resources be preserved and that this sample include properties associated with each occupational pattern of each subpopulation from each period. When a group maintained more than one seasonal pose—for example, working crops during one season and living in town during another—then properties representative of each pose should be preserved. Similarly, if a group experienced considerable change in occupational patterns through time—for example, from migrant laborer to landowner—then an attempt should be made to preserve properties representing points along the continuum of change.

The project suffered limitations, not the least being that it was my maiden effort at using the historical record anthropologically. It must be said that I used anthropology in the San Felipe study primarily for orientation, based on the discipline's concern for a holistic approach to the study of culture. The study did not result in a regional research design specifying what could be learned by studying the different types of properties. The study did identify subpopulations that represented social variety within the valley's history, and by doing so, it documented the biases of the inventories then in progress. I hoped that I would fulfill my responsibilities to future archaeologists and to the diverse groups that have contributed to the region's history by emphasizing the preservation of a sample of sites including those not normally considered significant by local groups and agencies. Anthropology was used more intensively as a body of theory in the next study described, at William Keys ranch in Joshua Tree National Monument, southern California.

## SIGNIFICANCE AS SPECIFIC RESEARCH VALUE: WILLIAM KEYS'S DESERT QUEEN RANCH

Williams Keys, an itinerant prospector-miner-cowboy, appeared in the area now encompassed by Joshua Tree National Monument in about 1910. By 1943, when he went to prison after a gunfight, his "Desert Queen Ranch" was a gigantic hodgepodge of buildings, dams, ditches, walls, and gathered-in tools, machinery, and artifacts of every kind. The collection and construction resumed upon Keys's return from prison; the ranch became a tourist attraction and Keys a local character until his death in 1969, when the ranch reverted to federal ownership. When I was asked by the Western Archeological Center of the National Park Service to assess the significance of Keys's ranch (Hickman n.d.a), I was working on an overview of the historical resources of Joshua Tree National Monument (Hickman n.d.b). I was able to base my study of the ranch on the knowledge of the region acquired during preparation of the overview. A regional approach to Keys's ranch was particularly appropriate because the Joshua Tree area, at least since earliest documented contact, has not produced an economically or socially isolated community. Social interaction has been centered in several loci, which I called nodes, within a network of relationships that connected the Joshua Tree area to the "outside"—primarily settlements along the California coast and the Colorado River. Keys's ranch had been one node of social interaction during various times in regional history; its function as such was eventually eclipsed by the permanent settlement and development of land around the nearby Twentynine Palms Oasis. I concluded that study of the ranch in this context of shifting interaction centers would be useful to an understanding of "frontier" situations in general; this guided my selection of data for evaluation.

The ranch was associated with the development of local cattle ranching, two or three phases of mining, homesteading, the creation of a rival community at Twentynine Palms, the depression economy of the 1930s, and the development of the retirement and recreation industries. These events reflected, in part, a pattern of increasingly "focused" social interaction with which the ranch was associated. This pattern of change, featuring a diminishing number of exchange nodes of increasing size, is typical of the passing frontier. The responses of ranch occupants to the ranch's diminishing role as an interaction node should be informative about how other groups will respond to similar changes on other "frontiers."

Keys's ranch had been nominated to the National Register of Historic Places; thus it was convenient to phrase my arguments concerning the ranch's significance in terms of the National Register criteria established by the Department of the Interior (cf. Advisory Council on Historic Preservation 1973). Although I used all of the National Register criteria in my discussion of significance, one criterion was most challenging, as it provided an anthropological entry into a discussion of history:

> The quality of significance in American history, architecture, archeology and culture is present in districts, sites, buildings, structures and objects of State and local importance . . . [t]hat are associated with events that have made a significant contribution to the broad patterns of our history [Sec. 800.10].

Events are often taken to mean discrete behaviors of individuals or groups at particular times and places that, when shown to be interrelated, form patterns. It is important to remember, however, that *event* and *pattern* are relative terms; their definition and use are products of particular historical analyses. The experience and interests of the researcher determine what is taken as an event and what kinds of relationships are seen as connecting events into a pattern. My commitment to a regional study led me to select as events those behaviors that linked the occupants of the ranch not only with one another but with residents of nearby communities and more distant settlements. In other words, events in this study were social interactions, and patterns were constellations of related interactions occurring during a particular time period.

I used the historical record to trace how occupants of the ranch were connected by social and economic links to surrounding communities and to more distant places. Changes in these social networks were interpreted in the light of regional culture change, such as periodic population shifts associated with "boom and bust" mining and the development of a permanent settlement at Twentynine Palms by veterans of World War I. I was interested in distinguishing kinds of behavior at the ranch that could be interpreted as reflective of these developments. In other words, I was concerned not only with how members of the ranch were linked to others outside the ranch, but with how changing relationships with surrounding communities affected behavior at the ranch.

I was guided in this approach by the methods of network analysts, such as J. A. Barnes (1972:1–3) and Mitchell (1974:280). My initial method of analysis was to arrange chronologically all documented interactions between ranch occupants and others and to map them. Of course the record is fragmentary, confined to those interactions noted in the documents to which I had access, but interactions and changes in interaction could be identified. Different kinds of interaction characterized different periods, periods being defined on the basis of regional economic and demographic developments.

Testable propositions regarding behavior within a network can be derived only if the network concept is integrated with some body of theory. Theoretical assumptions are required before the nature of relationships can be specified. I used a model from exchange theory in considering those documented interactions characterized by exchanges of goods and services. The model, proposed by Sahlins (1965), focuses on the expectations of mutual obligation, that is, reciprocity, that parties to an exchange have of each other. Expectations of appropriate reciprocal behavior (e.g., immediate repayment, deferred repayment, no expected repayment) vary according to the statuses of the parties to the exchange. I derived some propositions about the patterns of reciprocity that could be expected to characterize Keys's exchanges with individuals of different statuses. These propositions were based on documentary and oral sources, and their connection with the archaeological record is as yet untested. However, a basic assumption of my study was that the kinds, quantitites, and distributions of materials at the ranch would contain information relevant to a description of Keys's network of relationships, and of his perception of his role within this network. The idea that social relationships are embedded in material things is not new (cf. Polyani 1948); the general idea is that things acquire their value in terms of the social context of which they are a part. Keys's ranch is full of things that Keys hoarded, ranging from sparkplugs to stamp mills, arranged in large and small nonrandom clusters inside and outside the buildings. Old photos and documentary sources as well as archaeological methods should make it possible to determine how this arrangement has changed through time.

As Twentynine Palms became a larger and more complicated node in an expansive interaction system, the social and economic networks with which Keys interacted were shrinking. The depression ended, mining collapsed, and Joshua Tree National Monument began to regulate land use. Keys responded, according to the documents, by establishing distinctive patterns of reciprocity with particular groups; he opened up relationships with people in distant areas, he ignored and behaved in a hostile fashion toward Twentynine Palms, and he adopted a protective stance toward "outcasts" from Twentynine Palms society. The clusters of material that he hoarded at the ranch can be interpreted as a form of display. The visual impact of these clusters is directed by Keys's selection of items to comprise particular clusters; the organization of the clusters is a statement about Keys's wealth and social identity, designed to be interpreted by visitors. Description of the composition and organization of clusters, then, becomes in part a description of the information that Keys was trying to convey about himself and the ranch, and of the kinds of social relationships that he was trying to maintain or establish as the social environment about him shifted.

I assume that the organization of object clusters at the ranch is a physical manifestation of a system of order governed by principles. Given the documentary and oral data available on the ranch, as well as those obtainable from archaeology, it should be possible to ascertain the principles that underlie the system. If we can ascertain how Keys, as the central figure in an interaction node whose importance decreased while that of a neighboring node increased, tried to maintain and reorganize his systems of interaction, it will be a step toward defining the organizational principles that may be employed in similar situations at other places and at other times in history. Thus the ranch has research value as a location in which the organization of material remains can be studied in order to understand how an individual's perceptions of himself and his world change in response to changes in his position within a network of interaction.

## CONCLUSION

The two studies briefly described here illustrate some basic elements of an anthropological approach to the evaluation of historical properties. The anthropological significance of such properties depends on their representativeness of historical patterns and on the ways in which they can be used to study those patterns. Defining both kinds of significance requires intensive study of regional history, use of general anthropological theory to abstract and interpret broad patterns of cultural change and stability, and definition of the characteristics of sites whose analysis can contribute to an understanding of those patterns.

# 21

# Applications of Archaeological Resources: Broadening the Basis of Significance

KEITH A. DIXON

We have a relatively unexplored opportunity to broaden the basis of "significance" in evaluating archaeological resources. I refer to the many ways archaeological sites and their contents are data banks that contain vital information for applied and theoretical disciplines *other* than archaeology.

As archaeologists, we have a natural tendency to see these resources in terms of our own scientific research problems and in terms of humanistic values. This attitude is reinforced by the growing number of specialists in other fields who lend their knowledge and techniques to our anthropological and historical goals of analyzing the human past. Our collaborators are often not only willing but eager to bring us their own expertise in physics, chemistry, statistics, nutrition, botany, mechanical engineering, geography, ichthyology, musicology, hydrology, medical science, astronomy, pedology, meteorology—to pick a few at random.

Their projects have often stemmed from their own individual initiative. But sometimes such efforts are multiple, combined in a complex orchestration by an archaeologist-conductor; such a project is likely to be called interdisciplinary or multidisciplinary. There are hefty volumes on the subject written by individual authors. There are also large compendiums of papers written by specialists to show how new developments in other disciplines can be applied to help solve archaeological problems. New journals are devoted to the same cause. Even newspapers cover the more sensational new dating techniques and other applications.

It is understandable that archaeologists are overwhelmed by all this generosity. It is also understandable that they often feel a bit frustrated by the need to comprehend enough of these exotic sister sciences to direct their practitioners into worthwhile projects and to be able to interpret their results. No wonder, then, that archaeologists have tended to look inward instead of outward. We are at the focal point of the kinds of problems that also have proved to fascinate other kinds of experts. Therefore, it is both reasonable and correct that our attitude has been mainly to ask what they could do for us.

The opposite viewpoint has not as often been expressed, although it is important: What can we do for them? The answer has taken form, to a very limited degree so far, in what some have called applied archaeology. That is, the archaeologist works with archaeological data to produce information that is useful for other purposes than pure archaeological research. A good example is the testimony prepared by archaeologists for both plaintiffs and defendants regarding American Indian land-claims cases (N. A. Ross 1973). Some Indian groups have sued the federal government on the ground of inadequate or unjust compensation for lands that had been acquired from them in the past. Archaeologists, along with other specialists, provided information on traditional land occupancy and land-use patterns. This is an application of archaeological skills and research to practical purposes that are not in themselves primarily research oriented.

However, applied archaeology is not the subject of this chapter. What we are concerned with instead are the archaeological resources themselves and how they are pertinent to uses other than in archaeology or in applications of archaeological analysis. Certainly these other uses of the data may overlap with applied archaeology, but the relationship is not necessarily a dependent one when archaeological skills are not required directly.

In any case, our concern here is with the *other* values of the archaeological resources. This is what I meant in the chapter subtitle by "broadening the basis of significance."

The emphasis in this chapter is on those archaeological resources that either receive low priority or are found not to be of potential significance when evaluated in terms of archaeological research problems or research designs. The emphasis is also on resource preservation for the future rather than on data recovery by existing techniques.

The discussion is based on five propositions:

1. *All archaeological resources have potential significance unless proved otherwise.* I have never come across a reasonable denial of this proposition's fundamental intent. While it is obvious, the theme is basic to what follows and it is therefore worth restating.

2. *Our obligations are to preserve and protect as many archaeological resources as is feasible.* These obligations are fundamental in conservation archaeology and cultural resource management. In terms of the extent to which these obligations can be met, the key is the word *feasible.* Feasibility is determined mainly by cost—cost in time, effort, space, and money. Our task is to increase the scope of what is considered to be feasible by showing that preservation of the remaining archaeological record is worth the cost to the maximum degree that is in the public interest.

3. *The sample of preserved resources should be as representative as possible.* Because total preservation is not feasible, the archaeological resources that can be

preserved and protected should be not only as complete but as representative a regional sample as is feasible. It is obvious that the resources that have survived human and nonhuman agents of destruction prior to conservation efforts are distorted samples of what existed previously. We can do little about those biases except to try to assess what the agents and their effects were and to plan conservation efforts to lessen their future effects.

4. *Biases are introduced by archaeological research problems and research designs, which can decrease both the quantity and the representativeness of conserved resources.* In the course of pursuing the objective of conserving archaeological resources, the archaeologist himself may introduce biases. These biases can affect both the quantity and the representativeness of the sample because of the very nature of the research problems that govern conservation procedures and site evaluations. The kinds of problems and the specific criteria for evaluation often vary widely from one region to another, from one set of research interests to another, and from one tradition of archaeological training to another.

Here enters the concept of "significance." It is, of course, a common requirement in conservation and management procedures that archaeological resources be evaluated as to their scientific or other significance. At the worst, if the evaluation is not convincing to management or if the specific criteria are not seen to be relevant to established values, the result may be rejection of measures to protect a particular resource. Otherwise, priorities may be assigned in allocating costs of protection, some sites being designated as more "significant" than others. Note how examples of significance evaluation in this volume are often closely dependent on the author's experience and interests. Another investigator, faced with the same problem, would likely arrive at different solutions to the evaluation of significance. The same resources might not be ranked in the same priority order.

Whatever the criteria for evaluating significance, the result will always fall short of the ideal. When an archaeologist is successful in justifying the conservation of some sites in a region, there are usually other sites that are low on the priority list. Some sites will not be preserved at all, and some data will not be recovered from surveyed or excavated sites. The legacy of preserved sites is necessarily a biased and nonrepresentative sample of the original pattern of resources, as a result of the archaeologist's own efforts.

The archaeologist, of course, cannot anticipate future significance criteria and future research needs. The history of archaeological investigation is replete with examples of how sites once considered to be of little interest have turned out to be of critical importance for research problems or analytic techniques that were developed later. And we can predict with certainty that sites we now value only slightly or not at all will prove to be of critical importance in the future, once other questions are asked and other methods are developed. Therefore, as scientists we realize that *in the long view* attempts to assign priorities by means of significance evaluation may be virtually meaningless.

But regardless of the ideal, the reality now is that conservation priorities must still be assigned on the basis of significance, and therefore problem-oriented research designs and models are obviously necessary. They provide the means whereby the preservation of many sites is justified. They provide the guides to insure that at least some kinds of data from survey (and excavation, when necessary) are systematically preserved. And of course, research designs and models are vital both to interpreting and planning research and conservation strategies.

Nevertheless, it is also part of reality that the research problems generate the significance evaluations and introduce the biases as some data become more relevant than others to particular problems. That is, after all, a function of good research problems and designs.

Viewed from the idealistic perspective of this chapter, attempts to rank the research problems themselves in terms of scientific or other significance would not solve the problem.

Thus, we are still concerned with the sites that are left over from the archaeological research designs, whatever they might be—the resources that become the rejects, write-offs, or disposables. The conflict is clear: as always, we are brought full circle by the need, ideally, to preserve all sites versus the prohibitive costs of doing so.

As archaeologists, therefore, we are all interested in finding means to come as close to the goal as possible.

5. *The basis of significance evaluation can be expanded in order to increase support for archaeological resource conservation.* If the preceding four propositions are reasonable, then it follows that means should be found to compensate for the biases that archaeologists themselves may introduce into their conservation efforts.

When an archaeologist makes recommendations on archaeological resources, his approach need not be: How do the sites of this region fit into my research design? Instead, his orientation could be: What research problems and designs can I apply to *all* the sites of this region? The goal in conservation archaeology is to conserve resources, not to solve limited research problems.

Therefore, it follows that the broader the bases of significance that the archaeologist can use, the more thorough and less biased the results are likely to be from the standpoint of resource conservation per se.

It makes sense to search out purposefully other significance criteria in addition to those that are either standard operating procedure or specifically designed to serve the archaeologist's own research interest. The more good reasons for support, the more support there should be.

One obvious approach, which need not be discussed here, is the one that is already expected of professional archaeologists: the awareness of a variety of theoretical viewpoints and specific research problems in archaeology that are applicable to the resources in the area in which they are working. Schiffer and House (this volume, Chapter 18) have also discussed technical, methodological, and theoretical significance, areas that also can contribute strongly to our goals.

However, the very fact that the theoretical viewpoints and research problems are likely to deal with anthropological or historical problems means that other kinds of resource values will still be missed or will receive less attention than they might otherwise merit.

It is therefore proposed here that archaeologists reassess those resources that are found not to be significant or are given low priority in terms of their usual research problems. Reassessment may require the expansion of the areas of significance beyond their archaeological, historical, or other anthropological and humanistic values.

This kind of suggestion (in other context) is by no means new, but nothing systematic has ever been done, to my knowledge, to define and explore the possibilities. The attitude has seldom if ever been adopted as a consistent, wide-ranging effort to search out nonanthropological uses of archaeological data.

## SOME EXAMPLES OF OTHER USES OF ARCHAEOLOGICAL RESOURCES

The examples that follow are only a few of the cases that have come to my attention where archaeological data have been used for purposes other than the traditional kinds of research problems that involve archaeological, general anthropological, historical, or humanistic values. That is, the interest lies not in reconstructing or interpreting the human past, but in searching out practical ways in which the remains of the human past will aid us in present-day problems or help in planning our future. Of particular interest are the uses of archaeological resources that affect our wallets, our health, or our safety.

### Flood Control and Tax Dollars

In southern California as elsewhere, modern land uses are planned with reference to the possibilities of natural disasters. In certain areas unusual flooding can occur far beyond the normal expectations. Good planning must realistically evaluate the dangers to life and property. Not enough provision for flood control can spell disaster when unusual rainfall eventually occurs. But too big a flood control project, beyond what is reasonably necessary to provide the right margin of safety, can result in unnecessary environmental damage and the waste of millions of taxpayer dollars. Rainfall and flood records have been kept for too short a time to provide the time perspective adequate for reliable planning.

The U.S. Army Corps of Engineers was faced with such a problem in the area of Palm Springs, in the Coachella Valley, southern California. The city and outlying developments have long been a multimillion-dollar investment, and there is a potential for millions of dollars of further investment and great population increases. Needless to say, there is much at stake here.

The city is on a fan deposit below the mouth of Tahquitz Canyon. The canyon drains a portion of the San Jacinto Mountains on the rain-shadow side. The canyon stream is normally a small one, but if an unusual amount of rain falls in the mountains in a short time, the stream can be expected to fill rapidly and discharge large quantities of water and debris, like any other of the local desert canyon streams. The question is, what is the maximum amount of water and debris transport that should be responsibly planned for?

If there had been annual flood records expressed in cubic feet per second of flow for this canyon over the past several hundred years, the answer would be relatively simple. As it is, the lack of time perspective meant that the Corps of Engineers had to estimate.

As Wilke, King, and Hammond (1975) recount the story, the Corps of Engineers drew up plans for the construction of a massive dam and debris basin to be located at the head of the Tahquitz Canyon alluvial fan, on land owned by members of the Agua Caliente Band of Cahuilla Indians. The projected capacity "was based on a standard project flood of 17,500 cubic feet per second, somewhat larger than the mean annual flow of the unharnessed Colorado River between 1894 and 1911 inclusive [pp. 45–46]." The corps derived this figure from water discharge measured during a thunderstorm in 1939 at a place 20 miles away, when some 7 inches of rain fell in 3 hours. The largest recorded discharges from Tahquitz Canyon itself, apparently reached three times since around 1938, were only about 2,900 cubic feet per second. The question to be answered is whether or not the corps made an adequate assessment of the magnitude of their proposed project—especially, were there any data that they failed to take into account?

Meanwhile, it must be established that the corps prepared an environmental impact statement pursuant to requirements of the National Environmental Policy Act of 1969. However, the statement failed to include an assessment of the project's impacts on archaeological resources.

Members of the Tribal Council of the Agua Caliente Band of Cahuilla Indians requested the assistance of the Archaeological Research Unit, University of California at Riverside, to inspect the land that was to be impacted by the dam and debris basin. They found two cemetery localities and a large village complex. They reported to the Corps of Engineers that the entire area was archaeologically sensitive and that a full inventory and evaluation of resources was necessary before assessment of potential impact and recommendations could be made. The corps then issued a supplementary statement acknowledging the archaeological resources but denying that they would be disturbed.

The Agua Caliente Band's tribal council then arranged for, and also paid for, the detailed professional resource assessment which the Army Corps of Engineers had refused to do. (Later, as a result, the Tahquitz Canyon area was enrolled as a district in the National Register of Historic Places.)

Tahquitz Canyon and its cultural resources are of direct concern to the Cahuilla Indians as the traditional home of the spiritual being Tahquitz and the ancestral home of a prominent clan. In addition, the sites have scientific significance to the archaeologist for substantive settlement studies and also for theoretical issues having to do with changing human ecology. But these two kinds of values need not be described here. Instead, a third value is of importance for present purposes in that the archaeological study provided some surprising information of quite a different kind—the data served to test whether the canyon is subject to flooding and debris transport on the scale estimated by the Corps of Engineers.

Some of the archaeological sites are fragile midden deposits on or near the fan surface, near both major and minor channels of the Tahquitz Canyon outflow. A hearth with carbonized seeds, for example, lay 10 cm below the present ground surface and within 1 m above the base of the channel bottom; the radiocarbon date was 300 to 450 years old. It is apparent that "the maximum flow of water at any time during the past 300–450 years has never reached the volume necessary to fill the high water channel to a depth of 1 m. at Locus TC-27N. If it had, the deposits sampled there within 10 cm. of the surface would have been absent, deeply buried, or seriously disturbed [Wilke et al. 1975:69]." The fan must be considered to have been a stable environment, not threatened by floods beyond historically known normal flows, for at least 300 years.

I have recently been told that the Corps of Engineers has abandoned the plans to build the massive dam and debris basin at the mouth of the Tahquitz Canyon and will instead construct a series of small structures to control the stream flow farther up the canyon. The result should accomplish the objective of providing the necessary safety for life and property, yet not damage the cultural values or scenic beauty of the canyon.

The design for the dam and debris basin took years of planning, rock and soil testing, geological analysis, expert testimony in hearings, and the full panoply of effort. I heard one estimate that the cost to the government ran to hundreds of thousands of dollars, perhaps over $1 million, for the design study and planning alone. In contrast, the archaeological fieldwork, analysis, and report cost less than $1000.

One must wonder, if the Corps of Engineers had done the cultural resource analysis at the beginning of the planning process, when it was most appropriate, would some of that million or so taxpayer dollars have been saved? And if the archaeological analysis had not finally been done at the insistence of the Cahuilla, would many millions of dollars more have been spent unnecessarily?

I am told that the corps has made no official statement as to whether or not their change of plans was determined or influenced by the archaeological data. I have made no attempt to inquire of them, or to confirm the cost estimates, since it does not matter to the principle discussed here. The point is that the archaeological assessments should have been done early in the planning process, and the corps should at the very least have taken into account those data that are directly pertinent to flood control engineering.

While in this case it may have been the scientific and social values of these sites that actually led to the analysis, nevertheless the case does illustrate an important principle: *By their strategic locations and the evidence of past environmental characteristics preserved in them, it is possible for archaeological sites to be the only sources of data available to resolve completely different kinds of problems, often with highly practical applications.*

## Soil Genesis and Soil Management

G. W. Dimbleby, in his role as botanist, once tackled a practical problem of great significance to human survival—the relation of soils to plant growth. (The following is based on a convenient summary in Wilson 1975:283–286.) Dimbleby tried to find out why trees did not grow well in certain desolate moorlands and heathlands in Britain. The soil was the problem—a podzol from which the iron and mineral nutrients had been leached, leaving an impoverished soil above a hardpan layer. The standard explanation was that this was the natural and inevitable effect of interaction between climatic factors and original soil constituents, perhaps an incurable condition.

However, the clue to a different explanation appeared in the form of numerous earthworks and barrows in the same areas. Why were the works of man so numerous in such an inhospitable environment? Investigation under a barrow showed that the original soil surface had been protected from the leaching that produced the podzol; in other words, that soil had not been subjected to the natural forces that had previously been thought to have been in operation since the end of the Ice Age. Instead, the pollen showed that, at the time the barrow was built, the plant cover had been basically an oak-woodland. The soil deterioration must have followed the clearance of forest by humans for purposes of cultivation. The poor soils of today are the direct result of human influences starting in relatively recent prehistoric times. If the natural conditions alone are not to blame, it follows that if left undisturbed, the vegetation and soil "will gradually return towards the more fertile condition which previously existed [Dimbleby, quoted in Wilson 1975:284]."

Dimbleby concluded with an interesting observation: he subsequently learned that archaeologists had already had the significant information on record elsewhere. In the Netherlands archaeologists had found unleached soils under the Neolithic barrows but podzol under the Bronze Age barrows. The archaeologists had even been using this observation for archaeological purposes—to date barrows.

But the great significance lay in the fact that vast extents of land were stripped of their woodlands and lost their fertility because of increasingly intensive farming beginning in the Bronze Age, not because of inevitable or incurable natural processes of interaction between climate and soil chemistry. Had the ecologists and pedologists assimilated these facts, "it would have made a big difference to what was being taught as the fundamental principles of soil genesis, and I, working in an applied field, would have been saved a great deal of time in working out for myself the principles which I should have been applying [Dimbleby, quoted in Wilson 1975:285]."

Once again, the archaeological sites proved valuable beyond archaeology and history: they provided the clue for an important principle of soil science that should have significant practical applications.

> Dimbleby concluded, "I am not suggesting that studies of the past conditions will solve present problems, but I do believe that, taken with what we know and are still learning about ecological processes, they may tell us where things have gone wrong. Until we know this, efforts at restitution will be of a hit-or-miss nature and much expenditure of money and effort may be stultified [Wilson 1975:286]."

Once again, these barrow sites also had archaeological and other values. The point, however, is Dimbleby's attention to significant nonarchaeological evidence preserved with the barrows. Evidence for related kinds of studies elsewhere could well be preserved under sites that would ordinarily be given low priority or even be written off if evaluated by the usual archaeological criteria.

## Floodplain Origin and Development

Archaeological sites can be useful in the study of the dynamics of river erosion and deposition, as demonstrated in the Delaware River valley. According to Ritter, Kinsey, and Kauffman (1973), there has been general agreement that two main processes, working simultaneously, are responsible for the construction of flood-plains. One is sideways migration of the river channel, which results in lateral accretion of sediment spread fairly evenly across the valley bottom. The other is periodic flooding, which overtops the channel banks and leaves sediments in vertical accretion.

The authors state that normally the overbank deposits are thin because rivers migrate over the valley bottoms in a way that redistributes the valley-floor sediments before thick accumulations of overbank material can build up. Further, overbank deposits build more and more slowly because it takes floods of ever-increasing magnitude to top the channel banks as the floodplain grows higher through time.

The authors point out that for these reasons some studies that have estimated the rate of overbank deposition have been based on relatively short time spans. And those studies that have been based on longer spans of time were often based on a small number of dates or involved a complex alluvial history lacking detail about the continuum of deposition. However, the available information did seem to suggest that overbank sedimentation is of minor importance compared to lateral accretion due to river migration.

Archaeological data provide an important basis for demonstrating that in some cases overbank deposition can be the dominant of the two processes. Excavations were conducted at 10 archaeological sites. One, which was most important, was located only 18 m from the Delaware River channel. There were at least 12 different cultural strata in sequence from about 6000 years ago to the present. The geologic context of the site was the silts and fine sands that form the surface of the youngest (lowest) terrace in the valley, about 7.6 m above the low water level. The cultural strata were radiocarbon-dated, and the thicknesses of sediments between each successive pair of dates were measured. It was also determined that the textures of the sediments show that they did not originate from lateral accretion and that the sequence is unbroken by any periods of erosion.

The authors conclude that this instance, the Delaware River, "demonstrates that a natural channel in unconsolidated material can be fixed for very long periods of time and that under those conditions overbank accretion becomes the dominant process involved in the development of the floodplain [p. 375]."

Quite aside from any archaeological interest, this case shows once again that past human activity preserves data for the study of basic processes in another field of science and that the resulting knowledge is of a kind that can have direct application to practical problems of land use and planning.

## Climate and Weather

Detailed records of past climate and weather patterns are essential for increasing our knowledge of processes and causes, which in turn may lead to prediction and modification. The more detail on past variation, the more secure the interpretation of trends. The issues are highly practical.

Are the recent strange changes in weather patterns temporary deviations from the norm, or do they reflect long-term climatic change that may affect much of the earth's surface? If the latter, the implications for regional decreases in agricultural productivity, large-scale starvation in some areas, strained international political relations, and even disruption of world peace are staggering. Paleoclimatologists need all the information they can get. One data source is preserved in archaeological sites.

The relation of climate and weather variation to sunspot activity was an interest of A. E. Douglass that led him to develop dendrochronology as a means of searching for cyclical weather phenomena in the past. Douglass succeeded in establishing evidence of cyclic phenomena by means of a long chronology that provided a record of yearly weather and climate variation over some 2000 years in the Southwest. A large portion of this success was due to the preservation of wood and charcoal in archaeological context. Some important specimens may well have been from sites that might have been written off as having little or no archaeological interest at the time (or even now, in terms of some research designs). The story is too well known to require repetition here (see, for example, Douglass 1929).

One of many other examples of how archaeological resources can be of direct aid to these issues is provided by Fairbridge (1976). In this case, analysis of the contents, distribution, and dates of preceramic middens in coastal Brazil was directly applicable to studies in the history of mean sea level, paleoclimatology, and coastal geomorphology.

The Brazilian middens represent adaptations to five different resource situations. In each type the site was adjacent to or very near the principal resource that was being exploited. The midden contents reflect immediately available food sources rather than a pattern of gathering from widely spaced, contrasting microenvironments. Archaeological methods of excavation and analysis yielded sequential patterns of occupancy and of gathering the immediately available shellfish. Further, the record was dated by radiocarbon analysis of shell and charcoal.

The result is considered to be a dated history of local environmental changes over the last 7000 years. This history has allowed the testing and refinement of reconstructions of late Holocene sea-level fluctuation that had been based on other data. The sea-level changes correlate with known climatic events and are therefore regarded as basically glacio-eustatic.

Such a record would presumably not have existed there under normal geological processes of deposition and erosion. The record was the product of ancient human action, preserved in deposits made by humans. It is an archaeological resource, but it serves geology and climatology.

Fairbridge stresses that the resulting curve cannot be taken as a world standard because there are a number of mechanisms that result in regional deviations: "Discrimination and evaluation of these disturbances should be receiving worldwide attention, and all that the Brazilian record can do is to offer certain basic generalizations [p. 359]."

It is therefore reasonable to expect that archaeological resources along the coasts of the United States also have significant raw data, regardless of their values to archaeological analysis.

One such case is reported on the coast of Alabama where people had camped near sea level on the banks of estuaries (Holmes and Trickey 1974). A carbon-dated stratigraphic sequence consisted of artifact-bearing layers of shell midden alternating with sterile deposits of alluvial clay. The interpretation is that the campsites were occupied during former periods of low sea level. Periodically the sites were flooded by a rise in the water level and then were reoccupied during each successive period of low sea level. The authors found that each period of site occupancy correlated with the "Fairbridge Curve" at times of low sea level, thus providing evidence tending to support the reconstruction of the eustatic curve. It can be added that there are also practical implications relative to estimates of geomorphologic stability in this region, as in the Brazilian case.

There are many other excellent examples of paleoclimatic studies using archaeological resources, involving a variety of site situations and data resources.

## Marine Mammals, Science, and Biopolitics

In a research proposal in marine zoology, Woodhouse (n.d.) states that the islands of southern California and adjacent mainland coast have a "diversity of fur bearing marine mammals in the region [which] is unique relative to other marine areas [p. 2]." There is, in fact, a mixed boreal and subtropical assemblage. This includes six kinds of pinnipeds: the northern fur seal, Steller's sea lion, California sea lion, Guadalupe fur seal, northern elephant seal, and harbor seal. In addition to the pinnipeds, the mammal that has generated the greatest public controversy is the California sea otter.

The sea otter was abundant along the coast until it was nearly hunted to extinction 200 years ago. It has been protected by state law since 1913 but has been expanding both its population and its range to the point where it now has generated passionate debate (reviewed in Gilbert 1976). The sea otter is part of a complex ecological system, in which various groups of humans are included. For example, the sea otter is useful because it feeds heavily on sea urchins, thereby helping control these creatures which, by feeding, reduce kelp beds. Kelp has many practical uses; the harvest and the products derived from it are valued in the millions of dollars annually. Kelp beds also serve as sanctuaries, habitats, and food sources for many species that themselves have economic value (California Coastal Zone Conservation Commission 1975:22–25). How big a role the sea otter actually plays or could play in this system is not known in detail. The sea otter has in fact won passionate devotees mainly because of its personality and charm. It is, in Gilbert's phrase, a "glamour species." It is seen by many as a useful and desirable species that should be encouraged to flourish. Opposition to the sea otter is nevertheless strong for still other good reasons. It is reputedly a great feeder on abalone and other shellfish; the abalone hunters believe that their livelihood is threatened by the competition, and they in turn are strongly supported by segments of the local fishing industries. Losses ascribed to the sea otter have been estimated at several million dollars annually. The whole controversy involves intense emotion, political action, conflicting views of civic responsibility, and serious legal questions. Some of the legal issues hinge on whether the California population is determined to be endangered, depleted, or threatened, under the terms of the Endangered Species Act and the Marine Mammal Protection Act.

Conservation groups and government agencies at both the state and federal levels are in the dilemma of having to balance protection, effective management, and varied public interests. Rational decisions must be based on detailed knowledge of the interrelationships of the sea otter and the other marine mammals in terms of the whole ecological system. Therefore, because the marine biologists find it difficult to resolve the issues with living animals alone, without time perspective on the variables that affect the total system, they are turning to archaeological data sources.

Woodhouse (n.d.) has recently observed that in prehistoric middens "skeletal parts of pinnipeds and sea otters occur frequently, but few studies have concentrated on the material in terms of paleobiology or paleoecology. Instead, emphasis has been placed on human cultures and the use these cultures may have had for the various body parts of marine mammals [p. 2]."

Woodhouse has proposed a project to study "the dynamics of a shellfish—sea otter—aborigine system. Analysis of the material of both pinnipeds and sea otter . . . may provide valuable insight to interspecific relationships and long term changes in species populations that would be useful in understanding and possibly predicting population trends in contemporary populations [p. 3]."

Some of the kinds of information that are expected to be derived from chronologically controlled midden-bone sources include such population information as relative abundance of species; reproductive information; age structure; interrelationships between species and food sources; and processes of species succession and competition, including possible correlations with changes in climate or water temperature. Zoogeographic information may be gained on both geographic and breeding-range boundaries for some species, including the possibility of identifying rookery or hauling ground sites that are not presently used. Obviously, any such data can be applied to understand and safeguard these marine mammal species in balance with other needs.

There are also more academic issues—for example, Are the southern sea otters a separate subspecies? This controversy has lasted over three-quarters of a century

(Gilbert 1976). Data derived from the middens will include the taxonomic analysis of skulls. This would serve to test or expand on one of the few such earlier studies (Lyon 1937). This should provide enough information to contribute materially to the solution of that taxonomic problem, with all the practical, legal, and moral ramifications discussed by Gilbert.

Clearly, archaeological resources usually do contain abundant data to provide an opportunity for pure biological studies, many of which could have important practical applications. While a few such studies have been done, biologists in general seem unaware of the potential. The sites that contain important information for them, it should be remembered, are not necessarily the ones most valuable to the archaeologist.

## The Fishing Industry and Paleoecology

Long-range planning for the fishing industry, involving complexities of resource management and conservation as well as efficiency in harvesting, depends on comprehending the intricate ecological systems in which fish are involved. Time perspective has been much improved through recent techniques for dating natural deposits. Furthermore, it is now recognized that along the coast of California, Indian middens are the only source of fish distribution information to fill the gap between Pleistocene deposits and historical records.

Because bone does not preserve well and often is not easily identifiable, John E. Fitch has developed methods of recovering fish remains that come far closer to being a representative sample of the piscine population. This was accomplished through the species identification of fish otoliths (the calcium nodules in the internal ear of vertebrates). Because they outlast bones and scales, they are the most abundant of fish fossils. The fossil and subfossil otoliths not only allow inferences of the presence of species but of their relative abundance as well.

> Information on paleotemperatures, fish distributions, life history, predation, catastrophic events, etc. can be gleaned from fossil otoliths . . . and used in conjunction with knowledge of today's happenings to help explain long- and short-term trends. Obviously, a complete history of *Sardinops* in time and space would permit speculation as to its future potential, and such questions as to whether it has been displaced by the anchovy, whether it was ever very important except during the 1930's etc., would no longer be academic [Fitch 1969:78].

Archaeological deposits fill an important gap in the natural records. Archaeological site sampling needs, however, might be quite different from the research sampling needed by the ichthyologist.

## SUMMARY AND CONCLUSIONS

The preceding cases are taken from a file I have been accumulating of examples that demonstrate useful nonarchaeological applications of archaeological resources. Other examples in the file, all relevant to public problems, include studies in:

disease, medicine, and dentistry; agricultural productivity and prehistoric land-use patterns; pollution studies with time perspective; geological phenomena including tectonic movements and erosion rates; tests of theoretical propositions in chemistry and physics; and perspectives on modern environmental impact.

In nearly all cases, the skills and training of the archaeologist are needed in order to do at least three things: first, to sequence or to date the deposits that contain the information; second, to interpret the circumstances that gave rise to inclusion of the data in human context; and third, to minimize the loss of the rest of the data in the site context during the data recovery process. Although everyone has a right to the information in the data bank, not everyone has the skill to draw it out.

This chapter on broadening significance has been written largely from an idealistic viewpoint. The problem now is how to make the recommendations feasible. I doubt that any systematic program can be developed because the resources, skills, and interests of all parties are so diverse and unpredictable. The answer must lie largely in being aware of what has been done and in being alert to further possibilities.

While this broad view of the utility of archaeological resources has slowly been growing more popular, it rarely receives more than casual mention. Given the frequency of formally organized multidisciplinary projects over the past 20 years and the concentration on ecological systems as a theme, this is hard to understand. Perhaps the reason is that our colleagues in other fields are accustomed to working without the kind of time perspective that archaeological context can provide. Perhaps the obligation is ours to spread The Word.

The main point here, however, is the principle that the broader the bases of significance that the archaeologist uses, the more chance there is to insure official cooperation and to increase the funds to protect a wider range of sites for the future, including some of those that would normally be written off or would be given low priority for protection. It never hurts to strengthen any evaluation of significance; it is part of the insurance that more archaeological resources will survive.

Finally, to repay others for past and future favors is a pleasant challenge for us that will develop our own field by the doing.

## ACKNOWLEDGMENTS

I want to thank my colleagues in archaeology and other disciplines who have taken an interest in this project; who commented on one or another part of the present chapter; and who have called my attention to examples of archaeological data applications, most of which will be used in a more extensive paper. To that end, I would appreciate having further examples brought to my attention. I especially want to thank Dr. Charles D. Woodhouse, Jr. (Research Associate, Marine Mammals, Santa Barbara Museum of Natural History) for his kindness in permitting me to quote from his unpublished research proposal, and also Don Brothwell (British Museum, Natural History), Paul Chace, Robert F. Heizer (University of California at Berkeley), the late Eric Higgs (University of Cambridge), and Dee T. Hudson (Santa Barbara Museum of Natural History).

# Part VII

---

# FORECASTING IMPACTS

---

For a variety of reasons, many conservation archaeologists have not taken seriously the task of forecasting the impacts of proposed land modification activities. Most investigators assume for any development that impacts on directly affected areas will lead to total site destruction and that other impacts will be inconsequential. As Scovill, Gordon, and Anderson (1972) rightly point out, however, information about impacts is extremely important for management purposes, and this information must rest on a solid foundation; after all, responsible proposals for mitigation rest upon the reliable prediction of impacts. The greatest obstacle to the forecasting of impacts, beyond the conservation archaeologist's indifference to the problem, is the impoverished state of knowledge about the effects of various activities and processes on archaeological resources. Fortunately, modification processes are now coming to be studied more widely—from theoretical, experimental, and ethnoarchaeological standpoints. Unfortunately, conservation archaeologists cannot afford to hold their predictions in abeyance until better knowledge is forthcoming; they of course must use what information is handy and, in many cases, confine their predictions to a general level. Chapter 22 by Price and Chapter 23 Schiffer and House illustrate how these state-of-the-art forecasts are made. The purpose of this introduction is primarily to provide a framework within which new information about impacts can be integrated.

A discussion of this sort usually begins with the distinction between direct and indirect impacts. Direct impacts occur from the immediate physical consequences of a project's planning, construction, or use, while indirect impacts are those that are not directly caused by the project's activities but that would not occur otherwise (King 1975a; McMillan et al. 1977; Scovill, Gordon, and Anderson 1972). In practice the distinction is not always clear; that is of little consequence so long as one can argue that damage to the archaeological resource base can reasonably be predicted to occur as a result

291

of some activity or process set in motion or accelerated by the land modification project being considered.

Before we proceed to the general framework for considering impacts, several other definitions are required. We identify what might be called *effects* and distinguish them from *impacts*. Effects are the events, activities, and processes related directly or indirectly to a project's planning, construction, or use that have *potential* for altering archaeological resources. Removal of ground cover, excavation of borrow pits, emission of gases from a power-generating plant, increases in pedestrian traffic, and intensification of agriculture—all may threaten the integrity of archaeological resources. Whether or not the potential for destruction is realized—that is, an effect becomes an impact—obviously depends upon the specific resources present and the nature of the particular disturbance processes. The construction activities of a nuclear power generating station, for example, have some specifiable mechanical effects on the ground, which become impacts only when archaeological resources are present. When resources are present, it is possible to predict that some adverse impacts will occur; but we are on far safer ground, and can be more exact in our forecasts, if we have independent evidence for the relationship between a project's effects and the occurrence of archaeological impacts. That is, we should be able to document with some precision the modifications and resultant losses of information that will take place. It is not sufficient merely to state that plowing will damage a site; one must relate the kind of plowing and conditions of plowing to the alterations of the deposits that they will cause.

Admittedly, the distinction between effects and impacts is adhered to rigorously neither by us nor the other authors in Part VII. Nevertheless, we believe it is important to keep the concepts separate, at least in principle, in order to outline the basic process of forecasting impacts. Impacts can be forecast accurately only when the following conditions are met:

1. The effects of all activities that occur during a project's planning, construction, and operating stages are delineated.
2. The nature and significance of the archaeological resources are known for all affected areas.
3. The relationships are understood between all expected effects and the archaeological resources.

When these conditions can be met only in part, then forecasts will necessarily be made in general terms and will have a lower degree of reliability.

Some may suggest that we have set an unrealistically high standard for forecasting impacts that smacks of a concern with rigor and precision for its own sake. While we grant that many applications, perhaps most, will fall short of our standard, they may still be perfectly adequate when judged against the particular circumstances of a project and the state of knowledge concerning the relationships between effects and impacts. Even so, we prefer stressing the eventual achievement of reliable predictions, rather than enshrining hopelessly vague and indefensible statements—the present situation—as a standard.

## PLANNING STAGE

In many projects, especially those that markedly alter the earth's surface, effects may begin long before the first construction contract is signed. Indeed, most large-scale projects involve a considerable number of preparatory engineering studies, some of which may impinge upon archaeological resources. For example, new roads may be bulldozed and trees cleared in forested areas to permit the operation of survey crews, and core drilling may be carried out in order to learn about the underlying geological strata. Sometimes, of course, the sponsor does not enlist archaeological expertise until some preliminary planning and engineering studies have already been completed. For example, Siegel and Bradford (1974:56) report the discovery of recent drill holes in a site. That unhappy situation, one hopes, can be avoided more often in the future. Insofar as the analysis of effects is concerned, planning-stage effects can be treated in the same framework as those occurring in the construction stage.

## CONSTRUCTION STAGE

The effects brought about by activities taking place during the construction stage of a project may be divided into primary, secondary, and tertiary. *Primary effects* are those obviously connected to a project's principal goal: for example, digging the footings of a dam, bulldozing trees in preparation for channel straightening, and removal of material from a borrow pit to permit elevation of a highway. *Secondary effects* are those connected with support activities, such as the construction of an access road, and the establishment of a tent or trailer camp for the temporary housing of a crew. *Tertiary effects* are those that occur during the project construction stage but that are not the direct result of construction or support activities. Examples of such effects include the collecting of artifacts by construction personnel and the use of construction equipment for pot-hunting.

The usual source of information about primary effects is the engineering plans for a project. Generally these can be readily secured from the sponsor in the form of area maps with intended modifications noted. In obtaining these data it is also worthwhile to become familiar with actual construction procedures; one should almost be able to visualize the spatial organization of people and machines in their usual and unusual tasks, as well as the flow of traffic in construction areas. When information about a project is available in this kind of detail, it may sometimes hold surprises about effects. Toney (1975), for example, learned that at least in one area clearing of the transmission line corridor and the stringing of the power lines disturb the ground far more than mere placement of the transmission poles.

Information about secondary effects is far more difficult to obtain from sponsors—partly because such activities are not considered to be impact producing, and partly because decisions about their exact nature and locations may not be made until a project is well underway. Persistent questioning of the sponsor, especially project engineers, and a general familiarity with the logistic and support requirements of similar types of projects will often provide satisfactory data.

Tertiary effects are necessarily more difficult to deal with; ironically, the sponsor is probably much better able to prevent than predict them. Recent experiences in northwestern Arizona (Laurance Linford, personal communication, 1976) and various projects in northeastern Arkansas and southeastern Missouri (Dan F. Morse, personal communication, 1975; Price et al. 1975:277) provide ample support for the generalization that construction personnel will vandalize archaeological sites unless strong negative sanctions are maintained against such activities by the sponsor and his contractors. It is a safe bet to predict that unless such precautions are taken, accessible sites will be damaged by construction and support personnel. Also, as Price notes in Chapter 22, local landowners may rent heavy equipment from the contractor during inclement weather or other periods of nonconstruction and carry out land-leveling or other potentially destructive procedures. Presumably one can learn from the sponsor whether they or their contractors permit the equipment to moonlight. The possibility of other tertiary effects should be considered, but at present they are difficult to identify and predict.

## OPERATING STAGE

Once construction has concluded and use of a facility begins, other activities and processes that may affect archaeological resources need to be documented. Thus a third set of factors, related to the operating stage of any project, must be considered. Operating-stage effects are readily discernible into basic types and do seem in principle subject to accurate prediction. *Primary effects* are those directly related to the basic function of the facility. For example, reservoirs serve to impound water and regulate its flow downstream. Effects in reservoirs may be caused by the natural and cultural processes that take place in bodies of freshwater and by fluctuating pool levels (see Garrison, Chapter 11). (It is perhaps best to think of the act of inundation itself, which makes sites inaccessible for scientific study, as a construction-stage primary effect.) The activity of strip-mining, of course, produces marked primary effects by bulldozers, draglines, and explosives. For other projects, primary effects can sometimes be quite subtle. Pilles and Haas (1973:44) suggest, for example, that stack emissions from a proposed power plant in northeastern Arizona may, if they combine with water in the air to form acids, attack nearby calcareous sandstones (into which petroglyphs have been pecked). Other projects, such as transmission lines or pipelines, create few noticeable primary effects. Knowledge about primary effects depends on the availability from the sponsor of detailed information on the functioning of the proposed facility and on knowledge gained elsewhere about similar types of projects.

*Secondary effects* are usually the result of other intended uses of a facility, or of other uses that might reasonably be expected. For example, while reservoirs do impound water for flood control and hydroelectric generation, they also are used frequently for recreation, as Price notes in Chapter 22. In considering effects of this sort it is well to keep in mind not only mechanical effects on sites but also the long-term damage that may result from greater accessibility. Reservoirs, for example, are used predominantly by boaters who will have water access to the visible archaeological resources along the entire shoreline (Perino 1972:19). Under most circumstances it is safe to predict that when sites become more accessible, they will undergo greater rates of unscientific collecting and excavation (see Pilles and Haas 1973:49). When, for example, fire roads are built into rugged areas of a forest, one can almost certainly expect that they will also be used by artifact collectors and pothunters. Information on intended secondary effects is sometimes readily obtained from the sponsor, while greater resourcefulness is required to predict unintended or unauthorized uses of a facility or related areas.

The last category of operating-stage effects, *tertiary effects,* includes an enormous range of processes that could themselves be profitably subdivided. Some of the impacts named by King (1975a:18; see also King, Hickman, and Berg n.d.) are tertiary effects. Tertiary effects are not caused directly by the use of a facility but are the result of project-induced changes in demography and land use. For example, construction of a dam may make it possible for housing developers to obtain floodplain insurance for downstream areas, thus leading to increased construction and a higher intensity of land use (King 1975a:18). Schiffer and House in Chapter 23 describe an anticipated trend toward greater agricultural usage of the Cache Basin as a consequence of the flood-control benefits of the channelization project. King also cites the case where the federal government "finances a new sewer system that provides sanitary facilities for 10,000 people in a town whose current population is 5,000. Eliminating a check on population growth will result in a general increase in housing and facility construction [p. 18]." It is sometimes surprisingly easy to obtain information on tertiary effects from the sponsor; for, in many situations, changes in land use and demography are included among the intended benefits of a proposed project. Ethnoarchaeological investigations (the study by archaeologists of living groups) can provide additional information that may be useful in identifying tertiary effects. Padgett (1976), for example, administered a questionnaire to a sample of landowners to learn if the construction of Dierks Reservoir in western Arkansas would lead them to change their patterns of land use. Some familiarity with principles of regional planning and growth may help to complete the roster of tertiary effects.

## EFFECTS AND CONTRACT NEGOTIATION

The consideration of effects within the present framework is useful, not only as a foundation for forecasting impacts but also in contract negotiation and research design. As we begin to understand the general range of effects expectable from projects of a certain type, we will be in a far better position to delineate the study area and to assign priorities in our research, surveying, and testing efforts. For example, the knowledge that the bulk of transmission line project effects occur during the relatively short construction stage suggests that considerably more lead time is needed for archaeological investigations, and that the environmental impact statement and mitigative work in the corridor itself must usually be completed before construction commences. With the knowledge that a flood control structure is likely to modify appreciably downstream patterns of land use, one will initially recognize the necessity of expanding the study area to include zones of tertiary effect. Already the literature of conservation archaeology abounds with apologetic statements to the effect that, although appreciable effects may take place in indirect impact areas, they were not investigated because the contract did not call for it (e.g., Asreen 1974). In such cases the failure to correctly determine the study area is as much the fault of the archaeologist as the sponsor. Hopefully, some simple procedures can help avoid these potentially disastrous errors. Although information on a project's effects is likely to require a good deal of careful research during the course of archaeological investigation, something as simple as a table of potential planning-, construction-, and operating-stage impacts filled with the words *none*, *some*, and *many* is a better basis for research design and contract negotiation than no information at all. Naturally the archaeologist should strive to obtain from the sponsor as much data on effects as possible. Attention to gross patterns of probable project effects *before archaeological investigations begin* makes the job much easier and lessens the probability that the archaeologist will find himself in the awkward position of having to admit that, because he failed to survey the right areas, information on the archaeological resources and the probable impacts on them cannot be produced in compliance with the National Environmental Policy Act (NEPA).

## EFFECTS AND IMPACTS

The demonstration that a project will involve specific disturbances of the land on which sites are located (during planning, construction, and operating stages) does not in itself constitute an adequate forecast of impacts. There still remains the problem of linking those anticipated effects to actual impacts on the archaeological resources. This linkage is established by means of two sets of archaeological principles, known as *c-transforms* and *n-transforms* (Schiffer 1976). C-transforms include the principles that describe the operation of cultural deposit-modification processes. For example, plowing is likely to move objects along the furrows, with smaller objects being carried farther and larger objects sustaining more damage (Baker 1974). Pedestrian traffic on a site reduces the size of frangible objects, damages the more durable ones, and subjects all of them to horizontal and vertical displacements (Ascher 1968; McPherron 1967; Schiffer n.d.; Stockton 1973; Trigham *et al.* 1974). Artifact collecting by relic hunters is likely to impoverish a site's surface of finished, whole tools in which a great amount of effort was invested in manufacture (Claassen 1976).

N-transforms specify regularities in the noncultural processes that also affect archaeological deposits. The effects of wind and water erosion on sites, submersion of sites in freshwater, siltation, and even the effects of currents are processes whose regularities can be systematized as n-transforms (see Garrison, Chapter 11, for some examples).

The study of formation processes and the formulation of n- and c-transforms represent one of the great frontiers of current archaeological expertise. Fortunately, a heightened theoretical interest in these processes (e.g., Binford n.d.b; Clarke 1973; Schiffer 1976; South 1977a) has coincided with the practical needs of cultural resource management. The happy result is that presently dozens of experimental, ethnoarchaeological, and theoretical studies of formation processes are underway. The conservation archaeologist need not wait for others to provide these principles. Often it is possible to build into conservation archaeology projects a specific subsidiary ethnoarchaeological or experimental research design to investigate a particular kind of process. For example, when reservoirs are drawn down and resurveyed, it has been possible to document the effects of wave action on sites (e.g., Neal 1974; Prewitt and Lawson 1972). Almost any survey may provide the opportunity to study collections in the hands of amateurs and relic hunters, which can help document the regularities in their behavior. Many of these studies can be carried out quite inexpensively and require little more than an ability to ask the right kinds of questions and make the critical observations, as Baker (1974) has shown in his creative study of the effects of plowing on archaeological deposits. We expect conservation archaeologists to make considerable contributions to our general understanding of formation processes in the near future.

Because our knowledge about formation processes is advancing so rapidly, only with great trepidation do we offer at the end of this discussion a partial list to extant literature; they are likely to be superceded rapidly by far more exhaustive and definitive studies.

Treatment of a project's impacts also includes discussions of nonsite archaeological resources, such as environments and living human groups (insofar as study of the latter will provide data for archaeological questions). Although the general framework presented above will handle these kinds of resources, it is far more difficult to offer useful generalizations about impacts on them than about those affecting sites. The two chapters that follow contain examples of how nonsite archaeological resources may be considered (see also Canouts 1975).

## ONGOING DESTRUCTIVE PROCESSES

In addition to documenting as much as possible the range of effects expected from a proposed project, it is also frequently necessary to investigate the destructive processes currently acting on the resource base. Knowledge of these processes can be of considerable utility in serving as a baseline for offering predictions about impacts. For example, the prediction that greater accessibility into an area will lead to more site destruction is bolstered appreciably by a demonstration that in or near the study area collecting and pot-hunting are already taking place in accessible areas (e.g., Donaldson 1975). Ongoing processes have also been documented by Morenon et al. (1976) and Raab (1974b), as well as by the authors of the following two chapters.

In some cases information about ongoing processes may be of particular interest to a sponsor, especially federal and state agencies charged with management or similar responsibilities. In one case, for example, the Army Corps of Engineers contracted with an archaeologist to determine the rate at which several partially excavated sites in Alaska were being eroded away by wave action (Hosley 1968). We might also note that treatment of ongoing destructive processes is especially important for studies at over-view and assessment stages, to the extent that such processes may be identifiable without field investigation. Strategies for studying these processes are developing rapidly, as more uses are being found for the information. Interviews with local inhabitants and other forms of ethno-archaeological research seem to provide a suitable framework for acquiring the relevant data.

## IMPACTS AND SIGNIFICANCE

When we are able to forecast impacts of a project reliably in specific terms, our task is still but partially complete. This is so because management evaluations of impacts also need to incorporate information on resource significance. Simply put, impacts vary with the significance of the re-sources. After making this assertion we are forced to admit that it is likely to be quite controversial. Clearly, there are two senses of signifi-cance that could be considered: potential and actual (Schiffer and House 1977). The concept of *potential significance* accommodates the uncomfort-able fact that all resources are potentially significant because we do not know what questions may be asked of them in the future. *Actual signifi-cance,* of course, includes the presently determinable types of scientific (and other types of) significance that are discussed in Part VI. Naturally, impacts cannot vary with potential significance, for we have no way to assess it. The concept of potential significance can only leave one with a uniform assessment of significance that provides no guidance for making recommendations (other than to treat all sites as being equal). This problem becomes especially acute at the preliminary and intensive field study stages, when it is necessary to choose the least destructive alternative project or to offer proposals for mitigating the impacts of one particular land modification activity. Thus, in the final analysis, adverse impacts to the archaeological resource base are not simply land disturbances or even modifications of cultural deposits; instead they are losses of values related to significance.

How best to integrate significance evaluations with forecasts of impacts (i.e., deposit modifications) is a subject seldom broached. One of the few investigations that has addressed this problem, dealing with the Mid-Ark

Project of eastern Oklahoma, is reported by Bell and Gettys (n.d.). They attempted to evaluate eight alternative waterway projects without conducting fieldwork. Thus their information on sites is limited to a few published sources, manuscript data, and consultation with other archaeologists. For each site 19 significance-related factors, representing depth of deposit, location or ecological setting, degree of disturbance, potential utility of data to outside disciplines, and others (see introduction to Part VI), were given scores that ranged from 4 to 9. Composite scores for each factor were examined as well as overall patterns. Comparison of alternate routes for least impact was based on the average factor values for the known sites. Needless to say, the data base on which this exercise rests is totally inadequate; nevertheless, the attempt was worthwhile. With better data (from a field study) and factors weighted more in the direction of research potential, one might achieve fruitful results from applying their technique elsewhere (see Metcalf 1973 for a similar attempt).


## CONCLUSION

It has become quite evident in the recent history of cultural resource management that no longer can one merely *assume* that a proposed land modification activity will inevitably destroy or leave intact all sites in an affected area. Because of the sometimes substantial costs for mitigation, sponsors justifiably have come to expect that forecasts of adverse impacts will be carried out impartially, rigorously, and by making use of the most dependable principles and data at hand (cf. Verner 1976). Fulfillment of the intent of NEPA involves, we believe, total adherence to this high standard. One hopes that the present introduction and the two chapters that follow may serve to highlight the important process of forecasting impacts in conservation archaeology.

(See References at end of volume for full citation.)

*Agricultural activities:* Baker 1974; Binford *et al.* 1970; H. A. Davis 1972; DeBloois, Green, and Wiley n.d.; Feagins 1975; Ford and Rolingson 1972; McGimsey and Davis 1968; Medford 1972; Roper 1976; Scholtz 1968; R. Williams 1968, 1972.

*Pedestrian traffic* (trampling): Ascher 1968; McPherron 1967; Stockton 1973; Tringham *et al.* 1974.

*Excavation of pits or similar disturbances:* Daniels 1972; Drucker 1972; Hole and Heizer 1973; Matthews 1965; Medford 1972; Schiffer n.d.

*Inundation* (freshwater): Carrell, Rayl, and Leinhan 1976; Crawford 1965; Dragoo and Lantz 1968, 1971; Garrison 1975, n.d., this volume (Chapter 11); Garrison *et al.* 1977; Goggin 1960; Jewell 1961, 1964; Lenihan 1974; Livesay 1974; Neal 1974; Neal and Mayo 1974; Padgett 1976; Prewitt 1974; Prewitt and Dibble 1974; Prewitt and Grombacher 1974; Prewitt and Lawson 1972; Ruppé and Green 1975; Schnell 1969, 1975; Skinner and Gallagher 1974.

*Artifact collecting behavior:* Claassen 1976; House and Schiffer 1975b; Morse 1973b, 1975a; Price, Price, and Harris 1976; Schiffer and House 1975e.

*Logging:* Price, Price, and Harris 1976.

*Off-road vehicles:* Wilshire and Nakata 1976.

# Anticipated Impacts of the Little Black River Watershed Project on the Finite Cultural Resource Base

JAMES E. PRICE

A cultural resource assessment of the Little Black River watershed located in southeastern Missouri on the Ozark Border, was conducted in the spring of 1975 for the U.S. Department of Agriculture's Soil Conservation Service. One important requirement of the cooperative agreement for the survey between the University of Missouri and the Soil Conservation Service was an assessment of the anticipated impacts of the Little Black River watershed project on the cultural resources of the area. Although the archaeologist cannot look into the future, he can make predictive statements based on his knowledge of an area and the current trends in land modification. I have conducted archaeological research within the Little Black River watershed for over a decade and am familiar with the agricultural and recreational economics of the area. It is this experience on which I base my predictive statements concerning the impacts of the proposed watershed project on the finite cultural resource base of the area.

## NATURE OF THE CULTURAL RESOURCE BASE

The cultural resource base of the Little Black River watershed consists of prehistoric archaeological sites dating from at least 10,000 years ago to ca. A.D. 1350 and historical archaeological sites dating from ca. 1810–1915 in the form of pioneer cabin sites, early homesteads, Civil War skirmish areas, ancient paths and roads, gristmills, churches, schools, moonshine still sites, lumber towns and camps, tramways and commercial railroads, and the oral and published folkway traditions of the area.

303

## DIRECT IMPACTS

Since the Little Black River watershed project is large in size and rather extensive in its modification of the earth's surface, it is necessary to assess its effect on the cultural resource base of the area. The direct impacts of the project on the cultural resource base are obvious. Cultural remains that lie in the permanent flood pools of the proposed basins, in the areas where the floodway will be widened and where levees will be constructed, and in the channelization area in Arkansas will be destroyed, damaged, or changed by the modification and resulting use of the land. Unless mitigation measures are employed in these areas, data concerning the extent and content of cultural resources will be irretrievably lost.

The most destructive direct impacts, as outlined in the Soil Conservation Service's *Draft Environmental Impact Statement, Little Black Watersheds, Butler, Carter, and Riply Counties, Missouri and Clay County, Arkansas* (U.S. Department of Agriculture, Soil Conservation Service 1974a:2), relate to the 24 floodwater-retarding structures and the multipurpose reservoir whose construction will destroy or badly disturb cultural resources within an approximate 1500-acre area. An equal number of acres will be affected by proposed channel modification, which will not only remove land from use but will change the existing land-use patterns. This channel modification will also destroy or greatly disturb cultural resources in these direct impact areas.

## INDIRECT IMPACTS

I anticipate that the indirect impacts will be as destructive or more destructive of the cultural resource base over the next 100 years than will the initial direct impacts during the construction modification. Indirect impacts are numerous and alarmingly destructive of the cultural resources. Several such impacts will result from the landowners' ability to improve their cropland. Conservation practices of land smoothing, irrigation land leveling, grade stabilization structures, diversions, and drainage structures (U.S. Department of Agriculture, Soil Conservation Service 1974a:7) especially the ground surface. Drainage field ditches, described by the Soil Conservation Service (1974c:55) as graded ditches that collect excess field. water, would have an obviously deleterious effect on surface and shallow subsurface culture resources.

Land-smoothing operations, as the name implies, produce a topographically uniform surface (U.S. Department of Agriculture, Soil Conservation Service 1974c:56) and are the most destructive of all mechanical agricultural activities. The prehistoric and historical sites in the lowland area of the Little Black River watershed almost all occur as midden mounds, and on old abandoned river terraces and natural levees. Many Barnes culture (Woodland) sites lie on the small "prairie blisters," or mounds, and land-smoothing operations could, if not controlled, destroy over half of all Barnes sites in the area. If land smoothing proceeds as planned without mitigation, entire prehistoric settlement patterns would be removed forever from the archaeological record.

In addition to the construction of drainage field ditches and land smoothing, irrigation land leveling and pond construction are also planned (U.S. Department of Agriculture Soil Conservation Service 1974c:56–57). Altering the surface grade for irrigation purposes will result in major disturbance and probable destruction of surface and shallow subsurface sites. Ponds developed through excavation or dams and embankments also seriously afflict archaeological resources.

A little over $1 million has already been expended on land treatment activities in three of the project counties (U.S. Department of Agriculture Soil Conservation Service 1974c:54). These activities have destroyed dozens, if not hundreds, of archaeological sites. No mitigation measures whatsoever have been initiated to collect data on these sites. Most alarming is a statement to the effect that land treatment will affect about 30,500 acres over the project period. Without planned mitigation there will be drastic modification or destruction of almost all archaeological sites within this acreage.

Other indirect impacts will result from the planned recreational use of the area. The Soil Conservation Service's draft work plan (U.S. Department of Agriculture, Soil Conservation Service 1974d) estimates that the number of annual recreational visitors will be 90,000. This estimate reflects the sponsors' intentions

> to increase water-based recreation opportunities in the watershed and provide additional public access to the Little Black River. . . . The design capacity (number of people on a Sunday afternoon during the normal heavy use season) will be approximately 1,763 people. In addition, a separate access area on the Little Black River will be developed to accommodate about 30 persons at one time fishing and picnicking. . . . Some individual farms will be developed for private and income-producing recreation [U.S. Department of Agriculture, Soil Conservation Service 1974a:6–8].

With the increased recreational use of the watershed area will come additional destruction of cultural resources. Treasure hunters, vandals, commercial pothunters, bottle diggers, and relic collectors will have access to areas that have previously been inaccessible. Unless strict state or federal regulations are imposed, I anticipate additional looting of archaeological and historical cultural resources.

With the development of individual farms for private and commercial recreational facilities, the subsequent site looting and destruction of cultural resources as a result of the construction of homes, hunting cabins, and summer cottages on reservoir margins will be difficult to control. Such development will likely involve construction of roads, power lines, parking lots, waterlines, sewer lines, septic tanks, basements, and underground cables. Such construction would obviously destroy or badly disturb surface and shallow subsurface cultural resources.

Another indirect impact will develop during actual construction phases of the project. It has been my experience in the past that local landowners often hire project contractors to do land modification while the heavy equipment is in the area and available at reduced costs.

It has also been my experience that some project workers and contractors collect archaeological specimens during the construction of similar projects. Even government employees have been known to do the same.


## ADVERSE IMPACT PROCESS

All anticipated direct and indirect impacts of the Little Black River watershed project on the finite cultural resource base of the area are presented in Figure 22.1. I anticipate that the Little Black River watershed project will accelerate the destruction of cultural resources through land-use intensification. I anticipate accelerated land clearing in the lowland area as a result of better drainage and lack of flooding, which will make presently wooded areas desirable for row crop production. After lands are cleared, areas that have never been cultivated will be plowed. Often land leveling will accompany the clearing, and lowlands will be chisel-plowed and subsoiled to aerate and drain the soil. Throughout the watershed area I also expect the private construction firms that construct the dams to perform additional land modification jobs for local residents in their spare time and during inclement weather.

Land-use intensification is also expected in the form of land and housing developments around the catchment reservoirs. In conversations with private landowners of the basin areas I found that some expect to sell lots around the basins. Housing developments will be in the form of permanently occupied dwellings as well as summer cottages and hunting cabins. During construction of such developments I expect accelerated indiscriminate destruction of cultural resources by the construction of power lines, sewer lines, basements, roads, and other landscape modifications.

There will also be an increase in recreational use of the area in the form of increased tourism. This is expected to put more people in contact with unprotected cultural resources than would otherwise have occurred. It can be expected that there will be looting of archaeological sites because of greater access to formerly remote areas. Wave action on reservoir margins is also expected to expose archaeological and historical remains, which will then be looted by vandals and curiosity seekers. If large amounts of artifacts are evident, the area will be descended on by commercial pothunters, bottle diggers, and historical site looters employing metal detectors.

I also anticipate construction of public and private recreational areas in the vicinity of the reservoirs. This would involve the construction of camp grounds, outdoor toilets, shower houses, waterlines, etc. If annual visits by tourists reach sufficient numbers, I anticipate additional construction of golf courses, resorts, liquor stores, bait stores, and souvenir shops.

Another adverse effect of the Little Black River watershed project will be the intermittent flooding and drying of areas above the permanent flood pools but in the flood control pools. Intermittent inundation of historical sites will probably accelerate the oxidation and corrosion of iron, brass, copper, and pewter artifacts.

All of the above land-use intensification practices are expected to cause accelerated destruction of the cultural resource base of the area. Destruction processes

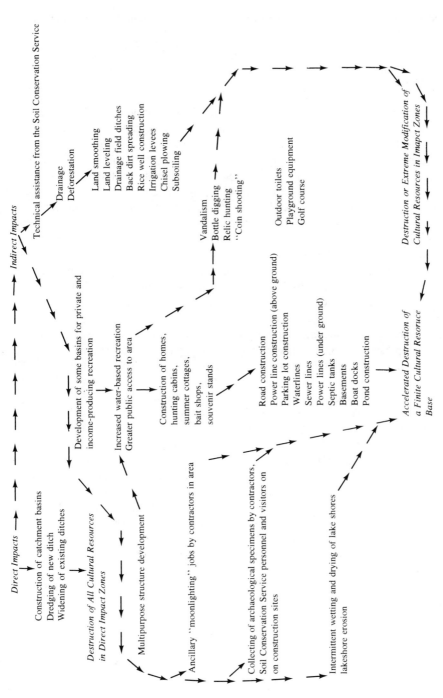

**Figure 22.1.** Anticipated impacts of the Little Black River watershed project on the finite cultural resource base of the area.

affecting the cultural resources that might otherwise take centuries will likely take place in a few decades.

## DISCUSSION

Consideration of these adverse impacts on the finite cultural resource base of not only the Little Black River area but also similar areas in the nation rest on important decisions that need to be made on local, state, and national levels. It is unrealistic for archaeologists or historians to demand excavation or preservation of all cultural resources. However, the professional community should insist that cultural resources be recognized and considered in terms of not only the direct impacts of such projects as that on the Little Black River watershed but also the ramifications of the future indirect impacts such a project will have. Difficulties arise, however, from many quarters. Many federal agencies do not control the subsequent modifications of areas after their initial project has terminated; and in the United States the view of private ownership of land and any cultural resources found thereon is a fundamental concept of the American individual's rights. The professional archaeological community has often been neglectful in educating the federal agencies and the general public in the stewardship of cultural resources.

It is important that archaeologists clearly indicate not only the range of cultural resources present in a given area but also the information or results that might be expected from investigation of this archaeological record through viable research designs. Likewise, the archaeologist would neglect his professional responsibility if he did not satisfy the demands of the funding federal agency while providing explanatory statements on the adaptation and behavior of man in prehistory and history. I feel that such an obligation includes statements of concern for the future preservation or study of cultural resources that will in time be modified as an indirect result of a given project. However, this concern does not require a totally dismal view of the future. Hopefully, by working together in complementary roles, the archaeological community and federal agencies can insure the preservation of a portion of this fragile entity known as cultural resources. Speaking on behalf of the archaeological community, I can say that significant gains in our understanding of the archaeological record in the Little Black River area have been made as a result of the present survey. It is my hope that continued cooperation between archaeologists and federal, state, and local agencies and individuals will insure that the rich evidence of man's utilization of the Little Black River area will be preserved and interpreted for appreciation by future generations.

# 23

# Assessing Impacts: Examples from the Cache Project

MICHAEL B. SCHIFFER
JOHN H. HOUSE

Assessment of the direct and indirect impacts of the Cache River Basin Project, an Army Corps of Engineers stream channelization undertaking in the 2000-square mile Cache Basin in northeastern Arkansas (see this volume, Chapter 14), was made considerably easier by the availability of a draft environmental impact statement (EIS) in which the construction activities and their direct and indirect effects on hydrology, plant and animal resources, land-use trends, and population distribution were discussed. Although most other cultural resource management projects may not have access in one convenient reference to other EIS data during the course of their investigations, it is always necessary to obtain as much up-to-date information on a proposed land modification activity as may be available from the sponsor and other sources.

In this chapter we present a largely verbatim coverage of our forecasts of direct and indirect impacts of the authorized channelization project, taken from the final report of the Cache River Archeological Project (Schiffer and House 1975c,e). We also mention how impacts of project alternatives were forecasted and conclude with a brief discussion of several shortcomings in our study.

## DIRECT IMPACTS

In lowland areas of the southeastern United States where rainfall is high and natural runoff is sluggish, channelization of existing streams and rivers is a favored procedure for increasing the drainage rate of many basins, thereby reducing the frequency and severity of flooding. Channelization involves the straightening, widening, and deepening of a stream or river and usually the construction of new feeder channels called "laterals." An artificial channel of the type proposed for the

Cache and its tributaries has a distinctive appearance. It consists of the channel proper, a flat area on either side of the channel called the "berm," and one or two elongated mounds of earth known as "spoil," or "spoil banks," formed by piling up materials excavated from the channel.

In assessing the direct effects of the proposed channelization project we are necessarily concerned not only with construction of the actual channel itself but also with all of the other land modification activities that accompany that construction. We will discuss each of these activities in turn and attempt to predict in a general way their impacts on the archaeological resources.

The federal portion of the Cache River Basin Project, to be carried out by the Corps of Engineers, consists of "improvement of 140.0 miles of the main channel of Cache River, 14.6 miles of its upper tributaries, and 76.9 miles of its major tributary—Bayou de View [U.S. Department of the Army 1973:2; Sec. 1]." In the upper reaches of the Cache and Bayou de View previously channelized segments will be enlarged, while in the lower reaches unmodified parts will be enlarged and realigned. Before channel modification can occur, areas must be denuded of vegetation to provide a zone for the operation of construction equipment (U.S. Department of the Army 1973:1; Sec. 3). This "clear-cut zone" extends beyond the spoil bank but does not always involve the entire width of the "direct impact zone." The width of the clear-cut zone will average about 390 feet for the entire project area but may be as wide as 700 feet in the lower reaches of the basin (M. B. Strohm, personal communication, 1974).

The area of major direct impact will be in the clear-cut zone, where trees are bulldozed; soil is disturbed by the repeated passage of heavy equipment; pits are dug for disposal of vegetation debris; the channel is widened, deepened, or dug anew by draglines; and spoil is piled up (U.S. Department of the Army 1974). In areas cleared for the first time, uprooting and sliding of trees will wreak havoc on vertical and horizontal distributions of archaeological materials. The passage of heavy equipment will break or modify artifacts, compress and disturb deposits, and scatter materials widely (Medford 1972). The excavation of the channel itself will destroy or severely damage all visible and buried sites in the immediate vicinity. And finally, the burying in pits of forest debris may adversely affect sites. In short, we believe the probability to be quite small that archaeological sites in the clearcut zone can survive with their information potential fully intact.

The survey of the direct impact zone recorded 53 archaeological sites in the nine sample units. Extrapolation leads to an estimated minimum site total for the entire direct impact zone of 477. Based on the average clear-cut zone of 390 feet, only about 30% of the direct impact zone will actually be affected by the channelization project. If construction activities take place as planned, then it is probable that a minimum of 143 sites in the direct impact zone will be damaged or destroyed by construction-related activities. It should be obvious that this impact can be reduced significantly by careful channel placement that takes into account the locations of archaeological sites.

In addition to activities in the clear-cut zone, other channel-necessitated construction and land modification will adversely affect archaeological resources, although it is not possible at this time to measure these effects quantitatively. The Cache River Basin Project requires, in addition to channel construction, the alteration of 61 highway and 5 railroad bridges, modification of 157 pipe, electric, and telephone lines, and relocation of 4.9 miles of roads (U.S. Department of the Army 1973:2–3, Sec. 1). Further, 14 water control structures will be placed in Dagmar and Bayou de View state game areas (pp. 1–2, Sec. 1). All of these activities could damage or destroy archaeological sites in the immediate vicinity. Because of the high costs of surveying for sites in the many small and widely dispersed areas that might be affected, and because project plans have not been finalized for most of the modifications, we cannot and need not precisely assess the extent of these additional adverse impacts at this time. However, we can predict that some archaeological sites will be destroyed or damaged by these land modification activities.

The data from the Cache survey indicate that many of the larger, more intensively occupied sites are located on high ground rather than within the floodplains of the Cache or the Bayou. Since the projected channels lie primarily in the floodplains rather than on the terraces, the probability of direct impacts on most of the larger, more prominent sites in the basin is reduced. However, the combination of high ground in close proximity to the main channel of a large stream seems to have made a location optimum for intensive habitation throughout prehistoric times. This topographical situation—terrace edges or terrace remnants in close proximity to the main channel of a large stream—was encountered frequently in the portions of the direct impact area investigated and was often the location of an intensively occupied site. Sites 3CY6, 3CY151, 3GE218, 3JA90, 3JA91, 3WO24–26, 3WO27, 3WO85, 3WO103, and 3MO40 are conspicuous examples of this phenomenon.

In addition, many of the smaller sites that are located in low-lying areas have only recently been cleared. Some of these sites on "new ground" may have an especially important research potential because they are not yet as severely eroded as are many of the large sites on higher ground that has been under cultivation for many years. Site 3GE219, a small middle Mississippian farmstead in the direct impact zone, is an example.

To this point we have discussed impacts mainly with regard to sites observable from the surface. As noted by Morse (1975b) and R. A. Taylor (1975), there is ample reason to expect buried sites in the Cache Basin. We have not assessed the probable extensiveness of such sites, nor can we predict exactly how many of them will be adversely affected by the channelization project. We can state that if encountered during land modification activities, buried sites will be subject to a variety of destructive forces and as a result may be severely damaged or destroyed.

Throughout this section we have used minimum figures for estimating the number of sites to be directly affected by the channelization project. It is necessary to underscore the many ways that these figures underestimate the actual number of archaeological sites. In the first place, only those sites visible from the surface in accessible (nonforest, nonswamp) areas are included in the estimates. Even in these areas the presently existing 1300 acres of spoil banks (U.S. Department of the Army

1973:5, Sec. 3) undoubtedly obscure some sites. Furthermore, long-buried sites may exist in the affected areas. And finally, recent silt deposition in the lower end of the basin has certainly reduced the visibility of a number of sites. We emphasize again: Because we have underestimated the actual site counts by an unknown factor, the adverse direct effects may be greater than our figures indicate.

Sites per se constitute just a part of the archaeological resource base of any region. Other environmental features whose careful scientific investigation can produce ancillary information needed for archaeological studies also comprise part of the resource base (Scovill, Gordon, and Anderson 1972:3,6). In the Cache Basin these include possible paleontological materials, and lowland forest and riverine ecosystems. The channelization project will have direct adverse effects on some of these resources. Paleontological specimens (useful for paleoenvironmental reconstruction) encountered during construction activities may be disturbed or destroyed. Other buried evidence of past environments, such as bald cypress logs and peat deposits, may be discovered and thereby disturbed or destroyed by project activities. If appropriate mitigation measures are taken, however, the discovery of these materials could prove to be a benefit of the channelization project. Construction activities will also reduce the rapidly diminishing wetland environment of eastern Arkansas (Holder 1970) by an additional 9500–10,500 acres of hardwood forest (U.S. Department of the Army 1973:4, Sec. 3). Aquatic ecosystems will receive direct but long-term impacts, especially in the loss of riparian cover, increased turbidity and siltation, and reduction of species diversity (p. 24, Sec. 3). These direct effects will reduce the value of the scientific information obtainable from study of the present natural environment as needed for paleoenvironmental reconstructions.

## INDIRECT IMPACTS

Alteration of the drainage patterns in the Cache River Basin will have indirect and long-term adverse impacts on the archaeological resources. By reducing the "frequency, depth, and duration of flooding and [improving] . . . drainage on adjacent tablelands [U.S. Department of the Army 1973:63, Sec. 3]," the channelization project will lead to the clearing of some of the remaining woodland and the conversion of this land into intensive agricultural use. Better drainage of already cleared areas will lead to the use of more intensive farming methods. Because agricultural practices are the single greatest cause of site destruction in the lower Mississippi Valley (Ford and Rolingson 1972; McGimsey and Davis 1968; R. Williams 1968, 1972), and especially in northeastern Arkansas (Medford 1972), one can expect the channelization project indirectly to cause the loss of scientific information obtainable from many sites. Losses of archaeological information from other indirect project impacts will also occur.

One of the proposed benefits of the Cache River Basin Project is the intensification of agricultural activities and the spin-off economic gains that it promotes.

> An increase in the acreage suitable for intensive agriculture will result in increased agricultural production and income. Improved agricultural productivity will be reflected by a higher standard of living for people living in the basin, an increase in the tax base, and subsequently improved municipal services in the rural and urban communities in the basin [U.S. Department of the Army 1974:51, Sec. 3].

The intensification of agricultural activity that makes possible these economic benefits results from improved drainage caused by the channelization project. This intensification occurs in two ways. First, many acres now in woodland will be cleared and converted to crop production. This will expose pristine archaeological sites to damage. Second, the lower frequency and severity of flooding will favor more intensive use of land already devoted to agriculture. Sites in such areas are presently being destroyed by farming; more intensive agricultural use will lead to an acceleration of the destructive forces. In this section we investigate the impacts of agricultural activities on archaeological sites, document the present extent of damage to sites in the Cache Basin, describe some of the impacts to be expected under more intensive agriculture, and predict the number of sites to be affected by increased agricultural use of the basin.

## Woodland to Agriculture

Woodland habitats that formerly could not be economically cleared and farmed because of high flood risk will be converted to agricultural use as a direct result of flood control benefits of the channelization project. The Corps (U.S. Department of the Army 1974:51, Sec. 3) anticipates that 18,368 acres of tableland will be cleared as an *indirect* impact of the channelization project.

Survey data from the Cache project and other archaeological work in the Western Lowlands indicate that large numbers of sites are present not only in the floodplain and on the terrace edges but, somewhat unexpectedly, also on the extensive interfluvial terrace areas. Site survey in areas that are just now being cleared of timber on the terraces between Bayou de View and the L'Anguille River is revealing the existence of numerous small but intensively occupied sites along small creeks. Many of these sites, especially those representing Woodland occupations, seem to reflect stable long-term cultural adaptations to the environment of the interfluvial terrace areas, seem to have some depth of midden accumulation, and for the time being, seem to be relatively well preserved. The same situation may be expected in similar portions of the braided stream terrace in the lower Cache Basin. Thus, many sites will be affected as woodland is cleared and land is converted to agricultural use.

## Land Clearing

The clearing of woodland will, in itself, have devastating effects on the newly exposed archaeological sites. We are fortunate in having available several recent studies on the general effects of both clearing and of farming methods on archaeological sites (Ford and Rolingson 1972; Medford 1972; R. Williams 1968). In the first place, the process of clearing itself damages archaeological sites directly and indirectly. Forests are cleared today with bulldozers that spread, grind, and compress cultural materials (Medford 1972:51-52). In areas where sand dunes occur (many are found in the upper end of the Cache Basin), clearing results in the shifting of dunes and wind erosion, which can bury or deflate deposits (p. 52). The adverse effects of clearing are more pronounced on small, shallow sites; clearing alone may eliminate much of their information potential, but even large sites will suffer damage.

### Cultivation

Once cultivation begins, additional destructive forces are set in motion that wear down and otherwise dissipate concentrations of archaeological materials. Plowing and disking of any kind move artifacts both horizontally and vertically, altering the integrity of deposits and their stratigraphic relationships (Medford 1972). For example, the Cache project testing program found that Site 3GE220 was almost entirely concentrated within the plow zone. Evidence as to whether or not the artifacts had been originally deposited on a distinguishable occupation surface has been destroyed. Naturally, subsoiling, chisel-plowing, and other practices that dig deeply are particularly hard on archaeological sites (Medford 1972; R. Williams 1968). Methods of cultivation can also indirectly result in damage to sites, as when crop rows follow the slope of the land, leading to rapid runoff and erosion. At 3CG230, another tested site, erosive farming reduced the depth of the deposit by as much as 25 cm in just 6 years. Morse (personal communication, 1974) also notes that intact house floors were once easy to find at 3CG230, but today they are difficult to come by. Ford and Rolingson (1972) describe the effects of various types of plowing on four kinds of sites: mounds, villages, hamlets, and camps. Their findings conclusively demonstrate the transitory nature of all sites in the face of persistent agricultural activity.

### Improved Farming Methods

In recent years farmers in northeastern Arkansas have not been content merely to till the soil, allow the rain to fall, and await a bountiful harvest; they have instead actively modified the surface of the land by various means and have begun to irrigate in order to increase productivity (McGimsey and Davis 1968; Medford 1972; Scholtz 1968). Land leveling and shaping, by grading and smoothing and by precision land leveling, are especially destructive practices because they remove part or all of a deposit and scatter materials in areas beyond the original site boundaries (Medford 1972:53-59). Needless to say, what clearing and ordinary cultivation fail to destroy, precision land leveling is likely to accomplish. Only small portions of even the deepest archaeological deposits can survive these remarkably destructive practices. All of these techniques are currently in use in the Cache

Basin, and there is every reason to expect that they will be used on freshly cleared lands. Their use is also likely to become more widespread in areas already being cultivated as a result of reduced flood risk.

The alteration of water distribution and drainage systems wreaks further havoc on archaeological sites. These activities include digging wells, often in high areas where sites are located (Medford 1972:59), constructing flumes, which damage the sites they run across, and the installation of drainage ditches. It should also be mentioned that additional channels will probably be constructed by local drainage districts to feed the newly improved Cache and Bayou de View channels. These laterals will have many of the same direct effects as the main channel itself. Other farming-related activities, such as the construction of levees, access roads, buildings, and digging of borrow pits, also will damage or destroy archaeological sites in the vicinity (Medford 1972).

## Extent of Present Agricultural Damage

Data gathered during the Cache survey can be used to estimate the extent of indirect impacts of the channelization project due to the intensification of agricultural activities on both newly cleared and already cleared land. Table 23.1 shows the present patterns of land use with regard to archaeological sites. Of the 184 sites from which data were obtained, 175, or 95%, were in cultivation. It should be recalled that all sites in cultivation have been subjected to at least two destructive practices: clearing and plowing or disking of some sort. Only two of the remaining sites were experiencing nondestructive uses.

Cache project data also illustrate an alarming pattern with regard to the erosion of sites. Only 4 sites out of the 168 on which we have data had not already undergone damage by erosion. But 120 sites, or 71% of the total, are slightly eroded. And fully 26% (44 sites) are already severely eroded. These figures on erosion serve to document only one of the ways that cleared sites are being destroyed in the Cache Basin.

**TABLE 23.1.**
**Present Patterns of Land Use for Archaeological Sites Recorded by the Cache Survey**

| Affected components and sites | Cultivation | Pasture | Forest | Residence | Industrial | Other |
|---|---|---|---|---|---|---|
| Paleo-Indian | 5 | — | — | — | — | — |
| Archaic | 121 | 1 | 1 | | 1 | 2 |
| Woodland | 75 | — | 1 | 1 | 2 | 1 |
| Mississippian | 33 | — | 1 | 1 | — | — |
| Historical | 3 | — | — | — | — | — |
| Undetermined | 19 | — | 1 | — | — | — |
| Total affected sites | 175 | 1 | 2 | 1 | 2 | 3 |

We also have some, admittedly limited, data on other destructive farming practices operative on the archaeological sites found by the Cache survey. The most frequently occurring damage (61% of all sites) results from the use of modern land-clearing methods (cf. Medford 1972), which are more destructive than earlier practices. The next most frequent kind of destruction (27% of all sites) is caused by erosive farming. Damage has also occurred from other farming-related activities and several miscellaneous land uses. Only 8 sites (less than 5%) did not appear to be damaged.

These figures indicate a consistent pattern of site destruction related to agricultural activities. Remarkably, when the Cache figures are compared with those obtained by Medford for all of northeastern Arkansas, sites in the Cache area seem so far to have undergone less destruction by advanced agricultural techniques. Actually, some major differences of this sort would be expected, since much of the land in the Cache Basin has been in cultivation for fewer years than other areas of northeastern Arkansas. For example, drainage projects have been present for over 50 years in some parts of the Saint Francis Basin; it is these very areas that show the greatest intensity of agricultural activity and site destruction.

## Sites to Be Affected in Already Cleared Areas

Removal of soil from plowed fields by flooding damages archaeological sites (Scholtz 1968); thus prevention of flooding might be viewed as a positive result of the Cache project. Unfortunately, modern farming practices are such that this potential benefit is completely negated. Actually, decreasing the flood risk in many already cleared floodplain areas would accelerate site destruction by making land leveling much more economically feasible. Even where flood control benefits do not lead to land leveling, other, more subtle processes will increase the rate of site destruction. For example, a field that is less frequently flooded can be cultivated more often; thus the rate at which archaeological remains are damaged and disturbed will increase.

Although it is not possible to determine exactly the number of sites that will be affected by land leveling and other intensified agricultural practices, we can provide some figures that may be indicative of the scale of this adverse impact. The corps estimates that 788,515 acres of farms (about one-half of the entire basin) will be benefited by the drainage project (U.S. Department of the Army 1973:64, Sec 3). If the average site density value for the direct impact zone of the lower end of the basin is used (2.15 sites per square mile), then one obtains an estimate of 2649 sites for the affected 1232 square miles. This count, however, is unrealistically low because flood control benefits will also accrue to farms in the upper end of the basin, where site density is greater. If the site density estimate for the entire direct impact zone is applied (7.18 sites per square mile), then 8846 sites are potentially affected. An average obtained from both density figures, 5748, would be a realistic composite estimate. The range of impacts to these 5748 sites is likely to be wide; on the one hand, sites already subjected to serious erosion or land leveling will probably suffer no significant increase in the rate of damage; on the other hand, sites on recently cleared land, of which there are many thousands of acres (U.S Department of Army 1974:23, Sec. 3), will incur appreciable adverse impacts.

## Unscientific Collecting and Vandalism

Besides the obvious direct effects, farming and clearing subject archaeological sites to the more subtle predations of unscientific collecting, pot-hunting, and grave robbing. Sites in northeastern Arkansas are notoriously vulnerable to unscientific collecting and even to organized groups of pothunters (Morse 1973b, 1975a). Morse (personal communication, 1974) reports that a variety of collecting and pot-hunting activities are presently occurring in the Cache Basin. One might reasonably expect that newly cleared sites will fall prey to collectors just as soon as word about them gets around.

Although no one has scientifically studied the effects on archaeological sites of different collecting and pot-hunting activities, some undocumented generalizations would not be out of place. In sites containing pottery, mounds and almost all other areas of the site are systematically probed for burials. When a burial is suspected, pits are dug in search of the often valuable grave accompaniments, and human bones are indiscriminately scattered about. If these activities continue for any substantial length of time, much of the research potential of these sites will be seriously diminished (not to mention the desecration of Indian cemeteries). On sites where no pottery is present, actual digging is carried out far less frequently. Instead, surface collections of selected artifacts (which are also made from sites with pottery)— usually bifacially worked chipped stone, bannerstones, beads, and other "goodies"—are taken. After long periods of collecting, these objects will become scarce on some sites. The longer a site is subjected to collecting, the more will common and less commercially valued objects, such as broken bifaces and unifacially worked scrapers, be removed.

Quite clearly unscientific collecting of one sort or another can markedly affect the contents of an archaeological site and render it useless for answering many questions about the past (Schiffer n.d.). It should be emphasized that only accessible sites can be collected. Because the channelization project will lead to more land clearing and more intensive cultivation—and thus greater visibility and accessibility of sites and artifacts—it will indirectly cause many more sites to suffer at the hands of unscientific collectors and excavators.

## Sites to Be Exposed by Land Clearing

Sites that are newly exposed on project-induced cleared lands will be subjected to all previously mentioned destructive forces. Although a precise total for the number of affected sites cannot be given, an estimate is readily obtained from survey data.

Most of the land to be cleared is in the lower end of the Cache Basin, much of it in Woodruff County. The files of the Arkansas Archeological Survey indicate that before the initiation of the Cache Project, 71 sites had been recorded in Woodruff County. By using ratios of previously known to Cache-project-discovered archaeological sites (U–D index), it is possible to estimate the probable site density of Woodruff County, and from that figure to obtain the likely minimum number of sites included in the area of induced land clearing.

Several U–D indices are available:

| | |
|---|---|
| Transect 1 | 9.67 |
| All random units in direct impact zone | 53.00 |
| Preliminary survey (direct impact zone only) | 7.00 |
| All sites, direct impact zone, Cache Basin | 10.67 |

The mean U–D index, 17.58, will be used in computations. The uncorrected site density for Woodruff County (71 sites in 591.9 square miles) is .12 sites/square mile. Adjusting this value with the mean U–D index yields a density of 2.11 sites/square mile, a figure remarkably close to the 2.15 sites/square mile for the direct impact zone sample units in the lower end of the basin. If one multiplies the estimated minimum site density of 2.11 by the forecasted 18,368 acres (28.7 square miles) of induced land clearing, a total of 61 sites is derived. We emphasize that this is probably a minimum figure for the number of sites to be exposed by land clearing: All U–D indexes and other survey data are based on observable, accessible sites. Others doubtless exist, especially in the lower end of the basin, where it is particularly difficult to carry out archaeological survey.

## Demographic Impacts

The increased emphasis on agricultural production in the basin will have several other socioeconomic impacts that will ultimately have indirect, adverse effects on the archaeological resources. One of these impacts will be demographic.

With increased production in agriculture and the expansion of cropland after the project is completed, population out-migration from the Cache River areas will be slowed. Thus, regional population will tend either to be stable or to increase slightly (U.S. Department of the Army 1973:63, Sec. 3). With increasing population comes more unscientific collectors and more demand for collections, and an increase in activities—road building and other construction—that can adversely affect sites. Not only are downward population trends expected to change, but urbanization in Craighead County, especially in Jonesboro, is expected to accelerate (U.S. Department of the Army 1973:63, Sec. 3). As Jonesboro expands in population, it will also expand spatially; thus sites in the path of that expansion may be damaged and destroyed.

## Environmental Archaeological Resources

In addition to the archaeological sites themselves, the Cache River basin contains environmental materials that can be used to enhance the study of the past. The woodland habitats to be reduced by indirect channelization impacts will become less suitable for the detailed ecological studies needed to support efforts at paleoenvironmental reconstruction.

## PROBABLE IMPACTS OF PROJECT ALTERNATIVES

In compliance with the National Environmental Policy Act, the Corps of Engineers also sought information on the probable impacts of structural and nonstructural project alternatives. In few instances, however, could the Corps supply us with very detailed information about these proposals. In addition, obtaining information on the archaeological impacts of these alternatives, none of which apparently were under serious consideration, was not listed as a high priority in our research program (see this volume, Chapter 14). As a result of these conditions the forecasting of impacts was done on a fairly casual basis.

The basic strategy was to determine as precisely as possible the amount of construction activity, induced land clearing, and agricultural intensification—relative to the authorized project—that would result if each alternative were implemented. We also considered other factors, especially the effects of a project on extant processes that are modifying the archaeological resource base. Using all available information, the aggregate adverse impacts of each alternative project were rated quantitatively relative to the authorized project. For example, the alternative "High-Level Floodway Channels" was a mix of channel enlargements and expanded floodways that would have led to far greater direct impacts because of a much wider clearcut zone (16,000 feet wide in some places). The amount of induced land clearing and agricultural intensification was expected to be about the same. Our guess was that the high-level floodway channel alternative would produce an aggregate adverse impact on the archaeological resource base of 25% over the authorized project. Each alternative was assessed in this manner, and a final ranking of all structural and nonstructural alternatives was produced.

## DISCUSSION

In retrospect one can easily point out where the process of assessing impacts could have been considerably improved. It is perhaps useful to indicate just a few of the weaknesses in our study.

Although the Cache project obtained data from its survey samples on the distribution of sites with respect to soil and landform variables, those data were not worked up into formal predictive models of differential density of site types in the environment, as was done, for example, by Fehon and Viscito (1974) in the neighboring Village Creek basin. Rigorous analysis of the data and formulation of predictive models of site location and density would not have changed the finding that sites are much more likely to occur on terrace edges than in the floodplains, but it would have elevated that statement from informed guesswork to scientific fact and provided a much firmer footing for discussion of the effects of channel placement and the impacts of project alternatives.

A major shortcoming in our treatment can be traced to the assumption implicit in the forecasts that all sites are of equal value. The forecasts, for example, are phrased in terms of undifferentiated "sites that will be damaged or destroyed." At the very least, sites should have been broken down by component and perhaps differentially weighted in terms of significance criteria.

A final problem concerns the lack of documentation for some ongoing destructive processes. Although several generalizations were offered about collector behavior, and they are probably accurate, rigorous ethnoarchaeological investigations among collectors are needed before such hypotheses can become widely accepted and used for predictive purposes. The studies of agricultural destruction referred to in this chapter are useful starting points but do not allow us to predict exactly what will happen to various sites subjected to different kinds of agricultural activity. Many more quantified and carefully controlled experimental and ethnoarchaeological studies are needed to provide investigators with the principles of formation processes on which to base accurate forecasts of impacts.

Although these and other problems inhere in our assessment of impacts, we did succeed in identifying the scale of destruction that would result from implementation of the authorized project or any of the alternatives. Future investigations should strive to remove whenever possible the element of informed guesswork and substitute hard data and valid generalizations.

# Part VIII

---

# MITIGATION

---

In just the few short years since its introduction to archaeology, the term *mitigation* has all but lost its original meaning. Despite the widespread tendency to use mitigate as a synonym for *excavate,* and even *militate,* the more appropriate, original meaning should prevail in conservation archaeology (Dixon 1976). In the context of environmental legislation mitigation is simply "the alleviation of impacts."

Recent writings have laid a foundation for development resources (e.g., Berg 1974; Lipe 1974; McGimsey 1973; McMillan *et al.* 1977; Moratto 1973; Price *et al.* 1975; Schiffer 1975g). Lipe's conservation model, which helped set the tone for the emergence of modern conservation archaeology, properly stresses that, among mitigation alternatives, excavation should be ranked as the last resort. The preferred methods of mitigation are avoidance or preservation of resources. As we shall see below, however, when factors of resource significance, ongoing destructive processes, and other archaeological values are taken into account, applications of the conservation model can become somewhat complicated—with no clear-cut solutions indicated.

## AVOIDANCE AND PRESERVATION

In accordance with the conservation model the archaeologist should first explore possible ways to preserve, or at least avoid destruction of, the archaeological resources. The nature of the recommendations naturally depends on the scope of the proposed project (if any) and its current stage, as well as predicted impacts on, and the significance of, the resources. When operating at the level of an assessment or overview, it is often desirable to fashion sensitivity maps that can serve as a coarse, preliminary guide to planners. King and Hickman in their contribution to Part VIII admirably discuss the role of sensitivity maps and other considerations in long-range regional planning. If sensitivity maps are based exclusively on data from extant site files, without additional fieldwork, it is usually difficult to determine if an absence of reported sites indicates an absence of sites or an absence of efforts to find them (Dixon 1974; Lipe 1974; Schiffer and House 1975d). This problem can sometimes be partially overcome by use of predictive models employing ethnographic and theoretical considerations (see Bettinger, this volume, Chapter 16; introduction to Part V).

As the early stages of specific projects are handled, it is frequently possible to recommend design changes that may lead to the avoidance of sites. The preliminary field study is an ideal way to evaluate alternative designs and suggest those that will have fewest adverse impacts (Vivian *et al.* 1977). An example is provided by Fehon and Viscito's (1974) work in the Village Creek drainage of northeastern Arkansas. On the basis of a 17⅔% stratified random sample of the direct impact zone of a proposed channel they were able to discern patterns of site location and density and to recommend design changes to the Army Corps of Engineers. They discovered a greater density and diversity of sites on the first and second terraces than on the floodplain of Village Creek. These findings led to the recommendation "that the proposed channel be confined to the present floodplain of the Creek [p. 30]."

Sometimes ill-conceived recommendations for design changes can actually result in greater site destruction. This can easily occur because avoidance per se does not insure preservation. For example, it is not uncommon for investigators to propose that sites in a transmission line corridor can be avoided simply by careful placement of the power poles (e.g., Stone and Opfenring 1975:12). In many situations this action would afford sites little protection. In fact, the destructive effects of construction activities (especially clearing the corridor, movement of heavy equipment, smoothing the terrain, and stringing of the line) and vandalism by construction personnel would probably be greater than the disturbance caused by erection of the poles (cf. Toney 1975:5–8; Weston 1974). A similar situation was encountered by Donaldson (1975) in making recommendations for management of Sitgreaves National Forest in eastern Arizona. Despite his documentation of a high rate of vandalism and pot-hunting in the area, he recommended that sites be flagged and avoided during juniper-push activities—risking increased visibility and accessibility of sites to vandals. Donaldson's judgment is apparently based on the assumption that juniper-push activities are highly damaging to archaeological sites. Clearly, precise information on the impacts of those practices would have made this recommendation much sounder (cf. DeBloois, Green, and Wylie n.d.). The solution to the general problem lies in a careful consideration of all destructive processes that may impinge upon sites, whether they are avoided or not, and selection of the least destructive alternative.

In some cases the archaeologist will want to propose that active preservation measures be implemented. Dixon (1971) thoroughly discusses this preservation alternative and illustrates it with an actual proposal he submitted to the Orange County (California) Planning Department to preserve the important Fairview Hospital site (Ora-58) and develop it into a public recreational and educational area. His advice on how to write preservation proposals, especially for urban sites, is sound and likely to be applicable generally. He lists (p. 56) several requirements that should be met in formulating proposals. These include specification of the long-term values held by preservation, thorough documentation of the significance of the site, demonstration that preservation is feasible, and enumeration of the immediate public benefits to be gained by preservation.

The probability that preservation proposals will be accepted may be increased by two other considerations. First of all, if there are recreational or scenic values in the immediate area, one should not hesitate to note how a preserved archaeological site, properly indicated and protected from vandalism, can enhance the overall qualities of the environment. The Corps of Engineers, for example, might be quite responsive to the argument that preservation of an undisturbed site in its natural setting will also provide an excellent opportunity for development of the recreational values of an area. Secondly, a close working relationship between the archaeologist and sponsor may sometimes pay rich dividends when it comes to implementing preservation proposals. McCormick (1973:2), for example, describes how Texas Utilities Services, Inc., rerouted a railroad in order to miss the last remaining Caddoan mound group in the country. In addition to saving the site, the utility company agreed to fence off the portion it owns and donate the land to Southern Methodist University.

Sometimes a recommendation of active preservation is highly warranted by special circumstances. In one project, for example, Rohn and Smith (1972:56) identified the presence of historical sites of known significance to the Delaware tribe and recommend the establishment of a Delaware Historic Park or locality to be used for educational purposes and to provide for the religious needs of the tribe (see also Grady, Chapter 24).

A somewhat controversial variant of active preservation is being increasingly promoted. This option involves taking "advantage of the preservative qualities of certain types of construction to stockpile sites for the future [Lipe 1974:224]." Highways and buildings are likely to preserve the sites they are placed over; but the latter will no longer be accessible for scientific study—in the short term. We return below to the implications of this problem. Suffice it to say, one should carefully determine if the proposed action will indeed preserve sites. For example, accumulating evidence indicates that many sites are drastically modified by processes operative in reservoirs (Garrison 1975).

Nomination of sites to the National Register of Historic Places does not by any means insure their preservation, but it does guarantee that they will be considered by the Advisory Council on Historic Preservation before any federal action is executed that threatens their integrity.


## MITIGATIVE EXCAVATION

After avoidance and active preservation alternatives have been exhausted, and when additional impacts remain unmitigated, scientific investigation—usually involving excavation—is the alternative that is frequently turned to. It is becoming clear that mitigative excavation must be conducted in accord with the highest standards of modern archaeology; this, after all, is the unambiguous intent of the Archeological and Historic Conservation Act of 1974. In projects of large scope this normally would include: multistage research throughout project duration; explicit, problem-oriented research designs; rigorous sampling programs; multidisciplinary collaboration; experimentation, simulation, ethnoarchaeology, and other activities as necessary to solve subsidiary problems in method, technique, and theory; and rapid publication and dissemination of the results to a wide audience (Schiffer 1975g:290). Projects of a lesser scope require careful tailoring of research problems to the specific resources. It would not be wise to recommend, for example, that a long-term multidisciplinary, settlement–subsistence research project be implemented to mitigate destruction of three Archaic surface scatters having little substantive research potential. It would, however, be quite appropriate to propose for the same sites an investigation of modest scale that could contribute to studies of lithic technology. What must be stressed is that regardless of the scale of the proposed project, it can and must endeavor to make a solid research effort.

One of the principal considerations in designing a mitigation investigation is to build in sufficient flexibility to facilitate multistage research and decision making. In far too many mitigation proposals the investigators provide, without benefit of a research design, fairly detailed specifications for the treatment of each site (e.g., complete excavation, major excavation, testing, surface collecting, etc.). This approach, which has been criticized in depth elsewhere (Schiffer 1975d:290), precludes multistage research and tacitly closes the door to innovative, problem-oriented investigations. Its primary appeal lies in the ease with which mitigation budgets can be prepared.

D. E. Fox *et al.* (1974) apply a more enlightened approach to recommending mitigative excavations. They propose a two-phase program for mitigating impacts on 357 sites. The first phase consists of exploratory testing, surface collecting, intensive survey of previously missed areas, and additional historical research. Based on the problems and hypotheses defined (and refined) in Phase 1, intensive excavations will be conducted. Naturally, the selection of sites for excavation and their specific treatment must await the results of Phase 1 research. Because research recommendations in a mitigation proposal are seldom more specific than problem domains (since the activity of research design has not yet been funded), it is also useful to suggest, as is some archaeologists' policy, that the first phase of any excavation project be devoted to detailed research design. The mitigative program proposed by Broilo and Reher (Chapter 25), oriented around problem domains, is an example of the kind of flexible strategy that is called for in proposing excavation projects (see also Cooley *et al.* 1975:56).

Although it is desirable to build into mitigation programs complete flexibility in the choice and handling of specific sites, it is sometimes helpful to assign excavation priorities to sites on the basis of significance criteria *and predicted impacts*. Bass and Hester (1975), for example, stratify their sites in terms of five impact areas in a reservoir project. Using this approach flexibility is largely retained, while sites that are in greatest danger— holding constant significance—receive a higher priority for excavation (see also Neal 1972; Nunley and Hester 1975; Canouts 1975).

As might be expected, there are no widely agreed-upon formats for constructing mitigation recommendations and formulating budgets. In the case of excavation, one is clearly faced with a dilemma when it comes to bringing a proposal down to specifics—that is, dollars and cents— especially if the capability of multistage research, with its inherent degree of unpredictability, is adhered to. Although one has identified areas of research potential and perhaps has assembled problem domains, there is still precious little upon which to erect a budget. Two basic solutions have been devised for this problem. The first is to argue, on the basis of the significance assessments and predicted impacts, that a research project is justifiable at a particular scale. This is an explicitly subjective procedure and is based on consideration of the likely range of research foci and research activities that might ultimately become involved in a mitigative undertaking (see Schiffer 1975f,g).

Another approach, exemplified in Grady's paper (Chapter 24), is based on assigning a dollar value to the affected resources calculated on the costs of "total data recovery." Since the latter is unattainable in practice, Grady's approach also depends on consideration of a wide range of potential research problems (although those considerations are not made explicit) and then designation of a (usually large) fraction of the dollar value as the appropriate level of mitigation. Both solutions are based on the need to preserve flexibility in research, and they do not differ substantially in underlying philosophy. In practice, however, Grady's method tends to produce higher and often ineffective estimates for mitigation costs.

In some situations the archaeologist will have an excellent opportunity to propose an excavation program that leads not only to scientific results, but also to enhancement of public educational and recreational values. In South Carolina, for example, T. M. Ryan (1972:181) proposed, after a survey of the 155-acre Columbia Zoological Park, that an integrated program of historical and prehistoric research be initiated and that the historic Saluda factory and canal sites be prepared as interpretive exhibits. As with preservation, one can sometimes make a stronger case for development of excavated sites (by display, stabilization, and restoration) if the immediate area already contains other educational and recreational attractions (see also Donaldson 1975; House and Schiffer 1975b).

## OTHER CONSIDERATIONS

One issue that has received scarcely any attention thus far is the advisability of proposing investigations outside of the direct and indirect impact areas of a project. Pilles and Haas (1973:47) offer the strong argument that any study area represents the remains of just a part of any past system of activities. The proper interpretation of a site requires knowledge of the larger system into which it once fit. Thus adequate mitigation may depend on the study of other (unaffected) sites (see also Lipe 1974:237; McMillan et al. 1977; Schiffer 1975f:296). Although this argument seemingly contradicts the conservation model, and is likely to be a controversial procedure, we believe that it can be justified by research needs and requirements for adequate mitigation.

To this point we have also skirted the issue as to whether mitigation should be proposed for indirect impacts. On this point conservation law is not specific, although precedents have already been set that support the view that a sponsor may be responsible for mitigating indirect impacts (e.g., U.S. Department of the Army 1974). From the standpoint of conservation archaeology the investigator ought to provide recommendations for mitigating all anticipated impacts on the archaeological resources. Whether any or all of the recommendations are acted upon is, of course, out of the hands of the archaeologist in any event.

It is likely that most mitigation recommendations, at least for projects of any size, will consist of a mix of measures, including avoidance, active preservation, and excavation. The conservation archaeologist should exercise his creativity to the maximum in tailoring the mix to the circumstances at hand. This becomes especially important if the environmental context of archaeological resources will also be adversely affected. At present, few investigators have given thought to how those losses may be responsibly mitigated.

## CONFLICTS IN ARCHAEOLOGICAL VALUES

Inevitably, well-intentioned and competent archaeologists may offer far different proposals for mitigating impacts on the same archaeological resources. Several recent examples point out the potential conflicts that can arise from giving different weights to preservation, conservation, and other archaeological values. In New York State, the Town Line Flats site, believed to contain data relevant to at least two important Woodland research problems in western New York prehistory, was to be adversely affected by highway construction. The consulting archaeologist to the state Department of Transportation recommended that the site be excavated (M. E. White 1974), while the state archaeologist offered the opinion that the site be preserved by elevating the roadbed above it (Lord 1974). In cases such as this where honest disagreements over the best means for mitigation arise, or may be expected to arise later, two potential remedies may be explored.

First, it might be worthwhile to obtain advice from a broad sample of investigators with established research interests in the area. This might lead to a consensus or to a possible compromise measure (e.g., partial excavation, and preservation of the remainder). Second, one might formulate the general principle that the preservation option (without further, immediate research capability) be reserved for nonunique sites. Thus portions of well-excavated sites and examples of common sites could be recommended for preservation, while rare types of sites—data from which are likely to be in demand for research questions in the foreseeable future—should be excavated using the best possible research design. Naturally, the cost differential will often make the preservation alternative more attractive to the sponsor; and this will require the archaeologist to construct convincing arguments about the meaning of adequate mitigation in particular situations. As Wildesen (1975) cogently argues, "The *preservation* of a site by not studying it now may in the long run cost us more than *using* it to increase our understanding of former ways of life [p. 11; emphasis in original]."

Another area of potential disagreement may surface when a proposal of excavation is preferred over avoidance. In some situations ongoing destructive processes (e.g., vandalism, farming, wave action, etc.) are destroying a resource base at a measurable rate. Under these circumstances, an avoidance alternative is based on the unrealistic assumption that, somehow, investigations will be carried out in the area prior to complete destruction of the resource base (S. Plog 1976b:278). As Stephen Plog (1976b) inquires, would it not be preferable to obtain some information now rather than possibly no information in the future? Arguments for the excavation alternative in similar situations will have to be tightly drawn, for they are likely to be appreciably more costly than avoidance.

Other painful choices may confront those who design mitigation programs. For example, Ahlstrom and Bradford (1974) surveyed two alternate plant-site locations in eastern Arizona. They found that sites in the vicinity of the Snowflake plant site were far less significant and more damaged than those in the St. Johns plant site. They recommended that the Snowflake plant be built and that excavation be carried out at affected sites, although they would have preferred—on purely research grounds—to excavate at St. Johns. Their proposal is a sound one in the framework of strict preservationist values, but one could have argued it the other way around as well, since avoidance of the St. Johns sites would not have guaranteed their preservation and availability for future research (see also McMillan *et al.* 1977).

In short, we can expect sometimes serious controversies to develop in the area of mitigation recommendations. These differences in opinion result from conflicts in archaeological values (King 1971) and cannot be readily—if ever—resolved. Our advice to conservation archaeologists is to provide a well-reasoned, thoroughly documented set of arguments for any mitigation proposal in the hope that they will be reviewed by those who, though they may disagree with the recommendations, do respect the pluralism in archaeological values.

## RESPONSIBILITIES TO THE SPONSOR

It is well to keep in mind that the archaeologist's primary task is to provide scientifically informed recommendations to those who, after weighing many factors, will make decisions effecting cultural resources. As a consequence of this advisory role, the conservation archaeologist assumes a number of weighty responsibilities.

First of all, the archaeologist's recommendations should always be based solely on archaeological considerations. Nothing can lower the credibility of a specialist faster than his attempt to go beyond his expertise.

Second, the archaeologist ought to become acquainted with the powers and workings of the sponsor agency. This enables the archaeologist initially to screen out mitigation ideas that *totally* lack feasibility. For example, the archaeologist would almost certainly lose credibility if he suggested to the Soil Conservation Service, a federal agency not empowered to own land, that they purchase sites for long-term preservation. Knowledge of the sponsor's limitations can help reduce embarrassing situations and misunderstandings and can lead to mitigation recommendations that have a measurable probability of being implemented.

In addition, consultation with project engineers to obtain detailed information about their procedures often can provide the archaeologist with mitigation ideas that might not otherwise occur. For example, in conversations with M. B. Strohm of the Corps of Engineers Schiffer (1975f) learned that although artificial channels usually have spoil piled on both banks, there is no technical reason why it cannot be piled on one bank only—thus it is possible to avoid covering sites. It was also learned that channel placement itself is somewhat more flexible than one might gather from viewing static project plans—thus there are some options for avoidance.

In the third place, the archaeologist should strive, whenever it is possible, to furnish the sponsor with a range of viable mitigation alternatives. This has seldom been done but, if tried, could perhaps improve relations between sponsors and conservation archaeologists. Needless to say, alternative mitigation plans should be ranked according to archaeological priorities.

And finally, we must bear firmly in mind that mitigation recommendations, above all other management information, will be read primarily by nonarchaeologists. This requires that mitigation proposals be lucidly and concisely written, be free of technical jargon, and be as specific and unambiguous as possible. A recent example from Arkansas illustrates how easily misunderstandings can develop when words are not chosen carefully. In proposing that the Arkansas Eastman Company protect several sites endangered by construction activities, Spears and Claassen (1974) recommended, at the urging of Schiffer, that the sites be covered with a layer of *sterile* soil. A communication problem was discovered later, after personnel from the company inquired plaintively about the required degree of chemical and biological sterility, while, of course, the archaeologists meant culturally sterile (Charles R. McGimsey, personal communication, 1975). Clearly the archaeologist is responsible for seeing to it that management recommendations are intelligible to the intended audience (see MacLeod, this volume, Chapter 3).

## CONCLUSION

In conclusion, we believe that mitigation needs to be viewed as an extremely broad concept. Impacts can be alleviated in many ways, only some of which we are now using. And let us not forget one of the simplest, most useful recommendations: Gather more data to permit the design of a detailed mitigation program. For example, when crops obscure part of the surveyed area, then revisits at more propitious times should be proposed. When dense forest prevents survey, then one should recommend that as areas are cleared for construction, survey should be carried out (e.g., Connors 1976; Skinner and Cliff 1973). If buried sites are anticipated, then efforts should be made to discover and evaluate them. As Schiffer (1975g:289) notes, the design of a mitigation program is predicated on the availability of up-to-date information on the nature and extent of the resources, their significance, and the impacts of the proposed action. When such information is not at hand, then the first task is to continue archaeological investigations until that level of knowledge is reached.

In reality, when archaeologists consider mitigation, they usually suggest a flexible plan that combines avoidance, preservation, and excavation. Avoidance and preservation and excavation are not necessarily mutually exclusive categories in most projects.

A final point needs to be underscored on the unavoidable losses that result from mitigative activities. Short of total preservation of the resources (or modification of a project so that it produces no adverse impacts), most mitigative measures do not totally alleviate impacts. Even creative and productive mitigative excavations must be viewed as incomplete; some scientific values always will be lost irretrievably. How can we ever mitigate doing what, in the long run, is premature destruction of sites? The realization that completely adequate mitigation is a chimera should alert us to the need for attending to our mitigation recommendations with the utmost care and reflection.

# 24

# Mitigation Recommendations for the Orme Reservoir Project

MARK A. GRADY

The following discussion is a synthesis and update of the mitigation chapter in the Orme Reservoir report (Canouts 1975). Although originally written by me, the chapter was partially revised by others in the Cultural Resource Management Section of the Arizona State Museum in order to comply with subsequent changes in the contract. The basic arguments and conclusions have not been altered; however, some pertinent recent information has been added, and several potentially confusing aspects of the original contribution have been clarified.

As indicated in an earlier chapter of this volume, Orme Dam, a Bureau of Reclamation undertaking, is proposed to be built at the junction of the lower Verde and Salt rivers, east of Phoenix, Arizona (Map 1, Chapter 19). The effects of project construction and water impoundment will disturb or destroy a considerable number of important cultural remains.

## THE CONCEPT OF MITIGATION

Mitigation can be defined as any action that results in reducing or eliminating the detrimental impact of land alteration activities on natural or cultural resources. Mitigation is thus implemented in a number of ways, at least three of which are generally recognized: (*1*) preservation of the resource base; (*2*) avoidance of the resource base; and (*3*) adequate study of the resource base. It is important to note that adequate study (or "salvage") of threatened cultural remains is not the only mitigative alternative available and in many cases is not the preferred approach.

The Cultural Resource Management Section of the Arizona State Museum recommended that the most responsible action to be taken with respect to the archaeological remains in the study area was to insure their preservation. However, in keeping with Section 102(C) of the National Environmental Policy Act as interpreted by the Scovill, Gordon and Anderson guidelines (1972), data study cost estimates were also derived. These estimates were developed on the basis of the research recommendations outlined in the significance discussion and projections relating to the ways in which dam construction and reservoir filling would impact the cultural remains.

## IMPACT OF THE PROJECT ON THE RESOURCE BASE

As currently proposed, the dam construction itself will affect several significant sites. In addition, the reservoir will partially, periodically, or permanently inundate most of the known cultural manifestations in the study area. Five major impact zones have been identified (see Map 1, Chapter 19).

### Dam Construction Zone (Orme Dam Site)

The sites in this area will be disturbed or destroyed early in the construction phase. Borrow pit establishment and development, slated to occur on the Salt River arm of the project area at the same time, will also result in damage to the archaeological record. Clearing and other terrain modification, which normally precede water impoundments, will be harmful to at least the surfaces of affected sites and will significantly reduce their information potential. The adjuncts of reservoir construction—such as heavy equipment access, movement, and storage; the temporary establishment of field construction buildings; and the deployment of a labor force—are relevant to the mitigation of cultural resources, although their consequences cannot be accurately predicted due to lack of available reservoir planning information.

### Minimum Water Surface Zone

This zone contains sites that will be inundated by, partially inundated by, or subjected to the wave action of the minimum water surface of the reservoir. The minimum pool will completely submerge several sites and partially inundate an additional one. Although no comprehensive studies of the effects of long-term inundation of archaeological sites have been undertaken, available data indicate that deflation of cultural and natural stratigraphy, sediment deposition, and decomposition of organic material are to be expected (Jewell 1961). Additional modifications would include alteration of the biotic communities subjected to inundation. Thus, cultural-environmental reconstruction following flooding would be rendered infinitely more difficult, if not impossible.

## Maximum Conservation Pool Zone

This is the part of the reservoir to be periodically submerged; the upper limit of this zone is the highest level the water will normally attain. A great many sites in the zone would be subjected to complete semiannual inundation, and several would face periodic partial submergence. Most of the information available on the effects of impounded water on archaeological sites deals with the results of sites exposed to wave action and fluctuating water levels—the fate of sites here. In almost all cases, erosion either completely destroyed or seriously damaged site contextual relationships (Husted 1973; Neal 1974). The effects of periodic inundation include the destruction mentioned with regard to permanent inundation, except that differential saturation and drying accelerates organic decomposition and stratigraphic deflation (Husted 1973; Jewell 1961; Prewitt 1972:6–11). Problems previously discussed in relation to cultural-ecological studies would also apply to the sites with this zone.

## Maximum Water Surface Zone

The effects of flooding in this zone will be somewhat different. As the upper limits of this level will only be submerged when extreme flood conditions prevail, the resources could be sporadically submerged or possibly not affected at all, depending on their location. Although the adverse results of reservoir construction would seem to be less in this zone, this is not necessarily the case. Even sporadic flooding of sites could destroy most, if not all, of the research potential (Leninan 1974:28–30). In addition, the maximum water surface area will be available for nonpermanent use, such as farming and recreation. The destruction of the archaeological record due to land modification activities and increased access will likely be as severe as with periodic inundation.

Many sites are present in the maximum water surface area, a number of which will be partially flooded. Sites closest to the maximum conservation pool limits and those in areas most suitable for reservoir-related exploitation will probably be the earliest affected. As traffic increases, however, most sites within this zone can be expected to suffer at least from vandalism.

## Indirect Impact Zone

Here adverse effects are related to land development and reservoir maintenance, both of which produce land modification and increased population pressure. Numerous sites are wholly or partially within the half-mile above the maximum water surface area, which was arbitrarily designated as the indirect impact zone; the amount of damage to these sites cannot be determined at present. Some assessment of predicted project results can be made only in those cases where developmental plans are available. In all such cases development will damage or destroy archaeological sites directly through topographical alteration activities and indirectly through resultant vandalism. Although these are largely privately sponsored activities, their presence will be in many cases a direct response to reservoir construction. The adverse impact that such private development will have on the archaeological record should be prevented if possible and mitigated if necessary.

## DATA STUDY COSTS

As has been previously discussed, cost is an incomplete indication of the cultural values in the project area that would be lost in the event that data study becomes necessary. Not only are certain aesthetic and educational considerations, among others, currently unquantifiable, but the data potential identified from a scientific perspective reflects primarily the research orientations maintained by the Cultural Resource Management Section personnel, as well as the current state of the discipline (Lipe 1974). Nonetheless, estimated cost figures for the study of the threatened data base are necessary for cultural resource management planning at this stage. Such estimates provide a comparison between the cost of conserving data and the projected monetary benefits of land alteration plans. They also provide a basis for emphasizing that adequate study of the resource base must take place if project implementation results. With these considerations in mind, the cost figures for investigating all the cultural remains in the study area were generated. These figures were derived from a series of data study formulas that are explained in the following pages. The resultant projected costs are based on complete information recovery, analysis, write-up, and report dissemination within the framework of research recommendations emphasized in Chapter 19. As such, they reflect currently applicable theory, method, and technique used to arrive at *responsible estimates* of funding requirements for the study of archaeological materials in the study region. The formula components therefore represent *averages* of the amounts of time and money to be allocated for these endeavors. Since the formulas were developed for use with a relatively large site population, general relationships hold between the formulas and intensive examination of sites in the study area. But individual estimates are likely to be slightly skewed with respect to very large or very small sites. Wage averages per laborer, for example, are somewhat disproportionate when applied to the extremes of site size in the Orme area. The greater number of medium-sized sites in the population, however, tends to even out this discrepancy, and the monetary evaluations as a whole are representative of the overall cost of contemporary data study.

It is difficult to account for all the factors that must be considered in recovering and analyzing archaeological remains. For one thing, surface survey information, even combined with testing, provides an incomplete indication of overall research potential. However, the formulas and estimates are believed to be applicable to the Orme area cultural manifestations and a range of research objectives appropriate to those manifestations. The time and labor estimates were developed through consultation with archaeologists having research experience in the area, as well as a review of pertinent documentary information. These data were derived from, among other sources, the Arizona State Museum, the Department of Anthropology at the University of Arizona, the Department of Anthropology at Arizona State University, and the Western Archeological Center of the National Park Service.

Three formulas for data recovery costs were developed. Each is applicable to a generalized site category for which certain research procedures are appropriate. For illustrative purposes only the habitation site category is included here (Table 24.1).

Analysis funding requirements were averaged based on the costs for the special analyses listed in Table 24.2. This figure was abstracted from information supplied to the Arizona State Museum by relevant professionals in these areas. Most of these figures vary with specific site conditions and are therefore not detailed in the text.

Write-up and publication procedures are standard for most archaeological reports. Again, average estimates for publication and dissemination costs were based on Arizona State Museum experience combined with information provided by local publication outlets.

It should be noted that these procedures do not include records and archaeological

**TABLE 24.1.**
**Time and Labor Estimates**[a]

*Habitation site components*

| | |
|---|---|
| Mounds | |
| (average for refuse and other plus backhoe time): | 1 person for 25 days |
| Pit houses (estimate of 10 per refuse mound) | |
| (average for 1 house plus backhoe time): | 1 person for 5 days |
| Ball courts | |
| (plus backhoe time): | 1 person for 100 days |
| Pueblo rooms | |
| (includes compounds plus backhoe time): | 1 person for 25 days |
| Historical rooms | |
| (includes Fort McDowell, corrals, latrines, plus backhoe time): | 1 person for 15 days |
| Additional features | |
| (includes extramural stripping, specialized sampling, other special activity areas, plus backhoe time): | 1 person for 20 days |

*Additional expenditure estimates*

| | |
|---|---|
| Aerial photographs | |
| (Approximately $1000/day): | 10 days |
| Data study research design | |
| (based on 1 person designing a specific research implementation strategy for adequate data study in the project area, including expenses and staff assistance—$20,000): | 1 year |
| Pre-project preparation | |
| (based on estimated costs for developing administrative and logistic support, planning and construction of field facilities, and other considerations necessary before full-scale fieldwork could be started—$480,000): | 1 year |

[a] Based on data recovery from single examples of site components.

**TABLE 24.2.**
**Procedures in Archaeological Site Study**

| Recovery | Analysis | Write-up/publication |
|---|---|---|
| Research design | Architectural studies | Report composition |
| Provenience control method | Archival research | Typing |
| Data collecting<br>  Aerial photography | Artifact typology | Drafting |
|   Copying (rock art)<br>  Environmental documentation | Burial/cremation studies | Photography |
|   Excavation<br>    (mechanical/manual) | Ceramic studies | Editing/proofreading |
|   Extramural stripping<br>    (habitation sites) | Data processing | Duplication |
|   Remote sensing<br>  Resistivity studies | Dating<br>  Alpha recoil | Peer review |
|   Specialized sampling<br>  Surface mapping<br>    (surface sites) | Archaeomagnetism<br>  Dendrochronology<br>  Fission tracking | |
|   Test excavation<br>  Topographical studies<br>    (agricultural features) | Obsidian hydration<br>  Radiocarbon<br>  Thermoluminescence | |
| | Geology<br>  Lithologic studies | |
| Data recording<br>  Photography | Soil analysis<br>    (chemical, etc.) | |
|   Drafting/illustration<br>  Data computerization | Depositional studies | |
| | Lithic artifact studies | |
| | Perishable studies<br>  Microfossil analysis<br>  Macrofossil analysis | |
| | Photogrammetry | |
| | Pollen studies | |
| | Shell studies | |
| | Trace element studies | |

materials processing and curation. It has recently been recognized that these activities, insofar as they are involved with contract research data, represent an expense that is legitimately charged to the contract sponsor.

The estimated costs for all the activities identified in these formulas, exclusive of those for labor (which were developed in 1973 and are now out of date), were prorated to provide a cost-per-day figure. This prorated estimate was then added to the cost of a single laborer in the field for 8 hours, yielding a unit cost per person per day of all necessary expenditures involved in archaeological data study (Table 24.3).

The data recovery and write-up/publication formulas personnel consist of not only the field staff directly responsible for work at an individual site but also the support staff involved in laboratory activities and overall project direction. No

**TABLE 24.3.**
**Total Site Study Formulas: Budget Elements**

| | | |
|---|---|---|
| Staff | | |
| Direction | | |
| 1 assistant director: | | $58.00/day |
| 1 supervisor III: | | $40.00/day |
| Laboratory | | |
| 1 supervisor II: | | $36.00/day |
| 1 laboratory technician III: | | $32.00/day |
| 1 laboratory technician II: | | $29.20/day |
| Field supervision | | |
| 1 supervisor II: | | $36.00/day |
| Specialized data collection and recording | | |
| 2 archaeological assistants II: | | $22.80/day |
| 1 photographer II: | | $36.00/day |
| 1 draftsperson II: | | $36.00/day |
| | Average | $34.88/day |
| Supervisors/specialists | | |
| 2 staff members/laborer-day: | | $69.76 |
| Labor | | |
| 1 laborer @ $22.00/day: | | 22.00 |
| Taxes and insurance | | |
| (17% of wages): | | 15.59 |
| Indirect costs | | |
| off-campus (30% of wages): | | 27.53 |
| Supplies | | |
| $15.00/day: | | 15.00 |
| Subsistence and lodging | | |
| $20.00/day/staff person: | | 40.00 |
| Transportation | | |
| estimate of 50 miles/day @ 13¢/mile + $3.00/day: | | 9.50 |
| | Total | $199.38 |
| | Rounded to | $200.00 |

(*continued*)

**TABLE 24.3.** (*continued*)

---

*Analysis*

| | | |
|---|---|---|
| Average analysis costs (includes travel or shipping costs where necessary; prorated to cost per person-day): | Total | $60.00 |

*Write-up/publication*

Staff
  Direction

| | | |
|---|---|---|
| 1 assistant director—½ time | $58.00/day: | 29.00 |
| 1 supervisor II | $36.00/day: | 36.00 |

  Write-up

| | | |
|---|---|---|
| 1 supervisor II | $36.00/day: | 36.00 |
| 2 assistant archaeologists | $32.00/day: | 64.00 |

  Report Preparation

| | | |
|---|---|---|
| 1 draftsperson II—¾ time | $36.00/day: | 27.00 |
| 1 editor—½ time | $54.00/day: | 27.00 |
| 1 typist—¾ time | $21.32/day: | 16.00 |

| | | |
|---|---|---|
| Taxes and insurance (17% of wages): | | 39.95 |
| Indirect costs on-campus (46% of wages): | | 108.10 |
| Supplies and operations: | | 20.00 |
| Publication estimated cost per person-day: | | 3.50 |

| | | |
|---|---|---|
| | Total | $406.55 |
| | Rounded to | $405.00 |

---

director is included in these estimates, as it is assumed that this individual is a permanent employee of the contracting institution.

Additional itemized expenses are largely specific to Arizona State Museum and the University of Arizona contractual policies and project-specific logistic considerations. These considerations are detailed in the report proper.

The estimates for complete study of archaeological features found in Table 24.1, combined with the formulas from Table 24.3, are multiplied by an estimate of the time it would take one person to do a thorough investigation of the site. Relevant site feature information is provided in the complete report. This figure, then, yields the total cost per site required to completely recover, analyze, and publish all data considered in the formulas.

For example, Site U:6:126 has two historical adobe structures, one of which has two rooms. These features make up the habitation site components. Referring to Table 24.1, note that it takes 15 person-days to recover the data from one historical room. Thus the historical structure data recovery time is 45 person-days (15 × 3). Multiplying this latter figure by the total data study unit cost per day ($200 + $60 + $405, or $665), yields the site study cost of $29,925 for the habitation site features.

The total cost-per-site figures for the Orme study area sites do not take into account additional implementation costs, which are listed in Table 24.1. These include the development of a detailed multistage regional research design, the planning and construction of field facilities, and other logistic preparations necessary before actual work can be started.

This evaluative approach, again, can only be employed in making *estimates* for funding archaeological studies. Nonetheless, the averages derived for total site study, given the current status of the discipline, the number of threatened resources, and the overall research orientations previously discussed, reliably approximate the expense involved in implementing responsible investigation of the complete resource base. This cost is calculated to be $53,875,510.

## Adequate Data Study Costs

Should data study become necessary in the Orme Reservoir impact area, the investigation of all available data is neither feasible nor desirable. Adequate data study should be directed toward the investigation of that percentage of the data base sufficient to meet project investigative objectives.

Yet the Orme Reservoir research recommendations did not emphasize any specific study program. Instead, a range of research approaches considered appropriate to the project area were proposed. A specific research strategy based on one or more applicable problems was to be developed prior to initiation of the fieldwork. Since it is not possible to establish particular investigation procedures in the absence of a research design, the sample size problem was dealt with in terms of precedents derived from recent archaeological sampling studies, the characteristics of the cultural resources in the study area, and the research orientations within which data study would most likely be undertaken.

The question of sampling has been a major concern of archaeologists for at least two decades (e.g., Judge 1972; Redman 1974; Redman and Watson 1970; Rootenberg 1964; Vescelius 1960). But little of this concern has been devoted to the question of sampling-fraction adequacy. And even less has been directed toward identifying a sample size applicable to a range of research approaches within a particular archaeological population.

The few archaeologists who have considered this problem (cf. Chenhall 1975:22; Fuller, Gregonis and Rogge 1976:102–117; Mueller 1974:57; Plog and Hill 1971:21; Ragir 1975; Texas Archaeological Salvage Project Staff 1971) have concluded essentially that a 40–50% sample or higher is necessary in order to satisfy the needs of many research requirements. This general position is supported in current publications on statistical applications in the social sciences (Blalock and Blalock 1968:285–286; Cochran 1963:8).

One recent study on archaeological sampling considered the effect of sample size on the validity of specific archaeological conclusions (Mueller 1974). One of the factors Mueller evaluated was sample size as it related to economy—the cost of archaeological research. He concluded that a 40% sampling fraction was the smallest that would provide a reasonably representative sample of population variability within a universe, given a minimum of stratifying parameters (Mueller 1974:66). Despite the problems with Mueller's conclusions (S. Plog n.d.), his argument was deemed relevant for defining the lowest acceptable sample fraction appropriate for the purposes of this project. In light of the fact that only a generalized research orientation is recommended at this level, the 50% figure represents the most responsible sampling fraction that can be advocated should mitigative data study become necessary. Adequate data study, therefore, will require between 40% and 50% of the cost of total data study.

It cannot be overemphasized that sampling considerations must relate to the problems being studied in the archaeological record and the character of the research universe. No one sampling design (or sampling fraction) will necessarily satisfy the requirements of all research approaches (Asch 1975; Cowgill 1975). On the other hand, there are occasions when sampling recommendations must be predicted on only generalized project goals (e.g., Lipe 1974:234). In these cases, particularly when the research potential allows for the consideration of complex questions, the sample must be relatively large (Cowgill 1975:274). Thus, for any site category identified in the research design for further study, the sample size should be great enough to allow mathematically valid sampling procedures to be applied. Such an argument does not necessarily indicate that 40–50% of every site will be sampled. Once specific research goals, sampling strategies, and confidence limits have been established, sampling requirements can be much more precisely defined. In some sites less than the overall sampling fraction will be adequate; in others a large sample size may be required.

The cost of the data study mitigation for the Orme Reservoir Project at 50% of the cost of total data study is estimated at $26,937,755. If we use a 40% sample, the estimated cost will be $21,550,204.

## MITIGATIVE DATA STUDY SCHEDULING

The proper implementation of adequate archaeological data study in the Orme Reservoir area would ideally require approximately 20 years and 10 full-time qualified archaeological supervisors. However, a multiphase program could be developed (cf. Redman 1973) that would maximize data study returns as well as coordinate with dam construction and reservoir-filling projections. Such a program would need a year of research strategy planning and logistic preparation before field research could begin. This program must also assume that land modification will occur in accordance with the phases discussed previously. If terrain alteration in addition to or out of sequence with the construction and water impoundment progression identified in the impacts zone discussion becomes necessary, alternative scheduling will have to be developed.

## Dam Construction Zone (Orme Dam Site)

Sites in the borrow pit areas and those immediately adjacent to the dam will be threatened first. Five sites are known to be in this impact area, with more potentially affected when borrow pit locations are finalized. Given current information, adequate data study will cost between $227,667 and $182,134, depending on whether the 50% or the 40% sample is used. A tentative estimate for the time required to recover the necessary data is 6 months to 1 year, with two to three supervisors needed in the field.

## Minimum Water Surface Zone

This zone, the area to be permanently inundated, will likely be partially or wholly flooded before completion of the dam proper. Thus it is recommended that this phase be implemented with the archaeological study of the previous zone. Five sites have been recorded in the minimum water surface area, and adequate investigation will cost from $236,737 to $229,389. Data recovery is estimated to take from 6 months to 1 year, requiring two to three field supervisors.

## Maximum Conservation Pool Zone

Containing 60 recorded sites, this zone will be subjected to semiannual flooding. As indicated previously, periodic flooding of sites may do as much damage as will permanent inundation, if not more. Adequate study of these records must therefore take place *before* any flooding occurs. More detailed priority decisions can be made once the research strategy is defined and reservoir planning is further developed.

Adequate sampling of the sites in this zone will cost between $8,284,290 and $6,627,432. The projected time period for completing data recovery is 5 years. As many as 10 full-time supervisors would be necessary to direct the work during this period.

## Maximum Flood Pool Zone

This zone is slated for use as a "safety margin" in controlling projected periodic flooding of the Verde and Salt rivers. The archaeological resources here would probably be subjected to occasional inundation. As occasional flooding and other activities will adversely affect cultural remains, ameliorative procedures should also be implemented in this zone. However, as flooding is not predicted to occur frequently, mitigative action here has lower priority.

Given the projected function of this zone, it is conceivable that preservation measures could be developed for some sites. Alternative solutions to data study include the building of dikes and berms to protect archaeological resources against flooding. Such alternatives would have to be carefully planned and executed, as similar approaches elsewhere have met with failure. Nonetheless, adequate long-term preservation would be preferable to investigation and would probably be less expensive.

The mitigative funding estimates for the maximum flood pool include all sites, as the decision as to which sites could be preserved cannot yet be made. A total of 68 sites are located in this zone. A 50% sample of total data study yields $12,838,295. The 40% estimate is $10,270,636.

With no Bureau of Reclamation constraints on mitigation time for this phase, completion of field data recovery and analysis will likely require 6 to 7 years. Seven to eight supervisory experts would be needed. In addition, some field restudies, analyses, and write-up from previous phases may be unfinished and should be dealt with at this time. This, of course, will not require additional funding. In total, this phase will take a minimum of 10 years to complete.

## Indirect Impact Zone

This area was surveyed in order to assess the archaeological resources potentially threatened by reservoir-related development and other indirect impact. Although the adverse effects cannot be assessed at this time, some resource loss is inevitable. As such loss would be a consequence of reservoir development, the cost of mitigating developmental zone sites is built into this budget.

Alternatives to data study should also be promoted during this phase. Sites in the indirect impact zone will not be exposed to inundation, and preservation measures would not have to include consideration of this problem. Protective steps such as fencing archaeological remains, guarding sites, or even burying cultural manifestations are viable alternatives to mitigative data study.

Although protection is preferable to site loss, there is no way of currently determining those sites that could be preserved. Therefore, as for the previous phase, data study estimates have been developed for all the sites located in the indirect impact zone.

The 50% figure for the 54 sites within this zone is computed at $5,035,416. A 40% sample would cost $4,028,333.

As this phase of mitigation need not be concerned with Bureau of Reclamation timetables, additional time can be spent on field studies. However, as permanent urban development is likely in this zone but will not be allowed in the maximum flood pool zone, parts of this phase should perhaps be considered of higher priority than the previous phase. Thus, if commercialization is imminent in certain locations, ameliorative action may be necessary before study is completed in all parts of the maximum flood pool.

## FINAL REMARKS

Prehistoric sites in central and southern Arizona are particularly susceptible to the effects of land alteration projects. Although literally thousands of such sites were once present in this region prior to Euramerican arrival, most of the archaeological knowledge concerning these peoples is derived from less than a dozen sites. Concentrated in the Salt–Gila Basin, a great many Hohokam–Salado sites succumbed to urban and agricultural expansion before they could be studied. In addition, systematic investigation of these sites has not kept pace with that of the other major prehistoric Southwestern cultures, and, as a result, much less is known about Hohokam–Salado development and adaptation. Thus the long-term archaeological productivity of the Orme Reservoir area is exceedingly relevant to the understanding of regional prehistory. Coupled with the fact that probably over half of all such sites along major drainages have now been destroyed, it is critical that short-term environmental modification be carefully weighed against the loss of this rapidly dwindling resource base. For it is only with the development of responsible conservation-oriented management approaches that the most productive and cumulatively beneficial use of our archaeological resources will have been achieved.

## ACKNOWLEDGMENTS

This chapter has benefited from refinements in the original report by Veletta Canouts and Lynn Teague. Any lack of sophistication herein should not be attributed to those individuals.

# 25

# Research and Mitigation Considerations in the Regional Contract Survey[1]

FRANK J. BROILO
CHARLES A. REHER

Increasingly the impacts of natural resource exploitation and other land alteration projects on the environment have become the concern of the public, federal and state governments, and, in this case, archaeologists as well. For, as a direct and indirect consequence of such activities, archaeological remains and their environmental context are subjected to damage or total loss. Specifically, this concern for the long-term productivity of cultural resources is manifest in both current legislation and a professional philosophy as phrased by Lipe (1974) and others (Gumerman 1973). The fragile and irreplaceable nature of the resource thus requires our awareness, as archaeologists, predicated upon several interrelated considerations; these include the implementation of a conservation ethic and the attendant necessity that research be conducted in accord with the highest professional standards.

Cultural resource management programs exhibit three broad spheres of responsibility: to the law, to the profession, and to the client. In this regard resource management programs occupy a pivotal point of articulation between the intent of the law and profession on one side and the needs of the client on the other. The former interests must serve to maintain the integrity of the resource base. However, it is argued here that such goals can only be affected by means of institutional research structures that efficiently meet contractual obligations, for ultimate failure to achieve adequate performance in any of these responsibilities constitutes an unsuccessful resource management project.

It is hardly necessary to point out that research conducted in the not so tranquil atmosphere of contract obligations often generates complex and demanding prob-

[1]This chapter was originally prepared for the Cultural Resource Management Symposium of the Society for American Archaeology, Dallas, Texas, May 1975.

lems for the archaeologist. We are all familiar with the engineer who requests that a 75-mile right-of-way be surveyed by next Thursday and that a report and letter of recommendation be submitted by the following Monday. Setting aside such extremes, we have a substantial basis for contending that the goals of professional research and the needs of the client are compatible and, in fact, function to serve both concerns. Based on this assumption, it is suggested that an inventory survey that is structured on an explicitly defined research design and incorporates interdisciplinary expertise should culminate in an efficient and economical mitigation program. The systematic collection of comprehensive cultural and environmental data during survey should provide a data base that permits sampling strategies to be employed in succeeding mitigation. Cultural resource management programs so structured serve the interest of both archaeologist and client.

For example, a recent inventory survey of approximately 68.5 square miles located on the Navajo Reservation in northwestern New Mexico implemented these considerations and may serve to illustrate our argument. The Coal Gasification Project (CGP) survey was undertaken to provide information on archaeological resources located on lands leased by Western Gasification Company and Utah International, Inc., for the purpose of developing an environmental impact statement. Let us briefly outline the relevant structural considerations as implemented in this survey and discuss some of its successes and failures as a resource management project.

## STRUCTURE OF THE COAL GASIFICATION
## PROJECT RESEARCH DESIGN

Fundamental in developing the research design for the CGP survey was the premise that archaeological survey can, in and of itself, contribute data to the formulation and testing of hypotheses that inform on cultural process (Judge, Ebert, and Hitchcock 1973:17). A second, related, consideration supposes that *no* assessment of scientific significance for a mitigation program can be formulated without a comprehensive understanding of the settlement–subsistence systems in the study area.

The initial phase of the CGP survey involved the usual gearing-up as well as an allotment of time and funds for the development of an explicitly defined research orientation. This phase is considered to be critical to the structuring of the survey, since it provides the basis for specifying what classes of data would be relevant to research questions and since it ultimately contributes to the overall efficiency of the project. Two basic assumptions were employed in the broad theoretical framework for the research design (Reher n.d.): (*1*) that culture is an adaptive system employing "minimax" strategies; and (*2*) that environmental determinants, that is, resources, would account for the nature and distribution of archaeological sites on the landscape. This research approach has been employed by the Southwestern Anthropological Research Group (SARG) (Judge 1971:40). The survey research design then structured hypotheses to be tested by survey data. These involved the consideration of settlement systems on a regional scale and were specifically focused to explicate relationships between intrasite variability and resource extractive behavior, and between site distribution and potential access to resources.

In accordance with these considerations, the survey was designed to gather data concerning a broad range of cultural and environmental variables. As such, the participation of researchers from several disciplines was incorporated into research development and implementation. Procedures involved in executing the survey consisted of employing an interval transect stratification that crosscut most, but not all, of the environmental variability observed by aerial imagery and ground truth verification. Survey of the interval transects proceeded in sample blocks of known percentage that permitted "data feedback" at predetermined stages (Redman 1973). This procedure not only served to "fine tune" the research strategy but also permitted an evaluation of the feasibility of undertaking research based upon new information. In addition, the multistage nature of the field survey provided critical information regarding site densities and field progress. This contributed to making necessary adjustments in the contract budget and the successful completion of the field phase of the project.

In all, the survey recorded 412 Navajo components, 190 Pueblo components, 5 Basket Maker components, 93 Archaic components, 3 Paleo-Indian components, and 5 unknowns. Intensive morphological and wear-pattern analysis was conducted on 12,000 pieces of debitage. In addition, 15,000 pottery sherds were subjected to attribute analysis.

## THE STRATEGY OF MITIGATION

From an economic perspective this survey format may require more initial cost, or need for "front money," for the client. Such may be the case; however, it is suggested that such an expenditure at this phase of the project results in a data base that permits the development of an elegant mitigation program, thereby substantially reducing cost during that phase. The reasoning underlying this strategy focuses on the implementation of sampling designs for mitigation purposes that are derived from comprehensive survey data. The use of this methodology can accurately delineate what proportions of the sites should be subjected to further investigation in a recommended program of mitigation. As such, the scientific significance of the resources may be defined in terms of sampling percentages within recommended research designs. Furthermore, the data provided by sampling indices enhance the archaeologist's decision-making ability in executing resource conservation recommendations whenever feasible.

Obtaining representative samples of sites from particular cultural periods was dependent upon the evaluation of several variables. These included such factors as statistical indices, site type, size, condition, and relationship to the overall settlement system.

The procedure employed the application of $\chi^2$ to interval transect data. The sample frequency was identified as the "observed" number of particular sites, and the corresponding population parameter for those sites constituted the "expected" variable. The $\chi^2$ statistic of $(O-E)^2/E$ was then calculated and used to measure the relative basis of accuracy for each sampling unit. This technique has been applied as a method of comparing the relative accuracy of various sampling designs (Judge *et al.* 1973:31). The use of this statistic is functional as a relative basis of comparison and has been referred to by Judge as an accuracy index rather than a $\chi^2$ value. The $\chi$-squares thus derived do not represent statistical significance, in that maximum values represent the more accurate sample. As such, the $\chi^2$ value is interpreted as an index of the percentage, or number, of sites needed to accurately predict the site population within the study area. In summary, the $\chi^2$ indices provide a generalization about the point at which sample size approaches the predictive power of representative proportions.

These indices, taken into consideration with other variables that reflect the amount of "information content" potentially available in particular sites, constituted the basis for the sampling percentages to be employed in the mitigation program. For example, in the case of the 190 Pueblo components recorded by the survey, 20 were habitation sites that generally exhibited a higher level of preservation and information content and were thus afforded a higher sampling percentage. In contrast, the majority of the 95 field houses were in a poor state of preservation and were thus assigned a lower sampling percentage.

Hypotheses generated by the research orientation and data of the survey provide the basis for structuring a research design for a program of mitigation. This design incorporates ongoing survey research, such as delineating the relationship between hunting and gathering Archaic adaptations and vegetational resources as measured by plant diversity indices, and investigating the relationship between Pueblo farmers and hydrological systems and other variables that may have affected agricultural systems in the past. Similar hypotheses were structured to gather information on Navajo sheepherding, Basket Maker, and Paleo-Indian adaptations.

These hypotheses and the specified sampling percentages provided the basis for developing mitigation *research packages*. The method allowed for suggested research orientations for the three main cultural periods encountered during the survey, and thus, flexible research strategies and attendant estimated costs were developed for the Archaic, Pueblo, and Navajo resources. Estimated cost figures were based upon an approximation of typical project expenditures. This cost index did not preclude other forms of research, such as resurvey, intensive surface collection, mapping, and ethnohistorical studies; rather it was designed to permit latitude in this area. It should also be noted that such figures were based upon current economic scales and served to approximate mitigation cost within a contemporary framework. As such, estimated general budgets were neither based upon the specific monetary value of a particular site (Schiffer 1975:289–301), nor were they of such a general nature as to possibly hinder the accurate consideration of alternatives for the client.

Let us conclude, then, with these more specific points:

1.  The intent of the law and the concern of the profession can only be effected by cultural resource management programs that exhibit research structures that efficiently meet contractual obligations. Such programs can serve the interests of both the archaeologist and client.

2.  Inventory survey can contribute to this goal by operationalizing explicitly defined research designs that monitor comprehensive cultural and environmental data, and by implementing sampling strategies that accurately reflect the information content of the resources. Research programs incorporating such sampling percentages provide the basis for an elegant and economical mitigation program.

3.  Mitigation programs based on research packages do not preclude evolving research perspectives by defining site-specific "problems" and costs; rather they function to offer judicious latitude in fugure investigations and "planning data" necessary to the client.

## ACKNOWLEDGMENTS

The authors express their appreciation to W. James Judge, Chaco Center, University of New Mexico; Richard Chapman and David E. Stuart, Office of Contract Archeology, respectively, for contributions to the research direction of this project and for editorial assistance.

# 26

# San Felipe: Designing a General Plan for Archaeology

THOMAS F. KING
PATRICIA PARKER HICKMAN

When a federal agency builds or helps build a water system, a sewage system, an airport, or a highway, its direct impacts on archaeology are relatively easy to identify: Construction destroys things. Such projects, however, also have indirect impacts. The provision of water may permit an expansion of irrigation and accompanying land levelling; the sewer may remove a constraint on urban growth; the airport or highway may cause growth to spurt into a new area. The federal agency involved in such an activity has a responsibility under the law to assess and, if possible, mitigate its indirect impacts (cf. Council on Environmental Quality 1973: §1500.8[a][3][ii]). In many cases, though, it is beyond what law or the traffic will bear to expect the agency to conduct a cultural resource survey of the entire area where indirect impacts may occur, and it is even less feasible to expect the agency to preserve or salvage all cultural resources that prove to be in danger from such impact. Where, then, is the happy medium that balances responsibility to cultural resources with fiscal reason? A study that we undertook in the Santa Clara Valley of California provides an example of what we think is a rational approach. This chapter briefly summarizes our study, which is presented in detail as "The southern Santa Clara Valley: A general plan for archaeology" (King and Hickman 1973).

## THE PROJECT

The San Felipe Division of the Bureau of Reclamation's Central Valley Project will provide water to the southern Santa Clara Valley, an agricultural valley south of San Jose and northeast of Monterey, California (Maps 26.1 and 26.2). The project is a complex of canals, pipe aqueducts, and small reservoirs. It was originally intended to service the coastal plain around the southeast edge of Monterey Bay

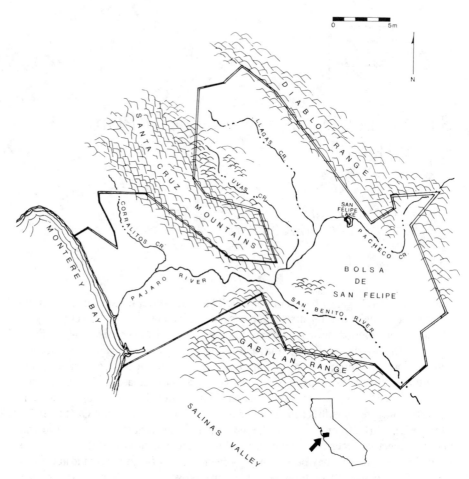

**Map 26.1.** Location and topography of the San Felipe project area.*

also, but this segment of the project has been deleted, and our study was primarily directed toward the southern Santa Clara Valley itself.

## THE STUDY

Before our study little was known about the archaeology of the study area. We undertook a straightforward survey of the canal and pipeline rights-of-way, reservoir locations, and other facility sites (King 1973), but to deal with the project's indirect impacts we went considerably further. We considered the entire service area

*Maps 1–8 were prepared by Ronald N. Melander and originally appeared in King, T. F. and Hickman, P. P., The southern Santa Clara Valley: A general plan for archaeology, *San Felipe Archaeology 1*, 1973.

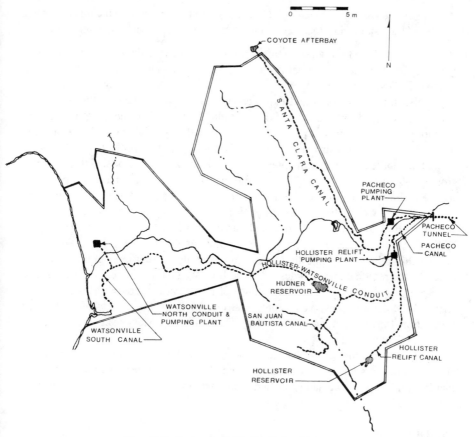

**Map 26.2.** Project facilities, San Felipe Division.

as our unit of study, since the introduction of new water would have broad regional impacts on land use (Chatham 1962) and hence on the region's whole range of historical and prehistoric resources. We organized the study around three general questions:

1. What is the general distribution of historical and prehistoric sites? What kinds of sites are there, and where are they likely to occur? Which are sensitive to environmental constraints, and therefore predictable from environmental data, and which cannot be mapped without further study?
2. What are the various kinds of sites good for? What questions about human social behavior can be answered using them? Which may be of sacred or special interest to particular groups? Which might be amenable to public interpretation?
3. What is the federal, state, and local administrative context within which the Bureau of Reclamation's preservation mandate must be fulfilled? In other

words, how can archaeological preservation be worked into the machinery of federal, state, and local government agencies pertinent to the service area?

We addressed the first question in several ways. Studying data on the distribution of soils, together with historical accounts describing conditions at the time of the Spanish conquest, we developed a picture of the prehistoric environment. A study of Spanish mission records and explorer accounts gave us data on the locations, sizes, and compositions of contact-period villages. Historical records provided information on early ranchos, postmission Indian villages, and other early historical sites. The nature and distribution of later historical sites was projected on the basis of land use indicated by documentary sources. Representatives of social and ethnic groups associated with special occupations and residence patterns provided additional information on the distribution of recent historical sites, up to an arbitrary cutoff point of A.D. 1940. Field survey addressed a random sample of about 25% of all stream drainage systems in the study area, stratified by stream rank (Plog and Hill 1971:17) and U.S. Geological Survey quadrangle.

To address the second question, we set up evaluatory criteria for prehistoric sites based on the regional research design of the Bay Area Archeological Cooperative, a local professional group. The significance of historical resources was discussed in terms of the need to preserve a representative sample of sites associated with each occupational group that had participated in the valley's history (See Hickman, this volume, Chapter 20).

Finally, we examined the land-use and development plans of all counties and cities within the study area and recommended changes to increase the probability that the kinds of sites we had identified or predicted would be protected or salvaged.

## RESOURCES

Map 26.3 shows the precontact environment as we reconstructed it; Map 26.4 shows the distribution of villages located from mission record analysis by C. D. King; Map 26.5 shows lands subjected to field survey. Three classes of prehistoric site were identified: large occupation sites, small occupation sites, and special-use sites. These represented at least two general time periods extending back 3000 years. Large occupation sites tended to occur in the mouths of canyons and on the margins of marshes. Small occupation sites were variable in location but concentrated around extinct marshes. Special-use sites—seed-grinding stations and flake scatters—occurred in the upper canyons of the surrounding hills.

The distribution of sites representative of each historical period was dependent on land use, location of major facilities (railroads, roads, etc.), and the social organization of each occupational group (See Maps 26.6 and 26.7 and Hickman, this volume, Chapter 20). Migrant labor camps, for example, were naturally close to the fields; but "Okie" laborers accompanied by their families during the 1930s tended also to establish shantytowns near local communities, while bachelor Chinese laborers in the 1880s did not.

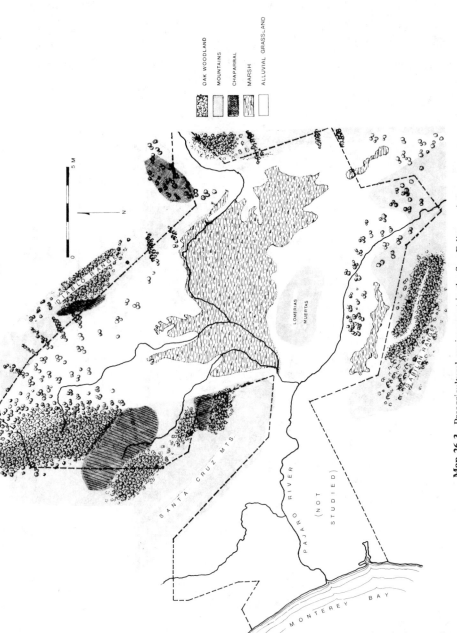

**Map 26.3.** Preagricultural environment in the San Felipe project area.

355

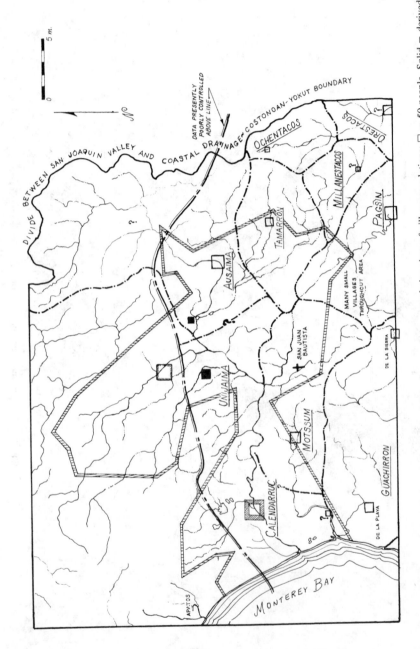

**Map 26.4.** Triblet boundaries and populations from historical data. Squares represent relative sizes of village populations: □ = 50 people. Solid = derived from house or population counts given by explorers. Outline = derived from interpretation of number and date of baptism. Locations based on interpretation of mission registers by Chester D. King.

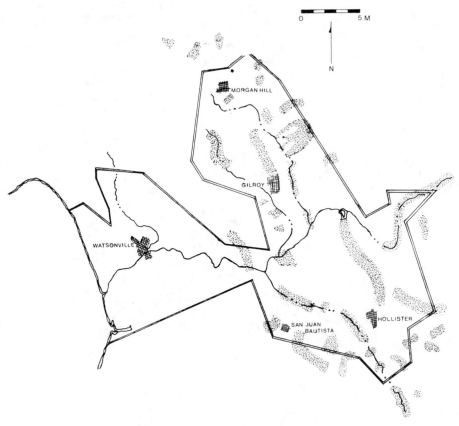

**Map 26.5.** Sample survey tracts in the San Felipe project area.

## SIGNIFICANCE

Prior to our study the Bay Area Archeological Cooperative had agreed to organize the varied research interests of its participants around the general question: "According to what principles do human social groups organize themselves in space? (King and King 1973)."

We developed a set of research questions based on this general topic for local prehistory. Our field data suggested that changes had taken place in the distribution of population, at least between the late prehistoric period and the time of Spanish exploration. Our consideration of possible causes for such change led to the posing of questions about how the area's prehistory might reflect the rise and decline of complex political organization among California hunter-gatherers (See King 1974). Answering such questions will require an understanding of social, settlement, and subsistence systems in the area during all prehistoric time periods. These requirements, in turn, provide bases for judging the research values of specific sites when they are threatened by future land uses.

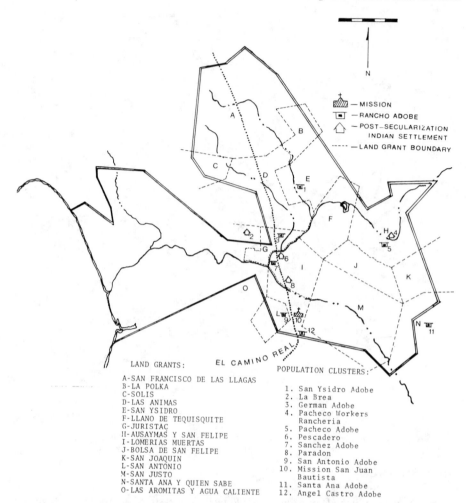

**Map 26.6.** Land grants and population clusters in the San Felipe project area, ca. 1845.

LAND GRANTS:

A-SAN FRANCISCO DE LAS LLAGAS
B-LA POLKA
C-SOLIS
D-LAS ANIMAS
E-SAN YSIDRO
F-LLANO DE TEQUISQUITE
G-JURISTAC
H-AUSAYMAS Y SAN FELIPE
I-LOMERIAS MUERTAS
J-BOLSA DE SAN FELIPE
K-SAN JOAQUIN
L-SAN ANTONIO
M-SAN JUSTO
N-SANTA ANA Y QUIEN SABE
O-LAS AROMITAS Y AGUA CALIENTE

POPULATION CLUSTERS:

1. San Ysidro Adobe
2. La Brea
3. German Adobe
4. Pacheco Workers Rancheria
5. Pacheco Adobe
6. Pescadero
7. Sanchez Adobe
8. Paradon
9. San Antonio Adobe
10. Mission San Juan Bautista
11. Santa Ana Adobe
12. Angel Castro Adobe

Historical archaeology in the area was entirely undeveloped; we had virtually no research base to start with. As Hickman (Chapter 20) indicates, our discussion of significance turned largely on the argument that a representative sample should be maintained of sites typifying all social, economic, and ethnic groups and their activities. We projected a series of general questions that could be asked about the ways in which the area's subpopulations—ranging from postmission Indians to pre–World War II Japanese agriculturalists—interacted through time under the influence of changing patterns of land use and ownership. Both the idea of representativeness and the specific research questions provided bases for judging the significance of particular sites.

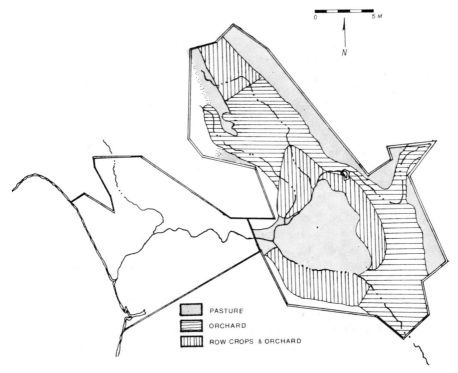

**Map 26.7.** Generalized land use in the San Felipe project area, ca. 1931 (after Broek 1932).

## THE PLANNING CONTEXT

In addition to the requirements of federal law, California state law places re-straints on land use and development in ways that are important for cultural resource management. Particularly important is the California Environmental Quality Act (CEQA), a NEPA-like statute that requires environmental analyses of undertakings over which any public agency has discretion. This covers all substantial private development, since such development requires permits from public bodies. Each of the four counties that impinged upon the study area, and each of the four cities within the area, had adopted general plans and/or guidelines for environmental review under CEQA and other statutes. With respect to cultural resource identifica-tion and evaluation under CEQA, the most common problems for local agencies lay in identifying potential areas of concern without requiring that absolutely every proposed use of the land be preceded by an archaeological survey. Federal agencies, such as the Bureau of Reclamation, could mitigate the indirect impacts of their activities only by encouraging responsible cultural resource management by their local partners, but they needed to do so without demanding fiscal irresponsibility.

## THE PLAN

Our study provided the basis for a projection of *sensitivity zones,* where prehistoric sites could be expected to occur in different densities. This projection is shown in Map 26.8. It is based on both our background research and field survey, and it identifies areas where modern land use would be differentially likely to conflict with the preservation of prehistoric resources. High sensitivity areas included canyons, riverbanks, and the reconstructed margins of extinct marshes. Moderate sensitivity zones included alluvial plains; low, broken, or rocky slopes; and ridge crests. Low sensitivity zones included marsh bottoms, steep nonrocky slopes, and recently heavily urbanized areas. Our first recommendation was simply that surveys for prehistoric sites always be required when projects were planned in high sensitivity zones, and that they need be required in low sensitivity zones only when some characteristic of the land involved indicated that prehistoric remains might be present. As a rule of thumb, we suggested that in moderate sensitivity zones such surveys be required only for large projects unless some characteristic of a small project area suggested sensitivity. Characteristics that might suggest sensitivity were specified.

Our data did not give us a basis for generating a *sensitivity map* for historical resources. On the other hand, historical resource "inventories" were underway in all the counties, albeit oriented toward standing structures. Accordingly, we recommended upgrading the inventories to include the whole range of predictable historical resource types in the area. We suggested that classificatory charts like the one shown in Table 26.1 be maintained as a guide to evaluation. This chart indicates the general time periods at the left and occupation types in the center. Sites representing each occupation type are inventoried as found at the right. Maintained over time, and used as a guide in inventory activities, such charts could lead to the recording of a more representative sample of historical sites than is the case under present conditions. Such charts can be elaborated as shown in Table 26.2, to take account of different predicted site types. Planners with access to such charts could note types of resources that were poorly represented and could plan surveys to identify such properties in connection with environmental assessment projects.

**TABLE 26.1.**
**Example of a Historical Evaluation Chart**

| Time | Occupation types | Sites |
| --- | --- | --- |
| Late American period (horticulture) | Large land owner | Bloomfield Ranch Dunne Home |
| | Small farmer | Burrell "Mountain Home" |
| | Tenant farmer | |
| | Regularly employed agricultural laborer | Zanger Work Camp |
| | Migrant laborer | |

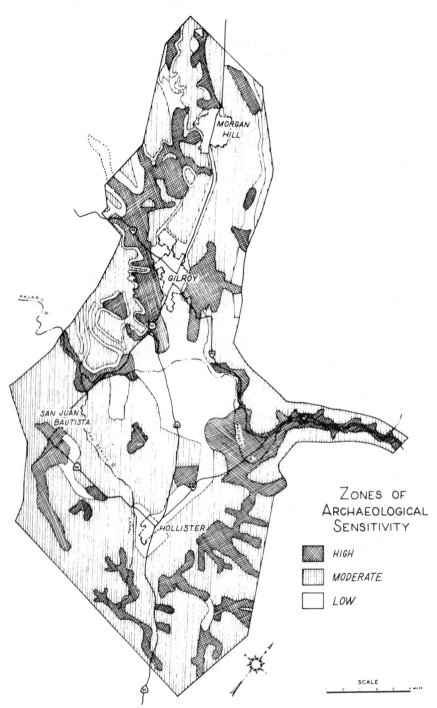

**Map 26.8.** Zones of archaeological sensitivity.

361

**TABLE 26.2.**
**Example of an Elaborated Evaluation Chart**

| | | Sites | | |
|---|---|---|---|---|
| Time | Occupation type | Individual structure | Settlement | Regional distribution of settlements |
| Spanish–Mexican period Stockraising Subsistence farming | Postsecularization Indians | Ruins of cabin on Pacheco Creek | Rancheria "El Paredon" | All known rancherias and single-family dwellings |

We also recommended use of our projections in the acquisition of land for open space and parks, and we offered suggestions for the mitigation of impacts on cultural resources when they were identified—including protective overfilling, construction over them on piles, relocation of potentially damaging construction, and salvage excavation. Finally, we argued that the impacts of expanding irrigation agriculture that would result from the project could be mitigated only by the support of a special survey and salvage team in the area. We recommended that such a team be provided by the federal government during the 10 years of agricultural growth predicted for the area once the project facilities were in place. This team could be supported by a modest increase of 50¢/acre-foot in the selling price of San Felipe water to local users.

We must note that the Bureau of Reclamation has not attended to any of our recommendations; in fact, in its environmental impact statement on the project it has consistently ignored, misused, and abused them. Project facilities have been relocated and rerouted without survey, and our recommendations for mitigation of indirect impacts have been uniformly ignored. The project has not been constructed as yet, however, and the bureau's insistence on taking the least responsible approach to archaeological planning may yet be called into question. In the meantime, local agencies have been making use of our material, particularly the predictive map (Map 26.8), in their general planning and environmental review activities.

We think that our study, imperfect as it was, points toward some useful directions for future research. No responsible local agency is going to mindlessly require an archaeological survey of every building lot, but when provided with a clear and defensible prediction of the locations of sensitive and less than sensitive areas, the agency is quite likely to take this prediction into account in the planning process. The trick is to make the predictions reliable, but a profession that has for several years been vitally interested in sampling as a means of predicting the distribution of archaeological phenomena should be able to cope with this challenge.

# Part IX

---

# RESEARCH CONTRIBUTIONS

---

In this, the concluding part of *Conservation Archaeology,* we provide examples of research contributions that have been made by cultural resource management studies.

## EARLY-STAGE PROJECTS

Despite conventional wisdom to the contrary, even the earliest stages of conservation archaeology in an area, the overview and assessment, provide ample opportunities for performing creative and useful research. Perhaps the easiest research task to accomplish is a history of prior archaeological investigations. Although many reports do include a section on "previous research," the discussions are usually too sketchy—consisting mainly of citations strung together by terse prose—and lack meaningful evaluations of what has been done. However, as Stacy and Hayden (1975) have shown, it is possible to write engaging critical histories (see also Fuller, Rogge and Gregonis 1976); one hopes that they will become more common.

A second kind of research that may be carried out in an early stage is the areal synthesis, which, sadly, is a species of archaeological document that is alarmingly endangered. Although areal syntheses necessarily have to be completed in cultural resource management studies, as part of the process of determining the nature and significance of the resource base, only a handful of investigators have accomplished the task with distinction. That a genuine areal synthesis needs to be more than a secondhand chronology stacked with traits and site names is a fact not widely enough appreciated. Those who do gain firsthand familiarity with the extant reports of excavations and surveys are able to assemble the disparate pieces into a coherent framework—however tentative—that is a contribution to knowledge, as shown by Debowski *et al.* (1976); Gumerman (1970); Gumerman, Westfall and Weed (1972); Hall and Barker (1975); House (1975d);

Moratto and Riley (1974); and Morse (1975b). In well-studied areas, the investigator may go appreciably beyond the synthesis by conducting advanced analyses of the available data, such as discerning patterns in site location or making systemic reconstructions. One hopes that the untapped potential of areal syntheses will not be overlooked much longer.

An adequate areal synthesis provides the foundation for a third type of early-stage contribution: the isolation of problem domains. The chapter by Moratto (Chapter 30) indicates how a thorough grasp of the local archaeology makes it possible to begin the process of identifying outstanding research problems.

A fourth opportunity is sometimes supplied by museum collections and old excavation or survey notes, which may make it possible to summarize the findings of unreported projects in an area. For example, Downing, Husted, and Jurney (1976) described collections made by previously unpublished fieldwork in Ozark bluff shelters. Although their work was accomplished as part of a field study, there is no reason why similar research cannot be undertaken at the overview or assessment stage.

A fifth type of research, involving the use of historical data, may also be carried out in early-stage investigations, although detailed analyses of primary data are usually reserved for more intensive studies. For example, in a field study D. E. Fox et al. (1974) creatively used historical records to reconstruct demographic and settlement trends in the area of the proposed Cuero I Reservoir in south central Texas. Reports by Price et al. (1975) and Price, Price, and Harris (1976) also include excellent examples of historical syntheses in field studies, relying both on primary and secondary evidence (see also A. A. Fox, Bass, and Hester 1976; Greenwood 1975; King and Hickman 1973). It should be possible to conduct early-stage projects so that similar anthropological analyses of historical materials may be carried out.

Innovative uses of historical data, while desirable at the overview and assessment stages, become necessary in field studies to provide a well-rounded view of the cultural resource base. Harris, Price, and Price in Chapter 29 illustrate some anthroplogical uses of historical data, focusing on the logging industry of the Little Black drainage in southeastern Missouri. In addition, using diverse examples, South shows in Chapter 32 that one can successfully pursue on contract a variety of methodological and substantive problems in historical sites archaeology. In fact, much of the relentless push that South and his colleagues are making on the anthropological frontiers of historical sites archaeology is taking place in the context of cultural resource management studies (South 1976a; the papers in South 1977c). House (n.d.), for example, has formulated a concept of regional study for historical sites archaeology that emphasizes the unique potential of archaeological data to contribute to an understanding of cultural process in historically known times (see also Shenk and Teague 1975).

## SMALL PROJECTS

The small project is ordinarily viewed as the least responsive toward efforts at producing research results—another facile judgment that seems unwarranted. We must admit to experiencing some surprise and not a little dismay when we are confronted by those who say, "What can you possibly do with this?" For, in our view, so much needs to be done in archaeology that there is no site or area, no matter how small or devoid of "goodies," that cannot provide information for some problem of current interest. The practical difficulty, of course, is in establishing a match between resources and research problems.

There are several ways to resolve this difficulty. A regional research design, if available, will hopefully furnish a framework for plugging in small areas (e.g., Grady 1976). In some localities institutions conduct ongoing research projects that allow work in the most barren area to make a contribution to knowledge. For example, James Schoenwetter has devised a simple regional research project for southern Arizona dealing with variability in the present-day pollen rain (described by Bair 1974:10–11). Each contract study takes surface pollen samples and collects standardized observations on the present-day environment. Similarly, the Arkansas Archeological Survey has been carrying out long-term studies of the efficiency of survey techniques (e.g., Claassen and Spears 1975). The Office of Contract Archeology at the University of New Mexico has formulated an umbrella research design covering patterns of site location by which one can even integrate areas having no sites (David Stuart, personal communication, 1975). Goodyear's (1975a) research design for highway-intercepted sites in South Carolina, focusing on site-specific behavioral reconstruction, provides another excellent example of this approach.

Even when regional research designs and ongoing projects are unavailable in the study area, the investigator may rely on his own familiarity with current topics in archaeology to devise a viable plan for research. The wide range of investigations being pursued in archaeological technology, methodology, and theory almost guarantees that something of interest can be done in any study area. As examples, one could empirically and theoretically investigate cultural and noncultural formation processes (e.g., Baker 1974, 1975; Hyatt and Doehner 1975; Schiffer 1975c,d; see introduction to Part VII), conduct experiments in lithic and ceramic technology (e.g.,

Flenniken 1975; House and Smith 1975; Million 1975; Spears 1975; Wyant and Bayham 1976), devise and test new excavation and survey techniques or strategies (e.g., DeBloois 1975; Klinger n.d.b; Morse and Morse 1976; Raab 1976b; Rodgers 1974; K. R. Williams 1976; Doelle, this volume, Chapter 15), experiment with computerized data storage and retrieval systems (e.g., Schoenwetter, Gaines, and Weaver (1973), carry out studies of lithic procurement and technology subsystems (e.g., D. E. Fox *et al.* 1974; Keller and Wilson 1976; Klinger n.d.b; Mallouf, Fox, and Briggs 1973; Skinner and Gallagher 1974; House, this volume, Chapter 27), or even erect or revise a typology (e.g., Braun 1976; House 1975b; Faulkner and McCollough 1973), among many other possibilities. Admittedly, not all of these types of research have yet been carried out in small projects, but most of them are easily adapted to those settings. In short, the failure of small projects (or, for that matter, of any project) to yield research results reflects less upon the characteristics of the resources than upon the competence, background, and interests of the investigators.

## FIELD STUDIES AND MITIGATION

Needless to say, the variety of research opportunities available to early-stage projects and small projects are also open to field studies and mitigative excavations. Additionally, one may also draw upon virtually the entire range of modern archaeological research questions for inspiration. For example, it is no longer unusual to find as a part of a field study ethnoarchaeological research (e.g., Doelle 1976; Price *et al.* 1975), methodological investigations (e.g., Fuller, Rogge, and Gregonis 1976), or tests of subsistence and/or settlement models (e.g., Banks 1975; Canouts 1975; Cheek *et al.* 1974; Doelle 1975, 1976; Goodyear 1975b; House, Klinger, and Schiffer 1975; Klinger n.d.b; McCormick 1973, 1974; McDonald *et al.* 1974; Price, Price, and Harris 1976; Reher n.d.; Reynolds 1974). Good examples of settlement–subsistence research are those by Cheek, *et al.* (Chapter 28) and Goodyear (Chapter 31). It should be noted that, while the Hecla project investigations reported by Goodyear took place during the mitigative stage, the surficial nature of the archaeological resources there (and in other parts of the Desert West) also lends itself to such research during field study projects. The lithic research in the Cache Basin reported by House in Chapter 27, is, like the settlement studies, applicable to many projects in the field study or mitigative stages.

## VIABLE LAST RESORTS

In the unlikely event that the conservation archaeologist has exhausted all avenues for productive research and has come up empty, a project may still be redeemed by two other possibilities: presentation of research designs and discussions of current issues in conservation archaeology. Research designs in themselves are often substantial contributions to knowledge because they succinctly summarize previous work on a subject and because they may furnish new ideas, hypotheses, and models applicable to future research. Klinger (n.d.b), McDonald *et al.* (1974), and Schiffer and House (1975b), include in their reports creative and potentially useful research designs. Any finally, if all else fails (and we expect that this would occur frequently), the investigator may wish to contribute to the ongoing discussions of major issues in conservation archaeology, including significance, survey methodology, mitigation philosophy, and the compatibility of research and management goals (e.g., Morenon, Henderson, and Nielsen 1976; Price *et al.* 1975; Schiffer and House 1975b).

## CONCLUSION

There is no doubt that, as a result of cultural resource management legislation, archaeological investigations in the United States have accelerated to an unprecedented pace. Never before in the history of American archaeology has so much money been spent nor have so many projects taken to the field. This prodigious activity has the potential for dramatically enriching our knowledge of the past and expanding our methodological tool kit. These benefits will be achieved, however, only as we begin to realize that sound research design and research results are not luxuries to be tolerated in conservation archaeology, but they are necessities to be demanded. We even suspect that, in the long run, today's efforts will be judged—not on the number of sites recorded, or reports written, or bulldozers halted—but on how much we contributed to archaeology. To this end, let us inquire of every project: Did we learn something about the past or ways to study it? Did we communicate this knowledge to our colleagues and to the public? If these questions are answered affirmatively, then one may rest assured that public funds for cultural resource management are being spent wisely, and that this judgment will be sustained by posterity.

# 27

# Prehistoric Lithic Resource Utilization in the Cache Basin: A Preliminary Analysis of Aboriginal Procurement and Use of Pitkin Chert[1]

JOHN H. HOUSE

One of the research designs operationalized by the Cache River Archeological Project was an investigation of prehistoric lithic resource utilization in the Cache basin. This research was undertaken by the Cache project to assess the potential of the archaeological resources in the Cache Basin for investigating processes of lithic resource procurement, utilization, and recycling. This problem domain is relevant to both the study of economic behavior in low-energy cultural systems worldwide and to reconstruction of the Dalton culture settlement pattern in the Cache basin (cf. Goodyear 1975c; House, Klinger, and Schiffer 1975; Schiffer 1975h), another of the problem domains investigated by the Cache River Archeological Project.

This research design entailed analysis of a spatially and temporally diverse set of collections of lithic artifacts from the basin and an attempt to identify the source of some of the raw materials present in the samples. Subsequently, visits were made to suspected source areas in hopes of locating prehistoric quarry and workshop sites representing procurement of the resource. In this way, investigation of lithic resource procurement in the Cache Basin took us to suspected source areas not only within the basin but outside the basin as well: to the foot of the Ozark escarpment on the western margin of the Mississippi alluvial valley.

During the archaeological survey of the Cache Basin, investigation of lithic resource utilization was concentrated on two of the many lithic resources known to have been used by prehistoric Indians in the basin: chert and quartzite gravels from

[1]The following chapter is a revised and abridged version of a chapter (House 1975c) of the archaeological environmental impact statement for the Corps of Engineers' Cache River–Bayou de View Channelization Project in northeastern Arkansas (Schiffer and House 1975b).

Crowley's Ridge and Pitkin chert from the Ozark Plateau. This chapter will review the results of the investigation of one of these resources, Pitkin chert.

## THE USES OF LITHIC RESOURCE
## UTILIZATION STUDIES

In almost all nonmetal-using societies, stone is the raw material of many tools used directly in exploiting the environment; it is also the raw material of tools used in the fabrication of most other tools. Lithic technology can be considered the technological cornerstone of such societies. Cultural systems with such a technology tend to produce large quantities of broken, exhausted, or lost stone tools and manufacturing debitage, which enter the archaeological record and are uniformly well preserved.

Since the lithic technology of a past society is articulated, directly or indirectly, with all other aspects of the past cultural system, lithic analysis need not be an end in itself but a means toward reconstruction of these other aspects as well. In this regard, knowledge of lithic resources and lithic resource procurement strategies becomes basic to a variety of research problems: Gould (1974) suggests, based on ethnographic data from the Western Desert of Australia, that manufacture of tools of nonlocal, "expensive" versus locally available raw materials usually takes place at base camps rather than at extractive loci. Analysis of raw materials in debitage samples, then, may be a source of information on site function in a settlement system. The mechanism of the movement of materials over long distances—whether by special expeditions for procurement, quarrying and preforming by local groups and exchange with other groups, or a market system—is presumably related to the overall economic and social organization of a society. And the development of new technologies in the course of major economic shifts often entails new tools with new requirements for raw materials.

The formulation of models to explain archaeological data pertaining to the movement of lithic raw materials through cultural systems requires a knowledge of the nature of lithic resources, their distribution and abundance, and the technological potential and limitations of each raw material. The Cache River Archeological Project undertook this preliminary investigation of lithic resource procurement in order to explore the research potential of the archaeological resources in the Cache Basin and to lay a basis for future studies involving prehistoric lithic resource utilization in lowland northeastern Arkansas.

## AVAILABLE LITHIC RESOURCES IN
## NORTHEASTERN ARKANSAS

Most of the land surfaces in the Western Lowlands and most of lowland northeastern Arkansas are of Late pleistocene and Holocene age and are entirely lacking in naturally occurring stone. All of the stone used by prehistoric peoples in the Cache Basin had to be imported from neighboring upland areas. Most of this stone came from two areas: Crowley's Ridge and the Ozark Plateau. The relevant lithic resources of these two areas have been summarized in a recent article by Morse (1969:15).

The only lithic raw materials commonly used in the Cache Basin in prehistoric times that did not come from one of these two areas are novaculite and clear quartz crystal, which originated in the Ouachita Mountains in southwestern Arkansas. Both of these materials are not uncommon at sites in the extreme lower Cache Basin. White River gravels, which might be considered an Ozark resource, seem to have been frequently used in the lower Cache Basin.

In the northern two-thirds of the basin, chert and quartzite from Crowley's Ridge gravels were the most common raw materials for chipped-stone tools. In many samples of chipped stone from the northern part of the basin they seem to be the only raw materials present. A great variety of Ozark cherts were apparently used. The chert resources of the Ozarks have been briefly discussed by Erwin (n.d.). One of the most prevalent types of Ozark chert used—especially in the lower part of the basin—is Pitkin chert, which originates in the Pitkin limestone in the Boston Mountains area of the Ozarks.

## PITKIN CHERT

### Description and Occurrence

The highly distinctive appearance of Pitkin chert has been described by Erwin (n.d.:7). It is most readily identified by its predominantly black color and by the presence of tiny, almost microscopic pits, where calcite inclusions have weathered out. These pits are characteristically lined with an orange film, which is probably iron oxide.

Erwin (n.d.:5–6) has also summarized the occurrence of Pitkin chert:

> Pitkin Chert occurs as nodules within the Pitkin Limestone. The Pitkin Limestone outcrops along the Boston Mountain Escarpment from near Oil Trough [Arkansas] in the east to near Muskogee, Oklahoma in the west.

### Quarry and Workshop Sites

Holmes's (1919) classic description of sites of prehistoric quarry activity throughout North America provides an extremely useful set of expectations for recognizing quarry and workshop sites. In February 1973, I visited sites 3IN24 and 3IN44 in the White River bottoms near Oil Trough, Arkansas, near the Ozark escarpment during the course of an environmental impact survey on the Black and White rivers. Intensive workshop activity involving Pitkin chert was evident from the extreme abundance of rejected biface blanks and debitage of Pitkin chert at these sites.

Even though the Oil Trough area is 20 miles to the west of the Cache Basin, data from source areas of Pitkin chert were considered crucial to any reconstruction of prehistoric procurement and utilization of this material within the basin. During the Cache project the area was revisited twice. Further collections were made at the two workshop sites, and a quarry site for Pitkin chert, 3IN73, was discovered on a hilltop on the Ozark escarpment about 1 mile southwest of the workshop sites.

The workshop sites are located in the White River floodplain just above the point where the White River leaves the Ozarks and enters the Mississippi alluvial valley. The hills immediately south of the workshop sites form the extreme easternmost tip of the Boston Mountains (Arkansas Department of Development and Planning 1973:3) and are the location of the easternmost outcrop of Pitkin limestone (Easton 1942:28). At the location of the quarry site, 3IN73, the Pitkin limestone seems to have eroded away, leaving behind residual nodule fragments and blocky chunks of Pitkin chert exposed on the hilltop. No chert-bearing limestone outcrops were observed on this hilltop or on the bluff between the hilltop and the river bottom. Pitkin chert nodule fragments are abundant on this hilltop, but probably only a small proportion were suitable for biface manufacture. These pieces of chert often have numerous seams and tend to break along these seams. Large solid pieces of Pitkin chert can, however, be found by searching.

In areas of the greatest density of Pitkin chert on this hilltop are occasional hammerstones, cores of Pitkin chert, and scattered debitage. The amount of quarry debris observed in this area seems rather small in comparison with the amount of chert at the nearby workshop sites. This quarry may be just one of several along this bluff area, or perhaps most of the evidence of quarry activity is below the present ground surface. No evidence of prehistoric excavation of pits through the subsoil to expose unweathered nodules was observed, even though this seems to have been the most prevalent quarry technique at many aboriginal quarry sites in North America (Holmes 1919:155–227).

Each of the two recorded workshop sites, 3IN24 and 3IN44, occupies an area over 100 meters in diameter on a sandy rise beside a former White River channel. The density of lithic debris is so great in most portions of both sites that it would be impossible to put one's hand on the ground without touching several pieces of chert.

Examination with the aid of a microscope reveals that the Pitkin chert from these workshop sites is virtually identical to that from the quarry site, 3IN73, and to most of the Pitkin chert from sites in the Cache, l'Anguille, and Village Creek basins in the Mississippi Valley to the east. Pieces of Pitkin chert from these workshop sites that bear cortex also indicate that the chert originated at 3IN73 or a very similar source.

The sample collected by the Cache project at the workshop sites includes a controlled collection from 3IN44 as well as a large sample of biface blanks, preforms, and other artifacts from both sites. No intensive analysis of these materials has yet been undertaken, but it is possible to make a few tentative statements about the data:

The Pitkin chert seems to have been brought to the workshops in the form of large, blocky blank flakes or tabular chunks, often still bearing areas of cortex. The blanks and preforms at the sites all seem to have been aborted and discarded. As such they represent all stages of manufacture from rough irregular blanks to thin, even-edged bifaces. A few preforms were even notched or stemmed prior to accidental breakage. Only lack of finished working edges distinguishes these from finished points that might have been broken during use.

Other artifacts that occur at these sites are evidently related to workshop activity. These include hammerstones and probable preform abraders, spokeshaves, and miscellaneous retouched and/or utilized flakes. Many of the spokeshaves are an unusual angular-notched variety virtually identical to some of those from site 3CG37 at the foot of Crowley's Ridge, an apparent workshop site for production of biface blanks from Crowley's Ridge gravels (House 1975c:82). The presence of midden staining and of large quantities of fire-cracked sandstone at 3IN24 and 3IN44 suggests that some habitation, in addition to biface manufacture, took place.

The cultural stage of most of the workshop activity at these sites is not readily determinable from the Cache project collections. The sites have reportedly been hunted by collectors for years, and large quantities of whole points have been picked up. The total absence of any prehistoric ceramics, however, argues for an Archaic stage affiliation, for the material and the few corner-notched and stemmed points found indicate late Archaic occupation. No Dalton point preforms (Morse 1973a:Figure 6; a,b) or other recognizable early Archaic materials have been found. The absence of early Archaic materials at these sites is somewhat puzzling in view of the frequent use of Pitkin chert by early Archaic people in the Western Lowlands. It suggests that in early Archaic times the inhabitants of the Western Lowlands were using other Pitkin chert sources—or at least other workshop sites.

An analysis of the debitage in the controlled collection from 3IN44 reveals the expected high frequency (13%) of obvious biface thinning flakes, but surprisingly, 43% of the flakes and chips exhibit some kind of edge damage. This is difficult to explain at a presumed workshop site, but it should be noted that on a great many of these specimens the edge damage is much more irregular and ambiguous as to origin than is typical of marginally utilized flakes in the Western Lowlands. A similar high incidence (roughly 40%) of flakes with apparent marginal utilization was observed in a sample of lithic debris from a novaculite workshop in the Ouachita Mountains in southwestern Arkansas by Mike Baker (personal communication 1974). Baker hypothesizes that much of this apparent utilization resulted from accidental crushing together of flakes where a high density of lithic debris existed. Indeed, the irregular, unpatterned edge damage on many of the Pitkin chert examples resembles that produced by "trampling" in edge damage experiments carried out by Tringham, Cooper, Odell, Voytek, and Whitman (1974:182, 192). The lack of such a high density of lithic debris—either underfoot in prehistoric times or in the soil in archaeological context—at most sites in the Cache Basin may account for the apparent absence of this phenomenon at the sites sampled in the basin.

## Transportation and Distribution

No detailed quantitative studies of Pitkin chert distribution in the Cache Basin have yet been undertaken, but the zone of greatest occurrence of this raw material seems to fall south of a line drawn straight east from the quarry and workshop sites to Crowley's Ridge. Pitkin chert is not uncommon on sites north of this line as far as Jonesboro, and a single biface fragment of Pitkin chert was identified in a collection from site 3CY5 on the Cache a few miles south of the Missouri state line.

Occasional pieces of black chert are found on sites east of Crowley's Ridge. Some of these may be Pitkin, but no samples of these specimens have yet been analyzed. Analysis of a large sample of middle to late Mississippian lithics from the Rose Mound, 3CS27, a large Mississippian village site in the Eastern Lowlands of Arkansas, revealed no specimens of Pitkin chert.

As I have already noted, Pitkin chert from the Cache basin and everywhere else in the Western Lowlands seems to be identical to that from the quarry and workshop sites in Independence County. Most of the Pitkin chert from sites in the lowlands is in the form of bifaces, steeply retouched unifaces, small biface fragments, and small biface thinning flakes. At some sites, however, biface blanks and flakes with cortex are also found. Virtually all of the specimens bearing cortex have come from outcrops or residual deposits similar to that at 3IN73 rather than stream gravels. A few specimens of Pitkin chert from sites in one of the sampling units on the Cache River near Newport, Arkansas, have stream gravel cortex and perhaps came from White River gravels.

## Utilization of Pitkin Chert

Present data suggest that two distinct subsystems of chipped stone tool manufacture can be distinguished for most prehistoric occupations in the Cache Basin. Subsystem 1 begins with extraction of the raw material and production of biface blanks and/or preforms at or very near the outcrop. These blanks or preforms were then transported to habitation sites in the lowlands where the biface tools were finished. Subsystem 2 begins with selection of appropriate cores (usually pebbles) with subsequent transport of entire cores to habitation sites where flakes intended for use as light-duty cutting and scraping tools seem to have been detached as they were needed for a particular task. The debitage associated with each subsystem is readily distinguishable. It seems apparent that Crowley's Ridge chert and quartzite gravels participated in *both* subsystems (see House 1975c:82–85) while Pitkin chert and other Ozark cherts participated almost exclusively in Subsystem 1.

Accordingly, almost all of the Pitkin chert in the lowlands is in the form of bifaces, unifaces, biface fragments, biface thinning flakes, and other small flakes. Small cores of Pitkin chert are found at some lowland sites but seem to be extremely rare. Observed examples are either from stream gravels or fragments of large biface preforms.

Utilization of Pitkin chert by prehistoric peoples in lowland northeastern Arkansas begins at least as early as the Dalton culture and persists through Mississippian.

Most of the utilization, however, appears to be associated with early Archaic, late Archaic, and perhaps Woodland. Mississippian artifacts made of Pitkin chert are not common in most portions of the Western Lowlands. Specimens of Pitkin chert that have cortex resembling that from the residual deposit at 3IN73 seem to be associated mainly with late Archaic occupations. The form in which early Archaic peoples imported Pitkin chert into the lowlands has not been determined. Cortex is not present on any of the rather small sample of early Archaic Pitkin chert artifacts collected by the Cache project, and no analysis of this problem has been undertaken using the early Archaic material in the Arkansas Archeological Survey collections at the Jonesboro Research Station. In view of the present evidence, it is possible that early Archaic peoples were mainly using stream gravels as their source of Pitkin chert. It may be, however, that early Archaic peoples went to greater trouble than did later peoples to remove all cortex from finished tools.

The rather intensive utilization of Pitkin chert by the Dalton culture is especially interesting. While Crowley's Ridge chert seems to have been the main material for adzes and flake tools in most parts of the Cache Basin, a very high proportion of the Dalton points and steeply chipped unifaces in Dalton assemblages are made on Pitkin or other Ozark cherts. In a sample of 106 Dalton point fragments from the Brand site in the L'Anguille Basin (Goodyear 1974), 19% were of Pitkin chert and many of the remaining specimens were of other Ozark cherts. Numerous artifacts of Pitkin chert were among the Dalton culture grave lots at the Sloan site, 3GE94 (Morse 1975a). These two sites are 40 and 50 miles respectively from the nearest source of Pitkin chert, and the pattern of consistent use of Pitkin chert and perhaps even more exotic Ozark cherts by the Dalton people may have important implications for our understanding of both the technological and the social aspects of the Dalton adaptation.

## CONCLUSIONS

### Research Potential: Substantive Research Designs

Pitkin chert is just one of many lithic resources used by prehistoric peoples in the Cache Basin. The preceding discussion of the procurement and utilization of this resource can be considered only preliminary, but it does demonstrate some of the research potential of the lithic resource data that could be obtained by further archaeological work in the Cache Basin.

The size of the basin, its long prehistoric sequence, and the varied kinds and locations of lithic raw materials used make the basin a suitable research universe for the study of a wide range of archaeological problems involving procurement and distribution of lithic raw materials. The lithic resource data from the basin can be considered to have a good potential for: (1) studying patterns of resource procurement in various cultural adaptations at various levels of sociocultural integration; (2) building and testing models involving the flow of lithic resources through various kinds of social distribution and/or exchange mechanisms; (3) testing hypotheses involving prehistoric modes of transportation in the lowlands; (4) locating the loci of various tool manufacture processes about the landscape; (5) delineating the boundaries of various cultural adaptations and changes in those boundaries through time; and (6) studying interregional interaction in this part of the Southeast in prehistoric times, with an emphasis on interaction between the ecologically diverse Mississippi Valley and Ozark Plateau. These are, of course, only a few of the kinds of substantive research problems that might be proposed. Research designs involving such problems should be integrated into any future multidisciplinary archaeological research program in the Cache Basin.

## Data Requirements and Further Background Studies

The data requirements for such research designs would, however, require much better understanding of the sources of raw materials used in the basin. More intensive geological and petrological background studies would have to be carried out.

J. Thomas Meyers' (1970) study of the chert resources of the lower Illinois Valley might serve as a useful model for further research involving raw material sources. Meyers emphasizes that answering archaeological questions about sources of raw material used by past societies requires not only a determination of the formation and outcrops of various types of chert- (or quartzite-) bearing bedrock and the locations of various types of potential sources of residual or redeposited material but also *sampling* of the "population" of chemically and physically variable chert that constitutes each source. He also emphasizes that the nature, distribution, and abundance of sources of chippable stone—just as much as corresponding data about plants and animals in the environment—represent important variables in developing settlement–subsistence models for various cultural phases in the region. The methods used by the Illinois Valley chert survey project are probably adaptable to the study of the chert and quartzite resources of the Ozarks and Crowley's Ridge.

Subsequent to sample collection, the analysis and comparison of samples from sources, on the one hand, and archaeological contexts, on the other, would require a number of specialized methods. During the Cache project examination of suspected Pitkin chert specimens under a binocular microscope was found to increase vastly the reliability of the identification of Pitkin chert. This method has the advantage of being convenient, inexpensive, and nondestructive, but in many cases various petrological techniques might be required. It should be borne in mind that archaeological lithic specimens are usually quite out of context, geologically speaking. They may not reflect modal tendencies in their parent outcrop but rather meticulous selection for certain qualities by past human beings. After this initial selection the materials may be altered in appearance by heat treatment to improve their chipping properties (cf. Crabtree and Butler 1964). David J. Ives (1975:8–10) has, indeed, recently concluded that for most lithic raw materials, only neutron activation analysis or a similar technique will permit reliable identification of sources.

It should be obvious that the accomplishment of such research would require the participation of persons with considerable geological as well as archaeological expertise. This consideration should be part of the organization of any research program involving intensive study of lithic raw materials procurement and distribution.

Other kinds of data requirements for such a study include better control over the technological potential of the various materials and better control over the processes of manufacture of various tools. These data requirements would be best fulfilled by experiments in *replication* of various tools in different materials and experiments in the *use* of these tools. The experiments in replication should focus not only on the advantages and disadvantages of various materials but also on the debitage and aborted preforms resulting from manufacturing processes. Not only would the qualitative attributes of debitage be of interest, but information on the quantitative transformations (cf. Schiffer 1976:63) involved in manufacture and modification processes could be used in building models for use in archaeologically recognizing the outputs of various stages in the manufacture, resharpening, and use of tools and could also be used in quantifying variables of past behavior.

## Research Potential: Cache Basin Lithic Resource Data and Cultural Theory

If we can achieve sufficient understanding of the systems of procurement and distribution of lithic resources existing during various stages in the prehistory of the Cache Basin, the Cache data may have a significant potential to contribute to the development of anthropological theory. Archaeological data indicate that the Western Lowlands, like all lowland northeastern Arkansas, was probably an extremely rich environment in terms of its potential, at least at certain times, to support large populations of people with technologically simple cultural adaptations. It might be considered ironic that, though the Western Lowlands contained a relatively high population density of "Stone Age" peoples at various times in the past, it is a region without naturally occurring stone.

Analysis of these data may play a role in the development of models pertaining to the role of exchange in technologically important raw materials in the development of increasing levels of sociocultural integration over wide areas—an important theme in the development of both metal-using and nonmetal-using societies throughout the world. There are also the little explored problems of the nontechnological—that is, ideological and sociotechnic—uses of exotic lithic raw materials in low-energy cultural systems. Specifically, the recent discovery of the use of exotic cherts in the manufacture of apparent sociotechnic artifacts by the Dalton culture 10,000 years ago in the Cache Basin (Morse 1975a) promises insights into band-level social organization in a rich environment.

# 28

# Settlement Patterns and Contract Archaeology: An Oklahoma Example

CHARLES D. CHEEK
ANNETTA L. CHEEK
STEVEN HACKENBERGER
KEVIN LEEHAN

Research generated by public-sponsored archaeology can be guided by a variety of theoretical orientations. One general orientation that has been usefully applied to archaeological data is a study of the interrelationships of archaeological populations and their environments. Such an approach seems appropriate, since publicly funded work is largely the result of legislation to protect the environment, and the development of information on past man–environment interaction may prove beneficial to both man and his environment in the future.

One particular environmentally oriented approach is the analysis of archaeological settlement systems. Such research can assist in the assessment of the scientific value of different types of sites. This is especially important in the case of small limited-activity sites with restricted assemblages that, considered individually, might be deemed unimportant but that might actually contain important information about a total settlement system. Unfortunately, all too often archaeologists doing publicly funded research have made just such a mistake and disregarded the potential of this type of site (e.g., see Perino 1972).

A major handicap to settlement pattern analysis derives from the structure of much publicly funded work. In general, individual projects are restricted to either the upper or the lower reaches of a drainage system, and unless other research has covered complementary areas, the archaeologist has difficulty analyzing the total settlement pattern, since it is likely to involve larger regions.

Beardsley, Holder, Krieger, Kutche, Meggers, and Rinaldo (1956) developed a conceptual typological model of community patterning that was the result of the relationship between the productivity of the subsistence system, the degree of mobility, and the impact of these two variables on the "organization of economic, socio-political, and cermonial interrelationships within a community [p. 134]." This typology of societies could be applied to both archaeological and ethnographic cultures and was not merely descriptive but also functional and evolutionary.

Two factors were considered important or "dynamic" in the development of types of community patterning. First, "the productivity of the subsistence resource" is the major determinant "in non-sedentary societies [p. 150]." The second is the degree of community mobility, which has an important limiting effect on the development of community complexity (pp. 151–152) when societies depend on domestication.

The typology produced was unusual for the time because of its explicit evolutionary approach that included what would today be considered both specific and general evolutionary statements (pp. 152–155). Another relatively unusual feature was the causal primacy given to the technoenvironmental complex, or subsistence pattern. The authors did not, however, separate the technoeconomic aspect, as did Steward (1955), who of course was writing at this time and who with L. White (1949) stirred interest in the evolutionary adaptational study of societies.

In spite of its straightforward statements of causal relationships between subsistence and other aspects of culture, this work seems generally to have been ignored by the historians of evolutionary and cultural-materialist thought (Dole 1973; Harris 1968) as well as by most archaeologists. However, similar kinds of analysis have been done by some archaeologists, such as Flannery (1972), MacNeish (1964), and Wilmsen (1973).

There are some problems with the Beardsley model, particularly in light of our increasing knowledge of band organization. In general it holds up remarkably well, possibly because of its emphasis on settlement types as defined by degrees of mobility. Some of these types can use refinement, an attempt at which follows, but the basic stages can be accepted. There are seven primary types and three additional types for pastoral nomads. The ten stages of the typology are as follows: (1) free wandering; (2) restricted wandering; (3) central based wandering; (4) semipermanent sendentary; (5) simple nuclear centered; (6) advanced nuclear centered; (7) supranuclear integrated; (8) incipient pastoral nomadic; (9) equestrian hunting; and (10) diversified pastoral nomadic. Types 2, 3, and 4 apply most frequently to the areas that we have studied, and the emphasis of this chapter will be on these three, with a few comments on 5 and 6.

The value of this typology to archaeologists doing survey work is that it provides a set of stages or types of community patterns that are reflected in site locations. In other words, it can be used in settlement system analysis. The model, with some minor modifications, supplies the archaeologist with a set of expectations for the distribution of archaeological materials (sites and artifacts) that allows more complete interpretation of the data.

## THE MODEL

*Restricted wandering* is an adaptation "to sparse, scattered, or seasonally available food resources [Beardsley *et al*. 1956:137]" by a group that lives within a territory that the group's members define as theirs and to whose food resources they have primary rights and access (p. 126). *Central based wandering* is an adaptation to special conditions that enables a community to live in one spot for "weeks or months." This is an adaptation to "one of three different types of subsistence resources: (*1*) a storable or preservable wild food harvest; (*2*) a locally abundant food source, such as shell fish; and (*3*) incipient agriculture producing a small harvest [p. 138]."

A *semipermanent sendentary* community "establishes itself in successive locations, occupying each for a period of years [p. 140]." The authors refer primarily to villages, although one or two family hamlets can be considered as a subtype of this kind of community.

There are a number of problems with the model that must be mentioned. In the two types characterized by hunting and gathering, what type of band is being discussed? Two possibilities exist: (*1*) a local band of 25–50 and occasionally as many as 100 people; or (*2*) a group of local bands here termed a *dialect band*. The latter averaged around 500 people (Birdsell 1968) and was composed of a number of local bands that spoke the same dialect and possibly came together occasionally. The dialect band is a significant unit because the individual local band is "sufficient neither for the social viability nor for the demographic survival of bands [Wilmsen 1973:13]." A third possibility, a band segment or task group, is just a part of a community pattern.

In discussing the restricted wandering communities, Beardsley *et al*. undoubtedly mean the first, given their conditions of sparse, scattered, or seasonal resources (p. 137). A dialect band could exist in one location perhaps, during particularly abundant times of the year. When they discuss central based wandering communities, it seems likely that they mean the larger extreme of the local band, but it is not likely that dialect bands were involved.

A second problem is the citation of a storable or preservable wild harvest (p. 138) as one of the defining characteristics of the central based wandering type. In temperate zones the winter and early spring months are potential hardship periods because the vast majority of the foods generally used by the members of a band are not available during this time (Schiffer 1975a:257–258). Thus almost any group in a temperate zone may have to store food to survive through the winter. The obvious question here is not is any food stored, but, is enough stored to support a local band for a sufficient period for the site to be considered a central base camp. This is a problem in quantification, which depends on local conditions, and it cannot be answered here.

A third problem needs to be considered. Beardsley *et al*. did not discuss small scattered farming hamlets. Such a settlement type is not really what they were considering under their Type 5, the *simple nuclear centered*. However, the attributes of the *semipermanent sedentary* type are similar enough that we can define both a village and a hamlet subtype. It could also be pointed out that the hamlet type may occur associated with both *simple* and *advanced nuclear centered*.

## ARCHAEOLOGICAL IMPLICATIONS

Archaeologically, the types of communities discussed in the model are said to be distinguished by the size of the sites, degree of midden accumulation, and kinds of artifacts present. During the following discussion, Table 28.1 should be consulted.

Restricted wandering sites would be small in size because of the small group size in environments with scarce, sparse, and scattered resources (Beardsley *et al.* 1952:137). The sites would tend to be located in different resource areas, especially in temperate climates where there is much seasonality of resources. Because of the small size of the sites and the possibility that they may not be occupied for long periods of time or often reoccupied, there is no midden buildup. However, in some areas where there are particularly abundant resources during part of the year several bands may join together and create larger sites, or numerous reoccupations may occur, generating sites with both resource-specific and tool maintenance artifacts as well as evidence of seasonal occupations if preservation conditions allow.

**TABLE 28.1.**
**Summary of Hypothesized Site Attributes According to Community Type**

| | Attributes | | | |
|---|---|---|---|---|
| Community types | Evidence of seasonality | Midden | Site size | Tool types |
| Restricted wandering | | | | |
| 1. Local band temporary camp | One season | No | Small | All types[a] |
| 2. Several-band camp | One season | No | Medium | All types |
| Central based wandering | | | | |
| 3. Secondary sites | One season | No | Small | Function-specific[b] |
| 4. Central base | One or more seasons | Yes | Large | All types, structures? |
| Semipermanent sedentary | | | | |
| 5. Secondary sites | One season | No | Small | Function-specific[b] |
| 6. Hamlets | All seasons | Possibly | Medium | All types, structures |
| 7. Villages | All seasons | Yes | Large | All types, structures |

[a]Inventory at such sites might vary with environmental zone.
[b]Such sites occupied for relatively extended periods might produce maintenance tools.

Central based wandering communities, as mentioned previously, occupy favored locations for significant parts of the year. These locations are frequently revisited and may have much more midden soil than the habitations of restricted wandering groups (see Table 28.1); they may also be larger, since a larger local band may have been in residence.

Because they were occupied for long periods, these sites would have higher frequencies and proportions of maintenance tools (Schiffer 1975a:260–261) and tools associated with a particular season. Associated with the central bases would be other sites, similar to those of the restricted wandering occupations, that are the result of activities away from the central base during those times of the year when it is not feasible to occupy that location, or that are associated with special activities at diverse locations (see Table 28.1). Such secondary sites may contain a much lower proportion of tool maintenance items than are found on restricted wandering temporary camps. Both central bases and secondary sites should have evidence of seasonal occupations if it is preservable under local conditions, although the former may contain evidence of having been occupied for a greater portion of the year.

It may be difficult for the archaeologist to distinguish restricted wandering sites from secondary sites of the *central based wandering* communities. However, sites in resource areas exploitable at the same season as a dated central base with evidence of special seasonal occupations may belong to a restricted wandering community of a different, generally earlier time period.

Another problem in attempting to identify the kind of site found is illuminated by the relatively new concern with cultural formation processes (Schiffer 1972b, 1975a). Schiffer points out that just because there are several definable areas of activity in the past, such as fishing camps or seed-gathering camps, there will not necessarily be the same number of definable kinds of sites in the archaeological record. A single site could have been formed in part by different task units or structural poses (Schiffer 1975a:260) of one local band, or even band segments. The result, of course, may be larger sites than one would expect and a blurring of evidence of seasonality.

The main implications of Schiffer's comment is for sites of restricted wandering communities and for secondary sites of central based wandering communities. The evidence at a restricted wandering camp used for a number of different tasks at different times of the year over a long period may suggest a central base rather than a temporary camp.

However, countering this is a generalization he makes from Yellen's (1974) work with the Bushmen that subsistence activities performed at or from a site vary with the environment being exploited (Schiffer 1975a:260). Thus, unless the archaeologist was studying an area where one location would be advantageous for the exploitation of resources available at different seasons, a site would probably primarily reflect activities associated with a single season, allowing a distinction between restricted and central based wandering. Additionally, sites continually revisited for seasonal tasks might be larger than expected under the conditions of "scarce, sparse, and scattered" resources.

Semipermanent sedentary communities are usually associated with horticulture or agriculture. Usually they have pottery as an aspect of their material culture assemblage, which differentiates them from the preceding two community types. Additionally, the sites may contain structures and be larger than the previous occupations due to the larger concentrations of populations (see Table 28.1). However, if the primary kind of site in the settlement pattern is the isolated hamlet type composed of one or two nuclear or extended families, these sites would likely be smaller in area than central bases but may have developed comparable middens depending on their length of occupation. The hamlet sites are sometimes associated, in our area, with simple or advanced nuclear centered communities.

Semipermanent sedentary populations would also generate secondary sites (see Table 28.1). The numbers and size of such sites would be determined in part by the importance of wild foods to the populations. If important wild foods could best be collected in a large group, then associated sites would probably be large, while food-procuring tasks that could be done by a few people probably left minimal archaeological remains. Such sites may be difficult to distinguish from restricted wandering camps and central based wandering secondary sites unless culturally diagnostic artifacts are present.

Two classes of activity sites that have up to this point been ignored must be discussed: quarries and kill sites. While both of these may be important in the technoeconomic subsystem of the society, their nature makes them difficult to relate to a specific settlement system. Quarries were often used over centuries and frequently contain no datable remains. Hunting sites in many regions of North America are extremely difficult to identify (Schiffer 1975a:262) because of the solitary habits of some game animals and resulting hunting patterns. On the other hand, kill sites that resulted from the drive and/or jump techniques are readily identifiable and relatively easy to locate.

This discussion of the archaeological implications of the settlement model of Beardsley et al. (1956) is admittedly very general; it would require specific test implications depending on the particular area in which it was applied.

## APPLICATION OF THE MODEL IN EASTERN OKLAHOMA

### Survey Data

The data recovered during a survey of the proposed Upper Muddy Boggy Watershed in south central Oklahoma (Cheek et al. 1974) were tested against three of the stages in Beardsley's model: restricted wandering, central based wandering, and semipermanent sedentary. This research was sponsored by the U.S. Department of Agriculture's Soil Conservation Service. Application of the model was restricted by two factors:

1. Not all sites could be assigned a temporal affiliation.
2. The proposed watershed was restricted to certain portions of the upper reaches of the area's drainage.

This second problem was in part offset by an earlier survey of the nearby proposed Parker Reservoir (Neal 1972), in the lower reaches of the area's drainage. These data, however, were not completely comparable.

The Muddy Boggy survey recorded 27 prehistoric and four historical components. Only the former will be discussed, although settlement pattern models can be applied to historical materials as well when the volume of data is sufficient. The Parker survey recorded 27 sites. All sites from both surveys either were assigned to middle Archaic (4000–1500 B.C.) or later stages or could not be assigned any temporal affiliation.

One definitely Middle Archaic site was identified by the Muddy Boggy survey. It was a small site on an intermittent stream and thus would have been either a seasonal site of a restricted wandering band or a specialized-activity site of a central based band according to the Beardsley model.

Four sites in the Muddy Boggy area were identified as Late Archaic (1500 B.C.–A.D. 500), and 14 of the 17 Parker sites were considered Archaic on the basis of the presence of various dart point types. Three of the former are on permanent water, and two of these are small sites, one is medium. The fourth is a large site on an intermittent stream. None showed the development of midden soil. The two small sites may have been specialized task group sites. Both larger sites on the permanent and the intermittent streams may have been seasonal, multiple function sites possibly occupied by the entire local band. These sites are located in far-flung parts of the watershed and probably represent portions of the settlement pattern of several different bands. No central base camps seem to be located in the surveyed area, and the sites found seem to suggest a restricted wandering settlement pattern with a few small secondary sites.

Ten of the Parker sites, Archaic in date and located in the lower reaches of the watershed's main stream, are substantially larger than the Muddy Boggy sites. They could represent repeated occupations of preferred locations. More likely, the sites could have been the gathering point for a number of local bands—perhaps a dialect band—during times of abundant food, or they could be central base camps; the absence of midden soils suggests the former. This area is a bottomland environment and provides denser, more diverse, and more dependable resources than any one ecozone in the upper reaches. Thus, it could have served as the gathering point for fairly large groups during times when upper-reach resources were limited. Again, this evidence suggests the existence of a restricted wandering settlement pattern during the Archaic.

Four horticultural stage (Caddoan) sites were located by the Muddy Boggy survey; none were recorded by the Parker survey. Of these four, three are tentatively dated to Early Caddoan, (A.D. 1000–1300). These three sites in the upper reaches were located where flooding is minimal and where arable land is available. They may all be small village or hamlet horticulture sites, or they may be horticulture-stage special-activity sites. In general they can be assigned to the semipermanent sedentary village or hamlet type.

One late Caddo site (A.D. 1300–1600) was located. It is a large site on a permanent stream, but it is located on a steep slope above abundant arable land. No midden deposits were found. Both plant-processing equipment and projectile points were found on the site, and it is more likely a secondary Caddoan site than a village site, although it may be a hamlet, possibly over an Archaic component. This can be classed as a semipermanent sendentary or hamlet community type also.

The remaining Muddy Boggy survey sites were small, undatable sites on both permanent and intermittent streams. They were probably either secondary sites or temporary camps.

Application of the Beardsley model to the data from the two surveys suggests that the Archaic populations were characterized by a restricted wandering settlement pattern and the village horticulture peoples possibly by a semipermanent sedentary pattern, although the data for the latter conclusions are scanty. Although these conclusions must be tenatative, they suggest possibilities for future research in the area.

## Excavation Data

In addition to its being used to assist in interpretation of data from regional studies, under certain conditions the Beardsley model can be employed in the study of single sites. The necessary conditions are the existence of comparable data from several other contemporary sites in the area that can be supposed to represent other portions of a settlement system. Such a study was made of two sites, Pw66 and Pw67, in Pawnee County, Oklahoma, northwest of Tulsa (Hackenberger and Cheek 1975).

The sites were assigned on the basis of projectile point types to the Woodland period (A.D. 600–1000). They occurred in an upland location on the upper reaches of the area's creeks. Other nearby Woodland sites in the Arkansas River valley proper, approximately 13 km to the north, had previously been excavated. The authors of the Pawnee report propose that these were secondary sites of a semipermanent sedentary community pattern. The assemblages of the various excavated sites can be compared in order to test this suggestion, specifically to determine whether the river valley sites could be interpreted as central bases, and the upland sites as secondary sites suitable for the exploitation of specific abundant resources. In general, the data from the sites are consistent with such an interpretation.

The river valley sites are larger and have denser depositions of cultural materials than the upland sites. The assemblages at the sites along the river are more diverse, containing proportionately more utilized flakes, knives, drills, scrapers, and other tools. Both types of sites contain similar projectile point types and some tools associated with the preparation of plant materials-manos, and metates. One significant difference is the presence of ceramics at the river valley sites and their absence at the upland sites.

The assemblages from the upland sites suggest that a narrower range of activities occurred there than at the river valley sites, and that at all sites some plant preparation and hunting occurred. Storage (as suggested by the ceramics) and maintenance activities (as suggested by the drills, scrapers, knives, etc.) appear to have been concentrated at the river valley sites, which may indeed have functioned as central bases. These sites can be considered under the hamlet type of semipermanent sedentary community. In sum, the use of the Beardsley model in this case allows a fuller interpretation of the data from two relatively small, isolated sites than would have been possible had the two sites been considered by themselves.

## Another Regional Research Program

Another discussion of the study of archaeological settlement systems (Southwestern Anthropological Research Group 1974) can be compared to the Beardsley model. The Southwestern Anthropological Research Group (SARG) scheme presents two hypotheses about the interaction of location and natural resources. Although in some areas, such as the proverbally well-studied Southwest, the SARG design seems oversimplified, in most parts of the country studies oriented by this model would improve the quality of area archaeological research.

The SARG design presents two basic propositions concerning the interaction of resources and site location:

1. Cultural activities were located with respect to critical on-site resources in order to minimize energy expenditure in the acquisition of required quantities of resources.
2. Cultural activities were located in positions intermediate to locations of critical resources in order to minimize energy expenditure in acquiring required quantities of resources existing in diverse locations.

From these propositions it can be seen that the emphasis of SARG is on the locations of sites in respect to the locations of environmental variables. No attempt is made to relate settlement pattern to different levels of mobility or to social organization. The utility of this scheme is discussed more fully shortly.

## CONCLUSION

Although more work needs to be done on the archaeological implications of the Beardsley model, we think it has three main benefits for archaeologists in general and contract archaeologists in particular.

The first of these is that the application of this settlement system model will enable the archaeologist to obtain some idea of the significance of a site, no matter how small it may be. As an example, if the archaeologist realizes that a restricted wandering system generates many small sites and very few large sites, he will have a theoretical basis for generating hypotheses concerning these smaller sites. If he does not consider such sites, he is ignoring most of the data about that particular society. Archaeologists have known for some time that small sites tend to be single-component or single-phase sites. Additionally, as Schiffer (1975a) has implied, small sites may also represent a restricted range of functions. The functions of occupations on larger sites may be obscured by multiple reoccupations at different times of the year. If the archaeologist has a bias toward large sites because his idea of prehistoric occupations does not include a recognition of the significance of smaller sites outside of the main drainages, then whole segments of prehistory, such as the Middle Archaic, which may have been typified by a restricted wandering system, may be misinterpreted.

Second, this model can be useful on surveys in which the area to be surveyed is restricted by boundaries of some arbitrary nature, such as often is the case with contract specifications. It can provide a way of relating results of disparate surveys in different but neighboring areas as was done on the survey of the Upper Muddy Boggy Watershed. It could also be utilized as a regional model for which a number of archaeologists could gather data and place them in an integrated structure. If this were done, the material gathered by various institutions and individuals would be made more comparable, and the relative value of a site could then be judged within this standardized framework. Such a use of this model would allow greater compliance with one of the primary purposes of any environmental impact statement: the evaluation of site significance with respect to what is known about the archaeology of a region.

A third point that can be made is that there are some similarities between the Beardsley community patterning model and the SARG approach. They can both be utilized for gathering comparable regional data and in assessing the significance of small or single-function sites. There are differences also. In some respects the Beardsley model is a conceptual model, a typology; but it is a typology built on dynamic changes in the relationship between people and their means of subsistence. Furthermore, Beardsley et al. (1956) point out that the typology is really the reduction of a continuum rather than a series of discrete points. The community patterning model is one of change over time, a historical and evolutionary model that has assigned the cause of change to technoenvironmental variables.

The SARG approach is somewhat unlike the Beardsley model in that it deals with different levels of explanation. SARG considers the explanation of site location per se within a settlement system, while the Beardsley model is intended to deal with the changes from one level of community organization to another. However, they both relate site location to similar technoenvironmental variables.

However, the utilization of the Beardsley model can be greatly aided by using SARG's proposed methodologies in identifying and measuring the resources relating to the location of a site or set of sites. Additional value is added to the conceptual model of Beardsley by the possibilities for quantifying and testing the hypotheses and methodologies put forward by SARG (see Hackenberger, Cheek, Leehan, and Purves 1976). These studies can identify a specific factor or set of factors that were responsible for the location of sites. This information can then be articulated with the Beardsley model to identify the community patterning of a particular society.

We do not mean to suggest that either way of studying regional settlement systems is better than the other, only that they are focused on different levels of explanation using the same kinds of explanatory variables and that they can be used complementarily with benefit.

In summary we have pointed out that the Beardsley community patterning and mobility model can be useful to archaeologists, especially contract archaeologists. It is a model around which regional research can be organized and it will result in comparable data suitable for addressing at least some problems. The primary utility to the contract archaeologist is that this approach presents him with a model within which he can assess the significance of the total range of sites that are found on any size project. We realize, however, that this model and our presentation of it can be, and needs to be, altered to fit individual regions and problems, and we hope that other archaeologists will assess this attempt critically and apply the model carefully in their own regions.

# 29

# The Archaeology of the Logging Industry in the Little Black River Watershed[1]

SUZANNE E. HARRIS
JAMES E. PRICE
CYNTHIA R. PRICE

In assessing the cultural resources of the Little Black River watershed relevant data were collected in accordance with a regional research design implemented in all archaeological research projects executed through the University of Missouri Department of Anthropology, American Archaeology Division, Southeast Missouri Archaeological Research Facility. This major research design, regional in approach and systemic in concept, is charged with the "explanation of man's changing role in the natural environment on the Ozark Border" or "man's changing utilization of a major ecotone [Price, Cottier, Harris, House, and Price 1975:75]." All archaeological research projects in the eastern Ozarks and Western Lowlands that are administered by the facility are consistent in goal definition and relevant data collected.

Data are placed in broad cultural context and viewed relative to all other archaeological and historical data available for the Ozark Border. In our opinion a research project that does not assess a broad spectrum of an area's cultural resources falls far short of its anthropological potential.

We likewise contend that recent historical data are just as anthropologically significant as data on the prehistoric millenia. We predict that archaeological and historical data from the last half of the nineteenth century will be considered more as archaeologists incorporate problems in social and economic history and cultural geography into their research strategies.

[1]Adapted from Chapter 21 of *An Assessment of the Cultural Resources of the Little Black Watershed* by James E. Price, Cynthia R. Price, John Cottier, Suzanne Harris, and John House. The assessment was the result of a cooperative agreement between the University of Missouri and the USDA Soil Conservation Service and was completed February–April 1975.

391

   The greatest social and economic impact on the Ozark Border following the Civil
War was the development of the logging industry. Today's settlement pattern and
population composition were greatly influenced by the arrival of this lucrative
capitalistic industry that chewed its wasteful paths across the Ozark Border, leaving
ghost towns and poverty behind as its ever hungry maws moved westward in search
of more virgin stands of timber.
   During the second half of the nineteenth century the lumber industry in the United
States successively moved through the virgin forests of New England, western New
York, Pennsylvania, and the Great Lakes states (L. G. Hill 1949:5). According to
Hill (pp. 14–21), the major reasons for the movement of the eastern logging companies into the forests of Missouri around 1880 were: (1) good local labor supply;
(2) mild climate permitting year-round logging; (3) good transportation (railroads
had been and were being constructed along margins of the Ozarks); (4) low cost of
timberland; (5) proximity to market, particularly the relatively treeless Plains states
of Nebraska, Kansas, and Oklahoma (then Indian Territory).

## LUMBER COMPANIES, TOWNS, AND CAMPS

   In the lowland area of the watershed several large lumber companies located in
Poplar Bluff, Missouri, extracted timber from the swamplands of the southeastern
portion of the watershed. Among the largest companies that began operating about
1875 were the Brooklyn Cooperage Company, which owned thousands of acres in
Butler County, Missouri, and Clay County, Arkansas; the Popular Bluff Lumber
and Manufacturing Company; and the F. G. Oxley Stave Company (Pottenger
1945:235).
   In addition to the lumber companies with headquarters in Poplar Bluff, the
following lumber companies also had headquarters located in the lowlands: the
Boyden and Wyman Lumber Company, the Horton Land and Lumber Company,
and the Ohio Hardwood Lumber Company. There were also several owner-operated
sawmills, often accompanied by small communities scattered along the railroads at
switches and spurs.
   Logging activities in the Ozark Plateau portion of the watershed were dominated
by the Missouri Lumber and Mining Company, which in 1888 built a large mill and
company in Carter County. This company was not locally owned but was organized
by a group of timber men in Pennsylvania (L. G. Hill 1949:22). Another large
company that operated on the northern edge of the watershed and beyond was the
Ozark Land and Lumber Company, based in Shannon County. Other smaller companies in the area were the Doniphan Land and Lumber Company, the T. L. Wright
Lumber Company, and the Culbertson Stock and Lumber Company, all located in
Ripley County. There were also several small owner-operated mills, such as
Seatstown, 23CT-H4, on the North Prong of the Little Black.
   During the lumbering period in both the highlands and lowlands, new towns
sprang up and existing villages boomed. Neelyville, Barfield (later Naylor), and

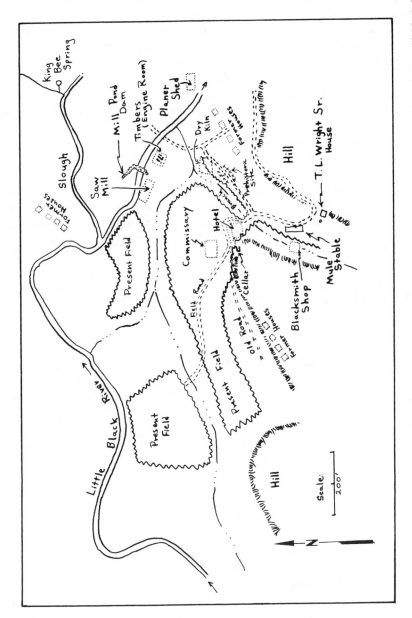

**Map 29.1.** The King Bee lumber village site, ca. 1895–1910. This sketch map was drawn February 28, 1975, from an on-the-ground inspection with Mr. J. S. Slayton.

Grandin then all had populations several times the present figures. Some of these once-thriving lumber towns now exist only as settlements of a few houses or have been abandoned completely.

Logging camps to house the loggers were set up in various valleys in the woods, usually at convenient places along the tram roads. In some cases, the houses were lined up and down the tram roads for as much as 5 miles (L. G. Hill 1949:50). Some of the larger camps—such as Mule Camp, 23RI-H34, on the Middle Prong of Beaverdam Creek, and King Bee, on the Little Black River (Map 29.1)—were functioning towns with a commissary, barracks, residences, blacksmith shop, and possibly a tram engine repair shop. The loggers rode back and forth from the camps to the cutting areas on the trams.

The entire logging and sometimes milling operations were portable. After an area had been cleared, whole camps were moved by placing the buildings on skids, loading them on flatcars, and transporting them by train to the new timbered area (Wihebrink 1974:50). Portable mills, even a large one that could cut up to 10,000 board feet of lumber per day, were transported into almost inaccessible areas (Hill 1949:36–37). Once an area was deforested, the tram roads were taken up and relaid in new locations. Some tram branches might be in place for only a single year (L. G. Hill 1949:53).

## LUMBERING LOGISTICS AND LOGGING METHODS

### Timber Cutting

Timber was procured either by individuals who delivered logs at a fixed price or by company logging and hauling (L. G. Hill 1949:42). In the woods the actual tree cutting was accomplished by two-man teams of fellers, using a measuring pole and either axes or saws and wedges. Logs were usually cut into 10-, 12-, 14-, or 16-foot lengths, the 12- and 16-foot lengths being the most easily sold (Deem 1940:97; Hill 1949:42). Before 1895 the Missouri Lumber and Mining Company cut only trees with a butt diameter of at least 12 inches, but after this date smaller trees were used. The average faller's day's work was expected to produce 10,000 board feet of lumber (p. 45). This company cut an average of 15,000–20,000 acres of timber per year (p. 210).

### Transportation of Timber

In the Ozarks the logs were moved to shipping points by rolling them out; by hauling them out with log wheels, log wagons, or tram roads; or by skidding them out with oxen or mules. Oxen were used by the Missouri Lumber and Mining Company primarily before 1892, after which mules were used (L. G. Hill 1949:45). The logs were then transported to the mills by rail, water, or both.

Tram roads were built connecting the various points of logging activity directly with the mills or with rivers on which the logs could be floated to the mills. In the highlands tram roads were built down many of the major hollows. The construction of only one tram road in the lowlands has been verified. It connected the Horton Land and Lumber Company's lumber camp at Blue Hole with the company head-quarters in Barfield (Naylor). Main tram roads lasted about 5 to 10 years, branches 1 year or as needed (p. 53). Most tram engines were fueled with unmarketable wood, however the Missouri Lumber and Mining Company used coal because it burned more efficiently than wood (p. 52). The logs were loaded on the tramcars by mules, which pulled chains attached to the logs and skidded them up two inclined poles into the cars.

In the mud and standing water of the lowlands oxteams were the major method of transporting logs from the cutting area. Oxen pulled a *lizard,* a large forked log with a crosspiece attached near the ends of the two sections protruding from the fork (Deem 1940:97). Logs to be so transported were chained to the crosspiece, and the loaded lizard was then dragged out.

Apparently log wagons, rather than tram roads, were the major method of long-distance transport both in the lowlands and in the Ozark foothills when water transportation could not be used. Very large logs in both upland and lowland areas were also transported by log wheels: 10-foot diameter wooden wheels attached to an axle with one end of the log suspended from the underside of the axle and the other end dragging along the ground.

Logs were transported down the Current River to the west of the watershed and down the Black River to the east. In the lowlands log rafts were made by fastening the logs together with wooden pins or iron spikes ("chaindogs" is the colloquial term used in the Ozarks for two flat iron spikes connected by a 6 inch piece of chain. Another term often employed is "raft shackle"). Rafts were then released at 20- to 30-min intervals to prevent jamming (Deem 1940:98). On the Current, due to the swiftness of the water, the logs sometimes could not be rafted; they floated freely and were followed by boats (L. G. Hill 1949:46). At other times they were rafted. Logs were pulled out of the water by a *hog chain,* a spiked, endless chain that ran up a V-shaped trough; the logs were then snagged by men with cant hooks (p. 46).

## Milling

Once at the mills, the logs were stored in millponds while they awaited sawing. The site of Grandin was selected for a major milling town because of a natural millpond there that covered 3.5 acres (L. G. Hill 1949:33). As a millpond, its capacity was 500,000 board feet of logs.

The actual milling operation was controlled by a sawyer, who was stationed near the main saw and determined the quantity, grade, and size of the lumber produced. Logs were first sawed into boards on a band or circular saw while they were carried on a conveyer belt, and bark was then trimmed off the edges. The boards were further trimmed and graded, and they were finally stacked and dried either in the open or, for the better grades of wood, in a kiln (pp. 57–59). Dried lumber was then either processed by a planing mill and sawed into building material (flooring, lathing, etc.), or processed by special-purpose mills, such as stave mills or heading (barrel top) mills.

The Grandin Mill, the largest of the Missouri Lumber and Mining Company mills, actually had three mill units. The "Big Mill" had one band saw and one circular saw; the second mill had one band saw, and the third was a lath mill producing lath and shingles (p. 55, 59). In 1892 the three mills produced 32 million board feet of lumber, and from the mid 1890s until the mill shut down in 1909, they produced about 60 million board feet annually. The daily production in 1901 was 192,000 board feet (p. 77–78). It is reported that in 1894 the Grandin Mill probably cut more timber than any other mill in the United States (p. 36).

### Tree Species Used by the Logging Industry

In the swampland forests of the southeastern portion of the watershed, the predominate trees cut were oak, cypress, ash, and sweetgum (red gum) (Deem 1940:97). In the Ozarks the Missouri Lumber and Mining Company specialized in yellow pine (now usually referred to as shortleaf pine, *Pinus echinata*). The trademark of the Missouri Lumber and Mining Company was a beaver, and "Beaver Dam Soft Pine," named for the Beaverdam Creek area, was known throughout the United States lumber market (L. G. Hill 1949:40). Most of the upland pine was sawed into building material (interior trim, veneers, window frames and sashes, siding, house framing and sheathing, lath, flooring, pickets, and boards for silos and barns) (p. 8) or railroad ties (p. 181). After 1907 oak was also cut for freight car manufacture (p. 191). Oak ties were cut by smaller companies (p. 191). In the lowlands, much of the oak was used in barrel making, particularly white oak bourbon barrels, and golden oak house interiors; decay resistant cypress was used for ships' masts, mine timbers, and railroad ties; sweet gum (red gum) was used in furniture manufacture (Settergren and McDermott 1962:33; 6; 66). Hickory, according to local residents, was used for oil well sucker rods.

### LUMBER MARKETS

Most of the Ozark lumber was shipped into the Great Plains, but some of it went east to Ohio, Illinois, and Indiana (L. G. Hill 1949:82). In 1898 the Missouri Lumber and Mining Company sold 39 million board feet west of the Mississippi River and 10 million board feet east of the Mississippi (p. 81).

Timberland in the lowlands cost about $1.25 per acre in the late nineteenth century. Similar or lower land prices prevailed in the uplands. A man who was later a major stockholder in the Missouri Lumber and Mining Company bought what became the nucleus of that company's Carter County timberland in 1871 for $1 per acre (p. 11). Tax delinquent land on which the land patent holders could not afford taxes was later purchased for as little as 25¢ and even 12.5¢ per acre (p. 19). This land averaged about 4,000 board feet of lumber per acre (p. 40). By 1899 "choice" timberland in Ripley County west of the watershed was sold for $5 per acre (Our sister towns 1899).

Profits from the lumber industry were high, although information on actual figures is sparse. When organized in 1880, the Missouri Lumber and Mining Company stock was valued at $150,000 by 1888 the capital stock was valued at $500,000 (L. G. Hill 1949:22–24). The mills began paying dividends in 1892, and by 1905 they were paying $490,000 per year and peaked in 1907 at $60,000 per month, or $720,000 per year (p. 219). During the period 1880–1909 demand for yellow pine steadily increased while production costs remained constant, therefore permitting high profits. During the period 1889–1909 workers' salaries began between $1.25 and $1.35 per day, and seldom exceeded $2 (p. 159).

## DECLINE OF THE LOGGING INDUSTRY

The timber boom ended in the lowlands about 1900 and in the uplands about 10 years later. Most marketable timber had been cut and profits made; however, no replanting or conservation practices had been followed. Cost of shipping to the local mills from more distant timberlands and high taxes on the cleared land resulted in the moving of the lumber companies and the closing of most of the smaller owner-operated mills. Land owned by the lumber companies was sold either to land speculation companies or to private parties.

The attitude of the day is typified by a front page article in the *Doniphan Prospect-News*, April 13, 1899: "It will be a lasting benefit to the towns Varner [Oxly] and Barfield [Naylor] when the last stick of timber is marketed and the attention of the citizens of the neighborhood is turned exclusively to farming." The same article had already described the depopulated town, dwindling business, and vacant houses in Barfield. This decline was a direct result of the burning of the Horton Land and Lumber Company mill the year before and the consequent unemployment of most of the town. A similar depression followed the collapse of the lumber industry throughout the watershed. However, the lowland sand ridges proved to be good farmland, and cotton, corn, and wheat farming soon became productive. Farming was possible only in the valleys of the Ozarks, but other income-producing activities developed in the highlands, such as raising livestock and moonshining.

## MODERN LOGGING

During the 1930s the U.S. Forest Service purchased vast areas of once-timbered land in the Ozarks and began replanting pines, while other species (oak, hickory, maple) were returning through natural regeneration. These areas are now a part of Mark Twain National Forest, and some commercial logging is presently conducted there. Clandestine logging has also been going on in the national forest since it was established. This practice is locally known as *grandmawing*, since individuals bringing logs to the lumber companies would claim the wood had come from their grandmother's woodlot.

According to Mendel (1961), a wide variety of species are currently being logged: shortleaf pine, cypress, red cedar, a variety of oaks, hickory, hard and soft maple, birch, black walnut, ash, elm, sweetgum, black gum, yellow poplar, cottonwood, and sycamore. The acres in timber for 1959 were as follows (abstracted from Mendel 1961:Table 1, p. 18):

TABLE A

| County | Acres in forest | Percentage of county in forest | Noncommercial forest (acres) | Commercial forest (acres) |
|--------|-----------------|--------------------------------|------------------------------|---------------------------|
| Butler | 245,300 | 53.7% | 1,800 | 243,500 |
| Ripley | 306,800 | 75.0% | 1,900 | 304,900 |
| Carter | 276,600 | 85.4% | 7,300 | 269,300 |

As of 1965 there were several sawmills and other wood-using plants in the watershed area that purchased stumpage or rough forest products (McCormick, Massengale, Smith, and Taylor 1965). Seven of these are located in the Neelyville and Harviell areas in Butler County. Twenty-nine ·are located in Ripley County, either in the watershed or just outside of it. Of the large lumber companies that operated in the watershed around the turn of the century only one remains, the T. L. Wright Company of Doniphan, and it now deals almost solely in gravel and ready-mix concrete.

## OBSERVED ARCHAEOLOGICAL EVIDENCE OF LOGGING ACTIVITY

During the course of the present survey, direct evidence (tram road beds and/or artifacts) of logging activity was found only in the upper Little Black River watershed, and with the exception of King Bee they were observed only north of the Little Black River. Of the 14 basins north of the Little Black River, 6 revealed evidence of logging, and 2 additional sites were so identified by local informants. Evidence of the most intensive logging came from the basins near Grandin, as was to be expected. The tram road beds were the most readily visible remains of the logging industry. Metal artifacts (railroad spikes and rail connecting hardware, nuts, bolts, coupling pins, large spikes, chaindogs, and saw fragments) were rarely on the surface, and a remote sensing device was a necessity for successful plotting and recovery of these specimens. Informants provided the location of Seatstown and the Old Company Farm.

No logging-related sites or artifacts were located in the lowlands in the direct impact zones of the proposed watershed project. The Blue Hole, south of Naylor, has been visited as well as the site of the Horton Land and Lumber Company Mill. Concrete foundations and rusting mill equipment of this mill remain in a thicket in a field in Naylor.

## SUGGESTED ADDITIONAL RESEARCH AND PUBLIC INTERPRETATION OF THE LOGGING INDUSTRY IN THE WATERSHED

The logging industry has been the only major industry in the watershed (with the exception of modern agribusiness). The "Work Plan of the upper Little Black Watershed" (U.S. Department of Agriculture Soil Conservation Service 1974b:14) notes the importance of the lumber activity centered at Grandin in Carter County. Under Point 12 of their "Elements of Environmental Quality Plan," the Soil Conservation Service suggests that it may "establish historic or nature trails to inform and educate. Subjects include: the Grandin sawmill [p. 4]." On the basis of our survey several suggestions can be made concerning specific topics of information that would be educational or of interest to the general public:

1. A stand of virgin pine trees marked for cutting by the Missouri Lumber and Mining Company in the early 1900s but never cut still stands on the south side of the B-9 Basin above the permanent or temporary flood pool. The pines were pointed out by Mr. Elmer Ward, who stated the marks designating the trees for cutting are still visible. Since the B-9 Basin will be developed as a state recreation area, this stand can be included in a nature trail or in some other similar way to educate the public, provided the trees are adequately protected from vandalism.

2. Several logs transported to the Grandin Mill but never used still lie at the bottom of the millpond on the east side of Grandin. Periodically some of the logs have been raised and salvaged by local residents. One or a few logs can be raised and used in an interpretive display.

3. Some of the old equipment, such as saws of various types and/or lumber wagons, used during the lumber period might be obtained for display purposes from local residents who possess such items.

4. Smaller artifacts (chaindogs, tram spikes, mule shoes) from the lumbering period have been collected by the survey team and may be used in an interpretive display as specified in the cooperative agreement between the curators of the University of Missouri and the Soil Conservation Service.

5. A section of tram bed might be set aside for public display. Unfortunately, no tram beds were encountered in the B-9 Basin, where the recreation facilities are planned.

6. Photographs illustrating various stages of the lumbering process (tree felling; transportation by mules, lizards, trams, or log rafting; a mill in operation; stacked drying timber; and life in a mill town) could be used in an interpretative display.

Several good photographs may be found in Leslie G. Hill's dissertation (Hill 1949), and other photographs might be obtained from local residents.

For a better understanding of the logging period in the watershed as a whole we suggest further research as time and funds permit. Aspects of the logging industry that require further research include such aspects as a more detailed study of the lumber industry in the lowland portion of the watershed comparable to that done by L. G. Hill (1949) on the Grandin Mill, the relationship of the timber operations of the large lumber companies to the smaller owner-operated mills (e.g., it appears that many of the smaller owner-operated mills were begun after 1900 [Hubbell, Speece, Townley, and Gaines sawmills], possibly after the larger companies had cut selectively and then moved on), a sociological study of life during the boom and bust period of the industry in the watershed, the settlement plans of logging camps and towns and the relative use of space in each for logging and residential activities, artifacts (ceramics, glass, utilitarian items) associated with camps and towns, and industrial material left behind when trams and camps were moved.

We propose that during the mitigation phase of the Little Black River watershed project that extensive research be conducted on changing settlement systems on the Ozark Border from the Civil War to World War I. During this period the area changed from an Ozark hillbilly economy to a lumber extractive economy in a very short time. The economy then changed to one similar to that of eastern Europe as the cutover lands were sold to Yugoslavians, Hungarians, and Czechoslovakians, who easily adapted to the rocky soils of the region. They built stone buildings and fences just as they had in the old country, and they changed radically the settlement pattern from what it had been 4 decades previously.

Yet another fascinating study we propose is the procession of lumber extraction with the first mills taking the best and most easily accessible timber. Later mills utilized smaller trees and larger numbers of tree species and manufactured more diversified products until the virgin stands of timber were depleted.

## CONCLUSIONS

The subject dealt with in this chapter is marginal to traditional archaeological research. However, with the coming of contract archaeology and the broadened scope of anthropological archaeology it becomes evident that archaeologists must deal with all important cultural resources in a region in order adequately to assess and explain past culture process. These factors prompted us to explore the role of the logging industry in the explanation of man's changing use of the natural environment of the Ozark Border.

# Research Prospects: New Melones Archaeological Project

MICHAEL J. MORATTO

> Above all else, archaeological resources are research resources. They may be beautiful or ugly, interesting to the public or supremely boring, unique or common, big or little, preservable or inevitably doomed by the forces of nature or man. Each of these distinctions provides a potential set of arguments for and against particular management policies, but the basic justification for managing archaeological resources at all is that such resources contain information of potential value to the human species and that they can be studied in order to extract such information and put it at our disposal [King 1975b:1].

The purpose of this chapter is to show that meaningful anthropological questions can be framed and tangible research results can be produced even in the earliest stages of a contract project. This premise will be examined with reference to the New Melones area, a 30-mile transect of the Sierra Nevada in California's historic mother lode country. Located in the Stanislaus River valley, the 25,000-acre study zone contains about 630 archaeological sites that are jeopardized by the development of New Melones Dam and Lake. Although this monumental construction project has been underway for a decade, the related archaeology has been limited to surveys and the preliminary testing of only 22 sites. Now, with less than 5 years remaining before the completion of New Melones Lake, I have been asked to design a realistic archaeological mitigative program, including both data recovery and *in situ* preservation (cf. Moratto 1976).

Any good mitigation proposal for such a large cultural district must take into account the constraints of limited budgets and demanding schedules (cf. Jennings 1963) as well as the complexity and potentials of the data in terms of current research interests. Here, however, I shall focus on questions of aboriginal archaeology and consider administrative problems and historical archaeology only in passing. In planning this research it should be remembered that the Indians of the New Melones area—the Central Sierra Miwok and their ancestors—functioned within a larger cultural and natural universe. Accordingly, we must look beyond the project confines for both data and hypotheses, and we should formulate our research in order to better understand culture histories and processes throughout the Sierra

Nevada and beyond. With this perspective, specific archaeological questions may be generated for testing in the "laboratory" of the New Melones district.

## EXPLANATION OF INITIAL SETTLEMENT

Elsewhere I have provided evidence for the apparent lateness of occupation in the western Sierra relative to adjacent parts of the Great Basin, Central Valley, and Cascade Mountains (Moratto 1972b). There is no known indication of settlement in the sierran foothills before ca. 1500 B.C. In view of the ethnographic importance of acorns as a dietary staple, one hypothesis is that the sierran piedmont was unsuitable for habitation until acorn-processing techniques were available to exploit its oak savannas. This idea is supported by noting that mortars, pestles, and other evidences of acorn use do not appear in the eastern Valley or the Sierra until ca. 1500–1000 B.C. Unlike the rich marshlands and riparian woodlands of the Central Valley (which provided an abundance of vegetal foods; bear, elk, antelope, and other mammals; and vast numbers of waterfowl and anadromous fish) the prehistoric Sierra would have offered no antelope or waterfowl and fewer, smaller, kinds of fish. Deer were more plentiful than in the Valley, but elk ventured only to the western margin of the hills. Lacking the technology to exploit the oak savanna belt, the Indians must have considered the Sierra far less attractive than the Valley.

Another reason for the "late" occupation may have been that harsh climates and glacial conditions prevailed until recently in the western Sierra, maintaining the oaks at low elevations. It is known that not less than five cycles of glacial activity occurred in the Sierra during the past 10,000 years, and these stadials can be correlated with fluctuations in climate and biotic zones (Birman 1964; Curry 1968). At times of glacial advance the Lower Sonoran life zone, with its oak parkland, may have been confined to the Central Valley, with concomitant shifts of all other life zones to lower elevations. In this regard the analysis of a stratigraphic section at East Meadow (elevation 6500 feet) shows a series of major fluctuations in the altitude of vegetation zones, changes in the fluvial regime, and variations in the processes of meadow development, "all of which implies a series of [Holocene] climatic changes that may have severely limited the areas of habitation for aborigines on the lower slopes of the Sierra Nevada [R. Faverty, personal communication, 1974]."

In this section I have presented two (mutually compatible) hypotheses to account for the apparently late initial occupation of the western Sierra. The New Melones project area, as a sierran transect, is a particularly good place to investigate these propositions. A basic objective of such studies would be to define a Holocene paleoclimatic sequence for the central Sierra and to relate this sequence to patterns of settlement and adaptation through time. A valuable first step in this direction was the 1975 discovery of two palynological sites—senescent lakes with stratified pollen deposits—near the New Melones project, for which basal radiocarbon ages of 7380 ± 245 and 9410 ± 315 years B.P., respectively, have been determined (Batchelder

1976). Lastly, the basic assumption as to the date of the first western sierran habitation needs to be examined critically with every effort being made at New Melones to discover possible archaeological settlements more than 3500 years old.

## THE ARCHAEOLOGICAL INVENTORY: A TEST OF SAMPLE VALIDITY

Because interpretations are seldom more reliable than the data from which they are derived, it is fair to question the New Melones cultural inventory as a valid sample. A total of 630 archaeological sites has been documented at New Melones: 223 aboriginal sites (see Table 30.1) and 407 historical non-Indian sites (e.g., homesteads, wagon roads, mines, ghost towns, ferry sites, cemeteries, etc.). To the extent that they have been studied, the historical sites of New Melones appear similar to their counterparts in other parts of the mother lode region (cf. Heizer and Fenenga 1948). However, the array of aboriginal sites along the Stanislaus seems quite different than the pattern in other foothill localities. To demonstrate this, we may compare the New Melones sites with those of the Buchanan Reservoir area on the Chowchilla River (about 65 miles south of the Stanislaus).

At Buchanan (2400 acres), 68 sites have been grouped into 7 classes: (*1*) isolated bedrock milling stations (BRM); (2) "campsites" (CS), with midden areas of less than 1000 m², 0–9 BRMs, and no house pits with diamters greater than 8 m; (*3*) "small village sites" (SVS), with middens of 1000–2000 m², 10–49 BRMs, and no house pits larger than 8 m; (*4*) "large village sites" (LVS), with areas of midden up to 5000 m², 50–99 BRMs, and no house pits over 8 m across; (*5*) "village community centers" (VCC), with areas up to 22,500 m², as many as 1000 BRMs, and one or more house pits with diameters of 9–20 m; (*6*) rock shelters (RS); and (*7*) petroglyphs (P) (cf. Moratto 1968, 1972a). Now we may compare the proportions of these site types found at New Melones and Buchanan (see Table 30.1).

**TABLE 30.1.**
**A Comparison of Archaeological Sites in Two Sierran Areas**

| Site type | Buchanan Project | | New Melones Project | |
|---|---|---|---|---|
| | No. | % | No. | % |
| BRM | 4 | 6 | 134 | 60 |
| CS | 20 | 30 | 27 | 12 |
| SVS | 24 | 36 | 11 | 5 |
| LVS | 15 | 22 | 16 | 7 |
| VCC | 3 | 4 | 2 ? | 1 ? |
| RS | 1 | 1 | 31 | 14 |
| P | 1 | 1 | 2 | 1 |
| Totals | 68 | 100 | 223 | 100 |

The most striking conclusion to emerge from Table 30.1 is that there were far more very large sites (LVS and VCC) at Buchanan (26%) than at New Melones (8%). This is probably due to the fact that the Buchanan area was virtually undisturbed at the time of survey, as opposed to the New Melones vicinity, which was greatly modified. It is highly probable that most of the LVS and VCC along the Stanislaus were obliterated by the hydraulic mining of the Gold Rush and by the later construction of old Melones Reservoir. It is also possible, though not likely, that the Indians of the Stanislaus operated with social and demographic patterns appreciably different than those of the Chowchilla River Indians and that there were fewer sizable villages on the Stanislaus to begin with.

Available data support the former postulate. Ethnographic reports by Barrett and Gifford (1933) and Merriam (1955, 1967) clearly state that the Central Sierra Miwok, as well as their more southerly kin, were organized with large central villages and subsidiary hamlets. It is known, moreover, that great numbers of foothill sites were washed away along with the auriferous gravels during the Gold Rush. The discovery of 134 BRMs without associated middens at New Melones, compared with only 4 at Buchanan (which was never affected by mining), suggests the enormity of the data lost to the flumes and monitors of the Stanislaus.

The point of this comparison is to show that the remaining archaeological sites in the New Melones district may not reflect the full range of aboriginal settlement forms. It would be worth the effort to survey portions of the Stanislaus drainage undisturbed by mining to learn whether physical traces of the village community settlement system have survived. This approach could produce a more complete understanding of the Stanislaus archaeological "universe" and the degree to which the New Melones sample may be skewed. Such an understanding would be a prerequisite for interpreting the cultural resources that have survived.

## DEMOGRAPHIC QUESTIONS

The size, density, and distribution of aboriginal populations may be investigated at New Melones. As a hypothesis concerning sierran demographic trends over the last 3000 years, I propose that:

1.  The earliest sites were located at favorable ecotones along the major rivers.
2.  Populations in these initial settlements gradually expanded and intensified the exploitation of their catchments.
3.  Later, subsidiary villages were settled by groups budding off from the primary sites until the corridors of the rivers and their largest tributaries were densely occupied.
4.  After 1500 A.D. demographic changes included the establishment of small, seasonal camps on minor watercourses, absolute population increases, and new levels of sociopolitical integration that permitted even larger aggregates in the influential central villages.

5.   As a result of Euramerican incursions and pressures, displaced Indians from the coast and from the Central Valley sought refuge in the Sierra after 1770.

This model, which fits the Fresno River and Chowchilla River sequences (Fenenga 1973, 1975; Moratto 1972a), may be tested on the Stanislaus. Johnson (1973) has noted that protohistoric to historic components form the majority of all sites sampled at New Melones and that the sudden proliferation of these late components is not explicable by an *in situ* population increase. Thus, even at the preliminary testing stage, it is clear that the New Melones country was a refuge for Indians disrupted by the invasion to the west. To evaluate other aspects of the model, research at New Melones should: (*1*) classify sites according to age and criteria that may reflect sociopolitical distinctiveness; (*2*) apply locational analysis (cf. Hole and Heizer 1973:384 ff.) to components of various ages and types to seek possible correlations between natural and cultural variables; (*3*) determine whether populations expanded between 1500 and 1770 A.D.; (*4*) identify "ethnic markers" that might reflect the influx of Indian refugees into the New Melones district after 1770; and (*5*) seek explanations for the demographic changes observed in the archaeological record.

Similarly, archaeology at New Melones may be employed to assess ethnographic population estimates critically. Kroeber (1925) set the number of Sierra (three divisions) and Plains Miwok at 9000, of which about 2250 people were assigned to each of the four dialect groups. Kroeber's figure of 9000 should be taken as an educated, but conservative, estimate. S. F. Cook, who has undertaken the most exhaustive studies of California demography, believed that the true population levels were nearly twice as great as those advanced by Kroeber. Using Cook's (1971) values, one may calculate that 15,000 to 20,000 Miwok occupied interior California in 1770. Assuming that the Central Sierra Miwok population was roughly one-fourth of the total or about 4375, and allowing them a territory of 2439 square miles, the density would have been approximately 1.79 persons per square mile. With this figure, the Stanislaus watershed (905 square miles) would have supported some 1620 Miwok. However, this does not indicate directly what the population may have been within the New Melones area. The density was certainly greater there than it was at higher altitudes; major, permanent villages would have been situated in the foothills below the snow line; and the resources near the river would have been more bountiful than in the hinterland. Collectively, these factors suggest a density of perhaps 5 to 10 persons per square mile within the New Melones vicinity and 200 to 400 as the population for the 40-square-mile project area, an estimate that may be evaluated both archaeologically and ecologically.

Baumhoff (1963) used the availability of resources (acorns, deer, salmon, etc.) to calculate carrying capacity and population densities for defined regions of California. Values of 0–2 persons per square mile in the high Sierra and 5–7 per square mile in the foothills were computed. The latter gives 200 to 280 as the New Melones population, which compares well with the hypothetical range of 200 to 400 (supra).

Another approach to population estimating is based upon longevity curves and the size of mortuary populations. The study area contains 56 known middens with a total volume of about 72,113 m³. Initial random testing of 63 m³ at 22 sites revealed the skeletal remains of 19 individuals. If this frequency is validated by an adequate sample, one would expect 30 graves per 100 m³, or 24,037 as the total for New Melones. Applying a life expectancy of 28.6 years (cf. Moratto 1972a) and a span of perhaps 2500 years for Stanislaus River occupation, we obtain 87.4 generations with mean populations of 275. The early populations were probably considerably smaller, and the late ones a good deal larger, than the mean. This estimate and those previously mentioned, while mutually consistent, must be taken as conjectural until they can be evaluated in the light of more extensive archaeological data from the New Melones project area.

## ETHNOHISTORICAL CONSIDERATIONS

A. L. Kroeber recorded the names of some 50 Central Sierra Miwok villages, of which 15 are near the New Melones project (1925:Plate 37). He cautioned that "some [villages] are in doubtful or conflicting records, others are vaguely located, and in general the condition of knowledge concerning the settlements of the group . . . is far from satisfactory [p. 444]." Nonetheless, there is an appreciable correspondence between the location of 5 of the named villages and archaeological sites (Moratto 1976:64). It is suggested that certain ethnographic settlements might be represented by New Melones area middens and that, once sensitized to this possibility, archaeologists may broaden their research scope to include ethnohistorical questions. In brief, some of the middens may contain data concerning activities or events noted, but poorly documented, in historical accounts. A case in point is 4-Cal-s565, a large, buried midden on the bank of the Stanislaus at the old town of Melones. This location fits *Wüyü*, where, in 1848, a man named Murphy reportedly controlled the gold-mining labor of an entire native village of "600 warriors" (W. R. Ryan 1973:40). History also records that the Indians of *Wüyü* were exceptional fishermen who took advantage of the excellent riffles adjacent to their village. If Cal-s565 and *Wüyü* prove to be the same, this site would be a valuable source of information regarding both the mining activities of the Miwok during the earliest months of the Gold Rush and specific aspects of acculturation. What kinds of equipment and methods did the Miwok employ in their mining? What sorts of goods did they exchange for their gold? Did Murphy's presence influence the social organization or stimulate the growth of *Wüyü*? To what extent were native economic pursuits disrupted by the early contact with Murphy and other whites? Excavations at Cal-s565 might also shed light upon the reported fishing specialization and clarify the relationship between the growth of Melones (town) and the demise of *Wüyü*. These queries show the advantages of conducting the New Melones fieldwork according to the interests of both archaeology and ethnohistory, and they underscore the need for the New Melones data recovery program to be a well-integrated multidisciplinary effort.

The case of *Wüyü* illustrates the derivation of archaeological questions with respect to a single ethnographic settlement. On a more general level, Hall (1976:103 ff.) has raised a series of problems suitable for study at any of the historical-era Indian sites in the New Melones locality. Hall notes that glass trade beads, which have appeared at numerous sites, probably reflect the entry of whites into the area, even though such items are often found great distances from their original source. Miwok artifacts made from foreign materials, such as the bottle glass projectile point from Cal-s330 and the glass scrapers from Cal-s326 and Tuo-s316, are more secure indicators of native occupation contemporaneous with the local presence of whites. Archaeological testing at New Melones has thus far yielded very little conclusive evidence in terms of Miwok ethnohistory except that there are several sites that were definitely occupied (and many more that were probably occupied) by Indians during the historical period. The area of Clarks Flat, which is quite far removed from the zones of heavy mining, has been intensively tested. One Clarks Flat midden contained sections of charred and unburned pine bark in a pattern that apparently represents a lean-to structure (Peak 1973:42). The presence of rusted metal under the bark indicates a recent habitation, and the secluded location hints at a refuge village of some sort (Hall 1976).

A study of the cultural sites in the Stanislaus River valley could support or refute some of the proposals advanced in Miwok ethnohistory. Can the seasonal movements into the higher elevations be documented? How does site location relate to defensive position, accessibility, and visibility? The tendency to form larger village aggregates has been documented in the histories; is this trend reflected in the archaeological record? Is there a change in the communal structures or in ceremonial paraphernalia that might represent new intravillage social organization? Can any evidence of refugees from the Yokuts or other groups to the west be identified? Is there any record of warfare? Can changes in authority patterns be discerned through changing status differentiation or other means. Do the more recent sites show a shift in diet?

In addressing these questions, it should be kept in mind that aboriginal middens are not the only sources of archaeological evidence for Miwok ethnohistory. Historical sites of white occupation may contain suggestions of contact with the Miwok, and it is also possible that some cabins of supposed white occupation were actually inhabited by the Indians at an early date (Hall 1976:104). One may conclude that the ethnohistory of the Stanislaus Miwok is largely an untold story. The general features of the contact period are known, but the details and the acculturative processes are poorly understood. The archaeological sites of the New Melones district comprise a significant resource for augmenting research into Miwok ethnohistory.


## POLITICAL ORGANIZATION

The historical Miwok of the New Melones area were politically organized into systems of major villages with clusters of satellite hamlets. Merriam (1967) observed that there were two classes of Miwok settlements: "(*l*) those in which the 'Royal Families' or families of the chiefs reside; and (2) those inhabited solely by the common people. . . . The head chiefs are men of high standing, power, and influence in the tribe, and are recognized as head chiefs by the tributary villages [p. 340]."

The archaeological implications of Miwok community organization are of considerable interest. First, a careful investigation of prehistoric settlement differentiation may illuminate the processes by which the political structure evolved and became increasingly complex through time. It is expected that community houses, grave lot variability, and other sociotechnic traits would permit archaeologists to recognize "royal" and "common" villages and to trace their origins into the past. Also, the concept of rank ascription appears to have been highly developed among the Miwok, with nonegalitarian statuses being defined in terms of wealth, prestige, political power, and a measure of control over religious activities. Both status ascription and intervillage political differentiation have been identified in the prehistory of the southern Sierra Nevada (cf. King 1976a). Any sort of comprehensive archaeological research at New Melones should also be designed to test models concerning the development of nonegalitarian society, rank ascription, and other facets of prehistoric political organization.

## THE ENIGMATIC MORTUARY CAVES

Artifacts and great numbers of human bones have been found in 12 endogene caverns in the New Melones vicinity, and many questions have emerged with respect to these mortuary chambers. So little is known of the cultures of the people who placed their dead in these natural tombs that explanations for the skeletal remains have ranged from the use of caves as prisons to their being sites of accidental deaths. It is also uncertain whether entire bodies were placed or cast into the often vertical shafts or whether only disarticulated skeletal parts were left in the chambers as secondary disposals. While primary burial is a possibility in some caves, most of the evidence points to secondary interment: The bones tend to be in very poor condition, fragmented and scattered (with very rare instances of articulation), and cremated bone is also present (Moratto 1976; Payen 1964; Payen and Johnson 1965). The matter of chronology is also of interest. Although the problem of dating the mortuary deposits has not been resolved entirely—estimates vary from 12,000 years B.P. to historical times—the artifacts indicate that the caverns were in use only from ca. 2500 B.C. until A.D. 300. This raises the possibility that the caves may have been used by "outsiders" before the New Melones locality was actually settled, or at least before major centers of occupation were established.

Thus, the caverns of the Stanislaus evidently served as ossuaries for the secondary disposal of bones and cremated remains at a time before A.D. 300. Some of the caves also functioned as quarries for calcite and alabaster, which were fashioned into ornaments, pipes, charmstones, etc.—items often found with Windmiller culture burials in the Great Central Valley. Further anthropological studies at New Melones could materially enhance our knowledge of when, by whom, and why these mortuary caverns were used.


## NATIVE BURNING PRACTICES

Lewis (1973) has assembled a large body of data to show that California Indians managed their resources through the seasonal, controlled burning of selected vegetation tracts. He has proposed that the Indians "molded the Sierra landscape with fire for more than 3000 years" in order to increase the yield of desired plants, facilitate the harvesting of seeds, drive game, improve visibility, and for other reasons (pp. 5, 41). Lewis has further demonstrated that the maintenance of certain plant communities depended on systematic burning. This fact should concern any archaeologist attempting to reconstruct and explain aspects of paleoecology and paleodemography in the Sierra Nevada.

Recent studies of systematic burning in Panama for purposes of savanna maintenance have confirmed that cyclical firing may be represented in the palynological record (J. West, personal communication, 1974). Therefore, an obvious problem to test at New Melones would be the possible presence (and the antiquity) of prehistoric systematic burning. It would be of great interest to learn the extent to which the modern biotic communities of the Stanislaus differ from the prehistoric condition and to investigate the prospect that the New Melones area's carrying capacity may have been increased significantly as a result of environmental modification by the Indians.


## ADDITIONAL RESEARCH DIRECTIONS

In this section I shall touch briefly on several other topics that might be pursued in the course of mitigative studies at New Melones.


### Warfare

Traditional ethnographies describe California warfare in terms of sporadic fighting of minor consequence; yet evidence accumulating in many parts of the state shows a very high frequency of violent death in archaeological societies. Taking this observation into account, the New Melones research should investigate the incidence of both violent death and nonlethal weapon traumas in the skeletal population, analyze imbedded weapon parts with the goal of identifying the source culture, and use these data to reassess the role and significance of warfare in Sierra Nevada prehistory.

## Seasonality

The origins and time depth of the seasonal transhumance could be investigated at New Melones by testing sites to collect dietary remains reflective of seasonal occupation. The Stanislaus River was a natural corridor for trade and for annual movements to and from the high country. It may be possible to learn which of the New Melones sites were abandoned during the summer months and which were temporary camps for specialized economic activities.

## Biological Anthropology

To better understand Sierra Nevada prehistory, the possibility of diachronic population replacement(s) should be investigated through analysis of skeletal remains. One might ask whether the Miwok and their ancestors were the first to occupy the New Melones district or whether they superceded some earlier group. Similarly, biological analyses might assist in the determination of population mixing during the protohistoric and historic periods. Lastly, an analysis of New Melones skeletal material may yield information on a variety of social, medical, actuarial, and related topics.

## CONCLUSIONS

Countless other subjects—prehistoric trade, subsistence activities, architecture, etc.—could be addressed. I shall not list such additional potentials here, as the overall direction of the New Melones research effort has already been defined. However, in conclusion, I wish to suggest certain guidelines by which any archaeological program at New Melones ought to be governed. Foremost, it is imperative that the agencies responsible for New Melones Dam and Lake recognize the magnitude of the data loss that will result from the project. The number and quality of entailed cultural resources are so significant that "adequate" mitigation of adverse effects is truly an impossible ideal. With the perspective that New Melones Lake will be completed at the cost of more than 600 cultural sites, no effort should be spared to program sufficient time and wherewithal for a high-caliber anthropological data retrieval program.

A *data optimization strategy* should characterize the archaeological work at New Melones. By this I mean that the efficient and economical recovery of nonredundant, problem-oriented data should be the primary criterion in planning mitigative work. Data optimization will govern both field and laboratory studies: Not all excavated material will be analyzed, and not all analyzed data will be published. Data will be processed to address as many questions as conceivable, but data that appear redundant or that do not clearly relate to research interests will be curated for posterity. The feedback between research problems (supra) and growing data inventories will determine how the recovery strategy evolves during the project. In this regard, flexibility becomes an indispensible element of sound research and management planning.

A related consideration is that the preservation of archaeological sites—by fencing, covering with a protective medium, stabilizing and flooding, or by other device—should be given high priority. Excavations ought to be kept to a minimum in cases where long-term protection is feasible, and as much as possible of the cultural deposits should be left intact. In brief, the objective will be to strike a fine balance between the systematic recovery of jeopardized data and the long-term protection of data that can be preserved *in situ*.

A matter often overlooked is the participation of local Indian people in the direction of mitigative programs involving the cultural and physical remains of their ancestors. At an early date project designers should meet with the nearby Miwok communities to seek a common understanding with respect to the cultural record of New Melones. Similarly, archaeologists are often (and justifiably) criticized for failing to communicate their findings to the interested public. It seems advisable, therefore, that both popular written accounts and exhibits interpreting Stanislaus River culture history be prepared as part of the New Melones mitigative work. Such products would ideally represent the cooperative input of the archaeologists, historians, Indians, and ethnographers concerned with the human story of the New Melones locality.

Lastly, I shall comment on potential contributions of the New Melones project to California archaeology in general. As Hanes (1976) has noted, earlier analyses of California cultures typically overlooked significant economic and social processes, complex aspects of political integration, surprisingly dense populations, extensive trade networks, frequent wars, and the fact that the Indians managed their environment through controlled burning and other mechanisms. The native Californians have often been presented as an exception to the ethnographic norm for hunter-gatherers or, in archaeology, as an anomaly caught awkwardly between the neat boundaries of the Archaic and Formative stages. The current view, however, is that California represented a normal situation on the socioeconomic progression from food collecting to producing. Yet little is known regarding the origins and development of the complex patterns that are identified with late California cultures. Thus, it is clear that not simply fresh questions, but new parameters on a more general level, will characterize future archaeology in California. The New Melones area is particularly important in this respect because of its great data potentials and the magnitude of the envisioned archaeological program. Thoughtfully designed research at New Melones—even in the matrix of eleventh-hour contract archaeology—could shed light on many of the fascinating problems concerning the evolution of complex cultures in California prehistory.

## ACKNOWLEDGMENT

I am grateful to Tom King and Lynn Riley, who provided helpful criticisms of an earlier version of this chapter.

# 31

# Regional Model Building in the Contract Framework: The Hecla Projects of Southern Arizona

ALBERT C. GOODYEAR

The Hecla projects were a series of mitigation-phase research efforts toward providing archaeological clearance to the Lakeshore Copper Mine property leased by the Hecla Mining Company from the Papago tribe. These mines are located in the Slate Mountains in the northeastern section of the Papago Indian Reservation in the extreme south central portion of Arizona. The research was conducted as three separate contract agreements from 1971 through 1973 on a part-time basis. Fortunately, the three impact areas abutted against one another proceeding downward from the upper elevations of the Slates. The final result was a contiguous series of survey tracts that formed a unified transectlike study area. The consecutive occurrence of contracts over a 3-year period resulted in a multistage aspect to our research, which was conducted in an area of sufficient size to allow the development and testing of regionally scaled models of settlement and subsistence (Goodyear 1973, 1975b; Goodyear and Dittert 1973).

## ENVIRONMENTAL SETTINGS

The Slate Mountains border on the eastern edge of the upper Santa Rosa Valley (Map 31.1). Physiographically this area is typical of the Basin and Range province as it is found in southern Arizona and northern Mexico. This region is typified by small mountain ranges that trend north and south surrounded by broad, alluvium-filled valleys (Bryan 1925:1; Haury, Bryan, Buerer, Colbert, Gabel, and Tanner 1950:22). The mountains and their colluvially derived pediments have distinctive topographical features that occur as a gradient. These include the rugged mountains proper, an upper bajada, or "bench," that intergrades into a lower bajada that in

413

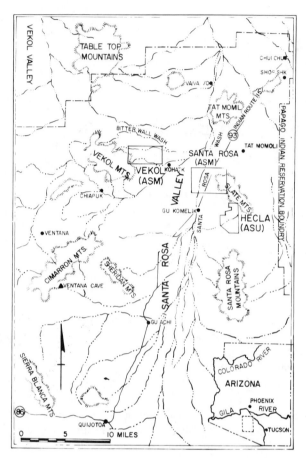

**Map 31.1.** Position of Hecla Mine study area and related projects within the Santa Rosa Valley region.

turn coalesces into the valley floor. These landforms are stable and have distinctive associations of flora and fauna due to changes along the gradient in elevation and substrate.

Climatically this part of the Lower Sonoran desert region is characterized by a low rainfall—less than 10 inches per year—with dispersion in a biseasonal summer-winter pattern (Green and Sellers 1964). Since this region is a true desert, the atmosphere is extremely warm throughout most of the year, with low humidity and high rates of evaporation. In the summer months temperatures reach lethal extremes on a daily basis. Water is the primary determinant of plant and animal life in the desert and accordingly has helped structure the form of human existence. Historically, the local Papago Indians obtained drinking water either in the seasonally flowing channel of the Santa Rosa Wash or in the mountain springs (cf. Stewart and Teague 1974:21–22). Ventana Cave, located 20 miles southwest of the Slates (Map 31.1), is probably the best known aboriginally occupied mountain spring in the

Papagueria (Haury *et al.* 1950). Presently, and ethnohistorically, there were no known naturally permanent water sources in the Slates.

Biogeographically the Slates are included in the Lower Sonoran desert life zone, with flora and fauna typical of the Arizona uplands (Lowe 1964; Shreve 1951). The upper and lower bajadas of the Slates and other similar desert mountains have a characteristic plant association known as the paloverde–saguaro community (Shreve 1951). The vegetation is typified by the familiar tall saguaro cactus, numerous species of other cacti, and a few species of arboreals. Plant distribution within the community is structured by variability in soil–water relationships, which are largely a function of substrate and elevation (Niering, Whittaker, and Lowe 1963; Yang and Lowe 1956). Because of this relationship, plant distributions are strongly organized by vertical zonation.

The paloverde–saguaro community contains numerous biotic resources that were historically critical to the overall adaptation of the Pima and Papago. The Hecla projects demonstrated that the subsistence uses of these species as described for the Pima and Papago have their antecedants among prehistoric societies as well.


## BACKGROUND OF RESEARCH

The Papago Indian Reservation, which forms the northern area of the ethnohistorical Papagueria, has for the most part remained an archaeological terra incognita. Excavation of a few large sites took place from 1930 to 1950, resulting in site reports and culture-historical reconstructions (Haury *et al.* 1950; Scantling 1939; Withers 1944). The monumental work of Haury *et al.* (1950) at Ventana Cave provided a major contribution toward defining the age, sequence, and artifactual content of prehistoric cultural systems in the Papagueria.

Beginning in 1970, a burst of archaeological activity occurred in the upper Santa Rosa Valley ushering in what I have referred to elsewhere as the "contract archaeology period [Goodyear 1975b:1]." The Santa Rosa Wash was under impact by the Army Corps of Engineers, who were considering a dam project. The Arizona State Museum conducted a survey on the Santa Rosa floodplain that resulted in a preliminary research design (Canouts 1972; this volume, Chapter 9), which was followed by a multiphase mitigation project equipped with a specially written research design (Raab 1973a; this volume, Chapter 13, 1974). Contemporaneous with these events, one preliminary report (Goodyear and Dittert 1973) and a specific research design (Goodyear 1973) were written for the Hecla projects in the adjacent Slates. On the western edge of the Santa Rosa Valley (Map 31.1), potential environmental impact by mining concerns on the Vekol Mountains resulted in a survey and report treating similar problems in cultural ecology as those formulated for the Hecla Mine study area in the Slates (Stewart and Teague 1974). All of these projects shared at a general level an interest in long-term human adaptation to the Sonoran Desert and provided complementary regional data toward that end. Research designs were written and exchanged, as well as methodologies and substantive findings, and publication was relatively rapid. Because of the cooperation between different institutions and their investigators, a mutually beneficial cumulative effect was created where each project had the opportunity to build upon previous research. The final Hecla Mine report (Goodyear 1975b) attempted to synthesize this new knowledge of mountain settlement–subsistence patterns as viewed from the Slates and to consider the role of Hohokam upland hunting and gathering in the complete regional settlement system.

## OCCUPATIONAL HISTORY OF THE HECLA MINE
## STUDY AREA WITHIN THE SANTA ROSA VALLEY
## REGION

Geological conditions of the desert mountains are such that open archaeological sites are rarely buried or buried deeply. The mountain substrate is formed by ablating and degrading talus and other coarse sediments. Soil-forming processes are slow and essentially mechanical. Although such conditions greatly aid regional sampling for archaeology due to the exposed ground, they hinder studies of chronology and generally necessitate dating by artifact crossdating. The Hecla studies took advantage of the basic reconstruction of cultural sequences at Ventana Cave (Haury et al. 1950) and those documented by Raab (1974) on the adjacent Santa Rosa floodplain. The latter studies were crucial not only for providing a framework for the occupational history of this locality but for establishing the whereabouts of the primary villages of gatherers who exploited the biotic and abiotic resources of the Slate Mountains.

While Archaic-stage occupations were present at nearby Ventana Cave, only slight evidence for them was found in the Slates (Goodyear 1975b:22), and no evidence was found on the alluvially formed Santa Rosa floodplain (Raab 1974a). The work of Canouts (1972) and Raab (1974a) on the floodplain established the existence of several villages with extensive trash mounds that were culturally identified by their diagnostic Hohokam red-on-buff ceramics. Based on ceramic styles, the Hohokam-related sites of both the Slates and Santa Rosa Wash floodplain appear to parallel the well-known Hohokam sequence of the Gila and Salt river basins dating from A.D. 300 to A.D. 1100. The Papaguerian Sells phase (A.D. 1200–1400) constituted the final prehistoric occupation of the Santa Rosa Valley (cf. Haury et al. 1950).

A long-standing problem in Papaguerian archaeology and ethnohistory concerns the existence of a protohistoric period that would historically link the Papago with prehistoric cultures (Haury 1950; Fontana et al. 1962). The Hecla studies revealed the existence of sites dating to a post-Sells, pre-Papago period that were identified by a characteristic thin brownware, a ware also reported from the top levels of Ventana Cave (Haury 1950:345). A structure manifesting this brownware was radiocarbon-dated at A.D. 1370 ± 100 years (Goodyear and Dittert 1973:62). Subsequent statistical analysis of technoenvironmental variables related to these sites has indicated they probably represent cactus extraction camps but with a different environmental distribution than earlier or later cultural groups (Goodyear 1977).

There were numerous sites in the Hecla Mine study area related to the occupation of the nineteenth- and twentieth-century historic Papago. The Papago used the native plant and animal resources of the Slates, especially for cactus fruit procurement, and some families from neighboring Gu Komelik, located at the foot of the Slates (Map 31.1.), until only recently maintained family cactus camps in the study area. Many of even the twentieth-century cactus camps exhibited a strong aboriginal character, since native ceramics were commonly used in fruit rendering, and ramada-type shelters were constructed of local vegetation. Practically all Papago sites date from the late 1800s to mid 1900s, with little or no evidence of eighteenth-century occupations. The Papago mountain settlement pattern and cactus extraction technology received special consideration in the final Hecla report with a study by Bruder (1975).

## THEORETICAL ORIENTATION AND RESEARCH DESIGN

The basic theoretical approach was that of human ecology as examined from a subsistence framework. The Hecla Mine study area was ideal for an intensive diachronic study of human utilization of the paloverde–saguaro community and its resources. The study area extended from nearly the tops of the Slates (2200 feet) down a southward-facing gradient, passed completely through the paloverde–saguaro community, and terminated in a creosote zone (1600 feet). The dimensions of the study area were about 3.75 miles in length and varied from .5 to 2.0 miles in width. The fact that the project area was situated on a south-southwest-facing slope was also to our advantage for ecological studies, since such slopes tend to be hotter and provide the optimum microclimatic situation for the growth of many desert plant species (Odum 1971).

The paloverde–saguaro community is of particular relevance to regional studies of subsistence in the Lower Sonoran desert region owing to certain of its biological properties. First, it has the *highest species diversity* per plant community (Halvorson 1970:15; Whittaker and Niering 1965:449). This translates into more subsistence alternatives to human consumers. Second, in a qualitative way, the community is of prime importance, since certain highly useful species can *only* be found within it. Nearly all the cacti, for example, are geographically restricted in their growth to the coarse-textured substrates of the mountains. Other aboreal species, such as ironwood and acacia, which produce edible seeds and wood raw materials, are either confined to the uplands or attain their maximum density there. Third, since all of the species important to aboriginal subsistence are drought-adapted perennials, food resources are available on a yearly seasonal basis, conforming to a predictable schedule. This dependability contrasts to a great extent with the *de temporal* method of floodwater agriculture practiced in the Santa Rosa Wash, which was subject to the vagaries of seasonal floods. Under these environmental conditions hunting and gathering formed the baseline of all groups, including those practicing mixed economies even throughout the historic period (Hackenberg 1964). Finally, because of specific adaptations by plants to various substrate and altitudinal conditions, community organization tends to be highly zonal. Such vertical stratification in turn has provided special ecological parameters around which human gatherers worked out adaptive strategies for efficient exploitation.

At its most general level the original research design was focused upon testing a hypothesis regarding the "carrying capacity" of the paloverde–saguaro community and its position in regional subsistence systems (Goodyear 1973). Raab (1973a) had prepared a research design treating the role of subsistence in determining settlement within the adjacent Santa Rosa Wash floodplain and related environs, and thus, it was expected that the two projects with their complementary environmental areas could provide a comprehensive regional approach to settlement and subsistence.

In order to explain differences in settlement between the mountains and the floodplain by reference to the biotic and abiotic resources of each, the mountain area

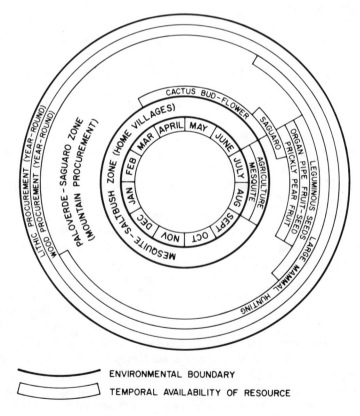

**Figure 31.1.** Temporal availability of major subsistence resources by environmental zone.

in this case was intensively examined for its natural resources. The properties of mountain flora just mentioned were considered along with other biotic variables for subsistence modeling. Analytically, the paloverde–saguaro community can be imagined to exist as a set of procurement subsystems within the macrocommunity system somewhat similar to those outlined by Flannery (1968). The biological components of these subsystems were comprised of single plant species and sets of them, the subsistence values of which have been well documented by prior studies in plant ecology, nutrition, and ethnobotany (see Doelle 1975; Goodyear 1975b). These procurement systems represent hypothetical components in the overall mountain portion of the regional subsistence system. These subsystems were arranged on a temporal basis as they would naturally unfold over a yearly season (Figure 31.1). It is necessary to organize the paloverde–saguaro community species into subsistence-related units, since people did not adapt to the ''community'' (a heuristic device to aid plant ecologists in the study and communication of biogeographic associations); rather, humans adapted themselves to *resources* of varying spatial and temporal loci that were commonly found as a mutually associated aggregate.

To analyze prehistoric subsistence activities empirically as a set of subsystems, it was necessary to construct testable archaeological models for each (Goodyear 1973). This was done by examining the literature of plant ecology for the temporal spans of availability of the target resources (e.g., buds, flowers, fruit), nutritional and caloric values (see Doelle 1975; Goodyear 1975b: Appendix H; W. Ross 1941), and the spatial growth pattern of relevant species. To determine the latter for the Slate Mountain study area, quantified vegetation mapping was performed (see Goodyear 1975b; Raab 1974a). The second major source of information for model building came from several highly useful ethnographic studies that have been performed for the Pima and Papago Indians, groups who relied heavily on wild foods commonly found in the desert mountains (Castetter and Bell 1937, 1942; Russell 1908; Thackery and Leding 1929). These sources contain many archaeologically relevant descriptions of both aboriginal technologies and the behavioral strategies associated with resource exploitation. Using information drawn from both plant ecology and ethnography, it was possible to set out a priori technoenvironmental predictions for the prehistoric existence of each subsystem (Goodyear 1973).

## OPERATIONALIZATION OF MODELS

In order to test each model, it was necessary to have representative quantitative data on plant growth distributions as well as archaeological data. To accomplish the former, vegetation mapping techniques were employed that were borrowed from methods of plant ecology. Two transects were used, which ran through the heart of the study area. These transects were composed of linearly aligned quadrats 30 m × 50 m, inside of which the frequency and cover value of 12 species of known ethnographic importance were recorded on specially prepared field sheets. Because of the strong vertical organization of plant growth on the mountain slope, the transects were extremely useful for determining the location and density of growth zones for the species of interest. The plant ecologist Oosting (1956) has described the utility of transects in similar situations where floral changes occur primarily on a gradient. Vegetation sampling also took place in smaller quadrats located inside randomly dispersed sampling circles coincident with a probability-based archaeological sampling scheme. The latter method was employed to gain both horizontal and vertical quantitative estimates of plant growth distributions. While not completely developed during the Hecla studies, the spatially dispersed method of vegetation mapping seems to offer the maximum amount of information on distributional patterns, the data of which can also be analyzed through three-dimensional computer mapping programs (see Goodyear 1975b:52–56, Figure 45).

When using present-day plant distributions as a functional attribute of archaeological loci, it must be assumed that contemporary growth patterns are similar to those of the past. In terms of species composition, pollen studies in the southern Arizona region (Martin 1963), as well as those in the Hecla Mine study area (Gish 1975), have indicated that the modern floral assemblage has been present for at least 2000 years, the period with which we are most concerned. The assumption of spatial similarities is more critical. In essence it is assumed that the spatial loci of contemporary flora maxima and minima are approximately the same as those of the past, due to the basically unaltered qualities of the mountain substrates. This assumption is supported by the strong species–substrate relationships well documented by plant ecologists (see Niering et al. 1963; Yang and Lowe 1956), and by the fact that there is no evidence of major climatic shifts of the scale necessary to alter these substrates. This assumption does not require that the biomass values of a species be the same throughout time, only their locations. Surely minor climatic fluctuations have occurred even within this century (see Hastings and Turner 1965). Finally, in every case but one of the subsystem models I discussed, there was a positive association between relevant archaeological loci and the growth zones of the hypothesized target species.

Due to the rocky desert pavement comprising much of the mountain substrate and to the relatively low density of plant cover, archaeological sampling was conducted under nearly optimum conditions. The Hecla projects used a mix of both intensive and probability sampling designs (Goodyear 1975b:37–52). The first two seasons were committed to intensive surveys attempting to map and surface-collect all observed archaeological manifestations. Due to time and budget constraints a specially derived probability sampling scheme was employed in the final season that consisted of a hypothetical grid system for the dispersion of randomized field sampling units. Sampling units consisted of circles 81.5 m in diameter, within which all remains were exhaustively mapped and collected, including proveniences such as isolated flakes and stone tools. This resulted in an extremely fine-grained spatial reconstruction of what would normally be considered rather ephemeral "sites," below the threshold of visibility for most regional surveys (cf. Mueller 1974). Such surveys have alternatively been referred to as "siteless" or "nonsite" (cf. Thomas 1975). In the Slate Mountains, most archaeological loci consist of isolated stone artifacts or sherd and lithic scatters only a few meters in diameter. Thus, such an intensive method of sampling and mapping allowed the collection of artifactual data preserving spatial integrity, further allowing these data to be related more closely to the behavioral systems that produced them.

## RESULTS OF MODEL TESTING

The testing of each hypothetical prehistoric procurement subsystem required that the associated exploitative activities be postulated and the relevant archaeological technoenvironmental variables be measured. A brief discussion of these test outcomes and the methods used in their evaluation follows.

### Bud–Flower Subsystem (March–June)

This subsystem was composed of the buds and flowers of certain cacti that begin their phenological activity in the early spring. The relevant species included most of the chollas, prickly pear, and ocotillo. The Pima and Papago relied heavily on these foodstuffs during the spring, since winter stores were running out by this time. The spring was also a period of nutritional stress on the Papago (Castetter and Bell 1942:45), and the cholla buds, while not particularly high in calories, provided excellent sources of vitamins and minerals, such as calcium. This procurement subsystem was critical, therefore, because it provided the first fresh floral foods since the previous fall. The Pima and Papago are described by several authors as roasting the buds in a specially prepared roasting pit (see especially Thackery and Leding 1929). Since no durable technologies were used in their operation, no other archaeological remains were expected except the roasting pits. Two subsurface roasting pits were excavated that conformed precisely in morphology to historically described cholla pits, and a small number of possibly deflated pits were recorded. The two subsurface pits failed to produce the predicted *Opuntia* pollen types, although pollen densities were very low for reliable counts (Gish 1975).

### Saguaro Cactus Fruit–Seed Subsystem (Late June–Early July)

Historically, the saguaro cactus fruit and seed occupied a significant socioeconomic role in Papago subsistence. Of all the cacti, saguaro fruit and seed are the highest in calories, protein, fat, and carbohydrates. The fruit is only available, however, for a short period of 3 or 4 weeks. Among the Papago whole families moved to temporary mountain extraction camps in order to maximize its subsistence input. Papago saguaro camps were seasonally revisited sites equipped with ramadas, jars for boiling and storing liquid products, and grinding stones for seed processing. Four major prehistoric concentrations of sherds and chipped and ground stone were found in the upper growth zone of the saguaro distribution. There was a predominance of jars (61%) over bowls, and the majority of all grinding implements found in the entire study area were concentrated within these four sites. The spatial distribution of saguaro was remarkably homogeneous in terms of biomass and density of individuals (Goodyear 1975b:Figures 22 and 23) and exhibited the typical abrupt termination in growth zone. A certain type of cobble facility referred to as rock rings hypothesized by Raab (1974a) to represent basket holders for cactus fruit picking were found to be spatially correlated with the distribution of saguaro. Where the saguaro ceased to grow was also the lower elevational limit of the rock ring distribution. This finding helped test the functional hypothesis for these cobble rings and also indicated that the lower elevational limit of the saguaro might have been relatively stable. Based on the dispersed spatial distribution of the rock rings and the fact that saguaro has a strongly homogeneous spatial pattern, the hypothesis was offered that the rock rings represent the center points of hexagonally arranged picking territories (Goodyear 1975b:118; Wilmsen 1973).

### Prickly Pear Fruit Subsystem (Late July–Early September)

This procurement subsystem was composed only of prickly pear fruit. The fruit has only half the caloric value of saguaro fruit and seed per unit volume but is relatively high in carbohydrates and calcium. Prickly pear also has a long fruiting period compared to other cacti and grows in a highly concentrated spatial pattern. The Papago and Pima made extensive use of the fruit for making jelly, preserves, and a beverage. The seeds were ignored (Russell 1908:75), and there is some evidence from ethnographic accounts that the consumption of seeds caused sickness. When processing of fruit took place in the resource zone, the only technologies required were jars for boiling and transportation of liquids, and wooden picking and cooking instruments. Archaeologically, only ceramic fragments would be preserved along the open hillslopes.

Archaeological loci that bore a predominance of jar fragments (83%) over bowls and a nearly complete absence of grinding tools were found concentrated in the maximum growth zone of prickly pear. A functional absence of grinding stones was critical to the identification of prickly pear–processing loci, since such tools were indicative of saguaro seed processing. These ceramic scatters, which also contained chipped stone tools and debitage probably related to wooden tool manufacture, were found to be statistically covariant with increasing and decreasing biomass values by prickly pear growth zones. These artifact scatters were smaller than the saguaro-processing camps, and more numerous, but they formed distinctive spatial clusters within the maximum resource zone. A nearest neighbor analysis was performed using the botanically defined maximum density zone as the area for calculation of the statistic. The results indicated that within the maximum resource zone loci were decidedly toward clustering $(R = .25, p < .001)$, indicating a highly agglomerative spatial distribution.

### Leguminous Seed Subsystem (July–August)

Four species comprise this subsystem: paloverde, ironwood, acacia, and mesquite. Mesquite, which is a common tree on the mesic floodplain, does not and probably never did constitute an important species in the study area, due to its well-drained higher elevation. All four species are morphologically similar in terms of their pods and seeds, the seeds being quite rich in calories and protein. The fruiting spans of these species overlap for approximately a 2-month period. Based on historical observations of the Pima and Papago, three strong test implications were derived. These are (*1*) the presence of grinding tools for seed preparation; (*2*) a high proportion of wide-mouthed bowls for parching seeds; and (*3*) a spatial correlation of this technology with the maximum growth zone of these species. All three implications were decisively confirmed. A large base-camp-like concentration of artifact scatters was found exhibiting manos, metates, and shallow bowl fragments, the latter dominating jars by nearly a 2:1 ratio. The spatial correlation of these remains and the maximum density zone of the target species was remarkably neat. The association was one-to-one, as this base-camp-like array was the only locus found to have the expected technological remains, which were located directly within the maximum biomass zone, a zone with nearly 3 times more leguminous cover than the next richest zone. This association in particular is considered strong evidence for the original assumption of spatial stability of plant growth zones.

### Organ Pipe Cactus Fruit–Seed Subsystem (July–August)

The exact period of fruit availability is not known, but observations within the study area indicate that the fruit ripens at a time after that of saguaro, thereby eliminating any scheduling conflicts. The organ pipe cactus has a highly restricted geographic range, and the Slate Mountains stand would appear to be something of a botanical rarity, since the normal distribution of the species is farther south (see L. Benson 1969:114;Figure 2.9). Organ pipe also grow at comparatively high elevations and the Slate Mountain examples were located at 2000 feet or higher up in the rugged mountaintops. Such a narrow adaptation by this species aids considerably the isolation of prehistoric remains related to its exploitation. The Papago usage of this species was primarily oriented toward the fruit and seed, which are morphologically similar to saguaro. The fruit was rendered in plainware jars and the seeds ground with manos and metates. Thus, the expected archaeological outputs for processing camps of both species were quite similar.

The critical difference that enabled the identification of organ pipe–processing loci was the relatively discrete spatial distribution between that species and saguaro. Organ pipe is biologically restricted to the rugged areas of the mountaintops, and accordingly, the location of processing camps was perforce confined to limited areas of flat usable terrain. A major concentration of artifacts characterized by a predominance of plainware jars (89%) over bowls and grinding tools was located in a mountain pass at elevation 2100 feet.

### Wood Procurement Subsystem (Year-round)

This subsystem included all arboreal species considered in the leguminous seed subsystem plus saguaro and ocotillo. The leguminous aboreals are characterized by sturdy trunks and branches, while the saguaro and ocotillo produce useful rodlike ribs and branches. The need of wood for various subsistence-related purposes was undoubtedly substantial in prehistoric times, and procurement probably occurred on a year-round basis. Some of the species, such as saguaro and ocotillo, which are useful for roofs and walls of houses, only grow in the mountains. Since all of the cactus exploitation activities require wooden tools for harvesting and rendering, it seems certain that wooden implements would have been manufactured on a need basis during the occupation of mountain extraction camps. Because metal and polished stone tools were absent among these prehistoric groups, the assumption was made that most, if not all, lithic remains on the mountain slopes represented tool manufacturing and/or tool using that was directly related to the extraction and modification of wood.

This assumption was supported by the small average size of lithic scatters (about 2 m in diameter), and by the fact that most of the lithic loci consisted of isolated flake tools, core tools, and debitage. Such archaeological outputs were highly suggestive of those created by a single individual making and/or using stone tools. The lithic remains were thus reflective of a very expedient system of production and use. The overwhelming majority of tools were simply use-modified flakes or minimally retouched cortically backed core tools. Loci containing debitage and tools were relatively uniform in their spread across the mountain slopes. This is explainable by a corresponding uniformity in the growth distribution of target wood species and by the equally coextensive spatial distribution of andesite, the naturally abundant raw material from which over 99% of all chipped stone tools were made.

The analysis design for wood procurement centered on two problem sets. The first was to rigorously identify lithic loci reflective of (1) tool manufacturing only; (2) tool using only; (3) and both activities in the same behavior space. The second problem was an attempt to determine if the structure of these activities varied significantly with changes in target vegetation by zone. The systemic processes responsible for archaeological outputs related to each of the three activities were modeled according to general cultural formation processes as described by Schiffer (1972a, 1976) and those associated with Australian aborigine wood extraction (Gould 1974).

Twelve quantitative variables were derived, treating locus morphology, debitage, and tool classes, which were expected to measure the degree of the three activities. These variables were factor-analyzed using the PA2 (varimax rotated) method from the Statistical Package for the Social Sciences (SPSS) programs (Nie, Bent, and Hull 1970), using 142 randomly chosen loci as cases. Separate factor runs were performed for two adjacent arboreal zones to search for possible shifts in the degree or presence of these activities. Although some differences in factor ranks were obtained, five significant factors were produced for each zone, which were roughly similar in variable composition. Factor analysis successfully identified groups of variables that were indicative of either pure manufacture or tool usage. Interestingly, the variable of locus density was consistently correlated with tool manufacture, while increasing locus diameter was correlated with tool use. This suggests that within this type of technoenvironmental system tool *manufacture* is a space-densifying event, while tool *usage* is a space-using activity.

## RESEARCH RESULTS

The overall success of the Hecla projects can be assessed in several ways. The models of procurement activities originally advanced in the research design (Goodyear 1973) were thoroughly tested archaeologically. Positive evidence for their existence was found in every hypothesized subsystem. These subsistence activities were confirmed primarily by specific technoenvironmental patterns predicted from information drawn from local ethnographies and from desert plant ecology. Based on these findings, there is now an archaeological system for *identifying* these prehistoric activities for ceramic-using peoples within open, unburied mountain sites. Papago and Pima subsistence activities described under aboriginal conditions appear to be rather good sources for archaeological model building. Their demonstrated relevancy in turn suggests long-lived patterns of procurement and processing for these plant species extending over the past 2000 years.

In order to obtain archaeological and ecological data necessary to test the procurement models, appropriate sampling strategies had to be developed. The use of quantified vegetation data toward testing archaeological hypotheses appears to be the first of its kind in this part of the Southwest (see Goodyear 1973, 1975b; Raab 1974a). Other applications of quantitative vegetation mapping are subsequently beginning to appear in the Lower Sonoran desert region (Sobelman 1973; Stewart and Teague 1974) as well as probability sampling designs that gather both archaeological and botanical data simultaneously (Doelle 1975; Rodgers 1974). These methodological experiments not only establish the feasibility of using modern vegetation for analyzing prehistoric subsistence activities vis à vis economically useful species but also provide information of interest to plant geographers for their concerns with long-term stability and change in desert plant communities (cf. Hastings and Turner 1965).

Diachronically, recurrent differences in utilization patterns were found between earlier Hohokam-related groups, identified by their red-on-buff ceramics, and the late prehistoric phase, known by red-on-brown pottery. The latter phase dominated nearly every procurement system. The fact that patterns of differential exploitation of these resources were observed indicates that significant changes transpired in the wider structure of settlement–subsistence systems. These shifts in resource emphasis documented in the mountain sector of regional subsistence require further explanations.

Future explanation strategies must include data drawn from both the mountain and floodplain zones on a unified regional scale. Such a systemic analysis must derive measures of the give-and-take relationships between the various natural and cultivated resources (cf. Bohrer 1970). The original research design (Goodyear 1973) attempted to evaluate observed differences between floodplain and mountain settlement patterns in terms of the "carrying capacity" of each respective environment. This strategy and hypothesis were abandoned early on in the analysis, due to methodological as well as theoretical limitations to such an approach. While both sets of environments have some inherent finite levels of productivity, measuring these biophysical values is exceedingly difficult even within presently dynamic systems (cf. Street 1969). It is more useful to concentrate on making resource estimates for variables of interest within and between zones and on studying changes in behavioral organizations applied to each.

In a theoretical vein the analysis of mountain biotic resources and the associated strategies of procurement and extraction lead to a consideration of certain etic variables of a timeless-spaceless nature relevant to low-energy economies. These refer to technobehavioral strategies and biophysical parameters affecting *resource accessibility*. Resource accessibility is a multifaceted concept that can be measured in various ways. Temporal span of availability, variability in the production curve of a species, energy–nutrition value, and the resource–space ratio are all aspects of accessibility. By knowing the values of these parameters it is possible to explain a procurement strategy for a given resource and determine how scheduling systems may have been worked out.

## CONCLUSIONS

The Hecla projects represent our first look on a regional scale at the archaeological record of Hohokam mountain gathering activities within the zones of procurement. Heretofore our knowledge of the hunted and gathered portion of subsistence had come from floodplain villages, such as Snaketown (Bohrer 1970), or from rare mountain spring sites, such as Ventana Cave (Haury *et al.* 1950). All of these sites are forms of habitation sites and do not directly indicate how wild resources were procured. The mountain subsystems played a heavy role in the total regional subsistence system of all prehistoric and historical groups and deserve study in their own right. In the early 1970s archaeology—contract archaeology—came into the Papagueria and found it as it was known in the 1950s. In the course of mitigating the loss of archaeological resources due to mining impacts, we examined a previously unexplored data base with modern method and theory and developed processual models and quantitative methods appropriate for their evaluation.

## ACKNOWLEDGMENTS

The Hecla projects were sponsored by the Department of Anthropology, Arizona State University. Professor Alfred E. Dittert, Jr., was the principal investigator and the author was in charge of all field investigations. L. Mark Raab aided considerably in the first two seasons of fieldwork. Research was funded by the Papago Indian tribe, the Hecla Mining Company, and the Office of Contract Archeology at Arizona State University.

# 32

# Archaeological Pattern Recognition: An Example from the British Colonial System

STANLEY SOUTH

Archaeology is rapidly expanding its role in cultural resource management through the examination of historical sites being developed for heritage-oriented goals. Sponsoring agencies are usually interested primarily in the discovery of architectural data for use in reconstruction activities planned for historical properties. A second area of interest is the recovery of artifacts for use in exhibits relating to the people or events of primary interest to the sponsor. The sponsors of such projects expect archaeological work to be relevant to questions they are asking. The fact that these questions are often limited in scope need not restrict the archaeologist in answering his own questions.

I would like to think that as sponsors of projects become more familiar with archaeologists' scientific goals of pattern recognition toward the purpose of explaining past human behavior and cultural processes, they will begin to write into their contracts more sophisticated questions than are now being asked of archaeological data. However, before this can happen, archaeologists themselves must ask better questions. Only when archaeologists demonstrate that their archaeological search for understanding past cultural processes has relevance to the sponsor's goals will there be a closer bond in the mutual quest for knowledge.

Although I have no hope that the goals of mission-oriented agencies will ever exactly coincide with those of scientific archaeology, I do see promise in educating sponsors of archaeology to understanding of the requirements of archaeological science. Those conducting archaeology within a scientific format have sometimes encountered resistance or interference by the sponsor in the archaeological process. To avoid misunderstanding and possible conflict in this area, the archaeologist has an obligation to let the sponsor know what to expect regarding scientific goals in relation to those sought by the sponsor. Such agencies, after having become accustomed to reports from archaeologists willing merely to discover foundation walls, dig a test pit, and describe the relics, are sometimes nonplussed by an archaeologist intent on recovering data relevant to a broad range of questions. In such instances it is imperative that the sponsor come to realize that the scientist's primary obligation lies with the data base, a basic cultural resource, and this responsibility will be fulfilled in the process of providing whatever answers are needed to satisfy the sponsor's needs.

It is up to the archaeologist to demonstrate that the results from scientific archaeology are capable of providing a far richer input into the archaeological data bank and the conservation of cultural resources than can ever be accomplished by a nonscientific avocational approach. It is in this area of educating the sponsor as to the requirements of, and benefits from, a quality archaeology project, as opposed to the results that would emerge from an effort oriented to meeting the minimal needs of the sponsor, that the greatest promise in conservation archaeology is held.

It is of utmost importance that sponsors and archaeologists as well understand that the greatest conservation of cultural resources comes from problem-oriented archaeological research deriving information from the data base that is relevant to questions being asked. This is totally in keeping with various federal laws, the intent of which is not merely to place a few pages of a routine, minimal report in a file as a clearance so that destruction of cultural resources can proceed, but rather to provide for the conservation of cultural resources through scientific study and mitigation. In addition to this professional and legal obligation to abstract the maximum relevant data from archaeological resources, the dedicated archaeologist invariably becomes personally committed to his role as a conservationist of important cultural values. This attitude of dedication contrasts vividly with that of viewing laws and regulations governing the conservation of cultural resources as impediments to progress to be dispensed with by the execution of *pro forma* procedures primarily designed to meet minimum legal requirements. In the following pages I will provide examples of the kind of pattern that can be derived from projects having sponsor goals relating primarily to architecture and the recovery of artifacts for use in museum exhibits. I hope to make the point that sponsor goals and archaeological goals can work together to produce maximum data retrieval.

## THE BASIC ARCHAEOLOGICAL TOOL KIT: TESTING OUR IDEAS ABOUT THE PAST

A primary function of archaeological analyses is the delineation of pattern in the material remains constituting the static record of past human activity and the explanation of why the pattern exists. Descriptive analysis of the by-products of past behavioral activities is a first step in the archaeological process, but too often it becomes the final statement as well. Pattern recognition and integrative synthesis of data are necessary activities in the archaeological process, composing an important part of the cultural resources to emerge from any archaeological site.

Archaeology on historical sites has long dealt with cultural resources as a means of interpreting past lifeways. This has focused on a search for greater accuracy, authenticity, validity, correlation, personalization, and interpretation of "historical reality" epitomized in the historical site preservation–restoration–reconstruction phenomenon. Archaeology does contribute toward these goals, but they should be secondary by-products of its primary scientific function: the explanation of cultural processes responsible for past human behavior.

The search for archaeological patterning requires a research design conducted with an emphasis on the archaeological record. Heritage-oriented research designs based on conclusions drawn from historical documentation, with the archaeological record used merely to fill in the gaps in preconceptions, are shortchanging the archaeological record as a valuable cultural resource. If archaeologists find that in dealing with the surviving historical record as well as the archaeological record they have drawn primarily on an existing body of knowledge, then the archaeological data have acted primarily as a mirror reflecting previous research and have contributed nothing new to our knowledge.

Archaeologists depend on archaeological as well as historical and ethnographic data. In using this broader data base, however, care must be taken not to lean too heavily on the historical data at the expense of archaeological analyses. To do so might result in a situation where there is no documentation to lean on and we may find that our archaeological tool kit is empty, or that we do not know how to use the tools we have available with which to make interpretative statements. Documentation is most useful as an independent control for archaeologically derived interpretations, not as a source from which archaeological interpretations are made. Archaeological data in the form of patterns reflecting culture process are no less cultural resources than the archaeologically impressive ruins of kivas, pueblos, earth lodges, and masonry foundations. No agency is likely, however, to finance voluntarily the saving of cultural resources in the form of only the empirically delineated artifact ratio patterns on which explanations of culture process are based. It is imperative, therefore, that archaeologists fulfill their obligations to *both* the sponsor of the research and to archaeological science by assuming responsibility for such archaeological goals.

In the following pages I will illustrate some of the ways this philosophy was demonstrated through a 10-week exploratory archaeology project carried out at the site of Fort Moultrie, South Carolina, through a contract between the National Park Service and the Institute of Archeology and Anthropology at the University of South Carolina (reported in detail in South 1974b).

## ARCHITECTURAL GOAL: FIND THE FIRST FORT MOULTRIE

Fort Moultrie is located on Sullivan's Island, South Carolina, at the northern entrance to Charleston Harbor, and was positioned so that its guns could protect the port at Charleston. There were three periods of major construction, with each fort being called Moultrie in honor of William Moultrie, the American leader of the

Second South Carolina Regiment of Infantry, who repelled the British fleet from Charleston on June 28, 1776 (Moultrie 1802:121–122). When first constructed in the early months of 1776, the fort was sometimes referred to as Sullivan's Fort in reference to its location on Sullivan's Island, but after the battle the name was officially designated as Fort Moultrie (Bearss 1968a,b,c; Drayton 1821:II, 304ff.).

The primary goal of the sponsors of the exploratory archaeology project at Fort Moultrie was to discover the location of the original fort and to determine its relation to two succeeding forts, the last of which, built in 1809, is still standing. Artifacts were also of interest for use in exhibits to be placed in a new visitor center to be built on the site as part of the interpretative program at Fort Sumter National Monument.

## ARCHAEOLOGICAL RESEARCH GOALS: TESTING METHODS AND IDEAS

Besides the obvious architectural goals centering around the discovery of the first Fort Moultrie, there were research goals set by the archaeologist beyond those specified in the contract. One of these was the testing of the mean ceramic date formula (South 1972:85), designed to produce a date approximating the median occupation date for the period during which the ceramic sample accumulated. A second goal was to determine whether a distinction between American and British occupations of the site could be made from archaeological data. If a distinction between these occupations could be determined, a third goal was the discovery of stratigraphic data reflecting the broad temporal range of occupation of the site from the Revolutionary War to the twentieth century. The exploratory phase of excavation at Fort Moultrie amply answered these questions, and provided some new insights relating to other areas of inquiry.

## STRATIGRAPHIC SEPARATION OF CULTURAL REMAINS: CULTURAL AND NONCULTURAL DEPOSITS

Exploratory trenches revealed a stratigraphic archaeological record varying from 3 to 7 feet in depth, with the Revolutionary War–period data below water level at the bottom, apparently as a result of sea level rise since that time. The soil had been built up by a series of hurricanes and construction activity during the Civil War, resulting in the stratigraphic separation of cultural remains from the Revolution, the War of 1812, the Civil War, post–Civil War, and twentieth-century occupations.

## ARCHITECTURAL ALIGNMENT:
## ARCHAEOLOGICAL AND HISTORICAL SYNTHESIS

Through discovery of the architectural remains of the first Fort Moultrie in the form of a water-filled ditch or moat, and the correlation of this with various surviving maps, the orientation of the first, and later, forts was determined (South 1974b:20,26).

In addition to the moat of the first Fort Moultrie a second architectural feature dating from the Revolutionary War period was discovered. This was a series of 1-foot-square timbers mortised together at diagonal angles forming part of a foundation for a bastion and curtain wall of a fort (p. 20). This was at first thought to represent a part of the original Fort Moultrie, but documentation and subsequent revealing of more of the timbers suggested that these were the footing timbers for a fort (Arbuthnot) traced out, but never completed, by the British in 1782 (pp. 91–92). From the timbers of this bonus contemporary British fort, and from an analysis of the documented descriptions of Fort Moultrie, reconstructive drawings of the appearance of the first Fort Moultrie were developed.

Historical archaeologists often focus on the architectural details of a site's structure and on the site content reflected by the variety of artifacts recovered in the process of locating the architecture. This is unfortunate in that the clues to site structure found in artifact density and dispersion are often very revealing, as are the patterns to be recognized in quantitative variability and regularity studies. In the sections to follow, the use of this approach to pattern recognition will be demonstrated.

## ARTIFACT DENSITY AND DISPERSION:
## ARCHITECTURAL ALIGNMENT VIA THE
## BRUNSWICK PATTERN

When the ditch for the first Fort Moultrie was revealed by exploratory trenches, an oyster shell midden was found to be heavily concentrated along the west side of this ditch, with the ditch itself filled with brick rubble and palmetto logs. The midden abruptly stopped at a point 10 feet from the edge of the ditch, and this has been interpreted as the point at which the palmetto parapet was located. This distribution of midden along this 10-foot-wide strip beside the ditch has allowed the berm of the fort to be identified. The berm is a shelf located between the parapet and the defensive ditch of the fort. As garbage and trash were discarded from inside the fort from the top of the palmetto log parapet, it landed on the berm. The identification of those responsible for this midden deposit along the berm was made from the buttons found in this midden, those on which a figure 2 in relief was seen. These were no doubt from the uniforms of William Moultrie's Second South Carolina Regiment of Foot, the defenders of the fort. No British military buttons were found in this midden (South 1974b:20,26). Clearly, this deposit of refuse was the result of occupation of the fort by Americans from 1776 to 1780.

The rubble and midden thrown into the ditch itself, however, reveals a different story entirely. Here buttons from seven British regiments were recovered, indicating that the British used the ditch as a repository of their refuse during their period of occupation of the fort from 1780 to 1782. The archaeologically recovered historical documents in the form of numbered regimental buttons reveal the fact that the British likely filled the fort ditch, apparently not considering it an important defensive feature. This is a different refuse disposal practice than that used by the Americans but one that still falls under the same broad British colonial pattern.

The density of midden within a 50-foot arc in the ditch and in an area on the berm was greater than elsewhere along the berm and in the ditch. This density of refuse deposition suggests a pattern demonstrated through excavation of British colonial sites at Brunswick Town, North Carolina, and elsewhere, to be expected at the entrances and exits of houses, shops, and military forts. This pattern has been called the Brunswick Pattern of refuse disposal (South 1977a).

If the increased density of refuse within the ditch and along the berm at Fort Moultrie can be postulated to represent the Brunswick Pattern, then the gateway to the fort should be immediately opposite this midden concentration. By positioning the map of Fort Moultrie over the angle of the ditch revealed by archaeology it is seen that the gateway to the fort was indeed located at this position (South 1974b:26). Architectural interpretation from artifact density and dispersion was necessary because of extensive disturbance from post–Revolutionary War–period construction of later forts in the area; the grave of the Seminole Indian Osceola; a commemorative monument; and existing sidewalks and highways, all restricting the area where eighteenth-century data could be recovered. The predictive value of the Brunswick Pattern was a valuable aid here.

The example presented here is only one of many allowing the interpretation of architectural, behavioral, and processual data from artifact density and dispersion patterns. Research strategies in historical archaeology are just beginning to tap this valuable resource for interpreting the archaeological record (South 1977b). I predict this will develop as a major methodological thrust in the decades to come.

By treating the refuse thrown onto the berm at Fort Moultrie as an "American" midden deposit and refuse recovered from the ditch itself as a "British" midden, we can examine the patterns characteristic of each. In the following sections I will focus specifically on the synthesis of artifact data from these deposits toward the goal of determining information about chronology (occupation periods), identification of military units (American, British, militia), status differences in a military context (officers and enlisted men), and function (buttons), on an intrasite and an intersite level.

## DETERMINING CHRONOLOGY THROUGH CERAMICS: THE FORMULA APPROACH

At historical sites in America ceramics are among the most useful artifacts recovered for chronological analysis. On British American sites, British ceramics predominate in the eighteenth century, and well into the nineteenth century they form the major body of the ceramic collection. Recently a formula has been developed for use with eighteenth- and early nineteenth-century British ceramics, to arrive at an *interpreted occupation period* represented by any specific ceramic collection. This formula provides a mean ceramic date that equates well with the median occupation date represented by the ceramic collection (South 1972:71). Using this mean ceramic date and the known end date for the occupation, or the known beginning date, an interpreted occupation period represented by the ceramic collection can be determined. If no end or beginning historical date is known, then the earliest manufacture date of the latest artifact, the *terminus post quem* for the collection, can be used along with the mean ceramic date to arrive at an interpreted occupation period represented by the ceramic collection.

The use of the formula for arriving at a mean ceramic date involves the use of a median date assigned to each numbered ceramic type (South 1972: 85). The number of sherds of each type is multiplied by the assigned median date for that type. The total of all sherds is then divided into the total of all the products derived for each type in order to obtain the mean ceramic date for the collection.

## THE MEAN CERAMIC DATE FORMULA

The mean ceramic date, $Y$, for the group of colonial British ceramic types from an historical site, taking into consideration the frequency of occurrence of fragments of the types, can be determined by a mean ceramic date–frequency formula as follows:

$$Y = \frac{\sum\limits_{i=1}^{n} \cdot X_i \cdot f_i}{\sum\limits_{i=1}^{n} f_i} - 1.1,$$

where

$X_i$ = the median date for the manufacture of each ceramic type,
$f_i$ = the frequency of each ceramic type, and
$n$ = the number of ceramic types in the sample.

The use of this formula has provided a mean ceramic date of 1774 for an occupation period by Americans on the site from 1776 to 1780. When we apply the formula to ceramics from the British midden deposit thought to represent the British occupation from 1780 to 1782, we obtain a mean ceramic date of 1781.8 (see Table 32.1).

This formula approach to chronology through ceramics has provided dates based

TABLE 32.1.
Derivation of the Mean Ceramic Date for the British Midden at Fort Moultrie[a]

| South type no. | $(X_i)$ Median date | Type name | $(f_i)$ Frequency | $(X_i \cdot f_i)$ Product |
|---|---|---|---|---|
| 56 | 1733 | Lead-glazed slipware (combed yellow) | 1 | 1733 |
| 49 | 1750 | Decorated delftware | 7 | 12250 |
| 21 | 1788 | Debased Rouen faience | 70 | 125160 |
| 43 | 1758 | White salt-glazed stoneware plates | 8 | 14064 |
| 44 | 1738 | Westerwald, stamped blue floral devices, geometric designs | 5 | 8690 |
| 54 | 1733 | British brown stoneware | 20 | 34660 |
| 46 | 1755 | Nottingham stoneware (lustered) | 1 | 1755 |
| 37 | 1733 | Refined red stoneware, unglazed, sprigged | 2 | 3466 |
| 31 | 1770 | English porcelain | 5 | 8850 |
| 15 | 1798 | Lighter yellow creamware | 98 | 176204 |
| 33 | 1767 | Green glazed cream-bodied ware | | |
| 36 | 1755 | "Clouded" wares, tortoiseshell, mottled glazed cream-colored ware | 2 | 3510 |
| 18 | 1788 | Overglaze enameled hand painted creamware | 7 | 12516 |
| 8 | 1805 | Marbled slip pearlware (polychrome slip-on creamware or pearlware) | 1 | 1805 |
| 14 | 1798 | "Annular Wares" creamware | 2 | 3596 |
| 17 | 1800 | Underglaze blue hand painted pearlware | 1 | 1800 |

Totals   230      $410059 \div 230 = 1782.9 - 1.1 = 1781.8$[b]

[a] From South (1972, 1974b).
[b] The mean ceramic date. Documented median British occupation date = 1781.

on the frequency occurrence of vessel fragments that is seen to correspond very well with the known occupation period for the American and British forces at the site. The use of this formula has been demonstratedd to be a valuable means for deriving an interpreted occupation date represented by a ceramic sample, and the concept has been expanded for use with prehistoric data as well as those from historical sites (South 1977a).

## ANALYSIS OF BUTTONS FOR IDENTIFYING THOSE RESPONSIBLE FOR THE MIDDEN DEPOSITS

Buttons from military sites often provide direct historical data in the form of regimental numbers stamped on the face to identify the regiment. Civilian buttons, on the other hand, are not nearly so productive of direct historical data, particularly in the eighteenth century, when there seldom were identifying marks on the backs to identify the maker (and thereby the time period of manufacture), as was the case in the nineteenth century (South 1964). The following frequency relationship between buttons from the fort ditch and the berm beside the ditch (Table 32.2) clearly reveals why these deposits of refuse have been identified as the American and British midden deposits.

Up to this point we have freely used the historical information supplied by the buttons themselves and existing documentary data on the regiments, both British and American, represented by the numbers on the buttons. In the section to follow we will examine these buttons as though we knew nothing about the specific regimental history represented, or the particular history of the site from which they were recovered. This procedure emphasizes the archaeological data base and places interpretive responsibility on the archaeologist and his manipulation of the data. This approach uses the historical data base as a check against archaeologically derived interpretations, rather than using the historical documentation as the means whereby such interpretations are constructed. In the following discussion, relating primarily to the British midden deposit, documented information is supplied in parentheses.

The fact that 17 of the 21 buttons recovered in the British midden deposit had numbers or letters—as opposed to plain or decorated buttons without numbers or letters—would, in itself, indicate a military association, that is, a classified, perhaps stratified, organizational base. The following figures were found on the bottoms: 2, 19, 23, 30, 37, 62, and 63. These figures might be considered to all belong to the same classification were it not for the wide spread between 2 and 19, and between 37 and 62. We might suggest, then, that 2 belonged to one system, 19 through 37 to

TABLE 32.2.
**Button Relationships from the British and American Midden Deposits**

| | British | | American | | | |
|---|---|---|---|---|---|---|
| | British | Loyalists | Continental | Civilian | Chronology range | Total |
| | | | The British Midden[a] | | | |
| Count | 13 | 2 | 2 | 4 | 1780–1783 | 21 |
| Percentage | | 71.5 | 9.5 | 19.0 | | 100.0 |
| | | | The American Midden[b] | | | |
| Count | 0 | 1[c] | 8 | 36 | 1776–1777 | 45 |
| Percentage | 0 | 2.0 | | 98.0 | | |

[a]*Terminus post quem* = 1781.
[b]*Terminus post quem* = 1776.
[c]Sleeve link.

another, and *62* to *63* to a third; but we have no way of knowing this from the figures alone, and such a hypothesis could not be supported.

When we look at the material from which the buttons were made, we see a difference between silver and less valuable white-metal buttons, and we might suggest that this reflects the difference between an upper socioeconomic or status group and a lower (officers versus enlisted men).

From the buttons we find that those with the figure *2* are made of a poor-quality pewter, whereas those with higher numbers are made of white brass and also show more technical sophistication in their manufacture. We also see that all except the buttons with *2* have some decorative element in addition to the number. The *2* buttons are different from the other numbered buttons in that the eye is cast along with the button in one-piece construction, whereas the other numbered buttons have a wire eye cast into the brass. From this combination of attribute differences it seems justified to separate the buttons with *2* from the others, typologically, and suggest that this button type is probably from a separate numerical group and thereby possibly a different cultural group than the higher-numbered buttons (Americans versus British).

Two of the buttons have the letters *RP* under a crown. A crown suggests royalty and thereby implies that the *R* may refer to the word *royal*. The *P* could, of course, stand for a number of alternatives, but we know from the documents that the correct word is *provincials* (loyalists), but from the archaeology alone we could not know this detail. We can, however, from archaeology alone, suggest that the buttons represent four separate groups, or classes, of individuals. One is a group that wore plain or floral device buttons (civilian). Another is a group that wore comparatively poorly made pewter buttons with a *2* in relief (Continentals). A third is a group wearing buttons with letters *RP* beneath a crown (loyalists). The fourth group wore numbered silver or white-metal buttons with some decorative motif accompanying the number (British). The fact that 13 of the 21 buttons in this context are from the latter group might suggest that was the predominant group, with the *RP* and *2* groups being less well represented (British military dominant, supported by loyalists, with American prisoners[?] during the British occupation). The plain buttons or buttons with floral devices apparently represent a fourth, less predominant group (civilian).

This examination, conducted without the benefit of direct historical documentation, suggests that four groups are likely represented by the buttons, with a structured, military, regimented, probably stratified group predominating. The variety and numerically high (*63,* etc.) numbers represented in this sequence would suggest that there are probably many units involved in the military sequence, suggesting either that a large number of companies, regiments, or corps are involved, or that each individual had a number. The latter possibility is more in keeping with a prison system, but the duplication of some of the numbers, the technologically sophisticated manufacture methods, and the expensive metal involved in the construction of the buttons would negate this possibility for interpretation. The large number of "companies, regiments, corps," etc., represented by the higher-numbered sequence would also imply a highly complex logistics base, and perhaps a long tradition is represented by this group of buttons (British military system).

The groups represented only by the 2 and *RP* buttons suggest less of a complex organization, one with possibly a tradition with less time depth, since 2 is low in the numerical sequence of "company, regiment, corps," etc. (Continental military system). The use of letters rather than numbers for the *RP* button, and the fact that this is the only one having a crown as part of its motif, might suggest that this group was a special one, perhaps not lending itself to inclusion within a numerical sequence designation (American loyalist military system).

From the buttons alone we have examined the possibilities for interpretation, and we have found four groups likely represented by the buttons. We have seen that military and nonmilitary units (civilian) are represented, and we have seen that there are two military units and a special group apparently involved. The chronological framework for these units on the site is not revealed in the buttons, and we must turn to history (of military regiments or the site), or to other archaeological data (ceramics, *terminus post quem*, coins, etc.) for this determination. Through the parallel control provided by the historical documentation of the buttons and the site we have been able to see that an archaeological examination of data along these lines is indeed a valid approach to identification of cultural variables represented by variability in the archaeological record. As more archaeologists realize the potential afforded by the broadened data base of historical archaeology, the prejudice against such data long endemic among those dealing with prehistoric data will begin to be dissipated within the scientific climate now having an impact in the field of archaeology.

## STATUS DIFFERENCES REVEALED THROUGH COLONO-INDIAN POTTERY: OFFICERS AND ENLISTED MEN

In the American midden deposit 37% of all ceramics recovered was Colono-Indian pottery, and from the British midden 38% was of this ware made by Indians in imitation of European forms (Noël Hume 1962; South 1974:181). Indians were with both the British and Americans at Fort Moultrie, but we know that this ware was being made by Catawba Indians and sold or traded in lower socioeconomic levels of British colonial society, particularly among Negroes (South 1974b:181).

It appears, then, that the Colono-Indian pottery from the American and British middens was the result of the presence of some group present during both occupations. One good candidate for such a group would be Negroes, who may have been on hand and who may have been with the British as captives or servants during their occupation. A more likely interpretation for the presence of this pottery would be that Catawba pottery was in the Charleston area during both the American and British periods of occupation as cheaply available wares, to be purchased by anyone with a few pennies to spend for a pot who might not be able to afford the imported wares. A low socioeconomic group that may well have taken advantage of such an opportunity to buy Catawba pottery from the Charleston markets was the enlisted men of both the American and British armies. The tin cup and plate were used by the Revolutionary War soldier to transfer his food from the iron mess pot to his stomach. He may well have supplemented this equipment at permanent-type fortifications, such as Fort Moultrie, by Catawba pottery bowls and cooking pots made in the form of the less easily obtainable iron pots (Moultrie 1802:213; Francis Lord, personal communication May 1, 1976). The presence of only two basic forms, the bowl and the pot, represented in Colono-Indian war from Fort Moultrie tends to support this interpretation.

It is suggested, therefore, that the Colono-Indian ware recovered from the American and British midden deposits at Fort Moultrie represents Catawba Indian pottery acquired by both American and British enlisted men during their tour of garrison duty at Fort Moultrie. When broken, the pottery was discarded in the midden deposit along with the broken dishes of British and European manufacture discarded by the officers.

From this study we would postulate that on military garrison sites of the Revolution, Colono-Indian or other locally made wares will be seen to represent refuse of the enlisted men, while European ceramics will reflect that of the officers. The more highly mobile nature of field encampments would act toward producing a lower frequency of Colono-Indian ware than found on the more permanent garrison sites.

## A FUNCTIONAL SYNTHESIS OF DATA FROM BUTTONS

A total of 117 one-hole bone disks and 480 fragments of bone scraps left over from the process of cutting the bone disks was recovered from the British and American middens at Fort Moultrie (South 1974b:188). The manufacture of such disks appears to be a characteristic of Revolutionary War military sites (Calver and Bolton 1970). In order to examine the relationship between these one-hole disks of bone and metal buttons as to function, a study of the metric size of these artifacts was undertaken. The hypothesis was that if the bone disks clustered in the same metric size range as metal buttons, a similar function might be indicated. This hypothesis was negated in that an inverse ratio was found between the major size represented by metal buttons and that for the bone disks. The results of this study are seen in Figure 32.1. The differences in size allowed interpretations suggesting that large metal buttons serve a different function than smaller metal or bone buttons, their size suggesting a large coat (greatcoat buttons). Metal buttons 16 to 18 mm in size apparently served a function exclusive of that served by bone buttons of the same size (waistcoat and uniforms). Bone buttons 12 to 15 mm in size obviously serve a function exclusive of that served by metal buttons of the same size (shirt, pants, and undergarments?). Bone disks 10 and 11 mm in size were found only in nineteenth-century contexts at Fort Moultrie.

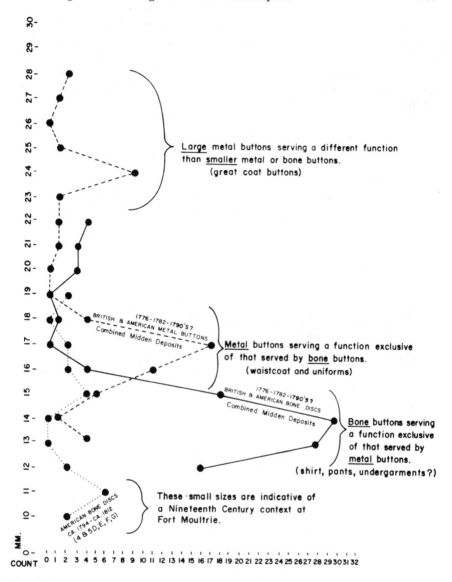

**Figure 32.1.** Comparative synthesis of metal buttons and one-hole bone disks from Fort Moultrie (38CH50).

In comparing the metal buttons with bone disks, as we have done here, the critical phrase is *of the same size*. A different view is placed on the comparison when we introduce the concept of the disks being cloth covered, in which case their size including the cloth may well be larger. If disks in the range of 12 to 15 mm in size were cloth covered, their increase in overall size might well allow them to function on garments with buttonholes designed to be used with metal buttons 16 to 18 mm in size. In such a case the function of all buttons, both bone and metal, from 12 to 18 mm in size could be interpreted as serving the same function, such as buttons for waistcoats.

The fact that the bone disks were not recovered in the large greatcoat size suggests that greatcoat buttons were most often of metal. The finding of evidence for the manufacture of waistcoat-sized bone disk buttons on military sites of the Revolutionary War period reveals a pattern of cloth-covered waistcoat buttons as opposed to those of metal. Too, the replacement rate of waistcoat buttons in relation to greatcoat buttons may have been far greater as a result of greater use in fastening and unfastening the waistcoat, which required fastening, whereas the great coat could be allowed to hang open. As metal waistcoat buttons were lost, if no matching metal buttons were readily available (perhaps as a result of interrupted supply lines during the Revolution), the necessary uniformity of the buttons could be achieved by means of cloth covering bone disks. Thus we may have the pattern of manufacturing of bone disks on military sites of the Revolution explained in terms of the need generated by strictures placed on supply lines during the war. This raises the question as to whether a higher ratio of metal waistcoat buttons to bone buttons are to be found on British as opposed to American sites of the Revolution. Since we have combined the data from both the British and American deposits for this study, we cannot answer this without a reanalysis addressing itself to this question. Another question raised by this study is whether a greater regimentation and concern for military orderliness and appropriateness can be seen revealed on British military sites as opposed to American military sites of the Revolution. Through analyses of artifact classes such as buttons, patterns relevant to such questions can be abstracted from archaeological data.

## QUANTITATIVE ANALYSIS OF ARTIFACTS: THE CAROLINA ARTIFACT PATTERN

By classifying the artifacts from a number of eighteenth-century historical sites in the Carolinas into eight groups and comparing the frequency of occurrence of these, a pattern range has been determined. This range has been designated as the Carolina artifact pattern (South 1977a). The artifacts from the middens at Fort Moultrie were used as two collections making up this pattern. These were expected to vary little, due to the fact that although political differences were dramatic between the British and Americans who occupied Fort Moultrie during the Revolution, the separation of these cultural systems on the basis of archaeological remains was not expected on the generalized level of the artifact group.

Although the artifact quantity from the American midden deposit was four times as great as that from the British midden, the artifact relationships were remarkably similar (see Table 32.3).

Through the use of these data and those from other sites in the Carolinas, the Carolina artifact pattern of relationships was delineated (South 1977a) (see Table 32.4).

TABLE 32.3.
Quantitative Comparison of Artifacts from the British and
American Midden Deposits

| Artifact group | American deposit | | British deposit | |
|---|---|---|---|---|
| | Count | Percentage | Count | Percentage |
| Kitchen | 4185 | 68.6 | 1208 | 69.2 |
| Architecture | 1510 | 24.8 | 344 | 19.7 |
| Furniture | 6 | .1 | 2 | .1 |
| Arms | 39 | .6 | 20 | 1.2 |
| Clothing | 136 | 2.2 | 69 | 4.0 |
| Personal | 4 | .1 | 4 | .2 |
| Tobacco pipes | 167 | 2.7 | 50 | 2.9 |
| Activities | 55 | .9 | 48 | 2.7 |
| Totals | 6102 | 100.0 | 1745 | 100.0 |

This expression of artifact pattern is based on 42 artifact classes composed of hundreds of artifact types. At the deeper artifact group level of analysis the military occupations at the Fort Moultrie garrison are seen to fall into the same pattern as eighteenth-century domestic sites from Brunswick Town, North Carolina, and elsewhere. However, when the ratio of military artifacts to all other artifacts is used as a means of comparison, the Fort Moultrie midden deposits cluster with other military, rather than domestic, sites (South 1977a). Recognizing pattern at the attribute level, the type level, the class level, and group level on an intrasite and intersite basis is a transformation process that progresses to increasingly deeper pattern recognition. Questions relating to status, chronology, function, and other behavioral variables in the past cultural system may well be answered more effectively on one level of data integration than another. Before archaeologists can hope

TABLE 32.4.
The Carolina Artifact Pattern: Frequency of Occurrence or
Eight Artifact Groups

| Artifact group | Mean percentage | Range | |
|---|---|---|---|
| Kitchen | 63.1 | 51.8 to | 69.2 |
| Architecture | 25.5 | 19.7 to | 31.4 |
| Furniture | .2 | .1 to | .6 |
| Arms | .5 | .1 to | 1.2 |
| Clothing | 3.0 | .6 to | 5.4 |
| Personal | .2 | .1 to | .5 |
| Tobacco pipes | 5.8 | 1.8 to | 13.9 |
| Activities | 1.7 | .9 to | 2.7 |
| Total | 100.0 | .9 to | 2.7 |

reliably to explain past behavior and cultural processes by means of the archaeological record, they must take these basic steps toward pattern recognition. Whether the pattern is being delineated from prehistoric Indian pottery fragments or abstracted from metal buttons should make absolutely no difference to the archaeological scientist.

## CONCLUSION

The examples of pattern recognition presented here using archaeological remains from the British colonial system as revealed in exploratory archaeology at Fort Moultrie are only a few of the patterns so delineated. It is hoped that these have been sufficient to demonstrate the contrast between this approach and the particularistic involvement with description and written history too often seen to emerge from an examination of sites of the historical period.

In this study we have tried to demonstrate how sponsor goals and archaeological goals can both be achieved through a testing of ideas about the past through the archaeological process of pattern recognition. By combining goals in this manner through a research design with a broad perspective, far more information can be abstracted from an exploratory archaeology project than is possible when particularistic, site-specific goals and descriptive reporting are the primary objectives.

Archaeologists should not expect sponsors of such projects to include within their site development plans goals oriented toward discovering culture process, testing archaeological methods and tools, delineating artifact patterning for the purpose of intersite comparative synthesis, or interpreting such patterns in terms of past human behavior and cultural systems. These goals are those of the archaeological scientists, and it is up to them to spell these out to the sponsor as part of the package to be executed under the terms of the contractual agreement to conduct scientific archaeology.

The sponsor, on the other hand, should make clear to the archaeologist those goals he has in mind, and these should be specified in the contract. The archaeologist should view these as important as the archaeological goals, but under no circumstances should he accept these as the *only* goals if he is to fulfill his obligation to his profession and to the cultural resources he is involved in conserving for posterity.

This attitude places responsibility on the archaeologist to spell out his scientific expectations, and on the sponsor for those goals of concern to the agency involved. This is a far more realistic approach than dreaming that someday sponsors may come to share the conceptual stance of the archaeologist. The archaeologist should strive, however, to demonstrate through archaeological science that adequate conservation of cultural resources can *only* come through combining the goals of sponsors with those of scientific archaeology.

Conservation archaeology combines a system of value judgments oriented toward the conservation of natural and cultural resources with a system of values determined by the concepts and methods of science. Both value systems work toward the most effective management of cultural resources through a combining of ideas, methods, and results of research carried out by means of agencies and individuals: administrators, lawyers, developers, builders, architects, engineers, historians, archaeologists, ethnographers, geologists, environmentalists, ecologists, etc. This being the case, it is imperative that those involved in this process be aware of the goals and roles being played in this drama. Only by such an awareness can we most effectively solve the problems that must be faced in efforts to conserve our cultural resources and increase our knowledge while planning and building for the future.

## ACKNOWLEDGMENTS

I would like to thank Leland G. Ferguson and Robert L. Stephenson for reading the transcript of this chapter and offering their comments.

# References

Advisory Council on Historic Preservation
1973 Procedures for the protection of historic and cultural properties. *In Code of federal regulations, Title 36*, Chapter viii, Part 800. Washington, D.C.: U.S. Government Printing Office.

Ahlstrom, R. V. N., and J. E. Bradford
1974 Bechtel Power Corporation 1978 Arizona plant site study, Salt River Project, state and private lands, Apache and Navajo counties, Arizona: Final report for Phase I archaeological and ethnohistorical research. Manuscript on deposit, Arizona State Museum, Univ. of Arizona, Tucson.

Allan, W. C., A. Osborn, W. J. Chasko, and D. E. Stuart
1975 An archaeological survey: Road construction right-of-way Block II—Navajo Indian Irrigation Project. In *Archeological reports, cultural resource management projects*, Working Draft Series, No. 1, edited by F. J. Broilo and D. E. Stuart. Albuquerque, N.M.: Office of Contract Archeology, University of New Mexico. Pp. 91–143.

Anderson, B. A.
1974 *An archaeological assessment of Amisted Recreation Area*. Santa Fe, N.M.: Division of Archaeology, Southwest Region, U.S. National Park Service.

Anderson, K.
1974 Contract standards for archaeological studies. In *Proceedings of the 1974 Cultural Resource Management Conference*, edited by W. D. Lipe and A. J. Lindsay, Jr. *Museum of Northern Arizona, Technical Series* No. 14:113–124.

Arkansas Department of Development and Planning
1973 *Atlas of Arkansas*. Little Rock, Ark.: Arkansas Department of Development and Planning.

Asch, D. L.
1975 On sample size problems and the uses of nonprobabilistic sampling. In *Sampling in archaeology*, edited by J. W. Mueller. Tucson, Ariz.: Univ. of Arizona Press. Pp. 170–191.

Ascher, R.
1968 Time's arrow and the archaeology of a contemporary community. In *Settlement archaeology*, edited by K. C. Chang. Palo Alto, Calif.: National Press Books. Pp. 43–52.

Asreen, R. C., Jr.
1974 An archaeological reconnaissance of the proposed Cooper River Rediversion Project, Berkeley County, South Carolina. *University of South Carolina, Institute of Archeology and Anthropology, Research Manuscript Series* No. 61.

Aten, L. E.
1972 Evaluation of the cultural resources of the Northgate Site, El Paso County, Texas. *University of Texas at Austin, Texas Archeological Salvage Project, Research Report* No. 5.
1974 Comments. In *Proceedings of the 1974 Cultural Resource Management Conference*, edited by W. D. Lipe and A. J. Lindsay, Jr. *Museum of Northern Arizona, Technical Series* No. 14:93–97.

Baily, W. C.
1971    Education of the public concerning the value of archaeological resources: Introduction of study materials into public school systems. Paper presented at the 36th Annual Meeting of the Society for American Archaeology, Norman, Okla.

Bair, G. A.
1974    An archaeological reconnaissance survey of the proposed Liberty–Parker 230 KV transmission line. Manuscript on deposit, Arizona State Museum Library, Univ. of Arizona, Tucson.

Baker, C. M.
1974    A preliminary archaeological field study of the Chicot watershed, Chicot County, Arkansas. Manuscript on deposit, Arkansas Archeological Survey, Univ. of Arkansas, Fayetteville.
1975    Arkansas Eastman Archeological Project. *Arkansas Archeological Survey, Research Report* No. 6.

Banks, K.
1975    *Prehistoric settlement in the Three-Mile and Sulphur Draw watersheds.* Dallas, Tex.: Archaeology research program, Southern Methodist University.

Barnes, E.
1967    Kaweah River archeology: Thoughts toward a public policy. Manuscript on deposit, U.S. National Park Service, San Francisco.

Barnes, J. A.
1972    Social networks. *Modular Publications in Anthropology* No. 26. Reading, Mass.: Addison-Wesley.

Barrett, S. A., and E. W. Gifford
1933    Miwok material culture. *Bulletin of the Public Museum of the City of Milwaukee 2* No. 4.

Bass, F. A., Jr., and T. R. Hester
1975    An archaeological survey of the upper Cibolo Creek watershed, central Texas. *The University of Texas at San Antonio, Center for Archaeological Research, Survey Report* No. 8.

Batchelder, G.L.
1976    Summary of exploration of potential fossil pollen records related to the New Melones project. In New Melones archaeological project—Stanislaus River, Calaveras and Tuolumne counties, California: Phase VI, edited by M. J. Moratto. Report submitted to the U.S. National Park Service, San Francisco. Pp. 457–461.

Baumhoff, M. A.
1963    Ecological determinants of aboriginal California populations. *University of California, Publications in American Archaeology and Ethnology 49:*155–235.

Beardsley, R., B. Meggers, P. Holder, A. Krieger, J. Rinaldo, and P. Kutche
1956    Functional and evolutionary implications of community patterning. *Society for American Archaeology, Memoir* No. 11:129–157.

Bearss, E. C.
1968    *The battle of Sullivan's Island and the capture of Fort Moultrie.* Washington, D.C.: U.S. National Park Service.
1968b   *The first two Fort Moultries, a structural history.* Washington, D.C.: U.S. National Park Service.
1968    *Fort Moultrie, No. 3.* Washington, D.C.: U.S. National Park Service.

Bell, R. E., and M. Gettys (Compilers)
n.d.    A consideration of the archaeological and historical resources involved in the Mid-Ark Project. Manuscript on deposit, Arkansas Archeological Survey, Univ. of Arkansas, Fayetteville.

Benson, C. L.
1976    Assessing the adequacy of a regional sampling design: Cedar Mesa, Utah. Paper presented at the 41st Annual Meeting of the Society for American Archaeology, St. Louis.

Benson, L.
1969    *The cacti of Arizona.* Tucson, Ariz.: Univ. of Arizona Press.

Berg, G.
1974    Secondary impacts of the proposed Bodega Bay public utility district sewerage facilities: A discussion of alternative approaches to mitigating the long-term impacts of the project on

archaeological resources. Unpublished report submitted to the Environmental Protection Agency and the Advisory Council on Historic Preservation.

Billings, W. D.

1970 *Plants, man and the ecosystem.* Belmont, Calif.: Wadsworth.

Binford, L. R.

1962 Archeology as anthropology. *American Antiquity 28:*217–225.

1964 A consideration of archaeological research design. *American Antiquity 29:*425–441.

1968 Archeological perspectives. In *New perspectives in archeology,* edited by S. L. Binford and L. R. Binford. Chicago: Aldine. Pp. 5–32.

1968b Methodological considerations of the archeological use of ethnographic data. In *Man the hunter,* edited by R. B. Lee and I. DeVore. Chicago: Aldine. Pp. 268–273.

1972 Evolution and horizon as revealed in ceramic analysis in historical archaeology—A step toward the development of archaeological science. *The Conference on Historic Site Archaeology, Papers,* 1971, *6* Part 1:117–126.

1973 Interassemblage variability—The Mousterian and the "Functional" argument. In *The explanation of culture change: Models in prehistory,* edited by C. Renfrew. London: Duckworth. Pp. 227–254.

n.d.a Forty-seven trips: A case study in the character of some formation processes of the archaeological record (in press).

n.d.b (Editor) *Theory building in archaeology.* New York: Academic Press (in press).

Binford, L. R., S. R. Binford, R. Whallon, and M. A. Hardin

1970 Archaeology at Hatchery West. *Society for American Archaeology, Memoirs* No. 24.

Birdsell, J. B.

1968 Some predictions for the Pleistocene based on equilibrium systems among recent hunters and gatherers. In *Man the hunter,* edited by R. B. Lee and I. DeVore. Chicago: Aldine. Pp. 229–240.

Birk, D. A., and D. C. George

1976 A woodland survey strategy and its application in the salvage of a Late Archaic locus of the Smith Mounds site, (21-KC-3), Koochiching County, Minnesota. *The Minnesota Archaeologist 35*(3):1–30.

Birman, J. H.

1964 Glacial geology across the crest of the Sierra Nevada, California. *Geological Society of America, Special Paper* No. 75.

Blalock, H. M., Jr.

1972 *Social statistics* (2nd ed.). New York: McGraw-Hill.

Blalock, H. M., and A. B. Blalock

1968 *Methodology in social research.* New York: McGraw-Hill.

Bohrer, V.

1970 Ethnobotanical aspects of Snaketown, a Hohokam village in southern Arizona. *American Antiquity 35:*413–430.

Braun, D. P.

1976 Rim form and ceramic vessel use: Results of an experiment with a central Arizona archaeological collection. Paper presented at the 41st Annual Meeting of the Society for American Archaeology, St. Louis.

Brauner, D. R., H. Hammet, and G. D. Hartman

1975 *Lower Granite Dam pool raising: Impact on archaeological sites.* Pullman, Wash.: Western Archaeological Research Center.

Brim, J. K., and D. H. Spain

1974 Research design in anthropology: Paradigms and pragmatics in testing of hypotheses. In *Studies in anthropological method,* cited by G. Spindler and L. Spindler. New York: Holt, Rinehart and Winston.

Broek, J.

1932 *The Santa Clara Valley: A study in landscape changes.* Utrecht, Holland: N. V. A. Oosthoek's Uitgevers-Mij. [1787–1849]

Brown, J. A. (Editor)
   1971    Approaches to the social dimensions of mortuary practices. *Society for American Archaeology, Memoirs* No. 25.
Bruder, J. S.
   1975    Historic Papago archeology. In Hecla II and III: An interpretive study of archeological remains from the Lakeshore Project, Papago Reservation, south central Arizona, edited by A. Goodyear, *Arizona State University, Anthropological Research Paper* No. 9: Appendix B, 271–337.
Bryan, K.
   1925    The Papago country, Arizona: A geographic, geologic, and hydrologic reconnaissance with a guide to desert watering places. *U.S. Geological Survey, Water-Supply Paper* No. 499.
Burnham, B. (Compiler)
   1974    *The protection of cultural property: Handbook of national legislations*. Paris: The International Council of Museums, Tunisia.
California Coastal Zone Conservation Commission
   1975    Preliminary Coastal Plan. San Francisco, Calif.: Hearing draft.
Calver, W. L., and R. P. Bolton
   1970    *History written with pick and shovel*. New York: The New York Historical Society.
Campbell, J. M.
   1963    Territoriality among ancient hunters: Interpretations from ethnography and nature. In *Anthropological archaeology in the Americas*, edited by B. Meggers. Washington, D.C.: Anthropological Society of Washington.
Canouts, V. (Assembler)
   1972    An archaeological survey of the Santa Rosa Wash project. *Arizona State Museum, Archaeological Series* No. 18.
   1975    Archaeological resources of the Orme Reservoir. *Archaeological Series* No. 92, Cultural Resource Management Section, Arizona State Museum, University of Arizona, Tucson.
Carpenter, J. I.
   1974    Archaeological contractual agreements. In Proceedings of the 1974 Cultural Resource Management Conference, edited by W. D. Lipe and A. J. Lindsay, Jr. *Museum of Northern Arizona, Technical Series* No. 14:39–43.
Carrell, T.
   1974    Effects of innundation. Research proposal for underwater archaeology, Univ. of California, Santa Cruz.
Carrell, T. S. R., and D. Lenihan
   1976    *A literature search on the effects of freshwater inundation of archeological sites through reservoir construction*. Santa Fe, N.M.: U.S. National Park Service, Southwest Region.
Castetter, E. F., and W. H. Bell
   1937    The aboriginal utilization of the tall cacti in the American Southwest. *University of New Mexico, Bulletin* No. 307, *Biological Series* 5(1).
   1942    *Pima and Papago agriculture*. Albuquerque, N.M.: Univ. of New Mexico Press.
Caws, P.
   1969    The structure of discovery. *Science 166:* 1375–1380.
Chalfant, W. A.
   1933    *The story of Inyo*. Los Angeles: Citizens Print Shop.
Chang, K. C.
   1967    *Rethinking archaeology*. New York: Random House.
   1968    *Settlement archaeology*. Palo Alto, Calif.: National Press.
Chapman, C. (Editor)
   1973    Archaeology in the 70's—Mitigating the impact. *The Missouri Archaeologist 35:* 1–71.
Chatham, R. L.
   1962    The geography of San Benito County, California: A regional plan for development. Unpublished PhD dissertation, Stanford University, Palo Alto, Calif.

Cheek, A. L., C. D. Cheek, S. Hackenberger, T. Jones, W. M. Jones, and K. Leehan
1974  *An archaeological survey of the upper Muddy Boggy watershed, Pontotoc, Coal, and Hughes counties, Oklahoma.* Tulsa, Okla.: Department of Sociology and Anthropology.

Chenhall, R. G.
1971  Positivism and the collection of data. *American Antiquity 36*(3):372–373.
1975  A rationale for archaeological sampling. In *Sampling in Archaeology,* edited by J. W. Mueller. Tucson, Ariz.: Univ. of Arizona Press. Pp. 3–25.

Claassen, C. P.
1976  Cultural formation processes of the archaeological record in the Aleutian Islands. Paper presented at the New England–New York Graduate Student Conference, Storrs, Conn.

Claassen, C. P., and C. S. Spears
1975  An assessment of site surveying, shovel testing and augering. In Arkansas Eastman Archaeological Project, edited by Charles M. Baker. *Arkansas Archeological Survey, Research Series* No. 6:123–127.

Clark, G.
1957  *Archaeology and society* (3rd ed.). London: Methuen.
1970  *Aspects of prehistory.* Berkeley, Calif.: Univ. of California Press.

Clark, J. D.
1968  Studies of hunters-gatherers as an aid to the interpretation of prehistoric societies. In *Man the hunter,* edited by R. B. Lee and I. DeVore. Chicago: Aldine. Pp. 276–280.

Clarke, D. L.
1968  *Analytical archaeology.* London: Methuen.
1973  Archaeology: The loss of innocence. *Antiquity 47:*6–18.

Cochran, W. G.
1963  *Sampling techniques.* New York: Wiley.

Coggins, C.
1972  Archaeology and the art market. *Science 175:*263–266.

Collier, B. D., G. W. Cox, A. W. Johnson, and P. C. Miller
1973  *Dynamic ecology.* Englewood Cliffs, N.J.: Prentice-Hall.

Connors, D. T.
1976  *An archaeological survey of the Salt River Indian Community Housing Project 14-6, Maricopa County, Arizona.* Tempe, Ariz.: Office of Cultural Resource Management, Department of Anthropology, Arizona State University.

Cook, S. F.
1971  The aboriginal population of upper California. In *The California Indians,* edited by R. F. Heizer and M. A. Whipple. Berkeley, Calif.: Univ. of California Press. Pp. 66–72.

Cooley, R. E., M. J. Fuller, M. Gilmore, G. Iffrig, R. Manes, R. Reuter, and S. Thompson
1975  *An archaeological and historical survey of areas to be affected by the Wilson's Creek sewer line, city of Springfield, Greene County, Missouri: 1975.* Springfield, Mo.: Center for Archaeological Research, Southwest Missouri State University.

Council on Environmental Quality
1971  Preparation of environmental impact statements: Proposed guidelines. In *Code of federal regulations, Title 40,* Chapter v, Part 1500 and *Federal Register, 36:*7724–7729, Washington, D.C.: U.S. Government Printing Office.
1973  Preparation of environmental impact statements: Guidelines. In *Code of federal regulations, Title 40,* Chapter v, Part 1500 and *Federal Register 38:*147, Washington, D.C.: U.S. Government Printing Office.
1976  Preparation of environmental impact statements: Guidelines. In *Code of federal regulations, Title 40,* Chapter v, Part 1500. Washington, D.C.: U.S. Government Printing Office. Pp. 754–777.

Cowan, R. A., and K. Wallof
1974  Field work and artifact analysis: Southern California Edison No. 2 Control–Casa Diablo 115 Kv transmission line. Manuscript on deposit at the Dry-lands Research Institute, Univ. of

California, Riverside.

Cowgill, G. L.
1964    The selection of samples from large sherd collections. *American Antiquity 29:*467–473.
1975    A selection of samplers: Comments on archaeo-statistics. In *Sampling in archaeology,* edited by J. W. Mueller. Tucson, Ariz.: Univ. of Arizona Press. Pp. 258–274.

Crabtree, D. E., and B. R. Butler
1964    Notes on experiments in flint knapping: I. Heat treatment of silica materials. *Tebiwa 7:*1–6.

Crawford, D. D.
1965    The Granite Beach site, Llano County, Texas. *Bulletin of the Texas Archeological Society 36:*71–97.

Culbert, T. P. (Editor)
1973    *The classic Maya collapse.* Albuquerque, N.M.: Univ. of New Mexico Press.

Cummings, C., and D. Lenihan (Compilers)
1975    Interagency cooperative research project to determine the effects of inundation on cultural resources in the United States. Prospectus manuscript on deposit, Division of Archeology, Southwest Region, U.S. National Park Service, Santa Fe, N.M.

Cunningham, B.
1974    Impact of another new archaeology. *Journal of Field Archaeology 1:*365–369.
1976    Risk control in archaeology. *Journal of Field Archaeology 3:*230–233.

Curry, R. R.
1968    Quaternary climatic and glacial history of the Sierra Nevada, California. Unpublished Ph.D. dissertation, Univ. of California, Berkeley.

Curtis, J. T., and R. P. McIntosh
1950    The interrelations of certain analytic and synthetic phyto-sociological characters. *Ecology 31:*434–65.

Dancey, W. S.
1974    The archeological survey: A reorientation. *Man in the Northeast 8:*98–112.

Daniels, S. G. H.
1972    Research design models. In *Models in archaeology,* edited by D. L. Clarke. London: Methuen. Pp. 201–229.

Davis, E. L.
1963    The desert culture of the western Great Basin: A lifeway of seasonal transhumance. *American Antiquity 29:*202–212.

Davis, H. A.
1972    The crisis in American archaeology. *Science 175:*267–272.
1976    CEQ to hold hearings. *American Society for Conservation Archaeology, Newsletter 3*(3):4.
1976b   The public and cultural resource management: Reaction and responsibility. In Symposium on dynamics of cultural resource management. *U.S. Department of Agriculture, Forest Service, Southwestern Region, Archeological Report* No. 10:50–54.

DeBloois, E. I.
1975    Elk Ridge Archeological Project: A test of random sampling in archaeological surveying. *U.S. Department of Agriculture, Forest Service, Intermountain Region, Archeological Report* No. 2.

DeBloois, E., D. Green, and H. Wylie
n.d.    *A test of the impact of pinyon–juniper chaining of archeological sites.* Ogden, Utah: U.S. Department of Agriculture, Forest Service, Laboratory of Archeology.

Debowski, S. S., A. George, R. Goddard, and D. Mullon
1976    An archaeological survey of Buttes Reservoir. *Arizona State Museum, Archaeological Series* No. 93.

Deem, D. B.
1940    *History of Butler County, Missouri.* Poplar Bluff, Mo.: Poplar Bluff Printing Co.

Derricourt, R. M., L. R. Peters, and E. Maluma
1976    Itezhitezhi: Archaeology and salvage in Zambia. *Current Anthropology 17:*497–500.

Dittert, A. E.
1975 An archaeological survey in the Gila River basin, New River and Phoenix city streams, Arizona project area. Report submitted to the U.S. National Park Service, Western Region, Tucson, Ariz. Manuscript.

Dittert, A. E., and M. Laughlin
n.d. A cultural inventory of the Salt River Indian Reservation. *Arizona State University, Anthropological Research Papers* No. 5. In preparation.

Dixon, K. A.
1971 Archaeological site preservation: The neglected alternative to destruction. *Pacific Coast Archaeological Society Quarterly 7:*51–70.
1974 Archaeological resources and policy recommendations, city of Long Beach. Manuscript submitted to the Department of City Planning, Long Beach, Calif.
1976 Hey, don't mitigate that site! *American Society for Conservation Archaeology, Newsletter 3*(3):2.

Doelle, W. H.
1975 Prehistoric resource exploitation within the Conoco Florence Project. *Arizona State Museum, Archaeological Series* No. 62.
1976 Desert resources and Hohokam subsistence: The Conoco Florence Project. *Arizona State Museum, Archaeological Series* No. 103.

Dole, G. E.
1973 Foundations of contemporary evolutionism. In *Main currents in cultural anthropology,* edited by R. and F. Naroll. New York: Appleton-Century-Crofts. Pp. 247–280.

Donaldson, B. R.
1975 An archeological sample of the White Mountain Planning Unit, Apache-Sitgreaves National Forest, Arizona. *U.S. Department of Agriculture, Forest Service, Southwestern Region, Archeological Report* No. 6.

Douglass, A. E.
1929 The secret of the Southwest solved by talkative tree rings. *The National Geographic Magazine 56*(6):736–770.

Downing, C., J. J. Husted, and D. Jurney
1976 1934 collections, an inventory-analysis. In Pine Mountain: A study of prehistoric human ecology in the Arkansas Ozarks, compiled by L. M. Raab. *Arkansas Archeological Survey, Research Report* No. 7:31–45.

Dozier, E. P.
1970 Making inferences from the present to the past. In *Reconstructing prehistoric pueblo societies,* edited by W. A. Longacre. Albuquerque, N.M.: New Mexico Press. Pp. 202–213.

Dragoo, D. W., and S. Lantz
1969 *Archeological salvage of selected sites in the Allegheny Reservoir in Pennsylvania and New York, 1968.* Pittsburgh: Carnegie Museum.
1971 *Archeological salvage of selected sites in the Allegheny Reservoir in Pennsylvania and New York, 1969–1971.* Pittsburgh: Carnegie Museum.

Drayton, J.
1821 *Memoirs of the American revolution.* Volumes 1 and 2. Charleston, S.C.: A. E. Miller.

Drucker, P.
1972 Stratigraphy in archaeology: An introduction. *Addison-Wesley Modular Publications in Anthropology* No. 30.

Dunnell, R. C.
1971 *Systematics in prehistory.* New York: Free Press.

Easton, W. H.
1942 Pitkin limestone of north Arkansas. *Arkansas Geological Survey, Bulletin* No. 8.

Erwin, S. L.
n.d. Some Boone chert versus Pitkin chert archeological relationships in northern Arkansas, or "Where did this black chert come from?" Manuscript on deposit, Arkansas Archeological

Survey, Univ. of Arkansas, Fayetteville.

Evans, D. R., and D. J. Ives
1976 The Meramec Basin archaeological research project. Paper presented at the 41st Annual Meeting of the Society for American Archaeology, St. Louis.

Fairbridge, R. W.
1976 Shellfish-eating preceramic Indians in coastal Brazil. *Science 191:*353–359.

Faulkner, C. H., and C. R. McCollough
1973 Introductory report of the Normandy reservoir salvage project: Environmental setting, typology, and survey. *University of Tennessee, Department of Anthropology, Report of Investigations* No. 11.

Fawcett, W. B., and D. Cleveland
1973 A survey of the archaeological resources: Parker Division, Colorado River Front Work and Levee System. *Arizona State Museum, Archaeological Series* No. 33.

Feagins, J. D.
1975 A most preliminary sketch of prehistoric site destruction in the Little Osage River Valley, Bourbon County, Kansas. *Kansas Anthropological Association, Newsletter 21*(4):1–6.

Fehon, J. R., and A. D. Viscito
1974 Archeological and historical inventory and preliminary field reconnaissance of Village Creek, Jackson and Lawrence counties, Arkansas. *Arkansas Archeological Survey, Research Report* No. 2.

Fenenga, F. F.
1973 *Archaeological work in the Hidden Valley reservoir area, Madera County, California.* Report submitted to the U.S. National Park Service, Western Region, Tucson, Ariz.
1975 The post-contact archaeological sites on the Fresno and Chowchilla rivers. Paper presented at the Annual Meeting of the Society for California Archaeology, Santa Cruz.

Fitch, J. E.
1969 Fossil records of certain schooling fishes of the California current system. *California Cooperative Oceanic Fisheries Investigations, Reports 13:*71–80. Terminal Island, Calif.: Marine Research Committee, California Department of Fish and Game.

Fitting, J. E.
1966 Archaeological investigations of the Carolinian-Canadian edge area in Michigan. *The Michigan Archaeologist 12:*12–32.
1970 *The archaeology of Michigan.* New York: Doubleday.

Fitzhugh, W. W.
1972 Environmental archeology and cultural systems in Hamilton Inlet, Labrador. *Smithsonian Contributions to Anthropology*, No. 16.

Flannery, K. V.
1967 Culture history vs. cultural process: A debate in American archaeology. *Scientific American 217:*119–122.
1968 Archeological systems theory and early Mesoamerica. In *Anthropological archeology in the Americas,* edited by B. J. Meggars. Washington, D.C.: Anthropological Society of Washington. Pp. 67–87.
1972 The cultural evolution of civilizations. *Annual Review Ecology and Systematics 3:*399–426.
1972b The origins of the village as a settlement type in Mesoamerica and in the Near East: A comparative study. In *Man, settlement, and urbanism,* edited by P. J. Ucko, R. Tringham, and G. W. Dimbleby. Cambridge, Mass.: Schenkman. Pp. 23–53.

Flenniken, J. J.
1975 Test excavations of three archeological sites in Des Arc Bayou watershed, White County, Arkansas. Manuscript on deposit, Arkansas Archeological Survey, Univ. of Arkansas, Fayetteville.

Flinders-Petrie, W. M.
1904 *Methods and aims in archaeology.* New York: Macmillan.

Fontana, B. L., W. J. Robinson, C. W. Cormack, and E. E. Leavitt, Jr.
1962 *Papago Indian pottery.* Seattle, Wash.: Univ. of Washington Press.

Ford, J. L., and M. A. Rolingson
1972 Investigation of destruction to prehistoric sites due to agricultural practices in southeast Arkansas. *Arkansas Archeological Survey, Research Series* No. 3, 1–40.

Ford, R. I.
1973 Archeology serving humanity. In *Research and theory in current archeology,* edited by C. Redman. New York: Wiley. Pp. 83–94.
1976 The significance of ethnobotany to archaeology. Paper presented at the 41st Annual Meeting of the Society for American Archaeology. St. Louis, Mo.: To be published in *Field Archaeology.*

Fox, A. A., F. A. Bass, Jr., and T. R. Hester
1976 The archaeology and history of Alamo Plaza. *University of Texas at San Antonio, Center for Archaeological Research, Archaeological Survey Report* No. 16.

Fox, D. E., R. J. Mallouf, N. O'Malley, and W. M. Sorrow
1974 Archeological resources of the proposed Cuero I Reservoir, Dewitt and Gonzales counties, Texas. *Texas Historical Commission and Texas Water Development Board, Archeological Survey Report* No. 12.

Freeman, L. G., Jr.
1968 A theoretical framework for interpreting archaeological materials. In *Man the hunter,* edited by R. B. Lee and I. DeVore. Chicago: Aldine. Pp. 263–367.

Frese, H. H.
1960 *Anthropology and the public: The role of museums.* Leiden: E. J. Brill.

Fritz, G.
1975 Matagorda Bay area, Texas: A survey of the archeological and historical resources. *Texas at San Antonio, Center for Archeological Research, Archeological Survey Report* No. 45.

Fritz, J. M.
1973 Relevance, archeology, and subsistence theory. In *Research and theory in current archeology,* edited by C. Redman. New York: Wiley. Pp. 59–82.

Fritz, J. M., and F. T. Plog
1970 The nature of archaeological explanation. *American Antiquity 35:*405–412.

Fuller, S. L., A. E. Rogge, and L. M. Gregonis
1976 Orme Alternatives: the archaeological resources of Roosevelt Lake and Horseshoe Reservoir. *Arizona State Museum, Archaeological Series* No. 98.

Funk, R. E., B. E. Rippeteau, and R. M. Houck
1973 A preliminary cultural framework for the upper Susquehanna Valley. *New York State Archaeological Association, Bulletin* No. 57, 11–27.

Garrison, E. G.
1975 A qualitative model for inundation studies in archeological research and resource conservation: An example from Arkansas. *Plains Anthropologist 20:*279–296.
n.d. A research design for quantitatively investigating the effects of inundation on archeological sites. Manuscript on deposit, Arkansas Archeological Survey, Univ. of Arkansas, Fayetteville.

Garrison, E. G., J. A. May, J. B. Newsom, and A. Sjöberg
1977 *A progress report on the effects of inundation on cultural resources, Table Rock Reservoir, Missouri.* American Archaeology Division, Department of Anthropology, University of Missouri, Columbia.

Gero, J. M.
1976 Archaeology tomorrow: The multiple-problem approach to site exploitation. Manuscript on deposit, Arizona State Museum Library, Univ. of Arizona, Tucson.

Gilbert, B.
1976 Dept. of Otter Confusion. *Sports Illustrated 45*(4):62–72.

Gish, J. W.
1975 Preliminary report on pollen analysis from Hecla I, II, and III. In Hecla II and III: An

interpretive study of archeological remains from the Lakeshore Project, Papago Reservation, south central Arizona, by A. Goodyear, *Arizona State University, Anthropological Research Paper* No. 9: Appendix A, pp. 254–270.

Goggin, J. M.
1960   Underwater archaeology: Its nature and limitations. *American Antiquity 25:*348–354.

Goodyear, A. C.
1973   Prehistoric settlement–subsistence systems in the Slate Mountains: A proposed study. Manuscript on file, Department of Anthropology, Arizona State University, Tempe, and Arizona State Museum Library, Univ. of Arizona, Tucson.
1974   The Brand site: A techno-functional study of a Dalton site in northeast Arkansas. *Arkansas Archeological Survey, Research Series* No. 7.
1975a  A general research design for highway archeology in South Carolina. *University of South Carolina, Institute of Archeology and Anthropology, Notebook 7:*3–38.
1975b  Hecla II and III: An interpretive study of archeological remains from the Lakeshore Project, Papago Reservation, south-central Arizona. *Arizona State University, Anthropological Research Paper* No. 9.
1975c  Research design for the study of Dalton settlement–subsistence activities in the Cache River basin. In The Cache River archeological project: An experiment in contract archeology, assembled by M. B. Schiffer and J. H. House. *Arkansas Archeological Survey, Research Series* No. 8:205–216.
1976   Current and future developments in archeological theory building within the contract framework. *University of South Carolina, Institute of Archeology and Anthropology, Research Manuscript Series* 101.
1977   The historical and ecological position of protohistoric sites in the Slate Mountains, south central Arizona. In *Research strategies in historical archeology*, edited by S. South. New York: Academic.

Goodyear, A. C., N. Ackerly, and J. H. House
1977   An archeological survey of the Laurens to Anderson connector route in the South Carolina piedmont. *University of South Carolina, Institute of Archeology and Anthropology, Research Manuscript Series* (In Preparation).

Goodyear, A. C., and A. E. Dittert, Jr.
1973   Hecla I: A preliminary report on the archaeological investigations at the Lakeshore Project, Papago Indian Reservation, south central Arizona. *Arizona State University, Anthropological Research Paper* No. 14.

Gorman, F.
1972   The Clovis hunters: An alternate view of their environment and ecology. In *Contemporary Archaeology*, edited by M. P. Leone. Carbondale, Ill.: Southern Illinois University Press. Pp. 206–221.

Gould, R.
1968   Living archeology: The Ngaratatjara of western Australia. *Southwestern Journal of Anthropology 24:*101–122.
1971   The archeologist as ethnographer: A case from the western desert of Australia. *World Archeology 3:*143–177.
1974   Ethno-archeology, or Where do models come from? (A closer look at Australian aboriginal lithic technology). Paper presented at the May 1974 meeting of the Australian Institute of Aboriginal Studies, Canberra.

Grady, M. A.
1975   Archaeological survey and the future of cultural resource management. Paper presented at the 40th Annual Meeting of the Society for American Archaeology, Dallas, Tex.
1976   Aboriginal agrarian adaptation to the Sonoran Desert: A regional synthesis and research design. Ph.D. dissertation, Univ. of Arizona, Tucson.

Grady, M. A., S. Kemrer, S. Schultz, and W. Dodge

1973 An archaeological survey of the Salt–Gila Aqueduct. *Arizona State Museum, Archaeological Series* No. 23.

Grady, M. A., and W. Lipe

1976 Conservation archaeology, research, and environmental law. Paper presented at the 41st Annual Meeting of the Society for American Archaeology, St. Louis.

Green, C. R., and W. D. Sellers (Editors)

1964 *Arizona climate*. Tucson, Ariz.: Univ. of Arizona Press.

Green, D. F.

1975 (Editor) The wilderness and cultural values: A symposium. *U.S. Department of Agriculture, Forest Service, Southwestern Region, Archeological Report* No. 7.

1975b The wilderness and cultural values: Introduction. In the wilderness and cultural values: A symposium, edited by D. F. Green. *U.S. Department of Agriculture, Forest Service, Southwestern Region, Archeological Report* No. 7:1–4.

Green, H. P.

1972 *The National Environmental Policy Act in the courts*. Washington, D.C.: The Conservation Foundation.

Greenwood, R. S. (Editor)

1975 3500 years on one city block. San Buenaventura Mission Plaza Project, Archaeological Report, 1974.

Greig-Smith, P.

1964 *Quantitative plant ecology*. London: Butterworths.

Gruhn, R.

1972 Letter on "The crisis in American archaeology." *Science 176:*353–354.

Gumerman, G. J.

1970 Black Mesa; survey and excavation in northeastern Arizona, 1968. *Prescott College Studies in Anthropology* No. 2.

1971 (Editor) The distribution of prehistoric population aggregates: Proceedings of the First Annual Southwestern Anthropological Research Group, edited by G. J. Gumerman. *Prescott College Anthropology Reports* No. 1.

1973 The reconciliation of theory and method in archaeology. In *Research and theory in current archeology*, edited by C. L. Redman. New York: Wiley (Interscience). Pp. 287–299.

Gumerman, G. J., and R. R. Johnson

1971 Prehistoric human population distribution in a biological transition zone. In The distribution of prehistoric population aggregates: Proceedings of the First Annual Southwestern Anthropological Research Group, edited by G. J. Gumerman. *Prescott College Anthropology Reports* No. 1.

Gumerman, G. J., D. Westfall, and C. S. Weed

1972 *Archaeological investigations on Black Mesa, the 1969–1970 seasons*. Prescott, Ariz.: Prescott College Press.

Hackenberg, R. A.

1964 Aboriginal land use and occupancy of the Papago Indians. Manuscript on file, Arizona State Museum Library, Univ. of Arizona, Tucson.

Hackenberger, S., and A. L. Cheek

1975 Test excavations at Pw66 and Pw67, lower Black Bear Creek watershed project. Manuscript on deposit, Oklahoma Conservation Commission and Archeological Research Associates, Tulsa.

Hackenberger, S., A. L. Cheek, S. Purves, and K. Leehan

1976 Preliminary report of ten percent archeological reconnaissance of the proposed McGee Creek reservoir. Manuscript on deposit, U.S. Bureau of Reclamation, Amarillo, Tex., and Archaeological Research Associates, Tulsa, Okla.

Hall, A.

1976 Ethnohistory. In *New Melones Archaeological Project—Stanislaus River, Calaveras and Tuolumne counties, California: Phase VI*, edited by M. J. Moratto. Report submitted to the

U.S. National Park Service, San Francisco. Pp. 81-106.

Hall, M. C., and J. P. Barker
  1975   *Background to prehistory of the El Paso/Red Mountain desert region.* Riverside, Calif.: Archaeological Research Unit, Univ. of California.

Halvorson, W. L.
  1970   Topographic influence on the pattern of plant communities, phenology, and water relations of a desert ecosystem. Unpublished Ph.D. dissertation, Arizona State University, Tempe.

Hanes, R. C.
  1976   Technological and social adaptations to the western foothills of the Sierra Nevada of California. Unpublished manuscript, Department of Anthropology, Univ. of Oregon, Eugene.

Hansen, M., W. N. Hurwitz, and W. G. Madow
  1953   *Sample survey methods and theory, methods and applications,* Vol. 1. New York: Wiley.

Hanson, J. A., and M. B. Schiffer
  1975   The Joint Site—A preliminary report. In Chapters in the prehistory of eastern Arizona, IV. *Fieldiana: Anthropology 65:*47-91.

Harris, M.
  1968   *The rise of anthropological theory.* New York: Crowell.
  1975   *Culture, People and Nature.* (second edition). Thomas Y. Crowell Company, Inc.

Harvard Law Review
  1975   The least adverse alternative approach to substantive review under NEPA. *Harvard Law Review 88:*735-758.

Hastings, J. R., and R. M. Turner
  1965   *The changing mile: An ecological study of vegetation change with time in the lower mile of an arid and semiarid region.* Tucson, Ariz.: Univ. of Arizona Press.

Haury, E. W., K. Bryan, E. H. Colbert, N. E. Gabel, C. L. Tanner, and T. E. Buerer
  1975   *The stratigraphy and archaeology of Ventana Cave, Arizona.* Tucson, Ariz.: Univ. of Arizona Press, and Albuquerque, N.M.: Univ. of New Mexico Press. [1950]

Heizer, R. F.
  1966   Salvage and other Archaeology. *The Masterkey 40:*54-60.

Heizer, R. F., and F. F. Fenenga
  1948   Survey of building structures of the Sierran gold belt—1848-70. *California Division of Mines, Bulletin* No. 141:91-164.

Heizer, R. F., and A. E. Treganza
  1944   Mines and quarries of the Indians of California. *California Journal of Mines and Geology 40:*291-359.

Helm, J.
  1962   The ecological approach in anthropology. *American Journal of Sociology 47:*630-639.

Hempel, C.
  1966   *Philosophy of natural science.* Englewood Cliffs, N.J.: Prentice-Hall.

Henderson, M.
  1976   An archaeological inventory of Brantley Reservoir, New Mexico. *Southern Methodist University, Contributions in Anthropology* No. 18.

Hester, J. J.
  1974   Guidelines for archaeological activities required under current Colorado and federal laws. *The Mountain Geologist 11:*127-130.

Hester, J. J., J. Musick, and M. Woolf
  1973   Archaeology and the law. In Archaeology in the 70's—Mitigating the impact, edited by C. H. Chapman. *The Missouri Archaeologist 35:*5-19.

Hester, T. R., F. A. Bass, Jr., and T. C. Kelly
  1975   Archaeological survey of portions of the Comal River watershed, Comal County, Texas. *University of Texas at San Antonio, Center for Archaeological Research, Archaeological Survey Report* No. 6.

Hickman, P. P.

n.d.a Country nodes: An anthropological evaluation of William Keys' Desert Queen Ranch. Report submitted to the Western Archeological Center, U.S. National Park Service, Tucson, Ariz.

n.d.b One hundred years of history in the California desert: An overview of historic archaeological resources at Joshua Tree National Monument. Report submitted to the Western Archeological Center, U.S. National Park Service, Tucson, Ariz.

Hill, J. N.

1966 A prehistoric community in eastern Arizona. *Southwestern Journal of Anthropology 22:*9–30.

1970a Broken K Pueblo: Prehistoric social organization in the American Southwest. *Anthropological Papers of the University of Arizona* No. 18.

1970b Prehistoric social organization in the American Southwest. In *Reconstructing prehistoric pueblo societies,* edited by W. A. Longacre. Albuquerque, N.M.: Univ. of New Mexico Press. Pp. 11–58.

1972 The methodological debate in contemporary archaeology: A model. In *Models in archaeology,* edited by D. L. Clarke. London: Methuen. Pp. 61–108.

Hill, L. G.

1949 History of the Missouri Lumber and Mining Company. Unpublished Ph.D. dissertation, Univ. of Missouri, Columbia.

Holder, T. H.

1970 *Disappearing wetlands in eastern Arkansas.* Little Rock, Ark.: Arkansas Planning Commission.

Hole, F., and R. F. Heizer

1973 *An Introduction to Prehistoric Archeology* (2nd ed.). New York: Holt, Rinehart & Winston. [1969]

Holmes, N. H., Jr., and E. B. Trickey

1974 Late Holocene sea-level oscillations in Mobile Bay. *American Antiquity* 39(1):122–124.

Holmes, W. H.

1919 Handbook of aboriginal American antiquities. *Bureau of American Ethnology, Bulletin* No. 60.

Hoover, M. M., M. A. Hein, W. A. Dayton, and C. O. Erlanson

1948 The main grasses for farm and home. In *Grass: The yearbook of agriculture 1948.* Washington, D.C.: U.S. Department of Agriculture. Pp. 639–700.

Hosley, E.

1968 Archeological evaluation of ancient habitation site, Point Hope, Alaska. Manuscript on deposit, Arizona State Museum Library, Univ. of Arizona, Tucson.

House, J. H.

1975a The Cache River Archeological Project: Survey methods and contract archeology. *Southeastern Archeological Conference, Bulletin* No. 18, 98–107.

1975b A functional typology for Cache Project surface collections. In The Cache River Archeological Project: An experiment in contract archeology, assembled by M. B. Schiffer and J. H. House. *Arkansas Archeological Survey, Research Series* No. 8:55–73.

1975c Prehistoric lithic resource utilization in the Cache Basin: Crowley's Ridge chert and quartzite and Pitkin chert. In The Cache River Archeological Project: An experiment in contract archeology, assembled by M. B. Schiffer and J. H. House. *Arkansas Archeological Survey, Research Series* No. 8:81–92.

1975d Records check and summary of prior archeological knowledge. In The Cache River Archeological Project: An experiment in contract archeology, assembled by M. B. Schiffer and J. H. House. *Arkansas Archeological Survey, Research Series* No. 8:29–34.

1975e The testing program. In The Cache River Archeological Project: An experiment in contract archeology, assembled by M. B. Schiffer and J. H. House. *Arkansas Archeological Survey, Research Series* No. 8:121–129.

1977 Survey data and regional models in historical archeology. In *Research strategies in historical archeology,* edited by S. South. New York: Academic.

House, J. H., and D. L. Ballenger
  1976  An archaeological survey of the Interstate 77 route in the South Carolina piedmont. *University of South Carolina, Institute of Archeology and Anthropology, Research Manuscript Series* No. 104.

House, J. H., T. C. Klinger, and M. B. Schiffer
  1975  A test of the Dalton settlement pattern hypothesis using Cache project survey data. In The Cache River Archeological Project: An experiment in contract archeology, assembled by M. B. Schiffer and J. H. House. *Arkansas Archeological Survey, Research Series* No. 8:93–101.

House, J. H., and M. B. Schiffer
  1975a  Archeological survey in the Cache River Basin. In The Cache River Archeological Project: An experiment in contract archeology, assembled by M. B. Schiffer and J. H. House. *Arkansas Archeological Survey, Research Series* No. 8:37–53.
  1975b  Significance of the archeological resources of the Cache River Basin. In The Cache River Archeological Project: An experiment in contract archeology, assembled by M. B. Schiffer and J. H. House. *Arkansas Archeological Survey, Research Series* No. 8:163–186.

House, J. H., and J. W. Smith
  1975  Experiments in replication of fire-cracked rock. In The Cache River Archeological Project: An experiment in contract archeology, assembled by M. B. Schiffer and J. H. House. *Arkansas Archeological Survey, Research Series* No. 8:75–80.

Husted, W.
  1973  Effects of inundation on archeological sites. Memorandum to the U.S. National Park Service, Southwest Region, Santa Fe, N.M.

Hyatt, R. D., and K. Doehner
  1975  Archaeological research at Cooper Lake, Northeast Texas, 1973. *Southern Methodist University, Contributions in Anthropology* No. 15.

Ives, D. J.
  1975  The Crescent Hill prehistoric quarrying area. *Museum of Anthropology, University of Missouri, Museum Brief* No. 22.

Jennings, J. D.
  1957  Danger Cave. *Society for American Archaeology, Memoir* No. 14.
  1959  Operational manual: University of Utah–National Park Service upper Colorado River basin archeological salvage project. In The Glen Canyon archeological survey, edited by D. D. Fowler and others. *University of Utah, Anthropological Papers* No. 39, Part 2, 677–707.
  1963a  Administration of contract emergency archaeological programs. *American Antiquity 28:*282–85.
  1963b  Anthropology and the world of science. *University of Utah Bulletin 54* (18).
  1974  Comments. In Proceedings of the 1974 Cultural Resource Management Conference, edited by W. D. Lipe and A. J. Lindsay, Jr. *Museum of Northern Arizona, Technical Series* No. 14:25–28.

Jewell, D. P.
  1961  Freshwater archaeology. *American Antiquity 26:*415–416.
  1964  Limnoarchaeology in California. In *Dividing into the past: Theory, techniques, and applications of underwater archaeology,* edited by J. D. Holmquist and A. H. Wheeler. St. Paul: Minnesota Historical Society. Pp. 27–31.

Johnson, P. J.
  1973  *The New Melones Reservoir archaeological project, Calaveras and Tuolumne counties, California: Phase IV.* Report submitted to the U.S. National Park Service, Western Region, Tucson, Ariz.

Judge, W. J.
  1971  An interpretative framework for understanding site locations. In *The distribution of prehistoric population aggregates: Proceedings of the First Annual Southwestern Anthropological Research Group,* edited by G. J. Gumerman. *Prescott College Anthropological Reports* No. 1, 38–44.

1972   An archaeological survey of the Chaco Canyon area, San Juan County, New Mexico: Final report. Report submitted to the U.S. National Park Service, Southwestern Region, Santa Fe, N.M. Manuscript.

Judge, W. J., J. I. Ebert, and R. K. Hitchcock
1975   Sampling in regional archaeology survey. In *Sampling in archaeology,* edited by J. W. Mueller. Tucson, Ariz.: Univ. of Arizona Press. Pp. 82–123.

Keller, D. R., and S. M. Wilson
1976   New light on the Tolchaco problem. *The Kiva 41:*225–239.

Kelly, J. H.
1963   Some thoughts on amateur archaeology. *American Antiquity 28:*54–60.

Kelly, R. E., and R. A. Frankel
1974   *An annotated bibliography for "public archeology" in the United States.* Northridge, Calif.: Department of Anthropology, California State University.

Kemrer, S., S. Schultz, and W. Dodge
1972   *An archaeological survey of the Granite-Reef Aqueduct.* Tucson, Ariz.: Bureau of Reclamation, Arizona State Museum, Central Arizona Project. Multilithed.

Kershaw, K. A.
1964   *Quantitative and dynamic ecology.* London: Edward Arnold.

King, C. D., and L. B. King
1973   General research design: Bay Area Archaeological Cooperative. In The southern Santa Clara Valley: A general plan for archaeology, edited by T. F. King and P. P. Hickman. *San Felipe Archaeology 1:*III-1-4.

King, T. F.
1968   County antiquities legislation, New hope for archaeological preservation. *American Antiquity 33:*505–506.
1971   A conflict of values in American archaeology. *American Antiquity 36:*255–262.
1972   A cooperative model for archaeological salvage. Paper presented at the 37th Annual Meeting for the Society for American Archaeology, Miami Beach, Fla.
1973   The direct impacts of San Felipe Division facilities on archeological resources. Unpublished report submitted to the U.S. National Park Service, Western Region, Tucson, Ariz.
1974   The evolution of political differentiation on San Francisco Bay. In *'Antap: California Indian political and economic organization.* Ramona, Calif.: Ballena Press.
1975a  *Cultural resource law and the contract archaeologist: Methods of evaluation and reporting.* Buffalo and Albany, N.Y.: Archaeological Resource Management Service, New York Archaeological Council.
1975b  *Fifty years of archaeology in the California desert: An archaeological overview of Joshua Tree National Monument.* Tucson, Ariz.: U.S. National Park Service, Western Region.
1976a  Political differentiation among hunter-gatherers: An archaeological test. Unpublished Ph.D. dissertation, Univ. of California, Riverside.
1976b  (Review of *Public archeology,* by C. R. McGimsey III). *American Antiquity 41:*236–238.

King, T. F., and P. P. Hickman
1973   The southern Santa Clara Valley: A general plan for archaeology. *San Felipe Archaeology 1.*

King, T. F., P. P. Hickman, and G. C. Berg
n.d.   *Cultural resource management: An anthropological approach.* New York: Academic (in press).

King, T. F., M. J. Moratto, and N. N. Leonard III (compilers)
1973   *Recommended procedures for archaeological impact evaluation.* Society for California Archaeology in cooperation with the Archaeological Survey, Univ. of California, Los Angeles.

Kish, L.
1965   *Survey sampling.* New York: Wiley.

Klinger, T. C.
1975   State support for archaeological research programs in the early 1970's. *American Antiquity 40:*94–97.
n.d.a   The problem of site definition in cultural resource management. *Arkansas Academy of Science,*

*Proceedings* (in press).

n.d.b (Editor) Village Creek: An explicitly regional approach to the study of cultural resources. *Arkansas Archeological Survey, Research Series* (in press).

Klinger, T. C., and C. M. Baker

1975 Contract archaeology: Salvage or science? *Anthropology Newsletter* 16(4):2,12.

Kluckhohn, C.

1940 The conceptual structure in Middle American studies. In *The Maya and their neighbors,* edited by C. L. Hay. Salt Lake: Univ. of Utah Press.

1961 *Mirror for man.* New York: McGraw-Hill.

Knapp, M. L.

1972 *Nonverbal communication in human interaction.* New York: Holt, Rinehart and Winston.

Knudson, R.

1973 Organizational variability in late paleo-Indian assemblages. Doctoral dissertation, Washington State University, Pullman.

Kroeber, A. L.

1925 Handbook of the Indians of California. *Bureau of American Ethnology, Bulletin* No. 78.

1947 *Cultural and natural areas of native North America.* Berkeley, Calif.: Univ. of California Press.

1952 *The nature of culture.* Chicago: Univ. of Chicago Press.

Lazerwitz, B.

1968 Sampling theory and procedures. In *Methodology in social research,* edited by H. M. Blalock, Jr., and A. B. Blalock. New York: McGraw-Hill. Pp. 278–328.

Leatherman, T.

1975 Conservation archeology reports: An evaluation. Manuscript on deposit, Arkansas Archeological Survey, Univ. of Arkansas, Fayetteville.

Lenihan, D. P. (Editor)

1974 *Underwater archeology in the National Park Service, a model for management of submerged cultural resources.* U.S. Department of Interior, National Park Service, Southwestern Region.

Lenihan, D. J., T. Carrell, T. J. Hopkins, A. W. Prokopetz, S. L. Rayl, and C. S. Tarasovic

1977 The national reservoir inundation studies project preliminary report. U.S. Department of Interior, National Park Service, Southwest Cultural Resources Center, Santa Fe, New Mexico.

Lewis, H. T.

1973 Patterns of Indian burning in California. Ecology and ethnohistory. *Ballena Press, Anthropological Papers* 1:1–101.

Lipe, W. D.

1974 A conservation model for American archaeology. *The Kiva* 39(-4):214–245.

1975 The wilderness system and archeological conservation. In The wilderness and cultural values: A symposium, edited by D. F. Green. *U.S. Department of Agriculture, Forest Service, Southwestern Region, Archeological Report* No. 7:7–21.

Lipe, W. D., and A. J. Lindsay, Jr. (Editors)

1974 Proceedings of the 1974 Cultural Resource Management Conference. *Museum of Northern Arizona, Technical Series* No. 14.

Lipe, W. D., and R. G. Matson

1971 Human settlement and resources in the Cedar Mesa area, southeastern Utah. In The distribution of prehistoric population aggregates, edited by G. J. Gumerman. *Prescott College Anthropological Reports* No. 1:126–151.

Livesay, J. A.

1974 Swift Creek Reservoir sites. *The Archeological Society of Virginia, Quarterly Bulletin* 29:21–30.

Longacre, W. A.

1968 Some aspects of prehistoric society in east-central Arizona. In *New perspectives in archeology,* edited by S. and L. Binford. Chicago: Aldine. Pp. 89–102.

1970a Archaeology as anthropology. *Anthropological Papers of the University of Arizona* No. 17.

1970b (Editor) *Reconstructing prehistoric pueblo societies.* Albuquerque, N.M.: Univ. of New Mexico Press.

Longacre, W. A., and R. G. Vivian

1972 Reply to Gruhn. *Science 179:*811-812.

Lord, P., Jr.

1974 *Informational report,* PIN 5115.01, Contract No. Paste 73-7, Section 5D Southern Tier Expressway. Albany, N.Y.: State Museum and Science Service, State Education Department.

Lovis, W. A.

1976 Quarter sections and forests: An example of probability sampling in the northeastern woodlands. *American Antiquity 41:*364-372.

Lowe, C. H. (Editor)

1964 *The vertebrates of Arizona.* Tucson, Ariz.: Univ. of Arizona Press.

Lyon, G. M.

1937 Pinnipeds and a sea otter from the Point Mugu shell mound of California. *Publications of the University of California at Los Angeles in Biological Sciences 1*(8).

Lyons, T. R. (Assembler)

1976 Remote sensing experiments in cultural resource studies: Non-destructive methods of archeological exploration, survey, and analysis. *National Park Service, Chaco Center, Report* 1.

MacDonald, W. K. (Editor)

1976 Digging for gold: Papers on archaeology for profit. *University of Michigan, Museum of Anthropology, Technical Reports* No. 5, *Research Reports in Archaeology, Contribution* No. 2.

MacNeish, R. S.

1964 Ancient Mesoamerican civilization. *Science 143:*531-537.

Mallouf, R. J., D. E. Fox, and A. K. Briggs

1973 An assessment of the cultural resources of Palmetto Bend Reservoir, Jackson County, Texas. *Texas Historical Commission and Texas Water Development Board, Archeological Survey Report* No. 11.

Martin, Paul Schultz

1963 *The last 10,000 years: A fossil pollen record of the American Southwest.* Tucson, Ariz.: Univ. of Arizona Press.

Martin, Paul Sidney, and F. T. Plog

1973 *The archaeology of Arizona: A study of the Southwest region.* Garden City, N.Y.: Doubleday (Natural History Press).

Matheny, R. T., and D. L. Berge

1976a Some problems pertaining to cultural resource management. In Symposium on dynamics of cultural resource management, edited by R. T. Matheny and D. L. Berge. *U.S. Department of Agriculture, Forest Service, Southwestern Region, Archeological Report* No. 10:1-7.

1976b (Editors) Symposium on dynamics of cultural resource management. *U.S. Department of Agriculture, Forest Service, Southwestern Region, Archeological Report* No. 10.

Matson, R. G., and W. D. Lipe

1975 Regional sampling: A case study of Cedar Mesa, Utah. In *Sampling in archaeology,* edited by J. W. Mueller, Tucson, Ariz.: Univ. of Arizona Press. Pp. 124-143.

Matthews, J. M.

1965 Stratigraphic disturbance: The human element. *Antiquity 39:*295-298.

McCall, J. W., III

1972 Cultural evaluation of the proposed Aquilla Creek Reservoir. In *The natural and cultural environmental resources of the Aquilla Creek watershed, Hill County, Texas,* assembled by S. A. Skinner. Dallas, Tex.: Southern Methodist University. Pp. 71-147.

McCormick, L. E., F. W. Taylor, R. C. Smith, and R. Massengale

1965 Sawmills and other wood using plants in Missouri. *Cooperative Extension Service, Extension Division, University of Missouri, in Cooperation with the Missouri Conservation Commission, Circular* No. 834.

McCormick, O. F., III

    1973    The archaeological resources in Lake Monticello area of Titus County, Texas. *Southern Methodist University, Contributions in Anthropology* No. 8.

    1974    *Archaeological excavations at Lake Monticello.* Dallas, Tex.: Archaeology Research Program, Southern Methodist University.

McDonald, J. A., D. A. Phillips, Jr., Y. Stewart, and R. Windmiller

    1974    *An archaeological survey of the Tucson Gas & Electric El Sol-Vail transmission line.* Tucson, Ariz.: Cultural Resource Management Section, Arizona State Museum, Univ. of Arizona.

McGimsey, C. R., III

    1971    Archaeology and the law. *American Antiquity 36:*125–126.

    1972a  *Public archeology.* New York: Seminar Press.

    1972b  Regional overviews and archaeological priorities. Paper presented at the 37th Annual Meeting of the Society for American Archaeology, Miami Beach, Fla.

    1973    *Archeology and archeological resources.* Washington, D.C.: Society for American Archaeology.

    1974    The restructuring of a profession. In Proceedings of the 1974 Cultural Resource Management Conference, edited by W. D. Lipe and A. J. Lindsay, Jr. *Museum of Northern Arizona, Technical Series* No. 14:171–179.

    1975    Peer reviews. In The Cache River Archeological Project: An experiment in contract archeology, assembled by M. B. Schiffer and J. H. House. *Arkansas Archeological Survey, Research Series* No. 8:325–326.

    1976    The past, the present, the future: Public policy as a dynamic interface. In *Anthropology and the public interest: Fieldwork and theory,* edited by P. R. Sanday. New York: Academic. Pp. 25–28.

McGimsey, C. R., III, and H. A. Davis

    1968    Modern land use practices and the archeology of the lower Mississippi alluvial valley. *The Arkansas Archeologist 9:*28–36.

    1977    *The management of archeological resources: The Airlie House report.* Washington, D.C.: Society for American Archaeology.

McGimsey, C. R., III, H. A. Davis, and J. B. Griffin

    1968    *A preliminary evaluation of the status of archeology in the Mississippi alluvial valley.* Fayetteville, Ark.: Arkansas Archeological Survey, Univ. of Arkansas.

McKinney, C. M.

    1976    Cultural resource planning in federal project and land management activities. In Symposium on dynamics of cultural resource management, edited by R. T. Matheny and D. L. Berge. *U.S. Department of Agriculture, Forest Service, Southwestern Region, Archeological Report* No. 10:24–32.

McMillan, B., M. Grady, and W. Lipe (compilers)

    1977    Culture resource management. In *The management of archeological resources: The Airlie House report,* edited by C. R. McGimsey III and H. A. Davis. Washington, D.C.: Society for American Archaeology. Pp. 25–63.

McPherron, A.

    1967    The Juntunen site and the late Woodland prehistory of the upper Great Lakes area. *University of Michigan, Museum of Anthropology, Anthropological Papers* No. 30.

Medford, L. D.

    1972    Agricultural destruction of archeological sites in northeast Arkansas. *Arkansas Archeological Survey, Research Series* No. 3:41–82.

Meighan, C. W.

    1955    Notes on the archaeology of Mono County, California. *University of California, Archaeological Survey, Annual Report 28:*6–28.

Mendel, J. J.

    1961    Timber resources of the eastern Ozarks. *Missouri Agricultural Experiment Station, Bulletin* No. 779.

Mendenhall, W., L. Ott, and R. L. Scheaffer
1971 *Elementary survey sampling.* Belmont, Calif.: Wadsworth.
Merriam, C. H.
1955 *Studies of California Indians.* Berkeley, Calif.: Univ. of California Press.
1967 Ethnographic notes on California Indian tribes, III: Central California Indian tribes. *University of California, Archaeological Survey Reports 68*(3).
Metcalf, M. D.
1973 Final report for Phase II, archaeological impact study, Arizona Nuclear Power Project transmission lines study. Manuscript on deposit, Arizona State Museum Library, Univ. of Arizona, Tucson.
Meyers, J. T.
1970 Chert resources of the lower Illinois Valley. *Illinois State Museum, Reports of Investigations 18* and *Illinois Valley Archeological Program Research Papers 2.*
Miller, D. S.
1974 Certification for archaeologists and amateurs. In Proceedings of the 1974 Cultural Resource Management Conference, edited by W. D. Lipe and A. J. Lindsay, Jr. *Museum of Northern Arizona, Technical Series* No. 14:145-153.
Million, M. G.
1975 Research design for the aboriginal ceramic industries of the Cache River Basin. In The Cache River Archeological Project: An experiment in contract archeology, assembled by M. B. Schiffer and J. H. House. *Arkansas Archeological Survey, Research Series* No. 8:217-222.
Mitchell, J. C.
1974 Social networks. *Annual review of Anthropology 3:*274-299.
Mooney, H. A.
1973 Plant communities and vegetation. In *A flora of the White Mountains, California and Nevada,* edited by R. M. Lloyd and R. S. Mitchell. Berkeley, Calif.: Univ. of California Press. Pp. 7-16.
Moratto, M. J.
1968 A survey of the archaeological resources of the Buchanan Reservoir area, Madera County, California. *Treganza Anthropology Museum Papers 4:*1-121.
1972a A study of prehistory in the southern Sierra Nevada foothills, California. Unpublished Ph.D. dissertation, Univ. of Oregon, Eugene.
1972b Paleodemography in the western Sierra Nevada, California. Paper presented at the 37th Annual Meeting of the Society for American Archaeology, Miami Beach, Fla.
1973 Archaeology in the far west. In Archaeology in the 70's—Mitigating the impact, edited by C. H. Chapman. *The Missouri Archaeologist 35:*19-32.
1975a (Compiler) Conservation archaeology: A bibliography. Sources dealing with public archaeology, archaeological law, ethics in archaeology, cultural resources management, and the relationship between American Indians and archaeologists. *San Franciso State University, Archaeological Research Laboratory, Conservation Archaeology Papers* No. 1.
1975b On the concept of archaeological significance. Paper presented at the Annual Northern California Meeting of the Society for California Archaeology, Fresno.
1976 *New Melones archaeological project—Stanislaus River, Calaveras and Tuolumne counties, California: Phase VI.* Report submitted to the U.S. National Park Service, San Francisco.
Moratto, M., L. Aten, V. Bellancourt, J. Brecher, C. R. McGimsey III, and M. Woolf
1977 A consideration of law in archeology. In *The management of archeological resources: The Airlie House report,* edited by C. R. McGimsey III and H. Davis. Washington, D.C.: Society for American Archaeology. Pp. 8-24.
Moratto, M. J., and L. M. Riley
1974 *An archaeological overview of the New Melones Reservoir project area, Calaveras and Tuolumne counties, California.* San Francisco: Archaeological Research Laboratory, San Francisco State University.

Morenon, E. P., M. Henderson, and J. Nielsen
  1976  The development of conservation techniques and a land use study conducted near Ranchos de Taos, New Mexico. Dallas, Tex.: Fort Burgwin Research Center, Southern Methodist University. (This is also in press in *U.S. Department of Agriculture, Forest Service, Southwestern Region, Archeological Report*.)

Morse, D. F.
  1969  Introducing northeast Arkansas prehistory. *Arkansas Archeologist 10:*12–28.
  1971  Recent indications of Dalton settlement pattern in northeast Arkansas. *Southeastern Archaeological Conference, Bulletin* No. 13:5–10.
  1973a Dalton culture in northeast Arkansas. *Florida Anthropologist 26:*23–38.
  1973b Natives and anthropologists in Arkansas. In Anthropology beyond the university, edited by A. Redfield. *Southern Anthropological Society, Proceedings 7:*26–39.
  1975a Paleo-Indian in the land of opportunity: Preliminary report on the excavations at the Sloan Site (3GE94). In The Cache River Archeological Project: An experiment in contract archeology, assembled by M. B. Schiffer and J. H. House. *Arkansas Archeological Survey, Research Series* No. 8:135–143.
  1975b Research potential in terms of questions of regional prehistory. In The Cache River Archeological Project: An experiment in contract archeology, assembled by M. B. Schiffer and J. H. House. *Arkansas Archeological Survey, Research Series* No. 8:187–198.

Morse, D. F., and P. A. Morse (Assemblers and Editors)
  1976  A preliminary report of the Zebree Project: New approaches in contract archeology in Arkansas, 1975. *Arkansas Archeological Survey, Research Report* No. 8.

Moseley, M. E., and C. J. Mackey
  1972  Peruvian settlement pattern studies and small site methodology. *American Antiquity 37:*67–81.

Moultrie, W.
  1968  *Memoirs of the American revolution.* Volume 1. Reprint. New York: Arno Press. [originally printed by D. Longworth, 1802]

Mueller, J. W.
  1974  The use of sampling in archaeological survey. *Society for American Archaeology, Memoirs* No. 28.
  1975a Archaeological research as cluster sampling. In *Sampling in archaeology*, edited by J. W. Mueller. Tucson, Ariz.: Univ. of Arizona Press. Pp. 33–41.
  1975b (Editor) *Sampling in archaeology.* Tucson, Ariz.: Univ. of Arizona Press.

Neal, L.
  1972  *An archaeological survey and assessment of the prehistoric resources in the Albany and Parker reservoirs, Oklahoma.* Norman, Okla.: Univ. of Oklahoma Press.
  1974  A resurvey of the prehistoric resources of Tenkiller Ferry Lake. *University of Oklahoma, Oklahoma River Basin Survey Project, General Survey Report* No. 13.

Neal, L., and M. B. Mayo
  1974  *A preliminary report on a resurvey of Wister Lake.* Norman, Okla.: Oklahoma River Basin Survey, Univ. of Oklahoma.

Neuschwander, K. M.
  1976  The concerns of industry. In Symposium on dynamics of cultural resource management, edited by R. T. Matheny and D. L. Berg. *U.S. Department of Agriculture, Forest Service, Southwestern Region, Archeological Report* No. 10:44–54.

Nie, N. D., H. Bent, and C. H. Hull
  1970  *Statistical package for the social sciences.* New York: McGraw-Hill.

Niering, W. H., R. H. Whittaker, and C. H. Lowe
  1963  The saguaro: A population in relation to environment. *Science 142:*15–23.

Noël, H. I.
  1962  An Indian ware of the colonial period. *Archaeological Society of Virginia, Quarterly Bulletin 17*(1).

Nunely, P., and T. R. Hester
  1975  An assessment of archaeological resources in portions of Starr County, Texas. *University of*

*Texas at San Antonio, Center for Archaeological Research, Archaeological Survey Report* No. 7.

O'Connell, J. F.
1976   *The prehistory of Surprise Valley.* Ramona, Calif.: Ballena Press.

Odum, E. P.
1971   *Fundamentals of ecology* (3rd ed.). Philadelphia: Saunders.

Oosting, H. J.
1956   *The study of plant communities.* San Francisco: Freeman.

Our sister towns
1899   *The Doniphan* (Mo.) *Prospect-News.* April 13, 1899.

Padgett, T. J.
1976   Dierks Lake: A problem study in cultural resource management. Manuscript on deposit, Arkansas Archeological Survey, Univ. of Arkansas, Fayetteville.

Parcher, F. M.
1930   The Indians of Inyo County. *Southwest Museum Masterkey 4:*146–153.

Parl, B.
1967   *Basic statistics.* Garden City, N.Y.: Doubleday.

Pastron, A. G., P. S. Hallinan, and C. W. Clewlow, Jr. (Editors)
1973   The crisis in North American archaeology. *The Kroeber Anthropological Society, Special Publication* No. 3.

Payden, L. A.
1964   ''Pipe'' artifacts from Sierra Nevada mortuary caves. *Cave Notes 6:*25–32.

Payden, L. A., and J. J. Johnson
1965   Current cave research in the central Sierra Nevada Mountains: A progress report. *Sacramento Anthropological Society, Papers 3:*26–35.

Peak, A. S.
1973   New Melones Reservoir archaeological project, Calaveras and Tuolumne counties, California: Phase III. Report submitted to the U.S. National Park Service, Western Region, Tucson, Ariz.

Perino, G.
1972   An historical cultural assessment of the proposed Birch reservoir, Osage County, Oklahoma. Manuscript on deposit, Arkansas Archeological Survey, Univ. of Arkansas, Fayetteville.

Peterson, N. A.
1970   The importance of women in determining the composition of residential groups in aboriginal Australia. In *Women's role in aboriginal society,* edited by F. Gale. Canberra: Australian Institute of Aboriginal Studies. Pp. 9–16.

Phillips, B. S.
1966   *Social research—Strategy and tactics.* New York: Macmillan.

Phillips, P., J. A. Ford, and J. B. Griffin
1951   Archaeological survey in the lower Mississippi alluvial valley, 1940–1947. *Peabody Museum of American Archaeology and Ethnology, Harvard University, Papers* No. 25.

Pielou, E. C.
1969   *An introduction to mathematical ecology.* New York: Wiley.

Pierson, L. M.
1976   Rangeland archeology and the BLM. *Rangeman's Journal 3:*79–80.

Pilles, P. J., Jr., and P. Haas
1973   Cultural resource impact statement for archaeological, ethnohistorical and historical resources of the Cholla Power Plant proposed expansion area. Manuscript on deposit, Arizona State Museum Library, Univ. of Arizona, Tucson.

Platt, J. R.
1965   The step to man. *Science 149:*607–13.

Plog, F. T.
1974a  Settlement patterns and social history. In *Frontiers of anthropology,* edited by M. Leaf. New York: Van Nostrand. Pp. 68–92.
1974b  *The study of prehistoric change.* New York: Academic.
1975   Archeology and cultural resource management: Issues in archeological training. Paper pre-

sented at the 74th Annual Meeting of the American Anthropological Association, San Francisco.

Plog, F. T., and J. N. Hill
1971 Explaining variability in the distribution of sites. In The distribution of prehistoric population aggregates, edited by G. J. Gumerman. *Prescott College, Anthropological Reports* No. 1:7–36.

Plog, F., and M. Stewart
1974 Methodological issues in the SUNY-Binghamton salvage program. Manuscript on deposit, Public Archaeology Facility, State University of New York at Binghamton.

Plog, S.
1976a The relative efficiencies of sampling techniques for archaeological surveys. In *The early Mesoamerican village*, edited by K. V. Flannery. New York: Academic. Pp. 136–158.
1976b Review II. In Orme Alternatives: The archaeological resources of Roosevelt Lake and Horseshoe Reservoir, edited by S. L. Fuller, A. E. Rogge, and L. M. Gregonis. *Arizona State Museum, Archaeological Series* No. 98:277–281.
n.d. Sampling in archaeological surveys: A critique of Mueller. Manuscript submitted for publication.

Polyani, L.
1948 *The great transformation*. New York: Rinehart and Co.

Poole, W.
1974 *An introduction to quantitative ecology*. New York: McGraw-Hill.

Pottenger, C. A.
1945 Place names of five southern border counties of Missouri. Unpublished M.A. thesis, Univ. of Missouri, Columbia.

Prewitt, E. R.
1972 An assessment of the archaeological and paleontological resources of Lake Texoma, Texas-Oklahoma. *Texas Archaeological Salvage Project, Survey Reports* No. 10.
1974 Upper Navasota Reservoir: An archeological assessment. *Texas Archeological Survey, Research Report* No. 47.

Prewitt, E. R., and D. Dibble
1974 The San Felipe Creek watershed project, Val Verde County, Texas: An archeological survey. *Texas Archeological Survey, Research Report* No. 40.

Prewitt, E. R., and K. A. Grombacher
1974 An archeological and historical assessment of the areas to be affected by the proposed Twin Oak and Oak Knoll Project, east-central Texas. *Texas Archeological Survey, Research Report* No. 43.

Prewitt, E. R., and D. A. Lawson
1972 An assessment of the archeological and paleontological resources of Lake Texoma, Texas-Oklahoma. *Texas Archeological Salvage Project, Survey Reports* No. 10.

Price, J. E., C. R. Price, J. Cottier, S. Harris, and J. House
1975 *An assessment of the cultural resources of the Little Black watershed*. Columbia, Mo.: Univ. of Missouri.

Price, J. E., C. R. Price, and S. E. Harris
1976 *An assessment of the cultural resources of the Fourche Creek watershed*. Columbia, Mo.: Southeast Missouri Archaeological Research Facility, Univ. of Missouri.

Raab, L. M.
1973a A research design for the field investigation of archaeological resources recorded in the Santa Rosa Wash project area: Phase I. Manuscript on deposit, Arizona State Museum Library, Univ. of Arizona, Tucson.
1973b AZ AA:5:2: A prehistoric cactus camp in Papagueria. *Journal of the Arizona Academy of Science 8*:116–118.
1974a Archaeological investigations for the Santa Rosa Wash project, Phase I preliminary report. Manuscript on deposit, Arizona State Museum Library, Univ. of Arizona, Tucson.
1974b Test excavations at AZ U:8:8 (ASU), Roosevelt Lake, Arizona: Final report. Manuscript on

deposit, Arizona State Museum Library, Univ. of Arizona, Tucson.

1975    A prehistoric water reservoir from Santa Rosa Wash, southern Arizona. *The Kiva 40:*295–307.

1976a   Archeological sample survey of the Caddo planning unit, Ouachita National Forest, Arkansas. Manuscript on deposit, Arkansas Archeological Survey, Univ. of Arkansas, Fayetteville.

1976b   A methodological note on excavations in bluff shelters. In Pine Mountain: A study of prehistoric human ecology in the Arkansas Ozarks, compiled by L. M. Raab. *Arkansas Archeological Survey, Research Report* No. 7:171–175.

1976c   (Compiler) Pine Mountain: A study of prehistoric human ecology in the Arkansas Ozarks. *Arkansas Archeological Survey, Research Report* No. 7.

1976d   Results of the 1975 survey and testing program. In Pine Mountain: A study of prehistoric human ecology in the Arkansas Ozarks, compiled by L. M. Raab. *Arkansas Archeological Survey, Research Report* No. 7:52–84.

1976e   The structure of prehistoric community organization at Santa Rosa Wash, southern Arizona. Ph.D. dissertation, Arizona State University, Tempe.

Raab, L. M., and T. C. Klinger

n.d.    A critical appraisal of "significance" in contract archaeology. *American Antiquity* (in press).

Ragir, S.

1975    A review of techniques for archaeological sampling. In *Field methods in archaeology* (3rd ed.), edited by T. R. Hester, R. F. Heizer, and J. A. Graham. Palo Alto, Calif.: Mayfield. Pp. 283–299.

Rahtz, P. A.

1974    *RESCUE archaeology.* Middlesex, England: Penguin.

Read, D. W.

1975    Regional sampling. In *Sampling in archaeology,* edited by J. W. Mueller. Tucson, Ariz.: Univ. of Arizona Press. Pp. 45–60.

Reaves, R. W., III

1976    Historic preservation laws and policies: Background and history. In Symposium on dynamics of cultural resource management, edited by R. T. Matheny and D. L. Berge. *U.S. Department of Agriculture, Forest Service, Southwestern Region, Archeological Report* No. 10:15–23.

Redman, C. L.

1973    Multistage field work and analytical techniques. *American Antiquity 38*(1):61–79.

1974    Archeological sampling strategies. *Addison-Wesley Modular Publications in Anthropology* No. 55.

Redman, C. R., and P. J. Watson

1970    Systematic, intensive surface collection. *American Antiquity 35:*279–291.

Reher, C. A. (Editor)

n.d.    *Settlement and subsistence along the lower Chaco River: The CGP survey.* Albuquerque, N.M.: Univ. of New Mexico Press (in press).

Reher, C. A., and D. Witter

n.d.    Archaic settlement and vegetative diversity. In *Settlement and subsistence along the lower Chaco River,* edited by C. A. Reher. Albuquerque, N.M.: Univ. of New Mexico Press. Pp. 000–000.

Reid, J. J.

1973    Growth and response to stress at Grasshopper Pueblo, Arizona. Ph.D. dissertation, Univ. of Arizona, Tucson. (University Microfilms No. 73-28786)

1975    Comments on environment and behavior at Antelope House. In Environment and behavior at Antelope House, edited by J. T. Rock and D. P. Morris. *The Kiva 41:*127–132.

Reid, J. J., M. B. Schiffer, and J. M. Neff

1975    Archaeological considerations of intrasite sampling. In *Sampling in archaeology,* edited by J. W. Mueller. Tucson, Ariz.: Univ. of Arizona Press. Pp. 209–224.

Reid, J. J., M. B. Schiffer and W. L. Rathje

1975    Behavioral archeology: Four strategies. *American Anthropologist 77:*864–869.

Renfrew, C.

1969    Trade and culture process in European prehistory. *Current Anthropology 10:*151–160.

1973   Social archeology. An inaugural lecture presented at the University of Southhampton, England, March 20, 1973.

Reynolds, W. E.

1974   *Archaeological investigations at Arizona U:9:45 (ASM): A limited activity site.* Tucson, Ariz.: Cultural Resource Management Section, Arizona State Museum, Univ. of Arizona.

Reynolds, W. E., S. Sobelman, M. McCarthy, and G. Kinkade

1974   Archaeological investigations at Jackrabbit Mine: Preliminary report. Manuscript on deposit, Arizona State Museum Library, Univ. of Arizona, Tucson.

Ritchie, W. A., and R. E. Funk

1973   Aboriginal settlement patterns in the Northeast. *New York State Museum and Science Service, Memoir* No. 20.

Ritter, D. F., W. F. Kinsey III, and M. E. Kauffman

1973   Overbank sedimentation in the Delaware River valley during the last 6000 years. *Science 179:*374–375.

Ritter, E. W., and H. Hanks

1976   Archaeological probability sampling and multiple-use planning in the California desert. Paper presented at the 1976 Annual Meeting of the Society for California Archaeology, San Diego.

Rock, J. T.

1975   The Canyon del Muerto study. Paper presented at the 40th Annual Meeting of the Society for American Archaeology, Dallas, Texas.

1976   *The Klamath archaeological program: A position paper.* U.S. Department of Agriculture, U.S. Forest Service, Klamath National Forest, California.

Rodgers, J. B.

1974   An archaeological survey of the Cave Buttes dam alternative site and reservoir, Arizona. *Arizona State University, Anthropological Research Paper* No. 8.

Rohn, A. H., and M. R. Smith

1972   *Assessment of the archaeological resources and an evaluation of the impact of construction of the Copan Dam and Lake.* Wichita, Kans.: Archaeology Laboratory, Wichita State University.

Rootenberg, S.

1964   Archaeological field sampling. *American Antiquity 30:*181–188.

Roper, D. C.

1976   Lateral displacement of artifacts due to plowing. *American Antiquity 41:*372–375.

Ross, N. A. (Compiler and Editor)

1973   *Index to the expert testimony before the Indian claims commission: The written reports.* New York: Clearwater.

Ross, W.

1941   The present day dietary habits of the Papago Indians. Unpublished M.A. thesis, Univ. of Arizona, Tucson.

Rothschild, N. A.

1976   Stranger in a strange land: A consideration of survey and sampling. Paper presented at the 41st Annual Meeting of the Society for American Archaeology, St. Louis.

Rudy, J. R.

1976   National Environmental Policy Act and cultural resources. In Symposium on dynamics of cultural resource management, edited by R. T. Matheny and D. L. Berge. *U.S. Department of Agriculture, Forest Service, Southwestern Region, Archeological Report* No. 10:38–43.

Ruppé, R. J.

1966   The archaeological survey: A defense. *American Antiquity 31:*313–333.

Ruppé, R. J., and D. F. Green

1975   Feasibility study: Effects of inundation on cultural resources. A research proposal for Roosevelt Lake, Arizona. Tempe, Ariz.: Arizona State University and Albuquerque, N.M.: U.S. Department of Agriculture, Forest Service.

Russell, F.

1908   The Pima Indians. *Bureau of American Ethnology, Annual Report 26:*3–390.

Ryan, T. M.
1972 Archeological survey of the Columbia Zoological Park, Richland and Lexington counties, South Carolina. *University of South Carolina, Institute of Archeology and Anthropology, Notebook 6:*141–183.

Ryan, W. R.
1973 *Personal adventures in upper and lower California in 1848–9.* New York: Arno Press.

Sahlins, M.
1965 On the sociology of primitive exchange. In *The relevance of models to social anthropology,* edited by M. Banton. *Association of Social Anthropologists Monographs* No. 1.

Saucier, R. T.
1974 Quaternary geology of the lower Mississippi alluvial valley. *Arkansas Archeological Survey, Research Series* No. 6.

Scantling, F. H.
1939 Jackrabbit run. *The Kiva 5:*9–12.

Schiffer, M. B.
1972a Archaeological context and systemic context. *American Antiquity 37:*156–165.
1972b Cultural laws and the reconstruction of past lifeways. *The Kiva 37:*148–157.
1975a An alternative to Morse's Dalton settlement pattern hypothesis. *Plains Anthropologist 20:*253–266.
1975b Archeological research and contract archeology. In The Cache River Archeological Project: An experiment in contract archeology, assembled by M. B. Schiffer and J. H. House. *Arkansas Archeological Survey, Research Series* No. 8, 1–7.
1975c Arrangement vs. seriation of sites: A new approach to relative temporal relationships. In The Cache River Archeological Project: An experiment in contract archeology, assembled by M. B. Schiffer and J. H. House. *Arkansas Archeological Survey, Research Series* No. 8:257–263.
1975d The effects of occupation span on site content. In The Cache River Archeological Project: An experiment in contract archeology, assembled by M. B. Schiffer and J. H. House. *Arkansas Archeological Survey, Research Series* No. 8:265–269.
1975e Introduction. In The Cache River Archeological Project: An experiment in contract archeology, assembled by M. B. Schiffer and J. H. House. *Arkansas Archeological Survey, Research Series* No. 8.
1975f Mitigating adverse impacts of the channelization project. In The Cache River Archeological Project: An experiment in contract archeology, assembled by M. B. Schiffer and J. H. House. *Arkansas Archeological Survey, Research Series* No. 8:293–297.
1975g The philosophy of mitigation. In The Cache River Archeological Project: An experiment in contract archeology, assembled by M. B. Schiffer and J. H. House. *Arkansas Archeological Survey, Research Series* No. 8:289–292.
1975h Some further comments on the Dalton settlement pattern hypothesis. In The Cache River Archeological Project: An experiment in contract archeology, assembled by M. B. Schiffer and J. H. House. *Arkansas Archeological Survey, Research Series* No. 8:103–112.
1976 *Behavioral archeology.* New York: Academic Press.
n.d. Toward a unified science of the cultural past. In *Research strategies in historical archeology,* edited by S. South. New York: Academic Press (in press).

Schiffer, M. B., and J. H. House
1975a The Cache River Archaeological Project: Archaeological research and cultural resource management. Paper presented at the Annual Meeting of the Society for American Archaeology, Dallas, Texas.
1975b (Assemblers) The Cache River Archeological Project: An experiment in contract archeology. *Arkansas Archeological Survey, Research Series* No. 8:289–301.
1975c Direct impacts of the channelization project on the archeological resources. In The Cache River Archeological Project: An experiment in contract archeology, assembled by M. B. Schiffer and J. H. House. *Arkansas Archeological Survey, Research Series* No. 8:273–275.
1975d General estimates of the nature and extent of the archeological resources. In The Cache River

Archeological Project: An experiment in contract archeology, assembled by M. B. Schiffer and J. H. House. *Arkansas Archeological Survey, Research Series* No. 8:147–151.

1975e  Indirect impacts of the channelization project on the archeological resources. In The Cache River Archeological Project: An experiment in contract archeology, assembled by M. B. Schiffer and J. H. House. *Arkansas Archeological Survey, Research Series* No. 8:277–282.

1977  Cultural resource management and archeological research: The Cache project. *Current Anthropology* 18:43–68.

Schiffer, M. B., and W. L. Rathje
1973  Efficient exploitation of the archeological record: Penetrating problems. In *Research and theory in current archeology,* edited by C. L. Redman. New York: Wiley. Pp. 169–179.

Schnell, F. T.
1969  Reservoir resurvey: A relatively unexplored potential. *Southeastern Archaeological Conference, Bulletin* No. 11:55–57.

1975  An archaeological survey of Lake Blackshear. *Southeastern Archaeological Conference, Bulletin* No. 18:117–122.

Schoenwetter, J., S. W. Gaines, and D. E. Weaver, Jr.
1973  Definition and preliminary study of the Midvale site. *Arizona State University, Anthropological Research Paper* No. 6.

Scholtz, J. A.
1968  Archeological sites and land leveling in eastern Arkansas. *The Arkansas Archeologist 9:*1–9.

Scovill, D. H.
1974  History of archaeological conservation and the Moss Bennett bill. In Proceedings of the 1974 Cultural Resource Management Conference, edited by W. D. Lipe and A. J. Lindsay, Jr. *Museum of Northern Arizona, Technical Series* No. 14:1–11.

Scovill, D. H., G. J. Gordon, and K. M. Anderson
1972  *Guidelines for the preparation of statements of environmental impact on archeological resources.* Tucson, Ariz.: Arizona Archeological Center, U.S. National Park Service.

Settergren, C., and R. E. McDermott
1962  Trees of Missouri. *University of Missouri Agricultural Experiment Station, Bulletin* No. 767.

Shenk, L. O., and G. A. Teague
1975  Excavations at the Tubac Presidio. *Arizona State Museum, Archaeological Series* No. 85.

Shreve, F.
1951  Vegetation of the Sonoran Desert. Volume 1. *Carnegie Institute of Washington, Publication* No. 591.

Siegel, D. N., and J. E. Bradford
1974  Salt River Project, Coronado Generating Station Project, state and private lands, Apache and Navajo counties, Arizona: Final report for Phase I and II archaeological and ethnohistorical research. Manuscript on deposit, Arizona State Museum Library, Univ. of Arizona, Tucson.

Skinner, S. A., and M. B. Cliff
1973  *Archaeological survey of the Blue Hills Station, Newton County, Texas.* Dallas, Tex.: Archaeology Research Program, Southern Methodist University.

Skinner, S. A., and J. Gallagher
1974  An evaluation of the archaeological resources at Lake Whitney, Texas. *Southern Methodist University, Contributions in Anthropology* No. 14.

Skinner, S. A., and G. K. Humphreys
1973  The historic and prehistoric archaeological resources of the Squaw Creek Reservoir. *Southern Methodist University, Contributions in Anthropology* No. 10.

Smith, V. L.
1972  Dynamics of waste accumulation: Disposal versus recycling. *The Quarterly Journal of Economics 86:*600–616.

Sobelman, S.
1973  Archaeological survey in the Vekol Mountains, Papago Reservation. Manuscript on deposit, Arizona State Museum Library, Univ. of Arizona, Tucson.

Society for American Archaeology
1961   Four statements for archaeology. *American Antiquity 27:*137–138.

Society of Professional Archeologists
1976   *The Society of Professional Archeologists.* Washington, D.C.: Society for American Archaeology.

South, S.
1964   Analysis of the buttons from Brunswick Town and Fort Fisher. *The Florida Anthropologist 17*(2):113–133.

1972   Evolution and horizon as revealed in ceramic analysis in historical archeology. *The Conference on Historic Site Archeology Papers 1971.* Volume 6. Columbia, S.C.: Institute of Archeology and Anthropology, Univ. of South Carolina.

1974a  Historical archeology reports: A plea for a new direction. In Historical archeology papers: Method and theory, by S. South. *University of South Carolina, Institute of Archeology and Anthropology, Research Manuscript Series* No. 64.

1974b  Palmetto Parapets. *University of South Carolina, Institute of Archeology and Anthropology, Anthropological Studies* No. 1.

1977a  *Method and theory in historical archeology.* New York: Academic.

1977b  *Research strategies in historical archeology.* New York: Academic.

1977c  Research strategies in historical archeology: The scientific paradigm. In *Research strategies in historical archeology,* edited by S. South. New York: Academic.

Southwestern Anthropological Research Group
1974   SARG: A co-operative approach towards understanding the location of human settlement. *World Archaeology 6:*107–116.

Southwood, T. R. E.
1966   *Ecological methods.* London: Chapman and Hall.

Spears, C. S.
1975   Hammers, nuts and jolts, cobbles, cobbles, cobbles: Experiments in cobble technologies in search of correlates. In Arkansas Eastman Archeological Project, by Charles M. Baker. *Arkansas Archeological Survey, Research Reports* No. 6:83–116.

Spears, C. S., and C. Claassen
1974   Tennessee Eastman Archeological Project, Phase I preliminary field survey of direct impact zone. Manuscript on deposit, Arkansas Archeological Survey, Univ. of Arkansas, Fayetteville.

Stacy, V. K. P., and J. Hayden
1975   *Saguaro National Monument: An archeological overview.* Tucson, Ariz.: Arizona Archeological Center, U.S. National Park Service.

Stacy, V. K. P., and W. Palm
1970   Partial archaeological survey of the proposed Tat Momolikot Dam and Lake St. Clair, Papago Indian Reservation. Manuscript on deposit, Arizona State Museum Library, Univ. of Arizona, Tucson.

Stephenson, R. L.
1975   An archeological preservation plan for South Carolina. *University of South Carolina, Institute of Archeology and Anthropology, Research Manuscript Series* No. 84.

n.d.   A strategy for getting the job done. In *Research strategies in historical archeology,* edited by S. South. New York: Academic.

Steward, J. H.
1933   Ethnography of the Owens Valley Paiute. *University of California, Publications in American Archaeology and Ethnology 33:*233–350.

1934   Two Paiute autobiographies. *University of California, Publications in American Archaeology and Ethnology 33:*423–438.

1938   Basin–Plateau aboriginal socio-political groups. *Bureau of American Ethnology, Bulletin* No. 120.

1955   *Theory of culture change.* Urbana, Ill.: Univ. of Illinois Press.

Stewart, Y. G., and S. Purves
1975 Coronado National Memorial survey report. Manuscript on deposit, Arizona State Museum Library, Univ. of Arizona, Tucson.

Stewart, Y. G., and L. S. Teague
1974 *An ethnoarchaeological study of the Vekol Copper Mining Project.* Tucson, Ariz.: Cultural Resource Management Section, Arizona State Museum, Univ. of Arizona.

Stockton, E. D.
1973 Shaw's Creek Shelter: Human displacement of artefacts and its significance. *Mankind 9:* 112–117.

Stone, L. M., and D. J. Opfenring
1975 *An archaeological reconnaissance survey near Heber, Arizona.* Tempe, Ariz.: Archaeological Research Services.

Street, J. M.
1969 An evaluation of the concept of carrying capacity. *Professional Geographer 21:* 104–107.

Struever, S.
1968a Problems, methods and organization: A disparity in the growth of archeology. In *Anthropological archeology in the Americas,* edited by B. J. Meggers. Washington, D.C.: Anthropological Society of Washington. Pp. 131–151.
1968b Woodland subsistence–settlement systems in the lower Illinois Valley. In *New perspectives in archeology,* edited by S. R. and L. R. Binford. Chicago: Aldine.
1971 Comments on archaeological data requirements and research strategy. *American Antiquity 36:* 9–19.

Sullivan, A. P.
1976 The structure of archaeological inference: A critical examination of logic and procedure. Manuscript on deposit, Arizona State Museum Library, Univ. of Arizona, Tucson.

Sullivan, A. P., and M. B. Schiffer
n.d. A critical examination of SARG. In Investigations of the Southwestern Anthropological Research Group, edited by R. C. Euler and G. J. Gumerman. Flagstaff, Ariz.: Museum of Northern Arizona.

Swartz, B. K., Jr.
1967 A logical sequence of archaeological objectives. *American Antiquity 32:* 487–497.

Taylor, R. A.
1975 Survey for buried Paleo-Indian sites in Arkansas. In The Cache River Archeological Project: An experiment in contract archeology, assembled by M. B. Schiffer and J. H. House. *Arkansas Archeological Survey, Research Series* No. 8: 199–203.

Taylor, W. W.
1967 *A study of archeology.* Carbondale, Ill.: Southern Illinois University Press.

Texas Archaeological Salvage Project Staff
1971 Archeological resource valuations, Laneport and Wallisville reservoirs, Texas. Texas Archaeological Survey, Univ. of Texas, Austin. Manuscript.

Thackery, F. A., and A. R. Leding
1929 The giant cactus of Arizona: The uses of its fruit and other cactus fruits by the Indians. *Journal of Heredity 20:* 400–414.

Thomas, D. H.
1972 A computer simulation model of Great Basin Shoshonean subsistence and settlement patterns. In *Models in archaeology,* edited by D. L. Clarke. London: Methuen. Pp. 671–704.
1973 An empirical test for Steward's model of Great Basin settlement patterns. *American Antiquity 38:* 155–176.
1975 Nonsite sampling in archaeology: Up the creek without a site? In *Sampling in archaeology,* edited by J. W. Mueller. Tucson, Ariz.: Univ. of Arizona Press. Pp. 61–81.

Thompson, J. H.
1966 *Geography of New York State.* Syracuse: Syracuse University Press.

Thompson, R. H.
1974 Institutional responsibilities in conservation archaeology. In Proceedings of the 1974 Cultural

Resource Management Conference, edited by W. D. Lipe and A. J. Lindsay, Jr. *Museum of Northern Arizona, Technical Papers* No. 14:13–24.

Toney, J. T.
1975 Archeological evaluation of the Garner–Pangburn Tap Line construction project. White County, Arkansas, by Arkansas Power and Light Company. Manuscript on deposit, Arkansas Archeological Survey, Univ. of Arkansas, Fayetteville.

Tringham, R., G. Cooper, G. Odell, B. Voytek, and A. Whitman
1974 Experimentation in the formation of edge damage: A new approach to lithic analysis. *Journal of Field Archaeology 1:*171–196.

Trubowitz, N. L.
1974 Instrumental and chemical methods of site survey and testing in the Allegheny and Genesee River valleys. *Eastern States Archeological Federation, Bulletin* No. 33, 12–13.

Trubowitz, N. L., and P. E. Snethkamp
1975 New evidence of the Frost Island phase in the lower Genesee Valley. *New York State Archeological Association, Bulletin* No. 65:19–26.

Trubowitz, N. L.
n.d. The persistence of settlement pattern in a cultivated field. In *memorial volume for Dr. Marian E. White*, edited by W. Engelbrecht and D. Grayson.

Tuck, J. A.
1971a The Iroquois Confederacy. *Scientific American 224*(2):32–42.
1971b Onandaga Iroquois prehistory. Syracuse: Syracuse University Press.

Tuggle, H. D., A. H. Townsend, and T. J. Riley
1972 Laws, systems, and research designs: A discussion of explanation in archaeology. *American Antiquity 37:*3–12.

UNESCO
1970 *Protection of mankind's cultural heritage: Sites and monuments.* Paris: UNESCO.

U.S. Department of Agriculture, Forest Service
1941 *Annual report.* Tucson, Ariz.: Southwestern Forest and Range Experimental Station.

U.S. Department of Agriculture, Soil Conservation Service
1974a Draft environmental impact statement, Little Black watersheds, Butler, Carter, and Ripley counties, Missouri and Clay County, Arkansas. Prepared by the U.S. Department of Agriculture, Soil Conservation Service, Columbia, Mo.
1974b Work plan, upper Little Black watershed. Unpublished work plan prepared by the U.S. Department of Agriculture, Soil Conservation Service, Columbia, Mo.
1974c Work plan for watershed protection, floor prevention, agricultural water management and nonagricultural water management (recreational development), lower Little Black watershed, Butler, and Ripley counties, Missouri, Clay County, Arkansas. Prepared by the U.S. Department of Agriculture, Soil Conservation Service, Columbia, Mo.
1974d Work plan for watershed protection, flood prevention and recreational development, upper Little Black watershed, Butler, Carter and Ripley counties, Missouri. Prepared by the U.S. Department of Agriculture, Soil Conservation Service, Columbia, Mo.

U.S. Department of the Army
1972 *Final environmental statement, Cache River basin feature, Mississippi River and tributaries project, Arkansas.* Washington, D.C.: Office of the Chief of Engineers.
1973 *Draft environmental impact statement, Cache River Basin Project, Arkansas.* Memphis, Tenn.: Corps of Engineers.
1974 *Final environmental impact statement, Cache River Basin Project, Arkansas.* Memphis, Tenn.: Corps of Engineers.

U.S. Department of Interior
1976 National Register of Historic Places: Criteria for statewide surveys and plans. Draft regulation circulated for comment by the Office of Archeology and Historic Preservation, National Park Service, Washington.

U.S. National Park Service, Interagency Archeological Services Division
1976 *A status report to the archeological community,* by R. L. Wilson, Washington, D.C.

Vayda, A. P., and R. Rappaport
    1968    Ecology, cultural and noncultural. In *Introduction to cultural anthropology,* edited by J. A.
            Clifton. Boston: Houghton-Mifflin. Pp. 277–297.
Verner, R. S.
    1976    Problems in resource management. In Symposium on dynamics of cultural resource manage-
            ment, edited by R. T. Matheny and D. L. Berge. *U.S. Department of Agriculture, Forest
            Service, Southwestern Region, Archeological Report* No. 10:33–37.
Vescelius, G. S.
    1960    Archaeological sampling: A problem in statistical inference. In *Essays in the science of culture
            in honor of Leslie A. White,* edited by G. E. Dole and R. L. Carniero. New York: Crowell. Pp.
            457–470.
Vivian, R. G.
    1970    An inquiry into prehistoric social organization in Chaco Canyon, New Mexico. In *Reconstruct-
            ing prehistoric Pueblo societies,* edited by W. A. Longacre. Albuquerque, N.M.: Univ. of
            New Mexico Press. Pp. 59–83.
Vivian, R. G., K. Anderson, H. Davis, R. Edwards, M. B. Schiffer, and S. South
    1977    Guidelines for the preparation and evaluation of archeological report. In The *management of
            archeological resources: The Airlie House report* edited by C. R. McGimsey III and H. A.
            Davis. Washington, D.C.: Society for American Archaeology. Pp. 64–77.
Wait, W. K.
    1976    The Star Lake Archaeological Project: A progress report. Paper presented at the 41st Annual
            Meeting of the Society for American Archaeology, St. Louis.
Wasley, W. A., and A. E. Johnson
    1965    Salvage archaeology in Painted Rocks Reservoir, western Arizona. *Anthropological Papers of
            the University of Arizona* No. 9.
Watson, P. J., S. A. LeBlanc, and C. L. Redman
    1971    *Explanation in archeology.* New York: Columbia University Press.
Webb, M. C.
    1974    Exchange networks: Prehistory. In *Annual review of anthropology 3:*357–383.
Weide, M. L.
    1973    *Archaeological inventory of the California desert: A proposed methodology.* Riverside, Calif.:
            Univ. of California, Archaeological Research Unit.
    1975    Research design in northeastern prehistory. Manuscript on deposit, Public Archaeology Facil-
            ity, State University of New York at Binghamton.
Weston, D. E.
    1974    An archaeological survey of the proposed Quanicassee nuclear power plant transmission line
            routes. *Michigan History Division, Archaeological Survey Reports* No. 3.
White, J. P., and D. H. Thomas
    1972    What mean these stones? Ethno-taxonomic models and archaeological interpretations in the
            New Guinea highlands. In *Models in Archaeology,* edited by David L. Clark. London: Me-
            thuen. Pp. 275–308.
White, L.
    1949    *The science of culture.* New York: Grove.
White, M. E.
    1974    A response to *Informational Report* of September 24, 1974, on Section 5D of the Southern
            Tier Expressway. Buffalo, N.Y.: Department of Anthropology, State University of New
            York.
Whittaker, R. H., and W. A. Niering
    1965    Vegetation of the Santa Catalina Mountains, Arizona: A gradient analysis of the south slope.
            *Ecology 46:*429–452.
Wihebrink, R.
    1974    *History of Whites Creek and the Irish Wilderness.* Mark Twain National Forest, Missouri. U.S.
            Department of Agriculture, Forest Service.

Wildesen, L. E.
1974 Archaeologists and planners: The uses and misuses of predictive models. Paper presented at the 1974 Annual Meeting of the Society for California Archaeology, Riverside.
1975 Conservation vs. preservation of archeological sites. *American Society for Conservation Archeology, Newsletter 2*(2):9–11.

Wilke, P. J., T. F. King, and S. Hammond
1975 Aboriginal occupation at Tahquitz Canyon: Ethnohistory and archaeology. *Ballena Press, Anthropological Papers 3* (Part 2).

Williams, K. R.
1976 A preliminary assessment of techniques applied in the FAI-255 survey. Paper presented at the 40th Annual Meeting of the Society for American Archaeology, St. Louis.

Williams, R.
1968 *Southeast Missouri land leveling salvage archaeology: 1967.* Columbia, Mo.: Univ. of Missouri, Archaeological Research Division.
1972 *Land leveling salvage archaeology in Missouri: 1968.* Columbia, Mo.: Univ. of Missouri, Archaeological Research Division.

Wilmsen, E. N.
1973 Interaction, spacing behavior, and the organization of hunting bands. *Journal of Anthropological Research 29:*1–31.
1974 *Lindenmeier: A Pleistocene hunting society.* New York: Harper & Row.

Wilshire, H. G., and J. K. Nakata
1976 Off-road vehicle effects on California's Mojave Desert. *California Geology,* June 1976, pp. 123–132.

Wilson, D.
1975 The new archaeology. New York: Knopf.

Windmiller, R.
1975 Archaeological investigations for the Two Forks Dam and Reservoir Alternative, Colorado: Third progress report and recommendations for mitigation. Manuscript on deposit, Arizona State Museum Library, Univ. of Arizona, Tucson.

Wither, A. M.
1944 Excavations at Valshni village, a site on the Papago Indian Reservation. *American Antiquity. 10:*33–47.

Witty, T. A.
1973 Sites destroyed by inundation. *Newsletter of the Missouri Archaeological Society 270*(April 1973):3.

Wood, D. G.
1971 A summary of the recorded archaeological sites on the Gila River Indian Reservation. Manuscript on deposit, Arizona State Museum Library, Univ. of Arizona, Tucson.
1972a Archaeological Reconnaissance of the Gila River Indian Reservation, Phase II. Manuscript on deposit, Arizona State Museum Library, Univ. of Arizona, Tucson.
1972b Archaeological reconnaissance of the Gila River Indian Reservation: Second action year (Phase III). Manuscript on deposit, Arizona State Museum Library, Univ. of Arizona, Tucson.

Woodall, J. N.
1972 Prehistoric social boundaries: An archeological model and test. *Bulletin of the Texas Archeological Society 43:*101–120.

Woodbury, N., C. R. McGimsey III, L. Brennen, B. Fagan, F. Hole, and A. Kehoe
1977 The crisis in communication. In *The management of archeological resources: The Airlie House report,* edited by C. R. McGimsey III and H. A. Davis. Washington, D.C.: Society for American Archaeology. Pp. 78–89.

Woodhouse, C. D., Jr.
n.d. An analysis of historic and prehistoric marine mammal populations in the Channel Islands of California. Research prooposal to the Marine Mammal Commission, 27 May 1976. Santa Barbara, Calif.: Santa Barbara Museum of Natural History.

Wyant, J., and F. Bayham
  1976  An experimental study of lithic use wear. In Desert resources and Hohokam subsistence: The Conoco Florence Project, by W. H. Doelle. *Arizona State Museum, Archaeological Series* No. 103.
Yamane, T.
  1967  *Elementary sampling theory*. Englewood Cliffs, N.J.: Prentice-Hall.
Yang, T. W., and C. H. Lowe
  1956  Correlation of major vegetation climaxes with soil characteristics in Sonoran Desert. *Science* *123:*542.
Yellen, J. E.
  1974  The !Kung settlement pattern: An archaeological perspective. Unpublished Ph.D. thesis, Harvard University, Cambridge, Mass.
Zubrow, E. B. W.
  1975  *Prehistoric carrying capacity: A model*. Menlo Park, Calif.: Cummings.

# Subject Index

# STUDIES IN ARCHAEOLOGY

*Consulting Editor: Stuart Struever*

Department of Anthropology
Northwestern University
Evanston, Illinois

*Lewis R. Binford.* **Bones: Ancient Men and Modern Myths**

*Richard A. Gould and Michael B. Schiffer (Eds.).* **Modern Material Culture: The Archaeology of Us**

*Muriel Porter Weaver.* **The Aztecs, Maya, and Their Predecessors: Archaeology of Mesoamerica, 2nd edition**

*Arthur S. Keene.* **Prehistoric Foraging in a Temperate Forest: A Linear Programming Model**

*Ross H. Cordy.* **A Study of Prehistoric Social Change: The Development of Complex Societies in the Hawaiian Islands**

*C. Melvin Aikens and Takayasu Higuchi.* **Prehistory of Japan**

*Kent V. Flannery (Ed.).* **Maya Subsistence: Studies in Memory of Dennis E. Puleston**

*Dean R. Snow (Ed.).* **Foundations of Northeast Archaeology**

*Charles S. Spencer.* **The Cuicatlán Cañada and Monte Albán: A Study of Primary State Formation**

*Steadman Upham.* **Polities and Power: An Economic and Political History of the Western Pueblo**

*Carol Kramer.* **Village Ethnoarchaeology: Rural Iran in Archaeological Perspective**

*Michael J. O'Brien, Robert E. Warren, and Dennis E. Lewarch (Eds.).* **The Cannon Reservoir Human Ecology Project: An Archaeological Study of Cultural Adaptations in the Southern Prairie Peninsula**

*Jonathon E. Ericson and Timothy K. Earle (Eds.).* **Contexts for Prehistoric Exchange**

*Merrilee H. Salmon.* **Philosophy and Archaeology**

*in preparation*

*Vincas P. Steponaitis.* **Ceramics, Chronology, and Community Patterns: An Archaeological Study at Moundville**

*William J. Folan, Ellen R. Kintz, and Laraine A. Fletcher.* **Coba: A Classic Maya Metropolis**

*James A. Moore and Arthur S. Keene (Eds.).* **Archaeological Hammers and Theories**

*George C. Frison and Dennis J. Stanford.* **The Agate Basin Site: A Record of the Paleoindian Occupation of the Northwestern High Plains**